ALSO BY DAVID DUBAL

Reflections from the Keyboard

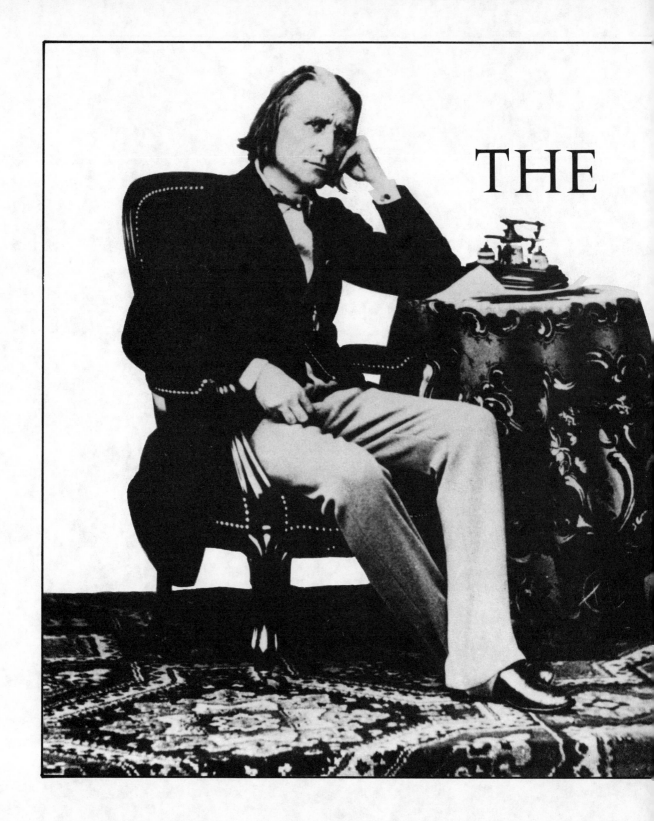

THE

Art OF THE Piano

Its Performers, Literature, and Recordings

DAVID DUBAL

SUMMIT BOOKS

NEW YORK • LONDON • TORONTO • SYDNEY • TOKYO

SUMMIT BOOKS
Simon & Schuster Building
Rockefeller Center
1230 Avenue of the Americas
New York, New York 10020

10 9 8 7 6 5 4 3 2 1

Library of Congress Cataloging in Publication Data

Dubal, David
   Art of the piano: the performers, literature, and
recordings
David Dubal.
      p.   cm.
   Includes index.
   ISBN 0-671-49238-1
   1. Music—Bio-bibliography.   2. Pianists.   3. Piano
   —Performance.
I. Title
ML105.D8   1989
786.4'041'09—dc19   89–4379
                                              CIP
                                              MN

TITLE PAGE: *Liszt during his Weimar period, around
the time of the composition of his Sonata in B minor.*

Acknowledgments

I AM especially grateful to Ileene Smith, senior editor at Summit Books, for her enlightened editing and encouragement during the various stages of the book; James Silberman, Summit's president and editor-in-chief, for his continuing support; Alane Salierno Mason, assistant editor, for her good will, patience, and excellent help; Sarah Gold, for her advice on the manuscript; James Stoller, for his searching reading; Jo-Ann Siegel, for her painstaking work in preparing the typescript; James Raimes, for his contribution to the book's conception; and Edith Fowler, for its design. I would also like to thank Carol Bresner, Sedgwick Clark, Florence Falkow, Lola Cantor, Sydney Wolfe Cohen and Jerold Ordansky for their invaluable help. Finally, I would like to express my deep gratitude for those many writers from whom I have borrowed quotations, as their special insights have enriched this book.

Contents

Acknowledgments • 7

Preface • 13

Introduction • 17

PART ONE • *27*

THE PIANISTS

PART TWO • *277*

THE PIANO LITERATURE
WITH LISTS OF EXCEPTIONAL RECORDINGS

Index • 448

Preface

THE ART OF THE PIANO consists of two sections. Part One is an assessment of history's best-known concert pianists, ranged in alphabetical order. Part Two is a listing of significant works in the piano literature, solo and concerto, in alphabetical order by composer.

In describing the work of pianists of the pre-recording era, my method, for the most important figures, is to use quotes by the best "ears" of the time. For example, it is important to know what Liszt thought of John Field's playing, what Clara Schumann felt about Mendelssohn's, or what Wagner wrote about Liszt at the instrument. We may understand Tausig's style of playing through the writings of the important critic Eduard Hanslick, or that of Rafael Joseffy, Tausig's and Liszt's great pupil, in the penetrating writings of James Huneker.

In the case of pianists who have benefited from the invention of recording, and/or whom I have heard in public performance, I write from my personal fund of knowledge and feeling. In my assessments, I have always kept in mind the words of the ancient sage Marcus Aurelius, who said, "Those who criticize have their own reason to guide them, and their own impulse to prompt them." My qualification then for establishing my opinions of these artists is a lifetime of passionate enthusiasm for the piano and its literature. For me the world is divided into two groups: those who love the piano and those who see it as simply another musical instrument. For the first group, nothing is as wondrous as great piano playing.

All criticism begins subjectively, but as one devotes a lifetime of listening to piano playing, there emerges a kind of aesthetic truth, a set of values and standards. The connoisseur will come to hear the uniqueness of a pianist's individual sound, his pianistic resource, his interpretive gifts, his temperamental affinities. No pianist has everything. One learns what is permissible in an interpretation, what is imaginative, what is eccentric, what is routine. It takes many careful comparisons to know, for instance, that nobody has ever played *Paganini* in Schumann's *Carnaval* with the swiftness and the verve of Rachmaninoff in his celebrated recording of nearly six decades ago. In addition, the critic must have practical ability in order to understand what are the outer limits of the nervous system in a technical feat. I could not possibly write a book about singers, flutists, violinists, or conductors. In writing, I draw on my own experience of piano playing, performing, recording, and teaching. Without that practical knowledge, my writing would lack authenticity. This grounding in practical knowledge doesn't mean my judgments do not change or that certain pianists do not confuse me (and such confusion is always interesting). I never judge an artist by one recording or live recital. Just as many pianists undergo vast changes during their careers, so I find my own ears always changing, learning, and finding more to hear in the greatest of all instrumental literatures. The book pretends to no completeness, and doubtless many important names have been left out. Such composers as Grieg, Fauré, Schumann, Chabrier, Balakirev, Szymanowski, and many more who were good pianists are not included as such since their playing was seldom made public.

Similarly in Part Two, space does not permit a listing of all the important or interesting works in the piano literature, and many for which I feel enthusiasm are not represented. Indeed, several of my choices, such as the Bridge or Bloch Sonatas, could have been changed for others. The major masterpieces of the literature, however, are all here. These are the works that should be in every record collection. These are the works that every student, teacher, and lover of the instrument is constantly dealing with.

I have also listed recordings of these works. For over two decades, as Music Director of the New York twenty-four-hour-a-day classical music station WNCN, I have been in a unique position to listen to thousands of recorded performances. The phonograph was a great invention, and its impact on music has mainly been for the good. As critic Roland Gelatt said, "A partisan historian could perhaps be forgiven for claiming it as the chief marvel and solace of the century." As a result, however, much that is mediocre and homogenized has entered the marketplace. The beauty of the greatest masterworks has been drowned in a sea of competently conventional and dreary playing.

The most dangerous aspect of recording is that it freezes and mummifies a musical work, imprinting on us one performance, one sound, one tempo. A recording has nothing to do with a live performance. Indeed, the compact disc is so seductive in its distance from reality, from real sound, that, for many, being at a live concert is often not only disappointing but irritating. (Seldom does a pianist care to listen to his own recordings. One reason is that they are always the same; the flow of life is gone. How I have longed to hear details of a pianist's playing that were captivating in live performance but missing from the recording.)

In this way, the masterpieces of music may become stale sooner rather than later. The phonograph has certainly helped wipe out amateur piano playing, and there are fewer in an audience who have the kind of discrimination that alone can give rise to "aesthetic ecstasy." The "gifted listener" is dying out, the listener who can lose all imprinting, who has a whole library of knowledge of a work, who has attempted to play it, who has lived with it, who has the freshness of ear to know when a performance is a revelation.

And yet a great recording can have a universality and an artistic truth which remain passionate and which can change as the listener grows musically. It can seem different and equally valid at dawn or dusk, like a masterpiece of literature, sculpture, or painting; it begs for many hearings. Each masterpiece demands lifelong study. As the adage goes, "Life is short, art is long." If we deal with a great work of art in a cursory way, it will yield little. It takes time and energy to get to know even fairly well Beethoven's *Diabelli* Variations or Chopin's B minor Sonata. The listener needs to build a relationship with each work, just as the interpreter does. The printed page is merely a blueprint; each player, to the best of his or her ability, tries to present what is in the music, what the composer means. "The written page," Aaron Copland wrote, "is only an approximation; it's only an indication of how close the composer was able to come in transcribing his exact thoughts on paper. Beyond that point the interpreter is on his own." Pablo Casals said, "Sometimes, looking at a score, I say to myself, 'What marvelous music. But I must make it so.'"

No matter how genuine one's intention to fulfill the composer's wishes, the performer cannot bring to a work any more or less than the qualities of his own temperament. One cannot manufacture a passionate, lyrical, or pastoral trait if one does not have it. On the other hand, one may be both forthright and elegiac, but not at the same moment. The art of interpretation is an art of sacrifice. This is its first law. Two players may, however, separately bring various traits to a score. For example: Horowitz plays the Rachmaninoff Third Concerto with an unbearable nostalgia—it is a memorial to his own lost Russia. His performance is like a wail of despair. On hearing Rachmaninoff himself in his recording of the score, however, one hears a drastically different content. The atmosphere loses its thickness, the tempi are faster, the composition becomes lithe, panther-like in its elegance. The *creator* of the work need not play with nostalgia; he does not tell the whole tragic story. Though expressive and Romantic, he holds his emotion in check. His very coolness becomes beguiling. An aristocratic musical mind is at work. The approach is perfectly planned and all the notes are chiseled. Rachmaninoff's extraordinary and subtle rhythmic propulsion does not shock us, as Horowitz's does. Rather, he gives a purely musical reading and the heavy languor evaporates.

There are many fine Rachmaninoff Third Concertos. Byron Janis brings to it a feeling of steely acidity; Victor Merzhanov is fascinatingly dry; and Tamás Vásáry is relaxed and autumnally glowing. No one performance can possibly contain all that these pianists reveal through their separate visions. The composer himself cannot transcend this limitation, cannot give a "definitive" reading. Here lies the endless glory of the performer's art, and here lies also one of the special values of recordings. Through them, you may hear many different performances of a work, over and over, to your heart's content. Creative comparative listening is at your bidding, with a legion of artists ready to play for you.

In Part Two, I have chosen performances on either record or compact disc which show a composition in its most diverse moods, giving us a score's largest range and possibilities. (In the text of the book, the words *disc* and *recording* are used interchangeably.) If listening to music becomes a serious way of spending time, then owning different interpretations of a work will be enlightening and will forever change one's musical life. In fact, without such listening the serious composer and interpreter have little to say.

Introduction

GEORGE BERNARD SHAW wrote: "The pianoforte is the most important of all musical instruments; its invention was to music what the invention of the printing press was to poetry." The piano is the most suggestive of all musical instruments, with the power to evoke the illusion of a singer, a French horn, a flute, a cello—indeed, the orchestra itself. Actually, the highest notes on the piano are higher than on any orchestral instrument, as the lowest notes are lower than any in the orchestra. Just as the printing press gave to the whole of humanity the literature of every nation, so the piano became the keyboard instrument of the world. Its growth in popularity as a musical instrument began with the French and American revolutions. The piano would ultimately supplant the aristocratic harpsichord and become a symbol of democracy, self-reliance, and personal expression. From a coal miner's humble dwelling to the President's mansion, a house was not a home without a piano in the parlor.

The piano's perfection and dissemination also coincided with the rise of the middle class and the era of Romanticism, when great pianists were heroes. Thousands emulated these troubadours of the keyboard, and the nine-foot concert grand, with its thousands of parts, became a cultural symbol of the luxuriant materialism of the Industrial Revolution. The piano also became the chief instrument of most of the great composers, from Mozart to Debussy, and was responsible for the enormous song literature of the nineteenth century. Imagine a Schubert, Wolf, Mussorgsky, or Fauré song with a harpsichord accompaniment.

By around 1700, polyphonic and religious music were on the wane. Music's emotional range was expanding and becoming personal and secular; people wanted to be entertained by simpler music with a singable melody, filled with sentiment. Thus there was an increasing need for a keyboard instrument capable of producing vocal expression, pure sentiment, and tonal gradation. The harpsichord could not produce a *piano* and *forte,* and the human emotions, which were bursting in the eighteenth century, needed an instrument to weep human tears and sing a melody. The great Stradivarius violins being made then were not adequate for this because they needed harmony. And so the piano was born out of necessity: an instrument that looked like a harpsichord but in every way was different from the plucked instrument; paradoxically, an instrument capable of producing song. Although there were various attempts to make such an instrument, the person acknowledged as the true inventor of the piano came from the same region of Italy as Stradivarius.

He was Bartolomeo Cristofori (1655–1731), a genius who died unsung. I know of no pianos called the Cristofori. From 1709 to 1726, he laboriously made twenty or so instruments, which differed radically from the plucked mechanism of the harpsichord. He called his hammer instrument *gravicembalo col piano e forte*—a harpsichord with soft and loud. The instrument was immediately recognized as special, and one Scipione Maffei wrote in an Italian journal in 1711: "The production of greater or less sound depends on the degree of power with which the player presses on the keys, by regulating which, not only the piano and forte are heard, but also the gradation and diversity of power." However, there was no interest in Italy in the new instruments. The piano's destiny lay in Germany, where Bach's friend, the organ builder Gottfried Silbermann, in the 1720s, happened on Maffei's article, translated into German, along with Maffei's diagram drawings of the mechanism. Silbermann had long wanted to make a keyboard capable of *inflection,* and the Maffei article seemed heaven-sent. He set to work and, by the late 1720s, showed his first instruments to Bach for his approval. But Bach disliked them. The treble, he said, was too weak, and the action seemed hard to play. Silbermann, though, undaunted, continued to improve his pianos.

By the 1740s, Frederick the Great had stocked his palaces with fifteen Silbermann pianos. In 1747, Frederick asked to meet Bach and so it was that Bach tried the king's new pianos. He was happy with them now, and a testimony from Bach was especially valued. But the still polyphonically-minded Bach was not about to embrace the new instrument. He, Couperin, and Scarlatti had been creating a magnificent literature for the harpsichord, which was now at its perfection. Voltaire, upon first hearing the early piano, was revolted. "This newcomer," he piped, "will never dethrone the majestic harpsichord. . . . The pianoforte is an ironmonger's invention compared with the harpsichord." However, the new instrument was becoming liked by the musical public, and it fit the musical mood of the time; *galant* music sounded *sweeter* on the piano.

By the 1760s, piano making had moved from Germany to London and Vienna. During the Seven Years' War, twelve keyboard makers, many of them disciples of Silbermann, immigrated to England from Germany. They were dubbed "the Twelve Apostles." The most successful was Johann Zumpe, who constructed a little square piano that became all the rage. Soon, piano sales were exceeding harpsichord sales.

The two finest pianists during the 1770s were Clementi and Mozart. The latter represented the Viennese school of playing, which was distinguished for its precision, rapidity, and clarity, the sound having more of a ping and a crisp radiance. Clementi played the English pianos which, with their heavier action and larger sonority, seemed to represent more of the might of the Industrial Revolution. By 1800, harpsichord building had practically ceased. It is no coincidence that the piano grew up during the *Sturm und Drang* movement, and that its improvement coincides with the Napoleonic era. "The Little Corporal" was exiled to Elba in 1815, and during a ruthless Paris winter, many gorgeous harpsichords, which had already been relegated to the basement of the Paris Conservatoire, were used for firewood.

The exhilarating and grandiose spirit of Napoleon had to be translated to the more pacific world of the arts. In literature, Napoleon became Byron, and in music the awesome image of Beethoven appeared—disheveled, inspired, improvising godlike harmonies on his battered piano; deaf, but undeterred. Beethoven was the first great Romantic pianist; he triumphed even over disability. He became the prototype for the Romantic genius and has remained so.

By the time of Beethoven's death, the piano was clearly the favored instrument of the growing middle class. Every family aspired to have one. Only one nonpianist performer, outside the field of opera, was held in awe by the public in those halcyon days of

Romanticism—Paganini, the wizard of the violin, whose appeal lay in the supernatural aspects of Romanticism. His art was akin to, say, Mary Shelley's *Frankenstein*. Paganini's demonic quality was soon to become assimilated into the many-sided genius of the greatest pianistic marvel of the time, whose reputation surpassed even Paganini's—Liszt. Liszt symbolized the artist as Romantic hero. The nineteenth century had quelled the Napoleonic spirit into the figure of a magnificent entertainer. In fact, Liszt was often called the Napoleon of the Piano.

Schiller said, "The gods never come singly," and a flood of piano geniuses came into the world around the same time as Liszt (1811): Chopin, Heller, Hiller, Mendelssohn, Schumann, Alkan, and a host of lesser lights were all born within a five-year period. These first-generation Romantics reached maturity in the early 1830s, precisely at the time when the piano, as we know it today, became more or less a finished product. The earlier differences between the English and the Viennese pianos were smoothed out in the grand pianos of Bösendorfer, Erard, Pleyel, Broadwood, and others. The instrument, with its cast-iron frame, achieved a range of 7⅓ octaves, utilizing eighty-eight keys. A piano made by Cristofori weighs less than the iron plate alone of the modern piano. In the 1830s, the piano could accomplish the lightning-quick shades of dark and light which the Romantics needed to spend their passion. The piano could sigh or shiver, quiver and swoon, as no instrument had ever done. Aldous Huxley pointed out, "Mozart's melodies may be brilliant, memorable, infectious, but they don't palpitate, don't catch you between wind and water, don't send the listener off into erotic ecstasies." The sound the Romantics wanted was, in Arthur Loesser's words, "a vague, mellow tone-cloud, full of ineffable promise and foreboding, carrying intimations of infinity . . . harboring the mystical suspicion that anything might merge into everything."

The piano became the quintessential Romantic instrument, and the public wanted virtuoso gods who could tame it, sing on it, and show them the stars. As the cult of the individual blossomed during the 1830s and 1840s, pianists far less gifted than Liszt thrived and prospered, with many of them achieving personal wealth from the power of music publishing, for performers also composed and their scores sold like wildfire. Piano teaching became a lucrative way of making a living; everyone needed to play the piano. One writer blasphemed that a new trinity had been formed "of which Liszt is the Father, Thalberg the Son, and Dreyschock the Holy Ghost." Frenzied hands flying over the keyboard thrilled people into believing that man could control nature and the machine. Virtuosity became a thing unto itself, and no other instrument could make virtuosity so attractive, so understandable, and so much a force to be emulated.

The pianist Charles Hallé one day found himself playing for the most erudite and revered art critic of the day, John Ruskin. But Ruskin, much to Hallé's disappointment, was overwhelmed by Thalberg's pot-boiler variations on "Home, Sweet Home." Ruskin explained to Hallé that he did not "care about the art of it . . . but I did care about having a million low notes in perfect cadence and succession of sweetness. I never recognized before so many notes in a given brevity of moment. . . . I have often heard glorious and inventive and noble successions of harmonies, but I never in my life heard variations like that. Also, I had not before been close enough to see your hands, and the invisible velocity was wonderful to me . . . as a human power."

Most of the Romantic pianists of all calibers, like the previous generation of Hummel, Czerny, and Kalkbrenner, were content to promote their own music. How else could it become known? In those early days of concert-giving, there were no impresario managements to speak of, and giving a concert was an

19

ordeal. If Chopin, for instance, wanted to give a concert, he booked the hall, took care of the piano, did the publicity, hired singers and other instrumentalists. A concert was more like a variety show. Although Liszt played his first solo recitals in 1839, such events were rare and were generally frowned upon by audiences and critics. The public wanted its money's worth, and the idea of playing alone was thought arrogant. In Chopin's short career, he played only one solo recital. Such an event also needed more educated audiences willing to focus on the music, as well as on the virtuosity of the performer.

It was the magnanimous Liszt who not only established the solo recital but broke the mold of playing only one's own music. From 1834 to 1847, he performed over the length and breadth of Europe, playing the music of the past and introducing the music of his contemporaries. As rapidly as new music was created, Liszt added it to his repertoire. Since program building was now possible with a fully realized piano literature, improvisation—once a staple of the programs of Mozart, Hummel, and Beethoven—was fast disappearing. Liszt, ever the consummate showman, needed to simulate the look of extempore playing without notes, and with Clara Schumann, began the habit of playing from memory. How could a Romantic tone poet be encumbered by the printed page? One needed to look inspired. Audiences remain in awe of the pianist who can play all those notes by "heart." Liszt's memory playing stuck at once. No other musician must play from memory, but pianists somehow seem incomplete if they have a score with them.

More important, however, was the fact that Liszt established the concept of the "interpretive" musician, and after his retirement, with few exceptions (such as the American Gottschalk in a still backward musical environment), pianists were now expected to perform a wide range of music. From that moment on, the chasm between composer and interpreters grew. After 1850, most pianists still composed, but the great demands of each activity took a toll. Liszt became exclusively a composer; his rival, Thalberg, having almost no repertoire but that of his own music, retired completely. Liszt also taught, spawning three generations of pianists who concentrated on piano playing above composition.

As piano music became ever more complex and difficult, and the public more educated to good playing, composing and performing could no longer mix. Could Robert Schumann, who desperately wanted to be a concert pianist, have in his short life created such a tremendous output if he had not paralyzed his fourth finger? Absolutely not, and it took his wife almost forty years to incorporate the Schumann literature, work by work, into her repertory. After Liszt retired from performing, Clara Wieck Schumann, younger than Liszt by eight years, became the high priestess of interpretive musicians. Although she composed well, it was her zeal, especially in the German classics dating back to Bach, that made her one of the most influential musicians of her time. For her, the composer stood first, and virtuosity for its own sake had no meaning. Her scrupulous respect for the composer stood in direct opposition to the willful "piano pounders" who, she felt, were influenced by the excesses of Liszt's youthful career.

Clara Schumann was the codifier of the German style of playing, and her influence has been felt down to our time. Hans von Bülow and Theodor Leschetizky (both born in 1830) were next in line as the most potent influences on piano playing. Von Bülow had studied with Friedrich Wieck, Clara's father, before going to work with Liszt. Bülow hardly bothered to compose, and he espoused Clara Schumann's high German seriousness with passion. Leschetizky, who studied with Liszt's teacher Czerny, may be called the codifier of the Chopin tradition. He set up shop in Vienna, where the pianistic world came to him. With a ravishing tone and high Romanticism, he was the most effective teacher of the nineteenth century. He preferred his students to be Slavic in origin, and from his stable came Essipova, Paderewski, Gabrilowitsch, Friedman, Moiseiwitsch, and hundreds of others. These pianists were primarily poets, dreamers at the keyboard, incomparable stylists, elegant, often wayward and exciting. At the center of their repertoire stood Chopin, a Chopin who could, in weaker moments, degenerate into a "Camille of the Keyboard."

Leschetizky founded an international marketplace of virtuosi. He taught more than two thousand pupils and the Leschetizky method (though he denied having one) was the golden path to pianistic stardom. Many of his lesser disciples developed the decadent *fin de siècle* style of playing, in which the composer was almost obliterated in an orgy of self-expression. The greatest Leschetizky pupils were primarily colorists and were at their finest in small forms. Anton Rubinstein, also born in 1830, became the roaring father of Russian pianism. An artist of unbridled temperament, his blood-and-thunder playing was a revelation to European audiences. No public performer had ever so exposed his soul, and he was capable of extreme sentiment. After Liszt's retirement in 1847, it was Rubinstein, with his animal magnetism, who symbolized to the world the power of which the piano was capable. His programs were marathons; he could give the Chopin *Funeral March* Sonata as an encore. Anton Rubinstein's name remains sacred in Russia.

America's greatest popularizer of the piano, Louis Moreau Gottschalk (1829–1869), had studied in Paris with Camille Stamaty, who was one of the founders of French piano playing. At the same time, Stamaty was teaching the astounding prodigy Camille Saint-Saëns, who, along with Francis Planté, represented French piano playing to the world. The *"style sévère"* had been developed from the very opening of the Paris Conservatoire. The French espoused perfect neatness of fin-

gerwork, *jeu perlé,* which came from Kalkbrenner, Zimmerman, Marmontel, Alkan, and indeed from Chopin himself. The French tradition is one of elegance, precision, sophistication, and emotional restraint. Saint-Saëns could have been speaking of French pianism when he wrote, "Art is intended to create beauty and character. Feeling only comes after, and art can very well do without it. In fact, it is very much better off when it does."

One might say that the French play on the tops of the keys, the Russians deep into the keys, and the Germans tried to figure out how much pressure should be applied to each key. James Huneker wrote, "I'm seriously studying tone-production, and trying to shake my Parisian staccato touch." Although French piano playing has lost some of its native flavor, the cool stylishness of Gallic playing remains strong.

History's next great pianist was Carl Tausig. Born in 1841, he died at the age of thirty. His teacher, Liszt, quickly helped realize his greatness, and from all accounts he was the most exceptionally equipped pianist of the era, blending the poetry and bravura of the Russian school, the perfection of the French, and the depth and scholarship of the Germans.

The earliest-born pianist to leave a body of recordings was Vladimir de Pachmann (1848–1933), an erratic, sensational miniaturist, born in the fabled musical city of Odessa. But a larger-spirited artist soon emerged to become the most important pianistic figure after Rubinstein's death. Ignacy Jan Paderewski (1860–1941), with Leschetizky's stamp of approval, carried on the tradition of pianist as Romantic hero. He united Byronic and Lisztian traits with an incomparable glamor and fierce patriotism, eventually becoming Premier of his beloved Poland. Paderewski was the darling of a new and growing world public; the geographical boundaries of his pianistic career were broad indeed. Paderewski became richer from playing the piano than any other player up to that time.

21

During the 1860s, a number of formidable and impressive pianists were born, including Arthur Friedheim, Emil von Sauer, Alexander Siloti, Eugene d'Albert, and Moriz Rosenthal, each of whom worked with Liszt. After Paderewski, however, the towering figure of Busoni (1866–1924) looms largest, and though his own music is valuable, it was as a pianist that Busoni was considered supreme. Like Tausig, he seemed to combine the qualities of all schools but with a monumentalism never before realized. Busoni seemed to stun all his colleagues, whether they liked his playing or not. Percy Grainger wrote, "Busoni was a twisted genius making the music sound unlike itself, but grander than itself—more super-human."

Busoni brought a new intellectual power to piano playing. He played with a symphonic, rhythmic sweep that had never before been heard, and he eliminated any trace of waywardness, mannerism, and sentimentalizing. He aimed for the mystical and the spiritual. Yet, as Egon Petri put it, Busoni seemed to "mould in flesh and blood." He must be considered the greatest pianist since Liszt and Anton Rubinstein.

During the 1870s, the Russian school produced a flood of great pianists inspired by Anton Rubinstein. Each was a superb technician. Godowsky, Rachmaninoff, Lhévinne, and Hofmann would all reside in the United States and enrich its pianistic culture greatly. Godowsky played, taught, and edited music; his playing was a pinnacle of perfection. Hofmann would direct the Curtis Institute of Music, and Lhévinne would teach at the Juilliard School. Rachmaninoff's prestige was vast; when he first toured the United States in 1909, American piano building was at its peak, with nearly four hundred thousand pianos a year produced by more than 350 makers. Player-pianos were popular and the most celebrated pianists made piano rolls as well as acoustical recordings. Paderewski recordings, beginning around 1910, did for the

popularity of the piano on early records what Caruso did for the voice.

As recording progressed, it changed the way pianists played. Soon they were listening to themselves for the first time. Max Pauer recalled:

When I listened to the first record of my own playing, I heard things which seemed unbelievable to me. Was I, after years of public playing, actually making mistakes that I would be the first to condemn in any one of my own pupils? I could hardly believe my ears, and yet the unrelenting machine showed that in some places I had failed to play both hands exactly together, and had been guilty of other errors no less heinous, because they were trifling. I also learned in listening to my own playing, as reproduced, that I had unconsciously brought out certain nuances, emphasized different voices and employed special accents without the consciousness of having done so.

Recording provided immortality itself. And yet, many pianists were wary of the medium. The Romantic pianist relied on the inspiration of the moment, and the idea of putting down one interpretation forever was widely disliked. Henceforth, music-making would become more cautious. Taking chances wasn't necessarily exciting on a record; it could be downright messy. The grand manner and rhetorical pretension of the era lessened immensely. Because of recordings, pianists were becoming a more "serious" species. They had to learn what sounded good on stage and what sounded good on record. This tremendous battle between live performance and recording has continued through the century. The technological breakthrough of electrical recording came in 1925, and Rachmaninoff was the first to produce an important body of recordings. He not only took recording seriously, but studied the medium closely.

The pianists of the early twentieth century, however, had nonintellectual, gracefully sensuous, charming qualities that were vanishing. Today we call Godowsky, Hofmann, Levitzki,

Lhévinne, Rosenthal, Friedman, Sauer, and others the representatives of a golden age of pianism. "Today," wrote Charles Rosen, "the style of the great pianists of the first quarter of this century and the air of casual elegance cannot be recaptured, and probably we shall never hear it again. Rosenthal, Hofmann, and Rachmaninoff combined technical perfection not only with spontaneity but with the appearance of improvising. Their technical mastery may still be found, but their ease of manner and their sense of high style have been lost forever: They played like gentlemen."

Many important figures born during the 1880s, such as Petri, Schnabel, Backhaus, Edwin Fischer, and Arthur Rubinstein—all German-trained—represent the trend away from the idiosyncratic to a larger and well-planned vision of the music they played. Each was a great influence on twentieth-century pianists, and they all took recording seriously, leaving a large recorded legacy. Of this group, only Arthur Rubinstein was eclectic, playing music of all styles. He placed a major emphasis on Chopin, but a Chopin that was respectful, virile, and structured. It took a long time to eradicate the standard melodramatic portrait of Chopin. No longer was Chopin merely an excuse for tortured rubato, altered texts, and the purple passion of de Pachmann and a host of others. In France, Cortot proved that Chopin could retain its glamor as well as its great poetic lyricism.

It must be understood how little music was generally known. Schnabel, in the 1940s, wrote: "During my educational phase in Vienna until 1899, I never heard, in this most musical city on earth, and in the midst of musicians, of the existence of the twenty-seven concertos by Mozart, or Beethoven's Opus 106 or the *Diabelli* Variations, or Bach's *Goldberg* Variations, etc." Rachmaninoff was once told about Schubert's sonatas, and he was surprised there were any. The spread of a literature takes far longer than one would imagine. When Schnabel completed the first

recording on 78s of the thirty-two sonatas of Beethoven, there were only a few hundred people ready to buy them. Today, hardly a month goes by without half a dozen recordings of Mozart concerti offered to a public that extends to Japan, Korea, and even China. Pianists are now expected to be literal museums of the past and present. They may have to play twenty different concertos a season, as well as several recital programs, flying all over the globe.

Pianists are no longer expected to compose, even during their studies; however, they have had to learn a performing repertoire that has grown enormously since the days of Liszt. It takes never-ending hours of toil to master the complexities of Scriabin, Granados, Debussy, Prokofiev, Bartók, Ives, Messiaen, Boulez, or Stockhausen. The twentieth-century pianist must be eclectic above all else. Arrau, Horowitz, and Serkin—three of the most influential pianists with careers spanning the century—performed huge repertories in their prime, including Scarlatti, Schubert sonatas, and Mozart concerti, which were all virtually new to the public.

Pianists of the Leschetizky atelier were prompted to play only what would be most successful in showing themselves off. When Horowitz played Scarlatti for Rachmaninoff, the latter did not like the music. Twentieth-century "interpreters," though, consider music not in terms of likes and dislikes, but rather in a historical context. One has only to look at the repertoire requirements of a piano competition to understand what awesome demands are made of each aspirant. The twentieth-century pianist must be a scholar. It is an age in which the document rules, the score is sacrosanct, the Urtext edition is supreme. Thanks to the medium of recordings, there are now, in every city, critics who grew up listening to all the Mozart concerti played by various artists. These critics sit in judgment, score in hand, peering at each marking. If the pianist dares overlook a marking or a staccato, 23 he or she becomes a ruthless liar, a defiler of the composer's intention; and of course wrong notes are sins.

In a competition today, an Anton Rubinstein or de Pachmann would be thrown out of the first round. Did Liszt *really* play all the notes in his *Transcendental Etudes*? How many slips of memory did he have? Nobody knew, nobody cared. However, each generation wears a new musical outfit. Yesterday's fashion often seems ridiculous to the present-day sensibility. Today, in fact, younger pianists are beginning to chafe at the often pedantic constraints of recent years. Even at competitions there are signs of a loosening up of the "standardized" performance, and a flight of imagination is not as suspect as before.

One thing is certain: the piano and piano playing are here to stay. More countries produce pianos than ever before—Korea, Brazil, Switzerland, Czechoslovakia, China, Thailand, Australia, and many others—while Japan has become the world's largest piano producer. The Orient, in its obsession with things Western, has been captivated by the instrument. Asian pianists are filling conservatories and winning competitions. The future of the instrument and its literature are becoming international. Had Beethoven or Liszt ever thought of a Japanese or a Korean pianist?

There are now nearly one million pianos made a year, an incredible number considering that the instrument cannot be mass-produced. The piano has come a long way from the age when Cristofori made his twenty pianos in twenty-five years. And although many think that composers no longer love the piano as they once did, the piano literature of the twentieth century gives abundant proof to the contrary. Indeed, one of the great challenges for the contemporary pianist will be to reveal the wealth of the twentieth century's piano literature to audiences worldwide.

The indefatigable pursuit of an unattainable perfection, even though it consist of nothing more than the pounding of an old piano, is what alone gives a meaning to our life on this unavailing star.

LOGAN PEARSALL SMITH (1865–1946)

PART ONE

The Pianists

A

LOUIS ADAM
1758–1848 — Germany

He went to Paris at the age of sixteen, and became one of the founders of French piano playing. Adam was a good pianist whose *Méthode de piano du Conservatoire*, published in 1804, contributed to the development of piano technique. He taught many pupils at the Paris Conservatoire, which through his prestige became a popular institution for piano study.

CLARENCE ADLER
1886–1969 — United States

A respected pedagogue and pianist who studied with Godowsky and had an influence on many pianists. He taught privately in New York for over half a century.

DANIEL ADNI
b. 1951 — Israel

Studied at the Paris Conservatoire. His recordings of the nocturnes of John Field and of pieces by Percy Grainger show a fresh lilt. Adni is also attuned to Chopin, especially such works as the Third Ballade.

GUIDO AGOSTI
b. 1901 — Italy

A student of Busoni, and one of the best pianistic minds of his country. He has made many editions and has composed effective transcriptions, including one of scenes from Stravinsky's *Firebird*, which the American pianist Robin McCabe has recorded. Agosti's teaching has been widely praised.

WEBSTER AITKEN
b. 1908 — United States

Studied with Sauer and Schnabel. He played a great deal of Schubert in the 1930s, when the sonatas were still neglected. He is a player with very strong ideas, verging on eccentricity. His recording of Beethoven's *Hammerklavier* Sonata is an intriguing one.

EUGENE D'ALBERT
1864–1932 — Scotland

One of the finest musicians of the late nineteenth century. Liszt called him "the astonishing d'Albert" and "the second Tausig." His playing possessed ardor, intellectual power, and Romantic rhetoric in full measure. Beethoven was his specialty, and he made an edition of the sonatas which is still valuable for its discriminating thoughts on phrasing and fingering. Around 1900, Arthur Rubinstein heard d'Albert play the Beethoven Fourth Concerto "with a nobility and tenderness," he wrote, which "remained in my mind as the model performance of the work." After 1910, d'Albert's playing became a jumble of wrong notes, but he continued to be venerated. In a 1913 letter, James Huneker relates: "Heard d'Albert play the other night—audience 2,000 delirious. Such playing, a smear, a blur, 100,000 dropped notes, rotten rhythms, but the whole like something elemental, an earthquake, a tornado, a collision of planets, the sun in a conflagration . . . I stood on my chair to yell with the rest (I was really standing on my head) . . . what a genius at the keyboard." At a similar concert, Busoni said to some students, "If only you could make such mistakes." Claudio Arrau, who also heard him at this time, felt that "d'Albert's playing was stupendous, his Liszt Sonata heroic." Unfortunately, the records he made give little indication of the qualities that made such a tremendous impression on his contemporaries. He composed a great deal, including piano music, but concentrated his energy on his operas, of which *Tiefland* was the best known.

DMITRI ALEXEEV
b. 1947—USSR

A prizewinner in several important competitions, he made his New York recital debut at Carnegie Hall in 1978. He has a sympathy for varied styles of music, and he plays much Chopin, a composer he is adept at.

CHARLES VALENTIN ALKAN
1813–1888—France

Studied with Pierre Zimmerman at the Paris Conservatoire. By the age of sixteen, he was advancing toward a successful career as a virtuoso. During the early 1830s he enjoyed the company of the Parisian intellectual and artistic elite and, for a time, lived at the fashionable Square d'Orléans, which was called "a little Athens." There he was especially close to Chopin and George Sand.

But Alkan's reclusive and rather misanthropic tendencies were too strong to contain. Gradually he disappeared from social life and public performance, preferring to be alone, teaching a few wealthy pupils, and composing assiduously while immersing himself in Talmudic and Biblical studies. He lived a sad, strange life with few notable events. His ending was tragic—as he reached for his beloved Talmud, which was resting on top of a massive bookcase, the structure toppled over, crushing the emaciated musician to death at seventy-five. While the story may be apocryphal, it suggests that his death was characteristic of his life.

Alkan was a pianist in what the French called *"le style sévère."* It was a precise playing, lucid, sparsely pedaled, and with little tempo rubato. He must have been impressive, as no less than von Bülow and Anton Rubinstein deeply admired him. (Rubinstein's finest concerto, No. 5, is dedicated to Alkan.) Liszt, too, always admired him, and once said that he was never nervous playing for anyone but Alkan. Yet, curiously, none of them ever played any of Alkan's work. After years of retirement, Alkan mysteriously emerged in 1874, and for several seasons played annual concerts in Paris which were remarkable for their diversity; yet he offered almost nothing of his own work. Vincent d'Indy heard him at this time, in Beethoven's Sonata Op. 110, and wrote that it "affected me with an enthusiasm such as I have never experienced since."

Alkan's leaving the pianistic arena early in his career may be the main reason for his overwhelming neglect as a composer, which remains an artistic tragedy. Most of the major Romantics were brilliant self-promoters, and in the great rush of the Romantic movement, Alkan's extensive output became buried. The publication in 1847 of his Grand Sonata, Op. 33 (longer than Beethoven's *Hammerklavier*), a work Raymond Lewenthal more recently called "a cosmic event in the composer's development and in the history of piano music," went all but unheralded at the time. Even worse, Alkan was called bizarre and unplayable, and the designation by von Bülow as "the Berlioz of the piano" stuck, as if Alkan had never written dozens of very playable miniatures. In his book *Around Music*, Kaikhosru Sorabji wrote, "Few remarkable and astonishing figures in music have been the subject of such persistent misunderstanding, denigration, and belittlement."

Only Busoni among early twentieth-century pianists was convinced of Alkan's worth, considering him—along with Chopin, Schumann, Liszt, and Brahms—one of the greatest of the post-Beethoven piano composers. Busoni at least attempted to rescue him from oblivion, but with little success. Later, Busoni put the task to his student Egon Petri, who took the challenge seriously and brought out some of Alkan's more important scores.

Not until the 1960s, however, did an important Alkan exploration begin to surface. In the United States, Raymond Lewenthal was deeply gratified by the fine audience response whenever he performed Alkan, and he pre-pared a long-overdue critical edition. In England, Ronald Smith devoted a prominent place in his programs to Alkan, in addition to writing a biography, *Alkan the Enigma*. John Ogdon, Michael Ponti, and others joined the cause, and a recorded legacy now exists. Ronald Smith has cautioned: "The very diversity and range of his composition has proved a frustrating obstacle to the filing-cabinet minds. Like Beethoven, he seldom if ever repeats himself. . . . These baffling pages, black with marching regiments of notes, become in performance a Pandora's box of demonic power to which only the most fearless player holds the key."

Without knowing something of his output, we lose a vital chapter of nineteenth-century piano music. No serious student of the keyboard can ignore Alkan's amazing writing for the piano, which extended its resources with an extraordinary understanding of the instrument. Alkan was one of the great temperaments of French Romantic art; his vision reminds one of the blazing passions of Géricault, Delacroix, Hugo, and Berlioz.

GÉZA ANDA
1921–1976 — Hungary

Although Anda played a good Liszt, a congenial Bartók Third Concerto, and a great deal of Schumann and Chopin, the last years of his life were spent mainly in the preparation and recording of the twenty-five Mozart concerti. In this magnificent achievement, Anda fulfilled his gifts. For these works he composed his own excellent and idiomatic cadenzas and also conducted the orchestra with control and subtlety, achieving a luminous homogeneity of sound. Anda plays with high polish, lovely tone, unforced tempi. Everything is refined and musical; it is a radiant, sunny, Italianate Mozart. On occasion, he misses the darker

31

strains of Mozart's genius, the undertow of passion, the stabs of pain, the momentary reaching for sublimity. In the slow movements, Anda plays with the taste and poise of a fine musical mind. It was Anda's gorgeous playing, with his widely arched phrasing of the slow movement, of the Piano Concerto No. 21, K. 467, that was used so strikingly in the film *Elvira Madigan*.

LUCY ANDERSON
1790–1878 — England

The first woman pianist to play at the Philharmonic Society in London, in 1819, in Hummel's B minor Concerto. Later, she taught piano to Queen Victoria and her children.

AGUSTIN ANIEVAS
b. 1934 — United States

Studied with Edward Steuermann and Adele Marcus at the Juilliard School. In 1961 he won the Mitropoulos Piano Competition. Though his playing is never profound, Anievas has the rare gift of intimacy. Rubato is natural to him and never applied after the fact. His recording of the Chopin Waltzes is ingratiating, and his twenty-four Chopin Etudes show his claim to virtuosity. He is not as satisfying in the Brahms *Handel* Variations, and he seems miscast in the Schubert Impromptus. His most ambitious assignment has been the recording of the *Rhapsody on a Theme of Paganini* and the four concerti of Rachmaninoff. Here we have a purebred, fluid pianism and a refusal to gild the lily in these lush concerti, which have all too often been cheapened in less aristocratic hands.

CONRAD ANSORGE
1862–1930 — Germany

One of Liszt's last pupils, a highly regarded pianist of his period in the "large" German style of d'Albert, Busoni, and Carreño.

ANNIE D'ARCO
b. 1920 — France

Studied with Marguerite Long. She is a typical representative of the slender, lithe, and elegant playing that still survives in French pianism, a style begun by Adam, Zimmerman, and Alkan ten generations ago.

MARTHA ARGERICH
b. 1941 — Argentina

Her early studies were with Vincenzo Scaramuzza; later training included working with Friedrich Gulda and Michelangeli. She was the winner in 1957 of the Busoni International Competition in Bolzano and, in 1965, of the Chopin International Competition in Warsaw.

Argerich is one of the most exciting pianists of our time. On stage her sultry appearance exudes mystery and electricity. In pianistic circles one constantly hears the question: Did you hear Argerich recently? Or: How do you like Argerich's new Schumann or Chopin recording? Do you know her Tchaikovsky concerto with Kondrashin? You can bet every pianist in town will be at an Argerich recital. Audiences are immediately aware of her passionate temperament, they drink in her musical vitality. Argerich has a restless nature and has taken a long time to come to grips with her tremendous talent, raw energy, and animal spirits. Often she has relied on her instinct and primitive strength to propel her through a concert. Although she has considerable musical intelligence, she finds it difficult to meditate on a work's design, its ultimate form. This has caused her to be rather inconsistent, often relying on the heat of the moment. Her inspiration can falter within a wonderful rendition, only to rise again on a surge of impulsive power. On stage, she carries the day, but defects show up in her recorded output.

Her Liszt Sonata is shapeless, too fast, with the left hand often murky. Her Chopin *Funeral March* Sonata bumps and belches. The Chopin B minor Sonata and the Schumann G minor Sonata rumble, and the slow movements sound artificial. I think she is bored in recording sessions. Even her Prokofiev Third Concerto, for all her hard-edged tone, is not as brilliant as it should be. But these are all earlier recordings. (Even among these, I have a favorite, a fabulous performance of Ravel's *Gaspard de la nuit*. The *Scarbo* movement, darkly hued and fiendish, is charged with a technical abundance that few can achieve.) Argerich also has the vital capacity for growth. Each season she shows increasing discipline and consistency without losing the high tension of white-hot creation. In Carnegie Hall I heard her play the Brahms Sonata Op. 2 in F-sharp minor, a work born of controlled fury—the first movement was steaming, like molten lava, and she uncovered in it a range of colors that I never knew the composition could display. At this same concert she played Prokofiev's own transcriptions from his ballet *Romeo and Juliet*. Her projection was so powerful, her color sense so deft, that there was no reason to long for Prokofiev's lavish orchestration. From the far simpler tone production of her early recordings, she has arrived at a sound that is rich and pliant. Her recordings of the Bach toccatas are well constructed and robust, and Schumann's *Kreisleriana* finds her at her most inspired. Let's hope that Argerich, who has a propensity for canceling concerts, will continue to let audiences all over the world hear her.

CLAUDIO ARRAU
b. 1903 — Chile

At the age of sixteen, he won the Liszt Prize, the first of many awards throughout his life. At twenty he made his American debut, playing with the Boston and Chicago symphony orchestras. Then, in 1927, he won the International Pianists' Competition in Geneva; in 1949 he was named "Favorite Son of Mexico"; in 1965 he received the Chevalier de l'Ordre des Arts et des Lettres. And in 1978, the Berlin Philharmonic awarded him its Hans von Bülow Medal. He has lived in the United States since 1941.

Arrau was born in Chillán, far from the great events that were shaping the century. His gifts were evident at a very early age, and his mother was his first teacher. Soon, however, it became apparent that he needed more advanced instruction and, with the aid of a stipend from the government, he went to Berlin. There he embarked on studies with the most enduring influence of his life—the long-time pupil of Liszt, Martin Krause. Krause nurtured the child, supervised his practicing, read to him, walked with him, taught him other subjects, and took him to concerts, where he heard everything and met everybody. The giants of his youth were Busoni, Carreño, d'Albert; "they were awesome in their scope," he remembers. Krause, conscious of the Lisztian "humanist" climate, taught Arrau a deep humility in his art, and he instilled in his young charge a fierce desire to play in public, a desire which has never abated. During those splendid years of guardianship of the young Arrau, Krause accepted not a penny. When his mentor died, Arrau was only sixteen. He was

33

crushed and did not want to work with another teacher, nor did he need to.

During the next decade, Arrau slowly began the process of career-building, while constantly adding to his repertoire. When he won the Geneva prize, Arthur Rubinstein was one of the judges. "It did not take two minutes of his playing," recounts Rubinstein in his memoirs, "before we began nodding to each other, smiling with satisfaction. . . . The competition was like a race between a thoroughbred and some cart horses."

By the 1930s, Arrau was performing worldwide, playing recitals of the complete keyboard works of Bach, Mozart, and Beethoven. In the last half-century, he has never rested, offering programs beyond the potential and potency of the average performer.

For this artist, pianistic frivolity or mere entertainment is never in order. "Wowing" an audience would be inconceivable. Arrau thinks of Art in the nineteenth-century sense, as sacred, mystical, spiritual. By temperament and education, he is from a vanished era, where Art was not a form of therapy or enjoyment, but a way of life. When this gentleman of dignity plays, I am taken back to a time when there was less noise and confusion, a time when value was placed on craftsmanship, and even on contemplation.

Arrau has had one of the major musical careers of the century. He is not, however, an artist beloved by all listeners. He is a problematic pianist, respected for his musicianly wisdom, but often irritating in his conceptions, which can be too ponderous, idiosyncratic in phrasing, or just tedious. His playing can indeed be heavy, and unrelentingly serious. There is always complexity in an Arrau rendering; there are seldom humor, lightness, or sensuousness for their own sake. It is especially interesting that many pianists, especially those with a Slavic bent, respond poorly to Arrau. Those who see the piano before the music find Arrau, no matter what the repertoire, just too stodgy.

Yet Arrau the pianist has not always been the lofty and serious-minded artist we have come to know. His early discs, from the late 1920s, show a pianist glorying in his technical power, thrilled by his athletic skills and glittering scales, playing with an elegance that he was later to forsake entirely. He plays Balakirev's *Islamey* with a lustful virtuosity, splurging in chordal and sonorous splendor. In Liszt's *Spanish Rhapsody,* he rides the high tide of virtuosity. Also spectacular are his Chopin and Liszt etudes. This was a period of sparkle and panache.

By the mid-1930s, a more dour Arrau emerged, an artist experimenting with the repertoire, finding his way in it, playing huge amounts of Bach and Mozart. But Beethoven was the rudder that set him on his ultimate course. He first played the cycle of Beethoven sonatas in Mexico City in the 1930s, and ever after made the master of Bonn his main concern. During the 1930s, Arrau emerged as a musical architect, with Fischer and Schnabel affecting him more deeply than any other pianists.

During and after the war years, Arrau's playing became even more austere. There was more angularity in phrasing, more definition, less pedaling for color's sake, and he became more objective in his conceptions. It is often rather bleak playing, such as his herculean Schubert *Wanderer* Fantasy, selections from Albéniz's *Iberia,* or the dry Chopin Etudes and Scherzos and a wiry Debussy. This period lasted a full twenty years.

In the last quarter-century, Arrau's art has crystallized. The bleakness of the postwar period has been left behind; there is more optimism in his vision, and the playing has never before been so imbued with lyrical sweep and monumentality of style. His recordings are a marvelous document of his art until around 1982, when such discs as his Schubert Op. 90 Impromptus, Chopin Waltzes and Scherzos, and others sound tired and faded, even plodding at times.

Arrau, like many older artists, has returned to Mozart for rejuvenation, but the kind of graciousness Mozart demands is not an innate part of his temperament. His recording of the C minor Sonata is too strenuous, the A minor Rondo too tortured, and the D minor Fantasy, needing simplicity, is too heartrending, full of pedal and torpor. Nor is he a successful player of the concerti. In Mozart there is always a tear beneath the smile, but Arrau searches only for the tear, unconcerned with the benevolence of style.

Arrau has committed Chopin to disc *en masse.* His conception of the Polish master is far from the Chopin of the French salon, far from the view of him as a "ladies' composer" (Arrau's words). I think that Arrau has been long in coming to terms with Chopin. I cannot pretend to care for all of it, but he has developed an authentic Chopin, in which he is, above all, a master of design; here structure is prime, but still sometimes the structure bursts its bounds. It is not a Slavic Chopin, but the essence of the Teutonic type, blended with his passionate Latin blood. Arrau's Chopin during the 1950s was skeletal, but in his later period it is often massive and colorful, possessing many interpretive depths. It is never "light," even in the most insignificant posthumous waltz or "pretty" nocturne. At times, the Arrau Chopin is an amalgam of mistreated or affected rubato and tortured pretension. His old versions of the Impromptus and Scherzos were stylistically uncomfortable, but the newer discs are bloated and structurally piecemeal.

He sees the Nocturnes as important music and attempts to play them as such, but somehow he gives them a transfusion of thick syrup. He emphasizes too many details, and the pauses seem endless—the inflections become harmonically and melodically pokey, while the hesitations border on mannerism. These Nocturnes have been stored in the hothouse; all their inherent voluptuousness has become moldy. Arrau would have been most uncomfortable in a Parisian salon, listening to the ethereal Pole introduce his amorous "night pieces" to fashionable society. His Chopin is most successful in the Third and Fourth Ballades, the F minor Fantasy, and the *Polonaise-fantaisie,* which has marvelous moments of depth. There are also many creative strokes in the Preludes, side by side with quirky passages.

Arrau's earlier Debussy is transformed in later years. He feels the Preludes are of visionary scope, with a "proximity to death," a phrase he often uses. Gone is the much-heralded Gallic clarity of this *"musicien français."* Here, the grace of simplicity rests uneasily in Arrau's music-making; his Debussy seldom has a moment's repose, and he finds in the music a labyrinth of mysterious murmurings.

The composers in whose work Arrau's genius truly blooms and flourishes are Schumann, Beethoven, Liszt, and Brahms. In recent years he has also become deeply involved with Schubert, whose music, he feels, poses the most difficult of interpretive problems. His recording of the B-flat Sonata shows many beauties of tone and feeling, yet it strays, lacking directness and charm. His best Schubert disc is a haunting reading of the great C minor posthumous sonata, with a chilling finale.

For many pianists and audiences, Schumann's large works, so discursive, daring, and thorny, are hard nuts to crack. But Arrau's creativity is perfectly wedded to Schumann's deep Romanticism. The denser the tapestry, the more involved Arrau becomes. His own metric clock fits closely with the seemingly barless music. Free to indulge and experiment, Arrau can actually become playful. Hands occasionally playing purposely slightly out of sync make for an unnerving effect. He brings out inner voices, subtleties of voicing and texture, and, above all, the vernal atmosphere of early German Romanticism. The Fantasy, *Symphonic Etudes, Humoreske, Davidsbünd-* 35 *lertänze,* the *Carnaval,* and others are filled with fire, a leaping, soaring spirit, but also with the dark overtones of Schumann's own nightmarish psyche on the brink of mental disaster. Arrau plays Schumann with the utmost compassion.

Brahms also has fared well with Arrau, whose interpretations of the two concerti are broadly conceived. They present a properly grand Brahms. In the F minor and F-sharp minor Sonatas and the Scherzo, Op. 4, Arrau is more remarkable than in the Variations on a Theme by Paganini or by Handel or in the smaller frame of the Ballades, Op. 10.

All pianists should study closely Arrau's Beethoven. He has been among the great disseminators of this composer's work, and in the time-honored tradition of von Bülow, d'Albert, and Schnabel, has prepared his own edition of the thirty-two sonatas. His playing offers an abundance of interpretive insight. Here is Arrau the master builder, fired with intellectual curiosity and passion. He sees in Beethoven a mirror of human aspiration, joy, and suffering. This music is Arrau's spiritual home. Playing Beethoven, he is never orthodox; the playing may not set everyone's blood on fire, but it offers a true listening adventure, which grows deeply on a listener.

In the Liszt literature, Arrau can be titanic. For him, Liszt is never small-minded or merely glittering. He finds in Liszt a large landscape—the nature poet, the gypsy, the inventor of an unprecedented technique, a Faustian, a religious ecstatic, and an impressionist.

Arrau's Liszt Sonata has always crowned his repertoire. His live performances of it are usually finer than his recording, which is nevertheless one that should be in any Liszt admirer's library. The twelve *Transcendental Etudes,* recorded when Arrau was seventy-four, are enormous conceptions carved from the piano's very innards, colorful and bold. Other Arrau landmark Liszt recordings include the Ninth Hungarian Rhapsody as well as *Les Jeux d'eaux à la Villa d'Este,* a fountain of golden inspiration in which Arrau is at the very height of his art. Also memorable are the trumpeting epic tragedy in his B minor Ballade; the large emotional span of his *Vallée d'Obermann;* and the long, flowering phrasing of the *Bénédiction de Dieu dans la solitude,* where the mystic Liszt is in harmony with Arrau's own penchant for contemplative states.

Arrau's career is an object lesson epitomizing the artist struggling with his daemon, digging deeply into the piano's repertoire, forever searching and studying, and, in his ferocious need to express himself musically, finally bringing his art to a world public. It has been a relentless, Faustian career. Playing the piano has been everything to Claudio Arrau.

VLADIMIR ASHKENAZY
b. 1937— USSR

He studied with the renowned teacher Anaida Sumbatyan and, at the age of eighteen, entered the Moscow Conservatory, where he worked under Lev Oborin. Ashkenazy quickly became the pride of the Soviet pianistic world. In 1955 he placed second in the Warsaw Chopin Competition, and the following year saw him triumph in the Brussels Queen Elizabeth Competition. From that moment on, his career prospered. By this time, he had already excited many connoisseurs with his finely grained Chopin F minor Concerto, of chaste and slender proportions. Soon after, his Chopin Etudes filtered to the West, announcing a breathtaking mechanism. His fingers were dauntless, double-notes were shaken from the wrist as if by magic, and in the lyric Etude Op. 25, No. 7, he revealed a passionate emotional makeup. In these early recorded specimens, Ashkenazy appeared to be a delectable Slavic miniaturist.

In 1962, Ashkenazy, who should have been beyond the competition circuit, was asked by the powers that be to enter the Tchaikovsky Competition. The already renowned pianist acceded and tied for first place with the British John Ogdon. Shortly thereafter, in 1963, the young virtuoso defected from Mother Russia. At the same time, he left the ranks of important young pianists, moving year by year into higher levels of artistry.

After his defection, Ashkenazy was intent upon musical growth. If he lost some of his Russian taste for musical titillation and quick excitement, he also gained a new knowledge of Classical composers, dedicating himself to the stylistic problems of Mozart, Beethoven, and Schubert. His accounts of the G major and D major Sonatas of Schubert are warm and insightful. In the late 1960s he began to perceive the might of Beethoven's mind, and he produced rich readings of Beethoven sonatas and the Concerti. His concerto performances showed a true instinct for orchestral collaboration. His *Hammerklavier* stands out as the highest achievement of this period.

During these marvelously inspired years of the 1960s, his Chopin took on more color and an emboldened tone. He made recordings of the Ballades and Scherzos, large in style and looking deep into the composer's spirit, while eschewing all mannerism. In such scores as the C-sharp minor Scherzo, the Barcarolle, the B major Nocturne, and the Second Ballade, Ashkenazy produced some of the best Chopin playing put to disc in the 1960s. During this period, he was active in promoting the Brahms concerti, and produced a library of recordings of Mozart concerti and sonatas, the finest being his A minor Sonata. He also recorded large amounts of Schumann, struggling to understand the German master's stylistic weirdness. He finds his target best in a marvelous reading of the *Symphonic Etudes,* while his other Schumann does not always fare so well, cramped often by a certain dullness. His Ravel *Gaspard de la nuit,* however, is shim-

mering, and his Liszt etudes are wonderful. In all that he touched there was a deep respect for the composers' wishes, together with a technique that was ravishing. In short, Ashkenazy had cross-pollinated Russian provincialism with cosmopolitanism, a unique mix that made him one of the most exciting and sought-after artists of the time. His career grew to astonishing proportions, and he seemed to be, indeed he was, all over the globe. He continued to play an excellent Prokofiev, and his Rachmaninoff kept expanding in its lyricism. He also added intelligent performances of Scriabin to his repertoire.

Throughout the 1970s and 1980s, Ashkenazy has remained furiously dedicated to his art. Recordings roll off the press—chamber music, Rachmaninoff song accompaniments, the ten violin sonatas of Beethoven with Itzhak Perlman, solo works and concertos, the complete Beethoven sonatas and the complete Chopin works. (How does he have the time to learn so difficult and ungrateful a score as the Chopin Sonata in C minor, Op. 4?) The breadth of his piano recitals remains staggering, from Schubert's *Wanderer* Fantasy to Scriabin's Sixth Sonata, and all of it is played impeccably. But in the last ten years Ashkenazy has lost something—a vitality, an adventurousness with the music. Perhaps even a boredom with the piano is setting in. When he turned to conducting, many felt this was merely to refresh himself, to relax from the rigors of the piano. But no, this restless, intelligent, formidable, and compulsive musical mind has kept at his conducting and is now turning out good readings of the established orchestral repertoire, and each season he grows more skilled in this adopted field.

Recently, some of his orchestral performances have been far more exciting than his piano playing, which sounds tired and tubby—Chopin valses without aroma, mazurkas without the wild wood note, so much seems manufactured. His Beethoven Sonatas are always correct and careful but played with little lust. It is extra-homogenized, the favorite Beethoven of the traditional, cautious conservatory student. When a pupil asks the teacher which Op. 2, No. 3 to listen to, the teacher says with confidence, "Hear Ashkenazy's. It is the most normal." And in actuality, the Ashkenazy way is what many audiences want today. High craft, stability, overwhelming professionalism, faithfulness to the text, infallible rhythm, and nothing that disturbs very much—like the clean plastic that pervades our sanitized environment. In this sense, Ashkenazy represents the last decade and a half admirably. He has been at the top of the class, and it is no accident that his career has been so enormously successful. He is stern and serious; one cannot imagine Ashkenazy resorting to the absurdities of some of his colleagues, who are heard on TV commercials and game shows, or in cheap "crossover" albums with "pop" musicians.

Yet Ashkenazy's piano playing seldom sounds inspired, and as there has been a slight change in taste recently, his straightforward objectivity is beginning to sound dull; or is it that we have heard the Ashkenazy "product" too often? He seems to have been playing by formula. At a recent recital, an Ashkenazy fanatic walked out shaking her head, muttering, "It's all there, but where is it?" This opinion is becoming prevalent with many pianists; they are unmoved. Yet they still admire him as one of the most all-encompassing pianistic talents of the present day. Perhaps a rest is due. He seems now to be conducting more than ever. Maybe, with time away from the instrument, a fresh urge to play the piano will bring him into a new chapter in his relationship with the literature he grew up with.

STEFAN ASKENASE
b. 1896 — Poland

A student of Sauer, Askenase has achieved a fine reputation in Europe, especially as a Chopin interpreter, and his discs are often poetic and never superficial. The Impromptus and Concerti are especially intriguing.

EMANUEL AX
b. 1949 — Poland

He studied at the Juilliard School with Mieczyslaw Münz. In 1973 he won the first Arthur Rubinstein Competition in Tel Aviv.

Ax never shouts, roars, or shows off. His conceptions are clear and direct. He breathes deeply, playing with confidence and spontaneity, unconcerned about hitting a few wrong notes. Style, balance, and good sense always inform his work.

Ax has an affinity with Chopin in all his genres. It's a very healthy, warm, but objective Chopin. The Ax brand never sighs or weeps, and there is never a morbid note. His *Polonaise-fantaisie* is firmly structured. The Nocturne in B major and the E major Scherzo are luscious, the two Concerti full-bodied, if somewhat too slick. The Ballades are rich with color, while his Mazurkas are among the best of his generation, so natural and arresting is his innate sense of rhythm in these dance-poems.

In Mozart he is weaker, not yet having found the key to this elusive music. The Mozart concerto readings are limited in emotional range, too tasteful and pleasing. Ax generally does not like to disturb; even the forbidding Schoenberg Concerto is somehow Romantically expressive and accessible.

In Beethoven, Ax is comfortable. He has produced fine readings of the *Waldstein* and *Appassionata* Sonatas, charged with Romantic drama. His Liszt is somewhat bland, well padded, and agreeable, with the supercharged flamboyance of this composer missing.

Ax is blessed with an exceptional singing tone, but maintaining this quality often appears to be his prime concern. There needs to be a dash of astringency in his playing. For instance, his plush reading of the Ravel *Valses nobles et sentimentales* could profit by being less Romantic, and his *Scarbo,* which is first-class technically, lacks the devastating sting and drollery of this music. In his desire to wrap everything in a beautiful package, he deprives much music of its true nature. After Liszt heard Henselt, who was renowned for his cantabile playing, he exclaimed, "Ah, I too could have had velvet paws." But Liszt opted instead for a variegated palette of sounds based on the character and needs of the music. All music is not beautiful, and perhaps this is why Ax has been admirably experimenting with a variety of contemporary music, possibly to relieve his ears of conventional harmony.

VICTOR BABIN
1908–1972 — Russia

He studied with Schnabel and married Vitya Vronsky; they would form a duo-piano team which became famous. Babin composed a great deal and late in life served as president of the Cleveland Institute of Music.

CARL PHILIPP EMANUEL BACH
1714–1788 — Germany

The second son of J. S. Bach was one of the most important musicians of the eighteenth century. His clavichord performances brought tears to the eyes of the historian Dr. Burney. C. P. E. Bach wrote his famous treatise on *The True Art of Playing Keyboard Instruments* in 1757. At Czerny's first lesson with Beethoven,

the boy was told to get a copy immediately. Later in his career, C. P. E. Bach realized that the piano would soon take pride of place over the harpsichord and clavichord. His sonatas were pivotal in defining the sonata form, and Haydn and Mozart deeply appreciated his work.

JOHANN CHRISTIAN BACH
1735–1782 — Germany

Known as "the English Bach." After J. S. Bach's death in 1750, Johann Christian was brought to Berlin, where his half-brother C. P. E. was court composer to Frederick the Great. Here the young Bach fell in love with the new pianofortes that the king had bought from Gottfried Silbermann. Later, in London, it was J. C. Bach who, on June 2, 1768, for the first time played a group of piano solos at a public concert, probably pieces from his

Op. 5 sonatas. It seems fitting that the piano's debut was given by Bach's youngest son. J. C. Bach was probably the best pianist of the day in London, and his advocacy of the piano was crucial at that early moment in its history.

GINA BACHAUER
1913–1976 — Greece

Bachauer brought to the concert hall a contagious excitement. She was a blood-and-thunder Romantic who had true bravura in her veins. She loved the meaty virtuoso works—from the Rachmaninoff Third Concerto to Stravinsky's three scenes from *Petrouchka*—and used large swatches of pedal in her quest for color. Some of her Chopin playing could be slapdash and overpedaled. In Classic works such as the Beethoven Sonata Op. 2, No. 2, she was overly cautious. A disc of the Scriabin Twenty-four Preludes Op. 11 finds her at her best. Her recording of Ravel's *Gaspard de la nuit* is played to the hilt; each piece is preceded by Sir John Gielgud reciting the Aloysius Bertrand poems that inspired Ravel's rapturous triptych. The important Gina Bachauer International Competition, held in Salt Lake City, Utah, is dedicated to her memory.

AGATHE BACKER-GRØNDAHL
1847–1907 — Norway

A student of Kullak and von Bülow, from all accounts she was an extraordinary pianist. George Bernard Shaw wrote: "A great artist—a serious artist—a beautiful, incomparable unique artist! She morally regenerated us all." Backer-Grøndahl played a large repertoire and her own piano music is Romantic, imaginative, and more pianistic than Grieg's.

WILHELM BACKHAUS
1884–1969 — Germany

He studied at the Leipzig Conservatory with A. Reckendorf. In 1899 he took lessons with d'Albert, and in 1905 he won the Rubinstein Prize.

Through seventy performing seasons, Backhaus established himself as one of the century's great German pianists. He was one of the first to record, doing so as early as 1909. Success came to him easily except in the United States, where he played yearly, only to give up trying to establish an American career during the 1920s. American audiences had been conditioned to the stars of Slavic pianism, many of whom had the tendency to place virtuosity and personality before solid musicianship. Backhaus bitterly wrote, "A little show of bravura will turn many of the unthinking auditors into a roaring mob. This is, of course, very distressing to the sincere artist who strives to establish himself by his real worth."

During his almost thirty years' absence from the United States, the American public grew immeasurably in musical sophistication, and the size of the record-buying public grew enormously as well. During that period, Backhaus was given many of the chief assignments in recording the literature, and his readings of the Schumann Fantasy, the Brahms *Paganini* Variations, and history's first set of the Chopin Twenty-four Etudes, peerless in execution, were "musts" in any collection. In 1954, Backhaus returned to Carnegie Hall, where he was at last hailed as one of the greatest of musicians. His all-Beethoven recital was recorded and preserved. Records had made him famous in his absence.

Beethoven was his main musical occupation. He recorded the complete sonatas twice, the second set much the same as the first. Backhaus was not an artist to change conception or to grow musically; all was formed early on. Backhaus heard the music simply; subtlety was not his concern, and his emotional range was limited. He was best with a brusque and bumptious Beethoven. In such pages as the arioso of the Sonata Op. 110, one can wince at his insensitivity to the score's suave fluidity and depth of emotion. In general his slow movements are faster than necessary—as though the kind of serious attention they required were beyond him. There is, as well, a definite tendency in such dramatic essays as the Sonatas Opp. 13, 57, and 111 to allow the drama to degenerate into lurid melodrama. Yet Backhaus's Beethoven still retains its great appeal. His playing has a wonderfully muscular animality in which a superb life force is at work. The vitality can be irresistible. Stephen Bishop-Kovacevich goes so far as to say that "Backhaus was the only person who ever truly understood Beethoven's *Hammerklavier* Sonata. . . . It's true he may not be faithful to the text in every instance, but the wildness of what he's attempting to do is quite wonderful."

Backhaus also basked in the Brahms repertory, having been one of the earliest advocates of the two concerti. His discs of the smaller pieces exhibit a lovely sound, but a curious blandness—the interior pathos is missing.

His Mozart is too earnest; it sounds square and lacks charm. His Schumann, at its best, although dry, was convincing. In Schubert, the dryness became parched, lacking in Viennese charm; it is a heavily made Schubert.

Backhaus was a German who was fond of Chopin. His 1928 recordings of the Twenty-four Etudes are still talked about by pianists. Backhaus delighted in technical finesse, more than in Chopin's puissant poetry. He walks through Chopin's exotic garden but seldom bends to smell the intoxicating blooms.

Backhaus was one of the technical giants of his time; his mechanism was never showy but was solid as rock. His finger dexterity was especially wonderful. He had great faith in scale practice and diligently worked at it his life long. Even at eighty-five, his technical health was impressive.

PAUL BADURA-SKODA
b. 1927 — Austria

At the dawn of the LP era, Badura-Skoda, an elegant young man from Vienna, became involved in studying the Schubert sonatas and Mozart concerti. He made many recordings and became one of the most listened-to pianists of his generation. Badura-Skoda is best suited to the German classics, but occasionally leaves this territory. His Ravel disc includes a rather tepid *Gaspard de la nuit*. When playing Chopin, most especially the Twenty-four Etudes, he is temperamentally far from his turf, and the technical material is too hot to handle with comfort.

He has recorded the entire Beethoven sonata cycle with the courage of a dedicated player, not quite up to every technical challenge, but always with astute intelligence. His Schubert is proficient; at its best it possesses charm and innocence, especially in the *Moments musicaux*. His Schumann gives off some heat, but is mostly too well-behaved. His finest work comes in Mozart, which is deft, careful, and balanced, and there is a Haydn sonata disc, played on a fortepiano, that is sparkling and witty, especially in the B minor Sonata. Badura-Skoda's cadenzas to Mozart concerti are invariably pianistic, effective, and imaginative.

41

ERNÖ BALOGH
b. 1897 — Hungary

He studied with Bartók and had a career as a pianist. He made recordings and settled in the United States.

ARTUR BALSAM
b. 1906 — Poland

A distinguished pianist and teacher and an excellent accompanist, in addition to having a wide solo repertoire. He has excelled in renditions of Carl Philipp Emanuel Bach, the Hummel Concerto in A minor, and Clementi and Haydn sonatas.

DANIEL BARENBOIM
b. 1942 — Argentina

He has had one of the outstanding musical careers of our time. His piano repertoire is based on the German classics, but he plays the Ravel concerto and the Bartók concerti with style. His playing of Liszt's Wagner transcriptions, or the *Rigoletto* paraphrase, is sincere and musicianly, if unexciting, and his reading of the Sonata is beautifully planned, while the *Sonetti del Petrarca* and *Liebestraum* are lyrically ripe. His disc of the Berg Sonata captures the languid neurasthenia so distinctive of turn-of-the-century Vienna. His first set of the Beethoven Sonatas, recorded in his twenties, strives for a dignity, almost a gravity, of utterance. They are played in the German Romantic tradition of the conductors Klemperer and Furtwängler. The slow movements,

replete with expressive devices, are somewhat heavy. His more recent set of the Sonatas is more youthful, more vigorous, more dynamic, but often superficial, and his complete recording of Mendelssohn's *Songs without Words* is too often perfunctory. His *Diabelli* Variations, however, shows Barenboim at the top of his form in a splendid and explosive performance. His Schumann *Carnaval* and Brahms *Schumann* Variations are dull, but his Schubert is often golden; especially warm is the B-flat Sonata. For this listener, his piano playing is far more important and absorbing than his conducting. For a time, I thought that the piano's severe exigencies would yield to the very different musculature of conducting, but not so. As a pianist, Barenboim continues to grow and prosper.

SIMON BARÈRE
1896–1951 — Russia

He was born in Odessa, the birthplace of many musicians. Barère died on stage in Carnegie Hall during a performance of the Grieg Concerto with Ormandy and the Philadelphia Orchestra. Glazunov said, "Barère is an Anton Rubinstein in one hand and a Liszt in the other." He studied with Essipova and Blumenfeld. Barère had one of the sleekest techniques of the century, casually tossing off the most breathtaking technical feats. When the music was right for him, and when it was difficult enough, he could make the listener's hair stand on end, playing in the grand manner with color and daring. At his worst, he was enamored of his own prowess, crass, or verging on vulgarity. Barère equated tempo with speed itself; he was happy playing fast, but he was never a musical moron, he was merely born with an unusual nervous system. A true Romantic, he performed according to whim and mood. He played the grandiose side of Liszt marvelously, and his recording of the Sonata is fabulous, as are the *Funérailles,* *Rhapsodie espagnole,* and *Don Juan* Fantasy, each one tremendous in scope, color, and presentation. His recordings of the Scriabin D-sharp minor Etude and the Etude for the Left Hand by Blumenfeld are invigorating in their verve.

His most celebrated interpretation, one that has become legendary in pianistic circles, is his spine-tingling *Islamey* of Balakirev. And to hear a double-note technique that will raise eyebrows, listen to Barère's Schumann Toccata. The writer Guy Murchie, in his book *The Seven Mysteries of Life,* calculated that "Barère plays Schumann's C major Toccata with its 6,266 consecutive notes in 4.20 at the astonishing average pace of better than twenty-four notes per second, which is slightly faster than the standard speed of movie frames that flash on the screen to create a non-flickering illusion of continuous motion."

DAVID BAR-ILLAN
b. 1930 — Israel

He has a large concerto repertoire, never fearing to play the lesser-known score. He plays the Robert Starer Concerto, has recorded a joyous performance of the Moszkowski E major Concerto, performs the Prokofiev Concerto for Left Hand Alone, and scores big in the Tchaikovsky Second. His high-gear virtuosity can be exciting, as in the Liszt *Mephisto Waltz* and B minor Ballade. His tempi are often very fast, his pedaling economical. His Beethoven *Waldstein* Sonata is vital and clipped, his Weber A-flat Sonata delightful throughout. Unfortunately, he has recorded too little given the quality of his bracing, forthright talent.

KARL HEINRICH BARTH
1847–1923 — Prussia

He studied with Reinecke and Tausig and had successful tours as a pianist in Germany and England; later he became an important teacher in Berlin. He taught Arthur Rubinstein without a fee. Rubinstein wrote: "Professor Barth was a formidable personality. . . . I was terrified by him. Nobody before had inspired so much fear in me as this sixty-year-old man. . . . He wanted to improve my sight-reading. At first I was indignant, but now, after all these years, I am able to appreciate, with deep gratitude, how nobly he sacrificed so much of his own free time."

BÉLA BARTÓK
1881–1945 — Hungary

The greatest Hungarian composer of the century studied piano with Liszt's pupil István Thomán. Bartók came in second to Wilhelm Backhaus in the 1905 Anton Rubinstein Competition. He was a most original pianist whose unusual freedom of conception and metrics can be heard on his complete recordings released in Hungary in 1981. Bartók's performances of such pieces as Scarlatti sonatas, the B minor Capriccio of Brahms, and his own music show a totally different kind of artistry from the usual percussive playing that passes for "Bartók." His lavish rubato and his beautiful singing tone, coupled with an elegant virtuoso mechanism, identify him as a pianist from the late-Romantic age, whose interpretations were never bound by the printed page. It is noteworthy that Bartók, as late as the 1930s, played "historical" recitals of the piano literature in Budapest, and that throughout his career he never taught composition, only piano.

HAROLD BAUER
1873–1951 — England

He began musical life as a violinist, but the urge to be a pianist proved irresistible. At the age of twenty he officially changed instruments. By 1900, he was making an American debut with the Brahms D minor Concerto. He obviously did things his way and was always an iconoclast. "Because our ancestors," he wrote, "were brought up to study the piano a certain way . . . along . . . rigid lines does not mean there are no better, broader, less limited ways of reaching the goals we seek. The only technical study of any kind I have ever done has been that technique which has had an immediate relation to the musical message of the piece I have been studying."

Bauer was a Romantic pianist, but with few of the mannerisms of his era. He was always dignified and mellow; grand surges and cavernous sounds were not his style. But he still had the Romantic's notion that the text is not sacred. After a performance of Franck's Prelude, Chorale, and Fugue, a listener showed up backstage telling the pianist, "I am glad to see that you play all the notes in that passage in the bass. So many pianists blur them." Bauer replied, "My dear sir, I didn't play them at all. I purposely leave them out. The passage sounds better that way."

In 1939, while still in fine technical fettle, Bauer recorded some small pieces, as well as one of his specialties, the Brahms F minor Sonata. In it, Bauer shows himself a stalwart and impressive molder of form, kindled by a warm and mature passion. His renderings of sonatas by Scarlatti, and Handel's *Harmonious Blacksmith,* are merely pretty; but in Chopin's Berceuse the pianist refuses to coo and swoon, and in Debussy's *Rêverie* one still hears the lustrous tone that was much remarked upon and compared to Paderewski's.

Bauer gave many premieres, including Debussy's *Children's Corner* Suite, and Ravel

dedicated his impressionist miracle, *Ondine,* to him. His many provocative but unscholarly editions of Schumann are now controversial and are seldom used today.

ELENA BECKMAN-SCHERBINA
1881–1951 — Russia

She studied with Igumnov and was a respected pianist who recorded music by Anton Rubinstein, Rachmaninoff, and Scriabin. She knew Scriabin and frequently played his own music for him.

LUDWIG VAN BEETHOVEN
1770–1827 — Germany

Beethoven spent his first twenty-two years in his birthplace, Bonn, a town of fewer than ten thousand, yet with a rich musical and literary life. Beethoven's father was a minor singer at court, and had an alcohol problem; his mother was sensitive, shy, and quiet. Beethoven's father tried to exploit the boy's talent, hoping to produce a second Mozart. Although Beethoven was a prodigy, his development was too slow to bring in the hoped-for financial results. But his father kept the young boy practicing, "stupendously," as Beethoven later put it, mostly past midnight after his father woke him from a deep sleep. All was not bleak, however, and the boy was fortunate enough to come under the tutelage of an excellent and sensitive musician, Christian Gottlob Neefe, who instructed him in several instruments. The young Beethoven soon joined the court orchestra and was appointed court organist, his first paying job. Equally important, Neefe nurtured him on Bach's

Well-Tempered Clavier, which he supposedly played from memory by the age of twelve. Only the most cultivated connoisseurs even knew, much less cared for, the "old Bach's" masterpiece. Actually, Beethoven had to learn it from a copy of the manuscript, since *The Well-Tempered Clavier* was not published until 1801.

The first important mention of Beethoven's musical gifts appeared in a magazine of the time: "Louis van Beethoven, a child of eleven, plays the clavier very skillfully, and with power, reads at sight very well, and . . . he plays chiefly *The Well-Tempered Clavier* of Sebastian Bach. . . . Whoever knows this collection of preludes and fugues in all the keys—which might almost be called the non plus ultra of our art—will know what this means. Herr Neefe is now training him in composition. . . . If he goes on as he has begun, he will certainly become a second Mozart." In the next few years, Beethoven composed a great deal. By 1786, the sixteen-year-old musician was traveling to Vienna, where he played for the thirty-year-old Mozart, whom he revered above all others. Mozart was impressed, telling friends, "Keep your eyes on him; some day he will make a noise in the world."

Beethoven's piano playing attracted considerable attention during his late teen years. Carl Junker, a Bonn musician, tells us that "I have heard the abbé Vogler on the pianoforte by the hour and never failed to wonder at his astonishing execution; but Beethoven, in addition to the execution, has greater clearness and weight of ideas and more expression. In short, he is more for the heart."

But Bonn was too small for Beethoven's talents and, in 1792, he moved to Vienna, where he lived the rest of his life. It was as a pianist that Beethoven gained admittance to the great houses of Vienna's cultured and musically proficient aristocracy. And there had never been a pianist with such power and energy, although many of his compositions seemed wild to his contemporaries. The pia-

nist Johann Tomáschek heard him in Prague in 1798, calling him "the giant among pianoforte players. . . . He played his C major Concerto (No. 1), the Adagio and Rondo grazioso from the Sonata in A, Op. 2, No. 2, and extemporized on a theme from Mozart's *Clemenza di Tito.* His grand style of playing, and especially his bold improvisation, had an extraordinary effect upon me. I felt so shaken that for several days I could not bring myself to touch the piano."

Beethoven lived during the final years of public improvisation. All pianists were expected to be able to improvise, and for the public it was often the most enjoyable part of the concert. His student Ferdinand Ries wrote of his extempore playing that "no artist that I ever heard came at all near the heights which Beethoven attained—the wealth of ideas which forced themselves on him, the caprices to which he surrendered himself, the variety of treatment, the difficulties, were inexhaustible." But Czerny found that "extraordinary as his extempore playing was, it was less successful in the performance of printed compositions; for, since he never took the time or had the patience to practice anything, his success depended mostly on chance and mood. . . . But when Beethoven was in practice, no one equalled him, not even Hummel, in rapidity of scale passages, trills, leaps, etc." In extempore playing, he had only two rivals, Hummel and Joseph Wölfl. Beethoven had previously demolished a number of pianists who had come through Vienna. Wölfl, however, several years younger than Beethoven, was a worthy opponent, of whom Beethoven's pupil Ignaz von Seyfried wrote, "Nature had been particularly kind in bestowing upon him a gigantic hand which could span a tenth [obviously a rarity then] as easily as other hands compass an octave, and permitted him to play double-notes . . . with the rapidity of lightning. . . . The combats of the two athletes not infrequently offered an indescribable artistic treat to the numerous and thoroughly select gathering. . . . In his improvisations Beethoven was transported above all earthly things—his spirit had burst all restraining bonds . . . triumphing over transitory terrestrial sufferings."

Wölfl himself was overwhelmed by Beethoven and later dedicated a sonata to him. This meeting took place around 1799, the period of the *Pathétique* Sonata. Beethoven's playing was now becoming distinct from the Classic poise of the Mozart school. During his so-called middle period, he continued to perform; his playing was often sloppy, but possessed a revolutionary and powerful emotionality never before dreamed of in piano playing. Beethoven was already asking Viennese piano makers for sturdier instruments that would withstand his force. He was delighted with a new Erard sent by the firm as a gift in 1803. Not everyone was impressed with his playing, however. Cherubini called it "rough," and Clementi felt it lacked polish, but admitted "it was always full of spirit."

During the first decade of the nineteenth century, with his hearing deserting him, Beethoven still continued to perform in public. He premiered all of his piano concerti, except for No. 5. In 1808 he played the first performance of his Fourth Concerto at a concert that also included first performances of the Fifth and Sixth Symphonies and the Choral Fantasy, as well as movements from his C major Mass and the concert aria "Ah! perfido." (Has there ever been such a concert since?) "He played with astounding cleverness and in the fastest possible tempi," J. F. Reichardt wrote. "The Adagio, a masterly movement of beautifully developed song, he sang on his instrument with a profound melancholy that thrilled me."

During the following years, Beethoven's depression deepened as his hearing loss grew, making his playing often incoherent. In 1815 the celebrated violinist Ludwig Spohr heard him: "Of the former so admired excellence of the virtuoso scarcely anything was left in consequence of his deafness. In forte passages, the poor deaf man hammered in such a way that entire groups of notes were inaudible. . . . I felt moved with the deepest sorrow at such a destiny. . . . Beethoven's almost continual melancholy was no longer a riddle to me now."

Around 1817, the Broadwood piano makers of London had sent Beethoven their newest instrument. It was the most powerful and loudest piano built at the time. Beethoven, in his feeble attempt to hear the sounds in his mind, played on it with a new relish, battering it out of shape. In thanking the Broadwood firm, he wrote: "I shall regard it as an altar upon which I shall place the most beautiful offerings of my spirit to the divine Apollo." Indeed, during this period, he worked on his late sonatas with a new enthusiasm, although he was forever complaining that the piano as an instrument was now inadequate for him. Beethoven had grown completely inward, and his music became an idealization as no other composer's had ever been.

If he was not pleased at being harnessed to the pianos of his day, still one wonders if the "modern" pianos of Bechstein, Steinway, Bösendorfer, Blüthner, and Erard, developed after 1850, would have come closer to his tonal dreams. Today, the idea of obsolescence in musical instruments is fast vanishing. The Viennese Classical grand piano was a perfect instrument in itself, quite different from the modern concert grand. It was the diaphanous elasticity of these pianos that had aroused the ears of Haydn, Mozart, Hummel, Czerny, Beethoven, and Schubert. They loved the instruments for their transparency, the crisp and grainy sounds they were capable of achieving. In reality the sound of the harpsichords of their youth lingered in their sonorous imaginations. The opulent-sounding modern grand is a far more homogenized instrument than perhaps Beethoven would have wanted.

Wilfrid Mellers argues in *Beethoven and the Voice of God:*

Nowadays Beethoven's piano music is usually played on large concert grands, and no one feels this needs justification, since the modern piano is regarded as the fulfillment of Beethoven's pianistic aspirations. There is a sense in which it is true that the *Hammerklavier* Sonata encouraged the development of an instrument capable of supporting its level of dynamic intensity; one cannot on the other hand assume that the instrument appropriate to mature Liszt and later nineteenth-century composers is the instrument Beethoven envisaged, and there is some reason to think that the fortepianos of Beethoven's day, however inadequate to the idealities of sound in Beethoven's head, approximate to those idealities more closely than do modern instruments.

Listening to or playing Beethoven on a fine fortepiano may well be an ear-opening experience, one that might alter a musician's way of thinking about Beethoven. Mellers tells of hearing Paul Badura-Skoda play the *Moonlight* Sonata on an 1815 Broadwood: "The Presto finale provides, on the Broadwood, the biggest surprise, for it sounds far more tempestuously terrifying than on any modern instrument, even though its dynamic level may be lower." Of a performance of the *Appassionata* Sonata on a Viennese Graf piano, Mellers discloses: "Only after I had heard this recording did I realize how startling to contemporary audiences the work must have been. Moreover, on this instrument it startles us today, as though we were hearing it for the first time: the deep arpeggios are more cavernous, the hammer-beats more minatory, the thickly syncopated chords more shattering, the arpeggios more lacerating, than on a modern grand, the big rich tone of which rounds off the corners, sacrificing bite and edge to volume."

If Mozart was practically lost to the nineteenth century, Beethoven was its chief obsession. Two early advocates, Czerny and Moscheles, mastered his Op. 13, the *Sonate pathétique,* by their tenth year. As interest in personal interpretation in performance grew, Beethoven's music became the backbone of the repertoire. The great interpreters of his piano sonatas would be Mendelssohn, Liszt, Clara Schumann, Anton Rubinstein, von Bülow, Sir Charles Hallé, Arabella Godard, d'Albert, Busoni, and, finally, Schnabel, who, in the 1930s, furthered the worldwide dissemination of the sonatas with his recordings of the complete set. This process of dissemination took roughly one hundred years after Beethoven's death to accomplish. "The essence of Beethoven," writes Louis Kentner, "perhaps the greatest artist ever produced by civilization, lies distilled in the piano sonatas."

The sonatas, variations, and concerti form one of the great creative documents of the ages; their humanity and breadth are perpetual challenges for the creative listener as well as the player. That Beethoven put at the command of one individual—the pianist—the greatest that music can offer is a blessing that has been appreciated by all serious pianists in every generation since.

ANNA CAROLINE DE BELLEVILLE-OURY
1808–1880 — Germany

She studied with Czerny for four years and toured Europe and Russia, where she was compared to Clara Wieck. She composed 180 pieces.

SIR WILLIAM STERNDALE BENNETT
1816–1875 — England

Both Mendelssohn and Schumann admired Bennett, who was the most honored English pianist and composer of the mid-nineteenth 47 century. His playing was considered remarkable, and his piano music is beautifully crafted and, although influenced by Mendelssohn, it has its own inherent value. His Third Piano Sonata, Op. 46, *The Maid of Orleans,* was the most respected English sonata of its period. His best music came early as a result of his Leipzig exposure to Mendelssohn and Schumann. Later, as H. C. Colles wrote, "his sensitiveness became fastidiousness and a delicate genius contracted into a narrow talent."

LUDWIG BERGER
1777–1839 — Germany

A pupil of Clementi, Berger was a good pianist and a teacher of renown. His students included Felix and Fanny Mendelssohn, Henselt, and Heinrich Dorn. He composed a large quantity of music; a set of twenty-seven etudes has exceptional merit. Frederick Marvin has recorded Berger's half-hour Grand Sonata, Op. 7, from 1815, a work exhibiting the *Sturm und Drang* of the period.

OSCAR BERINGER
1844–1922 — England

He studied under Moscheles and Tausig. In 1882 he gave the first English performance of the Brahms Second Piano Concerto, and in 1895, became professor at the Royal Academy of Music in London.

LAZAR BERMAN
b. 1930 — USSR

He was a pupil of Goldenweiser and won prizes in several competitions. In 1976, when the craze for Russian performers in the United States was at its peak, Berman, a spiritual descendant of Anton Rubinstein, who created the Russian mystique, made his American debut. Berman had become known through his recordings of the Liszt *Transcendental Etudes*—thrilling performances filled with a highly charged Romanticism. Indeed, never had the *Etudes* been played with such aplomb. Unfortunately, Berman's public performances have been disappointing, often wildly inconsistent; sometimes his playing is just shoddy, at other times he sounds like an automaton. Listening to a Prokofiev Eighth Sonata was an ordeal. But as more recordings were released, I realized that this artist does his best work before the microphones, though he never equaled those early recordings of the *Transcendental Etudes*, Rachmaninoff's complete *Moments musicaux,* or Scriabin's Fantasy. Berman has made records of the Rachmaninoff Third Concerto, Liszt's *Years of Pilgrimage,* and even Clementi's B minor Sonata, which offer playing of musical value, but without that added richness and excitement which were so apparent on the recordings early in his career.

LEONARD BERNSTEIN
b. 1918 — United States

The celebrated conductor-composer is also an expert and dynamic pianist in a rather wide repertory. He studied piano with Helen Coates, Heinrich Gebhard, and Isabelle Vengerova. His recording of the Copland Sonata is exhilarating but subtle. His rendering of the Gershwin *Rhapsody in Blue* has an irresistible tang, played with swing, heart, and abandon; and he was born to play the Shostakovich Concerto No. 2. Bernstein has also made excellent recordings of Mozart's Fifteenth Concerto and the Ravel concerto.

Bernstein's Symphony No. 2 for Piano and Orchestra, *The Age of Anxiety,* is an extraordinary synthesis of jazz and the symphonic form.

MICHEL BÉROFF
b. 1950 — France

A pianist who plays with skill and refinement. The French literature suits him best and his Debussy performances, especially the Preludes and Etudes, are a pleasure to hear. He has recorded with great care Messiaen's monumental *Vingt Regards sur l'Enfant Jésus*.

HENRI BERTINI
1798–1876 — England

Considered a superb pianist, he began touring at the age of twelve, and he later settled in Paris. He is best known for his Piano Studies.

MARIE BIGOT
1786–1820 — Germany

A remarkable pianist whom both Haydn and Beethoven respected. Beethoven was believed to have said to her, "That is not exactly the reading I should have given, but go on. If it is not quite myself, it is something better." She reputedly played the *Appassionata* at sight from the manuscript.

MALCOLM BILSON
b. 1935 — United States

A pianist and teacher who, in recent years, has become one of the best-known advocates of the fortepiano. He has given successful and enlightening classes on the early piano, and his playing of Mozart concerti and sonatas, as well as of some Haydn and Beethoven sonatas, reveals a sensitive musician who is technically adroit and who is not only a scholar but a passionate performer, with fire and a command of style and form.

IDIL BIRET
b. 1941 — Turkey

She is a remarkable virtuoso who plays a wide variety of often-neglected music. Her recording of Liszt's transcription of the Berlioz *Symphonie fantastique* is valuable and also fun to hear, while her Ravel *Gaspard de la nuit* and the Alban Berg Sonata display an unusual musical mind.

HANS BISCHOFF
1852–1889 — Germany

Studied with Theodor Kullak. He was a pianist, teacher, and scholar of repute. His Bach editions are still used frequently.

STEPHEN BISHOP-KOVACEVICH
b. 1940 — United States

A student of Myra Hess. Beethoven has been Bishop-Kovacevich's abiding interest. His readings are serious in tone, and he takes great care in setting up the building blocks in a large musical structure. His technique is solid, and he has an incisive rhythmic sense. In such epics as the *Diabelli* Variations, his monochromatic delivery and crisp tone give the music an unusual solemnity. He is not frightened of explosive sforzandos and his crescendi are tightly drawn. He is especially excellent in the Sonata Op. 101, where he brings out the exultant joy in the fugue.

Bishop-Kovacevich has also issued fine Bartók and Brahms performances, and his one recording of Chopin is largely convincing.

MARIE LEOPOLDINE BLAHETKA
1811–1887 — Germany

A well-known pianist and a composer who studied with Moscheles and Kalkbrenner. Her *Konzertstück* for Piano and Orchestra, Op. 25, was her best-known composition.

ÉMILE BLANCHET
1872–1943 — Switzerland

He studied with Busoni. An excellent pianist and a composer of very attractive piano music which is unfortunately never performed.

JOSEPH BLOCH
b. 1917 — United States

A pupil of Rudolph Ganz and Olga Samaroff, he made a New York debut at Town Hall in 1950, and has since had a distinguished career, playing on every continent. Bloch has been in the forefront of the Alkan revival, and wrote a monograph on the French composer. He has recorded and performed a variety of music. Virgil Thomson noted that Bloch "plays with grace and distinction." He was an honored member of the Juilliard faculty from 1948 to 1983.

MICHEL BLOCK
b. 1937 — Belgium

A student of Beveridge Webster at Juilliard, he received a special prize at the 1960 Chopin Competition in Warsaw. He is a pianist of considerable interest, with a large repertoire. His recordings include the *Iberia* of Albéniz. Block teaches at Indiana University.

FANNIE BLOOMFIELD ZEISLER
1863–1927 — Austria

Known as the Sarah Bernhardt of the piano, she was Leschetizky's most famous female pupil, and one of the most popular and respected musicians of her day. She played a Golden Jubilee concert in 1925. Unfortunately, she left no records to document her art, which was considered serious and technically accomplished.

FELIX BLUMENFELD
1863–1931 — Russia

A student of Anton Rubinstein, Blumenfeld was an able musician. His piano music is eminently playable; a set of Twenty-four Preludes, Op. 17, and a Sonata-Fantasy, Op. 64, are very interesting. He was the uncle of the teacher Heinrich Neuhaus and taught him, as well as Simon Barère, Maria Grinberg, and Vladimir Horowitz, who reveres his memory.

FELICJA BLUMENTAL
b. 1918 — Poland

She studied at the Warsaw Conservatory. During World War II, she went to Brazil, where she continued her career.

Villa-Lobos dedicated his Fifth Concerto to her, and she gave its world premiere. She has recorded many albums, notably of neglected works, including concertos by Ries, Clementi, and Albéniz; Szymanowski's *Symphonie concertante,* Op. 60; and many more.

JAKOB BLUMENTHAL
1829–1908 — Germany

He studied with Herz at the Paris Conservatoire and earlier with Bocklet in Vienna. After the revolution of 1848, he took refuge in England; he was one of the most popular musicians in London, becoming pianist to Queen Victoria. His piano music and songs were once well known.

CARL MARIA VON BOCKLET
1801–1881 — Czechoslovakia

A pianist who made a reputation as both performer and teacher. Beethoven had a high regard for him, and he knew Schubert personally; he was the first to bring Schubert's piano music to the public.

JORGE BOLET
b. 1914 — Cuba

He attended the Curtis Institute and studied with David Saperton and Abram Chasins. In 1937 he won the Naumburg Award.

Bolet is a pianist's pianist in the tradition of Godowsky, Hofmann, and Saperton; with Bolet, finesse and purity are the order of the evening. Each note must be in place; no effort is too insignificant. He spins iridescent webs of pianistic gold, cadenzas in colored sprays alight from the keyboard. His passagework is matched and evenly threaded. His digital skills are prodigious and he is capable of great tonal refinements. In concert he loves to charm audiences with his wonderful playing of fluff, such as the Weber-Godowsky *Invitation to the Dance.* Fluff it may be, but more dangerous for the pianist than a tightrope act. And how seriously he plays these frivolous items. He loves Godowsky, having played for him as a youngster, when he was brought to him by his teacher, Saperton.

A Bolet recital tells us that the piano has a luxuriant literature, full of challenge, adventure, amusements, and beauty for those willing to extend themselves without snobbery. Bolet can deliver all-"Ballade" programs—including Grieg's masterpiece, the Ballade in G minor, played with poignancy and playfulness. He plays transcriptions of all types, such as Wagner's *Tannhäuser* Overture in Liszt's amazing reduction. Here is the piano in full regalia, appearing to accomplish orchestral miracles.

Bolet is often thought of as a Liszt pianist, and indeed he is at his most exciting with Liszt. His Liszt Sonata is serious and spacious. He's willing to take chances in public: he rages in the *Don Juan* Fantasy and in the *Dante Sonata* his thunder is unequaled, and when he is really in the mood (for Bolet can be sadly out of the mood), he can truly be infernal. His sonority is suffocating. He plays an enormous amount of Liszt, from the concerti (his recordings are flabby) to the etudes, the Ballade in B minor, the Twelfth Hungarian Rhapsody, many transcriptions, and the Six *Consolations,* where he delivers the last word in ultra-pianissimos. At times he becomes so caught up in his tinting that the playing becomes more prissy than delectable.

He is not at home in the formal gardens of Mozart, Haydn, or Beethoven. He glides through them with a smoothness or a ponderousness that misses all points of tension. He is better equipped for a little Schumann, a little Mendelssohn, and some Chopin, though the last often sounds superficial. His best Chopin playing remains the Twenty-four Preludes. In Brahms he can be clumsy and in Reger's *Telemann* Variations he is tedious. He is always best when resurrecting some Romantic concerto, such as the Joseph Marx, or the Sgambati Concerto (which he has recorded). During his prime, Bolet, on the platform, was the very picture of power, but he has never quite managed to break through the barrier of recording. His records are always disappointing to one who has heard him on stage in the heat of battle. In the last several years a desire to be profound and weighty has marred many of these recordings, which as a result lack the stylishness of his earlier years, when his music-making had more happiness, naturalness, and flair. His recent recordings of the Tchaikovsky First and Rachmaninoff Second Concertos are tired and humdrum throughout, and the same may be said of much recent Liszt playing, especially his latest recording of the *Transcendental Etudes,* which are earthbound.

JOÃO DOMINGOS BOMTEMPO
1775–1842 — Portugal

The first Portuguese pianist of note; in 1833 he headed the Lisbon Conservatory.

ANTHONY DI BONAVENTURA
b. 1930 — United States

A student of Isabelle Vengerova at the Curtis Institute. He was a soloist with the New York Philharmonic at the age of thirteen.

He commissioned works from Nono, Ligeti, Ginastera, Persichetti, and others. His recordings of Scarlatti sonatas and Debussy etudes are the products of a refined and sensitive musical mind.

SERGEI BORTKIEWICZ
1877–1952 — Russia

A student of Alfred Reisenauer, he played and taught throughout Europe. His etudes and four piano concerti are masterpieces of slick pianism in an idiom laced with Russian Orientalism.

LEONARD BORWICK
1868–1925 — England

A pupil of Clara Schumann, he became a well-known pianist, playing throughout Europe, America, and Australia. He was an early advocate of Debussy and Ravel, and played the entire solo music of Brahms in 1923.

YURI BOUKOFF
b. 1923 — Bulgaria

Studied with Yves Nat and Marguerite Long in Paris. He has had many tours and recorded the nine Prokofiev sonatas.

YORK BOWEN
1884–1961 — England

He studied with Tobias Matthay. Bowen had a career as both pianist and composer. His piano music shows a gift for keyboard writing. It is, however, never performed. He was called the English Rachmaninoff.

GEORGE BOYLE
1886–1948 — Australia

He trained with Busoni. Boyle was considered a powerful pianist. His Piano Concerto in D minor deserves to be revived. He composed a body of brilliant piano music.

JOHANNES BRAHMS
1833–1897 — Germany

The great master from Hamburg was deeply grounded in piano technique by Eduard Marxsen. He made his debut in 1847. Although early on he gave up public performance of music other than his own, in his younger days he played a massive literature including the Beethoven *Eroica* and *Diabelli* Variations, Schumann sonatas and the Fantasy, and the Chromatic Fantasy and Fugue of Bach. Brahms also premiered his own D minor and B-flat major Concerti.

He had a fascination with piano technique and in the Variations on a Theme by Paganini, Op. 35, he produced one of the most subtly difficult works in the literature. He left the first performance of these fiendish "etudes" to Tausig. Ever since, they have been to pianists a touchstone of virtuosity. Later in his career, Brahms composed a volume of technical studies, which are not for performance, but are immensely valuable as a key to his unusual pianism.

ALEXANDER BRAILOWSKY
1896–1976 — Russia

He studied with Sauer and Leschetizky and had a long, successful, and even glamorous career. He played heroic programs, and was the first to offer the complete Chopin piano music in public, in Paris in 1924; he later repeated the cycle in other locales. Brailowsky was listened to by a huge public and made his career in an age of giants—such as Cortot, Rachmaninoff, Hofmann, Horowitz, and Rubinstein. He did this with far fewer natural endowments than his colleagues. At his worst, he could be square and stiff, percussive in tone, and lacking in either a large dynamic range or a true virtuoso mechanism. He was, of course, a thorough professional, and he always got through his task. Yet even when he fell into a rut, his playing had a Romantic allure. Everything was simplified; not one of

Brailowsky's interpretations had real imagination, yet there was a vigor and an absolute love for his instrument. He sold a lot of records during his career. The 78s of the 1930s and 1940s were more stylish than the later LPs. His discs prove that an indefinable alchemy may take place between performer and audience which is no barometer for the quality of the artist's recorded music.

LOUIS BRASSIN
1840–1884 — Germany

An important teacher and pianist. He studied with Moscheles and taught Safonov, Sapellnikov, and Arthur de Greef. He wrote many piano pieces, and his transcription of Wagner's Magic Fire Music was often attempted.

ALFRED BRENDEL
b. 1931 — Czechoslovakia

He studied with local teachers and in 1949 he received a fourth prize at the Busoni Competition in Bolzano, Italy. During the 1950s he made many recordings, including the first complete set of the Beethoven piano music. For this effort he was given the Grand Prix du Disque. His book *Musical Thoughts and Afterthoughts* appeared in 1976. Brendel has played the complete cycle of Beethoven sonatas in many of the world's major capitals, and in 1983 he was the first pianist since Schnabel to play all thirty-two at Carnegie Hall.

These recitals were the best Beethoven playing I have heard from him—intense and often moving; especially good were the earlier sonatas. The world now sees Brendel as one of its supreme Beethoven players. He has recorded the Sonatas twice; while both versions have points of interest, they are different in many respects. In the early set, there is a vital flow and an unselfconsciousness that is absent from much of the sonically superior second version. The lightness and lyrical gracefulness of the first edition give way to some unaccountably awkward readings later on. Indeed, this early set contains some of the finest Beethoven ever recorded. The earlier Brendel Beethoven also had a sense of adventure. Nobody has ever played with more charm the marvelous opening of the B-flat Sonata Op. 22. In it he captures the upward movement exquisitely; the same detail in the later version falls flat. Such points of comparison could be made throughout the Sonatas.

Yet if some naturalness is missing from the second recording, other qualities have deepened. There is more grit in the earlier *Appassionata,* for example, but his growing concern for line over color makes his late Beethoven more cerebral, less brooding. For this listener, his performances of the late Sonatas are schoolmasterish—stiff, clipped, and well-drilled. He spells out each phrase as if delivering a lecture. I find a kind of heart-chilling smugness in these late Sonatas. Of the last five, he is most successful in the Op. 110, where the fugue flows smoothly. His Op. 111 is just too facile, and Op. 101 sounds academic and clumsy. His best readings are the Op. 2, No. 1; Op. 10, No. 2, in a delightful and humorous performance; and a well-thought-out Op. 7, with a beautiful slow movement. His *Moonlight* lacks sensuous appeal, but his *Waldstein* has a wonderful sense of space; his Op. 31, No. 1 has comic appeal. There are a fine Opp. 78 and 79, Opp. 81a and 90.

His Beethoven Concerti, as good as they are, achieve little that is new. No. 4 lacks a necessary mystery; No. 5—the *Emperor*—lacks dramatic power. But his performances are well structured. I especially like Brendel's playing of some of the variations and small pieces. He is relaxed and takes a good deal of rhythmic leeway. But for this listener, his best Beethoven is his live recording of the *Diabelli* Variations. Here his fingers and heart are joined in a mighty penetration of Beethoven's world.

Brendel's Mozart is not nearly as interesting as his Beethoven. In the solo sonatas, he sounds airless and charmless. In his many concerto recordings, the playing is academic and much too dry; the magical melodies are square-cut and understated. In Haydn sonatas, however, Brendel plays with gusto, and he understands Haydn's kind of humor, but unfortunately his tone is often ugly.

Only recently has Brendel decided to accommodate Bach to the modern piano, where his good sense of line brings out the clarity and precision of each voice. How different are his conclusions on the Bach Chromatic Fantasy and Fugue from Edwin Fischer's, with his propulsive Romanticism. (Brendel took some master classes from Fischer.)

It has been said that Brendel has become Schnabel's successor in Schubert, but the two have little in common. Schnabel's Schubert was vocal; Brendel's is far more symphonic, less passionate, and the sound far less beautiful. Brendel's Schubert paints no rustic landscape. It is a large, tight, sometimes militant Schubert. Many "pretty" passages are weeded out, and Brendel, intent on clarifying everything he possibly can, leaves little to suggestiveness.

Brendel's discography is large and filled with performances of Schumann and Brahms, which are all good, but which miss the deepest fire and poetry. His Brahms concerti are too straight and bony. His Schumann never reaches the heights. He is too cautious, too serious.

In his youth, he recorded such works as Balakirev's *Islamey* and Stravinsky's *Petrouchka,* and some Chopin. He has been right to disregard this literature. Chopin is not suited to his temperament, and I cannot imagine him being convincing in a nocturne. The Romantic composer most suited to Brendel is Liszt, a composer he adores and promotes constantly. Brendel is not entirely born for this music because his technique is not quite large enough, not of the high virtuosity of an Argerich or Pollini. It is solid and highly functional, but it lacks, sadly, a real pianistic flexibility. Brendel can play loudly, but he is not a "big" pianist; moreover, he is always on guard against any extreme in his playing. However, he is now striving for the grand sweep and is trying with all his heart and might to triumphantly "throw off" all restraint. This was sometimes painfully apparent in his recitals of Liszt's *Years of Pilgrimage,* where I thought he manufactured an overblown style with an ugliness of tone and a lack of lyric freedom. The whole concert was a torture full of hand flaying, gesticulating, and facial grimaces, showing a desperate attempt to release himself from the confines of his highly intellectual frame.

Brendel is commendably trying to merge his intellectual and theoretical bent with a more convincing emotionalization of the music. He wrote, "Feeling is the alpha and the omega of the musician, the point where music comes from and the point to which it has to return." This feeling, the swell of human emotion, has not been fully realized in his art. The analytic has clogged him up, and it is now at odds with his ever more urgent desire to simply let the music speak. It is in Liszt's music that he is making his main attempts at liberation, and his newest recordings give many signs of a great pianist. In his recording of later Liszt, he expresses the true elegiac sorrow of these sketches. In many other pieces, including the Sonata, the Fantasy and Fugue on the Name *B-A-C-H,* the *Legends,* and the *Bénédiction de Dieu dans la solitude,* there is Liszt playing of some impact.

Brendel is a complicated and important musician, and audiences respond to his playing. He is an artist of the highest motivation who is deeply committed to the piano and its literature.

YEFIM BRONFMAN
b. 1958 — USSR

In 1973 he emigrated to Israel, where he studied with Arie Vardi at the Rubin Academy in Tel Aviv. Later, at the Curtis Institute, he worked with Rudolf Serkin. In 1982, Bronfman made a successful New York debut, and he has since had a worldwide career. He is a pianist of taste and power who is comfortable in many styles from Mozart to Prokofiev.

JOHN BROWNING
b. 1932 — United States

A student of Rosina Lhévinne at the Juilliard School. A winner of the Leventritt and other competitions, Browning is a perfect example of the eclectic American pianist, involved with many styles, brilliantly equipped both technically and intellectually. Indeed, few equal his level of preparation for a performance. Everything has been passed under the lens of a microscope. Browning knows exactly what he wants to do with every note. Occasionally a Mozart Sonata can be sterile.

He is gloriously suited to Ravel. Stravinsky called Ravel a Swiss clockmaker, and Browning loves each fine jewel; the Ravelian artifice glitters in his hands. The Left Hand Concerto soars, his *Tombeau de Couperin* is unrivaled, its Toccata golden and perfectly poised, the rhythmic formations breathtaking.

Browning's Prokofiev Concerti are deservedly celebrated, and few can equal him in the Third Concerto, which has always been one of his best stage works. He has recorded a very fine Barber Sonata, and his disc of the Barber Concerto with Szell is a collaboration whose quality surpasses the work's actual value. Of other twentieth-century repertoire, there is a remarkable set of twenty-four neo-Romantic preludes by Richard Cumming which are impeccably played. Browning's Chopin Etudes are cold, but in his technical treatment few could match him.

In Schumann, he is rather prosaic. His early recording of the Beethoven *Diabelli* Variations is masterful; a truly epic conception. Lately he has turned to Liszt with a new respect and understanding. His playing of the Sonata is pianistic and coolly patrician. His Rachmaninoff, too, glitters with cold intensity, and his recording of the Second Sonata is calculated to its boiling point. Browning is first and always a superb craftsman, with an unusual fastidiousness, musically and technically, and there is no such thing as a messy Browning concert. Indeed, Browning is always an amazing marksman who considers wrong notes to be practically inadmissible if not sinful.

LEONID BRUMBERG
b. 1925 — USSR

A student of Heinrich Neuhaus. He is a respected pianist and has recorded Romantic repertoire. He left the Soviet Union in 1981, and teaches at the Vienna Conservatory.

HANS VON BÜLOW
1830–1894 — Germany

He showed no sign of musical talent or interest until his ninth year. He was found to have an unusually fine ear, and was put under the direction of Friedrich Wieck, who was renowned for his teaching of his daughter Clara (Schumann). He later worked under Plaidy, an effective technique builder. To please his parents, he entered the University of Leipzig in 1848 to pursue a law career. But his attraction to music was too strong, and the newest German compositions fired him with the need to be part of that exciting moment in music history. After Liszt's celebrated first performances of Wagner's *Lohengrin* at Weimar, von Bülow left law for good. The decisive influence of his life was knowing and studying with Liszt, who also taught him the rudiments of conducting. He became, with Tausig, the favorite pupil of Liszt's Weimar period (1848–60). Liszt loved him and deeply admired his musical gifts. He said, "He has the most intimate insight into the music, as well as the nobility and perfection of beautiful style."

Liszt, who officially retired from the piano after 1847, gave von Bülow the honor of playing the world premiere of his Sonata in B minor in Berlin in 1857. (During that concert von Bülow also inaugurated the Bechstein concert grand for public performance.) It was also at that time that von Bülow married Liszt's daughter Cosima. Their marriage dissolved in 1869, when she left him for Wagner. Von Bülow continued to be a passionate Wagnerite, however, and conducted the world premiere of *Tristan und Isolde* at Munich in 1869. He now indefatigably pursued concertizing, becoming the foremost German pianist of his time (Tausig died in 1871).

In 1875 the Chickering piano firm brought him to the United States, in emulation of Anton Rubinstein's 1872 tour for the Steinway piano. He played no fewer than 139 concerts in the New World, and gave the world premiere of Tchaikovsky's B-flat minor Concerto in Boston. (The score is dedicated to Bülow.) It was an instant success there, and even more so when he performed it under Leopold Damrosch several weeks later in New York.

His career took place during the final stages of development of the piano-building art. Piano makers were in great competition with each other, and these firms did all they could to attract the best artists to their instruments. During Liszt's twelve years of whirlwind touring, he often played on pianos that no first-rate pianist today would deign to touch. But during the second half of the century, with an enormous increase in the public's musical education and the growing importance of musical interpretation, the piano's quality became of paramount concern to a pianist. Von Bülow was, to the public, the interpretive concert pianist *par excellence*. In his letters to Carl Bechstein he constantly tells the manufacturer what an artist needs from an instrument. He called Bechstein the "piano pope" but could admonish him on the quality of his instruments. In 1866 he wrote to him, of a Bechstein, that "I endured tortures at the concert through its inelastic touch and its bad repetition. In short, I had to make super-human efforts." Bechstein had a preference for softer-sounding instruments, and Bülow says, "You are growing very selfish—in making it sound soft and more pleasing to the audience you allow the individuality of the music and the player to go by the board. I was obliged suddenly to reject the interpretation of years and conform to the mood of the pianoforte action. Having made oneself master of the composition, one is to become the slave of the instrument! Much obliged!"

The last remark sums up the vexation of countless fine pianists during performance. Von Bülow was delighted with the American Chickerings put at his disposal during his American concerts, and rapturously wrote to his colleague Karl Klindworth, "I notice the most extraordinary transformation in myself. Whereas, before, I frequently played like a pig, I now occasionally play like a god. Chickering's gorgeous pianofortes—undeniably the best in both worlds—have made me into a first-rate pianist. Certainly I practice as I never did before."

Von Bülow's temperament was viewed as the opposite of Anton Rubinstein's animal magnetism. His interpretations were etched with a cold, scholarly intellect. He was often criticized for a lack of spontaneity and for being too analytic. In 1887 the composer Hugo Wolf wrote a scathing review, "Bülow—as Autopsist." Bülow was famous for his Beethoven and played all of the piano works from memory. But, Wolf objected,

unfortunately, he is on a rather strained footing with Beethoven. . . . Above all, he stands in awe of the living Beethoven. And so to get at him, he simply strikes him dead. . . . The corpse is carefully dissected, the organisms traced in their subtlest ramifications, the intestines examined with the zeal of a haruspex—the course in anatomy is under way. This dissected and sawn-up Beethoven belongs, however, in the conservatory, not in the concert hall. . . . Bülow gives the impression of one who would like to be a painter but can't get beyond anatomy. . . . The only gratifying thing about this Beethoven operation was the skill with which it was performed. Bülow's technical equipment is, indeed, astounding, his infallible knack of wounding or killing at the very first incision is absolutely hair-raising. But to breathe life and soul into the dead body he is utterly wanting in the requisite vaccine. He is merely a skilled surgeon. When Rubinstein and others deal roughly with the living Beethoven from time to time, and, carried away by their enthusiasm, give the mighty man a bloody nose, or do him some other injury, then Bülow is the man to mend the damage. None knows better than he how to patch and glue. This autopsist is forever directing his listeners' attention to liver and kidneys rather than to the pulsating heart.

Yet von Bülow was by no means a pedant; his mission was to convey to an audience exactly what he felt the composer wanted to say, and he proceeded to burn the piano literature into the public's consciousness. He

was well aware of his intellectuality, which indeed at times made him sound detached or icy. He was also aware that he was viewed as the prototype of the heavy-handed "serious" German school of piano playing. After an all-Liszt recital he wrote, "I played coldly and intellectually. . . . Berlin's chilling atmosphere and the animosity towards me which it engenders have always dried up my inner warmth, so that I invariably played like an advocate of my own 'classical' intelligence." The pianist Edward Dannreuther wrote of Bülow: "All details were thought out and mastered down to the minutest particle; all effects were analyzed and calculated with the utmost subtlety; and yet the whole left an impression of warm spontaneity."

Von Bülow, even more than Clara Schumann or Liszt, made playing from memory an obligation. (As a conductor, he ordered the orchestral members to perform from memory and standing up.) His impact on American musical taste was as great as Anton Rubinstein's. He astounded the American public on his second tour by playing all of Beethoven's piano music—sonatas, variations, and the smaller works—without a note of music. He probably had the largest performing repertoire of his time. He tirelessly promoted the composers he valued. (It was von Bülow who invented the celebrated phrase "the Three B's—Bach, Beethoven, and Brahms.") His editions of various composers, including the Beethoven sonatas, were the most valued of the time. Von Bülow's practicing always included preludes and fugues from Bach's *Well-Tempered Clavier,* which he called the pianists' "Old Testament," and the Beethoven sonatas, the "New Testament."

He was the apostle of high seriousness. Eduard Hanslick reported in 1881:

His arrival in a town is enough to quicken the hearts of all who want something more than merely pleasant musical entertainment. One always learns something new. . . . His restless, brilliant mind and his reckless energy flow like a north wind, brisk and refreshing . . . he is a born interpreter, one of the most remarkable I have ever known. . . . Bülow has just made his bow in Vienna. . . . He played the five last great Beethoven sonatas, one after the other, in a single recital. Nothing else. . . . It has only been within the past thirty years that anyone has dared to play one or another of them in public. . . . To play all five at one sitting was considered an impossibility until yesterday. Bülow survived the adventure, and so did the public. Only one who has tried to master these sonatas with his own hands can appreciate Bülow's extraordinary achievement. It is difficult to determine which is more admirable, his memory, his physical stamina, his technique, or the elasticity of his mind. . . . The total impression was fatigue mixed with admiration. If I correctly read the faces of the listeners going home, they said, "Beautiful but never again." Some chose to put it the other way around: "Never again—but beautiful."

Von Bülow was also an eminent teacher, and the list of his pupils includes Giuseppe Buonamici, José Vianna da Motta, Heinrich Barth, Hermann Goetz, Agathe Backer-Grøndahl, and countless others. To one student he said, "An interpreter should be the opposite of a grave digger. He should bring to light what is hidden and buried." At another lesson he declared: "Piano playing is a difficult art. First we have to learn how to equalize the fingers, and then in polyphonic music to make them unequal again; that being the case, it seems best not to practice the piano at all; and that is the advice I have given to many."

GIUSEPPE BUONAMICI
1846–1914 — Italy

A pupil of von Bülow, he was one of the most important Italian pianist-teachers of his time. He made many editions of Beethoven, Schubert, and Schumann.

DAVID BURGE
b. 1930 — United States

A pianist with a fine technique who has championed many contemporary scores. He plays with exactitude and the kind of commitment that is necessary for bringing to life difficult contemporary music by Boulez, Dallapiccolo, Berio, and others. Burge has a musical intelligence that finds its way into the most intricate reservoirs of the pieces he plays.

FERRUCCIO BUSONI
1866–1924 — Italy

He studied with his mother, Anna Weiss-Busoni, and thereafter was virtually self-taught.

Busoni, many believed, was the most important and creative pianist since Liszt. He was a colossus who struck a deep chord in the hearts of those who heard him. Arthur Loesser called him "unforgettable; shocking even . . . one could never forget his playing." Gunnar Johansen has recalled, "He outshone all others. In Germany, we didn't speak of Mr. Busoni, we spoke of Der Busoni, as if he were a monument. His presence on stage was immense." Egon Petri used to say that "the music became dematerialized; he brought it into another sphere. It had a mystical quality." Nadia Boulanger considered Busoni "a genius. To say that he played the piano in an extraordinary way is merely to state the blindingly obvious. . . . Above all, you sensed a unity in his interpretations. . . . He played with the air of composing as he played. Busoni's articulation was perfect, and came not only from the astonishing evenness of his technique, but above all from his prodigious sense of rhythm."

Busoni's conceptions seemed to possess a revelatory expressive power and a gigantic sweep. He projected the feeling that music had no boundaries or limits of expression. He once said, "Take it for granted that everything is possible on the piano." Edward Steuermann (commenting in the late 1950s) felt "Busoni's pianism would not be easily understood today, might even be bewildering compared with the perfectionism of today's playing (the avoidance of risks, spiritual or stylistic), his bold individualism . . . would appear revolutionary, almost rebellious, and so it was fifty years ago."

Busoni's pedaling was perhaps the most original in the history of the art of piano playing. "The potential effects of the pedals are still unexhausted," he wrote, "because they have remained the slave of a narrow-minded and senseless harmonic theory. The pedal is decried. Senseless irregularities are to blame for this. Let us experiment with sensible irregularities." The composer Otto Luening heard Busoni frequently and attested in his autobiography:

His pedaling was unique and set him apart from any other pianist I have ever heard. He sometimes used two or three pedals at the same time, setting sonority patterns that were somewhat veiled but within which he played with great, bell-like clarity. At times, he would raise or lower a pedal with great rapidity, even on a single note or chord, creating myriad tone colors and strange vibrations. His touch and attacks were always related to the pedaling he was using so that he could transform the piano sounds at will from a vaguely harpsichord resonance to a modern resonating box on which he could simulate singing and orchestral instruments. . . . Busoni avoided strict metrical playing in all performances. He was interested in projecting the form of each piece so that it could be remembered. . . . His performance of the Chopin Ballades went beyond brilliant piano playing. Sometimes he made the instrument sound like an Aeolian harp as described by the poets, or like sound floating from a box of electronic resonators with apparently no relationship to hammered-string

sound. Under his hands the piano became both a picture projector and a story teller, and in the Ballades Busoni became a bard.

Not that Busoni was immune from criticism. His Chopin was often condemned for bursting its form and exhibiting too much muscle. Busoni countered, charging that Chopin had been "prostituted, profaned, vulgarized." Some felt his Beethoven was too violent, but the pianist wrote: "I built up . . . an ideal of Beethoven which has wrongly been called 'modern' and which is really no more than 'live.' "

His Liszt playing, however, was the start of a new age in Liszt performance. Edward J. Dent, in his biography of Busoni, wrote: "The greater works of Liszt, which minor pianists turn into mere displays of virtuosity because their technique is inadequate for anything beyond that, often sounded strangely easy and simple when they were played by Busoni. The glittering scales and arpeggios became what Liszt intended them to be—a dimly suggested background—while the themes in massive chords or singing melodies stood out clear."

As a player, Busoni was simply inexhaustible; he could give nine Mozart concerti in three nights. And he liked to use his monumental repertoire to show the history of the concerto. In 1898 he played the Bach D minor, Mozart A major, Beethoven G major, and Hummel B minor during the first of four concerts. In concert two, he programmed the Beethoven E-flat, the Weber *Konzertstück,* Schubert-Liszt *Wanderer* Fantasy, and Chopin E minor. Concert three contained the Mendelssohn G minor, Schumann A minor, and Henselt F minor (the work with which he made his American debut). The fourth concert had the Rubinstein E-flat, the Brahms D minor, and the Liszt A major. In 1911, for the Liszt centenary, he played in Berlin six all-Liszt programs comprising more than seventy different works. It was his ambition to add a new work to his performing repertory each season. His consistency was admirable. This list includes merely a twelve-year period:

Six Paganini-Liszt Etudes—1892 (Boston)
Bach-Busoni Chaconne—1893 (Boston)
Weber *Konzertstück*—1894 (Hamburg)
Beethoven Sonata Op. 106—1895 (Berlin)
Grieg Piano Concerto—1896 (Copenhagen)
Chopin Twelve Etudes Op. 25—1896 (Berlin)
Weber Sonata in C major—1897 (Berlin)
Chopin Four Ballades (complete)—1899 (London)
Chopin Sonata No. 3 in B minor—1899 (Berlin)
Tchaikovsky Concerto No. 1—1900 (London)
Brahms Variations on a Theme by Paganini—1900 (Berlin)
Liszt Sonata—1900 (Berlin)
Weber Sonata No. 3 in D minor—1901 (Weimar)
Liszt Piano Concerto No. 1—1901 (London)
Alkan, various works—1901, 1902, 1903, 1908 (Berlin)
Saint-Saëns Concerto No. 5—1902 (Hanover)
Chopin Twelve Etudes Op. 10—1902 (Berlin)
Franck Prelude, Chorale, and Fugue—1902 (Berlin)
Schubert Four Impromptus Op. 90—1903 (Berlin)
Liszt Twelve *Transcendental Etudes*—1903 (Berlin)
Beethoven Sonata Op. 110—1903 (Berlin)
Busoni Piano Concerto (Karl Muck conducting)—1904 (Berlin)

Busoni hated the recording process of his time. His piano rolls give no indication of his genius. However, he recorded a few pieces at the end of his career. It is sad that this mighty artist left a recorded legacy that fits on one side of an LP, a taste that only serves to tantalize us. We get but a glimmer of his monumental art and great technical gifts in an abridged version of Liszt's Hungarian Rhapsody No. 13. There are also Bach's Prelude and Fugue in C major and a couple of Chopin works, including hu-morous touches in two versions of the *Black Key* Etude. But the recording hardly conveys the artistry commented on by the many experts who heard him.

Through his brilliant essays, letters, and compositions, we discover in Busoni one of the most complex musical personalities of his day. Prophetic yet perplexing, Romantic and modern, he was a person of the highest standards and idealism. "Anyone who will master the language of art," he wrote, "must have nurtured his life through the soul." He was a tireless worker, and courage is demanded by some of his technical dictums, such as: "Practice the passage with the most difficult fingering; when you have mastered that, play it with the easiest."

Busoni was a powerful and paradoxical intellect. On the one hand, he headed the avant-garde of his time as the founder of a radical neo-Classicism; on the other, he remained one of the last incarnations of Romanticism. Three distinct systems informed his mind and music: Bachian polyphony, Germanic Romanticism (with elements of Lisztian-Italianate melody), and his own personal theories of music—many far-out for their time—which he published as his *Sketch of a New Esthetic of Music*. Often the threads became tangled. But he was a fascinating creator, and his music is deep and valuable. His Piano Concerto of 1902–04, with its timing of sixty-five minutes for performance, is the ultimate Romantic statement in the form. It runs to five movements and the finale is scored for male choir, which makes the work difficult to mount. The concerto is a saturated conglomeration of originality and triteness, the Teutonic and the Italianate, theatricality and eloquence. His 1910 *Fantasia contrappuntistica* based on Bach's *The Art of Fugue* continues to fascinate pianists of intellectual bent and physical endurance. Some consider it a work of emotional beauty; others, like Peter Yates in his book *An Amateur at the Keyboard*, see it "as a phantasmagoria of styles and devices. . . . This was no longer the aristocratic complacency of Liszt amusing himself by writing for display a fantasy on the well-known melodies of an opera; here the highest and most discriminating judgment had grown crazed and tasteless." Such a work was needed, however, for Busoni to purge himself of his own nineteenth-century concept of Bach and counterpoint.

After this composition, Busoni became more comfortable with his polyphony and forged a twentieth-century Classicism, which brought liberation for many composers still in the grips of a stale nineteenth-century Romanticism. However, Busoni's piano music will never become popular. Among his most successful works are the Seven Elegies, from 1908; the bitter, driving, and despairing Toccata, from 1920; and, perhaps the truest synthesis in Busoni's piano music, the six sonatinas. The brooding No. 2 ranges from sensitive neo-Classicism to expressionist searching and free polyphony.

The serious yet entertaining No. 6 on themes from Bizet's *Carmen* uses Lisztian methods.

Busoni's music moves only certain souls, but that has fortunately been enough to keep a knowledge of his work quite alive. Of course, many pianists continue to play his mostly magnificent transcriptions of Bach. He was called Mr. Bach-Busoni. His legendary prowess as a pianist has echoed through the century. The most recent tribute by a great pianist was by Arthur Rubinstein, who wrote in his memoirs: "Ferruccio Busoni, the awe-inspiring master of them all! . . . with his handsome, pale, Christlike face, and his diabolical technical prowess, was by far the most interesting pianist. . . . Busoni remains a towering personality, a shining example to all musicians for the noble way in which he pursued his career so uncompromisingly, for the high standards he set for his own compositions and for his general culture, so rare among artists."

MICHELE CAMPANELLA
b. 1947 — Italy

A strong technician, he has earned a European reputation and has made recordings of Liszt and Busoni.

MARTIN CANIN
b. 1930 — United States

He studied with Rosina Lhévinne at the Juilliard School. He is an expert chamber musician, as well as a solo artist with a large repertoire. His recording of the Brahms F minor Sonata shows an aristocratic talent, with a beautifully polished mechanism, a lovely sound, and a keen ear for structure. In 1959, Canin became a member of the piano faculty at the Juilliard School, where his reputation as a teacher has flourished.

TERESA CARREÑO
1853–1917 — Venezuela

She was one of the most remarkable musicians of her time and a pianist of greatness.

Carreño was a prodigy who had a huge success in the United States. As a child in Boston, she played twelve recitals in a season. Gottschalk heard her several times and gave her valuable pianistic advice. Later, she played for Liszt, who was overwhelmed, telling her, "Don't imitate anyone. Keep true to yourself, cultivate your individuality and do not follow blindly in the paths of others." Anton Rubinstein taught her intermittently, calling her "my sunshine." She studied also with Chopin's pupil Georges Mathias, and for several years she played in the French *jeu perlé* style. Around 1875, she abandoned piano performance for a few years to pursue a quite successful singing career. She also conducted, and composed many charming salon pieces, as well as a string quartet. In 1892, Eugene d'Albert became her third husband. He was a great influence on her playing, which became deeper and richer. Her repertoire grew in stature, and Beethoven became one of her chief concerns.

She possessed a titanic technique, and few men could rival her animal vitality; she was second to none for sheer endurance. She often played Beethoven's Third, Fourth, and Fifth Concerti in a single evening without a shrug. She had a magnificent stage bearing, and her beauty was legendary. "Carreño," wrote James Huneker in his autobiography, "with her exotic coloring, brilliant eyes, and still more brilliant piano-playing, was like a visitor from another star. Her manner of playing for me has always seemed scarlet, as Rubinstein's was golden and Joseffy's silver." Claudio Arrau called her "epical," and decades later he still found her unforgettable: "She was a goddess. She had this unbelievable drive, this power. I don't think I ever heard anyone fill the Berlin Philharmonie, the old hall, with such a sound. And her octaves were *fantastic*. I don't think there's anyone today who can play such octaves. The speed and the power."

Carreño had lived a tempestuous life and during the war years she was charged with being a spy. She was in danger of execution and spent several months in a Tunisian prison. Her last recital took place in Havana, March 21, 1917. Unfortunately, she died before electrical recording, and the piano rolls she made, which were disowned by her, give practically no idea that "the Walküre of the piano," as she was often called, was one of the volcanic temperaments in late-nineteenth-century piano playing.

GABY CASADESUS
b. 1901 — France

A superb pianist who studied with Diémer. Her career as a duo-pianist with her husband, Robert, took her all over the world. Her solo recordings of his piano music are delightful.

JEAN CASADESUS
1927–1972 — France

The son of Gaby and Robert Casadesus was a pianist of distinction. His recording of Chabrier's *Pièces pittoresques* is a gem.

ROBERT CASADESUS
1899–1972 — France

A student of Diémer at the Paris Conservatoire, Casadesus came from a distinguished musical family. To a world public he became the absolute French pianist, his country's finest. Casadesus embodied the qualities of Gallic balance, unforced sound, style, and precision of technique. His sound was crisp, dry, and sparkling, like a vintage champagne. 63

Casadesus was a sophisticated musician, whose pianism was phenomenally supple. His range was wide and his use of the pedals simply astonishing. He composed admirable, pleasurable music, highly crafted and well worth performance. He could play a large-scale work with such concentration that if one was listening well, the performance seemed to be over amazingly soon, he simply presented it all so directly. His rubato in Schumann's *Carnaval* was so subtle that at first it sounded as if he never deviated from the metronome mark, yet it certainly never sounded tight. His pupil Grant Johannesen said: "He had a commanding ability to guide you through the music and it was so compelling. It's fascinating to consider, too, because his whole approach to music was simple. He was so concentrated that he produced a kind of inner musical excitement. . . . The man shed so much light on *all* the music he played. I can never forget his utter lack of pretension. He caught the spirit of the music and shared it with his audience as something supremely divine."

Casadesus had a large repertoire. His Scarlatti records are beaming, his Bach solid. He played and recorded Beethoven often. It was a cool French-styled Beethoven; the fierce *Sturm und Drang* was not his way. He played an ample amount of Chopin, and the B minor Sonata was architecturally superb. But he was not comfortable in the little pieces, where the deeply personal and darker tones were absent. His Schumann often had charm, but his style was too fastidious to indulge in the more dissonant side of the German's nature.

Casadesus was one of the superb concerto players. In his hands, the Saint-Saëns Fourth Concerto becomes lordly. His Mozart concerti will always be celebrated, and his own cadenzas are stylish. He could play Liszt's A major Concerto with spirit, and his disc with Szell of Weber's *Konzertstück* will always earn raves, as will his d'Indy *Symphony on a French Mountain Air* and the Franck *Symphonic Variations*.

This charming and civilized artist was at his peak in his interpretations of Ravel and Debussy. His recordings remain indispensable for those who love this literature. Casadesus uses a more economical, less purely sensuous approach to Ravel. His exquisite breeding brings to this music a cool poignancy. His playing may be restrained, but ardor always peeps in. The pianistic finish is high, and the sheer elegance attained in his complete Ravel is irresistible. Never was the adage "Less is more" so apt. The music forms a cohesive unity, with phrasing that is sculptured. Casadesus senses Ravel's antique spirit. For example, in the minuet of Ravel's *Sonatine*, he takes us back to the jeweled and graceful eighteenth-century French court.

Casadesus's Debussy is also near his very best work. Everywhere he plays with joy, scintillating brightness, and a rhythmic verve. It is a Debussy of taste. He brings to a score like the *Children's Corner* Suite the very springtime of life, each phrase affectionately shaped, and the humor is piquant. I wish he had recorded more Fauré, a composer born for Casadesus's hands. There is no finer Fauré than his recording of three preludes from Op. 103, or the exquisite traceries and refined passion he finds in the Ballade for Piano and Orchestra.

His life was filled with touring, recording, composing, and teaching. He played the two-piano literature with his wife, Gaby, as few such teams ever did—with élan and a rare musicianship.

ALFREDO CASELLA
1883–1947 — Italy

One of the important Italian musicians of his generation. He studied with Diémer at the Paris Conservatoire and later taught there. From 1915 on, he taught in Rome at the Santa

Cecilia Academy. He made editions of Chopin and Beethoven, and his compositions are often difficult, but stimulating, acerbic, and well worth investigation.

IGNACIO CERVANTES
1847–1905 — Cuba

He studied with Gottschalk and at the Paris Conservatoire with Marmontel. After returning to Cuba, he gave concerts and specialized in composing pieces utilizing Cuban musical elements. His twenty-one *Danzas cubanas* are his most important works.

CÉCILE CHAMINADE
1857–1944 — France

She studied with Félix Le Couppey at the Paris Conservatoire. Chaminade was a deft and stylish pianist whose salon music (more than two hundred pieces) was played for three generations. But her music went out of fashion as home music-making declined. Still, as Norman Demuth wrote, "in the days when domestic music-making was at its height, the name 'Chaminade' stood for an ideal. It is now an excuse for hilarity, but this attitude cannot detract from its importance in the 'Panorama.' . . . We wish that every writer for the piano had her innate gifts and that they could be equally musicianly in their own ways."

ABRAM CHASINS
1903–1987 — United States

A pianist who studied with Ernest Hutcheson and Josef Hofmann. He composed many piano pieces, including an admirable set of twenty-four preludes and a work, *Narrative*, recorded by his wife, Constance Keene. He was also a broadcaster, and for years was the Music Director of WQXR in New York.

SHURA CHERKASSKY
b. 1911 — Russia

He was born in Odessa but was brought early to the United States. He studied with his mother, Lydia Cherkassky, who had worked with Essipova; as a child, he also studied with Josef Hofmann. Cherkassky's early years were those of a highly visible child prodigy who absorbed a great deal of the Hofmann tradition. At the age of twelve, he played at the White House for President Hoover.

His career has had its ups and downs, and it was at a low ebb in this country from the 1940s until around 1975, when finally his appearances in the United States began to rival in success his recitals in London and other European capitals. His concerts have been a revelation for those who have heard him, and a whole generation of young Juilliard students has been inspired by his originality, his technique, his unrivaled command of voicing, rubato, and pedaling, and, above all, by his imagination.

Critics have consistently called Cherkassky a throwback to a bygone age, a pianist from the past, a reminder of Hofmann and Godowsky, an eccentric genius with a style closely related to that of the greater pupils of Leschetizky. But this assessment must irritate such an artist, who never thinks of the past or of Hofmann. He is entirely himself, a pianist blessed with a fascinating musicality, a man who works at the piano with a tireless hunger to achieve mastery within each measure. Endless dedication, total guilelessness, and a nonjudgmental view of the piano literature

65

permeate his life and his arresting programming. He can play Bernstein's *Touches* better than any young modernist, side by side with Paul Pabst's *Eugene Onegin* paraphrase; the Tchaikovsky or Grieg Sonata receives the same respect as Schumann's *Carnaval* or Liszt's Sonata. He plays Berg's Sonata with perfect understanding, and plays pieces by Mana-Zucca or Chaminade with the same thirst with which he plays *Islamey* or the *Don Juan* Fantasy.

In short, season after season this incredible-looking person, a leprechaun at the piano, develops, changes, and grows. Cherkassky is not a throwback, and his conceptions are not imitations of his past master, Hofmann, but vital interpretations in their own right, by a Romantic virtuoso imbued with a love for his instrument and its literature. Recently he decided that his playing was plagued by too many inner voices, which could come off well in concert but sounded cloying on disc. He simply did away with them. They may reappear, but they will always sound different, fresh, and uncalculated.

Cherkassky never remains static. It is impossible for him not to experiment; the stage is part of his life and a tremendous release for him away from his slow-motion practicing, which, he says, people would not believe if they heard it. Cherkassky is always his own best listener, and his stage concentration is formidable. Of course, his interpretations are highly personalized, highly colored. He loves to linger and relish the moment. He is an artist who takes enormous chances, and this can throw an audience, used to conservative playing, into a confused state until it gets used to his mercurial ways. And then again, Cherkassky, Romantic that he is, may not be entirely in the mood to inspire the multitude; or, on occasion, it may take him time to warm to his work. I heard him play a Chopin E minor Concerto as if he were half asleep. It was not until the finale that the pianist was ready to sing, but the wait was worth it, and a movement that had never seemed equal to its companions erupted and swelled magnificently.

At his best, his Chopin playing is fascinating. Here he becomes the Romantic poet of the keyboard. What a seductive, insinuating ring in the A-flat Ballade. His E major Nocturne, Op. 62, is translucent; some of his Chopin preludes are beguiling, the one in F-sharp major played as if upon a cloud. Few pianists can create so hushed an effect. "The characteristics of his Chopin," writes James Methuen-Campbell, "include a luscious tone, attention to the polyphonic side of the music, marvelously detailed phrasing, and a grasp of the overall shape of a work. It would be impossible to say that he favors fast tempos, because he never follows any rules. He is like a magician at the keyboard, conjuring up near miraculous sounds that the most assiduous listener may hear only once in a lifetime from another pianist." Cherkassky's Chopin repertoire is huge, and he plays many of the seldom-heard scores, such as the C minor Sonata, Op. 4; the *Là ci darem la mano* Variations for Piano and Orchestra; and the *Allegro de concert, Boléro,* and Tarantelle.

A unique Liszt player, he is mainly concerned with surface brilliance and charm. His *Rigoletto* Paraphrase is whipped into a silky froth. But in the Liszt Sonata there is a seriousness, if not a depth, of emotion. It is a rejuvenation of the score in which his imagination soars and his technique is staggering.

One of Cherkassky's chief traits is his elegance, and nowhere is this exhibited more perfectly and joyously than in the large collection of salon pieces and paraphrases he carries in his repertoire. Nobody can touch him in a work like the Strauss-Godowsky *Wine, Women, and Song,* where his fingers weave garlands in counterpoint. He is an exquisite stylist who never lets go of the pulse as he spins out these alluring ten minutes of intricate, sophisticated nostalgia.

Cherkassky often programs Schumann, but

these two quirky musicians do not mix well. His *Carnaval* usually sounds spasmodic, even ill-tempered, and the *Symphonic Etudes* are cluttered and nervous. He plays some Schubert, most notably the A major Sonata D. 664 (Op. 120), bucolic in mood and with a touching slow movement. Cherkassky is certainly not at home with the Classic masters, and his Beethoven is not thrilling. But one does not go to hear a Cherkassky concert for profundity or solidity. He is instinctive, fragmentary, an improviser and a troubador, an artist of half-tints, delicate pastels, Romantic vibrations, with a golden if somewhat piercing tone. He is often bubbling with joy, humor, and even shenanigans, and he is also a master of the grand statement, as in the Tchaikovsky Second and the Saint-Saëns Second Concertos. Recently, he played the Anton Rubinstein Fourth Concerto, and it sounded better and more coherent than the Hofmann performance on disc. The work had been heard only once in nearly forty years, at the New York Philharmonic concerts (played by Oscar Levant), and one wondered how such a masterpiece of the grand manner could have become neglected. The answer is that the piece is now faded and has been ousted by the Rachmaninoff concerti, but in the hands of an artist like Cherkassky, a necromancer of forgotten scores, it regained all of the pomp that attended its birth, when Anton Rubinstein himself mounted the platform, brought down the house, and claimed his place as the father of Russian pianism.

FRÉDÉRIC CHOPIN
1810–1849 — Poland

He made his debut in 1818, playing a concerto by Gyrowetz. In 1824 he entered the Warsaw Conservatory; the following year saw the publication of his Rondo in C minor, Op.

1. He premiered his own F minor and E minor Concerti in Warsaw in March and October of 1830. Late in that same year, he left Poland forever. He lived and performed in Vienna for eight months and in 1831 arrived in Paris, where he played his F minor Concerto and the *Là ci darem* Variations early in 1832. After 1835, his appearances as a concert pianist were infrequent. In 1837 he entered into his celebrated liaison with the writer George Sand, which ended in 1846. His main source of income was teaching. He gave his last recital in Paris early in 1848, and later that year arrived in Great Britain. He died in Paris in 1849. At his funeral, which was held at the Madeleine, Mozart's Requiem was given. He is buried at Père-Lachaise, where, according to legend, there has never been a day when flowers were not placed on his grave.

Chopin spent most of the first twenty years of his life in Warsaw. The Polish capital was rather provincial; still he was able to hear many of the best artists of the time perform there. Italian opera and singing in general had an indelible effect on him, through the performances of such great singers as Angelica Catalani. Long before Liszt heard Paganini, Chopin was learning from his violinistic feats. Hummel, too, played in Warsaw, and his tentative Romanticism and richly ornamented keyboard layout ignited Chopin's precocious genius. Other influences during his adolescence included Spohr's then strangely exotic chromaticism, Field's fragrant nocturnes, and the mysteriousness of Weber. Of equal importance were the dance forms of his homeland. From the age of eight, Chopin occupied himself with them, haunted by their rhythms, dreaming of an idealized Poland. The last page of music he wrote was a mazurka.

As a pianist, he was left to develop on his own. Warsaw had no piano teachers of importance, and Chopin's instruction was given over to a local violinist, Adalbert Zywny. Awestruck by his pupil's talents, he let Chopin sprout his own unique wings. To his credit, he instilled in him a love for Bach and Mozart, the only masters whom Chopin admired without reservation. There was also the fatherly guidance of his composition teacher Josef Elsner at the Warsaw Conservatory, who understood him and nourished him without too many strictures. When the twenty-one-year-old Chopin arrived in Paris, he was momentarily dazed by the old-fashioned perfection of Kalkbrenner, who tried to convince him to enter upon a three-year course of study with him. Opinions on the matter roared back to him from Warsaw: the pianist Maria Szymanowska screamed, "He is a scoundrel. . . . His real aim is to cramp his genius." Elsner, too, quickly realized that "they have recognized genius in Frédéric and are already frightened that he will outstrip them, so they want to keep their hands on him for three years in order to hold back something of that which nature herself might push forward."

Indeed, Chopin was a new and freer pianist, free from the conventional discipline of stiff bodily action. And his music was entirely new, demanding novel forms of hand coordination. Schumann was the first to understand this, ending his review of the Variations on "Là ci darem la mano," Op. 2, with the now-celebrated line: "Hats off, gentlemen. A genius!" Chopin was well aware of his own originality. At nineteen, he announced to a friend the creation of his Etudes: "I have written a big technical exercise in my own special manner." These would soon be known as his Twenty-four Etudes, Opp. 10 and 25. When first composed, they offered severe stumbling blocks to older players of the day. The German critic Ludwig Rellstab advised, "Those who have distorted fingers may put them right by practicing these studies; but those who have not, should not play them, at least, not without having a surgeon at hand." But the Chopin Etudes have come to rule the world of piano playing, forming an encyclopedic methodology, a summary of Chopin's enlarged vision of piano technique. They pro-

vide the equipment for the rest of Chopin's almost invariably difficult music, and give the key to music after Chopin. If only one set of piano etudes were to be preserved, these would be the unanimous choice. They contain all that Clementi, Cramer, Czerny, Berger, Moscheles, Hummel, Steibelt, and others were striving for technically, couched in music of incomparable beauty. They are a challenge for every generation of pianists, and few can feel equally comfortable in all. They are small in form; as each develops a single technical idea, they demand an enormous endurance, while musically they are as exposed as Mozartian writing.

Chopin was one of the most original harmonists in history, creating an exquisite chromatic garden. "Chopin's chromaticism," wrote Gerald Abraham, "marks a stage of the greatest importance in the evolution of the harmonic language. . . . [He was] the first composer seriously to undermine the solid system of diatonic tonalism created by the Viennese classical masters and the contemporaries in other countries." As a creator of ornamental *fioritura,* he is without equal in the nineteenth century. Chopin displayed an almost inexhaustible resource in discovering pianistic formations that are uniquely suited to the instrument. To transcribe Chopin or to change the medium in any way destroys the music's evocative power, more than with any other composer. It was born for the piano. Chopin extended the scope of the left hand to such a degree that it constitutes a miracle of imagination. Finally the entire range of the instrument was available for exploration. Just compare a Mozartian Alberti bass or a Field nocturne with a late Chopin nocturne. With Chopin, the impossible was achieved—singing upon the piano. The instrument was suddenly capable of iridescent and shimmering tone, where the pedal counts for all. It was widely noted how Chopin's feet were in constant motion. He was probably the first pianist to consistently use half and quarter pedaling.

Never had music been capable of such fluidity, such palpitation, such atmospheric effect.

Hearing Chopin play the A-flat Etude Op. 25, No. 1, Schumann imagined "an Aeolian harp that had all the scales, and these were intermingled by the hand of the artist into all sorts of fantastic embellishments. It was rather an undulation brought out more loudly here and there with the pedal, all gorgeously entangled in the harmony."

Chopin's influence, pianistically and harmonically, spans two centuries from Liszt to Scriabin and Rachmaninoff, to Debussy, Granados, and Szymanowski. His mazurkas and polonaises let loose the flood tide of ethnicity in music, which is having an impact even today. This delicate, ethereal being created, in the words of George Sand, "a revolution in the language of music and with only one instrument."

Chopin was consumptive, becoming more frail year by year. He scaled down his playing as a result, developing dozens of gradations of soft sounds. How he envied Liszt his power. Naturally he had a horror of large halls, and late in life he begged his friend, the Irish pianist George Osborne, not to attend a recital he had to give in Scotland. "My playing," he told him, "will be lost in such a large room, and my compositions will be ineffective." Nevertheless, his pupil Georges Mathias attested: "What power! Yes, what power, but it lasted a few bars; and what exaltation and inspiration! The man's whole body vibrated." His technique was flawless, and he always caused great excitement with the evenness of his scales and the careful manipulation of his legato. The pianist-writer Wilhelm von Lenz noticed him "changing his fingers on a key as often as an organ player."

The chief characteristic of Chopin's playing was his highly personal and wayward use of tempo rubato. In Chopin's view of this device, "the left hand is the conductor; it must not waver or lose ground; do with the right hand what you will and can." (Liszt's description of the much-discussed tempo rubato is more pictorial: "Do you see those trees? The wind plays in the leaves, life unfolds and develops beneath them, but the tree remains.") When Meyerbeer insisted that Chopin played his own mazurka in 4/4 time instead of 3/4, Chopin was furious and hotly denied it. Yet when his trusted friend Charles Hallé pointed it out to him, the Pole slyly called the rhythmic aberration a national trait. Berlioz, too, said that Chopin simply could not play in time. In truth, however, the freedom of his playing and his music was not fully understood. The Classicist Ignaz Moscheles, whose playing Chopin called "frightfully Baroque," could not understand Chopin's music until he heard him play it. Moscheles then confessed, "The harsh modulations which strike me disagreeably when I am playing his compositions no longer shock me, because he glides over them in a fairylike way with his delicate fingers."

Chopin's piano music remains the most frequently played in history. He is one of the few universal masters, and has never suffered an eclipse. Almost every note he wrote is in the permanent repertoire. Arthur Rubinstein confirmed: "When the first notes of Chopin sound through the concert hall, there is a happy sign of recognition. All over the world men and women know his music. They love it; they are moved by it. Yet it is not Romantic music in the Byronic sense. It does not tell stories or paint pictures. It is expressive and personal, but still a *pure* art." Anton Rubinstein called him "the Piano Bard, the Piano Rhapsodist, the Piano Mind, and the Piano Soul," declaring that "whether the spirit of the instrument breathed upon him, I do not know . . . but all possible expressions are found in his compositions, and are all sung by him upon this instrument." The world rightly knows Chopin as "the poet of the piano." Indeed, the instrument's very prestige would be in jeopardy without his contribution.

MARCEL CIAMPI
1891–1980 — France

He studied with Diémer at the Paris Conservatoire, and had many tours, some with Casals. He taught numerous pianists, including Cécile Ousset and Hephzibah Menuhin.

ALDO CICCOLINI
b. 1925 — Italy

A brilliant pianist who plays internationally and teaches at the Paris Conservatoire. He brings a robust, zestful feeling to his playing, which is colorful but never drenched in pedal. He is never niggling but shows instead a generosity of spirit. He is at his best in the French piano music of *La Belle Epoque,* standing as Chabrier's leading all-round interpreter. He has done the complete Satie on records, fully expressing the music's whimsy and satire. He has a taste for Saint-Saëns which gives to the five concerti a streamlined, nonrhetorical sensibility. His Scarlatti is admirable, clear, and joyous, but his Debussy is weaker, less focused, and his Albéniz *Iberia* leaves much unstated, achieving a Spanish flavor but without its deeper essence.

WILHELMINE CLAUSS-SZARVADY
1834–1907 — Czechoslovakia

She studied in Prague, and from the first, with her tour in 1849, her playing caused a stir. Her great reputation was based mostly on her playing of Bach and Beethoven; she played some Chopin as well.

MUZIO CLEMENTI
1752–1832 — Italy

Born four years before Mozart, he was, like Mozart, a child prodigy, playing both the harpsichord and the organ brilliantly. As a child, he studied with teachers in Rome. At the age of nine he became a church organist. By the time he was fourteen, he had composed several church works, and a mass was performed in Rome. His father, a passionate music lover, was extremely poor and unable to support his son, but a solution was found. At fourteen, Clementi was virtually sold off to a wealthy Englishman, Peter Beckwood, who brought him back to his country estate. For the next several years Clementi lived in a carefree atmosphere, with every possible advantage. Best of all, he had the new English Broadwood piano, and he experimented tirelessly on it, developing a far more muscular approach than anyone had attempted, with a new legato style.

At the age of twenty-one, he moved to London, where his playing was quickly appreciated as a great advance over that of J. C. Bach and other early players. From 1770 to 1780, he was keyboard player and conductor at the Italian Opera in London. In 1781, Clementi made his first European tour, during which his playing was recognized at once as entirely new. In Vienna, Clementi encountered Mozart in a grueling pianistic duel played before the emperor at court. The outcome was a draw, but Mozart was irritated and his letters are a rather brutal condemnation of his colleague. He called Clementi a mere mechanic, without a penny's worth of feeling or taste. Mozart was peeved at the Italian's brilliance, calling all Italians charlatans. He hated Clementi's loud, fast octaves, his overall boldness, his passages in thirds (a Clementi specialty), and he warned his sister not to touch Clementi's devilish music for fear of turning stiff. Actually, Mozart sensed in Clementi something wild and frightening. (It must be said that Clementi had nothing but praise for Mozart's singing tone and exquisite style.)

Upon his return to England, Clementi entered the business of making pianofortes. In the end, Clementi's pianos (and view of the piano) triumphed over Mozart's light, flutey-sounding Viennese pianos, whose tones were too Rococo and reminiscent of the metallic harpsichord for the stronger vibrations of the Romantic style.

In 1802, to promote his pianos, Clementi traveled with his pupil John Field to various European capitals, ending in St. Petersburg, where Clementi pianos made a particularly deep impression. They became revered both in Europe and in America, and Clementi himself grew wealthy. He enjoyed playing the part of a country gentleman who happened to be a genius. He once said, "I'm an old Englishman and a young Italian." He became an English institution, and when he died, in 1832, he received a public funeral and was buried in the cloisters of Westminster Abbey. The tablet reads: "Here lies the Father of the Pianoforte." Indeed, if any one person merits this epitaph, it is Clementi. Not only was he the world's first great pianist, but his sonatas of 1773 may be considered the first music composed for the young instrument's capacity to produce a wide dynamic range through the manipulation of varying pressures.

Clementi was not only a tireless promoter of the instrument, he also dramatically improved the art of piano building. He was a music publisher as well, and brought to the public a stream of new publications, including much of his own music. As a teacher, he helped produce the important pianists of the next generation, including Field and Cramer, and gave private lessons to a great many wealthy English aristocrats. He eventually charged the enormous sum of one guinea for a forty-minute lesson, and he could fit in a dozen lessons a day in his early years.

In the highly commercial climate of England, Clementi helped to establish respect for the musician and also for the teaching of music, a profession that at the time was deemed neither respectable nor gentlemanly. Haydn and most other musicians were accorded a status little higher than that of servants.

Clementi's enlarged view of piano technique was codified in his 1817 magnum opus, *Gradus ad Parnassum,* a set of one hundred pieces including etudes, slow movements, fugues, and canons. Clementi's pianism was still of the Classical period, but his work in many ways presaged what the piano would eventually be asked to do. Today, the *Gradus* is sadly neglected by teachers, though there is no work to compare with it for building a solid technique.

He also composed sixty-four solo sonatas from 1773 to 1820—the longest career of any sonata composer. Indeed, had Beethoven not lived, Clementi's sonatas would represent a high-water mark in the history of the form. Beethoven was deeply indebted to the Clementi sonatas and kept his volume of them always at hand. Brahms, too, admired Clementi's adventurousness and freedom of form. From the pianistic view, Clementi's etudes formed the foundation for the future of etude writing, culminating in the etudes of Chopin.

Clementi died at eighty, just as the twenty-two-year-old Chopin was putting the finishing touches on his etudes. It is worth noting that not one of Chopin's own pupils was ever allowed to touch these etudes until the student had a thorough grounding in Clementi's.

VAN CLIBURN

b. 1934 — *United States*

He began his musical studies with his mother, who in turn had studied with Arthur Friedheim. At eighteen, he arrived in New York to work with the celebrated Mme Lhévinne at Juilliard, where he became her favored pupil. The 1955 Leventritt Award started his career rolling. By the end of 1957, though, it was fading fast. Word of a great new Soviet competition was in the news for 1958. Thinking this could be his break, Mme Lhévinne encouraged him to prepare, and with classmate Daniel Pollack, he went to Russia. It was a tense time; the Cold War, a recession at home, and Russia's Sputnik were in the news. Although the Tchaikovsky Competition was designed to show the world the wonderful young artists of Soviet socialism, there just was no escaping the fact that Van was irresistible. This gangling, six-foot four-inch, curly-haired, homespun Southerner drove the Russians to fever pitch with his golden sound and relaxed but grand style. The competition had been reported measure by measure by the *New York Times*, and when Cliburn won the day for America, the country went wild. He returned home a hero of the Cold War, an American who played the piano better than the Russians.

This twenty-four-year-old was given a ticker-tape parade, an unprecedented welcome for a pianist. The Russians consoled themselves with the fact that Cliburn had studied with Rosina Lhévinne, wife of the great Russian master Josef Lhévinne. She knew all the secrets of tonal magic that had emanated from the St. Petersburg and Moscow conservatories. Van was at his best playing music by Russians; he was their spiritual kin. As a result of his victory, he made a recording with the Russian conductor Kiril Kondrashin of the signature piece of the Tchaikovsky Competition—the luscious Concerto No. 1. And what a beautiful reading it remains—sculptural, warm, grandly Romantic. The third movement is played much more slowly than usual, bringing Tchaikovsky's use of a folk song about a blind man to the fore. (If a household had only one classical concerto at that time, it was likely to be Cliburn's Tchaikovsky Concerto No. 1.)

Most of Cliburn's concerto readings from that early period display wonderfully Romantic, plush playing. The best is his Third Rachmaninoff Concerto, followed by the MacDowell D minor, Grieg, Schumann, both Liszts, the Prokofiev Third, and the Chopin E minor. They are all rather careful but also tasteful and musical.

For years after his competition victory, Cliburn played and recorded relentlessly. He has made some good Mozart discs, though his Beethoven may be just too tame, nailed firmly to a conservatory plan. He did make excellent displays of the Prokofiev Sixth Sonata, Rachmaninoff's Second Sonata, Barber's Sonata, a good Liszt Sonata, and much Chopin, such as the pianistically beautiful B minor Sonata, with a feathery scherzo.

But as the years went by, he lacked the time and energy to add to his standard repertoire. He became sloppy; the engaging lyricism and spaciousness were disappearing. The playing got severely predictable, the tempi stodgy, the emotion tepid. He built a piece to a climax only to lose it at its height. There was little doubt Cliburn needed a rest. He had become an institution. The Van Cliburn International Piano Competition that he had founded in Fort Worth seemed to be more important to him than playing the piano himself. He must have been weary of being a hero, on the move for twenty years, playing the Tchaikovsky concerto again and again. And so he quit playing for ten years, and although recently he has played at the White House, if Cliburn never returns to regular concertizing, he has written one of the most spectacular pages in the history of his instrument, and his accom-

72

plishment and his legend will live on. Cliburn has become the most famous American pianist of the century, even a household name.

FRANCE CLIDAT
b. 1932 — France

A student of Lazare Lévy, Clidat has great pianistic facility and a rare feeling for Liszt. In her many recordings of this master she is stylish and often grand. Her pedaling is sparse and her fingerwork clean and elegant.

HARRIET COHEN
1895–1967 — England

A student of Tobias Matthay, she developed into a very individual performer and toured widely. Her Bach playing was highly regarded, and although she had small hands, she was the major exponent of the thick and complicated piano music of Sir Arnold Bax. The Harriet Cohen Medal is given in her memory.

JEAN-PHILIPPE COLLARD
b. 1948 — France

He studied at the Paris Conservatoire and has become one of the most successful of present-day French pianists. He has a virtuoso technique and can play with bravura. His recordings of Fauré's piano music are beautifully planned and meticulous. He has a penchant for Rachmaninoff and frequently plays the piano concerti, especially Nos. 1 and 3. He has recorded No. 3 in a healthy rather than morbid style.

GEORGE COPELAND
1882–1971 — United States

Studied with Carreño and Harold Bauer and was an early champion of the modern French school. His name is most closely associated with Debussy. Copeland knew Debussy and worked with him on his exotic music.

ALFRED CORTOT
1877–1962 — Switzerland

He was brought to Paris by his French parents at an early age. He studied there with Descombes, a pupil of Chopin, and later with Diémer, in whose class at the Paris Conservatoire he earned the Premier Prix in 1896. This was followed by his debut with the Lamoureux Orchestra in the Beethoven Third Concerto. Soon after, he was appointed an assistant conductor at the Wagner festival at Bayreuth, and became a passionate Wagnerian. At Bayreuth he worked with the famous conductors Hans Richter and Felix Mottl. During this time, he was influenced by the French pianist Edouard Risler, who deepened Cortot's knowledge of Beethoven and veered him away from the lighter and drier style of French piano playing.

Back in Paris in 1902, the twenty-five-year-old conductor gave the first performances there of Wagner's *Götterdämmerung* and, later, *Parsifal.* Soon he was credited with many first Parisian performances, including the Brahms German Requiem, the Liszt *Saint Elizabeth* Oratorio, and even Beethoven's *Missa Solemnis,* and he was the champion of many new French works.

Along with Pablo Casals and Jacques Thibaud, in 1905 he founded perhaps the most famous trio in history. Fortunately, their art is captured in several recordings displaying chamber music playing of the highest quality. These include Beethoven's *Archduke* Trio, Schubert's B-flat Trio, and the Mendelssohn and Schumann D minor Trios, while Cortot conducted the Brahms Double Concerto with Casals and Thibaud as soloists.

In spite of these activities, it was the piano that most attracted his musical spirit. In 1907, Fauré appointed him Professor of the Pianoforte at the Paris Conservatoire, where he became one of the most important teachers of the century. He stayed at the Conservatoire until 1919, when he founded the Ecole Normale de Musique and became its director. Literally thousands of pianists came to his renowned master classes there, including Gina Bachauer, Dino Ciani, Samson François, Clara Haskil, Magda Tagliaferro, Ruth Slenczynska, Yvonne Lefébure, Dinu Lipatti, and Vlado Perlemuter. He implored his students to study intimately the lives of the composers, their letters, and everything regarding their music. For lessons, he required a written analysis of the music to be played—a "geographical map," as he called it.

Cortot prepared some eighty different editions of the music of Chopin, Schumann, Liszt, and others. These are among the most important and intriguing editions ever made, providing a fund of splendid annotations and ingenious exercises for overcoming technical problems. Cortot was one of the great piano minds, and his writings are sprinkled with his own constant wonder at the masterpieces he played. He also left a treatise on interpretation, as well as two books, *In Search of Chopin* and the invaluable *La Musique française de piano* (1932).

He made his first American tour in 1918, and during the 1919–20 season he played forty-nine recitals in less than ninety days, with four separate recital programs. At Carnegie Hall he performed the five Beethoven concerti and the Schumann Concerto, the Third Rachmaninoff, and the Saint-Saëns Fourth. During the 1920s and 1930s he made more than 150 recordings, becoming one of the best-selling recording artists of the 78 era. During those busy years Cortot also gave nearly 1,500 recitals in Europe, Russia, and South America, 282 concerts in the United States, and 292 in England, all in addition to his conducting and teaching.

Unfortunately, during World War II he became the High Commissioner of Fine Arts in the Vichy government and also played concerts in Germany. For one year following the war, Cortot, who was found guilty of collaboration with the enemy by a French governmental panel, was suspended from all public musical activity. But soon after the year was up, he was again playing more than a hundred concerts a season. Cortot gave his farewell performance on July 10, 1958, with Casals, and he taught his last master class in 1961.

With his many activities, Cortot was much too busy to sit at a piano for endless hours. He was certainly one of the sloppiest of the great pianists. His memory lapses and wrong notes were legion, and many concerts were badly blemished. He pursued his path with daring and flair and what happened, happened. But Cortot was a genius. There has never been anything like him. His phrasing could curl the toes, bring goose bumps to the flesh, send a chill down the spine—and when Cortot was in shape, he was a brilliant technician, with an astonishing left hand. The pianist Charles Timbrell interviewed Vlado Perlemuter, a pupil of Cortot's, who said, "He didn't just have one kind of technique. He constantly adapted his technical approach to the music." His pedaling was miraculous. Perlemuter explained, "It's a simple fact that the modern piano is often too harsh without the *una corda* [left] pedal, but too timid with it. So Cortot would often prefer the sound that one gets by playing strongly with the *una corda*, if he wanted a sonorous soft sound. It's a sophisticated concept that is not well understood even today." "At my lessons," relates another pupil, Guthrie Luke, "Cortot would often pedal for me, using quarter, half, and flutter pedaling."

Once one had heard Cortot's tone it could never be forgotten. Magda Tagliaferro thought "his sound was pure enchantment, whether the music was soft or loud." Yvonne Lefébure, who for years was Cortot's chief assistant, wrote, "When you listened to Cortot play, you realized that what he was doing at the piano was not like what other people were doing."

Cortot was one of the "originals" in the history of interpretation. He was highly unpredictable and relied heavily on inspiration. There was always a new flash of insight, a left-hand caress, even a countermelody of his own invention. The audience felt included in a special intimate moment. Everything was heightened with an uncanny elegance. He was so Romantic, truly the most youthfully Romantic of the great pianists. He had an inspired sense of rubato. For Cortot, music was aspiration, a reaching for the unknown. He searched for elusive lights and shadows. If ever a pianist had the power to seduce and intoxicate, it was Cortot. Magda Tagliaferro said, "The images that he conjured up were absolutely visionary." Musical ideas tumbled from his brain, and he seldom failed to communicate them to discriminating listeners.

Cortot's recordings are among the most fascinating in history, and many remain relatively easy to obtain. His discography includes a poetic 1941 version of the Weber Sonata No. 2 in A-flat, and a 1939 disc with Charles Munch conducting the Ravel Left Hand Concerto. His Ravel *Jeux d'eau* is luscious, pure poetry, and his playing of the *Sonatine* shimmers. Cortot was an admirer of Franck and recorded both the Prelude, Aria, and Finale and the Prelude, Chorale, and Fugue, as well as the *Symphonic Variations,* which he played frequently. His 1937 recording of the *Variations sérieuses* of Mendelssohn is strongwilled, and the Saint-Saëns Fourth Concerto,

again with Munch conducting, was one of his specialties.

In 1930 he recorded the *Malagueña* and *Seguidillas* of Albéniz; the plasticity of melody over the dance accompaniment, the sheer lift, the pride and Spanish flourish are a delight. His Twelve Preludes of Debussy, Book I, are stylish and tonally beguiling. He left a few smaller Liszt pieces, as well as a rather bombastic, flippant performance of the B minor Sonata, recorded in 1929. Of the Classic masters, there is next to nothing—no Bach or Beethoven solo music, no Haydn or Mozart, although he performed and taught all the Beethoven sonatas. The greater part of his recorded legacy centers on Schumann and Chopin. There are no fewer than four versions of the Schumann Concerto, the latest recorded at a live performance in 1951 with Ferenc Fricsay. There are three versions of *Carnaval,* the best being from 1928, which is all lighthearted fantasy. He recorded the *Kinderscenen,* an astonishing *Davidsbündlertänze, Symphonic Etudes, Papillons* (which is bewitching), and a *Kreisleriana* that has some moments of startlingly pure poesy. Cortot is concerned with extracting Schumann's lyricism. It is not a dark, disturbed Schumann, but a bright, animated, and chivalric one; above all, it is an impressionist, atmospheric Schumann, beautifully shaded in pastel tones. He remains the finest French interpreter of Schumann.

Cortot's greatest celebrity rests upon his Chopin. It was Chopin who gripped his heart and mind more than any other composer, and his contribution to the worldwide dissemination of the Polish master's works is significant. With the advent of electrical recording he began to record large segments of Chopin, beginning in 1926 with history's first complete version of the Twenty-four Preludes. James Methuen-Campbell wrote that Cortot was an artist who "possessed extreme virtuosity and one of the greatest musical intellects of all time, who managed to combine the two into a perfect blend, and who had a greater affinity with Chopin's music than any other pianist of our age. His discs are for me, and many others, the foundation of Chopin playing: subtle, melancholic, heroic, deeply communicative and 'full. . . .' This playing has a quality that transcends normal music-making—it is as if Cortot is revealing Chopin's soul." His Chopin recordings include various versions of the Four Ballades, Four Impromptus, Twenty-four Etudes, Three *Nouvelles Etudes,* Fourteen Waltzes, two scherzos, six nocturnes, two sonatas, Barcarolle, Berceuse, Fantasy, and the Prelude Op. 45. There are no fewer than four versions of the Twenty-four Preludes, Op. 28, the most celebrated being the profoundly moving interpretation of the 1933 recording. André Gide confided in his diary that he thought Cortot had an "absence of sensuality; in its place, grace and sentimentality." This is quite true of the 1926 Preludes, but in the 1933 issue a deep, almost guttural sensuality appears.

By this time, Cortot's Chopin had ripened and was far from the dry but "pretty" Chopin of many earlier French pianists. It is interesting to compare his 1933 disc of the Twenty-four Preludes with his 1955 live performance from Munich. The conceptions are quite alike, but in the later version one hears the desperation of an almost eighty-year-old artist in poor health, battling his frail body and sadly diminishing mechanism. I doubt that he ever knew this recording was to be released. The technical failings are devastating, and he finds the *appassionato* No. 24 in D minor practically unplayable. It is amusing to note that in the 1933 recording he has exactly the same technical problems; in 1955 they are merely multiplied. Yet despite these faults the musical imagination has become deeper and more human, and the sonority multicolored. In the slow preludes he is more glorious than ever. What depth of sound—a French horn here, a violin there, or a harp and a bassoon. As Eric Heidsieck said, "Cortot taught us to be in the habit of thinking of the piano as a 'little orchestra' or at times maybe a big one."

Perhaps it is the Etudes which best display Cortot's gift for Chopin. I once did a series of radio broadcasts in which I played dozens of performances of Chopin etudes to a panel of connoisseurs. In almost every instance, even with their smudges and wrong notes, Cortot's readings were favored. As Philippe Entremont said, "Even his mistakes were fabulous! Nobody has ever played the Chopin etudes the way Cortot played them. They are so immense, so gigantic; the nonconformity, the fabulous drive—the poetry of the music was airborne. I was absolutely spellbound by the courage of his playing."

Cortot's Chopin output is replete with magical moments, though also the most commonplace errors. Surely there are listeners who will be repelled by his fanciful and extravagant rubato, which in fact in many places borders on the banal and sentimental. His style of enchantment is foreign to the more standardized contemporary way of playing. Bar-lines disappear with a seemingly random freedom. His Nocturnes may border on affectation. His Waltzes are quirky, arrhythmic, dandified. However, since around 1975, pianists tired of the perfection and the sameness of most performances have been responding more and more to the charm, the soaring imagination, and the bold chance-taking of Cortot's recordings, which were the products of a dazzlingly Romantic nature, drunk on its own delirious temperament.

JOHANN BAPTIST CRAMER
1771–1858 — Germany

His first public performance took place in 1781. Cramer then studied with Clementi for two years. In 1824 he started a music publishing firm. He was a founder of the Royal

Philharmonic Society. Besides his well-known etudes, Cramer composed seven concerti, innumerable variations and rondos, and 105 sonatas.

Born in Germany and brought to London as an infant, "Glorious John," as the English called him, was one of the founders of piano playing, and one of the very important performers of Beethoven's generation. He was unusual in his day in that he revered music of the past, playing Bach and Handel whenever he could, and Mozart was his god. Cramer was also a fine improviser and was expected, as were all players of the day, to exhibit this skill at concerts. At thirteen, Cramer made piano history by appearing with his master Clementi in the first public performance of a work for two pianos. By the age of seventeen, he had begun giving regular concerts in England and on the Continent in a career that would last nearly sixty years. His colleague Moscheles described "his thin, well-shaped fingers which are so well suited for legato playing," and called his Mozart "breezes from the sweet south. He sings on the piano . . . he almost transforms a Mozart andante into a vocal piece."

In 1804, Cramer insured his immortality when he issued the first forty-two of his eighty-four etudes, a landmark in piano technique. Each of these etudes explores a specific mechanistic problem, but they are also interesting as music, and remain to this day worthy of study. Beethoven, who hated most pianists, deeply admired Cramer's playing and his etudes, which he recommended as technical preparation for his own music. He wanted them taught to his nephew and advised Czerny to that effect.

As a pianist and composer, Cramer outlived his time. The wooden pianos of his youth gave way to the huge iron-framed instruments bearing the names Blüthner, Bösendorfer, Bechstein, and Steinway.

In the 1830s, Liszt paid a respectful visit to Cramer, and they played a duet together. Liszt told Moscheles of the visit, roguishly saying,

"I was the poisoned mushroom, and I had at my side my antidote of milk." Cramer was considered dry and tame by the younger pianists of the time. He quipped, "Formerly, piano playing was mighty good (*fort bien*). Now it's good and mighty (*bien forte*)." The rich scent of Romanticism was not for Cramer, and he admitted the music was "too strong" for him. Nevertheless, he and his etudes were of vital importance in the development and growth of pianistic virtuosity.

HAROLD CRAXTON
1885–1971 — England

A pupil of Tobias Matthay, he had a fine career as accompanist and solo player, and was a distinguished teacher. His editions of Bach and Beethoven are noteworthy.

SIR CLIFFORD CURZON
1907–1982 — England

His early studies were with Matthay in London; later he worked with Schnabel in Berlin for two years and with Landowska in Paris. In 1939 he made his American debut, in New York, with the time-honored, but usually battered, Tchaikovsky First Concerto, which he always played with the greatest respect. During his career, he turned his hand mainly to the great German masters, whose works he clothed with new meanings, adding distinctly to our knowledge of them. His performances of Schumann, Brahms, Schubert, and Beethoven always possess breadth of conception, nobility, and passion. Curzon had the quality of universality in his playing, combining an unusual sense of formal design with an expressive simplicity.

Few have had his power to make clear the largest structures of Schubert. Reviewing a 1950 Curzon recital, Virgil Thomson noted this quality:

The Schubert Sonata in D, Op. 53 [D. 850] . . . he walked around in. He did not get lost in it or allow us to forget its plan, but he did take us with him to the windows and show us all its sweet and dreaming views of the Austrian countryside, some of them filled with dancing folk. The terraced dynamics and the abstention from downbeat pulsations . . . kept the rendering impersonal at no loss to expressivity. On the contrary, indeed, the dramatization of it as a form, the scaling of its musical elements gave it evocative power as well as grandeur of proportion. And its enormous variety in the kinds of sound employed, its solid basses, and a dry clarity in the materials of its structural filling prevented monotony from becoming a concomitant of its vastness.

Here is a description of the very ideal in large-scale Schubert playing. It would be equally true of Curzon's recordings of Schumann's Fantasy, Beethoven's *Eroica* Variations, and the Mozart concerti he so loved. In fact, in his last years Sir Clifford's world was exclusively devoted to Mozart. Each Concerto was refined, warm, playful, dignified, and deeply humane. He never lost the pulse or made a bad sound, and always found an inimitable freshness in these most subtle of all concerti.

He was a great Brahmsian, in the smaller scope as well as in the works of Brahms the giant. To my mind, his recording of the Brahms F minor Sonata is the greatest ever made, and I deeply admire the treasured performances by Bauer, Rubinstein, Kempff, and Arrau. Here Curzon's spirit soars. This diffuse, sprawling score is built up simply and majestically, with an almost unbelievable grasp of form. Never have mind, heart, and fingers so fused: the roll of Curzon's chords is oceanic, not an inflection goes wrong. Of the huge Andante espressivo movement, Curzon

wrote, "It is a picture of Romantic love perhaps not excelled in the whole literature of the piano." Curzon paints this picture with a consummate sense of space and atmosphere and overwhelming emotional power.

Curzon is not usually associated with Liszt, but his Liszt record is deeply satisfying, one to which I return often. It includes a finely spun Berceuse, a sadly neglected piece, played with murmuring pedalings. He gives us a sane *Liebestraum*, a beautifully formed *Valse oubliée*, and the *Dance of the Gnomes* played with ironic humor and with as much care as he lavished on a Schubert impromptu or a Brahms intermezzo. But the high point is a serious but sensuous reading of the great B minor Sonata. In it he achieves a large sonority combined with a deep tenderness, an unflagging rhythm, and an inexorable structural plan.

Curzon was an artist who worked for perfection. I can only imagine what pains he took to arrive at his tremendous achievements.

CARL CZERNY
1791–1857 — Austria

Czerny started playing the piano at three, composing at seven, and performed for Beethoven when he was ten years old, playing no less than Mozart's great Concerto No. 25 in C, K. 503, and Beethoven's own recently published *Sonate pathétique*. Beethoven grabbed Czerny as a pupil, instructing him with great diligence and regularity for three years, without compensation. Czerny repaid Beethoven by becoming one of the chief disseminators of his music. By the age of sixteen, Czerny was musically on his own, and flocks of students began coming to him. He was a pianist of the fleet Viennese school of playing, and his performances were considered fluid and brilliant. He never tried to imitate the volatile Beethoven, being a pianist in the neat Hummel tradition. He was extremely nervous about playing in public and did it seldom, but managed to give the Vienna premiere of Beethoven's *Emperor* Concerto in 1811.

As a composer, Czerny was a one-man industry. He could work on five or six pieces at a time, rushing madly from one music stand to another. He produced nearly one thousand opus numbers (some containing more than fifty pieces, such as his Op. 749—*The Art of Finger Dexterity*), all the while maintaining a ten- to twelve-hour teaching day. He wrote in many forms, but his renown rests on his etudes, which have been the pedagogical bread and butter for generations of students.

He made a fortune not only from his teaching, but by accurately gauging the taste of the day. Beethoven and Weber were not the average musical diet. The public wanted tasty opera tunes, well mannered and polite. Besides his etudes, Czerny concocted no fewer than 304 sets of variations and potpourris, based on eighty-seven operas of the time. These works had a worldwide consumption. As Arthur Loesser says: "His talent was extraordinary. Within the limits of a narrow harmonic scheme, he developed a prodigious understanding of the motion shapes feasible to keyboard-traveling fingers. . . . Rapid, feathery, well-articulated pianistic passagework, chiefly for the right hand, was his best product—just what the light, bouncing, leather-covered little hammer-heads of the Vienna pianos could deliver best . . . always smooth and pretty and rather ear-tickling when played fast."

Czerny was an outstanding teacher. Liszt adored him, modestly professing that "I owe him everything," and dedicated his *Transcendental Etudes* to him. Czerny was Liszt's only piano teacher, instructing him without fee. Theodor Leschetizky, the most famous piano pedagogue of the second half of the nineteenth century, studied with Czerny between ages eleven and fourteen. When he was asked about his own "method," he simply stated that he taught as Czerny did. Leschetizky auditioned for him with Czerny's own concertino and a set of variations by Herz. "His manner of teaching," Leschetizky later related,

was somewhat that of an orchestral director. He gave his lessons standing, indicating the different shades of tempo and coloring by gestures. Czerny insisted principally on accuracy, brilliancy, and pianistic effects. I played a great deal of Bach under him, some compositions by Alkan, some by Thalberg, and, above all, those of Beethoven. Czerny taught that Beethoven should be rendered with freedom of delivery and depth of feeling. A pedantic, inelastic interpretation of the master made him wild. He allowed me to play Chopin just as I pleased, and though he appreciated the great Pole, he sometimes said his compositions were sweetish. [Chopin met Czerny in 1829 and liked the man better than his music.] He understood Mendelssohn. I remember studying the *Songs without Words* almost as soon as they appeared.

Czerny, it seemed, had no personal life. He lived simply, with a house full of cats. Throughout his career, he helped many artists financially, and in his will he bequeathed a large part of his fortune to a school for deaf mutes.

HALINA CZERNY-STEFANSKA
b. 1922 — Poland

The co-winner, with Bella Davidovich, of the 1949 Chopin Competition in Warsaw. She is best known for her Chopin, especially her mazurka playing. A celebrated disc of the Chopin E minor Concerto thought to be by Lipatti has been discovered to be by Czerny-Stefanska.

GYÖRGY CZIFFRA
b. 1921 — Hungary

One of the most remarkable piano technicians of our time. His hands are boned and bonded for piano playing and he has breathtaking reflexes. His fingerwork alone is dizzying—tiny hot pearls falling on the proverbial red velvet. Intoxicated by sheer pianistics, he can weight a chord to its smallest ounce, and color whichever note he wants us to hear. But Cziffra just won't stop fooling with the score; he is a lapidarian who often makes the music rotten with artifice. He is a throwback to a madcap era when such playing was considered a sign of heaven-sent genius, when poetic license and a loose musical morality were often mistaken for freedom. Yet when Cziffra tries to temper himself, or plays a repertoire unsuited to his gypsylike temperament, he becomes earthbound and dull. He is at his best as a rarefied entertainer, and his transcriptions are wonderful. He often blends some trashy playing with delicious and elegant playing. His Liszt is sensational—listen to his set of the Hungarian Rhapsodies—and he can even be serious, as in the *Légende—Saint Francis of Paolo Walking on the Waves*. He plays a great variety of Liszt, from transcriptions (my favorite being the Polonaise from *Eugene Onegin*) to the concerti and *Totentanz*.

Cziffra finds Chopin an enigma. His Barcarolle is by turns nervous and too placid. The Polonaises are tawdry, and his recording of the Etudes is a compendium of bad habits and virtuosity for its own sake; nevertheless, he reveals fascinating perspectives on the music.

But enough carping. I don't listen to Cziffra for depth. I simply want to be dazed by one of the great piano trapeze acts. His octaves can only be termed fabulous. When I listen to his transcription in octaves of Rimsky-Korsakov's *Flight of the Bumblebee*, I ask, what would Alexander Dreyschock or Liszt say? In an age satiated with wonders, such a display is still dazzling, and not only to other pianists.

JOSEPH DACHS
1825–1896 — Austria

An eminent pianist who taught at the Vienna Conservatory. De Pachmann, Joseph Rubinstein, and Isabelle Vengerova worked with him.

KATHLEEN DALE
1895–1984 — England

A student of Fanny Davies and York Bowen. She was a fine accompanist and chamber player and the author of the book *Nineteenth Century Piano Music*.

EDWARD DANNREUTHER
1844–1905 — Germany

A student of Moscheles, Dannreuther settled in London, giving in 1863 the first performance there of the Chopin F minor Concerto. He taught James Friskin and Harold Samuel. His treatise on *Musical Ornamentation* was the standard work on the subject.

JEANNE-MARIE DARRÉ
b. 1905 — France

She studied with Isidor Philipp and Marguerite Long. Darré has had a distinguished career as a teacher at the Paris Conservatoire and as a concert pianist. She made her American debut in 1960, and her very smart playing was quickly appreciated. She thrives in objective scores, such as the Ravel G major Concerto, Weber's *Konzertstück,* or any of the Saint-Saëns concerti, for which she is famous. At her best, she is alert and glittering, possessing a dryness of tone that is characteristic of French pianism in general. At her worst, she sounds curt, even heartless. I heard her in recital with the Twenty-four Chopin Preludes, where she merely prattled without a smattering of involvement. Her Chopin is at its best in the Scherzos, at its worst in the tight-lipped and uncomfortable rubato displayed in the Waltzes.

Her playing at all times manifests an interest in neat, finely grounded pianism; each nut and bolt is squarely placed. Her prime achievement on record is a fascinating portrayal of Liszt's Sonata, which she spins out to 33:20. Darré has placed this complex puzzle under her microscope and dissected its every fragment. She strips the massive work of its usual Faustian rumblings and bombast, giving us the quintessential French Liszt Sonata: slim, linear, and controlled from first note to last. It is an abstract Liszt Sonata, and the playing is Flaubertian.

BELLA DAVIDOVICH
b. 1928 — USSR

A student of Igumnov and Flier, she shared first prize with Halina Czerny-Stefanska at the 1949 Chopin Competition in Warsaw. Davidovich had a successful career in the Soviet Union before emigrating to the West, where she has continued to receive acclaim.

Davidovich's pianistic diction is immaculate, each phrase being well tailored and finely calibrated. She has a poetic strain, but elements of rapture, giddiness, or humor are absent. There is a wholesome quality in her work, and her recordings of the four Chopin Ballades, several Beethoven sonatas, and the Saint-Saëns G minor Concerto are satisfying. She has an affinity with Scriabin, and her playing of the Second Sonata finds her at her best.

FANNY DAVIES
1861–1934 — England

Davies studied with Reinecke and later with Clara Schumann. She became one of the most celebrated of English pianists. During the 1888 season, George Bernard Shaw heard her and wrote: "Miss Fanny Davies was full of speed, lilt, life, and energy. She scampered through a fugue of Bach's with a cleverness and jollity that forced us to condone her utter irreverence."

The Beethoven Fourth Concerto was one of her specialties, and her Schumann playing was respected, deriving, as it did, directly from the great tradition of Mme Schumann herself. She also played the then all but unknown Elizabethan composers. In 1921, Davies was the first ever to give a piano recital in Westminster Abbey. Elgar wrote his Concert Allegro for her.

IVAN DAVIS
b. 1932 — United States

He studied with Carlo Zecchi and later with Horowitz for a short time. Davis is best in lighter music. His Gottschalk fairly bubbles. His Grand Scherzo, *Manchega,* and *Tournament Galop* are scintillating, as are such obscurities as Hoffman's *Dixiana,* Mason's *Silver-Spring,* or Bartlett's *Grand Polka de concert.* Here we have a freewheeling pianist who knows how to enjoy the music.

Davis also has an aptitude for Schumann, and his early recording of the *Carnaval* shows the music well fitted to his breezy action. He has recorded the *Norma* paraphrase by Liszt with a wide color wheel. In concerto work, his *Rhapsody in Blue* is too jerky, the Liszt concerti unaccountably ponderous, and his Tchaikovsky B-flat minor just too vulgar.

ÉLIE MIRIAM DELABORDE
1839–1913 — France

The son of Alkan and considered a formidable pianist. Saint-Saëns dedicated his Third Piano Concerto to him. Olga Samaroff studied with him.

ALICIA DE LARROCHA
b. 1923 — Spain

A pupil of Frank Marshall, she made her first public appearance when she was five. At eleven, she made her first orchestral appearance, in a Mozart concerto, with Fernández Arbós conducting. After World War II, she began playing throughout Europe. In 1955 she made her American debut with the Los Angeles Philharmonic. She has received numerous honors, including the Spanish Order of Civil Merit, the Paderewski Medal, and the Harriet Cohen Medal.

De Larrocha takes a rightful place as one of the instrument's greatest players. She is the most comprehensive and important of all Spanish pianists. Born with unusually small hands, she transcended her limitation, overcoming every problem. Yet those small hands were destined for the keyboard; they are sinewy and pliable and the tips are padded. Recordings of her playing at the age of seven reveal more than a prodigy: they show an intense, pure, innocent musicality that expresses Chopin as naturally as a lark sings. She has somehow retained this innocence into maturity. De Larrocha, at her finest, defies analysis. She is a player of pure instinct, guided by an acute musical intelligence. Her formal building is never flabby or spontaneous. She works within a precise time cycle and is never one to capriciously play a score three minutes longer or shorter.

When she performs, the house is packed. With great urgency, this exceedingly small woman, with black fiery eyes and an innocent face, begins a grouping of Scarlatti or Soler sonatas. The playing has a grandly Spanish flourish, the rhythm snaps, the grace and lust of her playing remind us that de Larrocha is blessed with one of the most perfect, kinetic rhythmic senses in the musical world. She performs Spanish music of every era and genre as if each author had composed for her alone.

She must tire of being cast merely as a Spanish specialist. Few pianists have a larger appetite, and this includes hearty portions of the great Schumann literature. She displays her candor, shyness, and range of color in the F-sharp minor *Novellette.* Her *Humoreske* and *Kreisleriana* are full of whimsy. Less forthright, though, are the *Carnaval,* which is a shade cool, and the Fantasy, which is too disjointed.

Her Chopin never whimpers; it is strong, unmannered, and unfettered. A false rubato, an excessive phrase would be anathema to de Larrocha. In Ravel, she is happy; French music in general is one of her chief domains, in which she is crystalline and suave. How she can captivate in a Fauré nocturne or the Poulenc *Suite française.* Or listen to her Mendelssohn *Variations sérieuses* and the neglected Capriccio in A minor, Op. 33—so perfect in their rhythmic symmetry and richness of tone. Mozart is another of her great loves, and her best Mozart is gallant and well structured yet also sassy and filled with life. She is happier in the solo works, where she is fully in command, than in the concerti. She is not always in sympathy with Liszt. Her version of the Sonata seems perfunctory, even dutiful, nor is she suited to such juicy concertos as the Third Rachmaninoff or the Khachaturian. But in Falla's *Nights in the Gardens of Spain* she is magnificent.

She remains the greatest interpreter of Spanish music. The daring and drama of Albéniz's *Iberia,* the poetry and amorous passion of Granados's *Goyescas* have found in her their ideal interpreter. In these works, her great gift for Spanish national rhythms of all types bursts forth. This music, so often condemned as picture-postcard nationalism, in her hands gains depth and power. She knows that within the scores lies music of mystical and mythic beauty. In her performances of *Iberia* and *Goyescas* there is a spiritualization that brings these works to the heights of epic national poetry.

Her perfectly controlled use of the pedal is an object lesson for all who play these pieces. Her instinct for the right color is unerring. Each line and sonority is woven into a complex tapestry. De Larrocha is not concerned only with producing a singing tone; she also knows when she must produce harshness. Her phrasing, too, is impeccable. She never dreams of throwing a line off kilter for the sake of a meretricious effect.

Her feeling is profound, her conceptions have a cumulative power. Every inflection is felt to the quick, each pause fraught with meaning, even with anxiety. Her *Fête-Dieu à Seville* erupts with pent-up violence. She employs a wide array of weights in voicing her chords; her fingers never fail to bring out whichever tone within a chord she wants highlighted. Liszt said nuance is the pianist's palette, and de Larrocha is a great painter in the Goya manner. One always hears the guitar, the castanets, the click of heels, and love sacred and profane. Through her art, she traces a history of the Spanish heart and landscape. Of all her composers, I think she most deeply and tenderly loves Granados, whether in the late *Danza lente* or the Twelve Spanish Dances; she attains dewy freshness in the early *Valses poéticos,* and plays the arresting, teeming *Goyescas* with more poetry by far than any others who have attempted this composition.

Ernest Newman wrote of Granados's *Goyescas* that "never before has an artist so profoundly entered into and colored the soul of a musician." De Larrocha, in turn, has entered the heart of Granados. Her performance of the great ballade *El Amor y la muerte,* in its fervent but noble melancholy, needs to be heard on a still summer's night, with the waft of lemon trees floating in the air, flooded by a luminous and ghostly moon. De Larrocha's playing has an extraordinary power of evocation.

JÖRG DEMUS
b. 1928 — Austria

He has had a busy recording career. His records, especially those of the late 1950s and 83

1960s, sound academic and dim, except for his admirable set of Bach's *Well-Tempered Clavier*. Without trying to imitate the harpsichord, he displays a scholarship, a subtle legato, and a fine use of the pedal. In the fugues, he handles the counterpoint with gentle ease. Schubert is the Classical master whom Demus plays best, with charm and affection, in fact. He is delightful in the G major Sonata. I also value his all-Franck disc, with a well-proportioned Prelude, Fugue, and Variation in the Harold Bauer transcription. Demus plays it with the right amount of Franckian fervor without ever getting sticky.

MISHA DICHTER
b. 1945 — China

Studied with Aube Tzerko in Los Angeles, and in New York he received instruction from Rosina Lhévinne. In 1966, Dichter won second prize at the Tchaikovsky Competition, where he was the popular favorite.

Dichter exemplifies the modern child of the age of the piano competition, where standardization is the first rule of survival. Pianistically, Dichter is highly adept, but he is careful to extremes. Nothing must disrupt anyone. When he is in the mood, he can be exciting; when not, he is bland indeed.

In his latest recordings, there are signs of an emerging confidence and individuality. He is capable of keeping interest alive in such big scores as the Brahms D minor Concerto and Schubert's posthumous A major and B-flat major Sonatas. His Beethoven is sturdy, but he is still finding his way with the sonatas. He has made several Liszt albums of quality, although his recent set of the complete Hungarian Rhapsodies shows little inspiration in the lesser-known ones. His Stravinsky *Petrouchka*

shows the extent of his large and padded sound.

LOUIS DIÉMER
1843–1919 — France

He studied at the Paris Conservatoire with Marmontel, whom he succeeded in 1888. He accumulated a long list of pupils, among them Cortot, Robert Casadesus, Yves Nat, and Edouard Risler. Diémer wielded a strong influence on French pianism of his time. Saint-Saëns dedicated his brilliant Fifth Concerto to him, and he gave the premiere of Franck's *Symphonic Variations* in 1886.

THEODOR DÖHLER
1814–1856 — Italy

An astounding child prodigy who studied with Czerny. Later he became a sought-after virtuoso. His own music reaches Op. 75, a set of etudes typical of the frippery he touted around Europe, music of immense difficulty with almost no content. The poet Heine called his playing "elegant impotence," but found he had "interesting pallor."

ERNÖ VON DOHNÁNYI
1877–1960 — Hungary

He studied with the Liszt pupil István Thomán. Dohnányi may be called the last in the line of virtuoso pianist-composers. In his early career, he was a storming thunderer of a virtuoso, and eventually became one of the most powerful forces in Hungarian music, the virtual czar of piano teaching. Not to have studied with Dohnányi was a distinct disadvantage. Bartók said that it was Dohnányi who revealed to him the greatness of the Liszt Sonata, and Mischa Levitzki worked with him for four years, saying, "I know of no greater teacher." The list of his students is impressive, featuring such names as Géza Anda, György Cziffra, Annie Fischer, Andor Foldes, Edward Kilenyi, Lajos Hernádi, Georg Solti, Imre Ungar, and dozens of other brilliant pianists.

Somehow he always kept up his own playing. Even when he was past eighty, he was a formidable technician, as his recordings attest, and his finger technique was phenomenal. His playing combines nobility and lusty peasantry, yet he also shows a curious turgidity, with rhythmic mixtures which suffer from years of neglect. His *Moonlight* Sonata, recorded when he was eighty, has a first movement that would have been in poor taste in any era. The slow movement is agonized—not the "flower between two abysses" that Liszt once described. But in the finale, there are flashes of his primal fire. His playing of Chopin is the old-fashioned and courtly playing of a melancholy improviser. He played his own music marvelously, recording several of his rhapsodies and a few of his valse transcriptions, which are delicious Viennese pastry. The most important of his discs is a masterly rendering of his B minor Concerto and his masterpiece, the Variations on a Nursery Tune for Piano and Orchestra, made with Sir Adrian Boult.

ANTON DOOR
1833–1919 — Austria

He was an eminent pianist-teacher who studied with Czerny; years later he taught at the Moscow Conservatory. Tchaikovsky dedicated his captivating *Valse-caprice*, Op. 4, to

Door, and Saint-Saëns likewise dedicated his Fourth Piano Concerto to him.

ANIA DORFMANN
1899–1982 — Russia

A brilliant instrumentalist born in Odessa, Dorfmann began her successful concert career in 1920 and recorded, among other works, the complete Mendelssohn *Songs without Words*. In her later years she taught at the Juilliard School.

JEAN DOYEN
b. 1907 — France

He studied with Marguerite Long. His performances of French music are always lucid and riveting.

ALEXANDER DREYSCHOCK
1818–1869 — Czechoslovakia

A pupil of Tomáschek, Dreyschock was a prodigy who became one of the kings of the piano. He played almost exclusively his own horrendously difficult music. Reputedly one of the towering technicians of the Romantic age, he specialized in pieces and arrangements for the left hand. He took Chopin's *Revolutionary* Etude in Octaves at an amazing tempo, to the disbelief of his audience. When Johann Baptist Cramer heard him in Paris, he cried, "The man has no left hand! Here are two right hands." He was compared to the titans of the piano. Heine said that he "made a hell of a racket. From Paris, one could hear him in

Vienna." He composed a great deal, but not a note remains in the repertoire, although his *Konzertstück* has been recorded by Frank Cooper.

ZBIGNIEW DRZEWIECKI
1890–1971 — Poland

A pianist and teacher of distinction and one of the founders and judges of the Chopin Competition in Warsaw. His many students include Felicja Blumental, Roger Woodward, Wladyslaw Kedra, Fou Ts'ong, Halina Czerny-Stefanska, Adam Harasiewicz, and Regina Smendzianka.

ALEXANDER DUBUC
1812–1898 — Russia

He trained with John Field and was an important figure in early Russian pianism. He taught Alexander Villoing and Nikolai Zverev.

FRANÇOIS-RENÉ DUCHABLE
b. 1952 — France

One of the bright lights of contemporary French pianism. In 1964 he entered the Paris Conservatoire, and in 1965 was awarded the first prize in piano playing. In 1968 he took the prize at the Queen Elizabeth Competition and immediately began concertizing on an international scale, appearing in Japan, Israel, Europe, South Africa, and the United States. In 1978 he made appearances with Herbert von Karajan, and he has appeared with the major orchestras of Europe. Arthur Rubinstein admired this young colleague and wrote, "He knows how to use his exceptional gifts to express music and convey intense emotion to his audiences."

Duchable has a wide repertory, but his Chopin playing has received the most attention. His recording of the Etudes is an exciting excursion into this literature, and his disc of the Second and Third Sonatas reveals an astute sense of form as well as an individual approach to these often-played scores.

JAN LADISLAV DUSSEK
1760–1812 — Czechoslovakia

Dussek was one of the most fascinating figures in the early era of the piano. His fame was widespread, and he was among the first pianists to take advantage of the newly emerging idea of giving concerts in public, to which he brought a showman's flair. Previously, keyboard players had played either with their backs to the public, or directly facing them. But Dussek, shrewdly aware of his handsome profile, exhibited it to his audiences. He was dubbed *"le beau"* Dussek. His innovation caught on, and from that moment forward, pianists, beautiful or not, have played seated in this manner. Yet Dussek's vanity served a musical purpose. *"Le Beau"* soon discovered that the piano turned to the side with lid raised transmitted a more direct sound to the audience.

It was immediately apparent that his playing was different. Mozart and Clementi cultivated a singing tone, but Dussek seemed truly to "sing" on the instrument. Johann Tomáschek, an excellent pianist reporting on a Dussek concert in Prague, relates that "after the opening bars, the public uttered one general ah! There was in fact something magical . . . his fingers were like a company of ten singers." Kalkbrenner, a pianist stingy with praise for anyone but himself, said of Dussek that "no other pianist I have ever heard more captivated his audiences." Dussek understood better than any of his contemporaries that the illusion of singing on the piano is dependent on a beautiful legato with judicious pedaling. Few pianists of the day fully understood pedaling, and Dussek was one of the first to notate pedal markings in his music, as well as to mark in his scores novel fingerings, which promoted legato. Dussek kept pestering the Broadwood firm to extend the instrument's range from the five-octave compass. Finally, in 1794, he played a six-octave piano for the first time in public. (It would eventually be extended to 7⅓ octaves.)

Dussek was a restless man, and his career included many adventures. The happiest years of his life were spent as friend and teacher to Prince Louis Ferdinand of Prussia (nephew of Frederick the Great). The prince owned thirteen English pianos and was a good composer and pianist. (Beethoven honored him with the dedication of his Third Piano Concerto.) Dussek would even occasionally accompany Louis on military maneuvers. These were the Napoleonic years, and the prince was killed in battle in 1806, at the age of thirty-four. Dussek was grief-stricken, but out of his loss he produced *La Consolation,* Op. 62, and the masterly two-movement sonata *Elégie harmonique sur la mort du Prince Louis Ferdinand* in F-sharp minor, Op. 61, a work of astonishing emotional range and daring. Indeed, upon hearing it one scarcely believes that Dussek could have been born a mere four years after Mozart and died thirteen years earlier than Beethoven, or that he was born half a century before Chopin and Schumann, whose music he sometimes anticipates in an amazing manner. William S. Newman, in his book *The Sonata since Beethoven,* writes: "Dussek's best sonatas are regarded here as close to the best of their day, including those of Clementi, Beethoven, Schubert, and Weber—a view that may well surprise all but the relative few who have had the opportunity to explore or re-explore them. . . . Their several innovational styles often go beyond Dussek's environment of high-Classicism and well into that of unequivocal, sometimes fully bloomed, Romanticism."

In his later years, the once-dashing *Le Beau* became obese and alcoholic. He found an influential patron in Talleyrand, who let the pianist eat, drink, and compose. Regardless of his physical state, Dussek showed continual growth in his last works, which culminated in 1812 in the Sonata in F minor, Op. 77, subtitled *L'Invocation*—a work of magnificent depth and power.

Dussek remains the finest Czech-born composer before Smetana, and in several pieces he also anticipates Czech nationalism. Unfortunately, his work has all but disappeared from the living repertoire. He was, however, one of the most important musicians of his era, and the best of his output should be explored by contemporary pianists. He left nearly three hundred works, including twelve concerti, showing him to be a composer who was deeply aware of the piano's potential.

VICTOR ALPHONSE DUVERNOY
1842–1907—France

A pupil of Marmontel at the Paris Conservatoire. His student pieces were played for several generations.

JOSÉ ECHANIZ
1905–1969 — Cuba

A pianist and teacher at the Eastman School of Music. He made a number of recordings.

YOURI EGOROV
1954–1988 — USSR

Studied with Yakov Zak and emigrated to the West. He made recordings of Chopin etudes and works by other composers, and had much success with his Schumann playing. His piano technique was well polished, and his conceptions were better planned than those of many of the Russian pianists of his generation.

ILONA EIBENSCHÜTZ
1872–1967 — Hungary

She studied with Clara Schumann. Brahms admired her playing, and she played many of his works in public.

SEVERIN EISENBERGER
1879–1945 — Poland

He was a student of Leschetizky and a pianist with a marvelous mechanism. He came to the United States in the 1930s.

JAN EKIER
b. 1913 — Poland

A teacher, pianist, and Chopin scholar who has recorded many of Chopin's works in a dry manner.

PHILIPPE ENTREMONT
b. 1934 — France

He studied with Marguerite Long at the Paris Conservatoire. Entremont has long been a favorite with American audiences. Since his late teens, he has been building an international career. If a town has a piano, Entremont will get there. Along the way, he has managed to become a fine conductor, with positions with the Vienna Chamber Orchestra, the New Orleans Philharmonic, and the Denver Symphony. As a pianist, he has an industrious discography—from luxurious concertos to Clementi and Kuhlau sonatinas, which are a model for young students.

His best playing is contained on his earlier recordings of such concertos as Liszt's Second, Falla's *Nights in the Gardens of Spain*, the Ravel Concerto in G, and Bartók's Second. In later years, he opted for the facile, glamorous gesture, and many discs pall in their artificiality and chunkish pedaling and general puffiness. The Chopin Ballades, for instance, become meandering narratives, and his polonaise playing does no honor to Chopin's patriotism. In these scores, Entremont cannot find "the cannon buried amongst flowers," to borrow a phrase from Schumann. Yet Entremont is a gifted musician, and lately his solo recitals and Mozart concerto readings show a renewed concern for details as well as an intense concentration that had been missing for many seasons.

JULIUS EPSTEIN
1832–1923 — Austria

For many years a well-known pianist and teacher at the Vienna Conservatory. His son, Richard Epstein (1869–1919), was an esteemed pianist and editor.

LONNY EPSTEIN
1885–1963 — Germany

Studied at the Frankfurt Conservatory and later with Carl Friedberg. For years she taught at the Juilliard School. Although she had a large repertoire, her Mozart playing was especially admired.

DOROTHEA ERTMANN
1781–1849 — Germany

She was a member of the cultivated Viennese social elite. Ertmann's playing was a constant delight to Beethoven. His great Sonata No. 28, Op. 101, is dedicated to her.

CHRISTOPH ESCHENBACH
b. 1940 — Germany

One of the finest German pianists of his generation. Eschenbach is singularly adapted to large forms and his recordings of the Schubert B-flat Sonata and the Beethoven *Hammerklavier* are spread to the limits of their time scale—the Schubert at 43:30, the Beethoven at 50:00. At times, especially in the central slow movements, Eschenbach becomes somewhat affected and prissy, doting over details. His recording of the Chopin Preludes is technically strong, but is sometimes marred by ridiculous pauses which serve only to detract from the music's urgency. He can play Schumann with purpose, finding nectar in the *Abegg* Variations, while lyricism and drama permeate his performance of the Intermezzi, Op. 4.

The Mozart concerti rank high for him, and he plays them while conducting from the piano. In recent seasons, Eschenbach has developed into an excellent conductor.

His finest recorded achievement is Mozart's solo Sonatas and Fantasies on seven discs. Eschenbach presides over these scores with sparkling dexterity; the slow movements are operatic, and the finales betray a humor that is often missing in these works. Occasionally his tone is too buttery for the idiom, and the rubato too strong; but overall it is significant Mozart playing by a pianist of exceptional musicianship.

VIRGINIA ESKIN
b. 1944 — United States

She plays a wide repertoire, but has become best known for her advocacy of women composers of the nineteenth and twentieth centuries. Eskin has recorded such neglected scores as Amy Beach's *Balkan Variations,* Louise Talma's powerful Sonata, and music of Fanny Mendelssohn.

ANNETTE ESSIPOVA
1850–1914 — Russia

A pianist of the first rank. She studied with Leschetizky, and was briefly married to him. She played throughout Europe and in America. Essipova helped Paderewski early in his career and premiered several of his compositions, including the Concerto and the now ubiquitous Minuet in G. She returned to Russia, where she was the most capable teacher at the St. Petersburg Conservatory. Her high level of technique and beauty of tone were keenly appreciated in Russian pianism. Her students included Simon Barère, Thomas de Hartmann, Isabelle Vengerova, Lev Pouish-

nov, Ignace Hilsberg, Sergei Prokofiev, and a host of others. In his memoirs, Paderewski wrote: "She was a charming pianist . . . very feminine. . . . Her playing in many ways was perfect, except when it came to strong, effective pieces—then she was lacking in real force."

MORTON ESTRIN
b. 1923 — United States

A pupil of Vera Maurana-Press and Rosina Lhévinne, he made his New York debut at Town Hall in 1949. Estrin is a strong pianist with excellent technical equipment. He is capable of playing the Scriabin Etudes Op. 8 and the Rachmaninoff preludes with brilliance and a modicum of poetry. He has made many recordings and has often performed neglected works such as Joachim Raff's impressive Suite in D minor, Op. 91.

EDITH FARNADI
1921–1973 — Hungary

She played throughout Europe and made many records, including a large number of works by Liszt. It was a careful, dry Liszt, lacking grandiosity and large technical mechanism.

LOUISE FARRENC
1804–1875 — France

A famous pianist and the only woman piano teacher at the Paris Conservatoire for over thirty years. Her editions of keyboard music from the sixteenth century to her time were invaluable. Schumann regarded her piano music highly, and her etudes are imaginative.

AMY FAY
1844–1928 — United States

Born in Mississippi, she studied in Europe with Tausig and many others before joining Liszt's class. Her letters home were published as *Music-Study in Germany,* which has become a minor classic. It is a volume filled with delightful observations on the sociological situation of a young American student in Germany, drinking in culture and genius. Her views of Liszt are especially revealing. She returned to the United States, where she had a long teaching career.

SAMUEL FEINBERG
1890–1962 — Russia

He studied with Goldenweiser at the Moscow Conservatory. Feinberg had a virtuoso technique, and his playing had a certain wayward Slavic feeling, especially in his idiomatic Scriabin. He composed a large quantity of difficult and intense music.

VLADIMIR FELTSMAN
b. 1952 — USSR

The winner of the Marguerite Long–Jacques Thibaud Competition in Paris in 1971, Feltsman was kept from emigrating from the Soviet Union until 1987, when he came to the United States with great publicity. He played at the White House and in November 1987 made an auspicious Carnegie Hall debut. In February 1988 he played the Brahms B-flat Concerto with Zubin Mehta and the New York Philharmonic. Feltsman is a pianist with musical gifts and solid technique who can rouse an audience to a standing ovation.

ALBERT FERBER
b. 1911 — Switzerland

An excellent pianist who is best known in England. He worked with Gieseking and Long. Ferber recorded many pieces; his best work is a recording of Rachmaninoff's Variations on a Theme by Chopin.

JACQUES FÉVRIER
1900–1979 — France

He worked with Long and Risler and was a pianist especially suited to the French literature. Ravel admired his distinctive playing. Together with the composer, he premiered Poulenc's Concerto for Two Pianos and Orchestra. The recording of it is a delight. Arthur Rubinstein wrote, "Jacques Février is a good pianist and an excellent musician and the best sight-reader I ever met."

JOHN FIELD
1782–1837 — Ireland

He studied with Clementi and performed in the major capitals of Europe, making a London debut in 1794 and a Paris debut in 1802.

As pianist and the inventor of the nocturne genre, John Field is an important figure in the early history of piano music. He was among the first to create small, self-contained pieces of a subjective nature. During his time, the sonata ruled the thoughts of most composers. Field escaped such formalism in his nocturnes, in which he accompanied his suave, Italianate melodies with a freer, more dispersed left hand, with the pedal blending the whole into an illusion of song. With the Field nocturne, intimacy and romance became part of the piano's vocabulary. Around the age of twenty, he settled in St. Petersburg. The musical life of Russia was as yet unformed, and Field established himself as a fashionable teacher despite his dozing through most of the lessons with aristocratic pupils. His eccentricities were the talk of the town. He charged exorbitant fees, and he lived, loved, and drank extravagantly. But his influence on Russian pianism was great. He gave Glinka piano lessons and taught the important pianist-teacher Charles Mayer, who himself had more than seven hundred Russian pupils.

Field's early-Romantic playing possessed a poetic allure. The great violinist Louis Spohr wrote of Field's "dreamy melancholy." Glinka said "his fingers fell on the keys as large drops of rain that spread themselves like iridescent pearls." In 1832, Liszt heard him in Paris and fell under his spell. He recalled that

Field did not so much play his own nocturnes but dreamed them at the piano. . . . His almost immovable attitude and but slightly expressive face attracted no attention. His eye sought no other eye. His execution flowed clear and limpid. His fingers glided over the keys and the sounds they awoke seemed to follow them like the foaming crest of a wave. It was easy to see that for him his chief auditor was himself. His tranquility was well-nigh somnolent, and the impression he made on his hearers was his least care. No abruptness, no shock, either of gesture or rhythm, ever supervened to interrupt his melodious reverie, whose fondly murmuring melodies, *mezza voce,* spread through the air with the most delicious impressions, the most charming surprises of the heart.

Field's first nocturnes were published in 1814, but were probably composed much earlier. Chopin so perfectly assimilated Field's style that the title *nocturne* has become synonymous with the Polish master, while Field's more naive and gentle night-pieces are now seldom played. Yet Busoni felt that to play a Field nocturne well required the highest art. Field was one of the first to divine the potential of the piano's "singing" capacities, and his still-fragrant nocturnes made him one of early Romanticism's most charming advocates.

KARL FILTSCH
1830–1845 — Hungary

The one genius among Chopin students. His sensitivity and perfectly polished mechanism prompted Liszt to say that when Karl was to begin touring, he would close up shop. Chopin wept when hearing his own E minor Concerto performed by the young pianist. Tuberculosis claimed Filtsch at the age of fifteen. Leschetizky, who was the same age, recalled many years later that "Filtsch was a handsome boy . . . a beautiful blond, really too refined and delicate for life's struggle. . . . As a parting gift he gave me an autograph manuscript copy of a Chopin Impromptu . . . saying that he believed I, of all his friends, would best interpret it."

SERGIO FIORENTINO
b. 1928 — Italy

He studied at the Naples Conservatory and won prizes in several competitions. His recordings of Liszt's late music are excellent.

RUDOLF FIRKUŠNÝ
b. 1912 — Czechoslovakia

He studied with Vilém Kurz and is the preeminent Czech pianist of the twentieth century.

In a Firkušný performance, one experiences undiluted tonal pleasure. His sound is rich and creamy and he is, above all, musical. Although he has given patrician readings of all the standard concertos, and premiered many works, such as the Howard Hanson Concerto and concertos by Martinů and others, Firkušný is at his best when he plays alone; then he yields to his reveries. When he appears with orchestra, he is weighed down by the orchestral apparatus. His temperament is Romantic, but guided by a precise intellect, and his hands are wonderfully well schooled. Firkušný's stage manner is appealing; he is an aristocrat and has no use for gesticulation.

When Firkušný is totally involved in the music, there is that rarest of occurrences: the merging of the artist with the instrument. When he is not, he becomes tight-lipped and merely sleek. Firkušný is essentially a lyric bard, who uses a wide color wheel. Especially in later years, he displays many soft hues. But he has power enough, and his playing always unrolls fluidly and logically in large-scale forms. He can make perfect sense of Dussek's half-hour Grand Sonata in F minor, Op. 77 (*L'Invocation*), a piece which would be incoherent in the hands of a merely average player.

Firkušný's Beethoven is well balanced, not a Teutonic Beethoven but Slavic to the core, and his Schubert readings are becoming some of his most esteemed interpretations. His Schubert Sonatas in A minor, D. 784 and D. 845, are both filled with beautiful impressionist tints. Firkušný's recording of the late Schubert Piano Pieces of 1828 is marvelously pliant. His deft rendering of the smaller Brahms pieces alternates between light and dark.

His playing of Mussorgsky's *Pictures at an Exhibition* is among the most impressive of his recordings. He is no casual viewer at a picture gallery, but a moved and observant visitor. Every rest, every line is objectively etched. His Chopin is without affectation, and while an early recording of the Third Sonata was rigid and plain, his Chopin has grown more intimate through the years. In whatever he touches, though, he always retains a reserve which is beguiling.

Throughout his long career, Firkušný has promoted Czech music of all periods. He has continued to champion Martinů and recently played that composer's Piano Concerto No. 2. (He has also played No. 3, which was dedicated to him.) The primary influence on Firkušný was his study and friendship with the greatest twentieth-century Czech master, Leoš Janáček. Firkušný plays the Concertino, the Capriccio for Left Hand and Orchestra, the Sonata, *In the Mist*, the Variations, and *On an Overgrown Path*. Every fiber of his being responds to Janáček's unique language. The Dvořák Concerto has toured everywhere with Firkušný, who makes this score sound even better than it is. He has also recorded Dvořák's Mazurkas and Humoresques, and gives a magical performance of his neglected A major Suite. His bravura is captivating in the pungent polkas of Smetana, whose work he also plays often.

ANNIE FISCHER
b. 1914 — Hungary

A student of Dohnányi, she is persuasive in a large and varied repertoire, with a rich sound and a big technique. Her Beethoven playing has special vitality. Fischer invests all of her interpretations with depth and feeling, but as a public performer she is not always consistent.

EDWIN FISCHER
1886–1960 — Switzerland

In Berlin, Fischer studied with Martin Krause; later, he taught at the Stern Conservatory for nearly a decade. He played chamber music, conducted, and wrote several books, including one on the Beethoven sonatas. His master classes were filled with students from all over the world, with Brendel, Barenboim, Badura-Skoda, Demus, and others in attendance.

Fischer, born the year of Liszt's death, was a contemporary of Schnabel and Backhaus, and like theirs his pianism was not characteristic of the arrogant virtuosity of the day. Fischer promoted the great Classical works and played Bach in the original, not in the pumped-up transcriptions that were so popular in his early days. To build a career on such a serious foundation was not easy. Nonetheless, Fischer's burning Classicism attracted Walter, Mengelberg, and Furtwängler, and these conductors constantly engaged him. Later, Fischer conducted his own chamber orchestra in Haydn and Mozart, and performed with the group as soloist in Bach concerti. These lean but passionate presentations were highly influential, and on disc they remain treasures of the recorded art.

Fischer the pianist was monumental, and it was impossible for him to play dully. He retained his nineteenth-century heritage, and although he was a transitional pianist, he sounds very different from a Badura-Skoda or a Brendel, who seem tame and academic by comparison. Listen to Fischer's celebrated recording of Bach's Chromatic Fantasy and Fugue, which is absolutely breathtaking in its white-hot Romanticism. More conservative, but thrilling in detail and regal in contrapuntal mastery, are his recordings of *The Well-Tempered Clavier*. Or hear his Handel Chaconne in G, with its ten degrees of shading, octave doublings, expressive pedaling, which have nothing in common with a modern harpsichordist's reading. I have played this record for scholarly harpsichordists, and they shake their heads in disdain. Fischer, in his Baroque playing, often phrases in Romantic gasps. His Baroque architecture is Venetian in splendor. But what spellbinding conceptions of Bach concerti and Preludes and Fugues he presents. It is not necessary to call such playing old-fashioned, or even lacking in correctness of style. Fischer's playing may not be to the letter, yet it may be more authentic in spirit than any cold and correct playing steeped in musicology.

He recorded the Schubert Eight Impromptus with the elusive breathing that gives these pieces their dewy freshness. His Mozart was famous, and his readings of the Concerti No. 20 in D minor, No. 22 in E-flat, and No. 25 in C are important recordings, to be studied and relished. His playing of slow movements shows an excruciating sensitivity.

Fischer was an inspiring teacher. Alfred Brendel describes him at a master class: "Fischer was electrifying by his mere presence. The playing of timid youths and placid girls would suddenly spring to life when he grasped them by the shoulder. . . . When Fischer outlined the structure of a whole movement the gifted ones among the participants felt they were looking into the very heart of music."

Badura-Skoda was convinced that "Fischer had all the bearings of genius. Everything he did was creative, different, touched by a different source. . . . And yet his massive gifts did not always come through in public. There were moments of agony in his concerts. He was so overly sensitive that he could sabotage his own recitals." Today there is a growing awareness of Fischer's immense musical imagination, and his recordings have never been more prized. Numerous young pianists are finding him to be a wellspring of inspiration, hearing in him a fearless interpreter with a musical integrity that shines through every note.

LEON FLEISHER
b. 1928 — United States

From childhood he was a student of Artur Schnabel. In 1952, Fleisher was the first American to win the Queen Elizabeth Competition in Brussels. Because of a muscular problem in the right hand, his solo career was ended in 1964. In the intervening years he has conducted a great deal and has appeared in concert in works for the left hand alone. At Baltimore's Peabody Conservatory, he has been an inspiring teacher.

At his peak, Fleisher was the model of clean-cut, intelligent American pianism. His playing offered a fresh, astringent, and at times brash sound, as in Copland's Sonata and Kirchner's First Concerto. Fleisher's motto seemed to be "First there is rhythm," and his rhythmic knife was sharp-edged, joyous, and bracing. He used the pedal sparingly, and his technique was on a high virtuoso level. His recordings of the Beethoven Concerti are masterly examples of solidity. He and conductor Szell romp in the rondos, are tight and precise in ensemble. The slow movements are expressive, but not subjective. It is a Beethoven without pretentiousness or metaphysics, the Second Concerto being the best ever recorded. His Brahms was just as successful, and the D minor Concerto has a mighty wallop. He recorded the Brahms *Handel* Variations with an objective frostiness and a ruthless energy that pointed up the work's structural wonders. In the tiny Brahms waltzes, he is entrancing.

Fleisher's playing is so direct that, on first hearing, it may seem somewhat cold. He seems to say, "Here now is the music. It is very good music." His Liszt Sonata is scrubbed clean of cloying sentiments. The Weber *Invitation to the Dance* becomes curiously modern under his hands, no longer the old-fashioned relic from 1819, which had always sounded better in Berlioz's orchestral setting. In Fleisher's rendering of Weber's Fourth Sonata in E minor, he sews together the still Classical form and the early Romantic material, with barely a seam showing. The minuet (one for witches) has a trio which shows off Fleisher's brilliantly controlled fingerwork, and the Andante is conceived with indescribable taste. With such playing, one wonders why this work is not part of the permanent repertoire.

YAKOV FLIER
1912–1978 — Russia

Within the Soviet orbit he had a distinguished career as both teacher and performer. He made an American debut with the Rachmaninoff Third Concerto in 1963. Flier possessed a warm virtuosity and his Chopin playing had heart. The Barcarolle and the E-flat minor Polonaise are very picturesque. Of special merit is a recording of a brilliantly colored Schumann Fantasy. He made a delightful recording of Kabalevsky's Twenty-four Preludes. He is uncomfortable with the style of Mozart's C minor Fantasy, K. 475, which is the case with a great deal of Soviet Mozart playing.

ANDOR FOLDES
b. 1913 — Hungary

A student of Dohnányi and the winner of the Liszt Prize in 1933. Foldes is the author of

Keys to the Keyboard. He made many recordings, some of the best being Bartók's solo music.

SIDNEY FOSTER
1917–1977 — United States

Studied with David Saperton and, in 1941, won the Leventritt Award. Foster was a highly respected teacher at Indiana University. His recording of Clementi sonatinas possesses a childlike charm.

FOU TS'ONG
b. 1934 — China

He has won prizes in several competitions, including the Chopin Competition in Warsaw in 1955, where he was also given the special prize for best mazurka playing. He went on to a fine career and is especially well known in England. He returned to the United States in 1987 with a successful recital at Alice Tully Hall in New York. His recording of Handel's G major Chaconne is an ideal transference of harpsichord music to the piano.

MALCOLM FRAGER
b. 1935 — United States

He studied with Carl Friedberg, won the Leventritt Award in 1959, and followed this by winning the 1960 Queen Elizabeth Competition. He recorded a superb Prokofiev Second Concerto early in his career. His recording of the twelve MacDowell Virtuoso Studies is a worthy contribution to the performance of American piano music, and his recordings of Chopin solo pieces and the Weber piano concerti are excellent. Frager is very much in demand and tours widely.

AUGUST FRANCKE
1870–1933 — Germany

A student of Anton Door in Vienna. He had a fruitful career as a pianist. In later years he headed the New York College of Music.

SAMSON FRANÇOIS
1924–1970 — France

A student of Cortot and Long, François achieved a strong European reputation. He also played in the United States and China. He was an always intriguing performer who could be very erratic and eccentric. His complete recordings of Ravel are among his best work. He composed, and his piano concerto was recorded.

CLAUDE FRANK
b. 1925 — Germany

A longtime student of Artur Schnabel, he came to the United States where he established a reputation as a valuable teacher and pianist. His Beethoven playing—fluid, suave, and often lyrical—is highly prized; he recorded the complete piano sonatas.

PETER FRANKL
b. 1935 — Hungary

He studied with Lajos Hernádi and Marguerite Long. In 1958 he won the Liszt Prize. Frankl has recorded a great deal, including the complete piano music of Schumann and Debussy. He is sensitive to Schumann's often thickly scored piano writing and is careful not to get stuck in *mezzo forte* when soft playing is required. Frankl's left hand is extremely solid and he often plays with gusto, bringing freshness to such often-played scores as *Carnaval* and *Kinderscenen*.

In Debussy, he opts for a middle road—neither a voluptuous impressionism nor a tightly fitted structure. Frankl's Chopin, such as the Ballades and F minor Fantasy, has shape and is without affectation. In his recordings of the complete polonaises, he is rather tedious in the famous ones, but quite stylish in the unknown and juvenile ones.

NELSON FREIRE
b. 1944 — Brazil

Freire studied in Vienna with Bruno Seidlhofer. He is a pianist of impeccable taste in Romantic music. His tempi are often quick, and his technique is sharp and diamondlike.

EMIL FREY
1889–1946 — Switzerland

He studied with Diémer. In 1910 he won the Rubinstein Prize. Frey taught at the Moscow Conservatory and later in Zurich. He had many successful tours and composed as well.

CARL FRIEDBERG
1872–1955 — Germany

In 1887 he played for Clara Schumann, who soon after became his teacher. Later, Brahms worked with him on most of his piano music. He made his orchestral debut in 1892, under Mahler. Friedberg had a distinguished career in chamber music, as a soloist, and was an inspiring teacher. In 1953 he recorded several works, including the *Symphonic Etudes* of Schumann.

ARTHUR FRIEDHEIM
1859–1932 — Russia

He was one of Liszt's most important pupils and a pianist of redoubtable powers, master of the Liszt Sonata, *Don Juan* Fantasy, the *Hammerklavier,* and the *Diabelli* Variations. In 1891, Friedheim was the first major artist to perform at the newly opened Carnegie Recital Hall, even as the main hall was still being built. That same year saw his New York concerto debut with the famous Theodore Thomas Orchestra at the Metropolitan Opera House in Beethoven's *Emperor* Concerto and the Liszt Second Concerto.

His programs were herculean. For example, a recital that included the *Hammerklavier* also featured his own three transcriptions from Wagner's *Walküre;* the C minor Nocturne, F minor Ballade, and *Polonaise-fantaisie* of Chopin; the *Mephisto Waltz* and the *Sonnambula* paraphrase of Liszt; as well as Balakirev's

Islamey, not to mention half a program of encores. In 1912, James Huneker wrote: "Those critics who cry for uncompromising artistic sincerity, a technical equipment that seeks not to display but only to interpret, and a penetrating insight into the purpose, method and moods of the composers—such exacting searchers have always found in Friedheim the actual embodiment of the ideal they profess to worship."

IGNAZ FRIEDMAN
1882–1948—Poland

His early studies took place in Cracow, and then he went to Vienna to study with Leschetizky. At first the great teacher told him, as he had told Paderewski, to give up the piano. Strange advice, since the mature Friedman had all the hallmarks of what Leschetizky most wanted in a pianist—an all-encompassing technique, beauty of tone, poetic feeling, and great projection in large halls. Indeed, Friedman became one of the most popular players of his day, giving more than three thousand concerts, and he had enormous success in Japan in the 1930s. He prepared some very special editions of Chopin and Liszt with fascinating pedaling. Friedman composed more than a hundred works, mostly for piano. He recorded several of them, such as *Elle danse,* which was danced to by Pavlova. The best known of his compositions are the Six Viennese Dances, little masterpieces of nostalgic waltz writing. During his last years, he was unable to play as a result of crippling rheumatism.

The complete Friedman recordings are marvels of the Romantic spirit. The Danish pianist Gunnar Johansen first heard him in Copenhagen, where Friedman was the pianistic hero during the First World War. "It was colossal," he wrote; "now, years later when I hear his recordings, I understand why. He had an individuality like nobody else—nobody plays like Friedman." Vladimir Horowitz told me that "Rachmaninoff was 'crazy' about Friedman's playing, but he could be guilty of playing to the gallery." At his worst, he strained for effect, as in the A-flat Polonaise, where he manages to be vulgar; or he could be eccentric and even dull, as in the Grieg Concerto, his only concerto recording. But the greater part of his recorded legacy is astounding—reckless and humorously tongue-in-cheek, as in the Second Rhapsody and *La Campanella* of Liszt. He throws caution to the wind and grins to himself throughout. His technique was as natural as breathing, and in certain technical realms, such as double-notes, he was incomparable.

His Chopin Etude in Thirds makes those of other pianists pale. Lhévinne's is the only one to equal his technically, but Friedman's is more nonchalant, more Romantically autumnal, with a living rubato. Friedman said that he practiced it five thousand times before he attempted it in public. He also recorded several other Chopin etudes: a disappointing *Butterfly* and *Black Key,* and a *Revolutionary* Etude that nobody has ever approached for originality and daring. His left hand and right are in two different spheres. The performance is barless and follows laws that only Friedman could follow. It would certainly be frowned upon in the conservatory today as a bad example for modern virtuosi. It is unique playing, however, and one may compare it with Pollini's grim, abstract reading to hear the two extremes of Romantic and modern interpretation. Pollini is literal and bleak; Friedman is flexible, imaginative, and original.

One other Chopin etude must be mentioned, the C major Etude Op. 10, No. 7, which, as a technical tour de force, is foremost among all performances of the work ever put on disc. It is stupendous in workmanship, courageous in conception—it is astonishing to think that he just walked into a studio on a winter's day in 1930 and tossed it off in an age before editing.

Chopin was the jewel in the crown of Friedman's repertoire. Other notable examples of his recorded output are a few Preludes, the best being the treacherous E-flat, No. 19. But the A-flat Ballade is far too precious. His disc of the Funeral March and Finale from the B-flat minor Sonata is superb. The march is uniquely pedaled, and the finale, "The Wind over the Graves," is as effective as Rachmaninoff's eerie version.

Friedman was a master of quarter and half pedalings, and his foot movements were as finely honed as those of his fingers and wrists. He used the piano as *his* way of expressing music; the composer's intention and other sacred cows of our era had no meaning for him. He understood that Chopin was beautiful and great, and he proceeded from there to imbue a work with his own personality. Sometimes he was simple; other times, impulsive; and above all, he used the piano as a singing instrument, an instrument to rival the voice and the violin in its ability to make a listener weep. Listen in a totally dark room to Friedman's recording of the Chopin Nocturne in E-flat Op. 55, No. 2. Here we have on disc the very acme of Chopinesque lyricism, a lyricism that transcends all fashion. Not a note is out of place. There is not a nervous motion to mar the lines, not a patch of purple passion to crush the delicate sentiment. It is, without doubt, the quintessential performance of a Chopin nocturne, the one I would choose above all others. Here is the perpetually singing tone, which alone can ravish the ear and heart.

This was what Leschetizky preached, and demanded from his pupils. Indeed, the further pianists have come from the Romantic tradition, the more Friedman's recordings

have become studied and valued. None have been more admired than the thirty-odd minutes of Chopin mazurkas that he recorded almost six decades ago. These Mazurka recordings are now mythic in the annals of the piano. His playing reveals a powerful authenticity, yet the interpretations have nothing even remotely in common with other mazurka playing. David Bar-Illan said, "The greater the interpretation, the more impossible to figure it out. A good example is Friedman's recordings of some of the Chopin mazurkas. I don't understand what he is doing. On purpose I try to imitate them—not to play like him, of course, but to understand what he does. And yet what he does with them remains an enigma." They seem to have a rhythmic life of their own. He pronounced the bass notes as never before. They are ruddy, fragrant, lusty, and filled with coquetry. They speak a universal language that resides deep within the ancient dance form.

One more segment of Friedman's art must be savored—his recording of a group of the Mendelssohn *Songs without Words*. In them, the very spirit of Mendelssohn is kindled. These pieces, so tortured by tyros of low sentiment, are warmed here in a radiant light; they melt the heart. In this performance we find the springtime of life; a sense that all will come in its time and its place. The playing enchants us in the sheer confidence of his phrasing, the lack of anxiety, the clarity of his many touches, the living staccato and smoothness of legato, the loveliness of the tone. Here, music plays Friedman—gentle and tremulous. He brings rapture to the *Duetto,* a velvety sound to the F-sharp minor *Venetian Boat Song,* mystery and bliss to the once-hackneyed G minor *Boat Song,* and joyous life to the *Hunting Song.* Friedman takes us away on a magic carpet. Although it occupies only one side of an LP, this playing alone would rank him as one of the great Romantic pianists.

JAMES FRISKIN
1886–1967 — Scotland

A student of Dannreuther, he settled in the United States in 1914. He was one of the original faculty members of the Juilliard School and taught there until his death. Friskin was a fine scholar who was best known for his precise Bach playing and excellent editions. He composed several chamber works.

ADOLFO FUMAGALLI
1828–1856 — Italy

Studied at the Milan Conservatory and made a debut in 1848. He had a brief but brilliant career. The best known of his many salon pieces is *Les Clochettes*, Op. 21. He had three brothers who achieved reputations as pianists.

OSSIP GABRILOWITSCH
1878–1936 — Russia

He studied with Anton Rubinstein at the St. Petersburg Conservatory and worked for two years with Leschetizky. In 1918 he was appointed conductor of the Detroit Symphony, building it into an exemplary ensemble. Gabrilowitsch was one of the most popular pianists of his time. His tone sang, and his legato was smoothness itself. Anton Rubinstein had said of him as a child: "Of course he must become a musician, for he will become great among the great." Much later, Olin Downes wrote: "Always the listener was fascinated, absorbed. Always he was responding, as he listened, to beauty, feeling, and a divine union of imagination and form. . . . He could have no imitators, and no rivals."

It is regrettable that so little of his pianistic art was recorded, either acoustically or electrically. He was also a wonderful chamber musician, and a beautiful performance of the Schumann Quintet with the legendary Flonzaley Quartet has been put on LP. With his friend Harold Bauer, he often appeared in two-piano recitals. Together they made a recording of the Arensky Waltz that is of an exquisite elegance; it is playing that has never been equaled for its lilt and perfect movement.

Gabrilowitsch occasionally gave cycles of piano concertos. His last Carnegie Hall venture, during the 1934–35 season, presented sixteen concertos in five evenings. In 1915 he gave a series of historical recitals consisting of eighty-five works. His father-in-law was Mark Twain. His wife, Clara Clemens, wrote a biography of him.

PAOLO GALLICO
1868–1955 — Italy

Studied with Julius Epstein in Vienna. He toured for years and taught in New York. He made instructive editions of Liszt's *Transcendental Etudes* and Henselt's Etudes.

RUDOLPH GANZ
1877–1972 — Switzerland

He worked with Busoni and was a champion of the new. In the course of his long career, Ganz played throughout Europe and the United States. In 1921 he was appointed conductor of the St. Louis Symphony. He was also head of the piano department of the Chicago Musical College. Griffes dedicated his *White Peacock* to Ganz, and Ravel honored him as the dedicatee of *Scarbo*. He also composed, and left some recordings.

ANDREI GAVRILOV
b. 1956 — USSR

Won the Tchaikovsky Competition in 1974. Later he left for the West. Gavrilov has a wonderful physical mechanism, but in public he can get carried away, often banging and playing too fast, and in such concertos as the Rachmaninoff Second, he does his best to vulgarize the score. On recordings, he is less ferocious and gives nicely turned out performances of Scriabin preludes and careful readings of Bach.

HEINRICH GEBHARD
1878–1963 — Germany

As a child, he came to the United States. Later, in Vienna, he studied with Leschetizky for four years. He frequently performed, and wrote a volume, *The Art of Pedaling*. His many students included Leonard Bernstein.

ABBÉ JOSEPH GELINEK
1757–1825 — Czechoslovakia

Mozart was struck by Gelinek's powers of improvisation. In Vienna he became a well-known piano teacher of the aristocracy. His variations, fantasies, and rondos were ready-made for easy consumption; not a note remains.

CECILE STAUB GENHART
1898–1983 — Switzerland

A student of Busoni and Emil Frey. In 1924, Genhart joined the piano faculty of the Eastman School of Music, where she spent her entire career, becoming the most sought-after piano teacher of that institution. She introduced the Brahms Second Concerto to Rochester.

ANTON GERKE
1814–1870 — Poland

He played and taught at St. Petersburg. Composed various genre pieces for piano, including *Ten Characteristic Pieces*, Op. 14.   101

WALTER GIESEKING
1895–1956 — France

He came from a cultivated family and played piano from an early age, but he was virtually self-taught until 1914, when, at the age of nineteen, he embarked on a course of systematic training. It was his good fortune to become associated with the unusual and experimental pedagogue Karl Leimer, with whom he worked until 1917. Leimer insisted on a visualization method which, when mastered, surpassed countless hours of physical drudgery at the instrument. Later, Leimer wrote of Gieseking: "He does not impress [pieces] upon his memory . . . by playing them over on the piano, but by visualizing them through silent reading. By further development of this idea, one acquires the ability even to prepare the technical execution through visualization, so that, without studying at the instrument itself, the piece can be perfectly performed and this in a most astonishingly short time."

Of course, this process was enhanced by Gieseking's innate genius and musical memory, among the greatest in history. He certainly spent fewer hours at the instrument than most pianists did. He was also a remarkable sight-reader, probably of the caliber of Liszt, Saint-Saëns, and Bizet. Stories about his wondrous musical facility are plentiful. He dared to play a premiere of a difficult piano concerto with only days of preparation—from memory! Gieseking also composed with immense ease a fair amount of music which has had no currency in the repertoire.

Gieseking's hearing was among the most sensitive of any musician's, and he was able to hear overtones that the average ear missed. One of the supreme wizards of the pedal, he seemed to have placed his ear next to the pedals themselves, creating effects that defy description, and his playing was perhaps the most ethereal of all time. Chopin would have adored him.

Gieseking's reflexes were split-second, and he achieved the illusion of a perfect and creamy legato more by calculated artful pedaling than through finger binding. After a chord, Gieseking's fingers were instantly detached rather than remaining bound to the piano. Such lifting off frees the vibratory power of the instrument. Few understood the piano's secrets as he did. His sound flowed through and out of the piano. Gieseking must never have known that the piano is officially called a percussion instrument.

There are many who would name Gieseking this century's greatest pianistic colorist. His dynamics included the subtlest pianissimos ever heard from a piano—as Huneker said of Chopin, "as ghostly as a lunar rainbow." He was a painter of music, and harmony was his color. He phrased with a unique pliancy coupled to a rhythmic awareness and a sense of forward motion. Nobody had ever brought to piano playing, especially in Debussy, such a feeling of inspiration, a sense of evanescent sound hovering in midair, vulnerable to the slightest breeze. Gieseking reveled in illustrating the elegant titles of Debussy's works, the mythological picturings—the fireworks displays, the scents and rhythms of Spain, the nymphs, the rains, the clanging of bells, the dancers, the desolation of snow, the shuddering west wind, and the child's own secret world; it was tone painting as never before effected or thought possible on the piano. If Debussy wanted the piano to sound hammerless, it was Gieseking who complied best. It's a pity that the French composer never heard his music painted by this artist.

Gieseking was also a great interpreter of Ravel, and his recordings of this French master are flooded with light. It is a Ravel of tremulous liquidity, although in many pieces lacking a needed focus and bite. It was Gieseking who put the seal on Ravel's pianistic fame, and his *Gaspard de la nuit* is a landmark recording. Gieseking's performance of the exotic repertoire of Debussy and Ravel is a major chapter in the history of world pianism. In his finest efforts, it was a kind of playing that had never before been imagined. With these composers, especially with Debussy, a symbiosis took place, a divination of the style. In the very spontaneity of Gieseking's approach, he overlooked many details of the composer's intentions. If one cares for a more solid and etched Debussy, then Gieseking will fail.

Though he produced fine interpretations of other composers and would never have thought himself an "impressionist" specialist, in no other branch of the literature would he experience the sense of comfort and identification he felt with Debussy. It was as though with Debussy he were on a heavenly journey while with other composers he was earthbound. Earlier in his career, he had played much Chopin, but soon relinquished him. He was attracted to Grieg and left on disc many of that composer's *Lyric Pieces,* which he played as precursors of impressionism or, as Debussy saw Grieg, "bonbons wrapped in snow." His Schumann is good work, often gentle, and his *Kinderscenen* a delight. In Schubert, he had an easygoing, graceful manner, and he enjoyed playing Mendelssohn's *Songs without Words.* Gieseking concentrated on Beethoven a great deal, and his recording of the Fourth Concerto is pretty Beethoven playing. He recorded as many as twenty-three of the Beethoven sonatas, and many of the slow movements are suavely lyrical. But much of the music is without grit and organizational power. His Beethoven is too refined; it lacks the lion's roar.

As for earlier composers, Gieseking is uninspiring in Bach and Handel, and his recordings of the complete piano music of Mozart are too rosy in hue. He was trained, basically, in the late-Romantic school, where Mozart was often heard essentially as a pretty pattern maker, a Rococo powdered doll. Gieseking's own natural elegance can certainly be heard, and in several of the Mozart concerti he is more satisfying by far than in the solo music.

He was better suited to the idiom of the late Brahms miniatures. His recordings of them, made in 1953, show Gieseking entering a new phase of growth. He bathes the cerebral, gray-bearded Brahms in a warm, golden glow, with tenderness, freedom of metrics, and a plangent tone. In his hands, the music quivers with ineffable sadness for the youth Brahms never had. The composer himself called these last pieces "the cradle songs of my old age"; each was sent off to Clara Schumann with the advice that even one listener was too many. Gieseking captures this intimate and solitary mood, and he sounds the tone of deep nostalgia in the pieces that recall Vienna. Gieseking was a great explorer of sentiment; he died too young at the age of sixty-one.

EMIL GILELS
1916–1985 — USSR

Born in Odessa, he studied with Berthe Ringold and later with Heinrich Neuhaus at the Moscow Conservatory. In 1938 he was the victor at the Queen Elizabeth Competition in Brussels. In 1944, Gilels premiered Prokofiev's Eighth Sonata, which was dedicated to him. In 1951 he became a professor at the Moscow Conservatory. In 1953 he made his first appearances in England; and in 1955, Gilels opened the "culture curtain" with a highly publicized tour of the United States, which had been for many years without contact with Soviet performers. American audiences cherished him from the moment he made his debut in the Tchaikovsky First Concerto, shortly after he recorded it with Reiner. Gilels liked playing in the United States, especially for New York audiences at Carnegie Hall, and he made nearly twenty American tours.

Gilels was born for the stage. He walked to the piano with supreme confidence, with a pride, it seemed, in the great tradition of Russian pianism. Just watching him was fascinating. With his Tartar features, eyes three-quarters closed, the shock of red hair of which he was always conscious, the ecstatic glances toward the heavens, hands lifted high, he was the very picture of the great virtuoso. And indeed he was a virtuoso, with enormous technique and a glorious sonority—a sound that stayed in the ear long after the concert had ended.

Gilels was a great public performer, and audiences knew something wonderful was happening. He was a galvanic concerto player, and he stormed the keyboard as few could; no orchestra could drown him out, and when he was inspired he could turn out the most reckless performances. Listen to the mad, animal excitement in his live recording of the Tchaikovsky Second Concerto with the Leningrad Philharmonic. Gilels had a primal urge to play the piano. At times he played it as though he were giving the instrument a bear hug. It was part of his attraction.

In his twenties and thirties, and even into his forties, Gilels displayed a streak of wildness. Scores were swallowed raw, and he could be quite helter-skelter, as well as a furious banger. His teacher Neuhaus said of the teenage Gilels that "he was very fond of playing very fast and very loud, and it was only beyond these prominent (though, it is true, captivating) qualities that one could make out the shape of the wonderful artist and virtuoso to be, the Gilels as we know him. I think that I did not point out in vain that the hardest, purely pianistic, task is to play very long, very loud and very fast. The true spontaneous virtuoso instinctively throws himself into this difficulty at an early age, and overcomes it successfully. It requires daring, persistence, temperament, passion, energy, and quick thinking." In fact, all of these are prime Gilels qualities, which made him one of the few pianists who could play at his best in the largest auditoriums.

As he grew and matured, Gilels went far beyond mere excitement in his music-making. He developed control and the ability to use color. He retained his elemental qualities, but developed into a deeper artist. Many of his interpretations were brooding, strange, and enigmatic, especially in live performance, where they sometimes grew formless, and often his pedaling was irritatingly blurred. He was not always successful, but he was always experimenting. And when it worked, he played divinely. I remember a Chopin Third Sonata with the great Largo movement of such meditative and dreamy introspection that time was suspended. His Brahms had a pensive flavor, and in later years it became more flexible and beautifully voiced, but also suggestive—his disc of the Brahms Ballades exudes an almost grotesque atmosphere in places.

Gilels played Beethoven more and more as the years passed. His set of the five concerti with Szell is fluid and plastic. Far more interesting are his interpretations of the sonatas. The playing is always in high relief, with a great deal of color, and Gilels elaborately orchestrates each work. His time cycle is long and often leisurely; his tone is especially large; and as sheer piano playing, the performances are always beautifully made and finely finished. In the late sonatas he is long-winded, yet fascinating, and many of the early ones seem sluggish, lacking forward motion. Quite frequently his presentations sound overpedaled and thick. In essence his Beethoven is not Germanic, but has been transformed into a Byronic Beethoven—or perhaps even "Pushkinian" would be apt.

Gilels had an enormous repertoire, and the world was blessed by the dozens of recordings he made. Of the Classic composers, he recorded a Carl Philipp Emanuel Bach sonata with its expressively "pathetic" slow movement; a sparkling Clementi C major Sonata; a group of brilliant and fetching Scarlatti sonatas; a joyful Haydn Concerto in D major. His disc of Schubert's *Moments musicaux* is memorable, his Chopin strong-willed. Schumann was one of his best composers, especially in Gilels's later period. He played Liszt with splendor, including the Sonata. His Grieg *Lyric Pieces* had a special charm. He cared for Medtner and championed him. He could be devastating in Stravinsky's *Petrouchka,* and equally so in Tchaikovsky's Sonata in C-sharp minor, a student piece that he charged with energy and played as if it were important.

He gave an aristocratic Third Rachmaninoff Concerto, and his recording with André Cluytens is technically ravishing and musically restrained. I remember when Gilels paid a visit to the Juilliard School and a student asked him how long it took him to learn the "Rock Third." He replied, "I began work on it at age eighteen. I am still working at it."

Gilels had one of the greatest careers of any Soviet musician, and his life's work will not be forgotten.

GREGORY GINZBURG
1903–1961 — Russia

He was an elegant Romantic stylist. Connoisseurs should seek out some of Ginzburg's records. At his best, he was one of the most delightful voices of Russian lyric pianism. His playing of such pieces as Liszt's *Rigoletto* paraphrase and *Faust* Waltz had a lightness of spirit, combining gallantry with a special sweetness of tone.

ARABELLA GODDARD
1836–1922 — England

The most famous English pianist of the 1860s and 1870s and a performer of extraordinary technical command. Shaw felt "nothing seemed to give her any trouble." As a child, she studied with Kalkbrenner, followed by Thalberg and then her future husband, the critic J. W. Davison.

Goddard was the first pianist to perform Beethoven's *Hammerklavier* in London, which she did at the age of seventeen, and the fact that she played everything from memory was often remarked. In 1857 and 1858, again in London, she performed Beethoven's last five sonatas. In 1872 she was the soloist at the inauguration of Royal Albert Hall, playing the *Emperor* Concerto of Beethoven.

Goddard was one of the first pianists to achieve a world career. In 1872 she left for a three-year tour, playing in Australia, New Zealand, India, China, and throughout America.

LEOPOLD GODOWSKY
1870–1938 — Poland

By the age of three, Godowsky was already finding his way around the piano. In 1879 he made his debut in his home town of Vilna. He denied ever having had a proper teacher, although he is reputed to have worked with Woldemar Bargiel and Ernst Rudorff at the Berlin Hochschule. In 1884 he made an American tour, staying for two years. From 1886 to 1890, he toured Europe and spent time in both London and Paris, where he gained the valuable friendship of Saint-Saëns. In 1900 his debut in Berlin proved sensational, and he was called *"ein Hexenmeister der Technik";* from that date, his pianism was heralded as incomparable. Hofmann and Rachmaninoff, two of the great technicians of history, were awed by his unprecedented digital independence. Arthur Rubinstein gasped: "It would take me five hundred years to get that kind of mechanism."

From 1909 to 1912, he gave master classes in Vienna, then went to live in the United States, where his reputation further flourished. In 1930, after recording extensively in London, he suffered a stroke which paralyzed him. Godowsky never again played. He had always been unhappy away from the instrument, never tiring of practicing, testing, and experimenting at the keyboard.

Godowsky was widely sought as a teacher and instructed many fine talents, including Heinrich Neuhaus, who in turn became one of history's great teachers. Neuhaus reminisced:

Godowsky, my incomparable teacher and one of the great virtuoso pianists of the post-Rubinstein era, once told us in class that he never practiced scales. Yet he played them with a brilliance, evenness, speed and beauty of tone which I believe I have never heard excelled. It was a delight to watch those small hands that seemed chiselled out of marble and were incredibly beautiful (as a good thoroughbred racehorse is beautiful, or the body of a magnificent athlete) and see with what simplicity, lightness, ease, logic and, I would say, wisdom, they performed their super-acrobatic task. The main impression was that everything is terribly simple, natural, beautiful and completely effortless. But turn your gaze from his hands to his face, and you see the incredible concentration: Eyes with lids covered, the shape of the eyebrows, the forehead, reflect thought, enormous concentration—and nothing else! Then you see immediately what this apparent lightness, this ease, costs; what enormous spiritual energy is required to create it. This is where real technique comes from!

Yet it was often acknowledged that on stage Godowsky was paralyzed by inhibition; only rarely did he have the power to move a large public. He seemed happiest when playing for a group of his friends and peers. Then he was the essence of subtlety. Perhaps the explanation can be found in his statement that "the deep things of our art are little understood by general students of the piano. The great artist is an aristocrat, a monarch; his work can only appeal to the few. They alone can understand." He simply had no faith in the ability of the large public to understand the musical and technical subtleties of his mind. "The piano is a marvel," he wrote, "perhaps the greatest instrument we have. It is so intimate, yet so impersonal." The instrument fascinated and tormented him, and for a select few he unlocked the secret labyrinths of his own compositions. His fifty-three arrangements based on many of Chopin's etudes "are absolutely transcendental in their difficulty," as Neuhaus wrote, "and incomparable for musical humor and inventiveness." James Huneker observed:

He belongs to the Joseffy-de Pachmann, not to the Rubinstein-Hofmann, group. I once called him the superman of piano-playing. . . . He is an apparition. A Chopin doubled by a contrapuntalist . . . The spirit of the German cantor and the Polish tone-poet in curious conjunction. He is a miracle-worker. . . . Dramatic passion, flame, and fury are not present; they would be intruders on his map of music. The piano tone is always legitimate, never forced. . . . His ten digits are ten independent voices recreating the ancient polyphonic art of the Flemings. He is like a Brahma at the piano. Before his serene and all-embracing vision every school appears and disappears in the void. The beauty of his touch and tone are only matched by the delicate adjustment of his phrasing to the larger curve of the composition. Nothing musical is foreign to him. He is a pianist for pianists, and I am glad to say that the majority of them gladly recognize this fact.

There are few excellent pianists who have not at least toyed with the demon at the heart of a difficult Godowsky composition, but few remain with the work, and only a fraction of those ever achieve concert pitch with it. Although highly pianistic, the music, because of its dense polyphony, is difficult to hold in the hand or memory. It shatters, splinters, and crumbles. Perhaps only an audience of pianists, who themselves have experienced the grueling tortures required, can appreciate the undertaking. It humbles the proudest technician, and so Godowsky's music receives few adequate performances. Earl Wild, a true Godowskian, has confessed, "Many of Godowsky's transcriptions are so difficult and complex that they may easily become an obsession. They plague you! . . . Because of their great physical demands, I find that I never have the total abandon that I wish for. They are even harder than they sound."

Godowsky was aware that he was leading piano music into uncharted technical terrain. In the preface to his Chopin Etude transfigurations, he indicated that "owing to innumerable contrapuntal devices, which frequently compass almost the whole range of the keyboard, the fingering and pedaling are often of a revolutionary character, particularly in the twenty-two Etudes for the left hand alone." Perhaps the ideal that Godowsky desired, the dissolving of hand into sound, was possible only in his most inspired moments alone with the instrument he so passionately believed in.

He pursued an almost philosophical elegance. For many, the Godowskian mold with its serpentine harmonics is too ornate, even decadent. His detractors consider his Chopin etude arrangements, in particular, the impieties of a fevered brain committing sacrilege on masterpieces. He could not, it seemed, help tampering with music. The simplest melody, such as Saint-Saëns's *The Swan,* was bedecked with frills and infused with a tinge of irony. Godowsky's ghostly and lavender harmonies, *Art Nouveau* patterns, and high nostalgia are now understood properly as a continuation of the Romantic's quest for individuality, a desire for color and compound texture. His works contain a figurational phantasmagoria, which only Godowsky's inner ear heard in all its coloration; they need from an interpreter a luxuriant aroma and a voluptuous rubato, with a radical use of pedaling. Many of his

pianistic concoctions opened a new realm of piano technique, although it remains a closed book for all but Olympian pianists.

Godowsky's recordings are rather disappointing; nor did he put on record any of his own significant works. He was as aloof in front of the recording machine as he was on stage. His playing sounds detached, but highly organized; there is never a hint of sentimentality. His Beethoven Sonata Op. 81a is businesslike and glib, the magnificence of his technical command apparent in the finale. The Schumann *Carnaval* is somewhat thin; it lacks comeliness, but has a winsome style all its own. The Chopin B-flat minor Sonata is slightly stilted, yet interesting in the Funeral March. His Chopin Nocturnes are poised, and the phrasing is finely threaded. He was a great believer in the Grieg Ballade and told Arthur Rubinstein to learn it. His recording of it exhibits coolness and technical finesse. Miniatures, such as the hackneyed *Rustle of Spring* by Sinding, sound plastic and pristine, with all semblance of their popularity vanished.

Godowsky will always remain a special and intriguing figure in the history of world pianism.

ALEXANDER GOLDENWEISER
1875–1961 — Russia

He studied with Siloti and Louis Pabst at the Moscow Conservatory and premiered several Scriabin pieces, including the B minor Fantasy, Op. 28, in 1908. He remained dedicated to Scriabin's music. He made many recordings, all very Romantic in conception. He was considered a great teacher. Lazar Berman, Samuel Feinberg, Oxana Yablonskaya, and Tatiana Nikolayeva were among his students.

ROBERT GOLDSAND

b. 1911 — Austria

Studied in Vienna, making his debut at the age of ten. Soon after, he worked with Moriz Rosenthal, who influenced him deeply. Goldsand has been before the public for sixty years. He is a superb technician who plays interesting programs. He teaches at the Manhattan School of Music.

HARRIS GOLDSMITH

b. 1938 — United States

A student of Robert Goldsand, Goldsmith made his New York debut at Town Hall in 1965. Subsequently he gained a strong reputation as a teacher and as a chamber and solo performer. He is also one of the most articulate music critics in the United States; for more than twenty-five years, he has contributed to the leading musical journals. His recordings of Schubert's B-flat Sonata and Beethoven's Op. 110, Op. 53, and Op. 31, No. 2 show a passionate musical nature.

STEFANO GOLINELLI

1818–1891 — Italy

Had a distinguished career as player and composer. His two hundred opus numbers are exclusively for piano, and include three sonatas, Twenty-four Preludes, Op. 23, and Twelve Etudes, Op. 15.

RICHARD GOODE

b. 1943 — United States

A student of Nadia Reisenberg and later of Rudolf Serkin. Goode won the Clara Haskil Competition in Geneva in 1973. He is a brilliantly equipped pianist with a fresh and rich musical mind and the sharpest musical sense. He is also a finely attuned chamber player. Goode is interested in a variety of music but does best with the Classical masters. His recordings of the Mozart Seventeenth and Twenty-third Concerti are of the first rank. Goode's Beethoven shows a musical thinker who sees the score as a whole. His Beethoven burns brightly, and the sound is full, limpid, and natural. In Schumann, Goode finds a touching intimacy, which is beautifully portrayed in the *Humoreske,* Op. 20.

He has found the time to dip into some contemporary music. Goode is sympathetic to George Perle's work and has recorded his beautiful Ballade.

KATHARINE GOODSON

1872–1958 — England

Studied at the Royal Academy of Music with Oscar Beringer and in Vienna with Leschetizky. She had a fine reputation and was especially popular with British audiences. She played mostly the standard repertory, although she ventured to perform novelties like the Delius Concerto and the Concerto by her husband, Arthur Hinton.

ALEXANDER GORIA

1823–1860 — France

He studied with Zimmerman at the Paris Conservatoire. He performed and composed extensively, including his Etudes, Opp. 15, 23, 39, and 43.

SASCHA GORODNITZKI
1905–1986 — Russia

He came to the United States as a child, studying with Edwin Hughes and Josef Lhévinne. In 1930 he won the Schubert Memorial Prize. His recordings of the Brahms *Paganini* Variations and the Chopin Etudes show a "big" technician. He was a celebrated teacher at the Juilliard School, and many of his students won prizes in the international competition circuit. His many students include Diana Kacso, Robert Preston, Edmund Battersby, André Laplante, Hai-Kyung Suh, Garrick Ohlsson, and Janina Falkowska.

LOUIS MOREAU GOTTSCHALK
1829–1869 — United States

He began playing piano at the age of three. His French-Creole mother took him to Paris in 1842, where he worked with Hallé and then with Stamaty, both pupils of Kalkbrenner. He had been denied even an audition at the Paris Conservatoire by Zimmerman, who, with typical French condescension, exclaimed that "America was a land of steam engines . . . the country of railroads but not musicians." (Ironically, Gottschalk's *Bamboula* would, in several years, be an entrance piece for a conservatory competition at which Gottschalk served as a judge.) By the time he was fifteen, everyone was impressed by him, including Kalkbrenner and Thalberg, and Berlioz became a supporter. He wrote: "Gottschalk is one of the very small number who possess all the different elements of a consummate pianist—all the faculties which surround him with an irresistible prestige, and give him a sovereign power. . . . There is an exquisite grace in his manner of phrasing sweet melodies and scattering the light passages on the top of the keyboard. The boldness, brilliance, and originality of his playing, at once, dazzle and astonish."

In 1845 he made a Paris debut and was soon making the rounds of the fashionable salons, where Chopin heard him and was pleased with the boy's playing of his E minor Concerto. The then thirty-five-year-old Pole was reputed to have told Gottschalk that he would be a "king among pianists."

His early success as a composer was equal to his acclaim as a pianist. At sixteen, he composed *Bamboula,* based on a Negro melody he had heard as a child in New Orleans, a city that had 465,000 slaves. The music of the Blacks made an indelible impression on him. Other Creole and Negroid-based compositions from his teen years were *La Savane* and *Le Bananier.* These and other pieces were instant hits throughout Europe. Their exotic beat proved irresistible.

The next stage of his career was a spectacular eighteen-month tour in 1851–52 through Spain, where his music took on a Spanish cast in works like *La Jota aragonesa, Minuit à Séville,* and the marvelous concert etude *Manchega.* His Spanish sojourn was capped with a decoration by the queen of Spain. But the sweet smell of American dollars wafted across the ocean and the luxury-loving Gottschalk came home to America in 1853, at the age of twenty-four. His native land was still in the infancy of music appreciation, and Gottschalk, sanctioned with Europe's highest credentials, took the United States by storm. He was big box office and rivaled even Jenny Lind, the "Swedish Nightingale," who had only recently stolen America's heart. P. T. Barnum had brought her to the United States, and now he wanted the languid, exotic Gottschalk, who refused his offer.

Like Chopin, Liszt, Mendelssohn, Herz, and Thalberg, Gottschalk, with his slim and pale good looks, embodied the Romantic ideal of the time. His seemingly carefree temperamental personality had great appeal and women went wild over him. He was often found in the most compromising circumstances; a scandal with a teenage girl in San Francisco received national coverage and sent him packing to South America.

Gottschalk was a great showman, full of ennui and disdain as he entered the stage, slowly peeling off his white gloves. Richard Hoffman, in his book, *Some Musical Recollections of Fifty Years*, wrote: "I have often seen him arrive at a concert in no mood for playing, and declare that he would not appear; that an excuse might be made, but that he would not play . . . but a little coaxing and a final *push* would drive him onto the stage, and after a few moments the fire would kindle and he would play with all the brilliancy which was so peculiarly his own." And play he did: Gottschalk performed ninety times in seven seasons in New York alone. Those were the days when multiple piano events were fashionable. (Sometimes eight pianos would grace a stage in Czerny's Fantasy on *William Tell*, or another blockbuster.) On one occasion in New York, Gottschalk and Thalberg contrived a two-piano extravaganza on themes from the hit opera of the day, *Il Trovatore*. Hoffman reported that "a remarkable double trill which Thalberg played in the middle of the piano, while Gottschalk was playing all over the keyboard in the 'Anvil Chorus,' produced the most prodigious volume of tone I have ever heard from the piano."

Gottschalk played throughout the United States, even touring during the Civil War. He often traveled with two Chickering grands— his "Mastodons," as he called them—and no town was too small to be blessed with a performance. He seemed to want to get to know his own country and his return home had inspired him to compose such extraordinary pieces as *The Banjo* and *Tournament Galop*. Gottschalk's diaries, later published as *Notes of a Pianist*, are a fascinating contribution to Americana of the Civil War period. He performed his *L'Union,* a major virtuoso piece, at a memorial service for Lincoln soon after the assassination.

After a while, though, Gottschalk's need for a more exotic landscape than Victorian America drove him to the West Indies, where he remained for long periods. He wandered throughout the Caribbean, living an almost wild existence, "giving a concert wherever I found a piano, sleeping wherever the night overtook me," as he noted in his diary. During his "Antillean" phase, he alternated between great bursts of inspiration and "madly squandered" times. In one of the most Romantic passages from his diaries, we find Gottschalk "living overlooking an extinct volcano. Perched upon the edge of the crater, on the very top of the mountain, my cabin overlooked the whole country. The rock on which it was built hung over a precipice whose depths were concealed by cacti, convolvuluses and bamboos. . . . Every evening I moved my piano out upon the terrace, and there, in view of the most beautiful scenery in the world, which was bathed by the serene and limpid atmosphere of the tropics, I played, for myself alone. . . . It was there that I composed *La Marche des Gibaros*"—the subtitle of one of Gottschalk's masterpieces, *Souvenir de Porto Rico*. And it was in Santiago, Cuba, that Gottschalk composed one of the most popular piano pieces in history—*The Last Hope*. It had "a melancholy character with which was connected a touching episode of my journey to Santiago, Cuba"—Gottschalk was describing an ill-fated romance—"that seemed to me to unite the conditions requisite for popularity."

For several generations, every well-bred young lady played *The Last Hope* together with Gottschalk's other best-known title, *The Dying Poet*. Gottschalk had a perfect understanding of the Victorian female piano public's demand for sentimental salon music. Gottschalk scholar Robert Offergeld calls it "his *style pianola*. This genre was also a calculated response to American taste, which liked sad titles, *vox angelica* melodies, pathetic barbershop harmonies, thrilling tremolos, sweepy harp effects, and lots of runs on cue." As Arthur Loesser put it: "By the rarefied monastic standards of latter-day high-brows, *The Last Hope* ranks as trash. However, if there is value in something because it has given satisfaction to a great many people for a long time, then *The Last Hope* must count as an important piece of music."

Gottschalk was a pianist of the Herz/Thalberg type, content to play his own music. Although he had been taught the classical composers by Stamaty, he gave in to the clamor for his own worst music, as well as the best of it. George P. Upton, in his *Musical Memories,* wrote: "How well I remember the last time I saw him! . . . He played for me in his dreamy way the so-called *Moonlight* Sonata of Beethoven . . . and some Mendelssohn *Songs without Words*. . . . I remember asking him why he didn't play that class of music in his concerts. He replied: 'Because the dear public does not want to hear me play it. People would rather hear my *Banjo,* or *Ojos criollos,* or *Last Hope*. Besides there are plenty of pianists who can play that music as well or better than I can, but none of them can play my music half so well as I can. And what difference will it make a thousand years hence, anyway?' " William Mason, as knowledgeable in music as anyone in America at that time, testified in his *Memories of a Musical Life:*

I knew Gottschalk well, and was fascinated by his playing, which was full of brilliancy and bravura. His strong, rhythmic accent, his vigor and dash, were exciting and always aroused enthusiasm. He was the perfection of his school, and his effects had the effervescence and sparkle of champagne. He was far from being an interpreter. . . . On one occasion, after hearing me play Schumann, he said, "Mason, I do not understand why you spend so much of your time over music like that; it is stiff and labored, lacks melody, spontaneity and naiveté. It will eventually vitiate your musical taste and bring you into an abnormal state."

But by the end of Gottschalk's career a higher level of musical taste was dawning in the United States. Anton Rubinstein's cross-country marathon of the classics would come in 1872. As music appreciation developed in America with a Germanic seriousness, Gottschalk's music disappeared. He was considered too lightweight and flighty, and his worst music drowned out the best. Recently, America has been discovering its past, and the best of Gottschalk is returning to the repertoire.

This troubadour of the piano spent his last years roaming South America, where he won the greatest acclaim. Gottschalk's life of only forty years reads like a biographical romance. Mystery and legend always surrounded him, and even his death was dramatic. He had just completed a new piece entitled *Morte*. While playing it during a concert in Rio de Janeiro, he fell unconscious at the piano, and died several days later.

Amy Fay, an American piano student studying in Germany, hearing of Gottschalk's death, wrote home: "What a way to die! . . . For the infatuation that I and 999,999 other American girls once felt for him, still lingers in my breast!" He was America's first great concert pianist and the instrument's chief popularizer during the 1850s and 1860s, when piano building in the United States was becoming a major industry. His music glorifies the piano with a dashing boldness, especially in the upper register, and the majority of his compositions require a virtuoso equipment. His is the fresh, scintillating, and brash art of a time when America itself was the most optimistic of places. In his music, one can hear circus bands, Sunday horse races, Caribbean tunes, hints of an emerging ragtime, sassiness, unabashed sentimentality, and good humor. Gottschalk's music should be considered a treasure of the Romantic literature, and the most important pianistic output by an American of the mid-nineteenth century.

GLENN GOULD
1932–1982 — Canada

He studied with his mother until he was ten. At three, he was at the piano; at five, composing. In 1938 he heard Josef Hofmann at his last recital in Toronto, which made a deep impression on the six-year-old prodigy. At ten, he entered the Royal Conservatory in Toronto. There he studied piano with Alberto Guerrero (1886–1959), a Chilean-born pianist, who was to have a major impact on Gould. He studied with Guerrero until 1952, although he had graduated from the Conservatory in 1946, at age fourteen, the youngest graduate ever.

Gould's debut took place, not as a pianist, but as an organist, in 1945. In 1946, playing the Beethoven Fourth Concerto, he made his debut as piano soloist with orchestra. In 1947 he made his recital debut, and in 1950, CBC broadcast a recital throughout Canada.

It was in 1955 that he made his U.S. debut at the Phillips Gallery in Washington, D.C., giving a typical Gould program, with works by Gibbons, Sweelinck, five three-part inventions by Bach and the G major Partita, Beethoven's Sonata Op. 109, the Webern Variations Op. 27, and the Berg Sonata. Paul Hume, Washington's best-known critic of the time, wrote: "Glenn Gould is a pianist with rare gifts for the world. It must not long delay hearing and according him the honor and audience he deserves. We know of no pianist anything like him of any age."

On January 11, 1955, Gould repeated his success at New York's Town Hall; the very next day, Columbia signed him to a recording contract. The young pianist chose Bach's *Goldberg* Variations. It caused an instant sensation. There was, after all, something new under the sun. Nobody had ever played Bach this way. Composed by the Leipzig cantor for an insomniac, the *Goldberg* Variations became in Gould's hands an eye-opening, ear-crackling, high-voltage experience—young, fresh, and brash. No amount of conservative criticism or musicological hair-splitting about playing Bach on the wrong instrument could quash the appeal of this recording. It put Gould on the musical map; fame came to him immediately and effortlessly, not through competitions or years of concert-giving, but through the singular power of recording.

His life became a marathon of concerts, beginning with his first big American tour in 1956. His American orchestral debut took place with the Detroit Symphony, and the following year he made his New York Philharmonic debut with Bernstein in the Beethoven Second Concerto. At his Berlin Philharmonic debut with von Karajan, he played the Beethoven Third. In 1957 he performed for two weeks in the Soviet Union, the first North American to play in Russia during the Cold War. His totally un-Slavic playing created a furor. Gouldomania sprouted everywhere, and the Russians have never stopped loving him.

During the next few years, Gould's playing, recordings, and madcap personality were everywhere. How he played and what he said caused controversy and delight. George Szell said, "That nut is a genius." However, he was unhappy; he grew to dread the live performances, which he saw as a narcissistic arena, a symbol of competitiveness, almost a blood sport. "At live concerts," he said, "I feel demeaned, like a vaudevillian." More and more he thought music should be a private experience. He felt he was forced to exaggerate dynamics in overly large concert halls. He found that he became too concerned with audience reactions, and worse, he could not repeat and correct what had not been good. He could not be the kind of artist he needed to be. He felt like Chopin, who wrote that he

could not "let myself become a machine and give concerts everywhere, grinding out the most insipid works devoid of any worth as long as it paid off." So, quietly, on March 28, 1964, at a recital in Orchestra Hall, Chicago, the not yet thirty-two-year-old Canadian commanding the highest fees retired from the concert stage, never to return. For eight years of his short life he had toured the world, making a sensation everywhere while hating the experience fiercely. Henceforth, he was to give his audiences their "dollars' worth," as he put it, in the kind of performances that he wanted, with the control that only a record could supply. Even years after his retirement, many people were bothered by what they considered his act of disdain for the public. It seemed selfish and arrogant—after all, how could you take the word *concert* away from the word *pianist?* Many of his fans were as eager for his return to the stage as Beatles fanatics were for their heroes'.

Meanwhile, a whole new generation of pianists grew up never hearing this legend in public. It didn't matter, though, because Gould was always present. He had become, through his seclusion and cleverness, a supreme manipulator of the media. He was the subject of a flood of articles. In fact, he became more famous than ever; everybody, including those who never went to a concert in their lives, knew the name Glenn Gould: "Oh, yes, the man who quit playing for people," or "the man who wears his overcoat in the heat." He became a folk legend, flaunting his phobias to the world. The rule that a pianist needed to play in public to sell records did not apply to Gould, who remained a best-seller.

Actually, Gould was the last in line of those artists depicted by Vasari, the biographer of Renaissance painters, when he wrote, "Love for his art makes an artist solitary and meditative . . . he who takes up the study of art should flee the company of men." But Gould was by no means a Michelangelo, who suffered agonies in seclusion; nor was he a Garbo,

who wanted to be left alone to no purpose. Gould wanted to have his cake and eat it, too. As he needed to control his performances, he needed to control his life, for there was a great deal to accomplish. But he needed people, too—on his terms. He spent an enormous amount of time, late at night, on phone calls all over the world. This writer spoke to him on occasion, and in those calls his contrapuntal mind let loose with an avalanche of concepts, stories (recounted in various accents), current events, and music criticism. He reveled in his verbal prowess. His voice was marvelously agreeable. He was probably the finest telephone conversationalist in the history of that instrument.

He died October 4, 1982, only a week beyond his fiftieth birthday. It had been a long time since the death of a classical musician had produced such worldwide sorrow. With the news of his death, at WNCN I programmed his recordings throughout the day. Calls and letters of grief kept pouring in. His death was felt by many as a personal loss. The playwright Tina Howe wrote to me, "I write my plays to Glenn Gould, I cook the kids' spaghetti dinners to Glenn Gould, I pay the bills to Glenn Gould. . . . What flattens me out about Gould is his style. It's so maniacal yet elegant. He's a true ecstatic like Proust, Nijinsky, or van Gogh."

For many others, he came to symbolize that rare person—someone who does exactly as he pleases. If he dared to say he hated Mozart, so be it! His irreverence was a tonic, and one got the feeling that he could have done anything, that if he had lived double his years, he would have become an Albert Schweitzer, a Dalai Lama, or the premier of Canada; or perhaps, if his beloved technology had moved fast enough, he would have come out of retirement to play on a distant planet, introducing Bach to the cosmos. Gould was a great Romantic personality, and Gould the artist was in the Romantic tradition. People bought Gould's ideas on Bach as they did Rachmaninoff's on Chopin, or

113

Horowitz's on Rachmaninoff. There was not a servile bone in his interpretive body. Had they heard him, the composers he played would have congratulated themselves on the flexibility of their idioms. Actually, Gould himself was an idiom, quite unrelated to conventional music-making. Edward Said, an English professor at Columbia University, wrote: "Gould playing Bach seems like a species of formal knowledge of an enigmatic subject matter."

He was adamant in believing that if you could not add anything new to a well-worn masterpiece, you shouldn't play or record it. No musician so practiced what he preached. If he could have, Gould would have let his public in on the orgiastic fun of editing records by issuing Glenn Gould kits containing all of his "takes," so that each listener could make his own Gould performance.

Of course, Gould will always be best known for his Bach playing, and he would not mind a bit. Bach on the piano had become a nightmare of boring, academic pattern-making, full of plushly pedaled, un-Baroque sonorities. Even with the onslaught of new Bachian musicology, which preferred Bach on the harpsichord, Gould's Bach continued to prosper. He was actually rethinking the Bach keyboard literature. It was a process that went far beyond quibbling about the correct instrument. Indeed, the timbre of the piano under Gould's hands became new and unexpected; each voice was a living organism; each ornament was felt with a new density. In short, it was the most creative, magical, and revolutionary playing of any literature. His Bach is re-creative genius of the highest order, and it transcends the question of likes or dislikes.

Gould was also the great contrapuntal pianist in history, with a hearing apparatus almost exclusively polyphonic and with the human voice always at the source of his inspiration. Even his celebrated humming was part of the texture—the chorus. Teachers have forever stopped their students from indulging in this natural outburst of guttural participation. It is not good playing manners, it is not in good taste; but good taste was of no interest to Gould. There was not a conventional thread in anything Gould ever played. His Bach did not stem from any Romantic notion à la Schweitzer, or from Landowska's heady and white-hot Bach, or from the many modern harpsichordists who washed Bach dry in supposedly correct performances devoid of passion.

Gould's Bach is sparse, abstract, yet mysterious. It is never pretty, certainly not sensuous. It is a northern Bach, piercing the listener like the cold. Nor is Gould's a friendly Bach. He is not the pianist to come home and relax to or be soothed by. Gould, with his quicksilver reflexes, is too astonishing for repose. He is after the revealing accent, the hidden hymn in the tenor voice. Gould surely understood Bacon's dictum, "There is no excellent beauty that hath not some strangeness in the proportion," and Bach never wrote a fugue according to the rule-book. Gould's vision of the *French* and *English* Suites, the Partitas, the Toccatas, the Two- and Three-Part Inventions, and, above all, *The Well-Tempered Clavier* has brought us closer to Bach's divine art. A year before he died, he re-recorded the *Goldberg* Variations. He had realized that his spirit as a man and his breadth as a musician had changed and grown since his first effort. Here, in the later recording, is a *Goldberg* infused with humanity, and the Aria has a terrible, withdrawn pain that is unforgettable.

If Gould's Bach is famous, then his Mozart is infamous. He disliked Mozart, yet spent much time on him, recording all the piano sonatas and the fantasies. Why? It is a Mozart that many rant and rage over. Gould is laughing at us, putting us on, some say. Or is he merely crazy? This is surely not our idea of dear, sweet Mozart: the Alberti basses sassing the melodies, slow movements without depth; no operatic *scenas* and all played with a perennial nonlegato touch, and everything too fast. Certainly this is a new sonorous imagery for Mozart. I can't pretend to love it. But I can prefer it to a Romanticized, sugary, or frilly Mozart. It is dashing and perverse and often sarcastic—a Mozart heard by a contrapuntist. Young students hearing it before others may become confused for life. But Gould had fun, I'm sure. He was truly irreverent here.

His Beethoven is another matter, and he recorded plenty of it—eighteen of the sonatas, the Bagatelles Opp. 33 and 126, three sets of variations, and the five concerti, the *Emperor* with Stokowski being the best known. There is no Beethoven quite like it—quixotic, too fast or too slow, sometimes petulant. Gould knows Beethoven is a great master, but the heroic aesthetic of Beethoven bothered him. He couldn't abide the overt emotionalism of some Beethoven interpreters. He wasn't interested in finding the metaphysical meaning in the slow movement of Op. 111. Gould was best in the biting, humorous works, such as the F major Sonata Op. 10, No. 2, with a finale amazing in its speed and dexterity. Mostly, Gould is beating his chest. But it is a fascinating Beethoven. He points up structures that have become blurred. His tempi let us hear new possibilities in the Beethoven kaleidoscope. His timbres are clearer, the big orchestral sonorities are gone from his economically pedaled Beethoven.

In 1960, Gould recorded ten intermezzi of Brahms. This is his most Romantic, wayward playing, quite different from the Two Rhapsodies and the Op. 10 Ballades that formed his penultimate recording, released shortly after his death. That is a stringent, serious Brahms, with many weird moments. Also available is the legendary Gould-Bernstein collaboration in a live performance of the D minor Concerto. Bernstein had made a public apology before the concert for the very slow tempo that Gould felt was correct. Today the interpretation sounds regal and original. (Many performances of the German classics are getting slower and slower, pretending to a misguided profundity.)

Gould was greatly attracted to music from before Bach, and his recording of Byrd and Gibbons is among his most satisfying projects. Byrd is the greatest of all masters of Elizabethan music, and Gould calls him "the patron saint of keyboard writing." But a pianist must choose this virginal music carefully. This Gould does in the First and Sixth Pavan and Galliards among others, giving performances that are captivating in the ornaments, and those supremely disciplined fingers—guided by a piercing intelligence—bring the music to life on the piano with great success.

Never was Haydn so sparkling, so clever, as in Gould's hands. The Haydn C major *English* Sonata and the famous E-flat are filled with laughter. How I wish he had played more Scarlatti than the three sonatas he recorded. (Gould called Scarlatti sonatas "popcorn.") There is also a marvelous reading of C. P. E. Bach's *Württemberg* Sonata No. 1.

Hilarity and wisecracking are part of Gould's personality and playing. His own composition, *So You Want to Write a Fugue*, tells us a great deal about this aspect of the man. His friend John McGreevy wrote, "All of those who caught a glimpse of this extraordinary phenomenon witnessed one of the most remarkable human performances of our time."

Gould couldn't resist the unusual. In his recording of Liszt's transcription of the Beethoven Fifth Symphony, Gould is nothing less than sensational, with his individualized sonority and sweep. Not to be outdone by Liszt, Gould himself was an epic transcriber, and his own piano transcriptions of Wagner's *Die Meistersinger* Prelude, *Dawn* and *Siegfried's Rhine Journey* and *Götterdämmerung*, and even the *Siegfried Idyll*, which he loved dearly, will amaze the listener. These are not mere piano reductions, but transcriptions that leave every detail intact.

Two other Romantic scores should not be overlooked. Gould considered Bizet's *Variations chromatiques* a masterpiece; it was once

115

orchestrated by Felix Weingartner, but has never received the attention it deserves. Gould plays it with consummate musicianship, if in a rather dry and straightforward way, well suited to the score. On the same disc is his tribute to his grandmother's first cousin Edvard Grieg. This performance of Grieg's only Piano Sonata, Op. 7, is unusual in every detail, and Gould takes about six more minutes than usual to present his view of Romantic melancholy. More memorable is Gould's last recording, of early piano pieces by Strauss and the Sonata in B minor from Strauss's sixteenth year. The music of Strauss was one of Gould's greatest loves. He recorded the *Ophelia* lieder with Elisabeth Schwarzkopf in 1968. He romped through Strauss's *Burleske* for Piano and Orchestra in the performance that I heard with Szell and the Cleveland Orchestra, though he never recorded it. In the Sonata for Piano, he saw a potential that nobody had guessed at. Gould transforms this student work into a breathtaking and momentous piece with his awesome originality, timing, and ability to voice.

One of the very largest segments of Gould's recorded legacy was his contribution in twentieth-century music. He recorded the Berg Sonata, the Křenek Sonata No. 3, the three sonatas by Hindemith, the Prokofiev Seventh Sonata, an album of Sibelius, Scriabin's Third and Fifth Sonatas, and two Canadians— Hétu's Variations and Morawetz's Fantasy— as well as Schoenberg chamber works, songs, the Piano Concerto, and the complete solo piano music. Of this mass of work, I would rank the Berg Sonata, the Křenek Third Sonata, the Scriabin Third Sonata, and the Schoenberg as high achievements. Gould's recordings of the Hindemith Sonatas are far too fussy, while his reading of the Prokofiev Seventh is not especially successful except in the third movement, marked *Precipitato*, where Gould's power of calculation makes for high tension. The Scriabin Third, however, while not suited to Gould's idiom, finds him better

able to contain the material. He keeps his attention on the placement of the figurations, highlighting the design of the work while stripping it of its lushness. Far better suited to Gould's analytic power is the music of Schoenberg. In the Concerto and the solo pieces Gould is very individualistic—his use of the pedal is taut and his phrasing intricate. The precision and projection of polyphony are stupendous, especially in the Suite for Piano (1924).

Gould never regretted his retirement for a minute. While his colleagues jetted over the entire planet, he lived in his splendid isolation, working on a myriad of projects. He made the musical scores for the films *Slaughterhouse Five, The Terminal Man*, and *The Wars*. He made films, and he wrote continuously, in prose as individual as his playing, producing articles, interviews, and liner notes. This work is collected in *The Glenn Gould Reader*. But most important are his more than ninety recordings of hundreds of scores: priceless examples of the recorded art. Gould's records stir me, rile me; they make me think, smile, and scowl, and he can move me in a way no other pianist can. It takes only one earful to know that it is a performance patented and sealed by Glenn Gould. He loved making records, and he knew that with his splicing tools, he could give his audience exactly what *he* wanted. (His second *Goldberg* Variations took a year of editing.) Indeed, Glenn Gould added more to the prestige of the medium than any other recording artist in history.

HANS GRAF
b. 1928 — Austria

A gifted pianist and a teacher at Vienna's Der Hochschule für Musik. Graf judges many international competitions.

GARY GRAFFMAN
b. 1928 — United States

He studied with Isabelle Vengerova at the Curtis Institute, and later with Serkin and Horowitz. After a successful international career, muscle damage in his right hand curtailed his playing, except for a few appearances in several works for left hand and orchestra. In 1986 he was appointed president of the Curtis Institute.

Graffman has a fine musical mind and is a superb craftsman. In a Graffman performance one knows where the music is going. His technique is brilliantly substantial in all departments. His discs of the Beethoven *Appassionata, Waldstein,* and Op. 111 have a stark drama. The finest of his excursions into the Classical literature is a taut conception of Schubert's great posthumous Sonata in C minor. His Schumann playing falls short of the quality of fantasy, for which his tone is too hard. In Rachmaninoff, Graffman is adroit and slick, and his Chopin recording is devoid of charm. But his Tchaikovsky First Concerto with Szell is crystal clear, and his Prokofiev Third Concerto is one of the best on records. Here and in his Prokofiev Second and Third Sonatas, Graffman's steely sound and tight-fisted rhythmic sense find an outlet. There is a powerhouse performance of the American composer Benjamin Lees's Fourth Sonata.

It seems to me that Graffman's prime motivation was to sound good, presenting the music with high gloss. He converted the grand manner into a modern American style, in which directness and effect took precedence over eloquence and originality of vision—a type of playing that was most prevalent in the 1940s and 1950s.

PERCY GRAINGER
1882–1961 — Australia

Grainger studied in Melbourne with Louis Pabst, and in Frankfurt with James Kwast. He later received valuable advice from Busoni.

He was a collector of folk songs and a dedicated champion of new music. He played many premieres, including the Cyril Scott Sonata Op. 66 and Nathaniel Dett's *In the Bottoms* Suite, with its famous Juba Dance which he recorded three times. He was also an early proponent of Debussy, Albéniz, and Ravel. Grieg was enthralled with Grainger, and thought him to be the best interpreter of his works. For the Norwegian, Grainger's playing was "like the sun breaking through the clouds." Grainger played Grieg's Concerto with an unforgettable pungency and brio. His ingenious edition of the Concerto should be consulted by all those studying the score.

Grainger's best days as a virtuoso were from 1900 until World War I. He played far and wide—throughout Norway, Denmark, England, South Africa, New Zealand, Australia, and later the United States.

Grainger played with an often overwhelming vitality and an earthy virility. His ruggedness surprised many on first hearing, but he usually won over his audiences with his freshness and verve. Perhaps his playing could be described as "of the great outdoors." Grainger personally was an unusual man. For those who knew him, his energy was alarming. He seems to have been one of history's first joggers, and could run and walk from town to town on his tours. He left a discography that attests to the spontaneity of his art. He recorded a good deal, and was the first pianist to record electrically the Chopin Sonata No. 3, in 1925. John Bird, Grainger's biographer, writes: "This performance has stood the test

117

of time and is the recording to which connoisseurs always turn when Grainger's greatness as a pianist is being discussed. It is played with a ferocity and wild abandon that is at times frightening."

The four other large solo works he recorded on 78s are the Chopin *Funeral March* Sonata, Schumann's G minor Sonata and *Symphonic Etudes,* and the Brahms F minor Sonata, all unorthodox yet each winning in its way.

In his own music, Grainger shines. Nobody else has played his *Mock Morris, Molly on the Shore, Spoon River, Handel in the Strand,* or the perennial *Country Gardens* with such rollicking good will. Grainger's greatest pianistic gift was his rhythmic dynamism. "Pianists," he once wrote—"with their alarming lack of rhythmic neatness, their inability to follow a conductor's beat, their inability to listen while they play—are more in need of some kind of musical teamwork (to offset their all too soloistic study activities) than almost any other class of musicians." During Grainger's heyday, musical leeway was the rule, and he was a fierce exponent of metronome practice, which he imposed on his students.

In recent years, his music has had its advocates, including Benjamin Britten. His output ranges from folk song settings to many cryptic works, making him a difficult composer to categorize. He wrote more than four hundred compositions in various media. Grainger was always the avant-gardist. He spent his final years developing an instrument that would help create a "free music." This was a pre-electronic machine of his own invention—called a Kangaroo-Pouch Free Music Machine—which was intended to liberate him from the "tyranny" of the division of whole tones and half tones that make up Western scales, enabling him to compose works using "gliding intervals," unusual rhythms, and a freer use of dissonance.

ARTHUR DE GREEF
1862–1940 — Belgium

He studied with Brassin at the Brussels Conservatoire. Later, he went to study with Liszt. His recordings of the *Hungarian Fantasy* and the Liszt Concerto No. 1, which he studied with the master, are important documents that have fortunately made their way onto LP. He was always a popular favorite in London. In 1889, Shaw heard him and wrote: "Mr. de Greef is a true Belgian, spirited, brilliant, neat, confident, clever, and intensely happy in the consciousness of being all that. His execution is extremely ambidextrous; and he has a prodigious musical gift, besides having a fair share of sense and taste."

MARIA GRINBERG
1908–1979 — Russia

Her teachers were Igumnov and Blumenfeld. Grinberg was a pianist of considerable but well-tempered power. Her playing had delicacy and she was blessed with a Romantic temperament. She was rather versatile, being at ease in the Franck *Symphonic Variations* or the snappy Shostakovich First Concerto. Her Brahms was warm, her Ravel Toccata golden, the *Symphonic Etudes* of Schumann filled with elegiac sorrow. But her best was given to Beethoven. Grinberg recorded all thirty-two sonatas in a Romantic, earthy style—a Beethoven that is impulsive and technically strong, full of light and dark and the swell of the heart.

COR DE GROOT
b. 1914 — Netherlands

An admirable pianist, dry and nimble. He has had much success and made many recordings. An arm problem ended his public career.

STEVEN DE GROOTE
b. 1953 — South Africa

Studied with various teachers including Horszowski. In 1977 he took first prize at the Van Cliburn Competition. His appearances show a good technician whose interpretations lack profile.

ALFRED GRÜNFELD
1852–1924 — Czechoslovakia

A student of Theodor Kullak. He settled in Vienna where his elegant, facile playing made him a popular favorite. His Strauss transcriptions were once often played. Grünfeld was pianist to the Imperial Courts of Austria and Prussia.

FRIEDRICH GULDA
b. 1930 — Austria

An excellent pianist who plays Mozart and Beethoven with special affection and insight. Gulda is an accomplished player of jazz. He is best known in Europe, where he also teaches.

HORACIO GUTIÉRREZ
b. 1948 — Cuba

Studied at the Juilliard School. He came in second at the Tchaikovsky Competition in 1970. Since his debut in New York in 1972, Gutiérrez has had a worldwide career. He is a pianist capable of virtuoso exploits in the Third Rachmaninoff Concerto. His Liszt is dazzling but never just for show. He can play Haydn's *English* Sonata in C major with many shades of tone without losing its Classical complexion.

MONIQUE HAAS
1909–1986 — France

She studied with Lazare Lévy and acquired a fine European reputation. Her excellent Debussy and Ravel recordings reveal her fastidious mind and very solid equipment.

ERNST HABERBIER
1813–1869 — Germany

Considered a splendid pianist, who in his compositions had a method of dividing the most intricate passages between the two hands, thus attaining great speed. His audiences were always delighted with his talent. Haberbier died during a recital. His Etudes Op. 53 are his best and most enjoyable pieces.

INGRID HAEBLER

b. 1926 — Austria

An artist who plays with polish and taste. Her Mozart is especially admired for these qualities. Her playing has refinement and gentility, as well as a very special tone quality. Haebler has made many recordings of merit.

ELSIE HALL

1879–1976 — South Africa

She had an enormously long career. Brahms admired her playing. She championed Medtner, whom she knew in Berlin. Hall had a spirited musical personality with a good technique, even past ninety. George Bernard Shaw heard her in 1889, when she was ten years old, and issued an important admonition for parents of prodigies: "Miss Elsie Hall is an infant phenomenon of the latest fashion, that is, a twelve-year-old pianist [sic]. She played . . . with all the vigor and enjoyment of her age, and as dexterously as you please, being a hardy, wiry girl, with great readiness and swiftness of execution, and unbounded alacrity of spirit. At the same time, there is not the slightest artistic excuse for exploiting her cleverness at concerts; I hope we may not hear of her again in public until she is of an age at which she may fairly be asked to earn her living for herself."

SIR CHARLES HALLÉ

1819–1895 — Germany

One of the venerable figures of nineteenth-century English music. He went to Paris in 1836, falling under Kalkbrenner's sway, but later became close friends with Berlioz and Chopin. He settled in London and was an early champion of Beethoven, playing the *Emperor* Concerto at Covent Garden in 1848. In 1861 he was the first pianist ever to play the complete cycle of Beethoven's thirty-two sonatas in eight recitals. His playing was described as "technically adroit, somewhat dry, and without the ability to truly let himself go." His general musicianship, however, was impeccable. Stephen Heller once said to him, "You have remained my ideal pianist, for you never exaggerate." Even after he founded the Hallé Orchestra of Manchester, he continued to perform the newest concertos of the day, and introduced the Grieg Concerto to Manchester in 1876, the Brahms Second in 1881, the Dvořák in 1885, and the Tchaikovsky Second in 1886—each a virtuoso work demanding huge resources of strength.

MARK HAMBOURG

1879–1960 — Russia

A popular virtuoso who had a big technique. His playing was supposed to have resembled Anton Rubinstein's, and his teacher Leschetizky told him, "You play more like Anton Rubinstein than any pianist I have ever heard." Schnabel admired his octaves, saying they were of "flesh and blood." Hambourg's discs show him to be a remarkable artist, temperamental, Romantic, and inquisitive. He gave the London premiere of the Busoni Concerto in 1910.

LEONID HAMBRO
b. 1922 — United States

A pianist with a prodigious memory and sight-reading ability. He brings to his interpretations a freshness and fluid technique. He plays Gershwin marvelously and was one of the first to record Griffes. For many years Hambro was the staff pianist for the New York Philharmonic.

CHARLES LOUIS HANON
1820–1900 — France

A pianist and teacher whose "Hanon exercises" are used to this day in every country in the world. These are a program of five-finger exercises in both hands which help to build finger equalization.

ADAM HARASIEWICZ
b. 1932 — Poland

For six years a student of Zbigniew Drzewiecki, he went on to win the 1955 Chopin Competition over an extraordinary field of contestants—Ashkenazy came in second. Harasiewicz has since recorded the complete Chopin. His is a structured Chopin with never a note out of place, but it lacks variety of tonal gradation.

SIDNEY HARRISON
1903–1987 — England

A concert pianist, writer on music, and teacher who was well known in England.

THOMAS DE HARTMANN
1886–1956 — Russia

He was a pupil of Essipova and played and recorded some of his own evocative piano music.

FRITZ HARTVIGSON
1841–1919 — Denmark

He studied with von Bülow and had a performing career with a sizable concerto repertoire. He taught at the Royal Academy of Music in London.

CLARA HASKIL
1895–1960 — Rumania

She studied with Dohnányi and Cortot and attended some master classes of Busoni. She was a distinctive artist in every sense. Her playing had a deep musicality and a vital intelligence. Her phrasing was always original, and in her work the listener sensed a maturity of feeling. Her metrical command infused the merest ornament with grace. Her flexibility was subtlety itself. Haskil scrutinized carefully all that she touched.

Mozart was her joy of joys and she played it with the freshness of morning dew. Depending upon the work, a slightly suppressed inner passion might appear. Her Schumann was played in the intimate vein, and her recording of the Schubert B-flat Sonata has a hushed majesty. In a minor-key Scarlatti sonata, Haskil managed a peculiar mystery and pensiveness. In the small amount of Chopin she played, she was serious, but poetic. Her Chopin F minor Concerto was simply ravishing, the work being one of her specialties. Haskil's art has a timeless quality. It is a pity that she did not record far more than she did. A piano competition in her memory is held in Geneva.

JOHANN HÄSSLER

1747–1822 — Germany

Early in his career he had a keyboard contest with Mozart which he lost. In 1792 he moved to St. Petersburg, becoming one of the dominant musicians in Russia until his death. He repudiated all of his early music written in Germany and began his Op. 1 in Russia. He performed in concert often, and was a strong advocate of the early piano. He left an effective Sonata-Fantasy, Op. 4 (1795), and twenty-four etudes in the form of valses. His *Grande Gigue* should be revived.

WALTER HAUTZIG

b. 1921 — Austria

After studying in Vienna at the State Academy of Music, he came to the United States in 1939 and attended the Curtis Institute, from which he graduated in 1943. That same year he made his New York debut at Town Hall. Hautzig has played throughout Europe, Latin America, and the Far East. His interpretations show a tasteful, careful approach to the Classical repertoire.

ERIC HEIDSIECK

b. 1936 — France

He studied with Cortot and Kempff. Heidsieck has made a fine career as a pianist, including appearances in the Orient. He teaches at the Conservatoire of Lyon, and he is best known in the French repertoire, although he has played complete cycles of the Beethoven sonatas, as well as Bach and Handel. He has recorded a great deal, especially French music, including deeply felt readings of the Twenty-four Preludes of Michel Merlet (b. 1939).

STEPHEN HELLER

1813–1888 — Hungary

A student of Anton Halm in Vienna, he settled in Paris, where his fine piano playing was admired. Heller's well-made compositions were loved by Schumann, and Heller's etudes and preludes were a part of every student's education. Today, unfortunately, the only remnant of his large output is the teaching-piece *L'Avalanche*. "Heller's music is ageless," wrote Maurice Hinson. "Freedom from sentimentality, impeccable workmanship, and refinement and simplicity of outlook go to the making of a miniaturist whose sole object was to perpetuate beauty." Heller was close friends with Berlioz, Chopin, and Hallé. "There was a singular modesty and reticence in his playing," wrote Hallé, "an indication only of expression and nuance, as if he felt shy of telling all the secrets of his heart."

HANS HENKEMANS

b. 1913 — Netherlands

A pianist who plays Mozart and Debussy especially well. He also composes.

ADOLPH VON HENSELT

1814–1889 — Germany

Henselt lived a long life but did relatively little to fulfill the wonderful talents he possessed. Pianistically, his prestige never wavered, and though he gave only three recitals during the last thirty-three years of his life, he nevertheless became a legend.

Schumann was the first to write of Henselt's pianistic glory, raving about his "equally developed hands of iron—his strength and endurance" and his "softness, grace, and singing quality." Henselt had a luscious tone and Liszt was overwhelmed by his "velvet paws." In London, the piano scholar Alfred Hipkins felt "Chopin never had a finer interpreter" and was amazed that "a German played Chopin so well." Von Lenz thought his Chopin playing was "touched by the wand of Oberon."

Realizing that modern piano sonority depended upon widespread chords and arpeggios, he became a fanatic at achieving legato by stretching his hands. Mendelssohn said that Henselt spent all day stretching his fingers over arpeggios played prestissimo. He accomplished with his finger legato what Chopin, Liszt, and Thalberg did with the pedal.

Henselt's music was played throughout the century. Anton Rubinstein included some of his etudes in his historical recitals (though he thought the left-hand extensions bordered on the freakish), and nearly everyone was fascinated by his Piano Concerto in F minor: Liszt loved it, Clara Schumann premiered it, and Busoni made his American debut with it. Other performers of the work included von Bülow, Sauer, Klindworth, Friedheim, Pachmann, Gottschalk, and Scriabin. Sadly, it fell into oblivion.

In 1889, James Huneker mused, "I refuse to give up my belief in the Henselt Etudes. . . . No, he must not go, for who may replace him? . . . his gentle, elegiac nature, his chivalry . . . his nights are moon-lit, his nightingales sing . . . what charming etudes are in Opus 2 and Opus 5. What a wealth of technical figures, what an imperative legato is demanded . . . and then, above all else—

touch, euphony!" But it appears that Henselt is lost to us. Huneker's ravings were about the last cries for Henselt. He was a poet who fell short of genius. Still, his piano layouts are masterful beyond question, and any student interested in building left-hand technique could utilize them with great profit. These pieces influenced the left-hand figurations of Rachmaninoff and Scriabin. His most famous etude, *Were I a Bird*, is a delight in double-notes and was once played by everyone. Rachmaninoff's recording is a masterly tribute.

LAJOS HERNÁDI
b. 1906 — Hungary

He studied with Dohnányi and Schnabel. Hernádi composed cadenzas to Mozart concerti and taught at the Liszt Academy in Budapest.

HENRI HERZ
1803–1888 — Austria

As a pupil at the Paris Conservatoire he studied with Louis Pradère. In 1818 he won first prize at the conservatory, the contest piece being Dussek's Twelfth Concerto.

By the age of twenty, the good-looking Herz was the darling of the popular Parisian salons, and was becoming the most popular pianist in Paris, even usurping Kalkbrenner's place. Herz was a clever musician, well aware of the ever-increasing popularity of the piano, and accurate in gauging the generally low musical taste of the pleasure-loving Parisian public. It wanted pieces that were easy but brilliant, preferably inoffensive pianistic embroideries based on the opera tune *à la mode*. His ability to create delightful tinklings at the keyboard made him the world's best-selling composer in the 1830s. Herz's pieces were in the parlor on the piano probably more than those of any other composer of the nineteenth century. The idealistic Schumann condemned him as a philistine, but Herz's music must be heard as a barometer of the public's taste, and one need not disdain such lighter music as his better sets of variations.

Herz was not content with only giving concerts and enjoying commercial success. He invented a ridiculous instrument of torture, which he named the "pactytion," and although one could not cross fingers under or over while using it, it was so designed to perfect "five-finger exercises" and thus to make the fingers a mechanism capable of supreme evenness. (This machine was probably conceived in response to Kalkbrenner, who also had developed his own device. These and other artificial means of acquiring finger independence were in vogue throughout the century.) Herz also became a piano maker, and a good one. And in Paris he opened a hall bearing his name.

Always full of daring and energy, one day in 1845 he set out for America without one concert booked in advance. He stayed until 1851, having success everywhere he went, playing his own music exclusively. P. T. Barnum saw dollars in Herz and wanted to sign him up, but Herz seemed to do splendidly on his own, playing throughout America, Mexico, and the West Indies. He even managed to establish a piano depot in California for the Herz piano, and began importing them to America. After retiring to Paris, he published a witty book titled *Mes Voyages en Amérique*. In fact, after Leopold de Meyer's visit, Herz was the next most important European piano virtuoso to play in America. He lived a long life, made lots of money and played lots of concerts, published reams of music, had many students, and never worried much about his place in pianistic history. Herz's music will never have a revival, but he must be seen as one of the most successful popularizers of the piano.

DAME MYRA HESS
1895–1965 — England

A student of Tobias Matthay. She developed into one of the most cherished and revered musicians of her time. She understood, as few have, that the making of a major career takes infinite patience, time, and strength both physical and emotional. Myra Hess never let up; season after season she crossed the oceans and traveled countless miles to attend to her work. The smallest American town would be graced by her presence. She was one of the few women whose performing careers equaled in success those of the male stars of her era. Her programs were serious; she never thought of playing down to an audience, no matter how provincial.

By World War II, she was one of the major pianists; by war's end, Hess became to the public more than a pianist—she was a heroine. From 1939 until the war's end, a time when musical life was almost totally curtailed, she helped organize, played in, and was the major force behind the National Gallery afternoon concerts. She was indefatigable in her own participation and played more than 160 works, including the complete cycle of Mozart concerti. And always she played, as only she could play it, her own "prayer"—the Bach-Hess *Jesu, Joy of Man's Desiring*.

Though she was physically small, her presence on stage was imposing. The public felt her eyes blaze with intensity. Hess had a gift for seriousness. After her recitals, one had that rare feeling that so few can inspire, that perhaps the human race was worthwhile if a Myra Hess existed.

After the war, her interpretive talent reached its full potential. She dropped the repertoire not suited to her. (A look at her early 78 discography reveals unexpected selections by MacDowell, Ravel, Falla, Palmgren, Granados, Griffes, and others not now associated with her tastes.) In the last seasons of her active musical career, audiences learned to expect a Hess program to include Beethoven's final three sonatas. In these compositions, she possessed a wholeness of spirit in which technique and mind blended into one.

She had an excellent, unobtrusive technique, quite capable of attending to the vicious awkwardness of the Brahms concerti and F minor Sonata, all specialties of hers, and she had plenty of power. She was a master architect capable of perceiving new depths in a score, and her quietly explanatory playing established an intimate bond with her audience. Hess looked for a "truth" in her performance, and perhaps for this reason she intensely disliked making records. The recording studio was too cold for her, and she felt helpless without an audience. Certainly her art on disc gives only an indication of her impact on concert audiences. Of course, her recordings are filled with great moments, and her Schumann *Symphonic Etudes* and A minor Concerto are aristocratic, yet they lack a certain tension. Her Beethoven Sonata Op. 110 is fervent, but for me her greatest recording— and one of the glories of Beethoven performance—is her incomparable rendering of the Sonata Op. 109, where she probes the very heart of this poem of humanity.

In a book of reminiscences of Hess, her friend the pianist Denise Lassimonne described a Hess practice session, exemplifying Dame Myra's search for her musical truth. Lassimonne was "all agog to hear how she practiced, so I sat down quietly on the other side of the music-room door with one ear glued to the keyhole. For a long time nothing happened, not a sound. Then there came the soft, soft playing over of a phrase. Again, silence, until a few more quiet notes were experimented with. Once more silence. After a

couple of hours of this, she emerged (I had rushed away just in time), and with a look of complete satisfaction said, 'I have had the most wonderful practice.'"

BARBARA HESSE-BUKOWSKA
b. 1930 — Poland

She studied at the Warsaw Conservatory with Margherita Trombini-Kazuro, and won second prize at the Chopin Competition in 1949. She has been applauded for her Chopin interpretations.

KATHERINE RUTH HEYMAN
1879–1944 — United States

A pianist who played a great deal of American music in Europe, and in America was a staunch believer in Scriabin when his work was seldom heard in the United States. Of a 1934 recital, Paul Rosenfeld wrote: "Miss Heyman again disclosed the fineness of Scriabin's art and the depth of the experience transmitted by it."

FERDINAND HILLER
1811–1885 — Germany

An important pianist-composer; a student of Hummel, at the age of ten he played a Mozart concerto in public. Hiller lived in Paris from 1828 to 1835, and gave (in 1828) the first performance of Beethoven's *Emperor* 125

Concerto in France. He was a scholarly pianist, admired by Mendelssohn, Schumann, and Chopin. He composed many worthy piano pieces, including twenty-four etudes, and his Piano Concerto in F-sharp minor was once a staple of the repertoire.

MAURICE HINSON
b. 1930 — United States

A pianist and teacher of note. He has played widely both in recital and lecture-recital formats, invariably offering imaginative programming. He has written considerably on the piano literature. His *A Guide to the Pianist's Repertoire* and *Music for Piano and Orchestra* are valuable source books.

ALFRED HIPKINS
1826–1903 — England

A pianist who was also a piano technician with the famed piano firm of Broadwood. He tuned Chopin's piano when the composer was in London in 1848, later writing a book on how Chopin played. Hipkins also had a career as a lecture-recitalist.

IAN HOBSON
b. 1952 — England

A student of Claude Frank, he also studied at the Royal Academy in London. Hobson has played extensively and has recorded Rachmaninoff transcriptions and Godowsky works with style and finesse.

LUDWIG HOFFMAN
b. 1925 — Germany

Has a fine reputation as a concert pianist, recording artist, teacher, and as a judge at international competitions.

RICHARD HOFFMAN
1831–1909 — England

A student of Moscheles, he settled in the United States when he was sixteen, and made a prominent career. Hoffman concertized frequently, and was the first to play the Chopin E minor Concerto in New York. He wrote an autobiography, *Some Musical Recollections of Fifty Years,* and composed a large quantity of piano music, some of it excellent. *In Memoriam to L.M.G.* (Louis Moreau Gottschalk), *Dixiana,* and the Impromptu in C minor are gems.

JOSEF HOFMANN
1876–1957 — Poland

He began the study of the piano at the age of three and a half. His father, Casimir, a good musician, then took over teaching the child, who made a debut at six. Anton Rubinstein heard him and was enthralled, calling him a "musical phenomenon." By the time he was nine, he was touring Europe. In 1887 the boy made his American debut at the Metropolitan Opera House. W. J. Henderson reported: "He is an artist, and we can listen to his music without taking into consideration the fact that he is a child." His sensational debut was the talk of the town, and he went on to play fifty-two concerts in ten weeks. The Society for the Prevention of Cruelty to Children was successful in stopping twenty-eight more engagements. In later years, the pianist always said that the tour had been no strain on him at all. However, Alfred Corning Clark gave the Hofmann family $50,000 to retire the prodigy from public life. It was agreed that he should go back to Europe for further study and not make another appearance until he turned eighteen.

Hofmann went to Paris to study with Moszkowski, which proved valuable, and at sixteen, he became Anton Rubinstein's only private pupil. Rubinstein became the musical center of his life. "His very manner of teaching," Hofmann wrote,

was such that it would have made any other teacher appear to me like a schoolmaster. . . . Rubinstein would always ask me the same question: "Well, what is new in the world?" and I would reply, "I know nothing new; that's why I came to learn something new— from you." He would follow every note of my playing with his eyes riveted on the printed pages. A pedant he certainly was, a stickler for the letter—incredibly so, especially when one considered the liberties he took when he played the same works! Once I called his attention modestly to this seeming paradox, and he answered: "When you are as old as I am now, you may do as I do—if you can."

Rubinstein told the boy, "Do you know why piano-playing is so difficult? Because it is prone to be either affected or else afflicted with mannerisms; and when these two pitfalls are luckily avoided, then it is liable to be— dry! The truth lies between those three mischiefs."

Hofmann returned to the concert platform in 1894 at Hamburg, in Rubinstein's D minor Concerto with the composer conducting. He was a major success, and from that moment, Hofmann was considered to be Rubinstein's heir. Rachmaninoff thought him the greatest of living pianists, "with the ability of investing each composition with an individual and characteristic charm." By his early twenties, Hofmann was one of the main concert attractions throughout the world. From Mexico to St. Petersburg, he filled auditoriums with large-scale programs. Before World War I, the Russian people considered Hofmann the supreme pianist, and his tours were legendary. In 1913 he played, within days, twenty-one sold-out recitals in St. Petersburg alone, in the Salle Noblesse, which seated 3,200. He played 255 compositions before 68,000 people. Such statistics give quite a good idea of the hunger for piano playing at a time when world piano production was at a peak and every proper home had a piano.

In 1898, Hofmann made the United States his headquarters. From 1901 to 1914 he wrote a series of articles for the *Ladies' Home Journal* which became one of the most popular features of the magazine. In 1924 the Boks, a prominent Philadelphia philanthropic family, founded a new conservatory to be called the Curtis Institute of Music, and Hofmann became its director, bringing some of the world's great musicians to teach there. They included Fritz Reiner, Marcella Sembrich, Efrem Zimbalist, and Leopold Auer. Hofmann gave a great deal of his energy to the school, curtailing his European concert-giving and concentrating his art in the United States. In 1933 he again played extensively in Europe, but he had played there so little that his legend had grown dim, and he drew only a small public.

On November 28, 1937, the fiftieth anniversary of his first performance in the United States, Hofmann gave a concert in which he returned to the Anton Rubinstein Fourth Concerto and played his own *Chromaticon* for Piano and Orchestra—an awful mismash of a piece. Fortunately, these and many encores were recorded, and the recordings show all of his worst as well as his best characteristics. The playing represents perfectly Hofmann's kind of willful, individualistic, self-centered approach to the composer—a style of playing which was beginning to collapse before a more respectful approach. The Chopin scholar Arthur Hedley, writing about the Golden Jubilee recording, decried the playing: "Those who wish to see summed up on a single disc the end-product of eighty years of 'tradition' need go no further than the Jubilee record of 1937, before an enraptured New York audience. Everything is there: the insane prestissimos, the wild fluctuations of rhythm (otherwise known as rubato)—in a word, the depths have been reached." Hedley diplomatically adds: "I am not suggesting that Hofmann invariably played Chopin like this." But the die is cast. Those elements of playing that disturbed Hedley are latent in all of Hofmann's playing of any composer. The critic B. J. Haggin thought Hofmann's performances "are contrived for their own effect of shock and excitement by their unexpectedness, their exhibition of daring willfulness and perversity." On the other hand, Abram Chasins, who worshipped Hofmann and studied with him, wrote of this record that "Hofmann's art was the adventure of technical perfection and imaginative insight. . . . Every Hofmann performance furnishes ample material for a treatise on the art of pianism and interpretation." For Harold Schonberg, Hofmann was "perfection plus." He dismissed the Hofmann dissenters as "old-maid critics."

Arthur Rubinstein, who had heard him through the years, wrote:

His magnificent grasp of the keyboard must have been inborn. Even in the playing of the masters, his chief interest lay in dynamics, in a slowly prepared crescendo ending in a volcanic outburst at the climax, and he felt great satisfaction in frightening the audience by using the violent contrast of a pianissimo followed by a sudden fortissimo smash. He liked to bring out accompanying voices which you never heard in the performances of others. And yet, he was a pianist of great stature because, in spite of all I have said, a musical personality emerged at every concert which I cannot lightly dismiss.

There is no doubt that Hofmann's art was distinct from all others. For years his playing so overwhelmed me that I discounted what bothered me, the blather and sheer superficiality. For all of Hofmann's gifts, an intellectual rigor was missing; he could not contain his almost diabolical desire to shock. In the concert hall, the inspiration of the moment carries the day. But on recordings those shattering surges, which on first hearing sweep one away, become—upon repeated hearings—nightmarish and ugly.

Almost all of Hofmann's performances left a feeling of unfulfillment. There was an electric personality, a forceful musical mind who refused to dig deeply. Yet when Hofmann was at his spontaneous best, he had a kinetic power that defied description. Although he considered himself small compared with Anton Rubinstein, he too had that elemental power which, when unleashed, could be so thrilling and supercharged.

But in mid-life and later, he began to feel bound to the piano and to music in general. He had become disillusioned with composing and doubtless knew his talent was far less than that of his friend Rachmaninoff, who had dedicated to Hofmann his third and greatest concerto—which Hofmann never performed. Hofmann was insecure about his music, and composed under the pseudonym of Michel Dvorsky.

Those rude awakenings, smashes, and perverted accents in his playing now sound nasty and extramusical to my ears. The many interesting "inner voices" have a fake originality. In his recording of Beethoven's *Waldstein* Sonata, the music is cut to shreds; the involvement is not real. It is surely not the heaven-storming Beethoven, but pretending to be.

He lashes out his selections from *Kreisleriana* without any suggestiveness or true passion. Actually, Hofmann is never warm, though he can charm with his many-colored tone, and the slow movement of the Chopin F minor Concerto is captivating. This is the best of his concerto performances that have survived. (All are taken from broadcasts.) His recording of the Anton Rubinstein Fourth is a glorious unrolling of the grand manner, with some exciting, reckless passages in the first movement, but the Beethoven Fourth and the Chopin E minor have only occasional flashes of insight, although I imagine that at his best he must have been thrilling in the Chopin, which was one of his specialties.

Hofmann possessed one of the massive technical equipments of all time. His trills and passagework are unique, with a sound that can only be called "Hofmannesque." He had a depth of sonority, and colors that ranged from bright yellow to bronze and pure black, reds, and purples. When I listen to his records, I close my eyes and the array of colors elicited by his playing is always startling. His climaxes, when they work right, never fail to thrill. His playing in the D-flat section of the F minor Ballade by Chopin is an ever-widening vista; it seems to grow beyond the music. It may be the most astounding moment in his whole discography; the coda of that work is a feat of playing that defies normal pianistic understanding.

Chopin was the composer he played most and there is nothing in his recordings of Chopin that does not excite, from the exquisite filigree of the D-flat and B major Nocturnes to the glamor of his *Minute* Waltz. His Chopin-Liszt *Maiden's Wish* is the most ethereal in history. His first movement of the Chopin B minor Sonata finds him at his most aristocratic, and his recordings of the *Andante spianato and Grand Polonaise* are endlessly fascinating. Like all geniuses, he had only *his* rules, and to imitate Hofmann's style would be disastrous. He could play with a kind of portamento where others play legato, creating a pointillistic effect, with ingenious pedaling, which is hypnotic. Hofmann was always the craftsman; he once wrote, "Technique is a chest of tools from which the skilled artisan draws what he needs at the right time for the right purpose."

His live performance on record of the G minor Ballade is a blending of courage, color, and abandon. Once I played the recording for my students at the Juilliard School, who went wild. These twenty-year-old pianists had no idea that such playing could exist, and in public too. Unanimously they regretted that styles today were so conservative that such playing was now impossible for them. But his magnetism was irresistible, and soon many students were searching for every Hofmann recording available. These young pianists were not interested in honoring the composer; they were interested in his daring individuality.

Hofmann was not the typical sentimentalist of the day. Indeed, he was often termed cold and lacking in emotion. Certainly his way with Romantic music was new. The laxity, the big ritards of the previous era are missing—he can sound glacial, and almost straightlaced. Hofmann used rubato, certainly, but it was structural in intent. His rhythm is uniquely imperial. Listen to the E-flat minor and A major Polonaises of Chopin, the invincible grasp of chordal mass in the Rachmaninoff G minor Prelude. Or try his *Spanish Caprice* by Moszkowski, with the cool elegance of its middle section, the machinelike perfection of the repeated notes, the coda tossed off with dynamite in his fingers, with a disconcerting nonchalance. Of this recording, the pianist Frank Cooper exults, "It is hair-raising, nearly frightening, to hear a piece played like this and to guess at the conceptual power behind so sybaritic a performance."

It is sad that Hofmann, a gifted inventor with approximately sixty patents to his credit, lives on records whose engineering quality is far below the standard of even his own time.

Perhaps the best of all his pre-electrical recordings are the acoustical discs of 1923. These included his favorite encore numbers—the Wagner-Brassin Magic Fire Music, the Beethoven-Rubinstein Turkish March, and the Gluck-Brahms Gavotte. All piano connoisseurs regret the lack of a large body of his work on disc, especially since it was the eleven-year-old master Josef Hofmann, in 1887, who was history's first recorded artist, making a group of cylinders for Edison's revolutionary recording machine. The cylinders, unfortunately, are lost to posterity.

LORIN HOLLANDER
b. 1944 — United States

Studied at the Juilliard School. Hollander has maintained a substantial career. His early recordings were serious and well played. There have been no recordings in recent years, and his public performances seem awkward and musically heavy.

HELEN HOPEKIRK
1856–1945 — Scotland

She studied with Leschetizky. Hopekirk espoused the music of MacDowell after she settled in the United States, and was a composer as well.

VLADIMIR HOROWITZ
b. 1903 — Russia

He studied with Sergei Tarnowsky and with Felix Blumenfeld, Anton Rubinstein's pupil.

At seventeen, he made his debut in a recital at Kharkov, thus commencing one of the most remarkable careers in twentieth-century music. During Horowitz's Russian years, he gave innumerable concerts. After the Revolution, he played eleven programs in Leningrad without repeating a composition. In 1925, Horowitz left Russia and played with overwhelming success in Berlin, Hamburg, and Paris, where he packed the Paris Opera in five recitals. The American impresario Arthur Judson heard him there and signed him for a U.S. concert tour. Horowitz made a spectacular American debut on January 12, 1928, in the Tchaikovsky Concerto No. 1; Beecham, who was also making his debut that night, conducted. Annual concert tours took place to the greatest acclaim until 1936, and then he did not play publicly until 1939. During the war years, however, he maintained a fierce schedule, which included raising money for the war effort.

In 1953, following a Carnegie Hall recital, he retired from the concert stage until May 9, 1965, when he made one of the great comebacks in the history of the performing arts. It was international news, and the anticipation of hearing Horowitz created unparalleled excitement. Music lovers waited for hours to get a seat. The recital fulfilled everyone's expectations, and fortunately the event was recorded.

During the next fifteen years, Horowitz made sporadic appearances throughout the United States, and in 1978, to mark the fiftieth anniversary of his American debut, he performed the Rachmaninoff Third Concerto with Ormandy and the New York Philharmonic. It was his first concerto appearance in a quarter-century. During the 1980s, Horowitz extended his concertizing to Europe and, for the third time, played at the White House. But it appeared that his playing was deteriorating, and performances in New York and Tokyo were alarmingly off form. Once again, however, he struggled to revive himself, and in 1986 he began playing with a vengeance,

Sunday Afternoon, May 9, 1965, at 3:30 o'clock

THE CARNEGIE HALL CORPORATION

presents

Vladimir Horowitz

Pianist

Bach-Busoni Organ Toccata in C major
Prelude
Intermezzo: Adagio
Fugue

Schumann Fantasy in C major, Op. 17
Fantastic and with passion
Moderato, energetic throughout
Lento sostenuto sempre dolce

"Through all the tones that vibrate about Earth's
mingled dream, one whispered tone is sounding for
ears attent to hear."

FRIEDRICH SCHLEGEL

INTERMISSION

*Scriabin Sonata No. 9 in One Movement, Op. 68
Poem in F sharp major, Op. 32

Chopin Mazurka in C sharp minor, Op. 30, No. 4
Etude in F major, Op. 10
Ballade in G minor, Op. 23, No. 1

---

*In memory of the composer on the 50th anniversary of his death, April 27th, 1915.

COLUMBIA RECORDS   STEINWAY PIANO   RCA VICTOR RECORDS

Net Proceeds for the Program Fund of The Carnegie Hall Corporation.

*The program for Horowitz's historic comeback recital
after his twelve-year retirement from the concert stage.*

making a triumphant return to Russia after more than six decades.

It was felt that Horowitz the artist had reached a new peak, and a worldwide television audience heard the octogenarian maestro playing from Moscow. He returned to Berlin, Hamburg, London, and Paris, where he was received as a cultural hero. After two grueling months on the road, he recouped his honor with a successful return to Japan. Wherever he performed, the world stood at attention. He was featured on the cover of *Time* magazine and received the Presidential Medal of Freedom, as well as decorations from the Soviet, Italian, and French governments.

In 1987 he recorded the Mozart Concerto No. 23, his first studio recording of a concerto since 1951, and played again in the major capitals of Europe, in June giving his first Vienna recital in fifty-three years. Horowitz's audiences sensed that this was music-making of a rarefied nature, poetic and singing, with phrasing of a unique individuality.

Horowitz has had to come to grips with the inevitable slowing down of his marvelous nervous system. A battle has always raged between his own virtuosity and the desire to be the most sincere of interpreters. For him there have always been three stages in his performance: first, the complete mastery of the text; followed by the art of interpretation; and finally, with all of its perils, the act of re-creation. The world has very often claimed victory for the great virtuoso, pronouncing him the greatest of them all. But in recent years, like a sublime but faded singer or an aging athlete, he has given up what he can no longer do—play like a lion—and the mighty roar, the floods of fortissimos, have been withdrawn. He has concentrated on new colors, colors such as Monet had realized through his near-blindness, a palette of incandescent pastels that even Horowitz had not dreamed of. In the mid-1980s, he began

playing—indeed became all but obsessed with—that most youthful master, Mozart, whose music he performs with indescribable nuance and relaxed beauty. It is a Mozart of Italian vintage, bathed in sunlight, fetching and flirtatious. Only the aged Horowitz could give such a young Mozart to the world.

From the moment Horowitz made his American debut in 1928, audiences went wild for him. Not since the early years of Paderewski had there been such a splash. Olin Downes reported in the *New York Times:* "A mob is a mob, blood is blood; the call of the wild is heard, whether it is a savage beating a drum or a young Russian, mad with excitement and physical speed and powers, pounding on a keyboard." News of Horowitz's successes in the capitals of Europe had traveled quickly, and Carnegie Hall was jammed with the most celebrated virtuosi of the "golden age," many of whom trembled as they went home to reassess their own technical equipment. One of them grumbled, "Our careers will never again be the same."

Horowitz was never dethroned; in fact, he became the yardstick of pianistic prowess. To this day, no review can be more exciting for a young pianist than one calling him or her "another Horowitz"—as if such a complex and towering musician could ever be duplicated. Pianists, of course, may not find congenial all that Horowitz plays, but, like him or not, every pianist in the world must come to terms with him. He has been the outstanding figure in the pianistic world for more than a half-century, as Heifetz was for violinists. I once asked the Polish violinist Wanda Wilkomirska if she thought there was such a thing as a "best violinist." She retorted, "There can be no best anything." But then she looked troubled and added, "I'm sorry. There is a best. It's Horowitz. He is better than anyone, any violinist, any singer, any pianist. Oh, but he is also not human."

When Horowitz burst on the scene, he was in danger of misusing his great powers of virtuosity. Two forces had a salutary influence during those early years: Toscanini, who shaped his intellectual respect for the composer's intent, and Rachmaninoff, who, with his almost cerebral approach to Romantic music, deemed mere showing off to be sinful. To exercise restraint when you know you can raise more excitement than anyone else takes an iron will. With his technical and temperamental gifts, Horowitz could have been the gallery player *par excellence*. And he was a born show-stopper. But an artist who engages in acrobatics soon finds himself having to top each effort. Slowly and painfully, Horowitz came to understand André Gide's words: "Any good execution must be an explanation of the piece. But the pianist, like the actor, strives for the effect. And the effect is generally achieved at the expense of the text. The player is well aware that the less I understand, the more I shall be impressed."

Whatever sins he might have committed in the concert hall, Horowitz took recording seriously, compiling the most listened-to, and studied, discography in the history of the art. Many of his recordings were pioneering efforts, and his great prestige and authority led many pianists to follow suit. Works that had been neglected began showing up on programs: Haydn's E-flat and F major Sonatas; Czerny's *La Ricordanza;* Clementi's F-sharp minor Sonata; Liszt's *Funérailles;* several Scarlatti sonatas; Kabalevsky's Third Sonata; Prokofiev's Seventh Sonata; Scriabin's Fifth, Ninth, and Tenth Sonatas; Schumann's *Humoreske;* Barber's Sonata; Rachmaninoff's Second Sonata—Horowitz's phenomenal success with these pieces was a powerful stimulus for other pianists to learn them.

The Horowitz discography reveals how little he recorded the war-horses of the literature. He has an abhorrence of the hackneyed. A trademark of his program-building in public and on disc is the delicate balance of timings, key relationships, and idioms. He selects his repertoire with great care, playing no work that he has not lived with for a long time.

Scarlatti is the only composer born in the seventeenth century that Horowitz has recorded. He has made an album of twelve of these priceless binary gems, with another dozen scattered throughout other discs. His interpretations are a lesson in the transference of harpsichord music to the Steinway grand. He employs a large set of dynamics, and the pedal is used ingeniously, in washes and dots and dashes. Horowitz packs these works with drama. One hears intrigue, gossip, the clatter of Madrid cobblestone, the pomp of court, the fetching fandango rhythms, all etched with a remarkable finger precision and spacing of notes. It is a living, breathing Scarlatti, which, once heard, can never be forgotten.

He refuses to play Bach in the original in public, believing that modern halls are too big for effective performance. I also suspect that, since he grew up during the decline of Russian Romanticism, "pure" Bach is not really much to his taste. But his recordings of some Bach-Busoni chorales are played to perfection, as is an especially coloristic performance of the large C major Organ Toccata in Busoni's wonderful transcription, which he played as the opening piece of his 1965 Carnegie Hall comeback.

Of Classical composers born during the eighteenth century, Horowitz recorded two Haydn sonatas, four Clementi sonatas and a rondo movement, five sonatas of Mozart, and five of Beethoven, as well as the *Emperor* Concerto and the C minor Variations. He has also recorded a set of variations by Czerny, and Schubert's posthumous B-flat Sonata.

The capriciousness of Haydn fits Horowitz well. His recording of the Sonata in E-flat is pianistically the finest ever made. Years later, he recorded the smaller Sonata in F major, playing the slow movement with a lavish expressiveness.

His Clementi sonata album from the early 1950s is vintage Horowitz and remains the 133 most effective all-around recorded example of any Clementi sonatas. He understands Clementi historically yet plays with stylistic freedom. The finales of the Sonatas in F minor and F-sharp minor bring out the latent passion in Clementi, and his recording of the large-scale Sonata in C major in the late 1970s pulls out all stops, while still remaining within the idiom.

Next in line chronologically is Mozart. Horowitz's 1947 recording of the celebrated Sonata in F, K. 332, is Italianate and operatic in style—a highly inflected and Romanticized Mozart, with a finale that reveals the composer in his most unbuttoned mood. Not as successful is the rather heavy interpretation of the A major Sonata K. 331, from a live concert in the 1960s; even the concluding Rondo *alla turca* misses the right kind of clangor. The Sonatas in C major, K. 330, and in B-flat, K. 333, are his latest recordings of Mozart, infused with a bewitching flexibility and tonal beauty. His renderings of the Rondo in D and the great B minor Adagio are incomparable. His recording with Giulini of the Mozart A major Concerto K. 488 has nothing in common with other performances of that work. Humor, bite, a brisk slow movement, and evenness of fingerwork are apparent along with a full-bodied freshness. It will hardly be to everyone's taste, especially the highly inflated second movement.

In 1944, Horowitz recorded Czerny's Variations on *La Ricordanza*. Czerny had turned the naive charm of Rode's aria into a *tour de force* of early Romantic piano music, and Horowitz displays devastating control and a ravishing sense of style.

Horowitz's nineteenth-century repertoire includes only one excursion into Schubert's sonata literature, the B-flat Sonata, written when the composer was dying. It is a controversial Schubert, without much depth, yet one that has a curious impact. The Horowitz Schubert Impromptus of the 1970s are oddly erratic. The E-flat and A-flat are tight instead of expansive, while the G-flat is pumped up into an overblown pool of sound. The Impromptu in B-flat major (recorded in 1986), on the other hand, is played with a beautiful limpidity. His interpretation of the Schubert-Liszt *Soirée de Vienne* No. 6 is all cream-puff, and the Schubert-Tausig-Horowitz *Marche militaire* is filled with humor and his characteristic sonority.

Although Horowitz has played Beethoven's Sonata in A major Op. 101 in public, he is not a lover of late Beethoven and finds only the early and middle periods congenial. The slow movement of the Op. 10, No. 3 has the pathos of a Greek tragedy, with a sound only Horowitz could achieve. The *Pathétique*, Op. 13, is large-scale and ripe. The *Waldstein* and *Appassionata,* while self-conscious, have a definite power and glitter, as does the *Moonlight* Sonata's finale. His C minor Variations are tightly packed, and the *Emperor* Concerto, with Reiner, is lean but heroically cast.

The first Romantic that Horowitz takes to heart is Mendelssohn. His account of several *Songs without Words,* including the *Spring Song,* is delightful and pithy; the *Variations sérieuses* is seething and impregnable technically. In 1981 he returned to Mendelssohn, recording the *Scherzo a capriccio* to rousing effect.

At times there is a clash of personalities between Chopin and Horowitz. At its worst, the pianist's phrasing sounds unnatural; sometimes it is touched with hysteria. He has delved deeply in the Chopin repertoire, and his earlier Chopin recordings, such as several Etudes and the Fourth Scherzo, are simple and refined. Later, however, his Chopin playing is often shredded and nervous—a public Chopin for gargantuan halls. The bubbling A-flat Impromptu is dour in Horowitz's hands, and the Nocturnes he has recorded are heavily made up and filled with a dense, musky atmosphere. Still, the famous F-sharp major Nocturne, Op. 15, No. 2, is fascinating in its languor, and the E minor, Op. 72, is overtly dramatic, even

Lisztian in its gestures. In the F minor Nocturne, Op. 55, No. 1, Horowitz whimpers and drools, and the celebrated E-flat major Op. 9, No. 2 lacks simplicity in both expression and shape. Yet these Nocturnes are filled with a passionate eroticism that can only be termed Horowitzian.

In both of his recordings of the *Funeral March* Sonata, Horowitz reveals a Byronic Chopin, full of burning frustration, willfulness, and bombast. Like a vampire, he extracts every drop of blood from the score, and violence suffuses its thick and murky atmosphere.

In other large Chopin scores, there is an irritable quality, as if he cannot tame the Pole. In the B minor Scherzo, he is most successful, properly gnarling his way to the heated coda. But Horowitz finds the G minor Ballade an inexhaustible problem. The great work fascinates yet evades him. Each of his four recordings is different and shows Horowitz fighting to make it his own. Yet each recording reveals startling pianistic creativity, a sense of sonority and tone color that is never less than fully projected and often unique. In the mighty triple fortissimo entrance to the coda on his 1940s 78 version of the Ballade, transferred to LP, there is a thunderclap unequaled for sheer drama in any performance of that Ballade ever recorded. His rendering of the Barcarolle makes me queasy: the waters are troubled, the crooning and warblings are uncomfortable. His early recording of the F minor Ballade is rather plodding and heavy, but his large-scale performance from the 1980s is very convincing, with many original moments.

In the area of the polonaise and mazurka, Horowitz often attains greatness. He has a real flair for the pomp of the polonaise, and his readings of the A major *Military*, the A-flat Op. 53, the A-flat *Polonaise-fantaisie,* and, most of all, the nerve-racking F-sharp minor are enthralling. He is surely one of the great mazurka players, impish and nostalgic, employing a pungent rubato. It is the Chopin genre he loves best and finds most conducive, and his playing is without ostentation.

Other memorable Horowitz Chopin performances include a regal *Andante spianato and Grand Polonaise,* Op. 22, and a Rondo Op. 16 which finds the pianist at his most infectious. There are also two performances of the famed *Revolutionary* Etude. The first one, from 1964, is staggering. It opens with the very "crack of creation" in Huneker's words. Here is the unique Horowitzian spirit with all of its controlled fury: the glistening chords with their gleaming tops; the swirling propulsive left hand, as wondrous as any could possibly be; all of the notes perfectly welded together, with the depth of nuance and that extra drive and cutting edge that only Horowitz can attain. All the while the artist's heart is alive to Chopin's despairing rage. The later Horowitz performance on disc is more casual, is lighter in weight and less colorful, and is more concerned with purely pianistic aspects, resulting in a far less powerful psychological imprint.

In Schumann, Horowitz's creative imagination is fired. Here he finds a kindred spirit, childlike but complex: thorny, caressing, fragmented, and full of trickery and whimsy. In no other composer has Horowitz so laid bare his heart. I think he loves Schumann more than any other German master.

His earlier recordings of Schumann—the Toccata, *Traumeswirren, Presto passionato,* and *Arabeske*—all have vitality, but are somewhat superficial. Later, his Schumann becomes darker. The second recording of the Toccata is far more spacious. The great Fantasy, Op. 17, is deep and tonally glorious; the first recording of the *Kreisleriana,* from the late 1960s, is an unforgettable experience. While Horowitz's rubato can be contorted in his Chopin performances, in Schumann its application is an instinctive drive. Sparks fly; it is a canvas of convulsion. In the 1986 recording, we hear a mellow, almost hallucinatory *Kreisleriana.* For me, the neglected *Humoreske* finds Horowitz at his best, in a performance that at last realizes the potential of this glorious masterpiece. Though he first learned it in the 1930s, Horowitz only brought it to public life in the late 1970s. In Alfred de Vigny's phrase, "A fine life is a thought conceived in youth and realized in maturity." Horowitz's disc of the Sonata in F minor must rank high in his Schumann contribution, it is so throbbing, fiery, and tender. And the *Kinderscenen* is never far from his fingers, although the children occasionally sound rather fiendish. He has long used *Träumerei* as one of his encores. One wit has said that he put too much trauma in the *Träumerei*. This is true at times, but as stated, Horowitz seldom plays a piece the same way twice.

Horowitz never played much Brahms, and has played none at all in the past forty years. He says he is not on good terms with him. However, Brahms's two concerti figured in his performing repertoire, and the 1940 disc of the Second, with his father-in-law Toscanini, is one of the five commercial discs of concertos that he has given us. It is a bitter, muscular, and taut performance, perhaps the most unidiomatic Brahms Concerto No. 2 ever recorded; one either loves it for its raw passion, or one hates it. There is also a charming recording of the A-flat Waltz and a convincing B-flat minor Intermezzo.

For the general public, Horowitz is possibly most identified with Liszt. His Liszt has often been accused of being narcissistic. This stereotype—of two great virtuosi outdoing each other—is put to rest by pianist John Browning, who writes: "I think Liszt is misunderstood in the same way that Vladimir Horowitz has been misunderstood by many people. In Horowitz's playing they hear the speed, they hear the glitter, but they don't hear the ten voices working at once, all separately, and they don't hear the incredible way Horowitz can unify a work that really has no structural unity. They don't listen to the beauty of the colors, so they hear the wrong things."

Horowitz has always chosen his Liszt carefully. Although the Liszt Sonata was prized by d'Albert, Busoni, Friedheim, Rachmaninoff, and Hofmann, it did not really enter the world repertoire until Horowitz's 1932 recording, which retains its importance and far exceeds the value of his torturous remake of the late 1970s, so full of exaggeration and grandiloquence. The Horowitz comprehension of the grief-stricken *Funérailles* has never been equaled. The range of nuance, the subtlety of his timing, the massiveness of his left-hand octaves have made this work Horowitz's own. My heart quakes when I listen to it. A pianist told me that he had always felt his own octaves so sluggish in this piece that out of curiosity he timed his and Horowitz's and found his own quite a bit faster. Horowitz's neuro-dynamic system cannot be clocked.

Other great Liszt performances include the piquant *Valse oubliée* No. 1, the *Sonetto 104 del Petrarca,* and *Au bord d'une source;* all have a special fragrance that only Horowitz can evoke. *Vallée d'Obermann,* with his own discreet touching up of the text, is a ripe expression of Horowitz's Byronic Romanticism. A recording of the D-flat *Consolation* captures the Horowitz sound wonderfully, but the temperature is too torrid for the piece's lyricism. His rendering of the *Mephisto Waltz,* with some Busoni additions, as well as his own retouching, is a Liszt with devilish humor. He is also in top form in his monumental performance of the B minor Ballade.

There are also Horowitz's own versions of four of the Hungarian Rhapsodies. Each is a reworking of the original, although No. 6 contains only a bit of touching up for added effectiveness. In this, the Horowitz octaves are unbelievable. His view of No. 2 is delicious— very spicy and irresistible; No. 15, the *Rákóczy March,* is greatly improved by Horowitz, while No. 19 is deliberate and serious. In these performances, which Liszt surely would have sanctioned, Horowitz displayed probably the most astounding muscular sonority in history. In Paganini's time, he too would have been accused of being in league with the devil. No matter the extent of this "virtuosity," however, it is his control, his very coolness, that is exciting. One hears everything clearly. His rhythmic sense seems so right, and his reflexes are peerless. Horowitz's use of the pedals is ingeniously calculated and often quite sparse: scales are partly pedaled, climaxes possess extra vibration, and all sorts of finesses are wrought with the *una corda* pedal. It is in Liszt that the sonorous imagery of his playing finds all of its variegated splendor. The Horowitz touch defies description. It is a sound that only a piano can make, and that only Horowitz can summon out of it.

Horowitz at his most stupendous can be found in his performances of the Russian literature. The Tchaikovsky First Concerto, which he played at his American debut, finds him kicking the turf like a stallion at the gate. The two early-1940s recordings with Toscanini are immortal: steely, edgy, with the reins tightly held. Nobody who listens can remain unaffected by his strength and raw nerve. A 1952 pirated recording with Szell and the New York Philharmonic at Carnegie Hall, taped in live performance, is totally different— wild and far less controlled, but soaring. Horowitz is having his way, rampaging through the work with a fearlessness that has never been approached in this most popular of all concertos. Horowitz's 1940 recording of Tchaikovsky's *Dumka* also should not be missed.

Perhaps the most controversial of his recordings is the Mussorgsky *Pictures at an Exhibition,* which Horowitz substantially amplified to bring out what he felt Mussorgsky really wanted to say pianistically. Purists persist in hating it, and some have sarcastically commented that Horowitz put graffiti on the score. But this pianism is awesome in its impact, and is so perfectly Horowitzian in manner that it must be judged as an extraordinary oddity, a pure melding of intention and realization. He recorded it twice—in the studio and live-in-concert—and I find the latter most thrilling.

From the very beginning of his career, Horowitz felt a bond with Rachmaninoff. The two developed a close friendship, and Rachmaninoff was dazzled by the younger artist's playing of the Third Piano Concerto, saying, "Horowitz swallowed it whole." Once, in an extremely uncharacteristic gesture, the composer mounted the platform to embrace Horowitz after a performance of the treacherous work. Horowitz has loved this concerto dearly, recording it three times. The 1930 version, conducted by Albert Coates, was severely truncated to fit onto nine 78 sides. Horowitz himself discounts the performance, available now on an LP transfer, but it is fine playing, unaffected and far less turbulent than his other recordings. The 1951 recording with Reiner is the pianist's most characteristic performance—demonic, searing, technically incomparable—with fewer, far more judicious cuts. By 1978, in the uncut, live-in-concert performance with Ormandy, Horowitz's Rachmaninoff Third had become marked by excess and self-absorbed melancholy.

In Horowitz's recordings of various solo pieces by Rachmaninoff, he concentrates on the epic side of the music far more than the composer himself ever did in performance. In the climax of the *Etude-tableau* in E-flat minor, for instance, Horowitz lifts one from one's seat. In the Etude in C major, his freedom of phrasing is exquisite, as is the shimmering light in the G-sharp minor Prelude. Horowitz's playing always evokes an orchestral instrumentation, but unlike many pianists who play orchestrally, he never leaves his audience longing for the actual orchestra, so completely does he understand the instrument and its plangent sonority. Listen to Horowitz's version of the Second Sonata, in which, with Rachmaninoff's permission, he worked out his own edition of the finale from

137

the composer's two versions. The whole endeavor is a *tour de force* of piano coloration inspired by orchestral sound.

If Horowitz relates well to Rachmaninoff's music and pianism, he is even closer spiritually to the mercurial and mystic impressionism of Alexander Scriabin, to whom Horowitz was taken to play as a child. If I had to choose my own favorite segment of the Horowitz art, it would be his Scriabin. Horowitz knows exactly how to bring to life that composer's flickering, flamelike spirit, its vertiginous, supercharged nervosity and quivering eroticism. Even on record his interpretation of Scriabin is ever-changing: one of his versions of the D-sharp minor Etude is convulsive, while another, from his late performance in Moscow, almost purrs before the demon sets in.

The early Etudes, Op. 2, No. 1 and Op. 8, No. 11, are filled with yearning, while later ones from Op. 42, especially No. 5, capture Scriabin's desire for breathlessness. The bouquet of sixteen Preludes is an indispensable disc for Scriabin lovers. Horowitz's recordings of the Sonatas Nos. 3, 5, 9, and 10 are the zenith of all Scriabin playing. These performances possess a devastating truth. The Sonata No. 3 is declamatory and spasmodic. One can see a blinding light in the trills of the Tenth Sonata. A diabolical sensuality is sparked in the Fifth Sonata, Scriabin's offshoot of the *Poem of Ecstasy,* while one can almost smell the sulphurousness of the Ninth Sonata, of which the 1953 recording is three minutes faster and more satanic than the 1965 performance. Horowitz draws from these scores every molecule of their meaning, and his very passion exhausts the listener. Other great Scriabin performances are the two wonderful *Poems* of Op. 69, played with capriciousness, and the extraordinary work entitled *Vers la flamme,* to which he brings an explosive, pent-up energy, a purification by fire.

Horowitz's survey of the Russians also contains an early-1920s recording of the *Danse russe* from Stravinsky's *Petrouchka,* and, more important, his well-known disc of Prokofiev's Toccata. He gave the first American performances of Prokofiev's Sonatas Nos. 6, 7, and 8, and the Seventh was recorded in 1945. Horowitz sent the record to Prokofiev in Russia, who sent Horowitz back the score, inscribed "to the miraculous pianist from the composer." In 1947, Horowitz made a dazzling recording of the clever Kabalevsky Third Sonata.

If Scarlatti is the firstborn in Horowitz's catalogue of composers, Barber, born in 1910, is the latest. In 1949, at a recital in Havana, Cuba, the pianist gave the world premiere of the Barber Sonata, which had been composed for him. One has only to listen to Horowitz's influential 1950 recording to understand why the composer was simply bowled over by it.

In the French literature, Horowitz has made a small but significant contribution. His efforts have included the Fauré Barcarolle in B minor and Fifth Impromptu. In 1932 he recorded the Poulenc Toccata—which was dedicated to him—along with the *Pastourelle.* His Debussy is a thorough delight: balanced and crisp. The Etude *Pour les arpèges composés* is a marvel of executant skill, the *Serenade for a Doll* and several Preludes are gracious, and the wonderful *L'Isle joyeuse* is positively orgiastic.

Finally, there are the fantastic discs of Horowitz's transcriptions and paraphrases. Besides the Liszt amplifications, there are further reworkings of Liszt's own paraphrases, of the Saint-Saëns *Danse macabre,* and the Mendelssohn-Liszt *Wedding March.* He also prepared his own Variations on a Theme from *Carmen,* and his patriotic tribute to his adopted land, an arrangement of Sousa's *Stars and Stripes Forever,* is played with a vital rhythmic explosiveness. During its vogue, Horowitz was called "a one-man band"; he certainly outdoes any band performance.

Horowitz has also played various pieces of fluff, such as the Moszkowski *Etincelles* and F major and A-flat Etudes, with exquisite polish and delectability. When I hear such playing, I am reminded of James Hilton's remarks: "If by some dispensation a man born deaf were to be given hearing for a single hour, he might well spend the whole time with Horowitz. Indeed, when I listened to Horowitz for the first time, it was almost like that—as if I had never heard the piano before—as if the instrument itself had never known what it could do until Horowitz came along."

It must be said that Horowitz has given to us on record only a fraction of his repertoire. Horowitz admirers would eat their hearts out if they knew how much he has not recorded that he could reel off in the most offhanded manner. Scores of Rachmaninoff and loads of Medtner, a composer he loves and plays with panache. Indeed, his Medtner repertoire is large, and he has played to me, from memory, long stretches from the concerti, sonatas, and *Fairy Tales.* If one mentions the Grieg Ballade, or *Islamey* or *Scarbo,* or the two Liszt concerti or the Chopin F minor, he has played them. If you mention Moscheles or Kalkbrenner, an etude sparks from his fingers. If you tell him you love his recording of the Kabalevsky Sonata No. 3, he plays to you a series of Kabalevsky preludes, and then the wonderful Second Sonata, of which he gave the American premiere, as he did of Barber's *Excursions.* If you discuss his transcriptions, he can play you others equally breathtaking from Rimsky-Korsakov operas, which have never been performed publicly or recorded. And there is his incomparable ability to sight-read, and when he is in the mood his improvisations are delights. For several years I have been privileged to be a constant visitor to his beautiful home, and I have almost always left surprised in one way or another, either by an unexpected performance or a dazzling piece of pianistic wisdom.

Throughout his career, Horowitz has given us indelible performances that have expanded our awareness of many works in the repertoire, always revealing new avenues of color and detail. His recordings are precious documents of the art of piano playing. Horowitz has shown us more completely than anyone else the glory of this instrument in all its range and sonority.

MIECZYSLAW HORSZOWSKI
b. 1892 — Poland

A child prodigy, he was called "the Mozart of his age." Early on, he went to Leschetizky and developed into one of the century's respected musicians. He settled in the United States in 1940, teaching at the Curtis Institute. Horszowski has had one of the longest performing careers in history and is still actively playing, not only with musical wisdom, but with a continuing command of his instrument. His great gift for chamber music has perhaps made the public less aware of his continuous solo career, and an artist of his stature should have been far more recorded than has been the case.

He has spent a lifetime exploring the Classical literature and Bach. His recording of *The Well-Tempered Clavier,* Book I, offers beautifully plastic examples of polyphonic playing, and the preludes are restrained and subtle.

Horszowski finds in Beethoven scope for never-ending development. In 1954 he gave New York audiences all of the solo output of that master. Though he does not always have a perfect technique, no detail escapes his searching mind.

Mozart is a composer in whom he thrives. Horszowski senses the essence of the Salzburg master. His Mozart is always glowing, suave, and lighthearted. In Chopin, Horszowski gives his Slavic temperament full sway. It is an affectionate yet serious Chopin, where the rhythm is forceful but the poetry apparent. His records of the E minor Concerto and the

Four Impromptus have a flavor of the past that stems not from old-fashioned playing, but from the kind of individual and personalized playing that Chopin so seldom receives today.

LESLIE HOWARD
b. 1948 — Australia

A fine pianist who has recorded with brilliance many neglected works, such as Anton Rubinstein's sonatas and pieces by Glazunov, Percy Grainger, and many others. He has played in public all of Liszt's original piano works.

EDWIN HUGHES
1884–1965 — United States

Hughes studied with Joseffy and Leschetizky. He played concerts and made editions of various classics.

JOHANN NEPOMUK HUMMEL
1778–1837 — Hungary

As a student of Mozart, Hummel lived in his home for two years, and made his debut in 1787 at a concert given by the master. The following year the young prodigy was playing through Germany, Bohemia, and Denmark. Soon after, he appeared in Edinburgh and in London, where he worked with Clementi and appeared in a concert with Cramer. By 1800, Hummel was considered one of the great musicians of his age. Hummel's studies with the two main keyboard masters of the high Classical era, Mozart and Clementi, were of great value to him. From Mozart he learned an assured and tasteful Classicism and the lightness of the Viennese school of playing, and from Clementi he gained a foothold into a more sonorous type of playing. Hummel's pianism was especially elegant and note-perfect, his pride being his pearl-like scales.

For a time in the early 1800s, he was considered Beethoven's rival. In the art of improvisation, he seemed to be as dazzling as Beethoven, who thought Hummel's playing was monotonous. However, Czerny, who idolized Beethoven, had some lessons with Hummel and admitted that his playing was phenomenal.

Hummel had a superb sense of piano sonority, and his compositions extended the piano's scope considerably, especially in the intricate ornamentation in his slow movements, where he would weave a fantastic tapestry of Romantic passagework. A particularly good example is the slow movement of his Sonata Op. 106. He was a great influence on the young Romantics. Mendelssohn, Schumann, Chopin, and Liszt all revered him, and Chopin was held spellbound by his playing in Warsaw in 1826. In Hummel's A minor Piano Concerto, one quickly detects this older master's influence on the Chopin E minor Concerto, composed in 1830. Liszt, as a youth, often played Hummel's difficult B minor Concerto, and the young Schumann was overwhelmed by Hummel's Sonata in F-sharp minor, Op. 81, which he called "epic and titanic," and he set out to conquer the piece. (He wanted to study with Hummel, but he could not afford his fee.) Indeed, the composition, published in 1819, served as a harbinger of Romanticism, as did his D minor Piano Septet, which made a great impression when introduced in Vienna about the same time.

In 1828, Hummel published an instruction book which was to be a pianistic bible for generations. He called it *A Complete Theoret-*

ical and Practical Course of Instruction on the Art of Playing the Pianoforte. It was Hummel's attempt to codify modern piano playing in such areas as fingering and ornaments. It included more than two thousand examples. The harpsichordist Ralph Kirkpatrick wrote: "I built up my own keyboard technique very largely on the exercises of Hummel's piano method which contains an admirably organized series designed to take care of nearly everything that the ten fingers need be expected to negotiate." Hummel's Twenty-four Etudes, Op. 125, from 1828, are also a superb summation of his pianistic technique.

Hummel continued to play publicly until around 1830, when he appeared in Paris to a rather cool reception. His immaculately clean-cut style, with very sparse pedal, now seemed dry; a larger, more colorful playing was taking its place. He lived in Weimar during his last years, and it is pleasant to know that the old Goethe often heard him play and was inspired by his improvisations.

BRUCE HUNGERFORD
1922–1977 — Australia

He was a student of Ernest Hutcheson and Carl Friedberg. Hungerford was a man of wide interests and unswerving idealism. His death at the very apogee of his musical powers deprived us of the fulfillment of his ambition to record the thirty-two sonatas of Beethoven. The twenty that he completed are statements of high-minded musicianship, wedded to an immense technical foundation and an extraordinary rhythmical framework. Each sonata

was treated as a universe in itself. He also did some of his best playing within the Schubert canon, and he left a glorious performance of the posthumous A major Sonata, terrifically strong and animated. His record of Brahms exposes many levels of dynamic gradation, and the A major Intermezzo, Op. 118, No. 2, is unusually beautiful in its fineness of voicing. He also made one Chopin recording, containing a powerful Sonata in B minor—firm and vigorous, large-scaled and deeply thoughtful, an intellectual Chopin B minor.

FRANZ HÜNTEN
1793–1878 — Germany

He studied with Pradère at the Paris Conservatoire. He later played and taught, and composed salon works, many of which were feeble, though they had a vogue and Hünten grew rich from them.

ERNEST HUTCHESON
1871–1951 — Australia

Hutcheson was a child prodigy who went for training at Leipzig, studying there with Reinecke. He made a New York debut in 1915, and became a faculty member at Juilliard, eventually becoming president of the school. He wrote a valuable book, *The Literature of the Piano,* and taught a legion of first-class players.

KONSTANTIN IGUMNOV

1873–1948 — Russia

A student of Nikolai Zverev, Paul Pabst, and Siloti. Igumnov was an excellent musician and a pianist of sensibility as well as one of the great teachers at the Moscow Conservatory for nearly half a century. Along with fellow teachers Goldenweiser and Neuhaus, Igumnov molded modern Russian pianism. Lev Oborin, Davidovich, Grinberg, Yakov Flier, and many others enjoyed his instruction.

EUGENE ISTOMIN

b. 1925 — United States

He was a student of Serkin and won the Leventritt Award. He toured as a soloist and as a member of the famed Istomin-Stern-Rose trio. From his earliest mature appearances, he was reckoned a pianist of importance. In the last decade, his solo career has suffered, but there are signs of revitalization.

His early recordings of the First Tchaikovsky and Second Rachmaninoff Concertos are steely and exciting investigations of these scores; when he performs them, I forget that they form the core of the most hackneyed concerto literature. His performance of the Brahms B-flat Concerto is huge in formation, reminding me of a great suspension bridge. Istomin feels sympathetic to Schubert's music, and there is a well-constructed D major Sonata on record. An early set of the Chopin Nocturnes finds him stiff and in the wrong climate.

JOSÉ ITURBI

1895–1980 — Spain

Iturbi worked for a time with the legendary Joaquin Maláts. Early in life, he had extraordinary success wherever he went, quickly becoming one of the most beloved pianists of his time. In the late 1930s and 1940s, Iturbi acted and performed in Hollywood films, which added immeasurably to his fame. He also conducted a great deal. He played the Romantics best, with Chopin occupying a large part of his repertoire. His 1940s recordings show a charming player with a good structural sense. In 1952 he was still in form when William Kapell called him "a wonderful pianist. The evenest playing I know."

Later on, Iturbi's work as an interpreter suffered, becoming shallow and less technically adroit. It was noted that his popularity as a movie celebrity hurt his reputation as a serious artist. Whatever the cause, Iturbi as a musician fell below his earlier standards. His sister, Amparo Iturbi (1899–1969), was a fine concert artist who played more atmospherically than her brother.

PAUL JACOBS
1930–1983 — United States

He studied with Ernest Hutcheson and Beveridge Webster. Jacobs was staff pianist to the New York Philharmonic. He was a formidable musician, and a pianist with a thoroughly competent equipment. His objective but probing style became a strong influence on many younger pianists. Jacobs was a meticulous performer and never feared to take the unknown road. His readings are cool and refreshing, his Debussy Preludes and Etudes a model of clarity.

In his last years, he fortunately put to disc a tremendous variety of repertoire—Busoni, Messiaen, Stravinsky, Schoenberg, Virgil Thomson, and a splendid version of the Elliott Carter *Night Fantasies*.

ALFRED JAËLL
1832–1882 — Italy

Jaëll studied with Moscheles, and later traveled incessantly, giving concerts in America from 1852 to 1854. He was called *"le pianiste voyageur"* and was considered a player of taste and elegance. He gave early performances of the Raff Concerto, and composed nocturnes, valses, and other Romantic genre pieces. His wife, Marie, was a good pianist who wrote a piano method, *La Touche,* which received considerable attention at the time.

BYRON JANIS
b. 1928 — United States

In his twenties and thirties, Janis shone brightly in world pianism. His art made a great stir. To the public, he was Horowitz's heir apparent, having studied for several years with the Russian-born master. Indeed, Janis had something of the Horowitz mystique, some of the Horowitz tension, and some of the poetry, too. Nor was it only imitative playing; Janis had his own sound, supported by a large and finely chiseled technical equipment, and he did some exciting, even breathtaking work; his Rachmaninoff First and Third Concerti and his Liszt *Totentanz* and two concerti sizzle with electricity. Because of an ongoing battle with arthritis, his performances in recent years have been infrequent.

NATALIA JANOTHA
1856–1932 — Poland

She studied with Clara Schumann and won many honors as a pianist who also composed piano pieces, including *Mountain Scenes,* which was dedicated to Mme Schumann.

143

GRANT JOHANNESEN
b. 1921 — United States

He was a student of Robert Casadesus. Later, he became president of the Cleveland Institute for several years. When Johannesen steps forward, the audience can count on a performance of the most distinguished bearing. He is an artist of uncommon curiosity, and he has delved deeply into virtually unknown literatures. He excels in French repertory, and the essential Johannesen blooms in his deep and affectionate playing of Fauré, where he lets the exquisite music unfold with leisure, but always with point. He knows every inch of its rich fabric, knows its nobility, but knows too when Fauré becomes fruity, and when that happens he can dissipate a stale sentiment or erase the effect of a trite modulation. In Poulenc, Chabrier, Roussel, and Dukas, Johannesen plays with sophistication and irony and, in the case of Poulenc, he extracts just the right amount of tongue-in-cheek sentimentality.

Johannesen is good in Schumann as well; especially lovely are his *Fantasiestücke* Op. 12. He also plays Grieg, and his rendering of the Norwegian master's *Ballade in the Form of Variations* is poignant. In Johannesen's Mozart and Bach, there is a tenseness and more of an academic feel, and his Chopin never glitters or boils. But when playing Castro tangos or Copland's Piano Variations, he finds himself totally at ease. Johannesen's unobtrusive patrician readings need sophisticated audiences.

GUNNAR JOHANSEN
b. 1906 — Denmark

He studied with Victor Schiøler and in Berlin with Frederic Lamond. His main influence was his work with Egon Petri. He toured Europe, and came to the United States, where he taught and was artist-in-residence at the University of Wisconsin. He has composed throughout his career.

Johansen is a large-spirited musician with a questing nature. He has performed in public the complete piano music of Beethoven, Mozart, Bach, Schubert, and Chopin. He has recorded the whole of Bach's keyboard music in playing that is highly personalized and not convincing to everyone. But it throbs with life and a wealth of detail; especially appealing are the dance movements.

Johansen has long been dedicated to Liszt. In the past quarter-century, he has recorded more than fifty albums of Liszt's music. Here we encounter stylistically brilliant playing, often refreshingly reckless, sometimes not fully formed, but with a fervent quality which endears these performances to many Lisztians. It is the playing of an artist who never got over the initial thrill of hearing Liszt's music, and his freshness is engaging. From Liszt, it was only a step toward Busoni. We may imagine those early lessons Johansen had with Petri, the Italian master's greatest piano student. Here was kindled Johansen's love for the dense and difficult music of Busoni, all of which he has recorded. Since Petri's death, Johansen has remained Busoni's most impressive all-around exponent.

ALBERTO JONÁS
1868–1943 — Spain

Jonás studied at the Madrid Conservatory and later with Arthur de Greef at the Brussels Conservatoire. He was a fine pianist and a well-known pedagogue. His *Master School of Modern Piano Playing and Virtuosity* in seven volumes is an important anthology featuring excerpts from one thousand examples of the literature, as well as original exercises by

Friedheim, Friedman, Goodson, Godowsky, Busoni, and others.

MARYLA JONAS
1911–1959 — Poland

As a young prodigy, Jonas studied with Sauer and Turczynski, with advice received from Paderewski. She had a successful career until World War II, when she had to escape to South America. She finally came to the United States, where she made her debut in New York in 1946. Jonas was one of the first pianists to be heard on the newly invented long-playing record. She was not a technical giant, but played with a profound sensitivity. Her recording of Chopin mazurkas displays a ravishing tone with a gracious and feminine sense of rubato.

MARTIN JONES
b. 1940 — England

Jones has made a reputation as a pianist and a teacher. His recordings of Busoni, Szymanowski, and Mendelssohn reveal refined musicianship, taste, and a good mechanism.

SCOTT JOPLIN
1868–1917 — United States

The father of notated ragtime was a wonderful pianist, and an inspiration to a whole school of ragtime pianists. His performing career was set in the lurid night-life of brothels and saloons in which he played ragtime throughout the Missouri Valley states—where ragtime was born. In 1899 the *Maple Leaf Rag,* in which he solidified the formal basis of the genre, made him "King of Ragtime." By 1904, it was the first piece of sheet music to hit the one million mark in sales. Although the white establishment looked down on ragtime, Joplin rightfully thought of his music as art. At Joplin's death, John Stark, his publisher, wrote: "Here is the genius whose spirit, though diluted, was filtered through thousands of cheap songs and vain imitations."

Not until the 1970s did Joplin's importance in American music find large-scale appreciation, with the appearance of such fine interpreters as Joshua Rifkin, William Bolcom, Dick Hyman, and others. His more than fifty rags have a uniform excellence. The joyous quality and the intoxication of such syncopated jewels as *The Entertainer, Ragtime Dance, Elite Syncopation,* and *Gladiolus Rag* are irresistible. Near the end of his sad life (he died insane from syphilis), Joplin made a few piano rolls which give no indication of his effectiveness as a pianist. He was concerned about the prevalence of bad ragtime playing, however, and composed a *School of Ragtime,* a set of six exercises which are now published with his complete piano works.

RAFAEL JOSEFFY
1852–1915 — Hungary

He worked with Moscheles and Tausig, and then with Liszt. Joseffy's success as a pianist was immediate. In 1879 he left Europe to live in New York, where he was well received. His editions of the complete works of Chopin were widely used, and although his fingerings are unorthodox, they are often ingenious. Joseffy also composed some brilliant etudes and transcriptions, but his most enduring work is an extraordinary volume of exercises, *School of Advanced Playing* (1902).

145

Joseffy left no recordings, but he was supposed to have been one of the color geniuses of the piano. James Huneker called him "that fixed star in the pianistic firmament, one who refuses to descend to earth and please the groundlings. . . . Rafael Joseffy . . . is for me the most satisfying of all the pianists. Never any excess of emotional display; never silly sentimentalizings, but a lofty, detached style, impeccable technique, tone as beautiful as starlight—yes, Joseffy is the enchanter who wins me with his disdainful spells. . . . His Chopin was as Chopin would have had it given in 1840. And there were refinements of tone-color undreamed of even by Chopin."

GENEVIÈVE JOY
b. 1919 — France

Joy studied with Yves Nat. She has played many contemporary French scores, including the premiere of her husband Henri Dutilleux's Piano Sonata.

EILEEN JOYCE
b. 1912 — Tasmania

A student of Max Pauer, Tobias Matthay, and Artur Schnabel. From the late 1930s through the 1950s, Joyce was frequently heard and admired in England and on the Continent. She tickled audiences by changing gowns between selections or concertos. Her recordings show her to be musically balanced, emotionally reticent, and endowed with a pliable finger technique that in sheer evenness was the envy of many pianists. Her discs of the Schubert E-flat Impromptu, Grieg's *Brooklet*, Fauré's F minor Impromptu, and many other works give pleasure in the purity of her manipulation of the keyboard.

ILONA KABOS
1892–1973 — Hungary

She studied in her native country and became a resident of London in the late 1930s. Kabos was a highly regarded teacher and performer. She made recordings, especially of Bartók, and later in life taught at the Juilliard School.

PÁL KADOSA
1903–1983 — Hungary

He was an excellent pianist, most notably in twentieth-century music. Many Hungarian pianists respected his teaching. Schiff, Jenö Jandó, Kocsis, and Ránki studied with him. He recorded his own Fourth Sonata and Piano

Concerto No. 3, which are derivative of Bartók but of high musical merit.

JOSEPH KALICHSTEIN
b. 1946 — Israel

Kalichstein is a superb pianist and a nourishing teacher at the Juilliard School. He won the Leventritt Competition in 1968, and has forged a successful career ever since, in both chamber and solo music. He has recorded Bartók, Prokofiev, Chopin, Schumann, and Brahms, all of it with depth. His Brahms has special appeal. A Kalichstein concert is always pleasurable; one feels that the artist is totally involved with his music and is himself enjoying every moment.

FRIEDRICH KALKBRENNER
1785–1849 — Germany

In 1798 he entered the Paris Conservatoire, where after four years' work with Louis Adam, he won first prize in piano playing. Kalkbrenner made a Berlin debut in 1805. From 1814 until 1823, he lived, played, and taught in London. Afterward, he made Paris his headquarters.

Kalkbrenner was one of the founders and popularizers of French piano playing. He was famous for his *jeu perlé*, an evenness of scales and arpeggios and elegance in passagework, much favored by generations of French pianists.

From 1824 until around 1830 when the young group of Romantic pianists poured into Paris, Kalkbrenner was considered one of the leading pianists of Europe. He was a transi-tional player who assimilated some of the new Romantic feeling, but whose playing retained a more Classical precision. Charles Hallé, who worked with him, found in Kalkbrenner's playing "a clearness, a directness, and a neatness that are astonishing." One observer called his execution "as polished as a billiard ball." It was playing of a deft perfection, and Kalkbrenner's evenness in fingerwork was ear-tickling.

When Chopin arrived in Paris, he quickly encountered Kalkbrenner and was very impressed: "If Paganini is perfection, Kalkbrenner is his equal, but in quite another style. . . . He is the only one whose shoelaces I am not fit to untie." He raved about Kalkbrenner's enchanting touch, his calm, and his "incomparable evenness." In another letter, he describes Kalkbrenner as "superior to all the pianists I have ever heard," but admits that nobody "can stand him as a man." Kalkbrenner in turn told the young Pole that he needed to study with him for three years to become a finished pianist. Chopin was more than tempted, but bowed out gracefully, explaining to Kalkbrenner "that I know how much I still have to learn but I don't want simply to imitate . . . and three years is too long." Kalkbrenner regretted this decision and told Chopin he had "not a perfect mechanism" and "after I die, there will be no representative of the great school of piano playing left." Chopin consoled him by dedicating his E minor Concerto to him. Other pianists flocked to Paris to study with him, however, among them Camille Stamaty, Marie Pleyel, George Osborne, Thalberg, and many more.

In Paris, Kalkbrenner's music was all the rage. He was expert at making music of tinsel and glitter designed for the musically superficial but piano-crazed public of the day. It provides a deluge of diminished-seventh arpeggiation, lickety-split passagework, and well-rounded *bel canto* tunes, as well as extensive octave passages. Kalkbrenner was proud of his untiring octaves. "Why has God

147

given us wrists," he asked a student, "if not to play octaves with?"

After his death, Kalkbrenner's music disappeared from the repertoire. It was jeered for its almost hedonistic superficiality and became a symbol of philistinism. Liszt refused to listen when a pupil brought in Kalkbrenner's *Sonate pour la main gauche principale,* Op. 42. Many sources indicate that the man was obnoxious and pompous, a true know-it-all, which certainly prejudiced some against playing his music. But after 1850, as pianists became increasingly occupied with the interpretation of masterpieces, even the better Kalkbrenner pieces were considered stale and old-fashioned, although his best-known work, the twenty-minute *Effusio musica,* Op. 68, has been recorded by Mary Louise Boehm.

Based on the *Grande sonate brillante,* Op. 177, William Newman feels that "Kalkbrenner's piano music has been deplored undeservedly." The main problem is "the cantilena themes are too similar to each other to have independent character and to serve as landmarks. . . . In short and at best, one is hypnotized mildly without being drawn, driven, or, in fact, moved." But the pianist surely can have a great time in the score, rippling the keyboard, relishing the pretty packaging.

Kalkbrenner also produced four concerti. They attest to a superficial mentality, with a touch of Weber and Hummel. Reviewing a Kalkbrenner concerto, Robert Schumann deplored its "manufactured pathos and affected profundity." Yet Kalkbrenner's Concerto No. 1 in D minor, Op. 61, is graceful and handsomely fitted for the hand. There is a kind of elegance to it, almost a dandyism. Nor would a teacher be remiss in looking at the Kalkbrenner Etudes, which are very resourceful pieces. Even Schumann had to admit that Kalkbrenner was "one of the most skilled and masterly piano composers for finger and hand."

LILIAN KALLIR
b. 1931 — Austria

She made a New York debut at the age of seventeen with Dimitri Mitropoulos conducting the New York Philharmonic; later she married Claude Frank, and has appeared with him in concert. She is a fine soloist and a respected teacher. She is also a dedicated chamber musician. Her recording of the Mozart Concerto No. 17, K. 453, shows her at her finest.

WILLIAM KAPELL
1922–1953 — United States

He studied with Olga Samaroff, won the Naumburg Prize at nineteen, and soon after, he made a New York debut. Kapell sprang to prominence early. By the age of twenty, he ranked as a mature artist of the first order with a rare passion that stood out like a beacon among pianists of his generation. He was killed at the age of thirty-one in an air crash near San Francisco, after a grueling concert tour of Australia. His early death continues to be mourned by the many concertgoers who were privileged to follow his artistic growth. His recordings are cherished as the finest examples of the modern unmannered style of piano playing— pure, passionate, large and clear in structure, and with a unique Romantic intensity. Leon Fleisher felt "without question Willy was the greatest pianistic talent this country ever produced. His raw talent was awesome. He had little time on this earth, but few used it like he did. He started out with the big success pieces, like the Khachaturian, Rachmaninoff, and Prokofiev concertos, but at the end he was coming around to Schubert's posthumous sonatas."

Kapell also had a great interest in the music of his time; even on his early programs he made room for contemporary composers like Prokofiev, Fuleihan, Persichetti, Copland, and many others. Such an undertaking was especially hazardous for a young career-builder at that time. As Virgil Thomson wrote in an obituary: "Few artists have ever battled so manfully with management or so unhesitatingly sassed the press. He was afraid of nobody, because his heart was pure. . . . Kapell had become a grown man and a mature artist, a master. He could play great music with authority; his readings of it were at once sound and individual. He had a piano technique of the first class, a powerful mind, a consecration and a working ability such as are granted to few, and the highest aspirations toward artistic achievement."

Indeed, if there was a place called perfection, and if it could be possessed by force, temperament, and an indefatigable energy, then Kapell would relentlessly pursue it. Several months before his death, he wrote to the pianist Shirley Rhoads, "I think greatness in art is something you *come upon,* after only yearning and pain, and a deep sense of being in a dark tunnel. Greatness in art is not something you *tell yourself* you have. It is the oasis, the greatness, the vision, or whatever you want to call it, after traveling the vast desert of lonely and parched feelings. After this, the oasis. And the older a musician gets who has once seen this oasis, the more he wants to live there all the time, so the more frequent are his attainments of greatness and vision."

Kapell was an American eclectic, fascinated by all styles, and as he grew his repertoire incorporated the suites of Bach, the sonatas and concertos of Mozart and Beethoven, the most sublime Chopin, and the bleak, industrial cityscape of Copland's variations. Kapell was a master of the miniature, as well, and could titillate the hearer in the tiny velocity prelude, No. 5 in D, of Shostakovich, or

penetrate to the very core of an intermezzo by Brahms. His *Evocation* by Albéniz is among the best of Spanish playing, slow-burning and sultry, as is his Falla *Nights in the Gardens of Spain.*

Kapell played Liszt with greatness. The *Mephisto Waltz* he recorded when he was twenty-two, with its atmosphere of erotic tension, is still unrivaled. His highly controlled Eleventh Rhapsody is also the best ever recorded. His Beethoven Second Concerto is a pearl. It is youthful and sharply contoured, with a ringing cadenza and a slow movement that is perfectly shaped.

He was also a master of the Russian school, and his Mussorgsky *Pictures at an Exhibition* was rightly admired. His Rachmaninoff Third Concerto blazed with intensity, and his recording of the Second Concerto is deeply lyrical. His recording of the Rachmaninoff *Rhapsody on a Theme of Paganini* remains my favorite; I even prefer it to that of Rachmaninoff himself. Kapell's performance has a modernity to it. It crackles and is technically astounding. His most famous recording will always be the Khachaturian Concerto with Koussevitzky and the Boston Symphony. What sumptuousness, bravura, and rhythmic drive!

Kapell was an important Chopin player, virile and large-scaled. No American-born pianist had ever entered quite so deeply into the spirit of Chopin's mazurkas. His recordings of this literature should be studied by performers interested in mazurkas without fancy rubato, but which reach deeply into the heart while clearly retaining the dance element. Kapell also left a recording of Chopin's great Third Sonata, Op. 58; it is magnificent and symphonic in scope—the playing of a great architect, perfect in its proportion. Overall, it is the greatest recording ever made of the sonata.

Aaron Copland dedicated his vast Piano Fantasy to Kapell's memory. The composer wrote of Kapell:

149

His questioning and demanding spirit gave off sparks of a youthfulness that never left him.... The search for artistic growth, the ideal of maturity was a central and continuing preoccupation with him.... What qualities were particularly his? There were brilliance and drama in his playing, songfulness and excitement; on the platform he had the fire and abandon that alone can arouse audiences to fever pitch. He knew his power, and I have no doubt was sometimes frightened by it.... No wonder he was unusually nervous before stepping on the platform. Like every basically romantic artist, he never could predict what was about to happen.... Characteristically, when playing on stage, Willy often turned his head from the auditorium, the better to forget us, I imagine. Nevertheless, even when most lost within himself, he instinctively projected his playing into the hall, for he was indubitably the performer. I cannot conceive of his ever having given a dull performance.

JULIUS KATCHEN
1926–1969 — United States

He studied with David Saperton. Although he died at forty-three, Katchen had been recording since he was nineteen, and left a large legacy on disc, from Chopin and Balakirev to Beethoven, Gershwin, Rorem, Ravel, Prokofiev, and Bartók. One of his last recordings is a magisterial conception of Beethoven's final sonata, Op. 111. Katchen will be remembered best, however, as his generation's preeminent interpreter of the piano music of Brahms. Brahms has been said to be a composer whom pianists should play to the public only in their ripe maturity. But the master of austerity and cerebral beauty became in Katchen's hands youthful and fiery. Katchen's Brahms is approachable and even friendly. He somehow glows with a brighter palette.

In the smaller pieces, he is not as secure as in the mighty works. Several of the Intermezzi are affected, even a bit prissy, but the Brahms *Handel* Variations are played with grit, and the Sonata in F-sharp minor, Op. 2, bursts with abundance and a Lisztian bravura. Katchen has all the virtuosity necessary for the hurdles of the Brahms *Paganini* Variations, and his Ballades, Op. 10, are mysterious, darkly lit, and filled with forest murmurs. In the Ballade in B minor, the goblins appear to be drenched in moonlight.

PETER KATIN
b. 1930 — England

Made his debut in 1948. Since that time, he has played in Europe, the United States, and Canada. His recorded output is quite large, ranging from such concertos as the Khachaturian to the complete preludes of Rachmaninoff and the complete nocturnes of Chopin. His work is reserved and musicianly, his technique equal to the demands of even the Third Rachmaninoff Concerto. Katin premiered and recorded the Grand Fantasy and Toccata by Gerald Finzi.

MINDRU KATZ
1925–1978 — Rumania

Katz had an extreme refinement of tone with many gradations. His technique was strong, and his interpretations from Bach to Fauré are always illuminating. He emigrated to Israel, where he was highly respected as a teacher. He had studied in Rumania with Florica Musicescu, Lipatti's teacher.

CONSTANCE KEENE
b. 1923 — United States

A student of Abram Chasins and a winner of the Naumburg Award, Keene has played hundreds of solo recitals, and appeared with such orchestras as the Boston Symphony, Berlin Philharmonic, and Philadelphia. She has had a long career as a teacher and is on the faculty of the Manhattan School of Music. Her recordings offer an interesting variety of repertoire. Among the high points are the three Mendelssohn etudes, Dussek and Hummel sonatas, a deep reading of the Griffes Sonata, a very stylish record of Chopin's Twenty-four Preludes, and the twenty-four Rachmaninoff Preludes, played with vibrancy and a fastidious musicality.

WILHELM KEMPFF
b. 1895 — Germany

He studied with Barth, held various teaching posts, composed many works, and slowly built his reputation as one of the world's finest musicians and the doyen of German pianists, with a major international reputation.

Kempff's recordings are marvelous products of a civilized, gentlemanly mind. He has a clear sense of organization, and I always feel warmed by his artistic generosity, keen intelligence, musical dignity and gentleness.

His Schubert playing is lovely and full of whimsy. He imparts that unique Schubertian amiability which makes for pure joy. He has recorded all the sonatas and various other pieces. His reading of the final Sonata in B-flat is angelic. Only in the *Wanderer* Fantasy does Kempff's playing lumber.

Kempff is often radiant in Brahms; his E-flat minor Scherzo and F minor Sonata are all heart, and the smaller pieces can be jewels in his hands. In Schumann, Kempff is even more successful. It is a compassionate, sympathetic Schumann. The darker recesses of the composer's soul are closed to scrutiny; instead, Kempff's Schumann is filled with fragrance and the apple-cheeked youth of early German Romanticism, all optimism and fancy. He is best in the *Davidsbündlertänze, Kinderscenen,* and a flickering *Papillons,* less successful in the *Symphonic Etudes* and *Kreisleriana.*

While Kempff is not known as a Chopinist, he has often played a variety of Chopin's music, including the F minor Concerto. He is not a blazing virtuoso, but his innate lyricism and sense of style are in harmony with the music of the Polish master. But ultimately, this idiom is not natural for him, nor is Liszt, though here, too, Kempff can be satisfying. He has a wonderful sense of poise in Liszt and produces a feeling of calm. Even in the bombast of Liszt's *Légende—Saint Francis Walking on the Waves*—the German pianist finds peace. He gets through Liszt's pyrotechnics by using good sense and slower tempi.

Kempff, who was also an organist, has given much time to Bach. His own Bach transcriptions are sensitive and beautifully tailored to the piano. In his recordings of the original works, such as the preludes and fugues and the *Goldberg* Variations, he offers a smoothly polished surface, a fine legato, and a rare qualification for counterpoint. But his Bach is somewhat stagnant and slow-moving, without pith.

Ultimately, Kempff's value for this listener is in his Beethoven—not the usual bugle-calling, heavy-handed Germanic Beethoven, but a Beethoven of grace, fullness, and air. It is a lighter-weight Beethoven; not monumental, but intimate and gracious. Kempff is not after huge rumblings, yet is able to produce large effects without forcing the sound. In fact, I suspect that the power of the contemporary keyboard at full throttle repels him a bit; extremes of sonority are not often heard in his playing. In Beethoven, Kempff's technique, although not virtuosic, somehow fits the music perfectly, and he exhibits the whole range of Beethovenian mechanism with perfect ease, everything as clear as a mountain stream. His interpretations are infused with imagination, depth of feeling, color, and suggestive power. Kempff has a faultless ear, and his phrasing is shapely and subtle.

For me, the highlights of Kempff's Beethoven come in Op. 2, No. 2; Op. 2, No. 3; Op. 10, No. 2; Op. 14, No. 1; Op. 27, No. 1; Opp. 53, 54, 57, 90, 101, 109, and 110; as well as in the Piano Concerto No. 4.

LOUIS KENTNER
b. 1905–1987 — Hungary

He studied piano with Arnold Székely and composition with Kodály. In the 1930s he settled in London. He made his American debut in 1956 with seven recitals at Town Hall, at which he played the complete sonatas of Beethoven. Kentner was never one to stay on the well-worn path, and he premiered the Bartók Second Concerto, Rawsthorne's First Concerto, and Tippett's Concerto. He was a musician of profound learning, and knew every corner of Beethoven's world. In the slow movements especially, he achieved a warm depth of tone and expression.

Kentner's admiration for Liszt sustained itself throughout his career. He played all genres of this complex composer and was an advocate of the more enigmatic later works. In Kentner's penetrating Liszt playing, there is never a tinge of triteness, no mere titillation, no speedy sprints. His discs of the often abused and much maligned Hungarian Rhapsodies are young and fresh and underscore the gypsy element in them. With his exceptionally powerful hands, Kentner could produce a big sound. His reflexes were not comparable to those of the greatest virtuosi, nor was his finger articulation pure; but Kentner knew marvelously well how to exploit his resources, and he was capable of mustering plenty of excitement as he scurried across the keyboard in Liszt's *Transcendental Etudes,* or produced grandiloquent drama in the B minor Ballade. He also made delightful recordings of the fascinating Balakirev Sonata in B-flat minor and the multicolored Liapunov Twelve *Transcendental Etudes,* which the composer aptly dedicated to Liszt's memory.

JOHANN KESSLER
1800–1872 — Austria

He was an esteemed pianist-composer. Chopin dedicated the German edition of his Twenty-four Preludes to him, and Liszt played some of his etudes, which occupy his Opp. 20 and 51.

EDWARD KILENYI
b. 1911 — United States

A pianist of repute who studied with Dohnányi. He is also a well-known teacher at Florida State University. His recordings reveal a highly musical nature, with a well-groomed technique. He is at his best in such works as Schumann's *Carnaval.*

JOHN KIRKPATRICK
b. 1905 — United States

He studied piano with Isidor Philipp and composition with Nadia Boulanger. Kirkpatrick is a scholar and editor of seventeenth- and eighteenth-century music. He was the pianist who premiered, in 1938, the Ives *Concord, Mass.* Sonata. His recording of this formidable work is a landmark in the recording of American music.

CLOTILDE KLEEBERG
1866–1909 — France

A product of the Paris Conservatoire, she was a successful concert artist whose playing was described as unaffected and vigorous. She was one of the first to revive the old French clavecinist composers.

JACQUES KLEIN
1930–1982 — Brazil

He studied with William Kapell. In 1953 he won the Geneva Competition, subsequently performing as well as teaching in his native country.

WALTER KLIEN
b. 1928 — Austria

Klien studied at the Vienna Academy and for a time with Michelangeli. He is a pianist who concentrates on the German-based repertoire. He has recorded the complete Brahms piano music with intelligent artistry, and his Mozart is often charming.

KARL KLINDWORTH
1830–1916 — Germany

In the early 1850s he studied with Liszt, who considered Klindworth, along with von Bülow and Tausig, to be the finest of his students from his Weimar period (1848–60). Liszt asked Klindworth to play his new B minor Sonata privately for Wagner. Later, Klindworth transcribed Wagner's *Ring* and *Tristan und Isolde* for piano. These arrangements are, in their way, the work of an amazing talent. His original compositions are difficult; the *Polonaise-fantaisie* may be especially interesting to pianists looking for a novelty. Klindworth made an edition of Chopin's works, which can be consulted with profit. In 1868 he became professor at the Moscow Conservatory, and from 1882 he resided in Berlin, where he was considered one of the best teachers of his time.

JULIUS KNORR
1807–1861 — Germany

A teacher and performer of reputation; his technical studies were once commonly used.

ZOLTÁN KOCSIS
b. 1952 — Hungary

He studied with Pál Kadosa and won prizes in several competitions, and began touring in his early twenties. Kocsis is also a composer, and has made transcriptions of Wagner, some of which he has recorded. He is a pianist of great vitality and a steel-like technical command, with an especially rare feeling for Bartók and Liszt. He plays the most demanding repertoire, from Bach's *Art of the Fugue* to the Rachmaninoff Third Concerto.

LOUIS KÖHLER
1820–1886 — Germany

Hermann Goetz and Alfred Reisenauer were among the many students of this honored pianist and teacher, who wrote numerous pedagogical works for piano.

ANTOINE DE KONTSKI
1817–1899 — Poland

He studied with John Field. "His wonderful execution," wrote Ernst Pauer, "created everywhere a sensation." He was a salon pianist and turned out hundreds of drawing-room pieces, including the once-popular *The Awakening of the Lion*. He had a long career, beginning a two-year world tour at the age of eighty.

LILI KRAUS
1905–1986 — Hungary

She studied at the Royal Academy in Budapest, later with Steuermann and Schnabel. Kraus was captured and interred by the Japanese during World War II and had no access

to a piano for more than three years. She made her American debut in 1949.

As early as the 1930s, Kraus made dozens of records. Her appearances always summoned a devoted audience. On stage she was the *grande dame* who had come to reveal the message of the masters. During the LP era she recorded many of the works she most revered, including the complete Mozart concerti, many solo sonatas, and a good deal of the Schubert repertoire, as well as some Bartók. She is heard to advantage in a nicely lyrical Schumann Concerto, the Beethoven Third Concerto, and a rather petite and engaging performance of Weber's *Konzertstück*. In the Mozart literature, Kraus was more comfortable in the *galant* sonatas than in the profound A minor and C minor Sonatas. Her recorded cycle of the Concerti shows stylistic authority, cadenzas of her own composition, and graciousness in the slow movements. But the overall impression is of plainness. In these recordings, the orchestral collaboration held her back; there is no symbiosis between orchestra and soloist. With Schubert, her structural planning of the big sonatas fails to integrate the composer's disparate elements, nor are the notes always played easily. In the B-flat Sonata she sounds sodden, and the A minor Sonata D. 845 is inflated, while her Impromptus are rhythmically and tonally flat. These works flowed more easily from her in the concert hall than in the recording studio.

MARTIN KRAUSE
1853–1918 — Germany

A student of Reinecke at the Leipzig Conservatory. In 1882 he met Liszt and worked with him. Krause was a good pianist and a teacher capable of inspiring the many gifted students who came to him, including Edwin Fischer and Arrau. Krause reveled in the grand tradition of Liszt and imparted to the young Arrau an awe for his art.

LEONID KREUTZER
1884–1953 — Russia

He studied with Essipova and, from 1908, was based in Berlin. Later, he made an edition of the works of Chopin. During the 1930s, Kreutzer was a respected teacher in Japan, where he was an influence on that country's immersion in Western pianistic culture.

ANTON KUERTI
b. 1932 — Austria

Studied with Arthur Loesser in Cleveland and with Rudolf Serkin at the Curtis Institute. In 1957 he won the Leventritt Competition.

Kuerti is a driven artist. His playing often displays compulsiveness and a fierce, lean power, even anger. I have heard him play the entire set of Scriabin's formidable Twelve Etudes, Op. 8, in tempi so fast that I thought a crack-up must be imminent. It was roller-coaster playing. But Kuerti sat there perfectly calm—only the audience was frenzied. One never feels at ease at a Kuerti recital, but the excitement he inspires is born of the involvement of an artist seized by the moment. On recording, he is less frenetic. He has filtered out the extraneous elements that make for his high-risk live performances. The records are still highly charged but in a more crystallized, more cerebral way. Of his many recordings, one can mention his Alban Berg Sonata, where every phrase is played *morbidezza,* yet clearly structured. He delivers the Scriabin Sixth Sonata as though it were a mystical message. His Schumann F minor Sonata is filled with characteristic Schumannian storm and stress, and his Liszt Sonata is icy, but of exceptional interest, played with chordal pomp and glittering preciseness.

Throughout his career, Kuerti has been partial to Mendelssohn, whom he loves to play lightly and fast. He refreshes war-horses like the *Rondo capriccioso,* and he makes the finale of the F-sharp minor Fantasy crackle and pop. But his finest achievement is certainly his stark and original reading of the thirty-two Beethoven sonatas. One may dislike his raspy conceptions, as I often do, but he plays Beethoven with a raw conviction that is compelling.

THEODOR KULLAK
1818–1882 — Germany

He was a student of Czerny, and a child prodigy who developed into an outstanding pianist and an effective composer. Kullak was one of the most successful and influential teachers of the nineteenth century. Moszkowski, Scharwenka, and Hans Bischoff studied with him, as did his son, the pianist Franz Kullak. His most famous pedagogical work is *School of Octaves,* which was once used by teachers everywhere.

VILÉM KURZ
1872–1945 — Czechoslovakia

He made his debut in 1890, and performed extensively. Kurz became the foremost piano teacher in Czechoslovakia. Rudolf Firkušný studied with him for years.

155

RADOSLAV KVAPIL
b. 1934 — Czechoslovakia

Studied in Brno and later with Heinrich Neuhaus in Moscow. He is a sympathetic pianist with a large repertoire, but he is chiefly known for his interpretations of Czech music, which include recordings of the complete piano works of Dvořák.

JAMES KWAST
1852–1927 — Netherlands

He studied with Reinecke, Kullak, and Brassin. Kwast settled in Frankfurt, where he became a noted teacher. Carl Friedberg and Percy Grainger were among his many pupils.

FERNANDO LAIRES
b. 1925 — Portugal

He studied with Isidor Philipp and James Friskin and has performed widely. He teaches at the Peabody Conservatory in Baltimore.

ALEXANDER LAMBERT
1862–1929 — Poland

A student of Julius Epstein in Vienna and also of Liszt. He settled in the United States, where he performed; and he taught Mana-Zucca, whose charming *Valse brillante* is dedicated to him. Vera Brodsky and Beryl Rubinstein also worked with him.

WANDA LANDOWSKA
1877–1959 — Poland

Landowska studied piano with Michalowski, but early in the century she turned to the harpsichord. Although there had been several attempts, as early as Moscheles, to revive the harpsichord in Baroque music, it was not until Landowska's arrival, with her keen personality and dazzling playing, that the musical world again took serious notice of the instrument and its rightful role in performing the works of the period. Peter Yates wrote of her early recording of Bach's *Goldberg* Variations that it "was an event as decisive for the future, and the recovery of the past of music, as the first performance of Stravinsky's *Rite of Spring* or the conception of the twelve-tone method." Later, she recorded Bach's *Well-Tempered Clavier,* her "last will and testament," as she called it, and one of the most gigantic interpretive feats ever put on records.

She was born in the Romantic era, and her performances burn with power and with an exciting virtuosity. On stage, Landowska was magnetic. Her concerts were consecrations from Bach, and her extraordinary face seemed illuminated by his wisdom. She once told a colleague, "You play Bach your way, I'll play him his way." Landowska never abandoned the piano, however, and her recordings of Mozart concerti and sonatas are Romantic and entirely individual.

ADELINA DE LARA
1872–1961 — England

A student of Clara Schumann who became well known as a Schumann player. She made recordings and also composed.

RUTH LAREDO
b. 1937 — United States

She was a student of Serkin at the Curtis Institute. Laredo has molded a fine career, and her numerous recordings include the ten Scriabin sonatas (which she has played in cycle in New York) garnished with smaller pieces, and seven albums offering the complete solo output of Rachmaninoff.

Laredo was nurtured on the Germanic literature, but by learning a great deal of Russian music later on, she entered the world of a quite different kind of pianism, which has extended her musical outlook, musicianship, and technique. Laredo has also made good recordings of Ravel, and her recording of Barber's *Souve-*

nirs is a sheer delight. She has a large concerto repertoire and plays Mozart concerti with the same enjoyment and skill which she brings to the Beethoven *Emperor* or the Rachmaninoff *Rhapsody on a Theme of Paganini.*

JACOB LATEINER
b. 1928 — Cuba

He studied with Isabelle Vengerova at the Curtis Institute, and later studied composition with Arnold Schoenberg. He made his debut in 1945, with Ormandy and the Philadelphia Orchestra.

Lateiner is a penetrating musician who blends fine craft with scholarship and feeling. His Beethoven playing is especially respected, and in such recordings as the last Beethoven sonata, Op. 111, and the Bagatelles of Op. 126, one hears a compelling musician. He has not recorded enough of the music that he has performed. He has taught at the Juilliard School since 1966.

SIEGMUND LEBERT
1822–1884 — Germany

A student of Tomáschek and Dionys Weber. He played in public frequently and was a founder of the Stuttgart Conservatory. He published many instructive methods and studies.

FÉLIX LE COUPPEY
1811–1887 — France

A student at the Paris Conservatoire. Le Couppey was a renowned pianist and teacher.   157

He received the Legion of Honor, and his educational works, such as the *Ecole du mécanisme du piano,* were once popular.

NOEL LEE
b. 1924 — China

Lee studied at the New England Conservatory. He has recorded extensively. Field nocturnes, Schubert sonatas, works by Moscheles and Stravinsky, all exhibit a solid technique and tasteful expression without much temperament. Lee has also composed a large amount of music in various forms.

THEODOR LESCHETIZKY
1830–1915 — Poland

He became the most famous piano teacher of the late nineteenth century, with an unrivaled list of students who came to Vienna from the world over. Not to have had Leschetizky's stamp of approval was almost a stigma. The longest-surviving of his pupils is Horszowski, who studied with him as a child. In 1884, Paderewski, already twenty-four, went to him. He later wrote, "He fulfilled my heart's desire. I had learned how to *work.* Yes, I repeat to you, how to work, and this is of the utmost importance. . . . Leschetizky, the lodestar of my early years, the greatest teacher of his generation. I do not know of anyone who approaches him now or then. There is absolutely none who can compare with him. He was in that respect a giant—all those I know at the present moment are pygmies, measured by his standards."

Certainly one of his standards was the quality of tone, which he insisted be beautiful and singing. Paderewski was renowned for his sultry, sensuous tone; yet when one listens to the recordings of any of Leschetizky's pupils, whether Moiseiwitsch, Friedman, Hambourg, or Schnabel, one hears in each an unforgettable sound. Leschetizky himself had it and was, as a pianist, a virtuoso, who studied with Czerny. His last appearance as a pianist took place in 1887, in Vienna, with Beethoven's *Emperor* Concerto.

THEODORE LETTVIN
b. 1926 — United States

A student of Rudolf Serkin. He won prizes at several competitions, including first prize in the Naumburg. Lettvin is a pianist with a broad spectrum, and he is particularly fluid technically. He has performed extensively and has taught successfully.

OSCAR LEVANT
1906–1972 — United States

He studied piano with Stojowski and composition with Schoenberg. Levant was best known as an exponent of Gershwin's music. In his middle years, he was famous as a wit, a radio personality, and a movie actor. An able musician, he wrote a piano concerto and a *sonatine* and made various transcriptions of such orchestral favorites as the *Sabre Dance* and *Lullaby* by Khachaturian. He wrote two droll volumes of autobiography: *A Smattering of Ignorance* and *Memoirs of an Amnesiac.*

Levant's many recordings include the Khachaturian Concerto, the Fourth Rubinstein Concerto, Gershwin's *Rhapsody in Blue,* and his Concerto in F, which Levant played with inimitable style and more character than it usually gets. His recordings of these works are essential on the collector's shelves.

MISCHA LEVITZKI
1898–1941 — Russia

A student of Michalowski, Stojowski, and Dohnányi. He had an international career, playing in the Orient and Australia. Levitzki was a favorite with American audiences. He played a fairly small repertoire in a cool-headed, rather detached, yet Romantic style. He was at his best in miniatures. His playing is meticulous; one feels in listening to his recordings that he was groping for a more modern approach to the Romantic literature. He was a transitional pianist who remained a Romantic stylist. His rubato is always fascinating; listen to his very slow reading of the Gluck-Sgambati "Melody" from *Orfeo* (one minute longer than Rachmaninoff's version), or his Chopin A-flat Ballade. Levitzki was always a curt but dashing Liszt player. The Sixth Hungarian Rhapsody shows some of the great octave playing of his time, and he was the first to record on 78s the Liszt E-flat Concerto. He recorded a few of his own delightful waltzes—bits of nostalgia tossed off by the pianist with a tongue-in-cheek nonchalance.

ERNST LEVY
b. 1895 — Switzerland

Studied with Petri and Pugno. Levy is an unusual and powerful pianist. His recordings of late Beethoven are grandly conceived, and his recording of the Liszt Sonata and *Bénédiction de Dieu dans la solitude* is major Liszt playing. In the Sonata, Levy throws all caution to the wind. There is a mocking spirit. It is nervous, lugubrious, recitativo playing—the very essence of the Faustian Liszt. His performance is an exhausting experience, but in the end, Liszt, Levy, and the listener find purification. His *Bénédiction* stands alone in its monumentality and its probing of the secret recesses of Lisztian Romanticism. Levy has also conducted and played organ, and has composed prolifically.

LAZARE LÉVY
1882–1964 — Belgium

A student at the Paris Conservatoire with Diémer. He was a brilliant executant and a teacher who helped produce such students as France Clidat, Lélia Gousseau, Monique Haas, Jean Hubeau, and Yvonne Loriod. He also composed interesting piano works.

RAYMOND LEWENTHAL
1926–1988 — United States

He studied with Olga Samaroff at the Juilliard School. Lewenthal was one of that rare breed who are endowed with endless curiosity, forever on the lookout for golden nuggets of the piano's past glories. He has been most productive in making many aware of music that tells us about the nineteenth century, its taste and values.

Of all the hibernating composers who interest Lewenthal, it is Charles Alkan who comes first. Lewenthal has devoted two recordings to this French master, and the playing is as varied as the composer's mercurial moods. There are the amazing and astringent *Sonatine*, the Barcarolle, played upon a mirrored lake, the breakneck virtuosity of the *Quasi Faust*, and the masterful and humorous *Aesop* Variations, plus a whole drawerful of other Alkanian drolleries. Of Lewenthal's other recordings, his performance of the treacherous and thrilling *Norma* paraphrase by Liszt is magnificent, and he has revived that weird collection of pieces titled by Liszt the *Hexaméron.*

Lewenthal has also given an admirable account of the important Henselt Concerto, as well as works by Thalberg and Scharwenka. In his last years he virtually disappeared from concert life.

JOSEF LHÉVINNE
1874–1944 — Russia

He was taken early to the Moscow Conservatory to study with Safonov. At fifteen, he had the honor of playing the *Emperor* Concerto with Anton Rubinstein conducting. He was awarded the coveted Gold Medal at the Moscow Conservatory in 1892. In 1895 he won the Anton Rubinstein prize, the most important piano competition of the time. In 1898, Rosina Bessie won the Gold Medal at the Conservatory, and soon after, Josef married her. Later they formed a two-piano team, which was one of the finest of the time. Lhévinne continued to pursue his solo career, and made his U.S. debut in 1906, using the Anton Rubinstein Concerto No. 5 as his vehicle. After hardships in Germany during World War I, the Lhévinnes came to America, where they were associated with the Juilliard School. Soon he became one of the most distinguished teachers of the era. He wrote a handbook called *Basic Principles in Pianoforte Playing* and continued to play concerts in the United States and Europe, although he played less than any of his colleagues with a similarly important reputation.

Lhévinne developed and matured in the competitive hothouse atmosphere of the Moscow Conservatory, where his octaves were the talk of the school. The main influence there was the overwhelming artistry of Anton Rubinstein, who heard the boy play, at the age of fourteen, Beethoven's *Eroica* Variations and several Chopin etudes. The great master "jumped to his feet," Lhévinne reported after his performance of the *Ocean* Etude, "kissed me, and wrung my hand. 'You are a big, big boy. Work hard and you will be a great man.' That was the first great moment of my life."

Lhévinne's approach to the piano was, first and always, pianistic: correctness of note and steadiness of rhythm foremost. The sheer control of the pianistic aspects of his art was chilling to his colleagues. His hands, like those of Rachmaninoff, were enormous. He could stretch from middle C to A—thirteen notes. His finger control was so great that Safonov entered him in a telegraph operators' competition, which Lhévinne won easily.

For the Rubinstein Competition, he played the Beethoven *Hammerklavier,* which Rubinstein called "the Ninth Symphony of the piano." Shortly after, in Berlin, the outstanding pianist-teacher James Kwast wrote of his Beethoven that "Lhévinne played with such perfection that it seemed to me I was hearing it from none other than Tausig, who had gone to the grave at an early age." In his biography of Josef and Rosina Lhévinne, Robert K. Wallace wrote: "As Tausig stood to Liszt, so did Lhévinne to Rubinstein. Josef admired Rubinstein above all other musicians, but did not completely follow his grand manner of interpretation. Lhévinne's temperament led in the direction of purity and perfection, and his playing, even when he was twenty, showed it." Especially in his early years, however, Lhévinne was a characteristic Russian pianist with temperament to spare, and capable of igniting a spark into a flame.

During the 1920s, when the Soviets allowed none of their artists to go to the West,

Lhévinne became one of the treasured links to the Russian grand manner of piano playing. After one of Lhévinne's concerts, the *New York Times* critic Olin Downes worried that "the Russian school of piano playing is vanishing. . . . If its traditions completely disappear the grand interpretive art of the pianist will weaken in favor of something neater and more puny." As Lhévinne matured, his small repertoire became ever more refined. There were some who felt his playing was calculated and cold or even exquisitely dull. Indeed, Josef himself felt Rosina was a warmer, more Romantic pianist.

By the 1930s, his style was confirmed. A typical program would include the Schumann Toccata, Beethoven's *Waldstein,* the Brahms *Paganini* Variations, Chopin's Fourth Ballade, several etudes, and Balakirev's *Islamey.* At his annual Carnegie Hall recitals every pianist worth his salt listened attentively. The recitals were object lessons in high pianism. Indeed, not one of his army of gifted students had anything like Lhévinne's technical equipment. J. W. Henderson of the *New York Sun* wrote in 1930: "In his youth he was a virtuoso and a magnificent stormer of the keyboard. He thundered his proclamations and sometimes stunned his hearers by sheer power and irresistible technique. This is not the Lhévinne of today. He is now a ripe and mellowed master who has found all the secrets of tone and who sheds the rays of a refulgent beauty through every composition he plays. . . . He sees laterally across the whole breadth of every composition and perpendicularly down into its depths. He makes the plans of his readings with brains and imagination."

Lhévinne was inherently musical, aristocratic, and possessed of poise and balance. His famous recording of Schumann's Toccata shows off his double-note mehanism, but without the frenzy of Barère's reading, which comes close to being a stunt. Lhévinne's recording of the Chopin Etude in Thirds, Op. 25, No. 6, reaches the heights of double-note technique. James Methuen-Campbell says it "silences any criticism. The opening tempo is extremely fast, and all the right-hand entries have an icy precision. . . . Lhévinne's bell-like clarity has never been surpassed on disc." Lhévinne's Chopin etudes, those that he played in public, were always the wonder of the pianistic world. His rhythmic gift was unleashed in his great recording of the *Winter Wind* Etude, Op. 25, No. 11, while the *Octave* Etude, Op. 25, No. 10, is unrivaled. Other pianists can only bow before such herculean octaves, and almost savage reserves of energy—like a panther ready to spring. When Lhévinne plays the luscious middle section in B major, unlike so many pianists who drool, he controls the structure and phrases with simplicity, knowing well that the general tumult of the composition must not be lost to sentimentality. The sheer power in this and in the *Winter Wind* Etude produces shivers. Lhévinne's great finger technique can be heard in his recording of the Chopin Prelude No. 16 in B-flat minor, which once again, with its control and delicacy of articulation, allied to a left hand that boils in agitation, remains, after more than half a century, the supreme playing of this treacherous work.

Lhévinne's octaves were legendary; they rank with those of Liszt and Tausig, Rosenthal, Levitzki, Rachmaninoff, and Horowitz. His octaves had a life of their own. On disc, they still live brightly in his reading of Chopin's A-flat Polonaise, which was one of his specialties. Another of Lhévinne's great pieces was the Schulz-Evler *On the Beautiful Blue Danube,* based on the celebrated Strauss waltz. Audiences refused to leave without hearing it. Lhévinne plays it without a drop of kitsch. Actually, he re-creates it as seriously as a Beethoven score. It is the playing of an unsentimental Classicist, and its tightness and rhythmic purity are cumulative; when he finally lets the listener breathe, one feels a sigh of relief. Even with all the advances in recording technology, this performance remains as vital today as it was in 1928.

My favorite of Lhévinne's recordings, which would be enough to immortalize him, is the starry Schumann-Liszt *Spring Night*. Here, musical mystery, the awe of youthful, romantic love, and the highest technical polish unite in an indescribable manner.

Lhévinne's attitude was an essentially modern one in that he lets the music speak for itself. He certainly had less creative imagination than Godowsky, Cortot, Hofmann, Rachmaninoff, Friedman, or Horowitz. Virgil Thomson wrote that "he made no effort to charm or to seduce or to preach or to impress. He played as if he were expounding to a graduate seminar: 'This is the music, and this is the way to play it. . . .' His concept of piano music is an impersonal one. It is norm-centered; it is for all musical men. Any intrusion of the executant's private soul would limit its appeal, diminish its authority. . . . If he seems to some a little distant, let us remind ourselves that remoteness is, after all, inevitable to those who inhabit Olympus." Although Lhévinne made too few recordings, they showed not merely an astonishing virtuoso, but one of history's greatest masters of the instrument.

ROSINA LHÉVINNE
1880–1976 — Russia

A student of Safonov at the Moscow Conservatory. She married Josef Lhévinne after graduation and proceeded to teach and to perform in a two-piano team with him. Her recordings of the Mozart Twenty-first Concerto and Chopin E minor Concerto, made in her eighties, testify to her tasteful, intimate Romanticism. Her passagework is beautifully even, and there is style in her phrasing.

In the 1950s, Mme Lhévinne replaced the late Olga Samaroff as the most famous piano teacher at the Juilliard School. Students flocked to her studio, where she was the standard-bearer of the golden days of Imperial Russian Romanticism. Her students won countless competitions in her name, the most famous to do so being Van Cliburn, the first winner of the International Tchaikovsky Competition. John Browning, Daniel Pollack, Misha Dichter, Garrick Ohlsson, Tong il Han, Howard Aibel, Jeaneane Dowis, and Olegna Fuschi are just a few of her students, many of whom hold posts at universities throughout the world.

ARTHUR MOREIRA LIMA
b. 1940 — Brazil

He studied in Paris with Long and Doyen, also for several years at the Moscow Conservatory. In 1965 he came in second to Martha Argerich at the Chopin Competition in Warsaw. Lima is best known for his engrossing and poetic Chopin interpretations.

DINU LIPATTI
1917–1950 — Rumania

He had a superb musical education. After early lessons from his parents, he studied at the Bucharest Conservatory from 1928 to 1932, with the respected piano teacher Florica Musicescu. Later he studied with Alfred Cortot, and with Dukas and Boulanger in composition. For conducting, he worked with Charles Munch. Georges Enesco was his godfather, and Lipatti constantly learned from him.

In the 1930s, he played in Germany and Italy. During the war, he was domiciled in

Geneva, where he taught at the Conservatoire. After the war, he became established as one of the most gifted pianists of his time. He played in England each year from 1946 to 1950. Tours of Australia and America had to be canceled because of illness—lymphogranulomatosis, which claimed his life at thirty-three. Still, Lipatti managed to record a small but treasured discography. He was also an estimable composer; his works include a Sonatina for the Left Hand and a Concertino in the Classic Style, both of which he recorded, and three nocturnes and a Fantasy for Piano Trio. All exhibit a delicate craftsmanship.

There seemed to be an aura surrounding Lipatti. Those who heard him were deeply stirred by his art. Poulenc called him "an artist of divine spirituality." There was a sweetness in his touch and an angelic temperament in his playing. He was a Raphael of the piano, poetic and youthful. There was never a trace of vanity in his style; for him music was a sacred responsibility, and he took the most minute pains in learning and digesting the piano literature. His record company gave him *carte blanche* as to what he would record, but he judged himself mercilessly and asked for three, four, and five years, depending on the work to be prepared. This responsibility to music was understood by all who knew him. He had never played Beethoven in public, considering himself not yet ready for the privilege, until finally with Artur Schnabel's encouragement, near the end of his life, he summoned the courage to give the public the *Waldstein* Sonata.

His recording producer, Walter Legge, wrote of him:

I do not believe that there has been, or will be, a pianist like Dinu Lipatti. It is not a matter of comparisons of quality, it is a matter of difference in kind. Hard as he worked and thought on purely technical problems of touch, sonority and pedaling, he was not a "virtuoso" in the word's modern and debased sense—but certainly in its Seventeenth Century application "a connoisseur." . . . He was a musician, a musician who used the pianoforte as a means of communication and expression. . . . The softness of his sound came through strength. He had enormous and powerful hands—the "little" finger as long as its neighbors—and the shoulders of a wrestler, quite disproportionate to his frail build. As he played, each finger had a life and personality of its own, independent of its neighbors, of his wrists and arms. Each finger seemed prehensile and the ten of them, when he played contrapuntal music, looked like a fantastic ballet danced by ten elephants' trunks each obeying the order of its own mahout. This visual impression of each finger having its own life is evident in the sound of his playing. Every note he played had a life of its own.

Lipatti was a lyric-Romantic pianist but with a cool and patrician sense of Classicism, and an extraordinary technique which was totally at the service of the musical essence. His left hand was peculiarly strong, and his superb rhythmic sense was apparent in every facet of his playing, no matter how Romantic the composition. His color sense was equally refined, and his pedaling was clean and artful, with legato playing as smooth as possible. He took a hackneyed score, such as the Grieg Concerto, and revived the pristine beauty. His Schumann Concerto breathes tenderness and chaste nobility.

Lipatti's finger control was perfect, as was his taste. His Bach B-flat Partita is gentle, precise but flexible, and moderate in tempo. His Mozart A minor Sonata is lofty; his Schubert G-flat Impromptu is an inspired song, simple and straightforward. His disc of the Hess transcription of *Jesu, Joy of Man's Desiring* is the work of a blessed musician, as is the heartfelt yet firm projection of the Kempff transcription of the Siciliano from a Bach flute sonata. The *Alborada del gracioso* of Ravel sparkles, and the Liszt *Sonetto 104 del Petrarca* is controlled but burning with passion. There is a 1943 radio broadcast of Enesco's Third Sonata. It is a complex work of

Rumanian folk elements, bound to an impressionist palette. The special care in its rendering, the subtle nuance, the fleeting colors, the flexible phrasing and transparent textures provide one of the great examples of piano playing on records.

Chopin was inevitable at Lipatti's concerts. His Chopin Sonata No. 3 in B minor will always be studied and discussed by pianists who seriously love this masterpiece. Lipatti's purity and sensitivity make for one of the great Chopin sonatas on disc. It is a refined, serious Chopin, always reserved, magnificently disciplined, yet with imagination and an inner fervor. One hears these traits also in his exquisite playing of the D-flat Nocturne, and his incomparable artistry in the C-sharp minor Mazurka, Op. 50, No. 3. For the highest refreshment, I constantly come back to Lipatti's recording of the Barcarolle, perhaps the greatest recording of it ever made. There is not a flaw in the filigree; the balance is impeccable. Lipatti left a disc of the fourteen Chopin Waltzes, which many regard as the finest Chopin Waltzes on record, though I find them a shade cool, lacking a vibrant spirit. There is also the poignant live performance of thirteen of the waltzes on Lipatti's last and most celebrated album, a two-record set of his final recital, at the Besançon Festival, September 16, 1950. The artist's strength was at its lowest ebb, the pain excruciating. Though his doctors begged him not to play, he had promised, and for him a promise was not to be ignored. Pumped with cortisone, he proceeded to play a demanding program, completing all but the final E minor waltz before his strength gave out. Lipatti lingered on for several months, passing away near Geneva on December 2, 1950. Nadia Boulanger felt, "Lipatti was an angel on earth. . . . Noble, profound, gay, right up to his death; he knew very well that there was a time-limit, a limit without remission. . . . He was one of the greatest pianists ever, the very image of a complete musician."

SEYMOUR LIPKIN
b. 1927 — United States

A student of Serkin and Horszowski. Lipkin is an exceptional musician who is active as pianist, conductor, and teacher. His playing of the classics is never rigid, and he is happy in such contemporary scores as George Perle's Serenade. He teaches at Curtis and Juilliard.

SAMUEL LIPMAN
b. 1934 — United States

He studied in San Francisco with Lev Shorr and later at the Juilliard School with Rosina Lhévinne. Lipman gave the New York premiere, at Carnegie Hall, of the Elliott Carter Piano Concerto in 1965. Since 1970, he has taught at the Aspen Music Festival. Besides his work as a pianist, Lipman writes criticism for various periodicals.

EUGENE LIST
1918–1985 — United States

A respected musician who studied with Samaroff at the Juilliard School. He made a debut in the Shostakovich Concerto No. 1 in 1934. He gave the world premiere of the Chávez Concerto in 1942. List played a variety of music and was helpful in bringing a great many Gottschalk scores back to public and recorded performance.

FRANZ LISZT
1811–1886 — Hungary

His earliest teacher was his father, Adam Liszt, a good amateur pianist who worked as a steward at the Esterházy Palace.

In 1820 the nine-year-old prodigy made his debut in Oedenburg playing a concerto by Ferdinand Ries. Soon after, funds were raised for the boy to study in Vienna with the city's best-known teacher, Beethoven's pupil Carl Czerny. In composition, he worked with Salieri. Both masters taught the young and poor Hungarian without a fee. Czerny was astounded by Liszt's native gifts, but was appalled by his lack of discipline. It was Czerny who laid the foundation for the revolutionary pianism that would soon burst upon the European musical world. Czerny was the dedicatee of Liszt's early etudes of 1826, which would eventually become the Twelve *Transcendental Etudes* of his mature years. But Liszt was to profit from Czerny's instruction for only eighteen months before his father became impatient to show off his son's worth and began a terrible exploitation of the young boy. Unlike Chopin and Mendelssohn, who were delicately nurtured at home, Liszt was now continuously on the move. He had even completed an opera, *Don Sanche,* which was performed at the Paris Opera late in 1825.

There was never any time for a formal education, and his life was a series of unprecedented successes. In London, he created a sensation and played before George IV; critics quickly understood his gifts. One writer felt that, at fourteen, Liszt "yields the palm to Hummel alone."

During these early years, when all of society petted him, Liszt—as no other pianist had done before him—learned how to play for and to the public. A large middle class was forming. Halls were being built for entertainment, and Liszt was now the youngest and best of a group of wandering "gypsies," who played, usually, less than the best music.

In 1827 his father died while they were on tour. Already the teenager was dismayed by his life, and now, without an aggressive father, and with an ever-increasing religious bent, the young virtuoso renounced that life and retired from the stage, instead teaching to support himself and his mother. "I would rather be anything in the world," he wrote at this time, "than a musician in the pay of great folk, patronized and paid for by them, like a conjuror or a clever dog." His virtual disappearance caused wonder, and there were even press reports of his death. Soon, however, he was romantically involved with one of his students, a sixteen-year-old aristocrat. Upon discovering their friendship, her father dashed any hopes that Liszt, a mere musician, might keep seeing her. He was completely devastated, and withdrew into religious books and hashish, seldom touching his piano. Some of the strongest traits of his personality were emerging: a love-hate relationship with performing, a deeply mystical attraction to religion, and a hatred for the lowly social level of musicians. His ennui was broken by the fighting on the streets of Paris during the political unrest in 1830.

His latent creativity was stirred, and he felt the urge to compose and play. He was deeply stimulated by three men of genius who were to make an everlasting mark on him. The first was Berlioz, with whom he had a budding friendship and whose epoch-making *Symphonie fantastique* he was soon to hear and to transcribe for the piano. The second was Frédéric Chopin, newly arrived in Paris. The Slavic genius's Etudes and the poetry and delicacy of his playing shocked Liszt into a new awareness of the piano and its technical possibilities. But the third influence—Paganini—was the catalyst that sent Liszt back to the keyboard with the goal of becoming "the Paganini of the piano." The infernal Italian violinist made his Paris debut in 1832, creating a public furor. "What a man, what a violin, what an artist!" wrote Liszt. "Heavens! What sufferings, what misery, what tortures in those four strings." With these concerts by Paganini, the only performer he could learn from, Liszt came to life, and the modern pianist was born.

Paganini became the spiritual father of piano playing. Liszt began transcribing Paganini's Caprices for the piano; he had to uncover the secrets of virtuosity. For two years, he worked with an unremitting savagery, reading Goethe's *Faust* with Berlioz, coming under the influence of the religious scion Lamennais, and practicing as no other pianist ever had. "My mind and fingers," he wrote, "have been working like two lost spirits—Homer, the Bible, Plato, Locke, Byron, Hugo, Lamartine, Chateaubriand, Beethoven, Bach, Hummel, Mozart, Weber are all around me. I study them, meditate upon them, devour them with fury. Besides this, I practice four to five hours of exercises, thirds, sixths, octaves, tremolos, repetitions of notes, cadenzas, scales, etc. Ah! provided I don't go mad you will find an artist in me! Yes an artist such as you desire, *such as is required nowadays*." When he reappeared, he would have a concert career more triumphant than even Paganini's. Indeed, Liszt may be called the father of the modern career, and the most idolized performer ever to play the piano. He virtually opened the concert corridor of Europe, playing more extensively than any other pianist of the first half of the nineteenth century.

During his "years of splendor," Liszt, with his special caravan, sixty suits of clothing, 360 cravats (one for each day of the year), and his shoulder-length hair, created the Romantic image of the pianist-hero—eyes heaven-sent, nostrils dilated, and held in the throes of inspiration. He was not above theatrics and, like Paganini, he had to be seen as well as heard. The dramatist Ernest Legouvé described Liszt "constantly tossing back his long hair. . . . With lips quivering, he swept the auditorium with the glance of a smiling master." A born showman, he began the finale of Weber's *Konzertstück* so fast that, unable to maintain the tempo, he conveniently fainted away. One writer saw "Liszt's countenance assume that agony of expression, mingled with radiant smiles of joy, which I never saw in any other human face except in the paintings of our Saviour by some early masters." Soon Liszt realized that to share the concert platform with other musicians was unthinkable—and so he invented the solo recital, even coining the term.

In 1839 he took the big step and played history's first solo public concerts, in Milan. The piano's solo function was finally proclaimed, and Liszt proudly said, *"Le concert c'est moi"* (the concert is myself). The piano had come a long way since the variety-show type of concert in which Johann Christian Bach first played a piano solo in public in 1768.

As he went from city to city, Europe was gripped by "Lisztomania." After Liszt wrote a rave notice of a Chopin concert, the Pole sarcastically muttered, "Ah, he is giving me a kingdom within his empire." And he was the "emperor" of the piano. Handsome beyond measure, he was likened to Dante, Napoleon, and Byron. If "Paganini had the evil eye," declared Sacheverell Sitwell, then "Liszt had the glamorous eye." Wilfrid Mellers states: "The impact of Liszt on Europe is, indeed, something for which there is no musical parallel. Only in Byron do we find the same combination of aristocratic elegance with Revolutionary force, of fearless sincerity with histrionic virtuosity." To the youth of Europe, Liszt symbolized democratic freedom. Stories quickly circulated regarding his pride and daring in his espousal of equality. When the dreaded Czar Nicholas I asked Liszt, "What are your politics?" the pianist answered, "I have none, sire, unless I have two hundred thousand bayonets accompanying me."

Liszt also elevated the piano to a new position of power and intimacy. "You see," he wrote, "my piano is for me what his frigate is to a sailor, or his horse to an Arab—more indeed: It is my very self, my mother tongue, my life. . . . I confide to it all my dreams, my joys and sorrows. Its strings tremble under my emotion, its yielding keys resound to all my moods." By the age of thirty-six, however, Liszt the performer was exhausted; he left the concert stage forever, although he would live to seventy-five. He now concentrated his great energies on composition and on making Weimar, where he was appointed court composer, the leading musical center of Germany, reviving the glory that it had had under Schiller and Goethe. Liszt now championed the newest in music, and from Berlioz to Wagner, Weimar promoted what was to be called "the music of the future."

From this period until his death, Liszt taught the torrent of pupils who came from everywhere to seek advice and learn from him the secrets of pianistic truth. Even before his departure from public playing, however, he had managed to have an unprecedented educative influence. His repertoire was the largest ever assembled by one artist. If Paganini and the majority of pianists played only their own music, Liszt played everyone's music, and he did this from Lisbon to St. Petersburg, from Edinburgh to Constantinople, with a zeal that defied description. He assimilated Czerny's Viennese light pianism, and at the same time his respect for Beethoven, with his orchestral coloring, was everlasting. It was Liszt who first brought many of the Beethoven sonatas to the recital stage. His early travels brought him in touch with all that Clementi, Cramer, and Hummel were doing. He incorporated the singing style of Field and the operatic virtuosity of Weber.

Liszt transcribed Schubert songs, as well as Beethoven's symphonies, and often played them before the public heard the originals. He brought Chopin's music out of the narrow confines of the Parisian salon, as Chopin himself could not do, and he proclaimed his friend to the world. Liszt grappled with the Romantic polyphony of the newest Schumann, and played all that was new of the "Romantic" school. Not one of Liszt's exact generation—including Chopin, Hiller, Heller, Alkan, Henselt, Herz, and Thalberg—played such an abundance of new music, while only Mendelssohn dug as deeply into the past.

It had become a commonplace in nineteenth-century criticism to call Liszt the greatest pianist who ever lived, yet the best ears of the time continually attest anew to his supremacy. His own greatest student, Carl Tausig, declared, "No mortal can vie with Liszt; he dwells upon a solitary height." Anton Rubinstein was convinced "we are all children compared with Liszt." Oscar Beringer conceded, "Words cannot describe him as a pianist—he was incomparable and unapproachable." Moriz Rosenthal said, "He played as no one before him, and as no one probably will ever again." Heine wrote, "The piano vanishes and the music is revealed. Liszt played quite alone, or rather accompanied only by his genius . . . the pianist of genius, whose playing often appears to me as the melodious agony of a spectral world."

Hans Christian Andersen marveled, "It did not seem to be the strings of a piano that were sounding. No, every tone was like an echoing drop of water. Anyone who admires the technique of art must bow before Liszt; he that is charmed with the genial, the divine gift, bows still lower. . . . The divine soul flashed from his eyes, from every feature; he grew handsome—handsome as life and inspiration can make one. . . . The instrument appears to be changed into a whole orchestra. This is accomplished by ten fingers, which possess a power of execution that might be termed superhuman."

When Liszt played privately to George Eliot, the novelist realized that "for the first time in my life I beheld real inspiration—for the first time I heard the true tones of the piano." The Russian critic Stassov admitted, "We had never heard anything like it before, never been confronted by such passionate, demonic genius," while the Russian composer Serov exclaimed, "How far the reality surpassed my expectations." For Siloti, Liszt's playing produced "music such as no one could form any idea of without hearing it."

167

Schumann observed, "But what is most difficult is, precisely, to talk about his art. It is no longer pianoforte playing of this kind or that; instead, it is generally the outward expression of a daring character whom Fortune has permitted to dominate and to triumph not with dangerous implements, but with the peaceful means of art. No matter how many important artists have passed before us in the last years; no matter how many artists equaling Liszt in many respects we ourselves possess, not one can match him in point of energy and boldness."

The critic Rellstab suggested, "It is not *what* Liszt plays, but *how* he plays it." Indeed, whatever music he touched seemed transformed. In a letter to Hiller, Chopin wrote, "Liszt is at this moment playing my Etudes and he transports me out of my proper senses—I should like to steal from him his way of playing my Etudes." In his diary, Moscheles recorded that "Liszt played three of my studies. . . . By his talent he has completely metamorphosed these pieces; they have become more his studies than mine." Berlioz hailed Liszt's *"sensibilité divinatoire"* and called him "the Pianist of the Future." The French master confessed to having found Beethoven's Sonata Op. 106, the *Hammerklavier,* an enigma until Liszt unraveled it for him. Actually, Liszt had learned the mighty work by his tenth year. He recalled that at that time he played the *Hammerklavier "fort mal, sans doute, mais avec passion"* (very badly, no doubt, but with passion). Of Liszt's own work, Berlioz wrote, "Unfortunately one cannot hope to hear music of this kind often. Liszt created it for himself—and no one else in the world could flatter himself that he could approach being able to perform it."

Concerning a performance of Bach's Prelude and Fugue in C-sharp minor, Wagner acknowledged, "I knew, of course, very well what was to be expected of Liszt at the piano, but what I heard when he played this piece I had not anticipated, although I had studied Bach thoroughly. This experience showed me how slight

is the value of study as compared with revelation." Debussy, who had heard the very old Liszt, spoke of his use of the pedal as "a sort of breathing apparatus." He had entirely changed piano playing, musically, mentally, and physically. The merely curved fingers, quiet body, light arms and shoulders had virtually no applicability to Liszt's music or playing. The pedagogue Rudolf Breithaupt observed, "What chiefly distinguished Liszt's technique was the absolute freedom of the arms. The secret lay in the unconstrained swinging movements of the arm from the raised shoulder, the bringing out of the tone through the impact of the full elastic mass on the keys, a thorough command and use of the freely rolling arm, the springing hand, the springing finger. He played by weight—by a swinging and a hurling of weight from a loosened shoulder that had nothing in common with what is known as finger manipulation. It was by a direct transfer of strength from back and shoulders to fingers."

He had transformed the piano's possibilities with his *Paganini Etudes,* his operatic transcriptions, and his monumental Twelve *Transcendental Etudes,* called by his first biographer, Lina Ramann, "an unparalleled, gigantic work of spiritual technique." Saint-Saëns considered Liszt's influence on the piano so enormous that he knew nothing comparable to it except the revolution in the mechanism of the French language brought about by Victor Hugo. There is no body of piano music so infallibly grateful and malleable for the hand. Liszt seems to gear his pianistic thinking to a universal hand. His music has a built-in playability no matter how difficult it may be.

He brought melody and accompaniment in the same hand to new heights of inventiveness. He divided between the hands colorful and daring chromatic passages. He laid out melodies in the most ringing registers, simulating the cello or French horn. He magnificently used the thumb as a melodic finger, instead of only as a fulcrum. He created worlds of tremolos, vibratos through pedaling. The simple trill was transformed into a stream of transparent light waves. His dense chordal masses were used for unprecedented dark coloring. He elevated octave technique to new heights, ranging in chromatic and diatonic scales, in broken chords, arpeggios and "blind" interlocking octaves. These "Lisztian" octaves are volcanoes of molten lava. He composes climaxes with the power of a tidal wave. He was almost inexhaustible in the creation of bejeweled cadenzas, sprays of sound; Liszt made these cadenzas into a structural device. In his music, they form a preparation for the next material, or they act as transitional moments before the new action takes place—a sumptuous sounded fermata, so to speak. Liszt was inimitable in imitating effects of orchestral timbre. He saw clearly the piano's latent coloristic and suggestive possibilities, and he called his efforts the "orchestration of the pianoforte."

Aaron Copland wrote:

The sonority chosen instinctively for its sheer beauty of sound . . . is partly the invention of Liszt. No other composer before him understood better how to manipulate tones so as to produce the most satisfying sound texture ranging from the comparative simplicity of a beautifully spaced accompanimental figure to the massive fall of a tumbling cascade of shimmering chords. . . . The profusion of his works and their variety of attack are without parallel in piano literature. He quite literally transforms the piano, bringing out, not only its own inherent qualities, but its evocative nature as well. The piano as orchestra, the piano as harp (*Un Sospiro*), the piano as cimbalom (Hungarian Rhapsody No. 11), the piano as organ, as brass choir, even the percussive piano as we know it (*Totentanz*) may be traced to Liszt's incomparable handling of the instrument. These pieces were born in the piano; they could never have been written at a table.

In all probability, Liszt was the best sight-reader ever to play the piano. The various accounts border on the incredible. When Grieg heard him sight-read his then manuscript Concerto, the Norwegian rejoiced, "He was literally over the whole keyboard at once, without missing a note. And how he did play, with grandeur, beauty, genius, unique comprehension. I think I laughed, laughed like an idiot." Ferdinand Hiller told Mendelssohn, "I have just seen a miracle! I was with Liszt at Erard's and showed him the manuscript of my concerto. He played it at sight—it is hardly legible—and with the utmost perfection. It simply can't be played any better than he played it. It was miraculous."

As a teacher, Liszt's influence has been incalculable. He gave no private lessons but used the plan of the master class with electric effect; here all could play for each other while benefiting from the master's wisdom. Technical matters were never mentioned. Practicing was "your own business." From the world over, students burst upon little Weimar (where the din of practice was so prevalent that a city ordinance demanded in those pre–air-conditioning days that windows be shut). There has never before or since been such a pianists' paradise. From von Bülow and Tausig to Friedheim, Rosenthal, Siloti, d'Albert, pianists of every nation nurtured themselves on him. Liszt never ceased helping his pupils, and instilled in them the courage to demand their due as artists. He never charged a fee for the countless classes. His motto was *"Génie oblige."*

His American student William Mason recalled: "He gradually got me worked up to such a pitch of enthusiasm that I put all the grit that was in me into my playing." Amy Fay, from Mississippi, "felt that with a touch of his wand he could transform us all . . . you feel so free with him, and he develops the very spirit of music in you." The pianist Alfred Reisenauer said, "Never have I met a man in any position whom I have not thought would have proved the inferior of Franz Liszt. . . . Liszt's personality can only be expressed by one word, 'colossal.' "

169

The nineteenth century craved idols, and Liszt gave Europe a bewildering variety of images to worship: the adorable child prodigy; later, the irresistible Don Juan (still later to be disguised as an abbé); and for much of his long career, the epitome of flaming Romanticism, the very personification of pianistic virtuosity. Even in old age (half-saint, half-Mephisto, looking for all the world like an aged Apache chieftain), his magnetism never failed to enthrall. The Grand Duke Carl Alexander of Weimar said that "Liszt was what a prince ought to be." Yet no mere prince ever ruled a dominion so wide as the Kingdom of the Keyboard—a realm in which Liszt's sovereignty was unchallenged through seven decades.

Busoni wrote, many years after Liszt's death, that "we are all descended from him radically. I am myself respectfully conscious of the distance which separates me from his greatness. . . . His aims are ascent, ennoblement, and liberation. Only one who is exalted strives to ascend; only one who is noble strives for nobility; only a master of freedom can bestow freedom. He has become the symbol of the pianoforte, which he lifted to a princely position in order that it might be worthy of himself."

HENRI LITOLFF
1818–1891 — England

A piano pupil of Moscheles, he made his debut at the age of twelve. He was a splendid performer whose compositions are often interesting and even original. Berlioz praised his five piano concerti, or *Concertos symphoniques,* of which a single movement, a scintillating scherzo from the Fourth Concerto, has been recorded by several pianists, among them Curzon. Also, Ponti has recorded the Third Concerto. Litolff started a publishing business, which was the first to issue inexpensive editions of the classics of the piano literature.

ARTHUR LOESSER
1894–1969 — United States

He studied with Sigismund Stojowski and made his debut in Berlin in 1913. Subsequently, he performed throughout the world. In 1926 he settled in Cleveland and became the head of the piano department at the Cleveland Institute of Music. Later he was music critic of the Cleveland *Press.* His book, *Men, Women, and Pianos,* published in 1954, is a social history of the piano and has become a classic. Loesser was a pianist of immense gifts. He was my own teacher and one of the best musical minds I have ever encountered. Loesser was never the pedant. He would say, "The music is not there on the paper. It's not in those black spots. I can't go along with people who believe they are supposed to be music typists. They are the Fundamentalists. They think they must speak only when Scripture speaks and be silent when Scripture is silent. It's all a misapplication of the Scientific Method, translated to music."

Loesser played all the Classical masters with the kind of aristocratic poise that one can only be born with. His Scarlatti, Clementi, and Haydn were bright and alive with wit. His Mozart was absolutely marvelous in its sense of humor. In Schubert's B-flat Impromptu, Loesser strutted and preened. In Bach's *French* Suites, he was incomparable and ingratiating. Actually, at a recital of the complete *French* Suites, he told the audience to forget that Bach wrote the B minor Mass and not to mind one bit if they found their feet tapping to Bach's rhythmic infectiousness. Loesser knew how to dance each Baroque dance and could show a student exactly how a sarabande, gigue, gavotte, or allemande really should go. Bach was his great love, and *The Well-Tempered Clavier* was sacred. His recordings of the forty-eight preludes and fugues should have a place of honor in any collection of great Bach playing.

He had a rare understanding of Schumann, and there is a 1937 recording of the Brahms F-sharp minor Sonata, Op. 2, which is full of Romantic ardor. He played Chopin with classic style, and a spirit of gallantry saturates his record of the neglected *Variations brillantes*, Op. 12. In James Methuen-Campbell's words, he played Chopin's B major Nocturne Op. 9, No. 3 "with a melancholy and exquisite pathos." His last major appearance was in New York's Town Hall in 1967, when he played a sumptuous program of forgotten gems. The hall was packed, and Loesser played such works as the E major Moszkowski Waltz and Busoni's Second Sonatina with a gusto and prodigious technique that brought the audience to its feet. Fortunately, this recital was recorded for posterity.

KATHLEEN LONG
1896–1968 — England

Studied at the Royal College of Music. She played both solo and in ensemble. Her performances of Fauré were admired. She wrote a well-known book, *Nineteenth Century Piano Music*.

MARGUERITE LONG
1874–1966 — France

A pupil of Marmontel *fils* at the Paris Conservatoire. She gave her first concert at the age of eleven, and her last at seventy-five. She had an enormous career, both as an interpreter, especially of the French literature, and as a teacher of hundreds of fine talents, such as Jeanne-Marie Darré, Bernard Ringeissen, Peter Frankl, Ludwig Hoffman, Nicole Henriot, and Philippe Entremont, to name only a few. She knew Debussy, Fauré, and Ravel, and studied their compositions with them. Ravel dedicated to her his G major Concerto, which she premiered with the composer conducting; they later recorded the score together. Her books *At the Piano with Debussy* and *At the Piano with Fauré* are especially informative. Her playing was distinguished by clarity, taste, and a general refinement that is rare in any era.

ALESSANDRO LONGO
1864–1945 — Italy

He studied at the Naples Conservatory, where he later taught. Longo was a concert pianist who composed some interesting piano pieces. His "complete" edition of Domenico Scarlatti's sonatas, for the publisher Ricordi, was a milestone in the resurrection and rediscovery of the great Italian keyboard master. The edition is a Romantic musician's conception of how Scarlatti should sound on the piano, replete with a wide dynamic spectrum.

YVONNE LORIOD
b. 1924 — France

A student of Lévy and Ciampi at the Paris Conservatoire. She married Olivier Messiaen and has been closely associated with his music, which she plays with virtuosity and understanding.

JEROME LOWENTHAL
b. 1930 — United States

At thirteen he made a debut with the Philadelphia Orchestra. He studied with Alfred Cortot and William Kapell, and at the Juilliard School with Edward Steuermann.

Lowenthal plays with breeding and intelligence, and possesses a fine technique. His recordings include Liszt operatic transcriptions and solo piano music by Sinding, as well as the Piano Concerti Nos. 2 and 3 by Tchaikovsky. A particularly astute performance is his recording of the six-movement Rorem Piano Concerto.

RADU LUPU
b. 1945 — Rumania

After an early debut, he was sent to the Moscow Conservatory, where he studied with the great teacher Heinrich Neuhaus. Lupu won first prize at the Van Cliburn Competition in 1966, and in 1969 he was the victor at the Leeds Competition.

Over the past years Lupu's career has been thriving both in concert and as a recording artist. He is a profoundly thoughtful artist and, at his best, possesses a deep insight into Beethoven. His technical apparatus is particularly fine, and one is seldom conscious of hands moving on a piano. He is fond of rather slow tempi, but his playing can often be turgid, as in his recording of the Brahms F minor Sonata, Op. 5. It is in Schubert that Lupu finds scope for his best work, and in the sonatas and shorter pieces we have playing of true stature.

MOURA LYMPANY
b. 1916 — England

She studied at the Royal Academy with Tobias Matthay and later with Mathilde Verne, making her debut in the Mendelssohn G minor Concerto at the age of twelve. Her career was extensive during the 1940s and 1950s. She let many seasons lapse without playing in New York; then, in November 1981, she returned to Carnegie Hall to find a still large following.

Her performances of Haydn's E minor Sonata and Schumann's *Symphonic Etudes* reminded me of the playing of Eileen Joyce, another Matthay student—it is smooth and on the surface with little structural development. But the second half of the recital was more suited to her talents as an objective lyricist. Here Lympany was charming in such water pieces as Debussy's *Reflets dans l'eau* and Ravel's *Ondine*. Her technique was deft and fluid, the playing slightly sweet while not extending to huge fortissimos.

In her memoirs, the writer Margaret Anderson wrote, "One of the landmarks in my musical life has been the discovery of Lympany's 'completely beautiful' playing. I knew at once, as she began Debussy's *Clair de lune*, that no one had ever played it so exactly in the right mood for me, the right breathing. Nearly all of Lympany's conceptions are marked by a rare responsiveness to great lyrical music."

NIKITA MAGALOFF
b. 1912 — Russia

A pupil of Philipp at the Paris Conservatoire. Magaloff has composed piano pieces, including a Toccata, dedicated to Horowitz. He has had a distinguished career as soloist and chamber musician. His most renowned playing is in the Chopin literature, which he has recorded complete. His readings are small in scale but distinguished in manner. Students from around the world have come to Geneva, where he teaches at the Conservatoire. He is often a judge at international piano competitions.

GUY MAIER
1892–1956 — United States

He studied at the New England Conservatory, then with Schnabel in Berlin. He was often heard with Lee Pattison in two-piano works. He edited many works and taught in California.

JOAQUIN MALÁTS
1872–1912 — Spain

He studied with Pujol in his native Barcelona and developed into the finest Spanish pianist of his time, much admired by all who heard his impeccable technique. He also composed, and his lightweight Serenade was once played frequently. It is a pity that this stimulating pianist, who was an inspiration to Albéniz, did not live long enough to make many records. He played the Spanish premieres of all twelve pieces of *Iberia*. The composer wrote to Maláts in 1907: "Since I was fortunate enough to hear you play my *Iberia*, I can truly say that I compose only for you. I have just completed, under the spell of your artistry, the third book of *Iberia*. . . . I think that in these pieces, I have taken the Spanish idiom and pianistic technique to their extremes, and I hasten to add, I hold you responsible for it . . . so brace yourself."

WITOLD MALCUZYNSKI
1914–1977 — Poland

A student of Turczynski at the Warsaw Conservatory. Later, he had coaching from Paderewski. Malcuzynski left a great many recordings, playing Debussy well and Franck's Prelude, Chorale, and Fugue with a feverish attitude. But he will be most remembered as a Chopin player who was immersed in a nostalgic and idiosyncratic style. He could be original and eccentric within the same piece; spontaneous and prosaic passages abound in his nevertheless fascinating playing. He had a fine career and was very effective as a stage personality. Invariably, the audience reacted favorably to whatever Malcuzynski did.

173

YEVGENY MALININ
b. 1930 — USSR

A fine pianist who worked under Stanislav Neuhaus. He has toured throughout Russia and Eastern Europe, recorded Scriabin and Beethoven, and was one of the teachers of Ivo Pogorelich.

ALAN MANDEL
b. 1935 — United States

A student of Leonard Shure and, at the Juilliard School, of Rosina Lhévinne. He now teaches at Catholic University in Washington, D.C. Mandel is a dedicated exponent of contemporary music. He recorded all of the Ives piano music, William Albright's *Sonata in Rag,* and music by Elie Siegmeister, all of which is played in a forthright and keen style. He also recorded forty pieces by Gottschalk; however, they lack flair and color.

ADELE MARCUS
b. 1905 — United States

Studied with Josef Lhévinne and with Schnabel in Berlin. Marcus won the Naumburg Award. Although she has performed often in public, she is best known for her years of work at Juilliard. Byron Janis, Agustin Anievas, Tedd Joselson, Santiago Rodriguez, Horacio Gutiérrez, and many others have worked with her.

174

ANTOINE MARMONTEL
1816–1898 — France

A student of Pierre Zimmerman at the Paris Conservatoire. In 1848, when Zimmerman retired, Marmontel became professor at that institution (a post Alkan desperately wanted). Marmontel became one of France's most respected piano teachers, and he taught an army of pianists. Bizet, Diémer, Théodore Dubois, Debussy, Planté, and Théodore Lack are but a few who achieved fame. He was given the Legion of Honor for his service to French art. He wrote many instructive compositions, as well as a book, *Pianistes célèbres.*

OZAN MARSH
b. 1920 — United States

He studied with Sauer and Petri, developing into a special pianist who continues to perform throughout the world. He is at his best in Romantic music, and his playing of the Liszt Concerto No. 1 and the Rachmaninoff Second Sonata displays grand conceptions, with broad strokes of color. His recording of the important Kabalevsky Second Concerto is an impressive achievement.

FRANK MARSHALL
1883–1959 — Spain

He was a student of Granados and a propagandist for his music and Falla's. A fine player whose only recording is accompanying the soprano Conchita Supervia. Marshall taught at the Granados Academy, where he was the only teacher of de Larrocha.

JOÃO CARLOS MARTINS
b. 1940 — Brazil

At the age of nine, he won a piano competition in São Paulo. Bach was his earliest love, and at twelve, he played the fifteen Two-Part Inventions in public. By the time he was eighteen, he was performing the complete *Well-Tempered Clavier*. In 1962, Martins made his New York debut, and soon after, he committed *The Well-Tempered Clavier* to disc to unusual critical acclaim.

A severe arm injury prevented him from playing from 1970 to 1975, but by 1976 he was slowly returning to concert life, and in 1978 he played to a sold-out house at Carnegie Hall. Since that time, he has re-recorded *The Well-Tempered Clavier*, in addition to recording the Partitas and the *Goldberg* Variations. Bach has continued to be his main concern, although there is also a recording of the Ginastera Piano Concerto No. 1, played to the hilt.

His Bach is unusual: lusty and teeming with life. There is not a pedantic note in Martins's makeup. It is a Bach technically astonishing, virtuosic, grandiose, and sensual. Martins is obviously not interested in Baroque conventions or in the harpsichord, and his Bach playing communicates in the grand manner.

GIUSEPPE MARTUCCI
1856–1909 — Italy

A pupil of Beniamino Cesi, he toured Europe as a first-rank pianist, also becoming a good conductor. Martucci headed the Bologna Conservatory and later the Naples Conservatory. His B-flat minor Concerto was admired by Anton Rubinstein, who conducted it with Cesi at the piano; d'Albert also played it, with the Berlin Philharmonic. Martucci wrote some of the best piano music by an Italian during an era when Italian opera was at its peak. A recording of his piano concerto was made by Horszowski with Toscanini.

FREDERICK MARVIN
b. 1923 — United States

A student of Rudolf Serkin. Marvin is also a musicologist. His recordings of Liszt, especially the B minor Ballade and the *Grand Concert Solo*, are large in scale. He recorded several Dussek sonatas in almost symphonic conceptions. He is best known for his scholarship in the music of Soler and has discovered and edited many Soler sonatas. His recordings of that composer's work, especially the unusual Fandango, are distinguished.

WILLIAM MASON
1829–1908 — United States

After early pianistic success in America, he went to Europe to work with Moscheles and later with Franz Liszt at Weimar. In 1855 he returned to the United States, where for the next half-century he was the leading piano teacher in New York. His brother was co-founder of the piano firm Mason and Hamlin. Mason composed some effective piano music, and his work *Touch and Technic* was long used by piano teachers. He wrote a valuable autobiography, *Memories of a Musical Life*.

WILLIAM MASSELOS
b. 1920 — United States

Carl Friedberg was his teacher, and he made his New York debut in 1943. A Masselos program is one of variety, but he has become known for his chivalry toward new music, devoting a great deal of time to the hard-to-sell wares of an unappreciated branch of the literature. Although his commitment to Scarlatti, Brahms, and Schumann is intense, I suspect his chief delight remains music of his own century—from Griffes and Copland to Ben Weber and Chávez. It was Masselos who gave the belated world premiere, in 1949, of the great Ives First Sonata. His recording is famous, but to hear him play it in public was truly to hear the work in its forty minutes of elemental fury. He emblazoned its bars in the audience's ears. During the playing, I thought Masselos might burst a blood vessel. Afterward, he was drained. The audience roared, and nobody squawked that the Ives was "ugly." Everyone in the audience became a convert!

GEORGES MATHIAS
1826–1910 — France

He studied with Chopin from 1840, and is—along with Karl Mikuli—the most important student of the Polish master. He taught at the Paris Conservatoire for thirty years, and Raoul Pugno, Carreño, Moriz Rosenthal, Alberto Williams, Isidor Philipp, and Ernest Schelling studied with him.

He composed a great deal of piano music and two concerti. James Methuen-Campbell wrote, "Mathias himself played in a manner which showed that his priorities were in the realm of delicate and sensitive nuances, such as had characterized Chopin's playing. Math-

ias forms a link between Chopin himself and the modern French school."

TOBIAS MATTHAY
1858–1945 — England

He studied with Sterndale Bennett and taught at the Royal Academy from 1880; later, he opened his own school. Matthay was a well-equipped pianist and composed many genre pieces, but his great fame was won through his work as a pedagogue. His books on piano playing, its theory and application, were considered by many to be gospel. He was undoubtedly the most celebrated teacher of his time in England. The list of his pupils is extensive and impressive; it includes York Bowen, Harold Craxton, Harriet Cohen, Eileen Joyce, Irene Scharrer, and Dame Myra Hess. Marian McKenna, in her biography of Hess, wrote: "Mr. Matthay was more than a teacher of the piano—he was an idealist and practical moralist, as much interested in shaping his pupils' character as in developing innate musicality. Music he conceived of as a great spiritual art, elevating and enriching life with beautiful thoughts, sounds, feelings and experiences. . . . His ideas about keyboard technique and a psychological approach to the study of the piano—something quite new for that time—proved just what was needed to unlock the rich potential in a pupil like Myra Hess."

DENIS MATTHEWS
b. 1919–1989 — England

A student of Harold Craxton at the Royal Academy. A pianist held in high regard, he was best in the music of Mozart and Beethoven. He wrote a book on Beethoven.

CHARLES MAYER
1799–1862 — Germany

He studied with John Field and taught hundreds of students while living in Russia. Mayer played frequently and composed prolifically, mostly for the piano. I have recorded his *Valse-étude* in D-flat, Op. 83, an amalgam of Weber and Schumann written with pianistic acumen.

JOHN McCABE
b. 1939 — England

An excellent pianist whose complete Haydn discs are well known. His own piano music has merit and he has recorded some of it, including his Fantasy on a Theme of Liszt.

ANNA MEHLIG
1846–1928 — Germany

A dynamic pianist, she was a pupil of Liszt and played in Europe, England, and America. Of her career in America, Liszt said, "Mlle Mehlig has blossomed so well and borne fruit."

HENRIK MELCER
1869–1928 — Poland

A student of Leschetizky. Melcer had a career as a pianist and teacher at Helsinki and Vienna, and became director of the Warsaw Conservatory in 1922. He composed a great deal of music in many forms. His early First Piano Concerto, recorded by Michael Ponti, is a smashing Romantic showpiece of undeniable effectiveness, expertise, and bravura, with a grand gesture thrown in every sixteen bars.

FELIX MENDELSSOHN
1809–1847 — Germany

Mendelssohn, after Mozart, was the most astounding child prodigy in the history of the art, but, unlike Mozart, Mendelssohn was not exploited. Indeed, few have ever been raised in such an atmosphere of wealth, culture, and love, saturated with an affirmation of the humanities and the arts (Mendelssohn's grandfather was the renowned philosopher Moses Mendelssohn).

His early compositions are unique in music. By the age of sixteen, he had written the Octet, and by seventeen, the miraculous Overture to *A Midsummer Night's Dream*. Mendelssohn seemed to be blessed with everything. He was handsome and charming, an excellent dancer and billiards player, an expert horseman, a superb watercolorist, an incomparable letter-writer, and a musical genius. He became one of the best conductors of his generation, and one of the greatest pianists of the age. The theorist Heinrich Dorn thought him the greatest of his era. His improvisations were miraculous. His playing was poised, crisp, and his technique was absolutely impeccable.

His first teacher was Clementi's pupil Ludwig Berger, who gave him a severely Classical background. Zelter, the boy's composition teacher, wrote in 1823, "I take his marvelous piano playing for granted." At fourteen, Mendelssohn took some "finishing" lessons from Moscheles. The older man, considered at that time the best pianist in Europe, was stunned by the boy's precocity. Moscheles noted in his

177

diary that he "gave these lessons without losing sight for a single moment of the fact that I was sitting next to a master, not a pupil."

All doors were opened to him, and at the age of twelve he was the invited guest of Goethe himself, who was deeply affected by the unaffected youngster. In a letter to his parents, Mendelssohn blithely writes: "Every morning I get a kiss from the author of *Faust* and *Werther.* Just fancy that! In the afternoon I played for him for about two hours, partly Bach fugues and partly improvisations." The powerful critic Ludwig Rellstab was at one of Goethe's gatherings, and left an account of Mendelssohn's playing of the overture to *Figaro:* "He began to play it with a lightness, sureness, roundness and clarity such as I have never heard since. At the same time he reproduced the orchestral effects so excellently, so transparently, and by little touches in the instrumentation produced so cunningly the illusion of accompanying voices, that the effect was utterly enchanting and I might almost say that it gave me more pleasure than any orchestral performance ever did."

Mendelssohn's repertoire was large. He played a great deal of Beethoven; one of his specialties was the Fourth Concerto. His interpretation of Weber's *Konzertstück* was considered the ideal. He played Bach and Handel as well as Mozart; especially wonderful was his performance of the Salzburg master's Concerto No. 20 in D minor. Of his playing, the important pianist Ferdinand Hiller attested: "He possessed great skill, certainly power and rapidity of execution—all, in fact, that a virtuoso could desire; but these qualities were forgotten while he was playing, and one almost overlooked even those more spiritual gifts which we call fire, invention, soul, etc. When he sat down to the instrument, music streamed from him with all the fullness of his inborn genius. He was a centaur, and his horse was the piano. What he played, how he played, and that he was the player—were all equally riveting, and it was impossible to separate the execution, the music, and the executed."

In an age when the piano was becoming the most popular domestic instrument, with an ever-growing audience wanting to be entertained, Mendelssohn was uncompromising. He refused to play any pot-boilers. It is well known that it was Mendelssohn who resurrected Bach's almost forgotten *Saint Matthew Passion,* and he was also a great proselytizer for *The Well-Tempered Clavier* and Bach's keyboard concerti. In 1831, when Mendelssohn premiered his dazzling G minor Concerto at Munich, he complained in a letter that "even the best pianists had no idea that Mozart and Haydn had composed for the piano; they had just the faintest notion of Beethoven. . . . I gave a long sermon to the leading pianist and reproached her for having contributed nothing towards the knowledge and appreciation of the works of the great masters and for having just followed the popular trend."

Clara Wieck Schumann perhaps knew his playing better than anyone else did. "The recollections of Mendelssohn's playing are among the most delightful things in my artistic life," she wrote. "It was to me a shining ideal, full of genius and life. . . . He would sometimes take very quick tempi, but never to the prejudice of the music. . . . He often told me he hardly ever practiced and yet he surpassed everyone."

Mendelssohn was the most famous musician of his age; it was his type of Romanticism that the public loved best and most easily understood. His art is picturesque, generally nonsubjective, and seldom disturbing as was the art of Schumann or Liszt. In his forty-eight *Lieder ohne Worte* (*Songs without Words*), Mendelssohn hit upon just the right kind of well-tailored, mild-mannered Romanticism, beautifully calculated for the needs of the Victorian drawing room, where the scores were always on the piano. Mendelssohn was a master of the staccato touch and the scherzando mood. He is irresistible in such airy works as the *Spinning Song, Rondo capriccioso,* Scherzo in E minor, and many others that were born out of Weber's *Momento capriccioso.* Mendelssohn created for the instrument a vision of a happy, sun-drenched world, full of good will and magical spells—his piano traveled on gossamer wings.

His sister Fanny, whom he adored, was a gifted musician who suddenly died at the age of forty. When told of her death, Mendelssohn collapsed; he died six months later, at the age of thirty-eight. Few artists have ever packed more into such a short life.

SOPHIE MENTER
1846–1918 — Germany

Menter studied with Tausig and then with Liszt. She had a tremendous career and was perhaps Liszt's greatest female student. He was devoted to her and entranced with her prowess, calling her "a pianist of exceptional virtuosity . . . an incomparable pianist . . . a pianist of the highest rank." Writing to Olga von Meyendorff in 1881, Liszt reports, "I spent only one day in Rome for Sophie Menter's concert. She played the whole program enclosed herewith superbly, so as to compare favorably with the three or four most famous male pianists. Her *bravura* is absolutely faultless; the rhythm and color are masterfully accented and blended. In the *Réminiscences des Huguenots,* a fantasia which in my years as a virtuoso I used to play only rarely because of the trouble it cost me, Sophie Menter astonished me." Ernst Pauer praised her "nobility of feeling, tenderness and warmth of expression. Her technical execution baffles description."

YOLANDA MÉRÖ
1887–1963 — Hungary

She studied with her father and then with a pupil of Liszt, Augusta Rennebaum. In 1910 she made her first tour of the United States, with great success. From that time on, she played mostly in the United States, and her many recordings reveal a fiery artist with a very efficient technical equipment.

FRANK MERRICK
1886–1981 — England

He worked with Leschetizky, performed, playing a great deal of John Field's music, and was a respected teacher in London. He wrote a little volume, *Practicing the Piano.* He also composed and recorded.

VICTOR MERZHANOV
b. 1919 — USSR

A winner of prizes in piano competitions in the Soviet Union and later a teacher at the Moscow Conservatory. He is greatly respected in the Soviet musical world. Merzhanov has played in Canada and South America, and has judged at the Queen Elizabeth Competition and Busoni Competition. His recording of the Scriabin Fifth Sonata is idiomatically morbid; his Rachmaninoff Third Concerto is dazzling and brittle; and his Brahms *Paganini* Variations has long been admired. For a deeper

179

Merzhanov, listen to his discs of the Grieg Ballade and Mussorgsky's *Pictures at an Exhibition.*

NOEL MEWTON-WOOD
1922–1953 — Australia

He studied in Melbourne and at the Royal Academy in London, and also had lessons with Schnabel. He made a London debut in 1940. Bliss dedicated his Piano Sonata to him. He had a passionate musicality and a formidable mechanism. At thirty-one, he committed suicide. Mewton-Wood recorded Tchaikovsky's Second and Third Concerti and the seldom-heard Concert-Fantasy of Tchaikovsky in tumultuous performances.

LEOPOLD DE MEYER
1816–1883 — Austria

A student of Czerny, he had an amazing career. De Meyer was one of the first piano-publicists, calling himself "the Lion Pianist." He roamed far and wide, playing in Constantinople in 1843, four years before Liszt arrived there. He was also the first important pianist to play in America, arriving in 1845, before either Herz or Thalberg. He played about sixty concerts, going as far as St. Louis. His publicity stunts and showmanship, as well as his highly demonstrative, muscular playing, electrified audiences. He played exclusively his own music, which, upon reading, reveals a poverty of creativity. In his journal, George Templeton Strong considered de Meyer to be "the most explosive musical bombshell ever to erupt upon the American scene" (at least in 1845).

ALEKSANDER MICHALOWSKI
1851–1938 — Poland

Studied with Moscheles, Reinecke, and Mikuli. He played with a beautifully molded, masterful technique and a rich tone. His Chopin playing had a sentimental elegance. He was the teacher of Antoinette Szumowska and Wanda Landowska, and he composed some salon pieces, which are charming and technically inventive.

ARTURO BENEDETTI MICHELANGELI
b. 1920 — Italy

Michelangeli has been thought by many to be the greatest Italian pianist to have been born in this century. In 1939 he won the International Piano Competition at Geneva, but World War II interrupted his work. After his discharge from military duty, Michelangeli quickly scored spectacular European successes, and he made his American debut with the New York Philharmonic in 1948. From the start of his public career, however, he was a quirky concertizer, prone to lightning-quick cancellations. Michelangeli's performing career has been characterized by fits and starts. For many music lovers, he has become a fascinating enigma. He is one of the few who can create a ticket stampede by the mere announcement of a recital. The question is: will he show up? But if he does appear, it will take only a few bars to establish that this will be an unusual musical experience.

At his best, Michelangeli is one of the most refined players in history. His secrets are in coolness and restraint. His realizations of Classical masters possess an uncanny purity. He delivers Clementi, Haydn, Mozart, Galuppi, and Scarlatti with the greatest delectability—all smooth, dainty, and rhythmically alert. They are worked at in great detail, and the pianistic finish is crystalline. He is a great colorist, too, as in his celebrated performance of Ravel's *Gaspard de la nuit*, which set new standards of technical finesse for that score. The piano becomes limp to Michelangeli's touch, issuing rare tonal treasures. His finger control achieves a glorious evenness, inhabiting a sphere quite above mere excellence. His performances are a merging of mechanism with music; his pedaling is the result of deep thought and the most sensitive ear.

When he plays, Michelangeli seems to be watching the proceedings with detachment. He is in his element with music that speaks objectively or that is stylistically elegant. As a programmer, he has always been refreshingly unhackneyed. If the work at hand is popular, his sympathy for it runs lower. For example, his Schumann *Carnaval* is finicky, but the *Faschingsschwank aus Wien* by the same composer is prankish and intoxicating in its brashness. I would think Michelangeli to be estranged from the more luscious atmosphere of Rachmaninoff's earlier concerti. His recording of the Rachmaninoff Fourth Concerto is played classically, almost prudishly. In the laconic Ravel G major Concerto, Michelangeli plays with an immaculacy which has never quite been approached, and the slow movement, with its chain of trills, is hypnotic musically.

In Beethoven, he is best when confronting the earlier works. The formal blocks of the E-flat Sonata Op. 7 or the First Concerto are sculptured. But the Op. 111, the final Sonata, seems contrived. The first movement is fine—it, too, has a solid structure—but he does not have a feeling for the variations. He does feel,

and in his own individualized way, the sensuous world of Debussy, as though he were swimming in cool water.

He seems insecure in Chopin and reacts moodily to him. There are moments of great beauty, and the shape of his phrasing is always thoughtful. But the organic element in large works is lacking, and the interpretation of the B-flat minor Scherzo droops in the trio, while the luscious long-limbed melody of the scherzo intimidates him. Even less successful is the performance of the G minor Ballade, which is a flight of oppressive eccentricity. His Mazurkas are very disappointing. The rubato is strained, by turns inhibited and outlandish. In some, he accentuates the dance element disproportionately.

Some scores, such as the Bach-Busoni Chaconne and the Brahms *Paganini* Variations, bring forth a demonic side of Michelangeli's nature. Here, tension is released with a cold and calculated fury, and his crescendi are formed to perfection. His Bach-Busoni Chaconne is the standard by which all others are measured. His building of the edifice becomes inexorable. Here Bach counts for little: it is Michelangeli paying homage to Busoni, his great compatriot. A parallel may be made with his famous version of the Brahms *Paganini* Variations. Brahms becomes merely the medium through which the two Italians commune, Paganini conveying to Michelangeli his dark and rarefied secrets of technique. Such playing has an element of mystery. For Michelangeli, music is a rite to be performed, an exorcism. When I listen to this performance, there is the ghostlike feeling that the piano is playing of its own accord.

Michelangeli has given far less to recording than his admirers would like. He is a perfectionist and does not easily authorize release of his recordings. No wonder that the pirated pressings of his live performances are quickly grabbed up by collectors who relish his highly original imprint. The albums should read, 181

"This playing can only be by Arturo Benedetti Michelangeli."

KARL MIKULI
1819–1897 — Poland

Had a distinguished career as pianist and teacher. He became a student of Chopin in 1844, and later made an edition of his master's works, which is still used.

SEBASTIAN BACH MILLS
1838–1898 — England

Studied with Cipriani Potter and Sterndale Bennett, also with Moscheles and Liszt. He had a successful career and first played in New York in 1860. His playing was widely recognized in the United States, where he eventually made his home. In 1866 he was the pianist at the first concert at Steinway Hall in New York.

BENNO MOISEIWITSCH
1890–1963 — Russia

Born in Odessa, he became a pupil of Leschetizky. When Moiseiwitsch touched his piano, the listener knew that here was a "tone poet." Rachmaninoff loved Moiseiwitsch's golden interpretations of his own music. Moiseiwitsch was primarily a lyricist, and his singing tone with its plasticity of line and colorful palette was the flowering of Leschetizky's ideal. Above all, he was relaxed, and his magnificently supple mechanism flowed with ease. He could discover delightful inner voices, and his sense of rubato was delicious.

Early in his career, like many Romantics of his day, he made "improvements" on the composers, but he later dropped most of these transgressions. His later LPs are suffused with a radiant light, and he paints lovely strokes in soft pastels. Moiseiwitsch said his favorite composer was Schumann, and his playing sang in *Carnaval* and the *Scenes of Childhood*. His best-known performances were in the Chopin repertoire, where his natural elegance and glistening virtuosity were equally at home in the preludes, ballades, or waltzes. In his later years, some of the sheen of his technique disappeared and the swiftness of finger velocity slowed somewhat. His best work is contained in his many 78 discs, and they are well worth locating—for instance, the Weber *Invitation to the Dance,* dressed in Tausig's ingenious arrangement, is piano playing of vivacity, high style, and melting tone.

GERALD MOORE
b. 1899–1987 — England

He developed into one of the finest accompanists of the century, collaborating with many of the best singers of his time, such as Schwarzkopf and, later, Fischer-Dieskau. His many recordings show a deep understanding of singing and Romantic lieder literature. He wrote several books, the best known of which is *The Unashamed Accompanist.*

IVAN MORAVEC
b. 1930 — Czechoslovakia

He studied with Ilona Kurz and with Michelangeli. He made a career in Europe and gave his U.S. debut in 1964. Since the 1960s, he has produced a wealth of recordings. Moravec is the finest Czech Chopin interpreter of his generation. His is a polished, aristocratic playing, harnessed to a technique of tremendous depth. His many virtues include the ability to sustain a singing line with a velvet tone, and to play a pure but vibrant pianissimo. He also has the smoothest legato, and his pedaling is a marvel—he always produces exactly the sound he wants. Moravec has an abundance of temperament, and he can rise to fever pitch in the rapturous codas of the four Chopin Ballades. Not all his playing is to my taste, though. Some of the Chopin Preludes bog down, becoming turgid, and Moravec—who revels in slow lyricism—may, in some Nocturnes, sound too slow; the perfume becomes too heavy. In public performance he tends to fidget with phrases and loses the continuity of shape.

His Beethoven is played with plasticity. His recording of the *Pastoral* Sonata, Op. 28, is rejuvenating, a breath of sweet country air. I also admire his spacious Franck Prelude, Chorale, and Fugue; a Debussy drenched in sunlight; a Ravel *Sonatine* of exquisite grace; a warmhearted Mozart Sonata in B-flat, K. 570; and a hushed rendering of Janáček's beautiful cycle *In the Mist*.

IGNAZ MOSCHELES
1794–1870 — Czechoslovakia

He studied from the age of seven with Dionys Weber in Prague; at fourteen he went to Vienna for extensive study. After 1815 he performed with great success throughout Western Europe. In 1826 he made his home in London, where he taught and played. He became one of the finest teachers of his time, commanding fees twice what Clementi had received. He taught a legion of famous musicians, including Mendelssohn, Thalberg, Louis Brassin, Sir George Henschel, Richard Hoffman, Rafael Joseffy, Sydney Smith, Max Vogrich, and many others. He left a penetrating autobiography and his music fills 142 opus numbers. In 1841 he translated Schindler's *Life of Beethoven* into English.

It is unlikely that any serious reader about music has missed the name of Moscheles. Through much of the nineteenth century, he was everywhere and he knew everyone. He was at the deathbed of Weber in 1826; he was at the sickbed of Beethoven even while preparing the piano score of *Fidelio;* he performed in private the first all-piano concerts in London in the 1830s. In Paris, he played duets with Chopin before Louis Philippe. When the revolutionary "double escapement" piano action by Sébastien Erard was ready, the piano firm first went to Moscheles for approval. When Mendelssohn founded the Leipzig Conservatory, he begged Moscheles to head the piano department. Later, Moscheles became director of the Conservatory and helped make the institution the most influential German school of music during the nineteenth century.

In 1831, Moscheles took the first train in England to play a concert at Manchester. "Words," he wrote in his diary, "cannot describe the impression made on me by this steam excursion . . . and the transports I felt with an invention that seemed to me little short of magic." With that trip was inaugurated the modern international concert career.

Moscheles represents the zenith of the Hummel school of refined virtuosity, and had also absorbed the depth, sonority, and brilliance of Clementi and Cramer. With Kalkbrenner, Moscheles was the most famous and most respected pianist in Europe around 1820. In his youth he was called "the Prince of Pianists." He was well aware of the improvements that had given new power and flexibility to the piano, bringing it out of the drawing room into larger halls. His fame was assured when, with perfect timing, he stormed the Congress of Vienna (1815) and won princely ovations for his Variations on the *Alexander March*. The young Moscheles knew that audiences were clamoring to hear and see what their now favorite instrument could do. Moscheles could supply "bravura" with the best of them. His *Alexander* Variations were attempted by all who aspired to dazzle at the piano.

But Moscheles was a musician of lofty aims and soon tired of only pleasing the public. He wanted to educate them and play the best music, including older music, which was seldom performed. He even introduced Scarlatti on the harpsichord.

As a composer, he fulfilled himself with such admirable works as the Twenty-four Etudes, Op. 70, of 1826; the 1820 G minor Concerto, which was popular for decades; and the *Sonate mélancolique* of 1821. By 1830, with the coming to maturity of the Romantics, Moscheles's influence paled. In their youth, Schumann, Liszt, Henselt, and Chopin were all inspired by Moscheles. The older Moscheles, however, was baffled by the execution and novel figurations of these young Romantics. He was correct when in his later years he saw himself as the link between the old and modern schools of piano playing. His fine pupil Edward Dannreuther wrote: "Moscheles was distinguished by a crisp and incisive touch, clear and precise phrasing, and pronounced preference for minute accentuation. He played octaves with stiff wrists and was chary in the use of the pedals." Of course, a creative use of pedaling was one of the hallmarks of the new piano style. But Moscheles complained that "all effects now, it seems, must be produced by the feet—what is the use of people having hands?"

Grieg, who studied with him at the Conser-vatory, wrote: "He could and did play beautifully. Specially fine were his renderings of Beethoven, whom he adored."

His etudes were once widely used. Von Bülow considered them an important stepping stone to the playing of the Chopin etudes, and Chopin himself always used them in his own teaching. Each of the Moscheles etudes possesses a genuine poetic impulse, which leads directly to the Chopin etudes. Moscheles proselytized for the best in music. In a period when mere keyboard banging was often heard, he stood as a force for moderation and good taste.

MORITZ MOSZKOWSKI
1854–1925 — Germany

He studied with Kullak and proceeded to play in public beginning in 1873. He was admired for his finished, graceful playing and for his compositions, which are great audience pleasers. The best of his salon music is of the highest caliber. He had a wonderful gift for composing music that seems molded to the hand. He was a delightful melodist, and his work can sparkle with humor. Virtuosi such as Rachmaninoff, Hofmann (who studied with him), Lhévinne, Horowitz, and Bolet always found a place for him in their repertoires.

In Paris during his last years, Moszkowski was ill and beset by poverty. A concert in Carnegie Hall on December 22, 1921, was arranged for his benefit. It was a veritable treasure-house of the Golden Age of Pianism. Harold Bauer, Ossip Gabrilowitsch, Fannie Bloomfield Zeisler, Yolanda Mérö, Alexander Lambert, Rudolph Ganz, Percy Grainger, Josef Lhévinne, Ernest Schelling, Ignaz Friedman, Germaine Schnitzer, and Sigismund Stojowski all took part in a multi-piano spectacle. Among the works on the program was Schumann's *Carnaval*, with each pianist playing one section. The concert was a great success and was repeated in Philadelphia.

JOSÉ VIANNA DA MOTTA
1868–1948 — Portugal

He trained with von Bülow and Scharwenka and was one of Liszt's last surviving pupils. Da Motta was a sterling pianist who had a huge influence on Portuguese pianistic culture. The piano competition in Lisbon is named for him.

He edited Liszt's music, taught, conducted, and composed. He was the first to play all of the Beethoven sonatas in Lisbon. His performance on record of Liszt's *Totentanz,* from 1945, shows him still in form and able to create excitement. He had an unforced manner in works such as Busoni's *Turandots Frauengemach.* In his own composition *Vals caprichosa,* Op. 9, he displays a succulent rubato.

WOLFGANG AMADEUS MOZART
1756–1791 — Austria

The most famous and amazing child prodigy in music history. His father, Leopold, a well-known musician, author of a notable violin method, and good composer, gave Wolfgang and his sister Maria Anna lessons in their early childhood. Both showed unusual talent, but more energy was spent on the boy, who was already composing little pieces at the age of five, as well as playing the harpsichord at sight. Mozart's infallible ear and prodigious memory were put to good use as he was exhibited on tour throughout Europe. It was an exhausting childhood. His first tour kept him away from his native Salzburg for three years. Indeed, Mozart spent nearly fourteen years of his short life on the road. The best that can be said of those years is that Mozart was kept in constant touch with the musical life of his time, and he absorbed and transformed all that came his way. Although piano playing was in its early stages, Mozart probably began changing from the harpsichord to the pianoforte in 1763, when he met J. C. Bach, the best pianist in London. Mozart was influenced by his music and playing, and when he was eleven, he transcribed sonata movements by J. C. Bach and several other composers into his first four piano concerti, K. 37, 39, 40, and 41. Mozart called them *"pasticci"* and performed them frequently.

By the age of seventeen, he preferred the piano to the harpsichord, and his Concerto No. 5 in D major, K. 175, was the finest Classical piano concerto thus far composed by anyone. This 1773 creation was to be a vehicle for his own constantly improving playing, and significantly, in an age when public performance was in its infancy, he scored it for one of his largest orchestras, using oboes, trumpets, horns, and timpani.

During the next years, he came in touch with one of the best piano makers of the day, Johann Andreas Stein, whose innovations were used by all the Viennese piano builders. A good indication of the aesthetic climate of the time can be found in a remark Stein made to Mozart, who wanted to try out a new church organ Stein had completed. The builder was "much amazed." "What? A man like you, such a great fortepianist, wants to play an instrument on which no tenderness, no expression, no *piano* and *forte* can take place, but which always goes the same?" This, of course, could also have been said about the harpsichord, which was, by 1780, losing ground to the piano.

In 1781, Mozart left a dreaded court post in Salzburg and moved to Vienna, which he called "Clavier Land." Although he had hoped for an imperial court position, he came to depend on the piano as his main source of a livelihood—teaching, and arranging subscription concerts around his own newly composed piano concerti. From 1782 to 1786, Mozart wrote no fewer than fifteen piano concerti, and from one concert he could earn nearly enough to cover his rent for a year. For each concert, Mozart paid a small fee for the hall rental, sold the subscriptions himself, engaged copyists, and hired and rehearsed the orchestra (the Vienna Philharmonic was not yet in existence). He also had to select the program, conduct the concert, and work with the solo singers. The concerts could take place only during Lent, when public concerts were permitted though the theaters were closed for plays and opera by law. Mozart's audiences were amazing in their splendor—everyone of importance in the imperial capital would arrive for his newest concerto: royalty, ambassadors, government officials, socialites, and every prominent musician, including, of course, Mozart's enemy at court, Salieri.

Mozart had recently been in a grueling piano contest with Clementi, before the Emperor Joseph II, and everyone was discussing the relative merits of the two artists. It may have been at one of these concerts that the emperor asked the eminent composer Karl Ditters von Dittersdorf if he preferred Clementi's playing to Mozart's. The composer humbly replied that "Clementi's playing is art alone. Mozart's is art and taste." Mozart, never the most generous colleague, condemned Clementi's music in a letter to his father: "As compositions, they are worthless. They contain no remarkable or striking passages except those in sixths and octaves. And I implore my sister not to practice these passages too much, so that she may not spoil her quiet, even touch and that her hand may not lose its natural lightness, flexibility and smooth rapidity." Of his own playing, Mozart wrote: "Herr Stein sees and hears that I am

more of a player than Beecke—that without making grimaces of any kind I play so expressively that, according to his own confession, no one shows off his pianoforte as well as I. That I always remain strictly in time surprises everyone. They cannot understand that the left hand should not in the least be concerned in a *tempo rubato*. When they play, the left hand always follows."

Mozart's dictum was "It should flow like oil." But his legato playing was probably not as smooth as Clementi's, and Beethoven told Czerny that Mozart still played in a clipped style. Very likely, during the 1770s and 1780s, legato was still the exception, and a detached "harpsichord" style was prevalent, especially on the pedaling systems of pianos of the period. To have a recording of Mozart's playing would answer so many questions of style, tempo, legato, ornamentation. Often, in the concerti, Mozart only sketched what he wanted to supply in the notation of the slow movements. And how thrilled pianists would be to hear Mozart improvising the cadenzas in the concerti, although in some, Mozart did write out cadenzas. But, as Tovey points out, "it is doubtful whether he would have regarded any of his written cadenzas to first movements as adequately representing his way of extemporizing."

At any rate, there is no indication that Mozart was displeased with the sonorous qualities of the Viennese five-octave pianos available to him and for which his piano writing was so deftly created. In the past decade there have been many performances of Mozart on fortepianos of his time, and they are becoming more prevalent. There is no doubt that the piano concerti can sound wonderful when played on a fortepiano. The voluptuous, palpitating, iron-framed piano often sounds slick when blended with Mozart's orchestra. Today's halls, however, are much larger than those of Mozart's day, and the contemporary piano will continue to be used in the Mozart concerti, which remain the most

186

important body of music for soloist and orchestra.

In the realm of the piano concerto, Mozart has no rival. In the nineteenth century, when played at all, he was usually treated as a frilly, Rococo doll, and performed in a mechanical style which passed for Classical "good taste." By 1920, things had changed considerably, and Mozart was heard in all of his depth, passion, humor, and humanity. Artists of the caliber of Busoni, Fischer, Tovey, and Schnabel began exposing large segments of his piano music in concert. By the LP era, pianists had become all but obsessed with this luminous literature. Seldom does a month pass without a slew of Mozart releases by pianists of all persuasions. The piano concerti constitute one of the most miraculous chapters in the history of music, and in the context of Mozart's total work, a miracle among miracles. Alfred Einstein wrote: "Mozart possessed a sensitiveness to sound that has remained altogether unique and was never again to be attained, and above all an entirely different sphere of emotion, at once sensuous and non-sensuous, hovering between grace and melancholy, indeed often changing color with a lightning-like abruptness."

MIECZYSLAW MÜNZ
1900–1976 — Poland

A student of Busoni, he played regularly to acclaim and came to the United States in 1922. He taught at Curtis and at Juilliard, as well as in Japan. His students include Ann Schein and Emanuel Ax.

ISTVÁN NÁDAS
b. 1922 — Hungary

A student of Bartók, he also studied composition with Kodály. Nádas is a major talent, especially in works which exhibit a monumental style. He has played many times over and in various cities the complete Beethoven sonatas and Bach's *Well-Tempered Clavier*. Nádas has a questing musical mind and an original way with whatever he touches. There is a feeling of the austere in his conceptions. There are also many moments of ponderous playing. Nonetheless, a tone of deep nobility infuses his best work. He most easily accommodates the German Classic school. The Beethoven piano concerti, the Brahms B-flat Concerto, the Beethoven *Hammerklavier*, and the *Goldberg* Variations are favorites of his. His recording of Schubert's *Wanderer* Fantasy is grand in scope.

Nádas has also recorded Bloch's and Stravinsky's sonatas, and Prokofiev's Seventh Sonata. In Chopin, he is interesting but not comfortable.

ALEXEI NASEDKIN

b. 1942 — USSR

He worked with Heinrich Neuhaus and won several prizes in competitions. Perhaps he is best known for his exceptionally lyrical Schubert playing. He has recorded some little-played Tchaikovsky, and in such pieces as *Rêverie,* Op. 8, and the *Valse-caprice,* Op. 4, he plays with a fine sense of rubato, grace, and tonal variety.

YVES NAT

1890–1956 — France

A well-known French pianist who studied with Diémer at the Paris Conservatoire. He recorded a great deal, composed some interesting piano music, and taught such students as Jörg Demus, Yuri Boukoff, and Geneviève Joy.

CHARLES NEATE

1784–1877 — England

He studied with John Field, played at Covent Garden at his debut in 1800, and was a founder of the Philharmonic Society of London in 1813. He was one of the first in England to appreciate the extent of Beethoven's genius, and traveled to Vienna, where he became friends with the great composer. Later, Neate introduced Beethoven's Concerti Nos. 1 and 5 to English audiences.

HEINRICH NEUHAUS

1888–1964 — Russia

He studied with Blumenfeld and Michalowski, and in Vienna with Godowsky. He taught at the Kiev Conservatory and later at the Moscow Conservatory. Neuhaus was the cousin of Szymanowski and the nephew of Blumenfeld. He became one of the most famous teachers of the century; his classes at the Moscow Conservatory were crowded with students hoping to gain inspiration. He taught some of the outstanding pianists of Russia, including Gilels and Richter, both of whom greatly acknowledged their debt to him. His warmth and great teaching instincts are evidenced in his book, *The Art of Piano Playing.* He recorded exquisite and intimate performances of Chopin mazurkas; a conservative but pure reading of the Chopin E minor Concerto, a specialty of his; and the Scriabin Concerto, which is the quintessence of that composer's early music and is played by Neuhaus with perfection of style.

STANISLAV NEUHAUS

1927–1980 — USSR

He studied with his father and was a hardier pianist than Heinrich, capable of full-bodied playing but lacking a restrained, delicate sensibility. His recordings of Scriabin, such as the Fourth Sonata, bring out the glittering aspects of the Russian's piano writing. In Chopin, Stanislav Neuhaus achieved a special urgency in the F minor Ballade and *Polonaise-fantaisie.*

EDMUND NEUPERT

1842–1888 — Norway

A student of Kullak. From all accounts, he was a marvelous virtuoso. Grieg entrusted him with the premiere of his A minor Concerto in Copenhagen. He left a considerable amount of attractive piano music.

WILLIAM NEWMAN
b. 1912 — United States

A pupil of Arthur Loesser. He has performed frequently, always playing refreshing programs. He wrote *The Pianist's Problems,* as well as the monumental three-volume work *A History of the Sonata Idea.*

ELLY NEY
1882–1968 — Germany

Ney, a pupil of Leschetizky, was a well-known artist who was at her best in the German repertoire.

LEONID NICOLAIEV
1878–1942 — Russia

He was a student of Safonov, a good pianist, and a respected teacher. Among his pupils at the St. Petersburg Conservatory were Shostakovich, Maria Yudina, and Vladimir Sofronitsky.

TATIANA NIKOLAYEVA
b. 1924 — USSR

A pupil of Goldenweiser at the Moscow Conservatory, she has had a major career in the Soviet Union. Nikolayeva played many premieres, including the Twenty-four Preludes and Fugues of Shostakovich, which she has brilliantly recorded. She has also composed.

BARBARA NISSMAN
b. 1945 — United States

A student of György Sandor, she made her debut in 1971 and has played with major orchestras. She has recorded music by Ginastera, who wrote his Third Piano Sonata for and dedicated it to her. Recently, she recorded the nine sonatas and smaller pieces by Prokofiev. During the 1988–89 season she performed three recitals of Prokofiev's piano music including all the sonatas. She is a propulsive player with a fine technique and a flair for large-scale playing.

MINORU NOJIMA
b. 1946 — Japan

One of the best-known Japanese pianists of his generation. In 1969 he took the second prize at the Van Cliburn Competition. Nojima has a fantastic facility and plays with fire and elegance.

GUIOMAR NOVAES
1896–1979 — Brazil

She had piano lessons from Luigi Chiafarelli until she was fourteen, when she went to Paris. Soon after, she entered a competition for foreign students to attend the Paris Conservatoire. She beat out more than two hun-

189

dred applicants with her playing of Schumann's *Carnaval* and the Chopin A-flat Ballade, among other pieces. The jury included no less than Fauré, Debussy, Moszkowski, and Isidor Philipp, and all were unanimously agreed that Novaes had a musicality of rare beauty. She proceeded to study with Philipp, who gently guided her persuasive individuality. At the age of twenty, in 1916, she arrived in New York and took the town by storm. After her fourth New York recital, she was heralded as "one of the seven wonders of the musical world." W. J. Henderson of the *New York Sun* wrote, "In the range of tonal beauties and immense vitality, only Paderewski or Hofmann could have equalled her." The inimitable phrasemaker James Huneker, with poetic and geographical license, pronounced her "the Paderewska of the Pampas." Another New York critic, the eminent Henry T. Finck, compared her to the great singers of the time. "Her tone," he wrote, "has the limpid purity and beauty that the world adores in voices like Patti's or Sembrich's or Caruso's; in runs these tones are like strings of perfect pearls."

Novaes's playing was first and always personalized. She delighted in details, leaving one wondering why others never saw or savored them. Novaes, although trained at the end of a self-indulgent era, was in her way a quite scrupulous musician. Even at capricious moments, she had that marvelous and indispensable trait of a great interpreter—the power to convince. She possessed a fabulous pianistic flexibility; her art was a compendium of the best Romantic characteristics. The terms *eccentric* or *idiosyncratic* never applied to her. The term *a natural* did. She was meant for piano playing; her hands belonged on the keyboard. Her playing, at its best, was as effortless as a bird in flight. She once said, "Piano playing for some is drudgery, for me it is the greatest joy," but she was also a pianist of unusual discipline. The pianist Allen Tanner told me that he overheard her even after sixty-five years of playing the *Waldstein* of Beethoven, practicing it slowly and scrupulously with the metronome ruthlessly beating.

Novaes was not a monumental musician, and she never played works not suited to her elastic temperament. She was divine in the Chopin F minor Concerto, Schumann's A minor, and Beethoven's Fourth. She played a large body of Schumann, and her *Carnaval* is fragrant with youth and ardor. Her recording of *Papillons* is another of the highlights of her Schumann playing. In little pieces like *The Prophet Bird*, she could make her listeners shiver. Her sense of nuance was very keen. In Beethoven she was stricter and more conventional, but she could "storm" in the first movement of Op. 111, and her readings of the *Moonlight* and *Les Adieux* were warm, though forgettable. She played very fine Debussy Preludes—not a French Debussy, but one that sounded rather Slavic somehow.

In whatever she touched there was a feeling of intimacy, and it was Chopin she touched most. A Novaes recital without Chopin would not have been tolerated by her large public. She was grand and original in the *Funeral March* Sonata. Her renderings of the Third Scherzo, the Second Impromptu, and the Fourth Ballade were alluring. In the Fourth Ballade, there seemed to be little planning for so large a composition, but her ravishing rubato carried the day. For this admirer, her Chopin B minor Sonata was heavenly; such imagination, poetry, velvety tone, command of nuance, and subtlety of rhythm are seldom encountered. Her recording of this is surely one of the best efforts in a recorded output that is dreadfully uneven. In later life, she made a series of records that are not always characteristic of her playing. Sometimes she is rough-edged and sloppy, as in the Chopin Etudes, and the Preludes are merely dull, as are many Nocturnes. She was not for the commercial world; she chose only what suited her best for public demonstration.

Still, she worked hard in her later years, and there are many discs to admire, from her Chopin mazurkas and Debussy preludes to her Mendelssohn recording of a dozen or so *Songs without Words*. Isidor Philipp had told her these last pieces were unduly neglected. Listen to her loving and tender playing of the beautiful *Duetto*, the daintiness of the usually simpering *Spring Song,* the warmth and passion of *May Breezes;* hear her as she trips the light fantastic in the *Spinning Song.*

But records could never yield the totality of Novaes's art; her spontaneous and instinctive music-making needed the immediacy of an audience. Her last New York recital, in 1967 at Avery Fisher Hall, was packed. An aristocratic-looking woman, with a nonchalant dignity, she was doing her job, as she had since childhood. The program contained her old standbys—the *Waldstein* of Beethoven, the *Funeral March* Sonata of Chopin. But what I will never forget was her last encore, the very long and ridiculously awful musically—but wondrously effective technically—Fantasy on the Brazilian National Hymn by Gottschalk. She was spellbinding in her bravura. When in the mood, the great Brazilian virtuosa could project the grand manner with a fascinating flair which brought the entire house, screaming, to its feet.

JAN NOVOTNÝ
b. 1935 — Czechoslovakia

He studied in Prague and teaches at the Prague Conservatory. Novotný has played in Europe, South America, and the Far East. His recordings of Smetana are lively and technically solid.

ERVIN NYIREGYHÁZI
1903–1987 — Hungary

A child prodigy who studied with Dohnányi and Lamond. He had a considerable career until the middle 1920s. During the next decades, he lived and drank, and married at least nine times. He seldom touched a piano until 1973, when his playing—touted as the great link to the Romantic era—caused an uproar wherever he was heard. He was heatedly discussed, made several records with a few remarkable moments, and dropped out of sight again, into the oblivion he obviously preferred. There is little doubt that when he was not being musically eccentric, his talent was compelling in sound and intensity.

LEV OBORIN

1907–1974 — Russia

He studied with Igumnov at the Moscow Conservatory. Oborin was the first winner of the Chopin Competition in Warsaw in 1927. He gave the premiere of the Khachaturian Concerto, which was dedicated to him. He was the teacher of Ashkenazy at the Moscow Conservatory. His performances were square and solid.

JOHN OGDON

b. 1937 — England

After studies at the Royal Manchester College of Music, he worked with Denis Matthews and Egon Petri. In 1962 he tied with Ashkenazy at the International Tchaikovsky Competition in Moscow. Ogdon also composes, and has recorded his own piano concerto—a splashy, eclectic piece of virtuosity.

Ogdon is a formidable talent of great power; he can play with elephantine strength. He is attracted by works that demand endurance. He can toss off a program that includes the twelve Liszt *Transcendental Etudes,* followed by smaller pieces and concluding with the Liszt Sonata. His propensity for the grandiose has led him to such compositions as Ronald Stevenson's eighty-minute *Passacaglia on D S C H* and Messiaen's two-hour-long *Vingt Regards sur l'Enfant Jésus,* or the Alkan Sonata and the colossal Busoni Concerto; he has recorded the latter with flair.

At his best, Ogdon plays in a lusty manner, though his stage playing is generally more representative of his powers than his recordings, which can tend to be a bit raggedy. He has consistently sought out worthy and neglected scores, such as the concertos of Cyril Scott, Michael Tippett, Peter Mennin, and Malcolm Williamson. His disc of Nielsen's piano music, especially the great Piano Suite dedicated to Schnabel, has an austere beauty.

ADÈLE AUS DER OHE

1864–1937 — Germany

A student of Kullak and Liszt. She pursued a successful concert career and also composed. She played the Tchaikovsky Piano Concerto No. 1 at the Carnegie Hall inaugural concerts in 1891, with Tchaikovsky conducting. The composer loved her performance; however, she refused to accept any applause for herself.

GARRICK OHLSSON

b. 1948 — United States

He studied with Sascha Gorodnitzki and Rosina Lhévinne at the Juilliard School. In 1966 he won the Busoni Competition, and soon after, he took the first prize at the Montreal International Competition. In 1970 he became the first American to win the Chopin

Competition. Ohlsson is thus assumed to be a prime Chopinist and, in fact, his Chopin discs are worth hearing, especially a spacious and free-wheeling E minor Concerto. In the Nocturnes we find a pretty Chopin, slightly dandified. His recordings of the Polonaises are strong but without any internal passion. In Liszt's *Funérailles* and *Mephisto Waltz* Ohlsson displays a large style, with little feeling of urgency. In the Brahms concerti, especially the D minor, he is convincing and at ease. His Brahms *Paganini* Variations is played with evident pleasure and a fine-tuned technique. There is a Rachmaninoff transcription album which shows him at his best—exuberant and technically light and airy in such difficult pieces as the Scherzo from Mendelssohn's *A Midsummer Night's Dream*. His performance of the Rachmaninoff Third Concerto is astounding in its note-perfectness, although it is dry and passionless. Recently, he gave a fabulous performance of the Busoni concerto, a blockbuster of a score, built for the extreme punishment required from a modern piano.

URSULA OPPENS
b. 1944 — United States

She studied with Rosina Lhévinne at Juilliard. Since winning the Busoni Competition in 1969, Oppens has toured in America and Europe, becoming best known for deft readings of contemporary scores. She gave the premiere of Rzewski's effective and huge set of variations, *The People United Will Never Be Defeated*.

NICOLAS ORLOV
1892–1964 — Russia

He studied with Igumnov at the Moscow Conservatory, and had a large European career. His best playing was in the Romantics.

LEO ORNSTEIN
b. 1895 — Russia

Studied at the St. Petersburg Conservatory and came to the United States in 1906. He made a New York debut in 1911, then toured in the United States and Europe, where his music was both denounced and defended fiercely. "His own music," said Henry Cowell, "startled the world with his unheard-of discords and his renunciations of form." Ornstein played his *Danse sauvage* for Theodor Leschetizky, who thought it was a bad joke. But the brilliant American critic Paul Rosenfeld, hearing Ornstein, wrote: "Always one senses the pavements stretching between steel buildings, the black hurrying tide of human beings, and through it all the oppressed figure of one searching out the meaning of all this convulsive activity." In addition to his own music, Ornstein programmed all that was new, including Ravel, Schoenberg, Busoni, Bartók, and Scriabin.

Ornstein made a big impression as a pianist, but retired from the concert stage before he was forty. He has continued to compose throughout his long life, his work varying greatly from his violent, "futuristic" early music. *A la chinoise,* Op. 39, dedicated to Rudolph Ganz, is a work with glissandi and clusters, and *The Three Moods* (1913) are considered by the composer himself to be "as graphic and exciting pieces as I have ever written." The Piano Sonata No. 4 harks back to the composer's Russian upbringing.

RAFAEL OROZCO
b. 1946 — Spain

He studied with Cubiles in Madrid, later receiving some lessons from Alexis Weissenberg. Orozco was the victor at the 1966 Leeds Competition. His recording of the Chopin

193

Preludes is expressive and technically excellent. His Third Rachmaninoff Concerto shows a real identification with the idiom.

CRISTINA ORTIZ
b. 1950 — Brazil

Studied in Paris with Magda Tagliaferro, later with Rudolf Serkin. In 1969 she was the winner of the Van Cliburn Competition, and has since appeared throughout the world. She plays with sparkle and graciousness.

GEORGE A. OSBORNE
1806–1893 — Ireland

In Paris he studied with Kalkbrenner and became a good friend of Chopin. Osborne held his own as a virtuoso in the glittering Paris of the 1830s. In 1843 he moved to London, where he became a fixture of the city's musical life. His well-written drawing-room pieces were popular. The best known of them is *La Pluie des perles*, Op. 61.

CÉCILE OUSSET
b. 1936 — France

She studied with Marcel Ciampi and won various prizes before embarking on a concert career. Ousset's recordings show a remarkable finger technique. Her Chopin has some graceful playing mixed with glibness. She is best in such scores as Saint-Saëns's *Allegro appassionato,* where her inherent dryness and nimbleness are heard to advantage.

LOUIS PABST
1840–1903 — Germany

He had an important career as a teacher and founded the Melbourne Academy of Music in Australia, where he taught the young Percy Grainger. In Russia, he was the teacher of Tina Lerner, Liapunov, Alexander Goldenweiser, and many others.

PAUL PABST
1854–1897 — Germany

The brother of Louis Pabst, a brilliant pianist, student of Liszt, and the teacher of Konstantin Igumnov at the Moscow Conservatory. He wrote beautifully for the instrument, especially transcriptions. A very elaborate one on Tchaikovsky's opera *Eugene*

Onegin was recently revived in recital by Cherkassky.

VLADIMIR DE PACHMANN
1848–1933 — Russia

He was mostly self-taught until he went to Vienna, at eighteen, to study with Joseph Dachs. Soon after, in 1869, he made a debut in his native Odessa, and continued to perform until he heard Carl Tausig, whose playing drove him into seclusion, where he worked with untiring fortitude. He emerged again in 1882, and developed a huge career. De Pachmann was among the half-dozen most famous pianists at the turn of the century. He was born one year before Chopin died, and he was the earliest-born pianist to have his fame substantially enhanced by a large number of recordings. His career was almost as successful in the United States as it was in Europe.

At his peak, from the 1880s until around 1905, de Pachmann was an elegant stylist, skimming over the keys, light as air. In Chopin, he played with an ethereal pianissimo, which he felt represented what Chopin's playing would have been like. "It was all miniature," wrote James Huneker, "without passion or pathos or the grand manner, but in its genre his playing was perfection, the polished perfection of an intricately carved ornament.... De Pachmann played certain sides of Chopin incomparably, capriciously, even perversely.... If in the mood, a recital by him was something unforgettable." Later, Huneker dubbed him the "Pianissimist" and also the "Chopinzee." De Pachmann had a perverse streak which often prevailed, and as the years went by, his recitals became a combination of eccentric and bizarre rhythmic aberrations, moments of inspiration, and all sorts of public antics, which audiences loved but which did him harm among his colleagues.

Sir Landon Ronald said to Rachmaninoff, who had somehow never heard him, "You ought to hear him once, because he is different from anyone else in the world." But the stern Rachmaninoff was by no means amused by de Pachmann's clownish persona. Even in an age when the composer's wishes were changed with ease, de Pachmann was a textual infidel. At his worst, he thought each new phrase demanded a new rhythm. The connoisseur must sift through his recordings, but the search is fascinating, for de Pachmann had a flair, a devilish humor—as in his own ending for Chopin's celebrated *Butterfly* Etude—but there was also a deeply poetic nature, a rarefied talent.

De Pachmann had the kind of mercurial temperament that has been largely eradicated in present-day piano playing. He took chances, and often they are musically miscalculated. Nevertheless, he was a fabulous craftsman, capable of playing the Chopin-Godowsky etude paraphrases. Although his best playing came before the birth of recording, his recorded output shows a finely tuned pianist who often lost his artistic equipoise.

IGNACY JAN PADEREWSKI
1860–1941 — Poland

In his youth, he taught at the Warsaw Conservatory, but played very little in public. In his twenty-fourth year, he decided to become a concert pianist, and he went to work with the famous Leschetizky, who tried to discourage him because, although he was a good pianist, Paderewski lacked repertoire and a virtuoso technique. But nothing could dissuade him from his goal, and he toiled relentlessly at the piano. He made his debut in Vienna three years after his first lesson with Leschetizky, appearing at a concert with the famous soprano Pauline Lucca—and he was a sensation. From that moment forward, Paderewski was to become the most fabled pianist of his epoch, one of the greatest performing artists ever, as well as the biggest box-office attraction in the history of the piano. To this day, no pianist has played live before more people than Paderewski.

From his first appearances in America in 1891, he was idolized, lovingly called "Paderooski." If the town had a piano, Paderewski, traveling in his private railroad car, would get there. As Liszt had broadened the concert life of Europe, it was "Paddy" who opened the doors to the large American public wanting "culture." Year after year people traveled for hundreds of miles to hear him. His arrival in even a small town sparked celebrations, mayor's speeches, brass bands in renditions of his Minuet in G. He played tirelessly and constantly, his huge programs often lasting up to three hours. Once, in a very small town, he played with a painful finger injury. Asked why he didn't cancel, Paderewski bluntly answered, "I may never come this way again. I couldn't disappoint them."

Paderewski's looks greatly contributed to his aura. In Australia, the young violinist Daisy Kennedy wrote, "This is the most poetic looking pianist I am ever likely to see." He possessed a Swinburnian beauty, with a halo of abundant auburn hair which crowned a presence that is exquisitely captured in Sir Edward Burne-Jones's silverpoint drawing of the pianist. He was the poet-pianist incarnate, the personification of the Pre-Raphaelite image of beauty. Never had there been a more glorious stage presence. He bewitched his audiences with his golden sound and his languorous rubato.

In the 1890s, he was accused of piano pounding and his fortissimos were considered

shattering and often ugly. "It is not his fault," said Henry T. Finck, the important New York critic, "but the fault of his instrument. No piano has ever been built, or ever will be built, which can be converted into the instrument Paderewski demands." During his early period, Paderewski produced, in Finck's words, "tidal waves of sound, cyclonic climaxes." Because of his popularity during those years, he was forced to play in auditoriums far larger than those in which his colleagues were accustomed to performing. During his best years, from 1890 through 1905, Paderewski possessed a seminal strength which he did not always channel. This, along with an inordinate desire to please the public, produced the banging effects. Most often, however, his playing was lauded. Perhaps this period was best summed up by the critic Richard Aldrich: "He touched the deepest and tenderest feelings and tugged irresistibly at the heart-strings of a whole people. He seemed to speak a new language in music; he raised its poetry, its magic, its mystery, its romantic eloquence, to a higher power than his listeners had known. There was a beauty of line as well as of color and atmosphere, a poignance of phrase, a quality of tone, a lyrical accent such, so it seemed, as to make of his playing something never till then quite divined."

By 1910, the endless rounds of touring made piano playing a burden for Paderewski, but he had formed and become dependent on a regal life-style, and only through performing was it possible for him to maintain it. During the early 1900s, though, he began to fulfill himself through composition, and he spent long periods of time on a Piano Sonata in E-flat minor, a massive opera, *Manru,* and a Mahler-sized Symphony in B minor, as well as other works, including a fine set of Variations and Fugue, Op. 23. But composing, too, was not enough for such a temperament, and he needed one great outlet to fulfill his destiny of Artist as Romantic Hero. From his earliest years, Paderewski had been a passionate patriot. He yearned for a free Poland. His Romantic patriotism was further inflamed by the failure of the Western European nations to understand Poland's plight. He had become a symbol to the throngs of Poles flocking to his concerts throughout the United States, and soon Paderewski perfected his oratory in ardent patriotic speeches. When the Great War broke out, Paderewski helped organize an army of twenty-two thousand Poles, who were trained in Canada and who would fight with the Allies. He spent his entire personal fortune on the Polish cause, and became the very spirit of his oppressed homeland. He achieved an extraordinary degree of world prestige. He was greeted with awe wherever he went. Wilson, Clemenceau, and Lloyd George admired his diplomatic powers. It was Paderewski who signed for his nation in the Versailles Conference, and his influence there was great in the organizing of a free Poland. After the war, he triumphantly became the first premier of Poland.

The strain of post–World War I politics became too brutal for him, however, and after an assassination attempt, he stepped down from office. He was now more than a musician: he was a world leader, a spiritual force, and no man ever played his part with greater nobility.

He returned to the piano after years of neglect. The piano had always been a monumental struggle for him. His mechanism was not a natural one, and he worked pitiably to achieve what he wanted. His playing was long past its glory; far greater technicians such as Hofmann, Rachmaninoff, Friedman, Backhaus, and Godowsky were at their peak, and soon the young Horowitz would compete for his market. But the crowds kept coming. He remained, in the words of Marguerite Long, "the sovereign of the piano . . . everything in his makeup, as in his art, was noble and grand." He played through the 1920s and 1930s; in 1936 he acted and played in a film,

Moonlight Sonata, which presented the first successful recording of the piano's sound on the screen.

Old and frail, Paderewski was still playing the piano when again catastrophe befell his nation in 1939. Everything he earned was poured into helping Poland during World War II, until his death in 1941. The funeral service at St. Patrick's Cathedral was attended by thousands. President Roosevelt ordered special burial at Arlington National Cemetery.

Paderewski the pianist lived in an age when individuality was prized; it was also musically an era of self-indulgence, when the performer was king. Most audiences were more concerned with personality than with great music. Lighter pieces by the great composers were often preferable to the difficult-to-digest works. It was easy for an artist simply to stop listening to himself when the majority in the audience wanted the shallow, cheap thrill, and charm at any cost. At his worst, Paderewski was almost as self-indulgent as de Pachmann, and his colleagues were often scathing in their comments. "Paderewski," a fellow pianist muttered, "did everything well except play the piano."

After 1910, his art painfully declined; he became stylistically artificial and insular. His interpretations were often marred by mannerisms, and by one in particular—not playing the hands together. However, many still heard the poetry that was always somewhere apparent. Pearl Records has issued five volumes of his recorded art. (He began recording in 1911, at the age of fifty-one, and was to the early days of piano performance on record what Caruso was to the vocal world.) Listening now to the many recordings he made, one can hear his subtle musicality in many melting phrases of sheer beauty, in small pieces by Schumann, for instance, such as *Warum?* and *Des Abends.* He was not the technical weakling his detractors liked to believe. One has only to listen to his Liszt F minor Concert Etude to hear his deft fingerwork. And there is

197

always a quality of heroism in his Chopin. The *Revolutionary* Etude was more to him than a turbulent "study" for the left hand; it meant faith in humanity. Paderewski had been called "the heart of Poland," and this quality comes through clearly on the ancient recording.

MARIA THERESA PARADIS
1759–1824 — Austria

She was blind from childhood. Paradis was an early pianist who attained considerable success. Mozart composed his B-flat Concerto K. 456 for her, and she was heard in France and England. She composed a great deal.

LEE PATTISON
1890–1966 — United States

He studied with Schnabel, played and taught, and was best known for his duo-piano work with Guy Maier. John Browning studied with him.

ERNST PAUER
1826–1905 — Austria

An important pianist who studied with Mozart's son, Franz Xaver Mozart (1791–1844). He made a reputation in London, where he taught at the Royal Academy of Music. He gave some of the first historical recitals and arranged a great many Classical symphonies for four hands. A. J. Hipkins wrote, "As a pianist, his style was distinguished by breadth and nobility of tone, and by a sentiment in which seriousness of thought was blended with profound respect for the intention of the composer."

MAX PAUER
1866–1945 — England

He studied with his father and developed into a fine artist, making many editions of the music of Schumann and Beethoven.

LEONARD PENNARIO
b. 1924 — United States

He studied with Guy Maier and with Isabelle Vengerova, making his New York debut in 1943. Miklós Rózsa dedicated his Piano Concerto to him; Pennario premiered it in 1967 and then recorded it. He has also played chamber music with Heifetz.

Pennario has been making records steadily since nearly the inception of the LP, and they have sold well. His repertoire is large and leans mostly to the Romantics, and he is rather colorful when exposed to the Khachaturian Concerto or other "juicy" Romantic staples. Pennario is musicianly, with a razor-sharp technique, but perhaps he is basically a remarkable sight-reader—able to devour a new score whole but unable to sustain his involvement with it. Often, a Pennario performance sounds just slightly bored—always extremely competent, yet musically held in check. There is something essentially glib in his work; he adds little of himself to the music. Still, when the music really suits him, especially in lighter fare like Saint-Saëns's *Etude in the Form of a Waltz,* Litolff's Scherzo, or Gottschalk, he can smile and have a jolly good time. He is especially well suited to the Gottschalk idiom. His performance of that remarkable piece of Civil War rhetoric, *L'Union,* Op. 48, dedicated to General McClellan, is played with dash and humor, as Pennario tosses off bushels of octaves with the greatest aplomb.

ERNST PERABO
1845–1920 — Germany

At the Leipzig Conservatory he studied with Moscheles. Later, he had a sizable career as a pianist and teacher in the United States, settling in Boston. He taught Amy Cheney (later to be known as the composer Mrs. H. H. A. Beach).

MURRAY PERAHIA
b. 1947 — United States

He studied with Jeannette Haien and Mieczyslaw Horszowski. In 1972 he won the Leeds Competition; in 1975 he was the first recipient of the Avery Fisher Award. He toured Japan for the first time in 1977. His career has blossomed into one of the largest and most important of his generation.

Among the pianists of his time, Perahia seems to be the most universally admired. His concerts invariably receive rave reviews, and his lyrical playing has been thought to resemble Dinu Lipatti's. His phrasing flows, bends easily, and flowers with a natural impulse. His work is never marred by idiosyncrasies, nor is there the slightest desire to "wow" an audience. Indeed, his art is best fulfilled in a more intimate setting, and he hates to overproject. Perahia has a subtle ear, and each sonority is pure; his pedaling is always clean and yet full. He displays a childlike quality in the *Papillons* of Schumann; a depth of understanding in the *Fantasiestücke* Op. 12; an elegiac beauty of expression in the *Symphonic Etudes*. His later disc of the Schumann Fantasy finds him a bit constrained in the wilderness of the first two movements, but in the finale he unrolls layers of tonal beauty with acute concentration and vocal plasticity.

Perahia is essentially a "vocal" artist and it is no wonder that he has a strong affinity with Schubert, which will undoubtedly deepen during his career. He plays the lyric Impromptus wonderfully, but is not at home in the dramatic thunder of the *Wanderer* Fantasy.

Chopin is one of the highlights of Perahia's repertoire. His early recording of the B-flat minor and B minor Sonatas is beautifully wrought, though still tentative stylistically. It is not really an intimate Chopin, nor does he capture the grandeur of these compositions. He hits his stride in the Preludes—the ideal Chopin for his poetic nature. In this recording, Perahia's technical mechanism is more refined than ever, perfectly honed. His later recorded Chopin, especially the Barcarolle, has a beautiful finish. James Methuen-Campbell, in his book *Chopin Playing,* writes: "Perahia is a near-perfect Chopin player. . . . His grasp of the vital place of counterpoint in Chopin's style also helps to give his playing a depth of understanding that many others lack."

Perahia's best-selling albums have been his luminous readings of the complete Mozart concerti. Here his singing tone, vocal phrasing, true feeling for chamber music, as well as his command of spacious form find their ideal outlet. Perahia is never afraid to play Mozart with depth of tone and warmth. His Mozart has a sense of satisfaction and well-being though it lacks any of the Mozartian operatic flavor.

In Beethoven, his finest playing is in the earlier sonatas, such as the Op. 7 in E-flat, Op. 10, No. 3 in D major, and Op. 22 in B-flat. Here everything is balanced and vibrant. His slow movement of Op. 7 is riveting—music built out of silence. With Perahia, each rest is as important as each note, and his pathos in the slow movement of the Op. 10, No. 3 can move an audience to tears. In later sonatas, as in Opp. 81a and 110, he is somewhat reticent, although there are signs in his live performances that Perahia is beginning to project a larger picture of many works that he has previously recorded.

Mendelssohn is another composer whom Perahia finds congenial. He puts on a delightful, zestful performance of the G minor Con-

199

certo, and his recording of Mendelssohn's little-known and impressive Sonata Op. 6 is played with weight and character. The recording also contains a dynamic and highly charged *Variations sérieuses,* a suave Prelude and Fugue in E minor, and a surprisingly earthbound *Rondo capriccioso.*

Perahia has not explored much modern repertoire. But his Bartók disc is unusual, nonpercussive, and his playing of the *Improvisations,* Op. 20, is soulful.

VLADO PERLEMUTER
b. 1904 — Lithuania

He studied at the Paris Conservatoire and with Cortot. He has had a long career in Europe and has continued to record the Romantic and impressionist repertoire. His performances of Ravel have been appreciated, and within the Chopin literature, many consider him a master. His interpretations have directness coupled with originality in phrasing. Unfortunately, he was never a big technician, and his late recordings, such as the Chopin Preludes and Etudes, show a sloweddown technique which hampers the execution of his musical intentions.

EDWARD BAXTER PERRY
1855–1924 — United States

A blind pianist who studied with Kullak, Clara Schumann, and Liszt. In the United States, he was famous for his lecture-recital format and was highly regarded.

JOHN PERRY
b. 1935 — United States

A student of Cecile Genhart. A prizewinner in several international competitions, Perry has performed extensively, and has achieved renown as a teacher at various institutions.

EGON PETRI
1881–1962 — Germany

He studied with Teresa Carreño as a child. In composition, he worked with Draeseke. His main influence was Busoni, with whom he was associated until Busoni's death. Petri made his debut in 1902. In 1905 he taught in Manchester at the Royal College of Music; thereafter he held various teaching positions.

In 1932, Petri made his American debut; he was revered in this country, teaching at Cornell University and Mills College in California. Like Busoni, Petri did not cultivate charm or sensuous beauty in his playing. His approach was clearheaded, black upon white, and always monumental. He played the large-scale works most happily, and he had an immense musical authority, which disregarded snobbery. When Liszt's transcriptions were frowned upon, Petri played them and was dazzling. Like Busoni, he had the greatest faith in Liszt's music. He was capable of the most fabulous deeds of technical daring in the *Transcendental Etudes,* which he programmed complete.

Petri was never afraid of the esoteric, and was an even greater champion of the gargantuan piano music of Alkan than Busoni had been. Of course, Petri played Busoni as an article of faith. The solo music and the Concerto were made for him, and his performances of the *Fantasia contrappuntistica* always caused excitement, displaying intellectual and musical powers of a high order. His recording is ideal.

Beethoven was the jewel in the crown of his repertoire; his mighty approach to music was naturally suited to this master. His Beethoven is carved in stone, with fierce determination. His interpretations of the Sonata Op. 90, of the *Hammerklavier,* and of Op. 111 are stark tonepaintings. He was inhibited and less successful in the songful late Sonatas Opp. 109 and 110.

In 1923, Petri visited the Soviet Union, the first Western musician to play there after the Revolution. During his first tour, he played thirty-one times in forty days. His playing had a real impact. Soviet audiences had never heard such a graphic rendering of materials; his forceful intellectuality was simply outside their tradition of Romantic emotive playing. Wise teachers such as Heinrich Neuhaus were deeply impressed. Even in old age, Petri's technique remained superlative. One of his last recordings was a performance of Busoni's piano reduction of Liszt's *Mephisto Waltz* in the orchestral version. Liszt, Busoni, and Petri—the three were perfectly in accord, confident that the piano could do anything.

ISIDOR PHILIPP
1863–1958 — Hungary

He was brought to Paris at the age of three, and studied with Georges Mathias at the Conservatoire, where he won first prize in piano playing in 1883. He received much good counsel from Stephen Heller and was influenced by him. In 1890 he played in London, and he also became a well-known pianist in Paris. But he became more interested in teaching and in the mechanics of piano playing, and in 1893 he accepted a professorship of the piano at the Paris Conservatoire. In the next half-century, Philipp became one of the most important piano teachers in history. His list of students includes such luminaries as Ania Dorfmann, Jeanne-Marie Darré, Nikita Magaloff, Beveridge Webster, and Guiomar Novaes. He lived and taught in the United States from 1940, performing his last recital in 1955, in New York, with considerable skill. Philipp's technical exercises for the piano have true originality, and his own piano music contains many charming pages.

MARIA JOÃO PIRES
b. 1944 — Portugal

The most famous Portuguese pianist of the present time; she trained at the Lisbon Conservatory, later going to Munich to study with Karl Engel. Pires won several prizes, including first prize at the 1970 Beethoven Competition in Brussels. She is a much sought after performer, especially in Europe. Her Schumann playing is quite flexible, bordering dangerously on affectation in such works as the *Arabeske*. Her Chopin Preludes are calmer, though her technique is not large enough to encompass the heaviest demands of several, such as the B-flat minor, or the formidable hurdles of the Twenty-fourth Prelude. But she possesses strong ideas in her Chopin playing.

It is in Mozart that she is most comfortable. It is a smallish Mozart, often of exquisite taste, always technically well groomed and unpretentious. Her concerto performances are tidy, with slow movements that sing. Her conception of the turbulent D minor Concerto, No. 20, is, however, curiously pallid. In the piano sonatas, she is generally excellent, and she has recorded the entire cycle.

JOHANN PISHNA
1826–1896 — Czechoslovakia

He studied at Prague, taught there and in Russia. His technical studies are still used in the training of many young players.

JOHANN PETER PIXIS
1788–1874 — Germany

Studied with his father. Pixis settled in Paris in 1825, becoming well known as a teacher and pianist. He composed voluminously and had a definite melodic gift. He wrote the third piece in the *Hexaméron,* a work titled by Liszt, with contributions by such pianists as Liszt, Czerny, Thalberg, Chopin, and Herz.

LOUIS PLAIDY
1810–1874 — Germany

He began as a violinist, and changed, in 1831, to the piano, becoming one of the best-known teachers of his time. Sir Arthur Sullivan, who knew him in Leipzig, wrote, "This popularity arose from his remarkable gift (for it was a gift) of imparting technical power. Were a pupil ever so deficient in execution, under Plaidy's care his faults would disappear, his fingers grow strong, his touch become smooth, singing and equal, and slovenliness be replaced by neatness." In 1843 he was asked by Mendelssohn to teach at the newly formed Leipzig Conservatory. His technical studies are still occasionally used today.

FRANCIS PLANTÉ
1839–1934 — France

He studied with Marmontel and developed into one of the most formidable French pianists. He played in public at the age of seven and continued into his nineties, with a style that was spontaneous and fresh. He was among the first to popularize Mozart and Schumann in France. In 1928 he made a group of recordings, which made him the earliest-born pianist to put his art on disc. When Planté was eighty-one, Arthur Rubinstein heard him play "the [Chopin] Tarantelle with a perfect control of his fingers and with the élan of a young man."

MARIA FÉLICITÉ PLEYEL (née MOKE)
1811–1875 — France

She studied with Moscheles, Herz, and Kalkbrenner, later with Thalberg. She had a splendid career and was deeply admired by Chopin and also by Liszt, who dedicated his *Norma* paraphrase to her. Chopin dedicated his Nocturnes Op. 9 to her. Berlioz fell in love with her, but she married the piano builder Camille Pleyel. The critic Fétis thought her the most perfect of any pianist. From 1848 until 1872, she was the best-known teacher at the Brussels Conservatoire.

IVO POGORELICH
b. 1958 — Yugoslavia

He studied at the Central School of Music in Moscow and later with Yevgeny Malinin at the Moscow Conservatory. He won the first prize at the Casagrande Competition in Terni, Italy, in 1978, and won the Montreal Competition in 1980. But it was his highly publicized loss at the 1980 Chopin Competition in Warsaw that put him into the limelight. His controversial playing aroused commotion and dissent among the adjudicators, with Martha Argerich walking out of the jury when Pogorelich didn't get into the finals. Through the power of controversy and his own knack for publicity, Pogorelich has become the best-known competition contestant since Van Cliburn won the Tchaikovsky Competition the year Pogorelich was born. His loss damaged the validity of the competitions (and there is an ever-increasing number of these events) as a means of bringing forward outstanding talent. Pogorelich has flourished, however, becoming one of the idols of the musical world.

The chief influence on his musical development has been Alicia Kezeradze, a teacher and pianist of uncommon ability. Pogorelich began working with her as a teenager, and subsequently married her.

He is a pianist interested in playing music of all epochs, and he has not yet become typecast in any specific repertoire. Bach and Prokofiev are equally important to him, and he chooses what he plays with great care. His programming is unhackneyed; Pogorelich can make a Bach suite just as much as a Chopin sonata the highlight of his program.

His repertoire, however, is limited, with much repetition season after season. Though he is careful in what he presents publicly, he has not had time to record or learn much new music, because of his constant touring. He also, if in the mood, likes to play a long encore session, which becomes tedious. He seems to want his audience to hear everything he has ever learned, from *Für Elise* to long Chopin polonaises, to impeccably but too rigorously played Scarlatti sonatas.

The pre-Romantic literature is the most interesting of his playing. His Bach is certainly unconventional, and he is not frightened to let it loose on the modern Steinway with all its colors. Nothing is dry or pared down. He plays with feathery lightness, individual tempi, and widely arching phrasing in his Sarabandes from the Bach suites. His Haydn B minor Sonata contains a variety of tonal values, and the finale, with its gutsy humor, is played with Mendelssohnian airiness.

Pogorelich's Beethoven is both fascinating and maddening. It is certainly serious, often grimly so, and his slow movements are intricate, and air-tight. Yet he has many strange ideas, which are unexpected and often startlingly convincing. His Sonata in E minor, Op. 90, is built on a large framework in the first movement, and he has an amazing talent for the manipulation of time. The second movement, with its many repetitions of the theme, is held together without resorting to twitches or tugs. Pogorelich's hard-boiled view of Beethoven's lesser-known but equally great sonatas is illus-

trated in the Op. 22 in B-flat, where he takes the listener beyond the apparent charm of the work. It is not a likable reading, nor is his *Tempest Sonata,* so slow and dull. His dry, objective performance of the Sonata Op. 111 leaves one unfulfilled. Pogorelich, a master of pianistic polish and effect, cannot use his artifice in the valedictory second movement, which is consequently stagnant and unfeeling.

Pogorelich is not comfortable in Romantic music. He is inhibited in it and relies on an unconventional, often overblown approach. His Scriabin Second Sonata, *Poems,* and Etudes are straightlaced, stiff, and tasteless, with no sign at all of the music's eroticism. Nor is he a master colorist, and his Chopin, while sometimes refreshing, is stern, even puritanical. It is seldom saturated with youthful verve, and it can be pedantic, as in some etudes or the C-sharp minor Scherzo. His Chopin Polonaises in F-sharp minor and C minor are gloomy conceptions.

He is more conventional in the B-flat minor *Funeral March* Sonata, self-consciously attempting to bring new light and dark to the famous and banal march. The trio section is straightlaced; there are no angels singing in these Elysian fields. Of more interest is his Chopin B minor Sonata. Actually, Chopin would probably be stunned by it. It is not a beautiful reading, not at all warm or tender. But his conception is massive, with the last movement swelling to an enormous climax that Chopin's own Pleyel piano could never have achieved. Indeed, Pogorelich can bang a piano mercilessly and without depth; yet his actual sound is not naturally large, and he is stiff in body. The best of his Chopin playing, or the least riddled with exaggeration or pedantry, is the C-sharp minor Prelude Op. 45, with its tonal painting, and the Nocturne in E-flat Op. 55, No. 2, with each strand of the Chopin polyphony beautifully articulated and carefully pedaled.

Schumann is still a closed book to Pogorelich. His *Symphonic Etudes* sound strangely

203

academic, while the Toccata, as marvelously played as it is, sounds pedestrian and removed.

He is more comfortable in the early moderns. The little Debussy he plays lacks sensuality, but his Ravel *Gaspard de la nuit* is incomparable. The high craft and perversity of Ravel's piano writing suit Pogorelich. His *Ondine* is beautifully laid out, but a shade bland; in *Le Gibet,* however, one can feel the sun beating down, the tragedy is real. It is in *Scarbo,* the finale of this score, that the Yugoslav pianist is at his acme. It is a startling pyrotechnical portrait of the infamous Scarbo—preening, ironic, a dangerous scamp, even a necromancer. This is Pogorelich's finest achievement on disc, and in concert performance it never fails to overwhelm.

Prokofiev is Pogorelich's favored twentieth-century master. He plays the Sixth Sonata often, better in public than on his two recordings, which are slightly rigid and dry. In a recital, I heard him play the Third Prokofiev Sonata better than I've ever heard it played. It was like a newly discovered work. He realized aspects of the score that others have overlooked.

He is not a truly successful concerto player. Pogorelich needs the stage to himself. Conductors can only get in his way. His recording of the Chopin F minor is quite dull, and his ever-so-long Tchaikovsky concerto is near to caricature. But, as Donal Henahan wrote in the *New York Times,* "there is a large talent there somewhere, hidden under the fondness of exaggeration and the self-conscious effort to be an original. And with his Van Cliburn height and rock-star sullenness, the Yugoslav is someone an audience cannot easily ignore. He presents a vivid picture on stage, with his long, spidery fingers and way of attacking the keys that suggests Dracula about to descend on a succulent neck. No one sleeps through Pogorelich's performances, at least."

Yes, he can rile the listener, and he does the unexpected. And at his best he makes many listeners feel that here is important playing, that his way is new and not a rehash of a thousand insipid interpretations one has heard over and over. He seems to be his own source, and this makes for a concert that one can either love or hate.

DANIEL POLLACK
b. 1935 — United States

He studied in Los Angeles with Ethel Leginska and later at Juilliard with Rosina Lhévinne. Pollack made his New York debut in 1957; the following year he was a prizewinner at the first International Tchaikovsky Competition, at which Van Cliburn won first prize. In subsequent years he has performed in the Soviet Union, China, and South America, and has made a number of recordings; especially notable are an energetic Barber Sonata, a heavily somber Liszt *Funérailles,* and a joyous Beethoven Sonata Op. 79.

FRANCESCO POLLINI
1763–1846 — Austria

He studied with Mozart and developed into a pianist with an excellent technique. In 1809 he became professor of piano playing at the Milan Conservatory. He produced a great deal of piano music and is credited with being the first piano composer to notate his music using three staves. This procedure is found in his 1820 *Trentadue esercizi in forma di toccata.* In his preface, the composer explains, "I propose to offer a simple melody more or less plain, and of varied character, combined with accompaniments of varied rhythms, from which it can be clearly distinguished by a particular expression and touch in the cantilena in contrast to the accompaniment."

MAURIZIO POLLINI
b. 1942 — Italy

He studied at the Milan Conservatory. In Warsaw in 1960, at the age of eighteen, he walked off with the first prize at the International Chopin Competition; the jury included Magda Tagliaferro, Heinrich Neuhaus, Nadia Boulanger, and Arthur Rubinstein. "Pollini," said Rubinstein, "showed a complete supremacy over the others." Later he worked with Michelangeli.

Pollini is the most important Italian pianist of the generation after the Second World War. Shortly after the Chopin Competition, he recorded a poetic Chopin E minor Concerto, which remains some of his finest Chopin playing, and which gave promise of even finer achievements. He withdrew from public performance for several years, however, and the Pollini who has since emerged is a very different artist from the one heard in the Chopin concerto. He developed into a ferociously abstract and hard-boiled player, with the most comprehensive technical equipment of our time, and a ravenous musical mind which can encompass all styles, from Bach to Nono. Indeed, for the younger generation of pianists, he is already a cult figure with an enormous influence. One may hear the obvious aspects of his style being imitated at competitions throughout the world, albeit without Pollini's aristocratic intellectual gifts. The modern pianist's ideal is not the leonine, heaven-storming artist stemming from Anton Rubinstein; not the expressive, intellectual, and snobbish player of the Schnabel school; nor the hypnotic poet-virtuoso exemplified by Paderewski, Rubinstein, and Horowitz. Today's ideal is Pollini—the cool and impassive striver for elemental perfection. He is the "state of the art" pianist. His playing is as sleek and elegant as a stainless-steel skyscraper.

Yet, in music that screams for a personal touch, such as Chopin's Preludes and Etudes, the Brahms concerti, Schubert sonatas, and all of Schumann, his unblemished playing sounds antiseptic and driven, with structures so tight that the concert room becomes airless. There is no pause for a moment of impulse. Pollini is never Italianate and, above all, never smiles. He seems to lack a vital imagination; everything sounds like a single conception—one style for all. However, his sense of architecture is great. In fact, there is no pianist today with finer organizational powers than Pollini. He can make Schubert sonatas, which wilt in the hands of many pianists, successful on a structural level, or realize the grandeur of Schumann's F-sharp minor Sonata without losing an audience's attention.

Pollini's programs are always intriguing, and never pander to popularity. He offers severe chunks of music, or one-composer programs. A constant and tireless learner, he has added to his public agenda an evening with Book I of Bach's *Well-Tempered Clavier*, which he performs flawlessly. For this listener, the humanity was missing, but surely the plasticity of the counterpoint and the purebred pianism were more than enough for satisfaction. After countless Pollini recitals, I no longer expect to be moved, but astonished by his intellect and coldly compulsive passion. Season after season, one hears relentless performances—his fingers are like laser beams. His playing presents no color, no sexuality, no brooding. I like best his prickly Debussy, his mordant Bartók, his Schoenberg, Webern, and an astounding Boulez Second Sonata, which can even bring down the house.

Pollini's audiences are among the best in the world. They realize that he is a great musician and that he sounds the note of authenticity. Pollini on stage is a lesson in high concentration. He is seated very low, and it seems that rays of energy emanate from his brow as he presents a Beethoven *Hammerklavier* of awesome dimensions, with an unequaled unraveling of the fugue. A great part of the satisfaction at a Pollini concert comes from his unbelievable technical security, reminiscent of that of the best high-tech CD recordings, edited to a hair. Modern audiences are used to this in their listening and find a profound and pure satisfaction in him. One never hears the comment "I like him better on recordings," which is heard so frequently regarding other artists. He can toss off an entire set of Chopin etudes without a scratch, while mere mortal pianists can only dream of the depth of his technical skill in Debussy's Twelve Etudes or in Stravinsky's *Petrouchka*.

JEAN-BERNARD POMMIER
b. 1944 — France

He studied in Paris at the Conservatoire. Pommier has a penchant for Chopin and Mozart. His playing has received acclaim.

MICHAEL PONTI
b. 1937 — Germany

Ponti studied in Washington, D.C. Early on he won prizes in several competitions, and in 1964 he took the first prize in Bolzano at the Busoni Competition. In 1970 he began a series of recordings of lesser-known composers, which earned him a reputation. His New York debut in 1972 included an encore sheet, from which encores were to be selected by audience request.

Ponti has prodigious strength; he must be a compulsive practicer. How else does one gulp down such meaty chunks of repertoire—so many unknown concertos, etudes, fugitive pieces, as well as the complete piano music of Tchaikovsky and Scriabin, albums of Rachmaninoff, Thalberg, Henselt, Moscheles, Scharwenka, and Alkan, and a truckload of piano transcriptions from Grainger to Pabst. I hope he had fun learning them. I know I find pleasure in listening to this harvest of goodies that had been stacked away and forgotten, and

this valuable music sheds light on the history of piano writing in the nineteenth century.

Ponti's performances are technically equal to the greatest demands, but he is dreadfully uneven. He does not always use his enormous strength and technique with wisdom, and musically he can be anxious and slipshod. Then, too, there is a nagging tendency to bang his instrument, resulting in ugly and brittle sound. His Scriabin Sonatas, for instance, were too quickly learned; they needed more time for maturation. Scriabin's essential nervosity becomes merely breathless in Ponti's rendering, which is nearly always too fast and flurried. This is a problem with many Ponti performances. In the course of extended listening, one will find that many works have a stylistic sameness in his hands. In his attempt to approximate a certain type of Romantic performance style of the past, he forgets to be himself. This is not always the case, and, surprisingly, in standard repertoire he comes out best. His *Petrouchka* or Brahms *Paganini* Variations, his Chopin Etudes, and his Liszt are well balanced and idiomatic. In recent years, he has also played much chamber music, which has helped harness his solo playing, giving it more point and discipline. Overall, Ponti plays with freshness and phenomenal bravura, and with a rare, often infectious enthusiasm for his work.

CIPRIANI POTTER
1792–1871 — England

He studied in London with his father and for five years with Beethoven's early rival Joseph Wölfl. He later befriended Beethoven, who thought he had talent for composition. Potter was a fine performer who gave the English premieres of Beethoven's Piano Concerti Nos. 3 and 4. He composed twenty-nine opus numbers, including two sonatas, two toccatas, and two sets of studies. In 1855, Wagner conducted one of Potter's works in London.

LEV POUISHNOV
1891–1958 — Russia

A student of Essipova, he won the Rubinstein Prize at the St. Petersburg Conservatory in 1910. He concertized and taught piano in Tiflis for several years. After the Revolution, he lived in England, touring in Europe and the United States. His specialty was Chopin, and much to the surprise of his colleagues, he advertised himself as "the greatest Chopin player in the world."

JOHN POWELL
1882–1963 — United States

He studied in Richmond, Virginia, and with Leschetizky in Vienna for five years. His debut took place in Berlin in 1907, followed by performances in Germany, France, and England. In 1913 he returned to the United States, where he established a career as both pianist and composer. In 1914 his sixty-minute *Sonata Teutonica* was premiered in London by Moiseiwitsch, and his 1919 *Rapsodie nègre* for Piano and Orchestra was the most widely performed work of its kind until Gershwin's *Rhapsody in Blue*.

LOUIS PRADÈRE
1781–1843 — France

Studied at the Paris Conservatoire, where he became professor in 1802. He was a father figure of early French pianism and was the teacher of Henri Herz. He composed sonatas and a concerto.

MENAHEM PRESSLER
b. 1928 — United States

A fine pianist with a dependable facility. His recording of the Shostakovich Preludes is characteristic of his best playing. He taught at Indiana University and is a member of the well-known Beaux Arts Trio.

ANDRÉ PREVIN
b. 1929 — Germany

Previn, the brilliant conductor and composer, is a pianist of quality, ranging from jazz to Mozart concerti, which he conducts from the piano. His performances of Gershwin's Concerto in F have flair and bounce.

SERGEI PROKOFIEV
1891–1953 — Russia

Prokofiev's contribution to the literature of the piano is of immense value. His Third Piano Concerto undoubtedly is the most often performed twentieth-century concerto, and his own recording of the work reveals Prokofiev as a brilliant performer, with strength, individual sound, and a virtuoso technique. The most characteristic aspect of his playing is a vibrant rhythmic sense. In public, he played only his own music—music which, of course, makes great demands on any pianist. Prokofiev's early training was at the St. Petersburg Conservatory, where he studied with the great teacher Annette Essipova, which means that Prokofiev was well grounded in the Leschetizky manner. For his graduation, his program included his own First Piano Concerto and Liszt's transcription of Wagner's *Tannhäuser* Overture.

JOSEF PROKSCH
1794–1864 — Czechoslovakia

A blind pianist who composed, played concerts, and founded a piano academy, which survived into the 1930s, in Prague. Smetana studied piano with him.

DIONYS PRUCKNER
1834–1896 — Germany

A student of Liszt, he was a well-known pianist, teacher, and editor.

ÉMILE PRUDENT
1817–1863 — France

He worked at the Paris Conservatoire with Zimmerman, winning first prize in piano playing. He became one of the most popular French pianists of the day—a brilliant and pleasing player of mainly his own works, which include many operatic fantasies, etudes, and a B-flat Concerto, premiered by Prudent in London in 1848.

RAOUL PUGNO
1852–1914 — France

He worked with the Chopin pupil Georges Mathias and developed into a pianist of world stature. Pugno was one of the first major exponents of Mozart in France, and his elegant style in this composer was much extolled. He played Chopin with a fleet-fingered virtuosity, and his interpretations are preserved on early recordings. He was the first to play Grieg's Concerto in France, as well as in St. Petersburg, and was a prolific composer in many forms. For piano, he composed a sonata and a set of four pieces, *Les Nuits*.

JUAN PUJOL
1835–1898 — Spain

The father of the Spanish school of piano playing and the most famous Catalán piano teacher; his pupils were Ricardo Viñes, Enrique Granados, and Joaquin Maláts. The Catalán tradition is distinguished by an overall sense of improvisation and color, yet with a stress on clarity as well.

ANNE QUEFFELEC
b. 1948 — France

She studied at the Paris Conservatoire, achieving the first prize in piano in 1965. A winner of prizes at the Leeds and Munich Competitions, she has toured extensively and recorded. Her Liszt playing is particularly appealing.

SERGEI RACHMANINOFF

1873–1943 — Russia

After early training, at the age of ten he went to study with Zverev. Later, at the Moscow Conservatory, he worked with his brilliant cousin Alexander Siloti. As a teenager, he played for Anton Rubinstein, whose own playing left an ineradicable impression on him. Although Rachmaninoff was one of the most brilliant pianistic talents at the Conservatory, his introverted nature turned more toward composition, and he achieved early fame with the success of his Prelude in C-sharp minor, Op. 3, No. 2, a work whose very popularity later plagued the composer. He called the piece the "It" Prelude, since after each concert the audience would chant "Play it." By 1905 he had written much exceptional music, including the glorious Second Piano Concerto, composed after several years of extreme depression. During the first decade of the century, he was also utilizing his conducting skills, and became a noted operatic conductor. In 1909 he began his first tour of the United States, for which he wrote his Third Concerto—a work of monumental technical difficulty, which Rachmaninoff said was composed for elephants. He dedicated it to Josef Hofmann, but the great pianist never essayed it publicly. Rachmaninoff premiered it in New York with Walter Damrosch and performed it later in the season with Mahler holding the baton.

In 1915 his classmate Scriabin died and Rachmaninoff learned some of his music to play in charity concerts for the benefit of his widow and children. It was the first time since his youth that he had played another's works in public. Besides the Scriabin Concerto, he performed an all-Scriabin program that included the Fifth Sonata. Constructing the recital program, Rachmaninoff found it needed another ten minutes, and consulted the pianist Alexander Goldenweiser, who advised him to look at the complicated Fantasy in B minor, Op. 28, which Goldenweiser had premiered and was fond of, but which Rachmaninoff had never heard. He liked the score, read through it, and learned it. The concert was three days later, and Goldenweiser would write, "His power of engraving in his memory the whole fabric of a musical work, and playing it with pianistic finish, was truly astounding."

Not until the 1917 Revolution, however, could Rachmaninoff be called a concert pianist. Even with the sudden loss of the property that had supported his family, he refused the lucrative conducting positions that had been offered to him in Boston and Cincinnati, and made a decision unprecedented for a man of forty-five. He set about learning a repertoire expansive enough for an international pianistic career, and never slackened from then until months before his death. Rachmaninoff continued to compose, but music now flowed slowly. Outside of Imperial Russia, he felt like a stranger. Western music had taken paths foreign to his nature and conditioning, and the few new works he composed were seldom greeted with bravos. But as a performer, he had become for many the cynosure of the world of the keyboard. His fingers seemed to burn the very keys, so intense was his playing.

A fantasy portrait of Rachmaninoff in pen and ink by David Dubal.

At first several critics were uncomfortable with his powerfully analytic mind. He lacked the casual and wayward sentiment of many of his Russian-trained colleagues. Even Prokofiev had rejected Rachmaninoff's reading of the Scriabin Fifth Sonata, missing the languor with which Scriabin had instilled it. "Behind every composition," Rachmaninoff wrote, "is the architectural plan of the composer. The student should endeavor, first of all, to discover this plan, and then he should build in the manner in which the composer would have had him build." For Rachmaninoff, the musical syntax had to be precise and clear, everything building toward a specific "point," as he called it, of climax. It was his main job as an interpreter to make that "point" clear to his audience. If he missed it, he considered the performance a failure, and he was known to be disconsolate after such concerts. In one season of seventy concerts, he could recall only two that he considered well played.

Rachmaninoff filed and polished every note. He worked untiringly; this greatest pianist-composer of the twentieth century slaved with relentless patience at a daily regimen of scales, arpeggios, octaves, and trills. Spontaneity was not for him. His recordings, unlike those of many of his colleagues, represent his true wishes. He recorded everything over and over until he got the results he needed; for example, his celebrated rendition of his own devilishly difficult transcription of Mendelssohn's *Midsummer Night's Dream* Scherzo was repeated forty-nine times (editing was not then possible). His concerts were jammed, and no pianist could afford not to hear him. The New York critic W. J. Henderson applauded a 1930 performance of Chopin's Second Sonata:

For one listener, this interpretation of the B-flat minor Sonata—in which even the Funeral March was played differently—closed itself with the magisterial quod erat demonstrandum which left no ground for argument. The logic of the thing was impervious; the plan was invulnerable; the proclamation was imperial. There was nothing left for us but to thank our stars that we had lived when Rachmaninoff did and heard him, out of the divine light of his genius, re-create a masterpiece. It was a day of genius understanding genius. One does not often get the opportunity to be present when such forces are at work. But one thing must not be forgotten: There was no iconoclast engaged; Chopin was still Chopin.

That year Rachmaninoff also recorded the sonata, and after nearly six decades it remains a towering interpretation of that composition. In whatever work he attempted, no matter how individual his statement, Rachmaninoff's way seemed the right one. Richard Baily, in an article, "Remembering Rachmaninoff," suggests, "It was like being in the presence of God himself. . . . Liszt's *Dante Sonata* was sublime in its sweep and emotional power. At the conclusion, I knew that Liszt was the greatest composer for the piano, and this was his finest composition." In his memoirs, Arthur Rubinstein writes:

Rachmaninoff was a pianist after my heart. He was superlative when he played his own music. A performance of his concertos could make you believe that they were the greatest masterpieces ever written, while when played by other pianists, even at their best, they became clearly what they were: brilliantly written pieces with their Oriental languor which have retained a great hold on the public. But when he played the music of other composers, he impressed me by the novelty and the originality of his conceptions. When he played a Schumann or a Chopin, even if it was contrary to my own feelings, he could convince me by the sheer impact of his personality. He was the most fascinating pianist of them all since Busoni. He had the secret of the golden, living tone which came from the heart, which is inimitable. In my strong opinion, he was a greater pianist than a composer. I fall, I have to admit, under the charm of his compositions when I hear them but return home with a slight distaste for their too brazenly expressed sweetness.

211

Rachmaninoff's piano works, however, have become increasingly popular with audiences and pianists alike. They present formidable muscular problems and are often dense in number of notes per measure, forming a tapestry of unusual effects and counterpoints. He loved the bells of Moscow, and he exploited the bass of his piano with rousing clangor.

Listening to Rachmaninoff in his own works, solo or concerti, is axiomatic for pianists learning them. Heinrich Neuhaus was once asked by a student for advice on a Rachmaninoff concerto, whereupon he ordered him to listen to Rachmaninoff's recording. In playing his own music Rachmaninoff was sublime, aristocratic, and fragrant, with an iron rhythm and the incomparable long line bathed in moonlight, limpid and pure. His recordings of his music fulfill the axiom "Less is more."

Listening to Rachmaninoff's enchanting recorded legacy, one realizes his kind of playing has little to do with the ideals of the present day. His playing, for all its formal logic, tonal gradation, and exquisite sound, makes literalists uncomfortable. The rubati at first seem out of character. His immense individuality in such works as Schubert's A-flat Impromptu or Chopin's C-sharp minor Scherzo sounds unidiomatic in a literal age, where caution is the watchword. Besides the Chopin *Funeral March* Sonata, Rachmaninoff's only other performance of a large-scale solo work on disc is his legendary *Carnaval* of Schumann, which is a marvel of control, chiseled phrasing, and infallible chordal technique. He was greatest in the large forms, and it's a pity that his Beethoven Op. 10, No. 3; Op. 31, No. 2; Opp. 57, 109, and 111; and the C major Concerto were never recorded. His repertoire was packed with Liszt, including what Shura Cherkassky calls "the mightiest of all Liszt Sonatas." He played mazurkas, waltzes, scherzos, polonaises, the Fantasy in F minor, the Rondo Op. 16, the Tarantelle, and the B

minor Sonata of Chopin. His recitals were spiced with Borodin, Rubinstein, Dohnányi, Scarlatti, Mendelssohn, Medtner, Moszkowski, Balakirev's *Islamey,* and even Godowsky's *Künstlerleben* and the *Alceste* Caprice of Saint-Saëns. He liked Grieg, admired the Concerto and the Ballade, and his recording of the Grieg C minor Violin Sonata with Kreisler is one of the great discs of ensemble playing.

John Browning feels: "Both Rachmaninoff and Kreisler had that thing which nobody has anymore—a type of elegance that seems to have died out. There's a certain kind of humanity in the performance that can bring tears to the eye. It happens very quickly—it can happen in a single phrase." "When he played a Liszt transcription of a Schubert song," wrote Harold Schonberg, "one immediately realized how unimaginative . . . most singers were. Only the very greatest vocal artists—a Lotte Lehmann or an Elisabeth Schumann—could shape a phrase with equal finesse and authority."

Rachmaninoff was an unforgettable stage personality. Tall as a tree, his hair very close-cropped, he seemed to have the worries of the world etched upon his stony face. He never smiled on stage. Stravinsky called him "a six-and-a-half-foot scowl" but, in fact, his face was expressionless during performance. Francis Robinson recalled, "The fall-out at a Rachmaninoff concert was high. . . . The shattering effect began almost with his first appearance, the austere frame which looked to be as long as his instrument and as gaunt, the angular gait unlike anything that has moved before or since, the withdrawn expression as remote as an icon before centuries of candle smoke."

Rachmaninoff's place in the history of the instrument must rank near the very top. He is the spiritual son of Anton Rubinstein, and along with Hofmann, he was the supreme artist of the early twentieth-century Russian school of piano playing.

JOSEF RAIEFF
b. 1908 — Russia

He came to the United States early and studied with Siloti and Josef Lhévinne, later going to Berlin to study with Schnabel. He made his U.S. debut in 1936, and has been a teacher at the Juilliard School since 1945.

DEZSÖ RÁNKI
b. 1954 — Hungary

He worked under Pál Kadosa and has toured worldwide since winning several competitions. He stands as one of the most acclaimed pianists in Central Europe. His repertoire is large, as is his musical intelligence. He plays with a fresh spirit, as well as an accurate and brilliant technique. His playing of Chopin is still superficial, but his Bartók is vital and sensitive.

JEAN HENRI RAVINA
1818–1906 — France

A good pianist, and composer of many light and effective piano pieces. He published four-hand arrangements of Beethoven's nine symphonies. In 1861 he received the Legion of Honor. As a child, the prodigy Josef Hofmann often played his *Etude de style,* and it was recorded by Arthur Loesser.

ALEXANDER REINAGLE
1756–1809 — England

The first American pianist of importance, Reinagle was born in the same year as Mozart and died the same year as Haydn. He came to Philadelphia in 1786, and established himself as a performer-impresario. He was also the foremost teacher in the city; George Washington's niece studied piano with him. His piano music is gracious and in the style of the Classical era.

CARL REINECKE
1824–1910 — Germany

Reinecke was a powerful figure in European music as a composer, conductor, pianist, and teacher. As a child, he studied with his father, Johann Peter, a respected theorist and teacher. The piano shared the stage with the violin through his teen years, but at eighteen, he began touring as a pianist. From 1846 to 1848, he was court pianist in Copenhagen to Christian VIII. During this period, he began a conducting career, which then propelled him to the leadership of the Leipzig Gewandhaus Orchestra, from 1860 to 1895. He also taught piano at the Leipzig Conservatory and became director of that institution, where he upheld the standards of his idol Mendelssohn. He was a conservative musician and, as a composer, he lived long past his day. Born at a time when Beethoven was writing his last quartets, in his later years he inhabited a world of music that was baffling to him. Debussy, Scriabin, Stravinsky, and Schoenberg were beyond his comprehension. Even in his heyday, if one considered oneself a "modern musician," then the advice was to avoid Leipzig.

As a pianist, Reinecke stemmed from Moscheles. Quiet hands and curved fingers sufficed for playing the music he respected. Yet an amazing number of important pianists worked with him and admired him, including Joseffy, Michalowski, Albéniz, Max Vogrich, Martin Krause, Julie Rivé-King, Robert Teichmüller, Fanny Davies, Karl Heinrich Barth, and Ernest Hutcheson, who thought Reinecke's playing was elegant and in the best taste and who noted that he was the best accompanist he had ever heard. The Swiss-born pianist Rudolph Ganz called his Mozart playing "delightful."

As a composer, he wrote clearly, with expert craft. His work is harmonically conventional, but not scholastic; his musical impulse is warm and genuine. He left much piano music, including four concerti; No. 1 in F-sharp minor, Op. 72, was often played by the composer with special success. He also left admirable cadenzas to Mozart concerti.

ALFRED REISENAUER
1863–1907 — Norway

A superb pianist who toured relentlessly. He studied with Liszt, and with Louis Köhler. Sergei Bortkiewicz and many others were products of his teaching.

NADIA REISENBERG
1904–1983 — Russia

She studied with Nicolaiev at the St. Petersburg Conservatory and came to the United States in 1922. Reisenberg was a musicianly pianist who recorded several neglected works, including the Tchaikovsky Sonata and the Paderewski *Polish Fantasy,* as well as many repertory pieces. She had a long career as a teacher at the Mannes College of Music, the Juilliard School, and the Rubin Academy in Jerusalem. There is a Nadia Reisenberg archive at the International Piano Archives at the University of Maryland.

FRANZ REISENSTEIN
1911–1968 — Germany

A well-trained pianist with a large repertoire, he studied piano with Solomon and composition with Hindemith. He taught a great deal and composed many substantial piano works.

ROSITA RENARD
1894–1949 — Chile

She studied in Berlin with Martin Krause, who was also the teacher of Arrau and of Edwin Fischer. Renard made a big impression as a pianist but retired to teach, emerging at Carnegie Hall only several months before her death; her recital was recorded. Her Chopin etudes were remarkable for their agility and their distinctive ideas.

THOMAS RICHNER
b. 1911 — United States

Best known as a Mozart interpreter. He has written a book on the Mozart sonatas, and his recordings reveal a Mozart that is mellow and flowing.

SVIATOSLAV RICHTER
b. 1916 — Russia

He came from a musical family, gave a debut in 1934 at the age of eighteen, and in 1937 went to the Moscow Conservatory to work with Heinrich Neuhaus. In 1949 he was awarded the Stalin Prize, and has since received most every honor that a Soviet artist may garner.

By the mid-1950s, some of his records had surfaced in the West, and piano connoisseurs were agog with admiration. Emil Gilels, whose resounding success in the United States whetted the appetite for other Russian performers, uttered the tantalizing phrase, "Wait till you hear Richter." The great impresario Sol Hurok took the cue, billing Richter "the Pianist of the Century," but could not get him to the West until five years after Gilels had first appeared. At last, in October 1960, Richter embarked on a great tour of the United States, both in solo recitals and with orchestras galore. Erich Leinsdorf was his first conductor, and nothing less than the mighty Brahms Second Concerto was played. Everywhere his success was overwhelming.

Of the twelve weeks during which he rampaged the American continent, his seven Carnegie Hall recitals were the high-water mark. The hall was overflowing, and there was an unequaled excitement from the pianistic community. The late Lonny Epstein of Juilliard raved to me that she had never heard Debussy the way she dreamed it until she heard Richter. The *New York Times* critic Harold Schonberg reported, "Certainly it was the most unparalleled triumph that this writer ever observed." And what a range of repertoire Richter fed his public. I was at each event and was staggered by the glory of his garden. From Haydn and Beethoven, to Debussy and Ravel, Chopin and Schumann, Scriabin, Liszt, Szymanowski, Prokofiev, and more, he played it all with an intensity and purpose never to be forgotten. Richter seemed to be an apparition. The "iron curtain" had risen, and for a lingering moment music appeared to bring us to peace and unity. A Richter concert produces such feelings of idealism; his motto seems to be "Above all, Art." He possesses a granitelike, almost authoritarian stage presence, best observed by the psychologist Allen Wheelis in his little book, *How People Change:*

Sviatoslav Richter strides out on the stage. His face is grim; there is anger in the set of his jaw, but not at the audience. This is a passion altogether his own, a force with which he protects what he is about to do. If it had words, it would say, "What I attempt is important and I go about it with utmost seriousness. I intend to create beauty and meaning, and everything everywhere threatens this endeavor: The coughs, the latecomers, the chatting women in the third row, and always those dangers within, distraction, confusion, loss of memory, weakness of hand, all are enemies of my endeavor. I call up this passion to oppose them, to protect my purpose." Now he begins to play, and the anger I see in his bearing I hear in the voice of Beethoven. It knows nothing of meanness or spite; it is the passion of the doer who will not let his work be swept aside. It hurts no one, it asserts life, it is the force that generates form.

This is Richter at his very finest. But there is another Richter: a great experimenter, sometimes inspired, other times doing weird things with pedaling and tempi. One never knows what to expect from this most mercurial, intellectual, exasperating, and profound of all Soviet pianists. When in form, he has one of the most all-encompassing techniques in the history of twentieth-century piano playing. He can be note-perfect in one piece, murky, turgid, and splattering notes in the next; sometimes he can be academic to the point of pedantry, or withdrawn and introverted. His complete Bach *Well-Tempered Clavier* shows him a master of contrapuntal control, but he plays with a variety of uncalled-for Romantic nuance, which negates the strength of the music. At times, his Chopin is Teutonic, and his Schumann sounds Slavic. Yet whatever he does, it is never arbitrary, never merely likable or homogeneous, nor is the result ever simple. Richter is a far-reaching

215

and inquisitive musical intelligence. He does not seem to have a "style," nor is he searching for one.

He has recorded extensively and, for the avid listener, Richter provides one of the most interesting of all discographies. I never tire of his Schumann Fantasy, G minor Sonata, or *Humoreske.* I am awestruck by his live performance from Sofia, Bulgaria, of the *Pictures at an Exhibition.* His Beethoven Sonatas Opp. 13 and 26, as well as the *Tempest* and *Appassionata,* are piercing. In Schubert, especially in recent years, Richter has attempted some of his most visionary interpretations. Tempi are so slow in the B-flat Sonata that the listener must breathe silently to follow its movement. Richter's lyricism is never flaccid; while the motion never quite breaks its inexorable course, the rhythmic power so seldom brought properly to the fore in Schubert is ever present. His playing of the *Wanderer* Fantasy is justly famous, and his recording of the posthumous C minor Sonata is majestic—the finale, a winter's journey. Or listen to his pulsating four-movement A minor Sonata (D. 845). And in the *Unfinished* C major Sonata, Richter's first movement seems boundless in scope.

In Liszt, Richter can be a refined miniaturist in the fearful *Feux follets* or *Valse oubliée,* or a Merlin in the concerti and the Sonata. His Scriabin Fifth was a landmark performance of the piece, and his recording of the Sixth Sonata is by far the most intriguing view of that elusive score ever recorded, while his Scriabin etudes are subdued but a wonder of technical control and variety of nuance. In the Russian repertoire, don't miss his definitive performance of the Tchaikovsky G major Sonata, with a grasp of design and chordal playing that makes this lumbering work sound important. What amazing hands—they seem to be made of marble; his fifth finger is fearsome in its physical strength. Some of his Rachmaninoff is imperial, and many of the Preludes are among the best recorded, as is his First Rachmaninoff Concerto. Richter has al-

ways been happy in Prokofiev, especially in the expansiveness of the sonatas, which he has done so much to champion. Prokofiev dedicated No. 9 to Richter, who makes quite a case for its quality.

Neuhaus, Richter's teacher, once wrote:

When I listen to Richter, very often my hand begins spontaneously to conduct. The rhythmic element in his playing is so strong, the rhythm so logical, so organized, strict and free and is so much the result of his total conception of the work he is performing, that it is impossible to resist the temptation to take part in it by gesture . . . strictness, co-ordination, discipline, harmony, sureness and mastery. This is the real freedom! With a performer such as Richter, two or three departures from strict rhythm are more effective, more expressive, more meaningful than hundreds of "rhythmic liberties" in a pianist in whom the feeling of harmony, this total concept, is absent.

HANS RICHTER-HAASER
1912–1980 — Germany

A pianist of value who made his debut in 1928. He had an international career, and was prized for his master classes. He was best known as a Beethoven player, and made several fine recordings of that composer's work.

ROBERT RIEFLING
b. 1911 — Norway

He worked with Kempff and took master classes with Edwin Fischer as well. In 1925 he made a debut in Oslo, and he has since played around the world. He is a sensitive artist in a variety of music, from Bach's *Well-Tempered Clavier* and Beethoven Sonatas to important recordings of the beautiful and austere music of his compatriot Fartein Valen.

FERDINAND RIES
1784–1838 — Germany

With Czerny, Ries was Beethoven's most important pupil, working with the master from 1801 to 1805. Beethoven cared deeply for him and helped realize Ries's substantial gifts. He was a deft pianist, whose playing was more akin to Hummel's elegance than to the ruggedness of Beethoven's style. Ries is a delightful composer, who contributed more than fifty sonatas, and many chamber and occasional pieces. His Third Concerto in C-sharp minor is admirable. In 1813 he went to London, where he became renowned, and did a great deal to propagate Beethoven's music.

BERNARD RINGEISSEN
b. 1934 — France

He studied with Long and Février. In 1951 he took first prize in piano playing at the Paris Conservatoire, and in 1954 won first prize at the Geneva Competition. He has played extensively, judged competitions, and recorded Alkan, Rachmaninoff, and others, with a very facile technique.

ÉDOUARD RISLER
1837–1929 — Germany

He was an extraordinary pianist with high powers of emotive projection. In 1889, as a student of Diémer, he won first prize at the Paris Conservatoire. After studies in Paris, he worked with Klindworth, Stavenhagen, and d'Albert, and became an exponent of Beethoven, giving the entire sonata cycle in London in 1906. He was also, perhaps, the first pianist to essay the complete oeuvre of Chopin in public, although Brailowsky gave himself credit for that feat. Risler presented the premiere, in 1901, of the monumental hour-long Dukas Sonata, as well as Dukas's Variations, Interlude, and Finale on a Theme of Rameau, in 1903. Chabrier dedicated to him the *Bourrée fantasque,* which Robert Casadesus called "the first truly modern French piano composition." In his memoirs, Arthur Rubinstein wrote of Risler's Beethoven: "To this day, I have never heard anybody play these sonatas as beautifully and movingly as Risler. He played them naturally, just as they spoke to him, revealing the highly romantic nature of these masterpieces. . . . The adagio of the *Hammerklavier,* the 'absence' in the *Les Adieux* Sonata, and the D minor, Opus 31, No. 2, made me cry when played by Risler."

THÉODORE RITTER
1841–1886 — France

A student of Liszt. His playing was suave and agile, as were the drawing-room pieces he turned out, such as *Les Courriers,* which became his favored composition.

JULIE RIVÉ-KING
1857–1937 — United States

A student of Reinecke in Leipzig, she also studied briefly with Liszt before she returned home, becoming one of the busiest concert artists in the United States. She gave more than four thousand concerts during her career.

RICHARD ROBERT
1861–1924 — Austria

He studied at the Vienna Conservatory, where he later taught. George Szell and Rudolf Serkin were his pupils.

PASCAL ROGÉ
b. 1951 — France

A pianist of quality who plays French music with style. He studied at the Paris Conservatoire, where he won a first prize. He also worked with Julius Katchen and, in 1971, was awarded a first prize at the Long-Thibaud Competition. He has made many worthwhile recordings.

JEROME ROSE
b. 1938 — United States

A student of Leonard Shure, Rose has been active as a teacher and performer. His many discs display his ability in Schubert, Chopin, and Schumann, as well as in many scores by Liszt, whose music he often performs.

HENRI ROSELLEN
1811–1876 — France

A pupil of Zimmerman at the Paris Conservatoire, he achieved popularity as player, teacher, and a composer of easily digestible etudes and miniatures.

CHARLES ROSEN
b. 1927 — United States

As a child, he worked with Moriz Rosenthal and Hedwig Kanner-Rosenthal. Rosen graduated from Princeton University in 1947, and received a Ph.D. in literature. He made a New York debut in 1951. He has written several books, the most important being *The Classical Style: Haydn, Mozart, Beethoven*. Rosen held the Charles Eliot Norton Chair of Poetics at Harvard in 1980–81.

I have long listened with great interest to Rosen's playing, especially to his earlier records, which have a coldly passionate climate. Rosen always has a strong point of view. He once stated that "a performance is more than a voluptuous noise or an historical echo from the past." His early record of the Beethoven *Hammerklavier* Sonata has a compelling hardness, a quality of bleakness, that fits this mountainous work. It is a performance with a headlong drive in the fugue, and a lonely vastness in the first and slow movements. His more recent Beethoven sonatas are not so eventful; they are stiff, arbitrary, and lacking in rhythmic intensity. The poet Stephen Spender heard him in a recital of late Beethoven sonatas and wrote: "Rosen plays with ice-cold precision, cutting up the phrases as though with a knife. At the same time in interpreting the music he communicates a kind of intellectual passion."

Rosen has done some of his best work in Liszt. In the *Don Juan* Fantasy, he confronts the terror buried within its pyrotechnics. And he has made Bach a large part of his musical existence. His *Goldberg* Variations are superbly focused; even more so is *The Art of the Fugue*, which he makes convincing on the contemporary piano. Rosen was the first pianist ever to record the Debussy Etudes, and he relieves Debussy's works of much of their shimmer, concentrating on their rhythmic boldness. As an interpreter of the modern repertory, Rosen is a musician of importance and courage, who has delivered some of the most durable interpretations of our time, giving life to many recondite works by Boulez, Stravinsky, Schoenberg, Carter, and Bartók. In his playing of Stravinsky's *Movements* or Bartók's *Improvisations,* one is made aware of every cell, every silence. His latest triumph is his disc of Carter's *Night Fantasies,* which finds in Rosen a penetrating advocate.

His live performances lately have been disappointing. There is a general feeling of awkwardness, boorishness, and tight patchiness. Instead of his usual highly organized playing, the music has been given in gulps and chunks, the dynamic range stinted, the sound quite shrill. But Rosen is ever a surprising artist, and his recent Schumann recordings of many major works are vintage, filled with persuasive lyrical moments and countless measures of imagination. This new Schumann is a distinct improvement on his earlier recordings, in which he was definitely inhibited by the composer's discursive expansiveness.

MORIZ ROSENTHAL
1862–1946 — Poland

He studied with Karl Mikuli, Chopin's pupil, followed by work with Joseffy and, finally, with Liszt for several years. He went to the University of Vienna, where he studied philosophy, and graduated in 1884. That was the beginning of a dazzling career in music. His playing was considered by many to be the ultimate in technical prodigiousness.

From the moment in 1884 when he stepped on stage at Vienna's Bösendorfersaal, his displays of technical daring caused wonder. The composer Hugo Wolf reported: "Rosenthal, in Liszt's appallingly difficult *Don Juan* Fantasy, brought off feats of pianistic athleticism designed to make a moderately accomplished pianist's hair stand on end. The audience was quite beside itself at this labor of Hercules." In 1886, Wolf, comparing him with d'Albert, felt that "the playing of the two virtuosos, in relationship of one to the other, was rather like a brilliant rocket and a glowing coal fire. Rosenthal's playing ignites, d'Albert's warms. The one inspires to deeds, the other to contemplation." Rosenthal, he said, "stormed over the keys like a roaring flood. He played godlessly (godlike sounds too commonplace), and demonstrated beyond the shadow of a doubt that the devil is the supreme authority in art. . . . When he finished, I had the feeling of having escaped from a frightful deadly peril." And Eduard Hanslick, the most powerful critic in Europe, gulped, "I have almost forgotten what it is to be astonished, but I found young Rosenthal's achievements indeed astonishing." There were also a few quibbles, and the matter of "the unlovely violence with which the keys were pounded in fortissimo passages . . . details characteristic of all the youngsters of the Liszt-Tausig school." But James Huneker, the foremost keyboard connoisseur in America, exclaimed that

the world of Pianism has never matched Rosenthal for speed, power, endurance; he plays his instrument magnificently, overwhelmingly. He is the Napoleon, the conqueror among virtuosi. His tone is very sonorous, his touch singing, and he commands the entire range of nuance from the rippling *fioritura* of the Chopin Barcarolle, to the cannon-like thunderings of the A-flat Polonaise. His octaves and chords baffle all critical experience and appraisement. As others play presto in single notes, so he dashes off double-notes, thirds, sixths and octaves. His *Don Juan* Fantasy, part Liszt, part Mozart, is entirely Rosenthalian in performance. . . . He is the epitome of the orchestra and in a tonal duel with the orchestra he has never been worsted. . . . His touch is crystal-like in its clearness, therefore his tone lacks the sensuousness of Paderewski and de Pachmann.

Unfortunately, Rosenthal did not record until after his sixtieth year. By that time, a great deal of the brilliance and power had been replaced by poetry and grace, a style of spontaneous elegance, though still mixed with impetuosity. He recorded about forty titles on 78s, and they are among history's great piano discs. There has never been a Chopin Etude Op. 10, No. 1 with more technical finesse, and as a Chopin mazurka stylist, Rosenthal ranks with Friedman. Paderewski thought nobody compared with Rosenthal in playing these exotic dance-poems. His Chopin playing became more and more rarefied and concerned with the softest colorations. Rosenthal wrote, "My teachers, Mikuli and Joseffy, delighted my ear with their almost infinite dynamic range from *piano* to *pianissimo,* and *pianississimo.*" He also said that his thirst for big orchestral effects was quenched by the "old thunderer" Liszt.

He recorded several of his own pieces, and in these his playing was unapproachable. Listen not to the piano-roll version, but to the 78 recording, transferred to LP, of his *Carnaval de Vienne,* based on Johann Strauss tunes. It has an improvisatory ease and aristocratic savoir-faire that seem to have disappeared from music-making forever. Such an impression is confirmed in his earlier disc of the Chopin-Liszt *My Joys*—playing of ethereal loveliness.

Rosenthal was captured on record in only one concerto, the Chopin E minor, recorded in Berlin in 1931. Its presentation is disappointing; the playing sounds somewhat stale and stilted. Of other large-scale works, we have only the Chopin B minor Sonata, made in 1939, but by that time his fabulous motor system had begun to crumble; though flashes of lyricism are apparent, his technique was no longer up to the taxing demands of the work.

It is a shame that most listeners since that time have known Rosenthal's playing by this performance, which was totally unrepresentative of his former glory. He was one of the master virtuosi born in the decade of the 1860s. The great conductor Hans Richter once introduced Rosenthal as "the king of pianists," and many would have bowed to that decree.

ANTON RUBINSTEIN
1830–1894 — Russia

After Liszt, Anton Rubinstein was the most written-about and idolized pianist of the nineteenth century. Rubinstein had a powerful mystique, and seated at his huge iron-framed piano, he was a virtuoso god, singing magically and pouring out emotional floods in the grand manner. With his smoldering temperament, Kalmuck features, and black, disheveled leonine mane, Rubinstein was the very symbol of the piano's power and pride. With Liszt's retirement from the concert stage, Rubinstein reigned supreme over the pianistic kingdom in an age that produced virtuosi of legendary status.

The countless words written of his playing echo one another in their praise. One listener reported, "The impression was so overwhelming, my nerves were so wrought up that I felt stifled. I glanced at my neighbor—she had left the room weeping. We all had a feeling of involuntary terror as if in the presence of some elementary power of nature." Even as late as 1919, James Huneker could write: "With the death of Rubinstein, no artist of his emotional caliber has appeared on the scene, nor is there likely to be one. . . . He was volcanic. He was as torrid as midday in the tropics. . . . The plangency of his tone, fingers of velvet, fingers of bronze, the sweep, audacity and tenderness of his many styles—ah! There was but one Anton Rubinstein." The great pianist Arthur

Friedheim likened Rubinstein's playing to the Old Testament, gloriously eloquent with the splendors of the world, and Rafael Joseffy said of Rubinstein's touch that it was not that of a pianist but the mellow tones of a French horn. The amorous Leschetizky, teacher of Paderewski, would bribe Rubinstein by saying, "Only play for me, and you may have all my wives and all my sweethearts."

His was probably the most tempestuous temperament that anyone ever brought to a piano. He was also immensely erratic, and he said that he often missed enough notes in one recital to make up yet another. A performer of such temperament needed ten times the technique of an average pianist, for he took daring chances. Later in his career, he suffered drastically "the tortures of the Inquisition," as he called them, because of constant anxiety, stage nervousness, and fear of memory loss. A true Romantic virtuoso, he relied on inspiration.

Rubinstein's playing deeply affected the players of his time, and he was the spiritual father of many of the great pianists of the early twentieth century. Paderewski, Rachmaninoff, Lhévinne, Scriabin, and so many others never got over his impact at the piano. Hofmann, his greatest pupil, thought of himself as small by comparison. Rachmaninoff said: "I stored up wonderful memories with which no others in my experience can compare. It was not so much his magnificent technique that held one spellbound, as the profound, spiritually refined musicianship, which spoke from every note and every bar he played, and singled him out as the most original, the unequaled pianist of the world. . . . One of Rubinstein's greatest secrets was his use of the pedal. 'The pedal is the soul of the piano!' said Rubinstein. 'No pianist should ever forget this.' "

As a teacher, Rubinstein asked his students to "will" to dream the sound they wanted and needed. He said, "You think the piano is one instrument? It's a hundred instruments." One of his students wrote: "Rubinstein's sense of touch was almost as keenly developed as that of a blind man. He loved to caress things with his hands. Where others smelled a rose, he touched its soft petals with his fingertips, much as he caressed a piano when drawing forth the witching sweetness of a Chopin nocturne."

He wrote an autobiography, but later summed up his life in six words: "I have lived, loved, and played"—and play he did, from the czar's palace to the mining town of Central City, Colorado. By 1872, America was ripe for a truly great interpreter. Under the auspices of Steinway and Sons, Rubinstein made a monumental tour of the United States, a marathon of incalculable importance in America's musical coming of age. Giving 215 packed concerts within the incredible space of 239 days, Rubinstein literally stunned the American public into an awareness of the piano literature. With his primeval force and elemental freshness, he gave programs of tremendous magnitude (on which his courtesy Variations on "Yankee Doodle" was the only lowbrow fare), and "how 'Ruby' played" became the topic of the day.

Rubinstein was a man of strong opinions: for example, "The human race does not deserve the finale of Beethoven's Sonata Op. 111." But he gave of himself unsparingly, and by 1881, he was codifying the interpreter's role in his great series of seven "historical recitals," publicly proclaiming the immense territories of the piano literature. These concerts surveying keyboard music from the sixteenth century to his own time were among the important musical educative ventures of the nineteenth century. He was an unusually brusque man who smiled seldom, but he was amazingly generous. In 1862 he founded the St. Petersburg Conservatory, and during his career he donated well over 300,000 rubles to charitable causes. But it was by his Conservatory that he said he wished to be remembered.

221

As a composer, there were those who thought his name would be enshrined among the immortals. Along with Brahms, he was regarded as one of the most important composers in the anti-Wagner camp. Even his appearance augured well for him—he was the very reincarnation of his supreme god, Beethoven. Some felt he must be the offspring of the great master, and Liszt dubbed him "Van II." Von Bülow gave him the appellation "the Michelangelo of Music." But the time has long since passed when Josef Hofmann stormed and swept the keyboard in his master's D minor Concerto, the only semisurvivor in a vast and proud output. The Fourth Concerto was regularly played, until the Rachmaninoff concerti ousted it; it still has great vitality and melodic appeal. Paderewski heard Rubinstein play it: "It was really overwhelming—impossible to describe. . . . The whole of the first movement is a masterpiece. It is just as if it had been born, like Minerva, from the brain of Jupiter." Now that the boarding-school piano is locked forever, no longer do young girls coo over the Melody in F, swoon to the Romance in E-flat, or dream of the exotic while exhibiting themselves in the *Kamenoi-Ostrow*. Nor do conductors give to their audiences the once popular *Ocean* Symphony. Rubinstein was a gifted melodist, but unfortunately he said nothing new. His own diatonic harmony would be buried under the spices of Russian nationalism. He is a tragic figure; his music is denied us, and what frustration for those of us who yearn to hear the Rubinstein force at work.

Anton Rubinstein's career ended only a few years before the advent of the phonograph. It was rumored that he had made a few early recorded tests; if so, they were never heard, never found. In any case, it would have been ludicrous to attempt to contain his titanic art within the confines of a primitive technology. Rubinstein unheard remains a legend that still resounds in the annals of the performing arts.

ARTHUR RUBINSTEIN
1887–1982—Poland

After leaving Poland, Arthur Rubinstein studied in Berlin with Karl Heinrich Barth. The first volume of his autobiography, *My Young Years* (1973), tells his remarkable story through his twentieth year. The second volume, *My Many Years* (1980), chronicles his adventures through the next seven decades of his life.

Rubinstein's career was one of the longest chapters in the history of piano playing. He played his final Carnegie Hall recital on March 15, 1976. It was a moving occasion. Afterward, he spoke briefly to the standing audience, who were unaware that this would be his last recital in the great hall where he had experienced so many personal triumphs. But Rubinstein knew he would never return. In June he would play for the last time in London's Wigmore Hall. On both occasions he played Schumann's *Carnaval*, performing with more passion and technical aplomb than I had ever heard from him in this work. Several days after the recital, I told him so, and the great pianist smiled. "I am now blind, I can't read my beloved Proust and Joyce, nor can I look at beautiful women. . . . I am bored," he exclaimed, "and so I am practicing, and I have been practicing the hardest spots in *Carnaval*, which I've neglected for years." And, he asked, "How did you like my *Paganini*?" Indeed, he had never played it with such speed and verve. Rubinstein continued, "I don't want the public or the critics to say that I am a doddering old man who should not be on stage."

In fact, it had been a recital of startling color and freshness, the embodiment of youth itself. He was certainly the most beloved pianist of his era. He said that he lived unconditionally, and so he played. And just as the man was approachable, so was his music-making. Everyone wanted to hear Rubinstein—and he seemed to be everywhere. If you were in Paris, Rubinstein was playing there; a week later if you were in Rome, he was there too. When the Rubinstein poster with its familiar line drawing appeared, everyone was glad that he was back in their town. Rubinstein was an exception among pianists—he loved his almost daily touring, the hotels, the bustle and grand whirl, which never tired him. Read the memoirs: he remembered every meal that was delicious, every performance he heard, and every person who was amusing. As Hans Christian Andersen said of Liszt: "Happy man! who can thus travel throughout his whole life, always to see people in their spiritual Sunday dress—yea, even in the wedding garment of inspiration."

When music lovers discuss Arthur Rubinstein's playing, they never speak of him as a virtuoso or a colorist, a scholar or a specialist. He was simply the pianist *par excellence*. There was a wholeness in his playing which defied analysis, and which ennobled whatever he played. After Rubinstein had performed, an audience looked fulfilled, musically well fed. He offered his feast with a unique gusto, and even a spray of wrong notes never marred the experience. Someone once said he preferred Rubinstein's wrong notes to many another's right ones. Of course, his occasional sloppiness never came from inattentiveness or technical weakness. For Rubinstein, the moment counted, and he could be seized with inspiration. A Rubinstein concert had the quality of complete authenticity. He had the grand passion for the piano and a blessed temperament. His playing was bracing, invigorating, without any hint of sentimentality or of morbidity. No emotion was ever faked. Nor did he ever play down to an audience. His musical nature was sane and balanced; he was the interpreter of normalcy. If one cares for self-absorbed or idiosyncratic playing, for cerebral or extreme playing, then one must look elsewhere. His art had no dark side. He could never have been the object of a cult.

Rubinstein had a wonderful legato, an amazing ear, his sonorities were clear; he had an unfailing steadiness in rhythm, colossal chord playing, and, of course, a golden, glorious sound—the quintessentially singing tone. He also played with perfect relaxation. I don't know if it came naturally or was learned through his many years of experience, but he was never tense or cramped. He never hit the keys, never pounded the piano. He utilized weight through his arms and shoulders. When he wanted a mighty sonority in chordal masses, he rose marvelously from the bench and then he swooped down upon the instrument with the grace of an eagle. Rubinstein played, it seemed, from a great pelvic thrust. And how he understood the halls' acoustics; hearing him pedal and envelop a hall in his sound was pure magic. Pianists wouldn't miss a Rubinstein concert: his excursions into the piano literature were worth a hundred lessons.

Rubinstein, a Polish Jew, was disciplined with long study in Germany, and was later nurtured in France. He was a cosmopolitan—a citizen of the world, an artist for all people. An amazing range of styles was ingrained in him. He played Debussy and Ravel when their music was hot off the press. Impressionism, from the first, was natural to him, as was most French music. Rubinstein's sense of balance and superb pedaling make his *Valses nobles et sentimentales* one of the most completely beautiful examples of Ravel on disc. He knew best what suited him in Chabrier, Fauré, Poulenc, Falla, Prokofiev, Villa-Lobos, and so many others. His recordings of the Franck Prelude, Chorale, and Fugue are technically magnificent and musically majestic. Franck's religious Romanticism can be easily tarnished with melodrama. Rubinstein, with his impeccable taste, is never cloying.

His 1960 disc of Grieg *Lyric Pieces* and the *Ballade in the Form of Variations* is fragrantly cool and brisk as a clear mountain stream. He triumphed in the Spanish repertoire and was adored in Spain. He went there, in 1916, for four recitals; he stayed to give 120. Inevitably, somebody would yell during encore time for the *Navarra* of Albéniz, or his hypnotic rendering of Falla's *Ritual Dance of Fire*. The same triumphs were recounted in South America. In Brazil he discovered the then unknown Villa-Lobos, and played him with sparkling vigor, introducing him to the rest of the world. He was also a close friend of Szymanowski, and he interpreted many of his compatriot's works for the first time. One of his early loves was Scriabin, whose music he eventually deleted from his repertoire, but not before giving the London premiere of the Fifth Sonata. He never deserted Brahms, and one could always hear him in rhapsodies, intermezzi, or the Sonata in F minor, rich and bronzed. His disc of Brahms solo music has never been surpassed for impeccable taste and veiled passion. His Brahms is never tainted by pedantry, nor were his Brahms concerti bloated. The D minor Concerto with Fritz Reiner is nobility itself.

I don't think he really loved Liszt, but he could play the *Valse impromptu* marvelously, seeming to glide across the ballroom floor, and the *Mephisto Waltz, Funérailles,* and *Valse oubliée* No. 1 have assured style. In performance the Sonata was virile, but the recording is not a success. The Liszt work he played in public with pomp and swing was the Twelfth Rhapsody, and his Liszt Concerto No. 1 contains fine work.

His solo repertoire of the Classic masters was skimpy. He did not play in public the sonatas of Mozart; but the soulful A minor Rondo, K. 511, was his favored solo Mozart work. (He loved several of the concerti and performed them with ease and simplicity.) Bach also was never played, except for the Bach-Busoni Chaconne, and the sonatas of Haydn did not seem to exist for him, although he played the poignant Variations in F minor admirably. He loved Schubert, and in several Impromptus he sang beautifully. In his later years he regularly performed Schubert's final Sonata in B-flat, though on disc it sounds wooden. Nor does the *Wanderer* Fantasy recording show him at his best.

Rubinstein chose his Beethoven carefully, but the five concerti were always on his agenda. His favorite was No. 4, which he first played with Arthur Nikisch conducting. In the concerti, he offered a cultured Beethoven, unpretentious and, especially in the slow movements, perhaps too Romantic for some tastes. Of the sonatas, he gave prominence to the concert favorites. His *Waldstein* was magnificent, and the *Appassionata,* to which he was faithful for three-quarters of a century, was resonant. He never failed to play it with élan and magnanimity. He could give fine readings of Op. 90, the *Pathétique,* the *Moonlight,* and *Les Adieux,* but this listener was most delighted with his performance of Op. 31, No. 3, which was pregnant with life, humor, and energy.

Schumann became, for Rubinstein, the ultimate Romantic. As he aged, his Schumann projected greater purity, and his late recording of the Fantasy captures a rare serenity; it is a milestone in his recording career. The *Fantasiestücke* were always played magically, and with the most rounded tone imaginable. They evoke the atmosphere of the springtime of Romanticism. His playing of *In der Nacht* is glorious.

Of course, the names of Chopin and Rubinstein will be forever linked. Yet early in his career, Rubinstein's Chopin playing was often considered unpoetic, if not cold. The "Camille of the Keyboard" view of Chopin was deeply entrenched, but Rubinstein felt Chopin's virile, Classical traits strongly. The pianist wanted to de-salonify him, to leave behind the often sickly, sentimental readings then prevailing and to give Chopin the status and stature he deserved. This was a Chopin new on the musical map, a Chopin that was full-bodied and unneurotic. And it was Rubinstein's perception of the Polish master that changed the attitude of twentieth-century pianists.

For many, Rubinstein's Chopin *is* Chopin. And what a public repertoire he possessed: the two sonatas, four scherzos, four ballades, four impromptus, the Fantasy in F minor, the Berceuse, six nocturnes, six polonaises, the

Barcarolle, the Tarantelle, five waltzes, most of the twenty-four preludes, and sixteen etudes—all of which he could play at the drop of a hat—not to mention the complete mazurkas, preludes, and waltzes, which he recorded. The etudes were never recorded because he felt he could not do justice to all of them. The least successful of his Chopin recordings are the Preludes, which are too careful, and consequently lifeless, and the majority of the Mazurkas, especially the last of the three sets he made, are academically played and literally stripped of their pungency. But one could write volumes about his best Chopin records. The Barcarolle, for example, is exquisitely paced, the phrasing arched, his breathing natural, his taste and simplicity utterly affecting. Rubinstein transforms even the rarely played Bolero, Op. 19, into something of a masterpiece; it becomes gallant, even regal, in his hands.

Rubinstein was at home in the chivalric style of the polonaises, and they are among the finest of his Chopin recordings. In these national tableaux Rubinstein was incapable of stopping the action to present a pleasing purple passage, and yet every page is infused with his specific and spacious style. Nobody who has heard him play the Polonaise in A-flat, Op. 53, will ever forget his verve and confidence. Rubinstein thrived in the Second and Third Scherzos, which were among his warhorses. Nobody played the Second Scherzo with more splendid spirit; the atmosphere in the concert hall was charged, the coda usually spattered with wrong notes, but the effect was exhilarating.

In the domain of the Romantic piano concerto, Rubinstein was king. Season after season he gave royal readings of the two Brahms concerti and the two Chopin concerti, the Schumann A minor, the Grieg and the Tchaikovsky, the Saint-Saëns Second, the Rachmaninoff Concerto No. 2 and *Rhapsody on a Theme of Paganini*, the Liszt E-flat, the Falla *Nights in the Gardens of Spain*. He never tired

of them. No performer in history extracted more juice from these time-honored scores.

Rubinstein's discography is a storehouse of treasures, though by no means the equal of his live performances, which had an irrepressible flow. In the studio, his inspiration was impeded by his fear of blemishes. This fight for cleanliness blunted him; he could not always come out of himself. His best recordings certainly testify to his greatness, yet future generations listening to them will never quite know his glory and the full majesty of his stage bearing and playing. Stravinsky wrote his *Three Scenes from Petrouchka* for Rubinstein, and nobody else has ever played it with such color and *joie de vivre*, even as he missed chunks of chords, yet it was never recorded, probably because he could never feel abandoned enough in a studio to make it come alive. Audiences were essential to Rubinstein; he sensed them to a startling degree, compelled them to participate in the event, and they heightened his art.

More than he loved music, more than he loved the piano—he loved life. He once said, "I am lucky to be a pianist. A splendid instrument, the piano, just the right size so that you cannot take it with you. . . . Instead of practicing I can read. A fortunate fellow, am I not?" For half a century, Arthur Rubinstein was the piano's most dashing cavalier, his joyous bravura proclaiming the grand manner. To an adoring public, he was an inspirational force, an expression of the very best in our civilization. There will never be another like him.

BERYL RUBINSTEIN
1898–1952 — United States

A pupil of Alexander Lambert, Busoni, and da Motta. He had a splendid academic career at the Cleveland Institute of Music, and be-

225

came its director. He was a composer of sparkling idiomatic piano works, wrote an outline for teachers called *Piano Pedagogy*, and often played in concert.

NIKOLAI RUBINSTEIN
1835–1881 — Russia

The younger brother of the great Anton Rubinstein, he studied with Alexander Villoing and then with Theodor Kullak. He was the founder of the Moscow Conservatory and the teacher of Sauer, Sergei Taneyev, Tchaikovsky, and Siloti. He composed some attractive trifles. His cool, classical, chiseled playing was the opposite of Anton's passionate intensity, yet he was deeply admired by his brother.

FRANZ RUMMEL
1853–1901 — England

He studied with Louis Brassin at the Brussels Conservatoire, making his debut at Antwerp in the Henselt Concerto. He had long-standing success as a teacher at the Stern Conservatory, and as a performer in many tours, including some in America.

WALTER RUMMEL
1887–1953 — Germany

The son of Franz Rummel, he worked with Godowsky and then began touring. He was a friend and early advocate of Debussy. Rummel is best known for his Bach transcriptions, but he also composed original works of quality.

VASSILY SAFONOV
1852–1918 — Russia

A very influential figure in Russian musical life. As a pianist, he had early success with his brilliant and finished technique. He was a teacher of renown, counting among his students Pressman, Medtner, Alexander Goedicke, Leonid Nicolaiev, Scriabin, and Rosina and Josef Lhévinne. They all worked with him at the Moscow Conservatory, of which he also became director. Safonov was also a conductor of special qualities, who dispensed with the use of a baton. He was a champion of Russian music and did much for Tchaikovsky's cause.

CAMILLE SAINT-SAËNS
1835–1921 — France

He studied with Stamaty and was trained in the precision school of playing exemplified by Zimmerman, Kalkbrenner, and Alkan.

Saint-Saëns was possibly the most astonishing prodigy in music after Mozart and Mendelssohn. He was playing Mozart and Beethoven by the age of five, and made his debut at ten in Beethoven's Third Concerto.

Saint-Saëns played throughout his long and illustrious career; composing for the piano came as naturally to him as did other branches of composition. "I produce music," he said, "as apples are produced from an apple tree." His philosophy was that music should please and satisfy. Emotion of a deep nature was alien to him, and it is unfair to ask more of him than he intended for his art.

He played the piano brightly, with a liking for very brisk tempi. Arthur Rubinstein, who often played the Saint-Saëns Second Concerto, heard him play the Chopin E major Scherzo, Saint-Saëns's favorite Chopin piece. "Too fast for my taste, but technically perfect." Isidor Philipp, who heard him often, thought, "It is impossible to play the piano with more strength and certainty, more spirit or rhythm, or naturalness. His interpretations are pure marvels of pianistic sculpture." He kept his piano technique in good shape. In 1920, at age eighty-five, he reported to Fauré, "You cannot imagine how hard I have been practicing your *Valse-caprice* in D-flat, but I have never got it off well enough to put it in my repertoire because I have never been able to practice it consistently enough. When I'm ninety, I shall perhaps be quite sure of it."

In 1915, Saint-Saëns made an edition of Mozart's piano music, which was often used. His own solo music, based on the pianism of Liszt, comprises some of the very best lighter pieces in the French repertoire. Liszt wrote to Olga von Meyendorff in 1877:

I know no one among contemporary artists who, all things considered, is his equal in talent, knowledge, and variety of skills—except for Rubinstein. However, the latter does not have the advantage of being an organist, in which capacity Saint-Saëns is not merely in the first rank but incomparable, as is Sebastian Bach as a master in counterpoint. You don't care much for the organ—the "Pope among instruments"—however, were you to hear Saint-Saëns play an organ worthy of his extraordinary virtuosity, I am convinced that you would be moved and amazed. No orchestra is capable of creating a similar impression; it is the individual in communion with music rising from earth to heaven.

His Toccata, *Allegro appassionato, Etude in the Form of a Waltz,* and many others are scintillating, and his five piano concerti, vulgar as they are in many pages, display a glittering pianism and an alluring feeling for the instrument. One of the finest of the concerti is No. 2, which Sigismund Stojowski quips "begins like Bach and ends like Offenbach." Perhaps a greater work is the more refined Fourth Concerto in C minor.

OLGA SAMAROFF
1882–1948 — United States

She studied with Ernest Hutcheson and at the Paris Conservatoire with Elie Delaborde. Samaroff was the first American woman to be admitted to the Paris Conservatoire. Her real name was Lucy Hickenlooper, but her manager was convinced that she needed a Slavic name to make a career.

She made a New York debut in 1905, and continued to play. Her dics on 78 show a very sensitive artist. She turned more to teaching in the mid-1920s, and became one of the world's most famous piano teachers. Claudette Sorel, Rosalyn Tureck, Eugene List, Raymond Lewenthal, and William Kapell studied with her. Alexis Weissenberg has said of Samaroff, "She was a brilliant woman who taught me in a marvelous way. She was one of the few teachers I have ever met whose pupils all played differently, and that you cannot say about many famous teachers. Individuality was

227

something she respected. She had great insight into the personality of her students, and she let people develop their own way."

HAROLD SAMUEL
1879–1937 — England

He studied first with Mathilde Verne and later with Edward Dannreuther. At his London debut in 1898, he played Bach's *Goldberg* Variations, which at that time were practically unknown. His solo career, however, was at a standstill until 1919, when he played an all-Bach program in London. He soon found a ready audience for large amounts of Bach's keyboard works in their original form. Few pianists played any Bach in public outside of organ arrangements. Samuel often gave, on consecutive days, five or six all-Bach recitals, in which he never repeated a work. He was reputedly able to play any Bach work from memory at any given moment.

In the 1920s he recorded a small segment of Bach: the B-flat Partita, the *English* Suite in A minor, the Chromatic Fantasy and Fugue, the Fantasia in C minor, and four preludes and fugues from *The Well-Tempered Clavier*. These discs display an impressive technique, swift and pliable, with interpretations that are very intelligible. Denis Hall wrote, "How modern the approach is to the music, the clarity of texture; the sense of rhythm, phrasing and rubato, the beautifully judged tempi and his highly individual use of dynamics. Samuel looked upon the clavichord's dynamic capabilities as an inherent part of the music, and it was therefore natural to transfer the interpretive qualities of the older instrument to the concert grand."

His Bach playing on the piano is stylistically less Romantic than that of Schnabel, Edwin Fischer, or Landowska, who chided Samuel for not playing on the harpsichord (Samuel

told her, "But Mme Landowska, I don't like the harpsichord"). It is very interesting and immensely profitable to compare the Samuel, Schnabel, Landowska, and Fischer recordings of the Chromatic Fantasy and Fugue.

Samuel was not a Bach specialist, however; he played a large repertoire from the Elizabethan composers to Ravel, and his Brahms playing was also respected.

PIERRE SANCAN
b. 1916 — France

Studied with Yves Nat at the Paris Conservatoire and has taught there. He is considered one of France's finest piano teachers. Sancan has played in public and has also composed.

SAMUEL SANDERS
b. 1940 — United States

He studied at the Juilliard School with Irwin Freundlich, later with Martin Canin. Very early in his career, he chose to be an accompanist. In this broad field, he has collaborated with many fine artists. Sanders is a subtle but rich accompanist whose musicianship is a boon to those he works with. His repertoire is extensive, and he has recorded dozens of albums.

GYÖRGY SÁNDOR
b. 1912 — Hungary

He studied with Bartók in Budapest and toured Europe extensively, settling in the United States just before the Second World

War. In 1946, Sándor premiered the Bartók Third Concerto with Ormandy, and he has, on occasion, played all three Bartók concerti in one evening. He is perhaps at his very best in Bartók, whose entire output he has recorded. His playing of this master is not always sensitive, but it is rugged, well planned, and filled with vitality. He understands the rhythms and his basically percussive tone is well suited to the style. One of his best discs is of Bartók's transcriptions of Baroque composers. Another good record is the piano music of Kodály, Sándor's composition teacher. Sándor has made recordings of the complete Prokofiev solo piano music; much of it is undigested, limited in emotional range, and tonally clangorous.

In Schumann, he is at his best in the Toccata and the *Carnaval,* but his *Kreisleriana* is stark and hollow, while his record of the Brahms Second Concerto, for all of its raw power, sounds loud, dull, and messy, with particularly ugly percussive chord playing. His Liszt playing is steely, tight-fisted, and can generate lots of excitement; his *Mephisto Waltz* moves like a whirlwind, and the Liszt Sonata, one of the fastest and flashiest on disc at 25:30, seems disjointed. Sándor has made many transcriptions, including Dukas's *Sorcerer's Apprentice* and the chaconne from the Bartók solo violin sonata. His book *On Piano Playing* was published in 1981.

JESÚS MARÍA SANROMÁ
1902–1984 — Puerto Rico

A student of Cortot and Schnabel, he had a long career as soloist and as an inspiring teacher both in the United States and in Puerto Rico. He played many premieres—including Parsi's Piano Sonata and Ferde Grofé's Piano Concerto—as well as the standard repertoire.

VASSILY SAPELLNIKOV
1868–1941 — Russia

He studied with Brassin and Sophie Menter at the St. Petersburg Conservatory, achieving a great reputation as a virtuoso. His specialty was the First Tchaikovsky Concerto. In a letter, Tchaikovsky wrote, "My great consolation is the pianist Sapellnikov, Menter's pupil. . . . My soul gets a rest with him." Shaw first heard him in 1890, in the London premiere of the Tchaikovsky Second Concerto: "It left me without any notion of Sapellnikov's rank as a player: he is, of course, swift and powerful with his fingers, but six bars of a Mozart sonata would have told me more about his artistic gift than twenty whole concertos of the Tchaikovsky sort." Shaw later wrote of his rendering of the Chopin A-flat Polonaise that the octave section "comes from his puissant hands like an avalanche." His few discs, including the Tchaikovsky concerto, show a wonderful left hand, as well as a simple and direct view of the music.

DAVID SAPERTON
1889–1970 — United States

He studied in the United States with August Spanuth. In Europe, he attended Busoni's master classes.

Saperton made his New York debut in 1905, with the Chopin E minor Concerto. In 1915 he met Leopold Godowsky, who became the paramount influence in his life, and also became his father-in-law. Saperton devoted a lot of time to conquering Godowsky's Chopin paraphrases, some of which he recorded in masterly fashion. Saperton was a major technician, and his influence as a teacher has been important. He 229 taught at the Curtis Institute from its early years, and his students included Abbey Simon, Jorge Bolet, Shura Cherkassky, Julius Katchen, Sidney Foster, and many others. His devotion to keyboard mastery and Romantic playing lives on in Bolet, Simon, and Cherkassky, who are descendants, through Saperton, of Leopold Godowsky. They represent, as Harold Schonberg put it, "a philosophy where the piano itself was the be-all and the end-all, less a musical instrument than a way of life."

In listening to Saperton, one is refreshed by the constant flow of musical ideas that today would be eschewed by many conservatory teachers and pupils as excessively mannered.

EMIL VON SAUER
1862–1942 — Germany

A student of Nikolai Rubinstein and one of the most successful pianists of the generation of Paderewski, Rosenthal, Freidheim, d'Albert, Carreño, and Busoni. Sauer also worked with Liszt, and we possess a wonderful disc of Liszt's two concerti, recorded when Sauer was seventy-seven, with another Liszt pupil, Felix Weingartner, conducting. It is the only collaboration on record of two Liszt students, and it shows Sauer still capable of excellent playing. His interpretations are slow but beautifully contoured and give us a clue as to how Liszt himself played them—unhurried, and grand in elevation.

Sauer, even in his prime, was never simply a bravura pianist, but one who played with great style and elegance, and with a beautifully even technique. Sauer was a combination of poet and virtuoso, and he played light music incomparably. His Chopin discs show a graciousness, but also elements of depth, as in the

B minor Sonata. To many ears, his playing sounds somewhat mannered, but it was much less so than that of a good many of his contemporaries.

Sauer was a delightful composer with many smaller works to his credit—Strauss transcriptions, as well as two piano sonatas and two concerti. He was universally considered a great teacher, and he left his mark on artists as diverse as Webster Aitken, Stefan Askenase, Maryla Jonas, Alexander Brailowsky, Ignace Hilsberg, and Elly Ney. Sauer made many editions, the most used being those of Liszt and Brahms.

IRENE SCHARRER
1885–1971 — England

A student of Matthay, she became famous for her brilliant playing. She appeared often with her cousin Myra Hess in two-piano recitals. She recorded a variety of music in straightforward, neatly balanced interpretations, representative of British pianism of the Matthay school.

XAVER SCHARWENKA
1850–1924 — Poland

He studied with Theodor Kullak, and went on to become one of the stars of European pianism. He composed prolifically, producing etudes, sonatas, and four piano concerti which are of considerable value, especially No. 1 in B-flat minor, magnificently recorded by Earl Wild. Scharwenka's Polish Dance in E-flat minor was one of the most popular piano pieces at the end of the nineteenth century. Its success obliterated his other works, as he feared it would. His compositions are quite strong and one may spend many delightful hours with him. He himself premiered his four piano concerti, and they served as part of the repertoire well into the early 1900s. No. 1 in B-flat minor is an outstanding Romantic concerto with fine themes, falling just short of the melodic magic necessary for survival. The working out of the material, however, is brilliant, and the last pages brim with glitter and excitement. His Theme and Variations, Op. 48, is a serious, estimable score of a dark quality, utilizing a variety of technical means, including plenty of octaves. The sixteen-year-old Arrau played it in Berlin in 1919.

H. V. Hamilton wrote: "As a pianist Xaver Scharwenka was renowned above all his other qualifications for the beautiful quality of his tone. If he was a specialist as interpreter of one composer rather than another, it was of Chopin . . . but of the other great masters his readings were always grand and musicianly, while to hear him play a waltz of Strauss was as dance-inspiring as the magic bells of Papageno."

ERNEST SCHELLING
1876–1939 — United States

He studied with Georges Mathias at the Paris Conservatoire from 1882 to 1885. As a prodigy, he was much discussed, but was plagued by poor health. He later studied for three years with Paderewski. As a pianist Schelling achieved a fine reputation, and his music, now forgotten, was often performed. There is a gorgeous reading by Paderewski of his *Nocturne à Ragaze*. On it one can hear why Paderewski hypnotized audiences—his tone is enchanting, with a delicacy in the

passagework. Schelling's finest work is a set of variations, *Impressions from an Artist's Life* for Piano and Orchestra, each variation being a portrait of a friend.

ANDRAS SCHIFF
b. 1953 — Hungary

He studied with Pál Kadosa at the Liszt Academy in Budapest. Later, in England, he worked with George Malcolm, who was a major influence on his general musicianship. He entered several competitions, but usually placed no higher than third or fourth. His reputation slowly grew, however, and he received widespread notice. In 1978 he made his Carnegie Hall debut, and ever since, his career has been of international scope.

Schiff is a refined player, uninterested in mere effect. His playing at times breathes a rarefied atmosphere that may or may not suit the idiom he is attempting. His Bach playing is unusual and tonally often ravishing; he can languish in Bach dances, yet he has such an unfailing sense of structure that all turns out well. He is one of a growing group of pianists who refuse to give Bach away to the harpsichordists. His performance on disc of the *Goldberg* Variations is lyrically conceived, and seems to move quickly even with all repeats. Schiff's piano tone is never anything but agreeable, often too much so. When he is carried away with himself, his tone sounds too sweet, like a soft marshmallow. When he pulls in the reins, he plays with poise, as in many Schubert pieces, where he feels very comfortable. His Mozart is tasteful, limpid, and beautifully played, and again his very individual approach can be hypnotic. Schiff is a Romantic by nature, and it is good to hear his lyricism flow deeply in Mozart. He is not always good in dramatic statements; the wild 231 floods of Beethoven are not suited to his gentle but high-strung temperament.

His Chopin playing can be both interesting and irritating. I heard a performance of the Preludes that was devoid of life. The pianist was playing as if the keyboard were made of eggshells. His best Chopin, however, is without affectation.

Schiff is not especially attracted to the showpiece repertoire, and his playing of the Tchaikovsky concerto, while distinctive in conception, remains a patchwork in performance. Lately, he has been doing splendid work in Dohnányi's *Nursery Tune* Variations, which allow his appealing sense of humor to be displayed. The twentieth-century composer he most esteems is Bartók, whose music he plays with sensitivity and a requisite boldness.

There is little doubt that Schiff is one of the most individual pianists of the present day and that he has the rare ability to express his own point of view in every phrase.

ALOYS SCHMITT
1788–1866 — Germany

An important pianist of the 1820s. His teaching was held in high regard, and he taught Ferdinand Hiller. He composed in many forms, and his etudes were often used.

E. ROBERT SCHMITZ
1889–1949 — France

He studied with Diémer at the Paris Conservatoire, taking a first prize. Subsequently he traveled widely, making a U.S. debut in 1919. He taught a great deal in North America and made numerous editions, including the Virgil Thomson Etudes. Schmitz gave the premiere, in 1946, of the Henri Barraud Concerto, and wrote a book, *The Piano Works of Claude Debussy,* which contains many valuable insights.

ARTUR SCHNABEL
1882–1951 — Poland

More than a century since his birth, and nearly four decades since his death, Schnabel's music-making remains deeply relevant to music lovers and musicians. "Schnabel represented in piano playing," said Glenn Gould, "something that was quite extraordinary, a way of looking almost directly at the music and bypassing the instrument." This procedure was revolutionary, and has made Schnabel one of the most potent interpretive forces of the century.

When Schnabel was growing up as a student of Leschetizky, the piano literature was mostly restricted to a specific branch of marketable Romantic music, which was beginning to be sold worldwide. Dozens of pianists were now performing in remote parts of the world, where audiences wanted to hear hackneyed Chopin pieces or Liszt's Rhapsodies. Very little Mozart, Haydn, Beethoven, or Bach was known at all.

Schnabel made his debut at the age of sixteen in Vienna's Bösendorfer Hall, playing the usual fare of the day. The program included pieces by Anton Rubinstein, Eduard Schütt, Moszkowski, and Leschetizky. But Leschetizky was certain that his serious young charge was not the usual marketplace concert aspirant. "You will never be a pianist," he said cryptically. "You are a musician." At that moment in history, the distinction was perhaps more evident than ever. Instead of stuffing him only with the standard virtuoso literature, Leschetizky introduced him to some all-but-unknown Schubert sonatas.

Schnabel started his career at the height of the craze for virtuosity; Clara Schumann, von Bülow, and Rubinstein had all died in the 1890s and taste was running at a particularly low level. To make matters worse, the musically underdeveloped areas on the concert circuit, such as Spain, Portugal, Italy, Latin America, and Australia, had atrocious audiences, who were often noisy and rude. Schnabel, however, had become convinced that his road was to play the great German classics, and his programs were unflinching in their demands, with no encores included. The road was often rough, but he persevered. He wrote to his wife, the lieder singer Therese Behr, "Some audiences in Spanish cities were so disappointed with my programs that I felt I was cheating them. Sometimes on the platform during my performance, I felt how unfair it was towards the audience—like in Seville while I was playing Beethoven's *Diabelli* Variations. I thought: 'Now, *this* is really unfair! I am the only person here who is enjoying this, and I get the money; they pay and have to suffer.' "

The turning point of his career came in 1927, with the Beethoven Centennial, where for the first time he played his Beethoven sonata cycle in London. By 1928, for the Schubert centenary, he made deep inroads into the Schubert literature, and he performed more and more frequently the neglected Mozart literature, especially the concerti. In 1931 he was asked to make the first recordings of the complete Beethoven sonatas. The project was finished in 1935. This achievement set the stamp on his celebrity. He became "the heavyweight title holder," as he put it. "As far as the public was concerned," Harold Schonberg noted, "Schnabel was the man who invented Beethoven." Indeed, his authority was such that the whole intellectual community understood Schnabel's Beethoven investigations as something profoundly important. The literary critic C. Day Lewis, for example, wrote, "When the critic has studied an author, lived with him in spirit over a long space of time, become saturated with him, an affinity may grow up between them so that some of the original power of the master is transmitted to the disciple. Like a great virtuoso, like Schnabel with Beethoven, the critic through his deep understanding may magnify the glory of his master: interpretation becomes an act of creation."

Schnabel once proposed, "It is unfortunate that the popularity of music is chiefly determined by the activities of the 'stars,' but it would be much better if we were to see the musician through music, rather than music through the musician." He never tired in his search for his ideal. Near the end of his career, he told his son after a recital that "for the first time I succeeded today in playing the last line of Beethoven's Sonata Opus 90 so that *I* found it convincing."

Schnabel dissected a score with both his head and his heart. "Music and musical art," he wrote, "are mysterious, inevitable, tangible and producible realities, cosmically related and individually fashioned; impersonal, personal and super-personal." His record producer Edward Crankshaw described Schnabel's questing nature:

He had to find out, to discover . . . removing with infinite application layer on layer of opacity, so that his performance of, say, the *Diabelli* Variations in his last years was like looking at the sun without dark glasses. . . . His trills (listen to the recording of the Variations of Beethoven's Opus 111) were not mechanical devices: They were variations of feelings, and always the same variation in the same place. He had a dozen quite distinct trills and could achieve through these more urgency and variety of expression than most musicians could achieve through the light and shade of a complete movement. His pauses were organic. Through them the music breathed. . . . When he played the arietta of Opus 111, time stood still.

The suggestion still lingers that Schnabel was a cerebral, cold pianist—a scholar and a pedant. On the contrary, he had more in common with his fellow Leschetizky students than with later Beethoven players like Brendel, Pollini, Bishop-Kovacevich, Anton Kuerti, Ashkenazy, or Glenn Gould, who pointed out that "Schnabel had certain trademarks, one of which was the tendency to use these extraordinary rushes in rather complicated stretti-like places. He would take the stretto, and, instead of simply coloring it harmonically, he would actually provide an acceleration almost automatically. It was very graphic, very gripping, but also very theatrical."

In a 1944 review of a Schnabel recital, Virgil Thomson contended: "There is too large a modicum of late nineteenth-century Romanticism in Mr. Schnabel's own personality to make his Beethoven—who was, after all, a child of the late eighteenth—wholly convincing to musicians of the mid-twentieth. No one wishes to deny the Romantic elements in Beethoven. But I do think that they are another kind of Romanticism from Schnabel's, which seems to be based on the Wagnerian theories of expressivity." Schnabel was indeed a full-blown nineteenth-century Romantic, with a tone as pellucid and haunting as Friedman's or Paderewski's. What he did was to wipe away a great deal of emotional and literary nonsense concerning Beethoven. He played without what he called "inside dynamics," which "were used as substitutes for genuine expression."

As he aged, Schnabel's tempi grew faster in the fast movements and slower in the slow ones. Some of this tendency came, no doubt, from the trauma of the recording process of his time, where he was confined to four minutes a side. In those years, Schnabel, I feel, was still insecure with the rather new "recording audience," and he overemphasized or underlined many things that more experienced listeners hear easily and naturally.

Despite his apparent disregard for the mechanical side of playing, it must not be thought, as has often been charged, that Schnabel had small technical means or that what he did have was faulty. That is absurd, and Schnabel—a child prodigy—was brilliantly equipped by Leschetizky. There is no doubt that he became lazy in technical matters. He let some basic aspects of his craft slip here and there, and he could splatter a performance with wrong notes. But as Eugene Istomin said, "After all, what do a few botched bars matter on the ascent to Olympus." Schnabel was a busy man, a teacher in the master-class tradition, and a highly serious composer of atonal music, which he himself refused to champion in performance. Certainly, practicing bored him. In his many records, I hear at times a kind of futility, even of torture, an artist of magnitude attempting to escape the exigencies of manual technique, of the hands themselves. Schnabel was, however, a very natural pianist, with a magnificent and inborn facility, and of course the most searching test of technique in its deepest sense is the musician's ability to sustain interest, structure, and breath in a long slow movement. In the slow movements of Op. 106 and indeed of many Beethoven sonatas, as well as several of Schubert's sonatas, Schnabel reached the loftiest regions manifested by hands upon a keyboard. Indeed, he was a genius at holding the listener's attention span in long structures. In fact, he helped make better audiences and better listeners.

Although he wore an inconspicuous suit, and played without ostentation, Schnabel's concerts became cultural status symbols. Not to attend almost amounted to philistinism. His students adored him and aped his programming. Schnabel had said, "I play only works that I consider better than they can be performed. It is a never-ending task, for they are so total and universal." Those works meant, to Schnabel, the Germans, and an unhealthy snobbery ensued, as many of his student-disciples pursued very little else, vying to cram as many Schubert sonatas as possible into a program. As critic Harris Goldsmith puts it, Chopin's Barcarolle and B minor Sonata are also "better than they can be played."

It is interesting to note that when the compact disc came on the market, people instantly asked, "When will Schnabel come out on CD?" It appears that in an era increasingly preoccupied with standardized virtuosity, Schnabel's flaming heart, even his insistence many times on being less than perfect, has become a measure of artistic conscience. As Bruno Walter marveled in his autobiography, "It is one of the encouraging symptoms of contemporary musical life that a pianist of so serious a bent, of so progressive an engrossment in his work, and of so strict an artistic morality, can continue to be eminently successful throughout a long career."

KARL ULRICH SCHNABEL
b. 1909 — Germany

The son of Artur Schnabel, Karl studied with Leonid Kreutzer and has had a long and distinguished career as a performer, a writer, and a teacher.

GERMAINE SCHNITZER
1888–? — France

A student of Pugno, she won first prize at the Paris Conservatoire. She had further studies with Sauer and commenced concert-giving. In 1906 she made her New York debut.

JOHANN SAMUEL SCHRÖTER
1750–1788 — Poland

A very important early pianist who made a sensation when his playing was first heard in London. He was among the first musicians to devote themselves entirely to the piano instead of the harpsichord. The celebrated historian Dr. Burney wrote: "He became one of the neatest and most expressive players of his time. It was graceful and in good taste, but so chaste as sometimes to seem deficient in fire and invention."

ANDRÉ-MICHEL SCHUB
b. 1953 — France

He was born in France but has lived in the United States since infancy. He studied with Jascha Zayde, as well as Rudolf Serkin. In 1974, Schub made a New York debut. He won the Van Cliburn Competition in 1981. He is a pianist of great solidarity. His concerts and recordings are rather brittle, but technically well executed.

JULIUS SCHULHOFF
1825–1898 — Czechoslovakia

He studied with Johann Tomáschek in Prague and appeared with success in the various capitals of Europe. He was still of the school that promoted playing one's own music, and he never developed a large public repertoire.

Leschetizky, as a young pianist, was deeply influenced by Schulhoff's ravishing tone, which became his ideal. Hearing him for the first time in 1846, Leschetizky wrote, "He began a composition of his, *Le Chant du berger*. Under his hands, the piano seemed like another instrument . . . not a note escaped me. I began to foresee a new style of playing. That melody standing out in bold relief, that wonderful sonority—all this must be due to a new and entirely different touch. And that cantabile, a legato such as I had not dreamed possible on the piano, a human voice rising above the sustaining harmonies! . . . Schulhoff's playing was a revelation to me. From that day I tried to find that touch. . . . I kept that beautiful sound well in my mind, and it made the driest work interesting." At that time, Leschetizky had not yet heard Chopin, Liszt, Rubinstein, Clara Schumann, Henselt, or Thalberg, all greater pianists who had brought tone production to the forefront. Leschetizky's revelation, however, is important as a barometer of the warmer, more colorful playing that was being newly demanded, rather than the drier, less pedaled piano playing still prevalent in Vienna at that time.

ADOLF SCHULZ-EVLER
1852–1905 — Poland

A pianist who studied with Tausig. The author of many compositions, Schulz-Evler survives in the annals of pianism only through his ingenious concert arabesques on themes of *On the Beautiful Blue Danube* by Johann Strauss, Jr. This elaborate network of pianistic machinations has been brilliantly recorded by Josef Lhévinne and more recently by Shura Cherkassky, Stanley Waldoff, Jorge Bolet, and others.

CLARA SCHUMANN (née WIECK)
1819–1896 — Germany

She studied exclusively with her father, Friedrich Wieck, whose one object in life was to produce a major pianist in his daughter. In

this he succeeded completely, for Clara Wieck became the most influential woman musician of the nineteenth century, and doubtless the greatest woman pianist of the age. Few women have had a more complicated life—she was a good daughter, a dedicated wife to Robert Schumann, a successful and devoted mother, and a glowing friend to Brahms for forty-five years, as well as a teacher of far-reaching influence and a worthy composer. But, as Joan Chissell writes in her monograph on Clara Schumann, "first and foremost, she was a concert pianist. Music-making was the great motivating force of her life, a mission from which any deviation, whatever the counterclaims of a warm and vulnerable human heart, was a betrayal. Nothing less than such a belief could have carried her through travails so arduous, and personal tribulation at times so bitter."

Indeed, Clara Schumann had one of the central careers of nineteenth-century pianism. It was through her valiant efforts that the great interpretive era dawned. Her performing career and the magnitude of her repertoire were equaled by no man: thirteen hundred printed programs have been preserved. She played in public from the age of seven, until 1888; only crippling arthritis stopped her restless career. Her hardest times were the sixteen years of marriage to Schumann, when she single-handedly raised eight children, bitterly resenting the curtailment of her concert life. At his death in 1856, she was only thirty-seven. Faced with the pressing need to support her family, she resumed her career, and with a vengeance. Many a physically strong man has bowed under the pressures of touring, but Mme Schumann could give up to five concerts in four towns within a week. And her programs were uncompromising. She was a great educator, and she is among the creators of the modern recital format. Her father, with his eye to the cash-box, gave Clara music by Hünten, Kalkbrenner, and Herz, as well as other pot-boilers, to play as a child. But Clara quickly outgrew such fare, and Friedrich Wieck was hardly pleased when his own student, Robert Schumann (nine years older than Clara), began inundating the impressionable teenager with Bach, Beethoven, Chopin, and, worst of all, his own "weird" music.

Soon, however, she would exclaim: "I will yield to popular demands only in so far as they do not betray my own convictions." Clara was a champion of the new Romanticism of Mendelssohn (she played the wonderful *Capriccio brillant* with the composer conducting in 1835) and Henselt (she loved his Etudes, and she premiered the F minor Concerto). At the age of twelve, she publicly performed Chopin's *Là ci darem la mano* Variations, Op. 2, and she added Chopin's new pieces to her repertoire literally as they were printed. Robert thought Chopin's playing was incomparable, "but Clara," he wrote, "is a greater virtuoso, and gives almost more meaning to his compositions than Chopin himself." However, she was repelled by Liszt's grand manner and unbridled temperament, although he dedicated his famous *Paganini Etudes* to her. She played some of his transcriptions of Schubert songs, but later abhorred all that she felt he stood for, including his son-in-law Wagner's "music of the future"; she thought *Tristan* the most repugnant music she had ever heard in her life.

Sad to say, she even suppressed Liszt's name from the dedication of Schumann's great Fantasy in her edition of her husband's works. She once said that Liszt had "the decline of piano playing on his conscience." Liszt retorted, "If you want to hear Schumann's music played as it should be, don't listen to Clara." Of course, Clara playing Robert's music became a tradition, and it was through her immense persistence that this great branch of repertory made its impact. Clara Schumann was an institution in England, and her performances of Schumann were sacred writ. On stage she always wore black, and she was dubbed "the professional widow." Paderewski, in his early London appearances, collided with her on Schumann. In his delightful memoirs, he rejoined:

The *Times* critic did not agree with my playing of Schumann, of course, because he belonged to Madame Clara Schumann's congregation. So my playing of Schumann displeased him very much. It was revolutionary for him, he was accustomed to that modest and very restrained Schumann-playing as performed by that very old lady! It was a tradition, and I was destroying, or disturbing, that tradition. I played it exactly as Schumann wanted it played—I mean not as to perfection, but as to the dynamics of the composition. When it was *fortissimo*, I played it *fortissimo*, which Madame Schumann, poor lady, could not produce. Therefore, in all these works, which were played in public by her, and which had established a certain tradition, I surprised the audience, and audiences do not like surprises.

But this was in 1890, and Mme Schumann had made her last London appearances in 1888, when she was racked by pain in her wrists and fingers. Nor had Paderewski heard her in her prime, as she was born forty-one years before he was. There had, however, grown up around her school of playing a kind of genteel Victorianism, which must have had little appeal to the vigorous virtuoso of the Leschetizky school.

A much more balanced view of Clara Schumann comes in a review by the great critic Eduard Hanslick. Clara played six concerts in Vienna early in 1856, containing Beethoven's *Emperor* Concerto, the Thirty-two Variations in C minor, the Sonatas Op. 31, No. 2, Opp. 81a and 101, and the *Hammerklavier,* besides works of Schumann, Mendelssohn, Weber, Chopin, Henselt, and the young Brahms, including the C major Sonata, Op. 1. Hanslick, reporting on her second concert, maintains:

As a young girl, she already stood above the insipid trifles of virtuosity and was one of the first to preach the gospel of the austere German masters. . . . Her penetrating understanding of every kind of music . . . is such that she can treat the whole range of technique as a matter completely dominated and utterly at her disposition. In one or another aspect of virtuosity, she may be surpassed by other players, but no other pianist stands quite as she does at the radial point of these different technical directions, focusing their respective virtues on the pure harmony of beauty. Although mere correctness is hardly her objective, it forms the essential basis on which she builds. To give a clear expression to each work in its characteristic musical style and, within this style, to its purely musical proportions and distinctions, is ever her main task.

Sir George Grove felt her place as a pianist was "indubitably in the very first rank; indeed she may perhaps be considered to stand higher than any of her contemporaries, if not as regards the possession of natural or acquired gifts, yet in the use she made of them." Bernard Shaw, upon first hearing her, "recognized, before she had finished the first phrase of Schubert's C minor Impromptu, what a nobly beautiful and poetic player she was. An artist of that sort is the Holy Grail of the critic's quest."

Clara Schumann brought to the concert stage an unprecedented seriousness. She did not consider herself only a performer, but an *interpreter* whose role was to shed light upon music of considered quality. As fine music began to be valued above mere displays of virtuosity, Clara Schumann's interpretations became yardsticks of musical integrity.

LUDWIG SCHUNKE
1810–1834 — Germany

A student of Kalkbrenner. By the age of ten, he could play concertos by Hummel and Mozart. He performed his own concerto in London in 1826, with Weber conducting. Later he developed a friendship with Schumann and they lived together. They were, in Schumann's words, "indispensable to each other," and he wrote of their friendship that they were "living out a novel the likes of which may never before have been put into a book." Schumann dedicated to him his great Toccata, which Schunke played magnificently.

Schunke died of tuberculosis before reaching the age of twenty-four. Some of his piano pieces have been recorded, and they display a considerable talent for piano writing.

EDUARD SCHÜTT
1856–1933 — Russia

He studied with Reinecke and Leschetizky, was soloist in his own piano concerto, frequently performed, and edited Schumann's piano music. Schütt composed salon music of charm and pianistic finesse.

MIKLOS SCHWALB
b. 1909 — Hungary

A student of Dohnányi. He made his debut in Budapest in 1923. He later moved to the United States, taught at the New England Conservatory in Boston, and made recordings.

LUDVIG SCHYTTE
1848–1909 — Denmark

An admirable pianist who studied with Edmund Neupert. Then, in Weimar, he worked with Liszt. Afterward, he resided in Vienna, where he played, composed, and taught. Schytte's works are beautifully crafted, lightweight music. He composed a piano concerto, Op. 28.

ALEXANDER SCRIABIN
1872–1915 — Russia

He studied with Nikolai Zverev and later at the Moscow Conservatory with Safonov. He and Josef Lhévinne were at the Conservatory at the same time, and the frail Scriabin once strained his right hand practicing Liszt's *Don Juan* Fantasy and Balakirev's *Islamey* in an attempt to compete with the strength of Lhévinne's virtuosity. It was around this time that he wrote his famous Nocturne for the Left Hand Alone. In 1892 he received the Gold Medal from the Conservatory and began concertizing. From 1898 to 1904, he taught at the Moscow Conservatory. In 1906 he made an American debut.

Scriabin was a fascinating and strange man, high-strung and excessive. He thought his art would help bring about a new world order. As composer and pianist, he became totally absorbed in his own work. Arthur Rubinstein, who greatly admired Scriabin's music, reported that when, as a young man, he met the composer, Scriabin asked him, "Who is your favorite composer?" "When I answered without hesitation, 'Brahms,' he banged his fist on the table. 'What, what?' he screamed. 'How can you like this terrible composer and me at the same time?' " Pianists inclined to Classicism or mental balance may have interpretive problems in Scriabin's rarefied world. With its erotic impulse, it is the kind of music which can become addictive. It is also the most original piano music composed in Russia during the first decade and a half of the century.

His compositions of the 1890s had been inspired by the purity and refinement of Chopin.

Later Scriabin added both a diabolical quality reminiscent of Liszt, but far more esoteric, and the hyperchromaticism of Wagner's *Tristan*. In his later music, he began using harmonic convolutions built upon fourths, which he termed "the mystery chord." Scriabin was a pianistic genius of a high order, and his work is a musical paradise, filled with the most inventive layouts—treacherous left-hand writing; novel widespread figuration; imaginative trill effects. He said he wanted his music to express the unheard tones between the keys, an effect calling for creative use of the pedals. This late music is the embodiment of ecstatic and trance-like states.

Although he deigned to play only his own music, Scriabin performed far and wide, and his playing was always controversial. He must have been a pianist of exceptional ardor—Alfred Swan described him as "all nerve and a holy flame." The writer Alexander Pasternak added:

His playing was unique. . . . It could not be imitated by producing similar tone, or power of softness, for he had a special and entirely different relationship with the instrument, which was his own unrepeatable secret. As soon as I heard the first sounds on the piano, I immediately had the impression that his fingers were producing the sound without touching the keys. His enemies used to say it was not real piano playing, but a twittering of birds or a mewing of kittens. His spiritual lightness was reflected in his playing: in his gait, his movements, his gesticulations, the way he jerked his head up when he spoke. Scriabin's nervous playing was one of his characteristics.

This nervosity of execution is apparent even in the few piano rolls he made, which have been issued on LP. He plays his D-sharp minor Etude, Op. 8, No. 12, in the heat of conflict; his wrists are rotary machines. It is arrhythmical, vertiginous, uniquely ecstatic, and faster than anyone else's. His spiritual descendants are Horowitz and Sofronitsky, and he passed on his tradition by instructing Goldenweiser, Elena Beckman-Scherbina, Konstantin Igumnov, Samuel Feinberg, and others, who continued to play and teach his music even after the Russian Revolution, when his orgiastic, super-sensuous, and harmonic adventurousness was considered decadent.

GYÖRGY SEBÖK
b. 1922 — Hungary

He studied and taught in Budapest, and settled in the United States. Sebok has recorded, and is a well-known teacher at Indiana University.

HANS SEELING
1828–1862 — Czechoslovakia

A very successful concert pianist who composed many character pieces for the piano which were popular, such as the Op. 10 Concert Etudes; *Memories of an Artist*, Op. 13; the Barcarolle; and the *Lorelei*, Op. 2.

ISIDOR SEISS
1840–1905 — Germany

A pupil of Friedrich Wieck, he went on to become a successful pianist, a teacher at the Cologne Conservatory, and the composer of many excellent piano pieces.

BLANCHE SELVA
1884–1942 — France

A student at the Paris Conservatoire, she made a debut at thirteen, and at twenty she performed the entire keyboard output of J. S. Bach in seventeen recitals. She was a remarkable musician who taught at the Schola Cantorum in Paris and at the Prague and Strasbourg Conservatories. She was also a brilliant scholar who wrote several books, perhaps the most important being *La Sonate*, published in 1913.

As a pianist, Selva dedicated herself to bringing to the public many works of the modern French school. She premiered and promoted Albéniz's *Iberia*. D'Indy dedicated to Selva his important Sonata, Op. 63, which she premiered in 1908, and Roussel dedicated his fine Suite for Piano, Op. 14, to her.

PETER SERKIN
b. 1947 — United States

The son of Rudolf Serkin. He began studying at the Curtis Institute of Music at the age of eleven. His teachers were his father, Horszowski, and Lee Luvisi.

The young Serkin appeared in concert early, and in his teens he toured the United States; in 1959 he made a New York debut. At sixteen, he was performing in public such monumental works as the Bach *Goldberg* Variations. I heard them at that time and was pleased with his wonderful feeling for them. Every note was in place, and while he played with seriousness of purpose, he also displayed charm. His early disc of the *Goldberg* without repeats is very congenial and well designed. Nonetheless, a much later recording made in Freiburg, Germany, repeats included, puts the earlier version in the shade. His later conception is that of a mature artist playing from his brain and his heart, while the earlier one is that of a greatly gifted student toying with the daemon of this testament to Baroque variation form.

From the first there appeared in Peter Serkin's work a very special gentleness. This quality is displayed in a pristine manner in a

1967 disc of Schumann's *Waldscenen* in which the famous *Prophet Bird* is played with exquisite care and tonal plasticity. On that same album is Serkin's delicately shaped and ethereal view of Schubert's seldom played early E-flat Sonata, D. 568. Serkin's openness and purity of feeling here are utterly captivating; he gives us Schubert's music at its most vulnerable.

Serkin has always warmed to Schubert and has a real connection to his music. It is surely a less weighty and "serious" Schubert than his father's. The only Peter Serkin Schubert-playing that has left me cold is a recording of Schubert dances played on a fortepiano that are too dry and cheerless.

He has made several curious Chopin discs; they are uneven and not instantly appealing. Certainly the waltz readings are unconvincing in tempo and in use of rubato. The Barcarolle hardly sails in smooth waters, but perhaps it should be rockier than we are accustomed to. The nocturnes provoke Serkin; though he gorges himself on the slowness of the F-sharp minor Nocturne, Op. 48, No. 2, his conception of the D-flat trio of that nocturne is the most convincing I have heard. His most fascinating Chopin performance is the *Polonaise-fantaisie,* which in its deep ominousness recalls Liszt's description of the work as pathological. In his Chopin, Peter Serkin never strives for lushness of sound, nor has he ever been interested in crashing sonority.

Beethoven is of importance to this deep-thinking artist. He plays many sonatas, but there is an odd cast to his Beethoven; his readings of the *Diabelli* Variations are stark, awkward, constipated, and even maddening. The performance feels like an eternity rather than fifty-five minutes.

Peter Serkin's Mozart is more memorable in concerti than in the solo works. In such pieces as the D minor Fantasy he gets bogged down in too much pedaling and profundity, and his D major Rondo doesn't bubble as it ought.

But even his Mozart concerti have not grown on me, though they are unconventional, and his piano sound is distinctive.

No American has been such an advocate for Messiaen's superstructures as Peter Serkin. He is exalted in this music, which stirs in him something deep and suggestive. His three-record set of *Vingt Regards sur l'Enfant Jésus* is certainly a great feat. The usual tendency in this music is to be muddy and smear the textures, or to provide a false ecstasy; Serkin's piercing musical intelligence avoids both of these pitfalls. He lets no rest go unnoticed; he feels purely. It is clean playing of the utmost honesty.

Few others perform the modern literature with such care. How different is his sparse Bartók Concerto No. 1 from his father's more vivid reading. The younger Serkin is ideally suited to the meditative nobility of Bartók's Third Concerto. In his beautifully stated performance of the Schoenberg Concerto, his prime concern is for perfect ensemble playing and control of shape. He has championed works by Stefan Wolpe, such as the Passacaglia, *Form IV,* and Pastorale, and solo pieces by Peter Lieberson: the Bagatelles, and the large-scale Piano Concerto with Ozawa conducting.

Serkin was a founding member of the chamber group Tashi, in which he participated in performances of works by Takemitsu, Berio, and others.

RUDOLF SERKIN
b. 1903 — Austria

Studied piano in Vienna with Richard Robert and composition with Joseph Marx and Arnold Schoenberg. Serkin made his debut at the age of twelve, and at seventeen he appeared in recitals with the violinist Adolf Busch. In 1939 he became a member of the faculty of the Curtis Institute, later becoming its president. He has been head of the annual summer festival at Marlboro, Vermont.

Serkin is one of the leading figures in the performing of music in our time. As a teacher at Curtis and as the guiding light at the Marlboro School of Music, he has inspired countless musicians to strive for the highest levels of artistic achievement. No other pianist today has so faithful a flock. As a performer and a teacher Serkin remains a fierce idealist who sees human grandeur in the greatest music. He has been a musical conscience to many piano students and concertgoers.

On the concert stage, Serkin appears slightly desperate. He has an inner drive that is almost frightening. The playing grips him, taking its toll in panting, sweat, and facial writhings; simply put, Serkin is spilling out his guts. He is forever looking within the score for a definitive version, his *vision*. But the music never seems quite conquered; it is always on the brink of something uncontrollable. This is what makes a Serkin performance so draining. I have seen audiences hushed and totally exhausted as they leave the hall. When Serkin is on, there is an exaltation that is like a blazing light. The performances take on an aesthetic truth.

Serkin knows well the musical results that his lofty conceptions can bear, but he is inconsistent in bringing them to fruition. He is a purging spirit, and when he is not achieving his ends, things can turn from bad to banging. His austerity turns ponderous, dry, and stilted, the bleakness of his sound turns brittle. He strives for a profound simplicity, and the effort can turn crude and thumpy, while his curiously untapered phrase endings give much of his work its peculiar angularity and tautness. There is always stress in a Serkin performance; it underlies all of his playing, from the slenderest of Mozart concerto readings to the Brahms B-flat Concerto. His style is unmistakable. Clearly, this master is not interested in being a colorist; he never luxuriates in either sound or conception. He is not a musical voluptuary, like his contemporary Vladimir Horowitz, but a worker in pen and black ink: a maker of large, lean, expressive forms. When listening to Serkin, I am often reminded of the lithographs of Albrecht Dürer.

An appreciation of Serkin's art does not come easily, especially for Slavic-trained pianists. The trappings are not pretty, and his monochrome palette and ascetic musicality are becoming more extreme in his late years, especially in his recordings.

It has often been said that Serkin is not a natural pianist. Indeed, he does royal battle at the instrument. His physical playing is unorthodox, and he is a pianist made and not born to the keyboard. He seems to will his hands not to fail him. Yet Serkin has an admirable technique and has performed the Chopin etudes publicly, though this music is more an emotional relaxation for him than an affinity.

Serkin's art is at its apex in Beethoven, whose anger and violence he captures. There is no *Pathétique* that matches his in intensity, and no other *Moonlight* Sonata has such Beethovenian wrath in the finale. His *Appassionata* is ruthless in its logic, with a finale that is scorching. He can whip chords into a scathing sound that is entirely Serkinian. Recently I was listening to his recording of the Beethoven Sonata Op. 101. Scalpel in hand, he grotesquely dissects its strange march movement. At first, I was revolted at its ugliness, but soon my mind was won over to his way. How well Serkin understands these cerebral but nerve-racking pages. His Beethoven playing has always been a mainstay for serious collectors, and with his powerful rhythmic sense, he is as successful in the Concerti as in the sonatas. The finale of the C major Concerto has a joyous motoric power; his recording of the Fourth Concerto with Toscanini has given untold pleasure; his

Emperor Concerto is might itself, and his *Diabelli* Variations possess a spectrum of drama that finds no equal.

Serkin naturally finds himself at home with Brahms, and his discs of the two concerti are vast in scope. Among my great musical memories are Serkin's performances of these concerti with Szell and the Cleveland Orchestra. They were titanic in the second movement of the B-flat Concerto, the movement Brahms called "a tiny, tiny wisp of a scherzo," while in the first movement of the D minor Concerto, one was reminded that Sir Donald Francis Tovey called the opening the mightiest utterance since the Beethoven Ninth Symphony. Serkin's recording of the Brahms *Handel* Variations is a fine example of his ability to create a cumulative effect. Unlike most who jauntily charge out with the theme in high relief, Serkin begins almost unpromisingly, if not tentatively, as if to say, let's see how pregnant with variational possibilities this slight tune really is.

I have always found Serkin's Schubert a shade less successful than his Brahms and Beethoven. He has achieved a mammoth structure in the great B-flat Sonata; however, his playing sounds too stubborn, too raw, lacking a delicate charm and flow. His greatest achievement in Schubert remains his performance of the posthumous A major Sonata (D. 959) where grandeur and grace are perfectly mated.

In Mozart, Serkin's superior organization makes for important readings of the concerti. They are always solid and serious. His discs of the concerti with Alexander Schneider are justly celebrated. Other outstanding Serkin performances of Mozart are the Rondo in A minor and the Sonata in C minor, which are deeply serious in tone.

Serkin has recorded a surprisingly broad repertory of concertos, ranging from the Bartók No. 1, the Prokofiev No. 4, the Reger F minor, in a powerful performance (he has championed Reger and has publicly performed and recorded his Variations on a Theme by Bach), and the Strauss *Burleske* (a favorite version of mine), to the bold recordings of the two Mendelssohn concerti. No. 1 in G minor is fresh and glittering, gleefully bursting its seams. Even at eighty-five Serkin continues to play in public with a somewhat impaired technique but with the same uncompromising commitment and fierce intensity.

GIOVANNI SGAMBATI
1841–1914 — Italy

An Italian pianist of great talent. His brilliant performances helped considerably to raise the taste of Italian audiences unused to hearing instrumental music, especially the German classics; he also introduced them to many new compositions by Liszt, Brahms, and Saint-Saëns. As a child, he studied with Amerigo Barberi. In 1860 he settled in Rome, where he played Beethoven, Schumann, and Chopin, as well as Bach and Handel. He gave the Roman premiere of the *Emperor* Concerto. During that period, he studied with Liszt in Rome, and Liszt admired him greatly. He traveled widely, conducting as well as playing. In 1882 he introduced his own piano concerto to England. While in London, he performed privately for Queen Victoria. In 1903 he went to Russia. Sgambati was honored in his homeland and was a founder of the Liceo Musicale, where he taught piano. His music is of a uniformly fine quality. He had a rare facility for writing for his instrument, and some of his work, especially the two piano quintets, deserves to be revived. Rachmaninoff, Levitzki, and Earl Wild have made recordings of his lovely transcription of the "Melody" from Gluck's *Orfeo;* Bolet recorded the Sgambati Concerto in G minor.

DIMITRIS SGOUROS
b. 1969 — Greece

He began playing at seven years old. The next year he made a debut. Ever since, this phenomenon has played publicly, showing a tremendous technique in the most stunning virtuoso music. He was performing a splendid Chopin E minor at the age of twelve, and at thirteen he was heard with Rostropovich at Carnegie Hall in the Rachmaninoff Third Concerto, playing it to the hilt with a real flair for the score. He has an assured stage presence and plays with a strength that seems to belie his slight physique. His performance, at age fourteen, of the Schumann *Symphonic Etudes* and the Brahms *Paganini* Variations at Avery Fisher Hall was full of temperament and musical to the core. Occasionally he forces too much and produces stiff playing, but it appears that, within large forms, Sgouros has an organizational mind far beyond his age.

ARTHUR SHATTUCK
1881–1951 — United States

He studied with Leschetizky for a long period, from 1895 to 1902, noting that Leschetizky "on some days would be harsh, critical, exacting; at other times indifferent." Shattuck toured throughout the world, playing in many far-flung places. He was the first to tour Iceland, and played throughout Egypt. For several months he practiced on his grand piano at an oasis deep in the Sahara. "For a pianist with a vivid imagination," he said, "and a real desire to work, it is an ideal place to study." Shattuck came back to the United States during World War I, and performed successfully for many years.

FRANK SHERIDAN
1898–1962 — United States

A student of Harold Bauer, Sheridan was an excellent pianist with a solid technique. His recording of Schumann's *Carnaval* is characteristic of his playing—conservative, but poetic. He was a well-known teacher at the Mannes College of Music in New York. It was habitual for him to make students learn the Chopin Etudes, followed by the Liszt *Transcendental Etudes*.

RUSSELL SHERMAN
b. 1930 — United States

A pianist of perception, beautiful tone, and sympathy in a varied repertoire; his Chopin Twenty-four Preludes are poetic, his Beethoven complete concerti and various sonatas are grand and often profoundly moving in the slow movements. His best-known discs are of Liszt's *Transcendental Etudes,* which are treated in a thoroughly musical manner.

Sherman studied with Edward Steuermann from the age of eleven. He made his New York debut at Town Hall in 1945. For some years he disappeared from the concert stage, but since the mid-1970s he has recorded and concertized extensively. For many years he was the chairman of the piano department at the New England Conservatory in Boston.

WILLIAM SHERWOOD
1854–1911 — United States

After studies in New York, he traveled to Weimar for finishing lessons with Liszt. In 1876 he returned to America to become one of the distinguished pianists and teachers of his time.

LEONARD SHURE
b. 1910 — United States

In Berlin, Shure studied with Schnabel, the most important influence of his musical life. He returned to the United States, where he has had a long career as a teacher in Boston, Cleveland, and elsewhere. His interpretations of Beethoven are remarkable for their depth of thought and their large scale. He taught Jerome Rose and Gilbert Kalish.

JEFFREY SIEGEL
b. 1942 — United States

He studied in Chicago with Ganz, in New York with Rosina Lhévinne and Ilona Kabos. He has recorded the music of Gershwin with flair and technical abundance, as well as the marvelous Sonata by Henri Dutilleux, in which Siegel is an expert craftsman. At a recent recital, Siegel premiered a very difficult Liszt paraphrase on *Ernani* which he discovered.

MARTIN SIEVEKING
1867–1950 — Netherlands

He had a fine reputation as a performer and teacher. His early studies were with Leschetizky. He was well known for his method of weight relaxation. His hand was extremely large, and he played with power and brilliance.

BÉLA SIKI
b. 1923 — Hungary

Studied at the Liszt Academy. He has since taught extensively and recorded. He exhibits a virtuoso mechanism and has a great knowledge of the piano literature.

ALEXANDER SILOTI
1863–1945 — Russia

He studied with Zverev and Nikolai Rubinstein, later with Liszt. His little volume, *My Memories of Liszt,* is valuable for its many insights into Liszt's personality, playing, teaching, and humanity.

Siloti was a brilliant musician, a dedicated teacher of Rachmaninoff, who was his cousin (and who dedicated his First Piano Concerto and the Preludes Op. 23 to him), as well as of Igumnov and Goldenweiser in Russia, and later a whole generation of young pianists who studied with him at Juilliard.

Siloti made many editions and transcriptions which show a rare perception of the piano. His editions must be looked at with care, as he takes many liberties with the text. He was a true late-Romantic, and the composers' intentions were seldom enough for him. Siloti never recorded, but his editions may give one a clue to his performances.

In his early years, he was one of the most influential musicians in St. Petersburg. He was a brilliant fixture of its varied musical life, both as a pianist and as a conductor. Mark W. Grant, in his introduction to Siloti's *My Memories of Liszt,* wrote: "In turn-of-the-century Russia it was Siloti who was a more famous pianist, and perhaps a more highly regarded one, than Rachmaninoff; whereas Rachmaninoff was considered precise and over-perfect, Siloti's playing was said to have more charm and sentimentality. This distinction would align Siloti in style with such players as Paderewski, de Pachmann, et al.; Rachmaninoff more with the later Hofmann and Lhévinne." Siloti's student Bernardo Segall has said of his playing that "it was the Romantic sense of adventure, very Lisztian . . . he played from the heart—direct, with great simplicity and nobility and a beautiful singing tone."

ABBEY SIMON
b. 1922 — United States

He studied with David Saperton at the Curtis Institute. In 1941 he won the Naumburg Competition, and he has received the Elizabeth Sprague Coolidge Medal and the Harriet Cohen Medal. His concert tours have taken him all over the world. He has been on the faculty of the Juilliard School since 1977. Chopin is the mainstay of his large repertoire, and he has been recording the complete works. All of his Chopin is pianistic, with just a hint of the Romantic influence of Saperton, his teacher. His disc of the Etudes is the product of a smooth, well-lubricated mechanism. He is straightforward and always musicianly in his somewhat small-scaled but adroit playing. His Chopin can have a few suggestive ideas, and his polished virtuosity is always pleasant. Simon is capable of blinding speed and precision, and has an unusually strong left hand. His Rachmaninoff Concerti recordings have an idiomatic ring, and no difficulty seems beyond him. He misses the quality of lushness in the Third Concerto, but is better in the leaner Nos. 1 and 4. His Ravel playing is convincing, the delivery assured. He is commanding in Liszt's *Don Juan* Fantasy, and his Strauss-Godowsky *Die Fledermaus* claims respect. Tonally, he offers little luster and indeed is often bland, but he plays with taste, if not

with the soaring imagination of the greatest artists.

RUTH SLENCZYNSKA
b. 1925 — United States

She studied with various teachers and had a career as a child prodigy, during which she was terribly exploited. Her autobiography, *Forbidden Childhood,* tells her story. After a retirement, she again appeared in concert with good result. She made numerous albums; the playing is secure, with a musician's mind always at attention. She teaches at the University of Southern Illinois and continues to perform publicly.

JOSEF SLIVINSKI
1865–1930 — Poland

A famous pianist in his day, he studied with Leschetizky. He played in Europe and America, taught in Riga and Warsaw, and was often compared to Paderewski. He was not always a dependable artist; he could begin a concert only to decide he didn't like what was coming out, close the piano, and depart well before completing the program. When he was in form, however, it was said he melted an audience with his "soulful" playing.

ALEXANDER SLOBODYANIK
b. 1942 — USSR

He studied with Heinrich Neuhaus at the Moscow Conservatory. Slobodyanik played in America several times. In New York, his cool virtuosity was appreciated, and he played with power and some charm. He has recorded a brilliant Prokofiev Sixth Sonata. His Chopin playing is facile, but has an attractive suavity.

REGINA SMENDZIANKA
b. 1924 — Poland

She studied with Drzewiecki, developing into an important teacher and pianist. Her recording of her compatriot Grazyna Bacewicz's Sonata No. 2 shows formidable playing, as does the set of the same composer's ten etudes, which receive impeccable readings by her.

JAN SMETERLIN
1892–1967 — Poland

A student of Godowsky. His success came early and he built a career that made him famous. He recorded very little considering the size of his reputation. A late-Chopin disc finds him unsatisfying, but he was especially honored for his playing of his compatriot. He also did loyal service for the music of Szymanowski.

LEO SMIT
b. 1921 — United States

He was a student of Vengerova. Smit has been identified with contemporary music, especially the music of Aaron Copland, whose piano works he has recorded superlatively.

These performances are vivid, beautifully proportioned, and poetic in such scores as the *Four Piano Blues,* which were premiered by Smit. Copland has said, "Smit's brilliant and perceptive performances of my piano works are absolutely outstanding." Although he has done great service for many contemporary scores, and is himself a composer, Smit also plays the Classical and Romantic literature with imagination. He has a beautiful sound, and a technique that is well oiled and always serviceable.

RONALD SMITH
b. 1922 — England

Studied at the Royal Academy. He made his London debut in 1942. In 1951 he won the Geneva International Competition. In 1954 he recorded Bach's Triple Concerto with Edwin Fischer and Denis Matthews. A wide-ranging musician, Smith plays the standard repertoire, but he has consistently wandered down the byways of the piano literature, playing worthy music by Balakirev and much by Busoni and Alkan. His Alkan discs have been very well received. He is sarcastic and lean in the *Sonatine,* Romantic and raging in the Grand Sonata. Nobody interested in Alkan can afford not to hear Smith's vital investigations of this fascinating, madcap literature.

SYDNEY SMITH
1839–1889 — England

A student at the Leipzig Conservatory with Moscheles. He returned to London, where he was much appreciated. As a composer, Smith gave the English piano-playing public dozens of pieces beautifully crafted for the hands. His operatic potpourris and E minor Tarantelle afforded much enjoyment. He had a talent for composing music that achieves the maximum in brilliance with a minimum of difficulty. His works are heirlooms from a Victorian parlor. Neely Bruce recorded his *La Reine des fées— Galop de concert,* three minutes of high-riding pianistic high-jinks.

VLADIMIR SOFRONITSKY
1901–1961 — Russia

He studied with Nicolaiev at the St. Petersburg Conservatory. Sofronitsky became a legend in Russia and was one of the signal forces in Soviet pianism. His recitals were highlights of the Moscow musical season and took on cult status. He lived a turbulently Romantic existence and played the piano with a lyrical passion possessed by few. He traveled little, playing in Paris, but not America. His many recordings, however, made their impact in the West, and Scriabin is most especially linked with his name. Indeed, Sofronitsky was a profoundly great interpreter of the Russian master. When he was in the mood, a merging of the pianist with Scriabin took place. He seemed born to Scriabin's sensibility, suggestiveness, and vertiginous qualities. In some of his interpretations, one feels he is about to faint away. Especially vaporous are his luscious, barless presentations of the Fourth and Fifth Sonatas; there is intense heat in the Tenth Sonata, and acid irony in the *Satanic Poem* and Ninth Sonata.

Sofronitsky was essentially an improviser, waiting for inspiration to lift him to the heights. His tone was round, limpid, and penetrating. His conceptions are often languid, and his original musicality is marked by an individual use of rubato. One feels his music-making in halftints, and he had a metric freedom which produced dreamlike glidings. His readings of such later Scriabin pieces as *Guirlandes, Flames sombres,* and the *Poème-nocturne* are the "liquifications" Scriabin said he wanted, music dripping between the keys. His pedaling is ravishing; for Sofronitsky, the pedal *was* the piano.

Sofronitsky also played mounds of Chopin, Schumann, Rachmaninoff, and other Romantics. He could be both inspired and uneven in the same composition. His Schumann Fantasy and *Carnaval* have beautiful and perfunctory measures side by side. There is one wonderful Chopin Mazurka for every three bored ones. In the Classical literature he was less successful. His discs of Schubert's Sonata in B-flat and Beethoven's Sonata Op. 111 are emotional and erratic. Sofronitsky was a true Russian Romantic, and his entirely un-Classical complexion lacked balance. He loved to make records at live concerts, where the audience could stimulate him. When the daemon struck, as in a Rachmaninoff *Etude-tableau,* or when he sulked in a slow and morbid Scriabin prelude, he was a unique and highly charged artist with a rarefied temperament. He had a big technique, though his equipment was by no means as comprehensive as that of Richter, Gilels, or Ashkenazy, and he often needed a dose of good, clean practicing, but there is always something intriguing in a Sofronitsky performance.

SOLOMON
1902–1988 — England

Known to the world only by his first name. He studied with Mathilde Verne and was a prodigy who made his debut with the Tchaikovsky First Concerto at the age of eight. During his career, Solomon gave the premieres of several works, including the Bliss Piano Concerto in 1939. He became one of the best known and loved of British pianists. In 1956 he suffered a massive stroke. The damage proved permanent, and we were denied his revelatory art for the more than three decades that remained of his life. Fortunately, Solomon left many recordings, which prove him to be one of the great British pianists of the century, ranking with Myra Hess and Clifford Curzon.

Solomon, like most English pianists, was eclectic in his musical attractions, with a predilection for the Austro-Germanic literature. Here he is a magnificent interpreter, combining brain-power with a splendid equipment of virtuoso caliber and a civilized musicality, which puts balance foremost but allows for plenty of color and excitement, too.

His Beethoven, Schubert, Brahms, and Schumann readings at times reach incomparable levels of musical awareness. He seemed to love these composers especially and equally. Many English pianists have never had Chopin in their blood, and perhaps Solomon was not born to him either, but he approached the Pole with a rare respect, playing him with a gorgeous tone and in the finest taste. It is a Chopin without frills or trumped-up virtuosity. Solomon's Waltzes, Fantasy in F minor, and Fourth Ballade have breeding and control. His Chopin is warmhearted and honest, without any superficiality of style. Solomon occasionally played Liszt, but this was not really his cup of tea, although we can hear his large technique in resounding performances of the *Hungarian Fantasy* and the Fifteenth Rhapsody.

In all that Solomon played, there was an even-tempered well-being and a hearty, throbbing spirit. When necessary, he could roar, and his chords are packed with solidity. His art had a full-blooded richness denied to most English pianists. His rhythmic sense was keen but flexible. He played with an unusual firmness and his phrasing was fresh and forthright. With his sovereign mastery of the keyboard, he could sustain a "hush" of pure

suspense in a slow movement, telling of intense and significant emotion. He could induce the most familiar music to pierce the heart anew; indeed, he seemed naturally to shed new light on whatever he played. The pianist Gerald Moore felt that "Solomon breathed such a magical freshness into his playing that the listener might almost be persuaded the inspired artist was hearing and revelling in the music for the first time. . . . Interpretation at his level . . . is fundamentally the same art as composition. He not only played—he created music."

Beethoven was one of Solomon's chief interests. It is a Beethoven of expansiveness and joy. He could be tender and humorous, but brilliantly exciting as well; in the *Waldstein* and *Appassionata,* for instance, he can be scalding. But there is never in his Beethoven a trace of mock heroics or metaphysics. It is an earthy Beethoven, full of the world.

Solomon was a majestic Brahms player, titanic in the Second Concerto, intimate in the intermezzi. His disc of the *Handel* Variations is one of the great recordings of a Brahms composition, and Schubert's A minor Sonata D. 784 (Op. 143) is grandly conceived, containing a deep sadness throughout. Solomon is a master of the large canvas, and the sweep of his emotion is never adulterated by petty detail. He was perhaps the century's greatest British exponent of Schumann; this composer touched Solomon's nature deeply. His recording of the *Carnaval,* for example, is peerless. The score swings and dances; there are glossy gowns, the movement rustles. With Solomon playing, *Carnaval* is far more than a string of vignettes, it is a whole and brilliantly living form. The pianist brings the auditor as a spectator to an evening's merriment—indeed, to an orgiastic *Carnaval.* Solomon whispers to the listener Schumann's many intrigues. One hears the music always as music, but Schumann the man— the multifaceted personality of this tragic figure—is revealed by Solomon, himself one   249 of the glorious and tragic pianists of the century.

YONTY SOLOMON
b. 1937 — South Africa

After early studies, he worked with Myra Hess. He has performed much, playing many offbeat works, including some by Sorabji, who lifted his "ban" on performing his works for Solomon.

HILDE SOMER
1930–1980 — Austria

She studied with Serkin and Arrau. Somer had a large musical appetite, and played a great deal of new music. Some of her finest moments came in the neglected Latin American repertoire. She is at her best in Juan José Castro's exceptional *Sonatina española*, whose finale is a rondo based on Weber's celebrated Perpetuum Mobile in the right hand, while the left is occupied with other material. Somer also helped popularize Ginastera, who composed his Second Concerto for her. She had previously recorded the Sonata and First Concerto. Somer had the right, refreshingly harsh, rugged sound for Chávez's *Poligonos,* a powerful, angular work which the composer called "a piece of piano playing music." She played the 1968 Antonio Tauriello Piano Concerto and made a good recording of the theatrical John Corigliano Piano Concerto.

She also made a disc of Czerny's Sonata in A-flat, as well as two albums of Scriabin's music, where she is rather heavy-handed. At Lincoln Center's Alice Tully Hall, she once gave a "light works" recital of Scriabin's music, using colored lights to highlight its psychedelic aspects.

CLAUDETTE SOREL
b. 1931 — France

She studied with Samaroff. Sorel has high-speed fingers and a good musical mind. She plays with an airy lightness such pieces as Raff's *La Fileuse,* which she recorded. She is attracted to Rachmaninoff and has recorded his Second Sonata and the three 1887–88 nocturnes. She has edited the work of other Russians, including the attractive Twelve Etudes, Op. 74, by Arensky.

GONZALO SORIANO
1916–1972 — Spain

He studied at the Madrid Conservatory; later he toured throughout Europe and the Far East. Soriano had a special way with Spanish music. His playing had a restrained elegance, an intimately hued tone. He convincingly used fascinating and almost imperceptible fluctuations of tempo in such Granados Spanish dances as the *Andaluza, Zarabanda, Jota,* and *Asturiana.* It was an inborn rhythmic knack. Soriano was once asked how one succeeds in Spanish music. He simply replied, "It's a question of accent, as with a foreign language."

CAMILLE STAMATY
1811–1870 — Italy

He was brought early to Paris but did not have a piano until he was fourteen. He studied with Kalkbrenner, developing into a superb pianist of the Kalkbrenner school, very polished and elegant. Kalkbrenner felt Stamaty was his best student, calling him his musical son. Like all of Kalkbrenner's pupils, Stamaty used the Kalkbrenner hand machine for the development of even playing, using his master's *Méthode pour apprendre le piano à l'aide du guide-mains.* Stamaty insisted that his own students use the guide, and since he was the prime piano teacher of two of the great prodigies of history, Gottschalk and Saint-Saëns, one can well believe that there may have been something valuable in Kalkbrenner's invention. Both of these young artists found Stamaty an inspiring teacher.

Stamaty had also spent some time in Leipzig, coming under the spell of Mendelssohn, who prodded him to introduce to Paris the Classical works of Bach, Mozart, and Beethoven, which he did.

As a composer, he produced some marvelous etudes, two piano sonatas, and a concerto, as well as twelve transcriptions, *Souvenir du Conservatoire.* Schumann reviewed some of his work with praise. In 1862 he was made Chevalier of the Legion of Honor.

BERNHARD STAVENHAGEN
1862–1914 — Germany

One of Liszt's last and favorite pupils. The master admired his piano playing as well as his billiard playing. His career was very successful. Writing in 1889, Shaw felt his fortissimo was "serious and formidable," not like Paderewski's which was "violent and elate." He played throughout Europe, holding various official posts. He composed as well. The 1894 Piano Concerto in B minor has been given a memorable recording by Roland Keller. It is one of the best post-Lisztian concertos, with an engaging piano part and a well-made structure. It deserves public performance.

DANIEL STEIBELT
1765–1823 — Germany

An early piano virtuoso whose reputation was so great that he was considered Beethoven's rival.

Steibelt was a colorful personality. The critic W. J. Henderson wrote: "He was arrogant, vain, affected, and even dishonest; yet his abilities were so great that he was welcomed everywhere. . . . He was a dazzling performer, but it is beyond doubt that he was deficient in the deeper and subtler power of art." Steibelt, however, was important in the early days of the piano, as an efficient promoter of the new instrument, especially of the English pianofortes with their foot pedals, which he utilized far more than the average player. Steibelt is credited with the invention of tremolo passages, which he used to excess. He composed fifty etudes; Nos. 3 and 8 have more than a hint of Mendelssohn. He was heard from London to St. Petersburg performing his eight concerti. The Third Concerto contained the *Storm Rondo,* a celebrated piece of the time; his Eighth Concerto has a choral finale. He also wrote more than eighty sonatas, many for violin and piano, and 117 rondos, as well as sonatinas which have a Classical grace.

PAUL ŠTĚPÁN
b. 1925 — Czechoslovakia

A well-regarded pianist who plays an abundance of Czech music, some of which he has recorded.

251

CONSTANTIN VON STERNBERG
1852–1924 — Russia

An influential figure of his time. He studied at the Leipzig Conservatory with Moscheles and Reinecke, later with Kullak and Liszt. He toured a great deal, finally settling in Philadelphia. He composed some brilliant etudes and taught George Antheil.

HERBERT STESSIN
b. 1922 — United States

Studied with Clarence Adler and José Iturbi, and at the Juilliard School with Sascha Gorodnitzki. He gave concerts in solo and with orchestra early in his career. Stessin has held master classes in the United States and in Japan and teaches at the Aspen Festival. A faculty member of the Juilliard School, he has had a large following as a teacher who understands how to integrate technique, tone, and interpretation.

EDWARD STEUERMANN
1892–1964 — Poland

Busoni was his teacher and later he studied composition with Schoenberg. He played concerts in Europe and came to the United States in 1936, teaching at the Juilliard School until his death.

He was a musician of great intellect who played the classic repertoire, but whose interpretive world included all the important Germanic trends of the twentieth century. The Schoenberg Concerto was premiered by him in 1944, with Stokowski conducting the NBC Symphony. His disc of Busoni, especially that composer's Elegies, is dry and somewhat puny, but of psychological profundity. He was revered as a teacher, passing on his knowledge to hundreds of pupils. He composed twelve-tone music, leaving a Suite for Piano (1954) as well as other small piano pieces.

RONALD STEVENSON
b. 1928 — England

He studied at the Royal Manchester College of Music. A good pianist, he has written extensively for his instrument. Stevenson is an artistic descendant of Busoni, whose work has engrossed him. His *Passacaglia on D S C H* is eighty minutes long and has become his best-known work. He once said, "My main interest in music is in the epic. This is an epic age it seems to me, and only epic forms can fully express its aspirations."

SIGISMUND STOJOWSKI
1870–1946 — Poland

A pianist and composer who studied with Diémer at the Paris Conservatoire. Later he worked with Paderewski, who said, "You are an improviser, with results good or bad attendant on caprice." In 1926, Paderewski recorded, with engaging style, Stojowski's *Chant d'amour* and *By the Brookside*. Stojowski settled in the United States, where he had much success as a pianist, a teacher who taught Oscar Levant and Arthur Loesser, and a prolific composer; he wrote two concerti, Opp. 3 and 32.

AUGUST STRADAL
1860–1930 — Czechoslovakia

He worked with Anton Door at the Vienna Conservatory before coming to study with Liszt, whose music he interpreted with special qualities of bravura and color. He wrote music and authored several books.

SOULIMA STRAVINSKY
b. 1910 — Switzerland

The son of the great composer, Soulima Stravinsky studied in Paris with Philipp. He made an American debut in 1948. He has often been heard in his father's music, and has himself composed and recorded.

HAI-KYUNG SUH
b. 1960 — Korea

She made a debut in Seoul at the age of eight in Mozart's Concerto No. 21. She studied with Nadia Reisenberg and at the Juilliard School with Sascha Gorodnitzki. Suh is the most brilliant pianist to emerge from Korea. She won the Busoni and Munich Competitions and is the recipient of Korea's cultural medal. She is especially captivating in the Russian repertoire, where her virtuoso powers dazzle in the Mussorgsky *Pictures*, the Tchaikovsky concerto, the Prokofiev Third Concerto, and the Rachmaninoff Third Concerto. Her extraordinary mechanism sends out sparks in works like the Brahms *Paganini* Variations.

ROBERTO SZIDON
b. 1941 — Brazil

A pianist with an enormous technique. He is heard to advantage in Villa-Lobos's music, especially the *Rudepoêma*, which was composed for Arthur Rubinstein. His recordings of the complete Scriabin sonatas have too harsh a sound and are too tense in some places, but display a remarkable mental command.

ANTOINETTE SZUMOWSKA
1868–1938 — Poland

From 1890 to 1895, she studied with Paderewski in Paris. Earlier, she was at the Warsaw Conservatory with Michalowski. She settled in the United States, where she played solo and chamber music as the pianist in the Adamowski Trio.

MARIA SZYMANOWSKA
1790–1832 — Poland

A very well-known pianist. She studied with John Field in Moscow. Szymanowska was often called "the feminine Field," and her nocturnes resemble his. The most captivating is the B-flat Nocturne, with its early-Romantic seed, which Chopin knew well. Goethe was infatuated with her, and rated her playing even over Hummel's, calling her "an incredible player." Schumann thought well of her twelve etudes. She also composed a set of twenty-four mazurkas.

T

GABRIEL TACCHINO
b. 1934 — France

A splendid pianist. His playing is buoyant and well planned. His career has taken him to the Far East, as well as throughout Europe. His recordings of Poulenc and Saint-Saëns have been well received. He studied at the Paris Conservatoire and took away prizes from the Busoni Competition and the Long-Thibaud Competition.

MAGDA TAGLIAFERRO
1890–1987 — Brazil

A pianist of distinction, Tagliaferro had one of the longest careers ever, continuing to play well into her nineties. In 1983, in Carnegie Hall, she astounded listeners with her fresh, captivating playing, filled with curves and color, and wrought with an amazingly loose wrist and fingerwork. She studied with Cortot, whose memory she revered. She knew Fauré well and toured with him. She remained a tiller of the Fauré garden, and her style of playing him is slim and elegant.

She made many recordings; Villa-Lobos dedicated to her his 1929 *Momoprecoce* for Piano and Orchestra. And there is a delightful collector's item, transferred from the original 78s, of Reynaldo Hahn's Piano Concerto of 1930, with Hahn conducting. The chic of the score is played with sophisticated demeanor by Mme Tagliaferro, who remained faithful to his music, programming his delightful Sonatina in her nineties.

YUJI TAKAHASHI
b. 1938 — Japan

A pianist of tremendous skill, especially in twentieth-century music, including brilliant performances of Messiaen and of Iannis Xenakis, with whom he studied composition. Xenakis's *Herma* was dedicated to him, and he premiered it. He has also composed a great deal. His composition *Maeander* (1973) was written for his sister, Aki Takahashi (b. 1944), also a brilliant concert pianist, who studied with Ray Lev.

Takahashi once wrote: "A musician serves people by filtering their collective imagination through his technical knowledge and bringing it back to them as a musical form."

CARL TAUSIG
1841–1871 — Poland

This short-lived favorite pupil of Liszt was by all accounts the most perfect and highly polished pianist of his time. Many felt that in certain branches of technique, he outshone his beloved master, who said of Tausig, "Men such as he are so rare that one does not know where to come across them." At his death, von Bülow eulogized: "Here is the whole history of piano playing from the beginning to this day."

Tausig prided himself on playing all representative works for the piano from memory. His programs were serious and stupendous, and in the short years of his concertizing, he did a great deal to celebrate the best in music. This is a characteristic program from 1870, when such a dose of piano music was still new and the institution of the piano recital was still young:

Sonata Op. 53, *Waldstein*	Beethoven
Bourrée	Bach
Presto scherzando	Mendelssohn
Barcarolle, Op. 60	Chopin
Two Mazurkas	Chopin
Invitation to the Dance	Weber-Tausig
Kreisleriana	Schumann
Serenade	Schubert-Liszt
Hungarian Rhapsody No. 6	Liszt

He once showed Wilhelm von Lenz how he could play "forever" the octaves in the Chopin Polonaise in A-flat. In refusing to show strain, he was akin to Thalberg, but unlike his great predecessor, who idealized only the singing touch, Tausig was master of a whole range of touches—from the crystalline to the dramatic. Amy Fay wrote, "I never expect to hear such piano playing again. . . . He was absolutely infallible." Wagner wrote, "His furious piano playing made me tremble." Not everyone loved his playing, though. In 1862, when Tausig was only twenty-one, Eduard Hanslick reviewed a Vienna recital: "What must one think of the ear of an artist who does not hear the howling metallic rattling of the abused chords or is not disturbed by it? And what a choking, squeezing, and strangling of tones you get when he finally sets loose his whole pack of hounds!" Hanslick reminded his readers that "Tausig again stuck to his trying practice of presenting himself alone the whole evening, admitting neither singing nor accompanying instruments."

Notwithstanding Hanslick, Tausig was to be the most idolized German pianist of that decade, a great interpreter first and foremost. He taught some important pianists in his short life, and opened a piano conservatory in Berlin. Karl Barth, Oscar Beringer, Joseffy, and many others came to work with him. But it seems his teaching could be as violent as some of his playing. "His idea of teaching," Amy Fay declared, "is to utter such cries of encouragement as 'Terrible, shocking, dreadful, Oh God, Oh God!' He would then push the pupil aside violently, play the passage himself, and tell the pupil to do it just so."

Tausig lives on as a composer of some fabulous piano transcriptions and paraphrases in the Lisztian manner, the most celebrated being his arrangement of Bach's Toccata and Fugue in D minor, and an exceedingly clever adaptation of Weber's *Invitation to the Dance*, a real lesson in transforming its "classical" pianism into a more "modernized" style. His Fantasy on themes from Moniuszko's opera *Halka* was once well-known and has been recorded by Michael Ponti, and his Strauss paraphrase *One Only Lives Once* is immortalized in Rachmaninoff's 1927 recording (the rhythmic fineness and sheer organization of this playing are wonderful).

His few original works, such as the two Concert Etudes, Op. 1, and the Ballade (*The Ghost Ship*), are genuinely wonderful pages of German Romanticism. The Ballade is fearsome, heavily octaved, and eerily pictorial. Tausig's monument to piano pedagogy is his set of Daily Exercises, which build finger dexterity.

Tausig set standards for the achievement of pure virtuosity, not for its own sake but as a means of penetrating to the core the masterpieces of the piano literature—an idea that he helped to spread. He remains a legend in piano lore.

FRANKLIN TAYLOR
1843–1919 — England

A student of Clara Schumann, Taylor became an influential teacher, made many editions, and was by all accounts a remarkable pianist.

IGNACE TEDESCO

1817–1882 — Czechoslovakia

A student of Tomáschek, he pursued a fruitful career as a concert pianist and salon composer.

ROBERT TEICHMÜLLER

1863–1939 — Germany

His chief teacher was Reinecke at the Leipzig Conservatory, where he later taught. He also played and made editions.

SIGISMOND THALBERG

1812–1871 — Switzerland

He studied with the most famous piano practitioners of the day: Hummel, Moscheles, and Kalkbrenner. Thalberg made a debut in Vienna in 1830. In 1834 he was appointed court pianist to the emperor of Austria. He toured Belgium, Holland, Russia, Spain, and England. In 1855 he gave concerts in Brazil; in 1857 he played in the United States to tremendous acclaim. He composed two operas, a piano concerto, nocturnes, etudes, valses, a sonata, and *L'Art du chant appliqué au piano*, Op. 70. His best-known compositions were the sixty fantasies on various operas.

Thalberg was one of the great stars in the Romantic firmament. He was aristocratic and handsome, his manners were perfect, his dress impeccable. He was the illegitimate son of a baroness and a count: even this blemish had an aura of romance. Everywhere he was the darling of the public. Indeed, Thalberg was the only pianist capable of threatening Franz Liszt's supremacy throughout Europe.

Unfortunately, Thalberg's celebrity now rests on his rivalry with Liszt. During the 1830s, the question of who was the mightier pianist was taken quite seriously by Romantic-minded and claque-ridden Paris. Finally, a contest of pianistic daring was devised, in which the two titans of the keyboard tested their prowess and played their choicest commodities. All of Parisian high society came to applaud for either the demonic Liszt or the gentlemanly Thalberg. The poet Heine reported: "Everywhere in the room were pale faces, palpitating breasts, and emotional breathing." But neither Thalberg nor Liszt could manage to win the day. The eccentric Princess Belgiojoso, who arranged the pianistic duel, decided for history when she gasped, "Thalberg is the best pianist in the world; Liszt is the only one." Later, Liszt said of Thalberg's singing tone that "Thalberg could play the violin on the piano." (In fact, Thalberg studied singing for five years.) The twenty-year-old Chopin heard him in 1830, and wrote to a friend that "Thalberg plays famously but he is not my man; he is younger than I, popular with the ladies, writes potpourris on themes from Masaniello, produces *piano* with the pedal instead of with the hand, takes tenths as easily as I do octaves, and wears diamond shirt-studs."

Thalberg possessed one of the most perfect mechanisms of his era. It was a point of honor with him never to show the slightest exertion during a performance. He was indefatigable in his striving for perfection and could practice through the night on one measure. A story circulated that an Englishman, having followed him from concert to concert for several years in the hope of hearing Thalberg play just one wrong note, finally blew his brains out in despair of ever hearing the long-awaited clinker.

Like Chopin and Liszt, Thalberg was of the new school of multitextured pianism. In his music, especially his many operatic fantasies, he employed a compositional technique that

256

to the simpler ears of his time sounded as if there were three hands playing. It was accomplished by highlighting his melody with clever use of the thumbs, surrounded by arpeggiated figures of various kinds. With the use of the sustaining pedal, he could keep both hands free, while the melody was singing out in bold relief. (He had probably learned much from the technique of the harpist Elias Parish-Alvars, 1808–1849.) Thalberg's arpeggio technique was so smooth and rounded that he was nicknamed "Old Arpeggio." In the early years of the development of virtuosity, it was not unheard of for some awed member of the audience to stand on his chair, trying to see where Thalberg's third hand came from.

In his heyday, Thalberg's music was played everywhere there was a piano to be played. Two of his supreme pot-boilers, the Variations on "Home, Sweet Home," Op. 72, and the Variations on "The Last Rose of Summer," Op. 73, were popular around the world. These have been recorded by Michael Ponti and show off Thalberg's superb talent for pianistic effect. He wrote a Piano Concerto in F minor, Op. 5, reminiscent of Hummel, Weber, and Rossini, all within a latticework of finely grounded pianism. The score was too derivative and trite to survive, yet an aroma of the period surrounds it. Of greater importance is the large C minor Sonata, Op. 56, a showy work with Classical intent, containing moments of nobility.

His most ingenious use of the piano, however, is in his operatic fantasies and paraphrases, which were cherished in a time of unashamed virtuosity. Clara Schumann in her younger years played several of these concoctions, as did Anton Rubinstein and the young César Franck, and Brahms too performed them. Actually, the calculation of effects in a Thalberg paraphrase amounts to a kind of genius. Indeed, Mendelssohn, who used Thalberg's three-handed effect in his E minor Prelude, wrote, "A Fantasia by him is a piling up of the choicest, finest effects and an astounding climax of difficulties and elegances.

Everything is so thought-out, refined, with such sureness and knowledge and in such good taste." Among Thalberg's characteristic fantasies are the Rossini-*Moses*, Op. 33, which rode a wave of popularity for decades; the Fantasy on Rossini's *Barber of Seville*, Op. 63; the Fantasy on Donizetti's *Don Pasquale*, Op. 67; and the Meyerbeer *Les Huguenots* Fantasy, Op. 20. Each one is highly fanciful and creative in its use of themes from the opera. The music makes no pretension, though, to anything more than the tinsel it is. It is an elegant and idealized pianism, magnificently notated. Daniel L. Hitchcock expresses something of Thalberg's intent: "Whatever else it may be, Thalberg's music is three-dimensional—existing within and without. Melody is the nucleus—whether great arcs of sound, undulations of harmony, or sparks of note fragments. Only a portion comes from the instrument, the rest hovers about it, or passes through as though coming from a great distance."

Unfortunately, Thalberg's harmonic imagination was far weaker than his purely pianistic invention; and in an age of growing chromaticism, his harmonic simplicity wedded to a complex pianistic fabric began to sound pale. Through his three-handed formations, however, Thalberg gave piano scoring another dimension—one which Liszt favorably utilized as part of his orchestrally conceived style, and which is part of the texture of the keyboard music of Franck, Fauré, Granados, and many others.

ISTVÁN THOMÁN
1862–1940—Hungary

One of the foremost piano teachers of his time in Hungary, Thomán taught Dohnányi and Bartók, and was deeply respected by them. Thomán was himself a pupil of Liszt from 1881 to 1885.

PART I.

MOZART'S IL DON GIOVANNI.

Terzetto.. "Ah taci ingiusto core,"

Miss RAINFORTH, Mr. WEISS, and Mr. BALFE.

CANTATA—Wind of the Winter Night, whence comest thou?

Mr. H. RUSSELL.

Words by Charles Mackay, Esq.

"Wind of the winter night, whence comest thou?   Sad, sad is thy voice, on this desolate moor,
And whither, oh whither, art wandering now?   And mournful, oh mournful, thy howl at my door."

BALFE'S ARIA,

"La speranza.".........Madame BALFE.

NEW FANTASIA, PIANOFORTE,

On Airs from Lucrezia Borgia (first time of performance)....Mr. THALBERG.

BISHOP'S SONG,

"Peace inviting.".......Miss RAINFORTH.

ROSSINI'S IL CONTE UGOLINO,

Aria, "Già il momento.".................Mr. WEISS.

"Già il momento s'appressava
Che a lor pane si ricava,
Ma ognun d'essi dubitar.
Chè di quella torre infame,
Ch'ora ha il titol della fame,
L'uscio udirono inchiodar."

Andante, Pianoforte, in D flat, Op. 32, followed by a **Grand Studio,**
Mr. THALBERG.

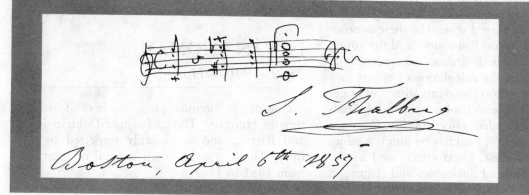

Boston, April 6th 1857

PART II.

BALFE'S FALSTAFF.

Duo, " Voi siete un uom di spirito."......Mr. WEISS and Mr. BALFE.

Fantasia, Corno,....Mr. MAYER.

BENEDICT'S BALLAD,

" The Sleeper,"...........Miss RAINFORTH.

Hush! from all voice, save of Music, forbear,
  Speak in low murmurs, tread lightly the ground ;
Let her sleep on, while her long auburn hair
  Waves o'er her shoulder in tresses unbound.
Lo! her lips open, as if in a prayer ;
  Mark how the shadow hath passed from her brow :
Ah! what a smile of contentment was there ;
  Surely she wanders in fairy land now.

She is at home with her sisters at play,
  In the hall meadow, around the yew tree ;
O, in all revel of Christmas or May,
  None was so airy, so lively as she.
Lo! she's joining their laughter again,
  Mocking the linnet aloft on the bough ;
All is forgotten, bereavement and pain ;
  Surely she wanders in fairy land now.

Now she smiles brighter—a voice at her heart
  Whispers the vows that she answered of old ;
How hath she yearned, since she saw it depart,
  Once again, waking, that face to behold !
Ah! 'tis in vain ; for the drear ocean wave
  Hides her belov'd in its chambers below.
Call her not back to remember a grave !
  Hush! let her meet him in fairy land now !

Grand Fantasia, Pianforte, on the Minuet and Serenade in Don Giovanni, *(by desire)* ....Mr. THALBERG.

Ballad, "The Ivy green,"....Mr. RUSSELL.

Written by Charles Dickens, Esq.

Oh! a dainty plant is the Ivy green,
  That creepeth o'er ruins old.

LOVER'S BALLAD,

" When first I o'er the mountain trod,"......Madame BALFE.

When first I over the mountain trod,
How fresh the flowers, how green the sod !
The breeze seem'd whisp'ring soft delight,
And the fountains sparkled like diamonds bright.

But now I wander o'er the mountain lone,
The flowers are drooping, their fragrance gone ;
The breeze of morn like a wail appears,
And the dripping fountain seems weeping tears.

And are ye changed, oh, ye lovely hills ?
Less sparkling are ye, bright mountain rills ?
Does the fragrant bloom from the flowers depart ?
No ! there's nothing chang'd but this breaking heart.

Pianoforte.

New Grand Capriccio on the 1st Finale and Introduction to Semiramide........Mr. THALBERG.

*This program of a Thalberg concert in London in 1842
is typical of the early Romantic period,
before the solo piano recital became entrenched in musical life.*

An autograph from Thalberg's second American tour.

VERA TIMANOFF
1855–1942 — Russia

A student of Anton Rubinstein, Tausig, and Liszt; he called her "an artist of rare talent." She made a few piano rolls, and lived and taught at St. Petersburg.

JAMES TOCCO
b. 1944 — United States

He has had a successful career. His concerto repertory is especially large, and he plays many concerts a season. Tocco has recorded the Griffes piano music, the four MacDowell sonatas, and an album of the solo piano music of Bernstein. Tocco also premiered John Corigliano's *Etude Fantasy.* His playing is brilliant and musicanly. He teaches at Indiana University.

JOHANN TOMÁSCHEK
1774–1850 — Czechoslovakia

A fine musician; a pianist, composer, and teacher of importance. He left 110 opus numbers. He was one of the first composers of his time to write expressive short pieces. His *Eclogues,* Opp. 35, 39, 47, 51, 53, 66, and 83, and *Dithyrambs,* Opp. 52 and 65, were esteemed by Schubert and Schumann. Julius Schulhoff, Ignace Tedesco, and Alexander Dreyschock were among his many students. He also taught the critic Eduard Hanslick.

ALEXANDER TORADZE
b. 1953 — USSR

Born in Tbilisi, Georgia, Toradze trained in Moscow with Yakov Zak. In 1977 he won a prize at the Van Cliburn Competition. In 1983 he emigrated to the United States, where his career has been highly publicized. Toradze is a lusty player with plenty of original ideas, and a style of playing that capitalizes on extremes of louds and softs. He is never fearful of making a grand gesture, and audiences respond often rapturously to his guttural artistry characterized by heat and terrific velocity.

SIR DONALD FRANCIS TOVEY
1875–1940 — England

A musical scholar, writer on music, composer, and an extraordinary pianist. The great violinist Joachim helped promote his talents. He said, "I have discussed music with Schumann and Brahms, but not with that young Tovey. He knows too much." Tovey's *Essays in Musical Analysis* have been staple reading for musicians. He composed Classical, austere music; a large Piano Concerto in A major has been totally neglected. "Like all the compositions of this amazing musician," wrote James Friskin, "this employs a classical musical vocabulary and technique. The Concerto is a work of great dignity, beauty and power with a command of resource that actually challenges comparison with its great models. The idiom, of course, belongs to a bygone day."

As a pianist Tovey had a huge repertoire, and his programs were uncompromising. He was a great teacher also. Myra Hess in her prime once asked him if she could play for him. "I shall never forget the inspiration of those two hours," she wrote.

DAVID TUDOR

b. 1926 — United States

A brilliant exponent of avant-garde music as well as a composer who utilizes electronic music. He has premiered many works, including Sylvano Bussotti's *Five Piano Pieces for David Tudor,* Cage's *Concert for Piano and Orchestra,* Stockhausen's *Kontakte,* and the American premiere of the Boulez Piano Sonata No. 2.

JOSEF TURCZYNSKI

1884–1953 — Poland

A student of Essipova in St. Petersburg and of Busoni in Vienna. In 1915 he taught at the Kiev Conservatory; he returned to Poland after the Revolution. At the Warsaw Conservatory, his fame spread as a teacher and as a fine interpreter of Chopin. His students included Ryszard Bakst, Malcuzynski, Czerny-Stefanska, and others of high caliber. Turczynski was one of the editors of the now established "Paderewski edition" of the complete works of Chopin, begun in 1941 and completed by 1949. It is now perhaps the most often used of any Chopin edition.

ROSALYN TURECK

b. 1914 — United States

In Chicago she studied with Sophia Brilliant Levin and Jan Chiapusso, and later at Juilliard with Olga Samaroff. At the age of twenty-one, she made a Carnegie Hall debut in the Brahms B-flat Concerto. She holds four honorary doctoral degrees and has been visiting professor at numerous universities. There is a Tureck Archive at the Library of the Performing Arts at Lincoln Center.

Although Tureck's fame is now exclusively tied to Bach playing, she has performed other repertoire in addition to premiering a number of modern compositions. Tureck presented her first all-Bach recital in 1937, and her appetite for the Leipzig master has never abated. In fact, each year her researches have brought her new light on Bach's music. Tureck's public has always been a dedicated group, and a Tureck Bach convocation sometimes has the look of a cult. It is certainly worship on a high level, and Tureck is an artist with a big personality. One does not leave unmoved. Every page she attempts has its own fascination, its own sense of timing. She has marvelous finger independence that colors each voice; each contrapuntal unit is delicately attenuated. Yet she is never idiosyncratic. Her Bach is the product of great erudition and toil. Her perfect legato, variety of touches, and rhythmic flexibility come from a saturation of scholarship. Nothing in her art happens quickly. When she plays the Chromatic Fantasy and Fugue, one may be certain that she has "studied the twenty-two extant manuscripts that circulated in the eighteenth century, as well as sixty editions." She worked for twelve years before bringing her performance to the public. Her recording of it is a magnificent blending of mellow interpretive maturity and a passionate investigation of the music's emotions. She is always involved, but there is also the feeling of great knowledge. "I do what Bach tells me," she has said. "I never tell the music what to do."

Tureck is proficient on the clavichord, fortepiano, and harpsichord as well, and often teaches other instrumentalists, including guitarists, her way with Bach. She is, however, primarily a pianist and still believes that Bach can be played convincingly on the contemporary piano. But she states emphatically that

I do not play the piano as a nineteenth century instrument or with current pianistic style and technique. Mine is a new piano technique, built from the established art of historical performance practices plus the structural requirements of Bach's music. The piano is capable of immeasurable tonal and stylistic approaches. It is not limited to or by the Romantic style of the nineteenth century or the percussive style of the twentieth. Given the combination of the knowledge of the scholar, the aesthetic sensitivity of the conscientious artist, and a technique emerging from eighteenth-century principles of music and performance, the piano is a valid and profoundly successful medium for the performance of Bach's keyboard music.

Students interested in her approach may consult her three volumes, *An Introduction to the Performance of Bach.*

One of Tureck's programs consists of the *Goldberg* Variations, played first on piano and then on the harpsichord (repeats included). An interesting comparison is between her older version of the *Goldberg* Variations on piano and her more recent disc on the harpsichord. The changes are many and suggest the long gestation period Tureck has gone through to arrive at her present conception. There are many who love her old discs of *The*

Well-Tempered Clavier from the 1960s. Indeed, nobody interested in that great work should forgo listening to them.

RONALD TURINI
b. 1933 — Canada

He took prizes in several competitions, including tying Pollini for second prize at the 1958 Geneva International Piano Competition. He later studied with Horowitz for a time. Turini toured the United States, as well as the Soviet Union. He plays with a refined craftsmanship.

AUBE TZERKO
b. 1908 — Canada

A pupil of Schnabel; an excellent pianist and a renowned teacher.

MITSUKO UCHIDA
b. 1948 — Japan

She trained in Japan and studied in Europe with Askenase and Kempff, later winning prizes at the Leeds and the Chopin Competi-

tions. She is a fastidious musician with a well-developed technique. Her Mozart playing is pliable, the phrasing well defined and always with vocal intent. She is at her finest in the slow movements of the sonatas, and in such scores as the A minor Rondo. Her Chopin, too, has many points of interest.

IMRE UNGAR
1909–1972 — Hungary

A brilliant pianist who was blind. He was a student of Dohnányi. He lost the Chopin Competition in Warsaw, in 1932, to Uninsky at the toss of a coin, each having acquired the same number of points from the jury.

ALEXANDER UNINSKY
1910–1972 — Russia

The 1932 winner of the Chopin Competition. He studied at the Kiev Conservatory with Sergei Tarnowsky, and at the Paris Conservatoire with Lazare Lévy. Uninsky was a less emotional pianist than many Russians. His playing was finished, but dry. His best recording is a precise and finely spun reading of the Chopin Etudes.

TAMÁS VÁSÁRY
b. 1933 — Hungary

He studied with József Gát and Lajos Hernádi. As a child, he received advice from Dohnányi. He also studied composition with Kodály. After the Hungarian uprising in 1956, Vásáry settled in London, where he added conducting to his career. He has made a distinguished series of piano recordings, essentially of the Romantic literature.

Vásáry is a poet-pianist, a dreamy bard. For him, music must first be beautiful. It must also be Romantic and emotional. In Vásáry at his peak, we have a luscious colorist replete with an exceptionally wide dynamic range, an artist capable of ravishing lighting effects. His pedaling is plush and creamy, the technique well oiled and balanced within its parts.

Chopin is never far from his field. His multicolored imagination depicts this artful literature with all kinds of felicitous lingerings. He can also become over-refined; Vásáry can suspend a note for so long that one wonders if the phrase will continue. In his quest for a free improvised art, he occasionally gets caught up in detail and hovers dangerously at the brink of arrhythmic action, where formlessness lurks. In recent years, however, this happens much less.

Vásáry plays a great deal of Liszt. In the Sonata, the *Legends*, the *Years of Pilgrimage*, and the *Don Juan* Fantasy, he appeals not to the virtuoso Liszt, but to Liszt the colorful tone poet. He has recorded all of Rachmaninoff's concerti, and they are warm readings filled with a ripe, unsentimental nostalgia. His Debussy is well formed, clean and without mannerism. In Schubert, he is fragrant and affectionate. His performance of Schubert's G major Sonata-Fantasy, D. 894, is luxuriant in its evergreen lyricism. Vásáry's searching spirit is always looking at the music from his own very individual point of view. His various Brahms pieces are among the most original and vital of his recorded output, and his several Mozart concerti find a Romantic and flexible interpreter.

ISABELLE VENGEROVA
1877–1956 — Lithuania

She studied with Essipova; also with Joseph Dachs, as well as with Leschetizky for an extended period. Vengerova taught at the St. Petersburg Conservatory. In 1921 she came to the United States, where she taught in New York, as well as at the Curtis Institute in Philadelphia from 1924. She was the teacher of Samuel Barber, Leonard Bernstein, Jacob Lateiner, Leo Smit, Sidney Foster, Ignace Hilsberg, Leonard Pennario, Lilian Kallir, and Gary Graffman, who discussed her at length in his autobiography, *I Really Should Be Practicing*. "Vengerova," he wrote, "was really only interested in the piano and how to coax the largest range of beautiful, subtle, dazzling, dramatic, velvety and singing sonorities from that intractable black beast." In short, she exemplified all of the qualities of the Russian school of pianism with which she grew up.

ILANA VERED
b. 1943 — Argentina

She studied in Paris with Perlemuter and Darré, and in New York with Rosina Lhévinne. Vered is a stylish virtuoso with great technical flair. Her recordings of the twenty-four Chopin etudes show a remarkable dexterity, as does her disc of Moszkowski's virtuoso etudes. Her recording of Mozart's A major Concerto K. 488 shows her to be equally comfortable in the Classic literature.

MATHILDE VERNE
1865–1936 — England

A pupil of Franklin Taylor, she then studied for six years with Clara Schumann. She took part in the concert life of London and opened a school for piano. Her sister Adela Verne (1872–1952) was an acclaimed concert pianist.

VLADIMIR VIARDO
b. 1949 — USSR

He received piano studies in Moscow, and was the winner of the 1973 Van Cliburn Competition. In Russia he has had a formidable career, and is respected as a creative teacher as well as a virtuoso player in the grand manner. In 1988 he returned to the United States in a series of triumphant appearances, crowned by a Carnegie Hall performance of the Rachmaninoff Third Concerto with the Dallas Symphony.

ALEXANDER VILLOING
1804–1878 — Russia

A student of Dubuc, he became the only teacher of Anton Rubinstein. His *Practical School of Piano Playing* was used for years in Russia.

RICARDO VIÑES
1875–1943 — Spain

He studied with Pujol and later at the Paris Conservatoire. He became one of the most persuasive interpreters of the Spanish and French modern schools. His playing of Falla, Debussy, Ravel, de Séverac, Poulenc, and so many others brought him great distinction.

Falla's *Nights in the Gardens of Spain* is dedicated to him. Poulenc studied piano with him and wrote, "I owe him everything; no one taught the pedal, that essential factor in modern music, better than Viñes. He could play clearly within a flood of pedal work, which seems paradoxical. And what a mastery of staccato touch!"

PANTCHO VLADIGEROV
b. 1899 — Bulgaria

The most distinguished Bulgarian composer and pianist, and the early teacher of Alexis Weissenberg. An international piano competition held in Sofia is named for him.

MAX VOGRICH
1852–1916 — Austria

A student of Reinecke and Moscheles at the Leipzig Conservatory. He lived, taught, and performed in Australia, London, and New York. He composed a piano concerto and edited Schumann and others. His *Staccato-Caprice* makes a brilliantly effective encore.

JAN VOŘIŠEK
1791–1825 — Czechoslovakia

He studied with Tomáschek, played concerts, and composed some good piano sonatas.

VITYA VRONSKY
b. 1908 — Russia

She studied with Schnabel, married Victor Babin, and achieved renown in the Vronsky and Babin piano duo.

ANDRÉ WATTS
b. 1946 — Germany

He studied in Philadelphia, and at the age of ten played a Haydn concerto at a Philadelphia Orchestra children's concert. In 1963 he made an overnight sensation appearing on national television in the Liszt E-flat Concerto, with Leonard Bernstein conducting. Bernstein was so impressed with the youth's pianistic finesse that he predicted "gianthood" for Watts. Immediately afterward, they recorded the Liszt concerto. In 1967, Watts made a world tour for the U.S. State Department. During this time he continued studies with Leon Fleisher. In 1973 he played in the Soviet Union. At the age of twenty-six, he was given an honorary doctorate by Yale University, the youngest person ever to receive that honor from Yale.

Watts never had to build his career through the drain of competitions. In his case, one TV exposure began the road to stardom, and Watts has never stopped since. He is a rugged professional with a deeply ingrained technique, which is very secure on stage. He is an especially fine concerto player, and the Liszt E-flat Concerto that he recorded as a youngster of sixteen is engaging and natural in its lyricism, unforced in its virtuosity, his scales smooth and the tops of his octaves glistening. It's all singularly elegant. From that period, there are also a delightful Haydn Sonata in E-flat, a fleet Paganini-Liszt Etude in E-flat, and a nicely balanced and restrained C minor Nocturne of Chopin, Op. 48, No. 1.

But as Watts developed, the elegance disappeared, and a harder, more lustful tone appeared. His conceptions became stolid. He recorded a Rachmaninoff Third Concerto, a respectable Schubert album, a journeyman's Liszt Sonata, and an electric Liszt *Totentanz*. His Gershwin album lacks style, with a lumbering *Rhapsody in Blue* in the solo version. His Chopin Sonata in B-flat minor and F minor Concerto display nothing more than competence; the heated drama of the sonata is missing, and the concerto is perfunctory.

After those discs, Watts literally disappeared from the recording studio for years. His public career thrived, and he continued to have great success with audiences, but the artist in him did not seem to grow. His recitals had more than a hint of vulgarity, with banging and other meretricious effects. He seemed convinced that these pieces, played more idiomatically, would not move an audience. He lost all semblance of his naturalness.

Just when I was about to drop Watts from my concertgoing, though, I did a double-take on listening to his disc "André Watts Live in Tokyo," where he is gallant in two Scarlatti sonatas, once again elegant in the Haydn Sonata No. 48 in C major, and quite childlike

in Debussy's *Children's Corner* Suite. Not one to give up on any pianist of talent, I went to several more Watts recitals at Avery Fisher Hall only to be disappointed again. Gershwin, Chopin, Liszt, all writhed in bloated playing. Where was the Watts of Tokyo? When two Liszt records were released, I gave a listen, and found a high level of Liszt playing, this new version of the Sonata being better by far than his early one. And even finer is the album containing a good selection of the "later" Liszt, played with genuine affection, dash, tenderness, and simplicity.

Watts may now be past the phase when he played down to his audience. These latest records show an honest musicality, and reveal that Watts may yet grow to the "gianthood" predicted for him by Leonard Bernstein.

CARL MARIA VON WEBER
1786–1826 — Germany

He studied for a short time with Michael Haydn, the great composer's brother, and later with the gifted musician Abbé Vogler. Weber the pianist, however, may be said to have been self-taught. He was one of the best conductors of the time and was the creator of German Romantic opera. He also had a pleasing singing voice until his vocal cords were partially destroyed when he took a glass of nitric acid that he had thought was wine. He had a literary bent, writing well-turned criticism, and he could draw well. In many ways he was the model for Schumann, but unlike that unhappy master who injured his hand in his feverish attempts to achieve pianistic virtuosity, Weber was a concert pianist, one of the most original of the first quarter of the nineteenth century.

Weber's career in Germany was a revelation for the budding young Romantics. He was distinguished looking, worldly, had a Byronic limp, and died of consumption at only forty, days after conducting his last opera, *Oberon*, in

London. His life was the stuff of which legends are made. Philipp Spitta wrote of the youthful Weber: "His life had been that of a wandering minstrel or troubadour. Roving restlessly from place to place, winning all hearts by his sweet, insinuating, lively melodies, his eccentricities making him an imposing figure to the young of both sexes, and an annoyance to the old, exciting the attention of everybody, and then suddenly disappearing, his person uniting in the most seductive manner aristocratic bearing and tone with indolent dissipation; his moods alternating between uproarious spirits and deep depression—in all ways he resembled a figure from some romantic poem."

Although Weber never studied with a major pianist, he prided himself on a thorough knowledge of all aspects of technique. He thought the school of Viennese pianists headed by Hummel were superficial, dry, and correct. Weber wanted the piano to have a music that spoke of mystery and poetry, of forest glens and chivalry, as he had achieved in his operas.

Weber's hands were enormous, possibly spanning a twelfth. He wrote some of the most complicated piano music of the early 1800s, with difficult left-hand figurations and chordal layouts of abnormally large stretches. His music calls for finger independence in new ways, such as having one hand play staccato and legato within a single passage. An excellent guitarist, he invented wonderful strumming effects for the piano. His music dashingly takes the most adventurous leaps until Liszt.

As a pianist, he performed in public primarily his own music, but privately he played Beethoven sonatas for his pupil Julius Benedict "with a fire and precision and a thorough entering into the spirit of the composer, which would have given the mighty Ludwig the best proof of Weber's reverence and admiration for his genius." This was in 1821, and Weber had already written his own four piano sonatas, the two concerti, and the *Konzertstück,* which became one of the war-horses of nineteenth-century virtuosi. John Warrack, in his biography of Weber, states the unique importance of the score: "The *Konzertstück* is a keystone work of Romantic piano writing, crowning the bridge that leads from Dussek, Hummel, Kalkbrenner, Prince Louis Ferdinand and their contemporaries into the mid-nineteenth-century and Mendelssohn, Schumann, Chopin and Liszt, while its influence was consciously acknowledged as late as 1929 by one of Weber's greatest modern admirers, Stravinsky, in his Capriccio."

When Liszt first heard Weber's music, he was beside himself with glee. Mendelssohn was mesmerized, and Chopin, who criticized almost everybody's work, sighed, "An angel passes through the sky," when his student Georges Mathias played Weber's A-flat Sonata for him. Brahms and Tchaikovsky were so fascinated with the celebrated Rondo from the C major Sonata, known as the Perpetuum Mobile, that for fun they were both impelled to transfer the right hand to the left hand.

It was in 1819 that Weber launched the dance form of the century—the waltz. His immortal *Invitation to the Dance* linked all the popular elements of Romanticism in piano writing of a poetic virtuosity. The *Invitation* was the most played piano work for decades after its composition.

Today Weber is seldom found on recital programs, nor are his two piano concerti and *Konzertstück* often heard in orchestral programs. Yet his music has a fresh piquancy and an endearing innocence. He was the richest genius among the transitional composers born in the early stage of Romanticism, and some of his music will always exert a special magic.

BEVERIDGE WEBSTER
b. 1908 — United States

He studied with his father in Pittsburgh and with Isidor Philipp at the Paris Conservatoire; later with Artur Schnabel.

Webster has had an important career as a soloist with major orchestras, an adjudicator of international competitions, and for more than three decades an eminent teacher at the Juilliard School, where he has taught Paul Jacobs, Michel Block, and Jeffrey Swann. He has been honored for service to American music and has received honorary degrees, including a Doctor of Humane Letters from Baldwin Wallace University in Ohio.

He has recorded a great deal: outstanding readings of works ranging from the *Hammerklavier* Sonata of Beethoven, and Weber and Schubert sonatas, to Copland's Variations, Rachmaninoff's *Etudes-tableaux*, Ravel's *Gaspard de la nuit*, and Elliott Carter's Sonata, in which Webster's performance is packed with intellectual control and hard, raw technical command. He also has one of the most impressive of concerto repertoires, and has investigated every idiom in his seemingly insatiable delight in the literature.

Webster is a spontaneous performer who can be spotless in one piece and quite messy in the next, but when inspiration strikes and all elements happen to blend, he is a deeply moving artist. I vividly recall a 1958 Town Hall recital, which ranks high in my recital experiences, where he played the most ravishing Schubert Sonata-Fantasy, Schumann's *Waldscenen*, Liszt's *Dante Sonata,* and other works, with unforgettable impact, precision, and tonal balance.

ALEXIS WEISSENBERG
b. 1929 — Bulgaria

He played a concert at the age of eight, while studying with Bulgaria's most famous musician, Pantcho Vladigerov. In 1946 he graduated from the Juilliard School, where he worked under Olga Samaroff. Weissenberg, in 1947, won the Leventritt Competition and made his American debut with the New York Philharmonic, with Szell conducting. For nearly ten years Weissenberg was busy with concertizing. In 1956 he left the concert stage for nearly a decade to study. He reappeared after this hiatus with great success, bringing the public a larger and rejuvenated solo repertoire, which includes Bach to Bartók and Stravinsky, with a considerable amount of Chopin, Debussy, Scarlatti, and a great deal of Schumann, as well as a big concerto repertoire, containing the Bartók Second; the two Chopin, Brahms, Tchaikovsky; the five Beethoven; the Prokofiev Third; the Ravel D major; and the Rachmaninoff Third.

On stage, Weissenberg is a presence of unusual magnetism. An air of high seriousness mingles with tension. Weissenberg is there to do battle with a dragon—he must vanquish the piano. He plays with extreme economy of movement; a smile never passes across his lips. His programs are invariably challenges for himself and the audience. Weissenberg must impose his will on the score. It is not Schumann's *Carnaval* but "his" *Carnaval.* I don't mean that Weissenberg has no respect for the composer; quite the contrary. But he has stated publicly that as an interpreter it is his responsibility to pass the masters through the filter of his own sensibility, a contemporary sensibility. Certainly the stamp of Weissenberg's personality is indelibly imprinted on his interpretations. One quickly recognizes a Weissenberg performance once one is familiar with his art.

Weissenberg is also a controversial artist. Some find his playing repellent, while others are visibly moved and deeply shaken by his work. I have never been less than fascinated by his self-confident performances, which are always deeply thought out to the last detail. Weissenberg's playing has not changed one note since his return to the stage more than twenty seasons back. He knows what he wants and ferociously goes after it. But it is always a battle. Each season he plays one hundred concerts and seldom fewer than four in New York. In one concert he may hit his mark, while three others can be lacking almost everything he desires. This pattern of hit-or-miss has become more pronounced in the last five years or so, and he seems once again to be feeling a weariness with the stage. For the Bulgarian-born virtuoso, public performance seems to be a life-and-death struggle, an act of love-hate.

While both fans and detractors agree that Weissenberg has a fabulous mechanism, this does not mean he doesn't miss notes. The listener who wants pretty playing and melting emotions need not attend his work. Phenomenal facility or not, Weissenberg would assuredly have been laughed off the stage in 1900. Once Arthur Rubinstein's Chopin was thought unfeeling and Rachmaninoff and Hofmann icy, and doubtless Chopin would be amazed at Weissenberg's granitic reading of his Third Sonata, but we must learn to listen to a re-creative artist in the context of his era. So today too one may consider Weissenberg's Chopin Nocturnes, if not brutal, at least unpoetic. Yet after several hearings, they emerge as not insensitive or abrupt, but rather quite musical on his terms.

Weissenberg is never interpretively irresponsible. He dusts off accumulations of literary affectation in the Nocturnes. His is not a languishing Chopin. He analyzes his Chopin and finds quite a bit of psychological disturbance, even violence. Actually, Weissenberg too is a Romantic, a present-day Romanticist, more blaring, more cruel than those of the nineteenth century. In his art there seems to be a sadomasochistic streak. When all is going well, however, he can fuse his relentless personality into Schumann's *Symphonic Etudes* (the five posthumous variations always included) and find in the score all that was latent in Schumann's personality, but that comes to the fore with electrical shock in Weissenberg's

staggering conception. By far, my favorite of his Schumann performances.

A characteristic Weissenberg program presented us with three large-scale works, beginning with Haydn's E-flat Sonata; if Weissenberg had played it on Haydn's own wooden piano, he would have demolished the instrument. Ah! if Haydn could have been sitting next to me—how I would have liked to see his face. (I don't want to give the impression that Weissenberg is devoid of all repose or color, or that he cannot play softly, and he certainly can play slowly.) For the next piece, Weissenberg launched into the Liszt Sonata, which in his hands is ruthless, steely, and elemental, with an almost gruesome power, so much so that he makes me realize how twentieth-century, in an emotional sense, this score can be. After intermission, the pianist offered the seldom-played thirty-five-minute Rachmaninoff First Sonata. Blocks of sound roared from his piano; it was pandemonium. He played as loud as anyone in the history of the piano. The contemplation of sonority is a complex issue. But those chords were not merely banged, or percussive either. Most important, this fairly problematic composition was compelling in Weissenberg's hands because of his belief in his own playing.

He is not an endearing artist, or conceivably even a deep one. But he burns with an intense flame. And I often leave the hall shaken up in one way or another.

ERNST WENZEL
1808–1880 — Germany

A student of Friedrich Wieck. He was friends with Mendelssohn and Schumann and was a well-liked pianist and the teacher, at the Leipzig Conservatory, of Grieg, Sir George Henschel, and Ernst Perabo.

FRIEDRICH WIECK
1785–1873 — Germany

The father of Clara Wieck Schumann and her only teacher. He was a superb musician and influenced all who studied with him. Robert Schumann learned much from him, and was deeply pained by the rift between them over his love for Clara. Clara Wieck was ever grateful to her father for his remarkable teaching and devotion during her formative years. Mendelssohn knew his value and tried to secure him as a teacher at his newly founded Leipzig Conservatory in 1844. Among his many pupils were Wenzel and von Bülow, in addition to Alwin Wieck, his son (1821–1885), and another daughter, Marie Wieck (1832–1916), whose final public appearance at the age of eighty-three was ironically in Schumann's Piano Concerto.

JOSEF WIENIAWSKI
1837–1912 — Poland

A well-known pianist and brother of the great violinist Henri Wieniawski. He studied with Zimmerman and Marmontel, and later with Liszt. He composed many worthy salon works and was a professor at the Moscow Conservatory.

EARL WILD
b. 1915 — United States

Wild studied with Paul Doguereau and Egon Petri. In 1939 he became the first pianist ever to give a recital on American television.

He is also a composer, and his transcriptions of Gershwin and Rachmaninoff songs show his special understanding of the piano. Wild has premiered many new works, including the Paul Creston Concerto, and his tours have taken him throughout the world. He has had a distinguished recording career and has recorded over two hundred solo works, as well as such concertos as the MacDowell Second, the Menotti, Scharwenka, and the Paderewski. In 1986, for the centennial of Liszt's death, he played three Liszt recitals in Chicago, New York, and other cities.

He made his reputation slowly. He was born at a time when Americans trusted only artists who were European-born and -bred. He won no competition, and he began his career during the Great Depression. He joined NBC as a staff pianist, survived there for eight years, and participated when needed as a member of the NBC Symphony under Toscanini. Later, in 1942, the great conductor asked Wild to perform with him in Gershwin's *Rhapsody in Blue*. In fact, he was the first American soloist to perform with Toscanini. For a long time Wild was typecast as a Gershwin performer because of the sassy verve in his performances of the *Rhapsody* and Concerto in F. Later, Wild composed a Grand Fantasy on *Porgy and Bess*.

Wild has one of the world's great piano mechanisms. He is a tireless worker who thinks constantly about the difficulties at hand. Few understand the instrument as well as he. He has delighted in uncovering exciting works that lay coated with dust, and the public responds with enthusiasm to his clever programming. He has even given all-transcription programs to a packed Carnegie Hall. Wild is an elegant stylist, tossing off the most difficult works as a magician shakes his rabbit out of a hat. He is lavish in his use of rubato. A witty man, he once told me that his performance of the Chopin Ballade in G minor one evening had had enough rubato to last for two years. (I remember thinking how ghastly the performance had been.) But he is a true stage personality, and he seldom plays the same way twice. He likes the danger and thrill of performance, and at times he can border on kitsch. On the other hand, he can also pull the reins in and play like a drill sergeant.

He has added immeasurably to our enjoyment of neglected composers like Balakirev, Godowsky, Medtner, d'Albert, and many others. His Brahms *Paganini* Variations sizzle, and he rejoices in Liszt. It is not a deep Liszt, and a goodly dose of vulgarity appears here and there. But his passagework has a kind of glossiness that only he achieves. That sound alone gives his playing a unique glow. His best Liszt record is called "The Daemonic Liszt" and in it he plays the *Faust* Waltz rhapsodically, and the *Valse infernale* wickedly.

I don't much like most of his Chopin, which is either trite or wimpy. What he does with Liszt cannot be done with a purist like Chopin. He glories, however, in Rachmaninoff, where he is first-rate in the preludes and Concerti, all played with gusto and a beguiling tone. He plays the French composers, too, although his Franck, Ravel, and Fauré are not memorable. The Wild that I find irresistible can be heard in such works as Thalberg's Fantasies on Donizetti's *Don Pasquale* and Rossini's *Semiramide*, where Wild amplifies and "improves" the score, as pianists did unashamedly in an earlier era. He delights in the delicious chromatic scales; he is dazzling in the frippery of the passagework. In these and other works, such as the Herz Variations on "Non più mesta" from Rossini's *La Cenerentola*, Wild gracefully jumps all the hurdles. He plays with aplomb and a twinkle in his eye, with light heart and hand. He has a simple athletic enjoyment in what hands can do at such high levels of discipline.

Wild is a superb Godowsky player. In a piece like the *Symphonic Metamorphosis on Themes from Johann Strauss's "Künstlerleben,"* he knows exactly how to voice those ghostly, sickly harmonies and how to untangle the excruciating labyrinth of notes into a luminous glorification of the piano. For Godowsky enthusiasts, this is the purest, most classically played Godowsky.

Wild is a true virtuoso of the old school, happy as can be when giving his transcription "fests," unconcerned about the pedant's frown, and truly enjoying his wonderful, unabashed Romanticism and his ability to galvanize audiences.

DAVID WILDE
b. 1935 — England

A pianist of repute, he has made recordings and written on music. He is best known for his Liszt playing.

ALBERTO WILLIAMS
1862–1952 — Argentina

The foremost Argentinian pianist and composer of his day. He studied piano at the Paris Conservatoire with Georges Mathias and composition with César Franck. In Buenos Aires he opened a music school and was popular as a pianist; his Chopin playing was particularly admired. Williams composed very well for the piano, and his pieces include a *Sonata Argentina*.

AUGUST WINDING
1835–1899 — Denmark

He studied with Reinecke and Dreyschock, making his debut in Copenhagen at twenty-one. He went on to a fine career as a pianist and composer. His cadenzas to Mozart concerti are still used.

PAUL WITTGENSTEIN
1887–1961 — Austria

He worked under Leschetizky and pursued his career as concert pianist until he lost his right arm fighting on the Russian front in World War I. He vowed to continue playing and learned the existing left-hand literature; also, he commissioned many concertos for left hand alone. The best of these are Prokofiev's Piano Concerto No. 4, Britten's *Diversions,* and the great Ravel Concerto for the Left Hand, which Wittgenstein premiered in Vienna on November 27, 1931.

AUGUSTE DÉSIRÉ WOLFF
1821–1887 — France

A pianist who studied with Zimmerman, later becoming head of the Pleyel piano firm.

KONRAD WOLFF
b. 1907 — Germany

A leading scholar and writer on the piano. A student of Artur Schnabel, Wolff has appeared in recital, lectured, and been a prominent teacher. His latest book, *Masters of the Keyboard,* is an examination of the keyboard

style of Bach, Haydn, Mozart, Beethoven, and Schubert.

JOSEPH WÖLFL
1772–1812 — Austria

One of Europe's leading pianists and a rival of Beethoven, whom he tied in a contest of improvisations.

Wölfl composed voluminously, including seven concerti, twenty-four sets of variations, and fifty-eight solo sonatas. Some of this output contains very good music. His C minor Sonata, Op. 25, is bold in outline, wide in emotional range, and quite skillfully bound together.

He lived in an age interested in exploring new avenues in piano technique, and Wölfl, who had a large hand, was in the forefront of this development. His once famed Sonata Op. 41, from 1808, is subtitled *Non plus ultra;* its variation finale is still technically mean. (Dussek was soon to write a sonata, *Plus ultra.*) Every important pianist of Wölfl's generation, such as Cramer, Berger, and Steibelt, was spinning out sets of etudes, and Wölfl's was called *Practical School for the Pianoforte,* consisting of fifty exercises.

HERMANN WOLLENHAUPT
1829–1863 — Germany

He studied with Julius Knorr and Moritz Hauptmann, emigrated to New York in 1845, and established himself as a brilliant performer, teacher, and composer of one hundred well-bred salon pieces.

ROGER WOODWARD
b. 1943 — Australia

A student of Drzewiecki in Warsaw for six years. He has made a Chopin disc but is especially noted for his exemplary readings of twentieth-century music. His best-known recordings are the Shostakovich Preludes and Fugues.

FRIEDRICH WÜHRER
b. 1900 — Austria

A highly acclaimed pianist who is especially known for his fine artistry in the Austro-Germanic repertory. He studied at the Vienna Conservatory and later taught there. His many recordings offer many interpretive insights, and his Schubert Sonatas have special value.

OXANA YABLONSKAYA
b. 1941 — USSR

She studied with Anaida Sumbatyan and at the Moscow Conservatory with Goldenweiser. She was the winner of the 1963 Long-Thibaud Competition. She made her American debut at Carnegie Hall in 1977, and now teaches at the Juilliard School.

such as Hindemith, Bartók, and Křenek, for whose Piano Concerto No. 2 she gave the Russian premiere. Shostakovich thought she "played Liszt like no one else," and in his memoirs he tells us that "I think Yudina plays my sonata badly [No. 2 in E minor]. The tempos are all off and there's a free, shall we say, approach to the text. But perhaps I'm wrong, I haven't heard the recording in a while."

MARIA YUDINA
1899–1970 — Russia

A legendary figure in Russian musical circles; a student of Nicolaiev at the St. Petersburg Conservatory. She was a fascinating and eccentric personality. Her concerts were always packed, and she can be heard on many Russian recordings. She played a large repertoire, with the courage to program moderns

MICHAEL VON ZADORA
1882–1946 — United States

A student of Leschetizky and then of Busoni, whose music he often played. His recording of Busoni's Sonatina No. 6, *Super Carmen,* is the work of a virtuoso.

YAKOV ZAK
1913–1976 — Russia

He studied at the Moscow Conservatory with Heinrich Neuhaus, later becoming professor there. He was an objective player, somewhat dry. His recording of Kabalevsky's Third Sonata is typical of his playing. He taught many first-rate artists, including Youri Egorov and Alexander Toradze.

JUANA ZAYAS
b. 1940 — Cuba

After studies in Paris, she settled in the United States. She has appeared in concert here and in Europe. Her playing is crisp, and she has enormous verve. Her disc of the Chopin Etudes exhibits high craft.

CARLO ZECCHI
1903–1984 — Italy

He studied in Rome, then with Busoni. He was a pianist of impeccable technique, with a fine sense of tonal values. He played Scarlatti with finesse, and Chopin with style and a beguiling elasticity of phrasing. Zecchi was also a famed conductor and teacher. He died during the 1984 Busoni Competition, where he was to be a judge.

IGOR ZHUKOV
b. 1936 — USSR

He was a student of Heinrich Neuhaus. He traveled to Paris, where he won a prize at the Long-Thibaud Competition in 1957. Since that time, he has had a busy career in the Soviet Union, where he has recorded prolifically. His Scriabin is special; he brings out the composer's mysticism in elongated and elastic performances.

GÉZA ZICHY
1849–1924 — Hungary

When he was seventeen, he lost his right arm, but continued his pianistic training, eventually studying with Liszt. He became a brilliant player with his left hand and wrote many works for his own purposes. Ernst Pauer wrote that "he reached so wonderful a degree of facility and technical perfection that his performances were received with bewildered astonishment and phrenetic acclamations."

KRYSTIAN ZIMERMAN
b. 1956 — Poland

He began lessons at five with his father, then proceeded to train under Andrzej Jasinski, a relatively unknown teacher-pianist who was Zimerman's only other piano instructor. In 1975 the eighteen-year-old student won the Chopin Competition in Warsaw. From that moment forward, Zimerman has played throughout the world.

His work possesses a fresh lyricism. His Chopin has a rare finesse; he presents a light-hearted quality in such works as the Waltzes and plays the mazurkas with some style and without exaggeration. He has a fine sense of form, with a vital feeling for plastic beauty. His repertoire is fairly eclectic, and he plays Brahms with rich color, Szymanowski with tremulous and exquisite contour, Mozart and Schubert with a pristine elegance. He has a tendency in his sheer gracefulness to overlook a certain pithiness in weighty music, such as the Brahms F minor Sonata, and in a work like Liszt's A major Concerto he skims over its theatricality to become absorbed mostly in its poetic issues.

At present, he is experimenting with his conceptions, and many of them are in flux; at times he distorts as he aims for an ever freer expression. However, Zimerman is one of the finest young pianists of his generation. His playing may lack fierce passion, but this emotional restraint combined with a highly Romantic and sensitive nature, as well as one of the most elastic techniques on the concert stage, make for luminous sound and piano playing of great appeal.

PIERRE ZIMMERMAN
1785–1853 — France

He studied the piano at the Paris Conservatoire from 1798, working with Boieldieu. In 1800 he took first prize in piano playing, beating out even Kalkbrenner, who placed second. In 1820, after much teaching experience, he became full professor of the piano at the Conservatoire, holding this post until 1848.

Zimmerman became one of the leading piano teachers of his time, with many eminent students to his credit. His best-known pupils were Alkan, Prudent, Marmontel, Ravina, Alexander Goria, Josef Wieniawski, and César Franck. He received the Legion of Honor and composed dozens of works.

AGNES ZIMMERMANN
1847–1925 — Germany

She was brought early to London, where she studied at the Royal Academy of Music with Cipriani Potter and then with Ernst Pauer. Subsequently becoming a well-known pianist, she was happiest with the Classical composers. In 1872 she gave the first performance in England of Beethoven's interesting transcription for piano of his great

275

Violin Concerto. She wrote a piano sonata, Op. 22.

NIKOLAI ZVEREV

1832–1893 — Russia

He studied with Dubuc and with Henselt, later becoming a prominent teacher in Moscow. He had one of the great piano classes in history, and as a molder of young talent he must have had special gifts. Indeed, he was considered a perfectionist and a demanding teacher. He trained many of his students through the formative teen years, and then they would go on to the Moscow Conservatory. These pupils included Igumnov, Scriabin, Rachmaninoff, Lhévinne, Siloti, and many others who rose to distinction.

PART TWO

The Piano Literature

with lists of
exceptional recordings

Introduction

ART Two presents a brief discussion of each composition. I often include the date of the work when available, and occasionally give timings of a work's duration when I think it necessary. When I say a concerto is thirty minutes long, I mean that this is the average timing of the work. Naturally there will be considerable deviation in this respect. One performance of the Liszt Sonata may be only twenty-six minutes while another may run to as long as thirty-three.

After each composition, I have listed various recordings which represent the widest diversity of interpretation. If, for example, listeners were to hear each of my selections for the Brahms Second Piano Concerto, they would form through such "comparative listening" a great knowledge of the work's potential and interpretive possibilities. From such listening one becomes open-minded, and always curious as to the next performance. In these selections I do not rank the performances. They are different, but always represent professional craftsmanship. Naturally the sonics of the recordings vary greatly.

I do not list 78s, although many have been transferred to long-playing records. But if one comes across, say, Cortot's magnificent performance of the Weber A-flat Sonata, one should not pass it up. Many splendid 78-era recordings are invaluable, and many of these are sonically more true to piano sound than many a CD. Even when not listed in my text, I would try to have any recordings by Cortot, Gieseking, Casadesus, Rachmaninoff, Rosenthal, Backhaus, Lhévinne, Godowsky, Hess, Barère, Friedman, Moiseiwitsch, Edwin Fischer, Hofmann, Kapell, Lipatti, Rubinstein, Rudolf Serkin, Schnabel, Arrau, Gould, Michelangeli, Gilels, de Larrocha, and Horowitz. In the case of the last ten, these pianists' lifework will be, all or in part, eventually on compact discs, or whatever new invention will take their place. All of the above-mentioned artists possessed unique musical personalities, and interpretive gifts of a high order. Present-day pianists should take it for granted to be thoroughly familiar with their respective styles. Jorge Bolet says, "I wish that every young pianist would really study—I don't mean just listen, but really study the performances of Rachmaninoff, Horowitz, Moiseiwitsch, Hofmann, and Friedman and really analyze what made their performances so great."

My selections of records include mono as well as stereo LPs (although I do not indicate if they are mono). If the score is on compact disc, the abbreviation CD is used. I have not used record numbers (catalogue numbers), which would needlessly clutter the text. Today many recordings are being transferred to CD, or have been remastered digitally. Some are reissued on cheaper labels, and many selections are also available on cassettes. The use of numbers is confusing; it is usually sufficient for the collector to know the work, the artist, and the record label.

Although a majority of the recordings listed are easily available, my concern is not what is temporarily available. This is a discography. Some labels (such as Dover or Remington) are now defunct, some labels are foreign, and many albums are out of print, temporarily or forever. Nonetheless, the world of the record collector is an exciting one. Never before have there been so many stores in major cities where one can locate gems that one has been yearning to have. Recently I found an old Westminster recording of Busoni's *Fantasia contrappuntistica* played by the great Egon Petri, which had been on my mind for some time. Record collectors, it seems, are now more numerous than book collectors. George Steiner points out: "Habits of the bibliophile—of the library cormorant, as Coleridge called him—have shifted to the collector of records and performances. The furtive manias, the condescensions of expertness, the hunter's zeal which bore once on first editions, colophons, the *in-octavo* of a remaindered text, are common now among music lovers. There is a science and market in old pressings, in out-of-stock albums, in worn 78s, as there has been in used books. Catalogues of recordings and rare tapes are becoming as exegetic as bibliographies."

There is a vast pianistic legacy ready to be listened to. Recording has given the performer immortality. What would we not give to hear Mozart, Beethoven, Chopin, and Liszt play! At least future generations will not have to guess how Cortot, Richter, Horowitz, or Gould played.

A

ISAAC ALBÉNIZ
1860–1909 — Spain

He composed 250 piano pieces, mostly of slight value. The composer disowned his early music. After 1890, he came into contact with Debussy, Fauré, and Dukas and forged a sophisticated impressionist art, which culminated in his masterpiece, *Iberia* (twelve pieces, 1906–09). Here Albéniz paints an idealized Spain, mostly set in Andalucía. The pieces are of immense technical difficulty, rich in textural fabric, intricate in voicing, and awkward in hand placement. One day, Manuel de Falla and Ricardo Viñes came upon Albéniz wandering the streets in despair. He told them, "Last night I came near to burning the manuscripts of *Iberia,* for I saw that what I had written was unplayable." Fortunately, some have mastered the cruel tasks and have revealed Albéniz's synthesis of Spanish moods and dances.

Iberia

Evocación: Marked Allegretto expressivo. Albéniz uses seven flats for most of its notation. It is technically the simplest of the *Iberia,* asking for tonal discrimination in its slow-burning lyric intensity. In form it is the Spanish dance known as the fandanguillo.

El Puerto: A depiction of the harbor of Santa Maria teeming with life. The rhythms are derived from such Andalusian dances as the polo, the seguiría gitana, and the bulerías. Albéniz asks the performer to play "très brusque," to play "toujours joyeux," and "très langoureux."

Fête-Dieu à Seville ("Corpus Christi Day in Seville"): A superb use of the piano, asking for excellent staccato and chord technique. Albéniz describes, with joy and pathos, a processional on this religious occasion. In nine minutes, Albéniz's sense of smoldering Spanish drama and repressed violence produces an overwhelming effect.

Rondeña: A lighter work but difficult to make coherent in its contrasting rhythms. It is also difficult to extrapolate the melodies from the web of texture. James Gibb writes, "The middle section of this piece shows specially subtle choice of harmony and skill in placing notes which suggest a vocal line with guitar accompaniment: Although the voice part is played in the middle register of the piano, it sounds as if the singer is straining in the upper range of his voice. Here the art of mimicry is transcended and we have a truly creative and individual contribution to piano writing."

Almería: A Spanish port town. In the composition we find the tarantas, which is a dance native to that city, as well as aspects of the jota. *Almería* is somewhat less demanding technically than *Rondeña*. It asks the interpreter to play with a lavish color-wheel and with imaginative freedom. The middle section touches the depths of the soul of Andalucía. *Almería* is perhaps the loveliest music Albéniz wrote.

Triana: The most famous piece of the cycle. The name is taken from a Seville suburb. *Triana* is a sparkling virtuoso piece with the beguiling rhythm of the pasodoble. The gypsy element is apparent throughout.

El Albaicín: The gypsy quarter of Granada. Albéniz marks the score Allegro assai, ma melancolico. Debussy admired the score. He explained that in *El Albaicín,* "one rediscovers the fragrance of the blossom-filled nights of Spain . . . the tone of a muted guitar which sings its sorrow to the night, sings with sudden awakenings and nervous starts." Albéniz attempts to make the performer aware of the great tonal variety he desires with different markings ranging from *piano* to *pp, ppp, pppp,* and *ppppp.*

El Polo: Andalusian song and dance. A sobbing chant persists throughout the piece, embedded in a tone of melancholy, bitterness, and irony.

Lavapiés: Working-class quarter of Madrid. A formidable work of virtuosity and rhythmic verve. Albéniz exploits the dance called the chulos. The lean, brittle chords have a dashing glitter.

Málaga: A difficult malaguena; hard-edged, full of vitality with a peculiarly Spanish sadness and fatality, which in the hands of an unsympathetic executant can become monotonous.

Jerez: The famous wine city, the home of sherry. Along with *Almería* and *Fête-Dieu à Seville,* the longest work of *Iberia.* Here Albéniz reaches the very essence of what he aspired to in his music. Debussy wrote that without actually using folk themes, "it is as if he had imbibed them, had so absorbed them that they passed into his art without it

being possible to draw the line of demarcation."

Eritaña: A tavern on the outskirts of Seville. Debussy stated that a "flowing tide of humanity bursts into laughter, accompanied by tambourines. Never has music achieved such differentiated, such colorful impressions, and the eyes close as though blinded by these pictures all too vivid in hue."

Iberia:
  ARRAU (Book I): Odyssey
  AYBAR: Connoisseur Society
  BLOCK: Connoisseur Society
  CICCOLINI: Seraphim
  DE LARROCHA: London (CD)
  REQUEJO: Claves (CD)
  URIBE: Orion

Navarra
Twenty-six measures were left unfinished at Albéniz's death. They were completed by de Séverac. *Navarra* is a pendant to the *Iberia* cycle, sharing its intense nationalism. Gibb writes, "The extremes of Spanish masculine pride and grandiloquence, almost toppling into self-parody, are presented with Lisztian brilliance and spaciousness."

  DE LARROCHA: Turnabout; London (CD)
  RUBINSTEIN: RCA (CD)

Cantos de España;
La Vega;
Azulejos
Other Albéniz compositions that are well known are the five pieces that comprise the suite *Cantos de España,* Op. 232. With its Moorish Prelude, description of *Córdoba,* and brilliant Seguidillas, the suite evokes an enchanted Spain. Even more popular is the Tango from the *España* suite of 1890, Op. 165. Of greater importance, but virtually unknown, are the very long (fourteen minutes) *La Vega,* and *Azulejos* ("Colored Tiles"), which was completed by Granados after Albéniz's death.

  DE LARROCHA: MHS

CHARLES VALENTIN ALKAN

1813–1888 — France

Alkan left some of the most inspired piano music of nineteenth-century France, and is finally coming to be appreciated as a visionary Romantic. His works have been feared by pianists because of their extreme difficulty and the physical strength necessary to play them. But in fact he created many smaller works which cover a wide range of emotions and technical skill.

Shorter Pieces

Alkan's "miniatures" include the haunting *La Chanson de la folle au bord de la mer* ("Song of the Mad Woman on the Seashore"), No. 8 of his Twenty-five Preludes; the magical *Petit Conte;* the piquant Barcarolle Op. 65, No. 6; *Les Soupirs,* a sensuous piece of impressionism; and *Le Tambour bat aux champs,* Op. 50, No. 2 ("The Drum Beats in the Fields"), which is, in Raymond Lewenthal's words, "one of the bitterest, most vehement and sarcastic commentaries on the folly of war that has ever been written." The composer Bernard van Dieren thinks it possesses "a depth of imagery, an incandescence of statement, and a universality of meaning which remind one of the most intense lines of Poe or Blake."

SMITH (25 short pieces): Arabesque (CD)

Sonatine, Op. 61

Surely the most grueling *sonatine* in the literature. Composed in 1861, it is in four movements, totaling eighteen minutes. There is nothing else like it from its era. The writing is lean, the sarcasm is devastating. Kaikhosru Sorabji calls it "vehement, droll, gargoyle-like, childlike and naive in turn . . . almost as if Berlioz had written a Beethoven sonata."

Sonatine and short works:
LEWENTHAL: CBS
RINGEISSEN: Harmonia Mundi
SMITH: Arabesque

Grande Sonate, Op. 33

Composed in 1847, this is a problematic and fascinating score, running to forty-five minutes. It is subtitled *Les Quatre Ages;* each movement depicts a man at a different stage of life—twenty, thirty, forty, and fifty years old. Only the second movement, titled *Quasi-Faust,* is in sonata form. Raymond Lewenthal plays only that movement in his recording. However, Ronald Smith has spent years exploring this weird and magnificent work, and his recording is a compelling document. In *Quasi-Faust* in particular, Alkan hurls all caution to the wind. Joseph Bloch writes of the Sonata that "as a conception it is astounding and without parallel in the Romantic piano literature." Lewenthal observes that in this work "Alkan deals with the hopes, triumphs, joys, and sorrows of a human being." He finds it "the most difficult piano sonata since Beethoven's *Hammerklavier,* and the strangest one before the Ives sonatas."

The composer went to extreme lengths to tell his would-be interpreters his intentions, and the score is strewn with adjectives and phrases such as "palpitant," "amoureusement," "avec désespoir," "sataniquement," "avec délices," "avec bonheur," "déchirant," and many more.

LEWENTHAL: RCA
SMITH: Arabesque

Twelve Etudes in All the Minor Keys, Op. 39

In 1847, Alkan composed Twelve Etudes in the Major Keys, Op. 35. Hans von Bülow reviewed them enthusiastically, calling Alkan "the Berlioz of the piano." The Op. 35 are of interest musically and technically, yet they remain etudes in size and intention. In the decade to follow, Alkan was practically silent. In 1857, however, his most monumental work appeared—the Twelve Etudes in the Minor Keys, Op. 39, which grew to absurd proportions, "rather like Frankenstein's monster," as Ronald Smith says. The Twelve Etudes span 277 pages of uncompromising, obsessive madness and a technical hardship never before seen in a work for the piano.

No. 1, *Comme le vent* ("Like the Wind"), is marked Prestissimamente. Smith calls it "a kind of nightmare tarantella which falls roughly into sonata form."

No. 2, *En rythme molossique,* is a harsh work in 6/4 meter. To play it demands the strength of an Olympic weight lifter. The ending, with its repeated low D's, is a study in monotony.

No. 3, *Scherzo diabolico,* is the shortest of these pieces. It includes very difficult finger-work with a mighty chordal trio of Byronic, blood-curdling melodrama.

Alkan's *Symphony for Solo Piano* occupies Nos. 4, 5, 6, and 7 of the Op. 39. Here the composer indulges his love for orchestral sonorities and creates a cogent work of pure musical effect. The first movement, in C minor, is concise and dignified. The second movement, *Marche funèbre,* conjures up an immense procession. Lewenthal suggests: "Think of soft-playing military band instruments through this wonderful trio, and bear in mind the first movement of Berlioz' *Symphonie funèbre et triomphale* throughout all of this movement." The third movement is, ironically, a menuet, of the least genteel quality. Cross-rhythms and irregular phrase groups (a characteristic of Alkan's style) are jaggedly flung against a lyrical trio. The fourth movement is, for Lewenthal, "like a wild ride in hell." This half-hour composition will amaze the listener with its anticipatory glances toward Bruckner, Brahms, Mahler, Nielsen, and others.

In Etudes Nos. 8, 9, and 10, titled *Concerto for Solo Piano,* Alkan evokes both soloist and orchestra; the work is gargantuan—121 pages in length. The first movement alone is 1,341 measures in 72 pages of a classical concerto

form, which takes about thirty-five minutes of playing time. Alkan is ingenious in raising the voice of his soloist above the roar of a great orchestral body. The movement is surely one of the splendid pieces of architectural planning. Smith speaks of "the far-flung tonal strategy that holds the vast construction together." He also notes "an uncanny anticipation of the arctic world of Sibelius's Fourth Symphony."

The slow movement, an Adagio in C-sharp minor, contains some beautiful writing, as well as what Smith calls "a grimly realistic episode over which the spirit of Mahler seems to preside." The finale is marked Allegretto alla barbaresca, a rondo in F-sharp minor. Bloch writes, "Its harmonic clashes, its barbaric rhythmic drive, its strange cross-rhythms give an almost Bartókian effect. And it is one of the real virtuoso pieces—a closing number guaranteed to have any audience sitting on the edge of its seats."

No. 11 is an Ouverture in B minor of tremendous scope—the longest of any of the etudes except the first movement of the *Concerto.* Bloch thinks it "perhaps the weakest member of Opus 39," but this recondite study becomes adventurous in Ronald Smith's heroic performance. He absolutely exults in Alkan's work.

No. 12 is a ten-minute set of variations, *Le Festin d'Esope,* which in Bloch's estimation "belongs among the important Variation-works of the piano literature. Its neglect by pianists is inexplicable."

Wilfrid Mellers speaks of "the necromantic quality of Alkan's pianism." The score is fraught with tension, wry humor, and mocking fury, producing a cumulative effect of startling power.

Twelve Etudes Op. 39:
SMITH: Arabesque

Selected Etudes Op. 39:
LEWENTHAL (Symphony for Solo Piano & Le Festin d'Esope): RCA
PONTI (Nos. 1–7, 12): Candide

JOHANN SEBASTIAN BACH
1685–1750 — Germany

In selecting the literature for Part Two of this book, I have not included works of pre-piano composers, except in the case of Bach and Scarlatti, simply because pianists seldom perform or record on the piano such keyboard works as those of the Elizabethan masters, the Baroque composers (such as Froberger or even Handel), or the great French master François Couperin. Even Bach, once indispensable to the pianist's world, has been largely displaced from the active repertoire by many more performances on harpsichord. Nevertheless, I have included a small survey of Bach's chief works.

Although pianists will not and should not give up Bach on the piano, and indeed for the fingers and mind there is nothing more nourishing, the great cantor of Leipzig may well sound better on his own instruments. Claudio Arrau has said, "Any shades of crescendo and diminuendo and other inflections which can only be achieved on a modern piano hinder Bach's meaning. These qualities of the piano's creep into Bach whether you like it or not." Today we find beauty in instruments once thought to be outmoded. Nineteenth-century sensibility thought of the harpsichord as an insufficient instrument: industrial progress had produced the piano, an instrument that Bach would automatically have saluted as superior. This attitude was summed up by the pianist Edwin Hughes, a student of Leschetizky, when he wrote, "On account of the limitations of the harpsichord, Bach doubtless did what any other good musician had to do in playing it or composing for it; in his mind's ear he imagined the nuances that he was unable to reproduce on its keyboard, just as in playing the clavichord he doubtless let his fancy expand indefinitely the tiny-toned dynamic range of that charming instrument."

Chromatic Fantasia and Fugue in D minor
The Chromatic Fantasy is one of Bach's most often performed larger works. Its emotional content remains "Romantic" for each generation.

SCHIFF: Hungaroton (CD)
SCHNABEL: Perennial Records
TURECK: CBS
WEISSENBERG: Angel

Concerto in the Italian Style
  (Italian Concerto)
Composed for the double manual harpsichord; the slow movement's expressive singing works well on the modern piano.

GOULD: CBS
SCHNABEL: Perennial Records
Y. TAKAHASHI: Denon (CD)

The Six English Suites, Six French Suites,
  and Six Partitas
These suites represent the most sophisticated use of Baroque dance forms. Bach gave his students the *French* and *English* Suites to learn after they had mastered the Two- and Three-Part Inventions. The Partitas are the most complex of Bach's keyboard suites and the

285

most frequently performed in the concert halls of the world. The *French* Suites are the least complex, lacking the first-movement preludes of the Partitas and the *English* Suites.

English and French Suites (complete):
GOULD: CBS (CD)

English Suites:
ARGERICH (No. 2): DG
POGORELICH (Nos. 2 & 3): DG (CD)

Partitas:
GOULD: CBS (CD)
LIPATTI (No. 1): Angel (CD)
MARTINS: Arabesque
SCHIFF: London (CD)
WEISSENBERG: EMI or Angel

Aria with Thirty Variations (The Goldberg Variations)

The peak of Baroque variation writing, this work is titanic in scope. John Gillespie calls it "the crowning achievement of the Baroque keyboard." Charles Rosen asserts, "The elegance of the *Goldberg* Variations is its glory: It is the most worldly of Bach's achievements, with the *Italian Concerto*. . . . Except for the *Saint Matthew Passion,* in no other work is the depth of Bach's spirit so easily accessible, and its significance so tangible." Nonetheless, its enormous length and contrapuntal mastery keep the score from the hands of tyros.

GOULD (Early and Late): (1955) CBS (CD); (1981) CBS (CD)
KEMPFF: DG
MARTINS: Arabesque
P. SERKIN: Pro Arte (CD)
TIPO: Angel (CD)

The Fifteen Two-Part and Fifteen Three-Part Inventions

These pieces in two and three voices are masterpieces of contrapuntal perfection. The Three-Part Inventions are quite difficult, and they thoroughly lay the foundation for the study of *The Well-Tempered Clavier.*

GOULD: CBS (CD)
NIKOLAYEVA: Harmonia Mundi (CD)
SCHIFF: London (CD)

The Well-Tempered Clavier, Books I and II—Forty-eight Preludes and Fugues

One of the landmarks in the history of music. In Bach's day, two systems of keyboard tuning were still used, the "mean tone" method and the newer "equal temperament" system. The equal tuning permitted far more ease in modulation from one key to another. Bach's advocacy of the twelve-tone chromatic system, through his preludes and fugues in the twelve major and twelve minor keys, gave added prestige to equal-tempered tuning. Ernest Hutcheson describes the work as "a treasury of musical scholarship, giving final definition to instrumental counterpoint and fugue." Arthur Loesser sees "its vast range through all phases of feeling, from a brisk delight in muscular playfulness through harrowing depths of personal introspection up to heights of grandeur unsurpassed in music."

E. FISCHER: Pathé
GOULD: CBS (CD)
GULDA: Philips (CD)
MARTINS: Arabesque
S. RICHTER: JVC/Melodiya (CD)
SCHIFF: London (CD)

MILY BALAKIREV
1837–1910—Russia

Islamey—Oriental Fantasy

Balakirev, a fine pianist, could never quite master the hardships of his own *Islamey.* Liszt was reputed to have sight-read it. It remains one of the wonderful works of Russian virtuoso pianism. The Rubinstein brothers, von Bülow, and Tausig played it frequently, and Ravel greatly admired it; his *Scarbo* stems directly from its pianism. Balakirev wrote a quantity of appealing, beautifully scored piano music, the finest being his neglected and unconventional Piano Sonata in B-flat minor.

Islamey:
ARRAU: Desmar
BARÈRE: Varèse/Sarabande
ZELTSER: CBS

SAMUEL BARBER
1910–1981 — United States

Sonata in E-flat minor, Op. 26 (1949)
Barber's major achievement for the piano and the most popular American sonata since its composition. The work is in four compact movements, concluding with a brilliantly jaunty fugue. Barber also composed a fine Piano Concerto, for John Browning, who has played it with success everywhere.

Sonata:
BROWNING: Desto
CLIBURN: RCA
HOROWITZ: RCA

BÉLA BARTÓK
1881–1945 — Hungary

The greatest Hungarian composer of the twentieth century. His contribution to the piano literature brought to the instrument an entirely new personality and sonorous language. The music contains asymmetrical phrase groups, irregular meters, keyless modal melodies, wonderful tonal clashes, the drone bass, block chordal accompaniments, much of it inspired by Magyar folk music. It sounds new, yet its roots are ancient. Bartók was a pianist of great originality, as may be heard on his complete recordings issued by Hungaroton.

Fourteen Bagatelles, Op. 6 (1908)
One of the finest sets of piano music of its decade. Unlike much of Bartók, these are not folk-inspired; each piece is ingenious in its application of sonority.

SILVERMAN: Orion

Three Etudes, Op. 18 (1918)
Extraordinary music, and technically hazardous. All three total only eight minutes. In No. 2, Bartók has assimilated Debussy's and Ravel's impressionism into his own style.

JACOBS: Nonesuch
ROSEN: Epic

Improvisations, Op. 20 (1920).
A subtly connected set of eight pieces based on Hungarian peasant songs.

KOCSIS: Philips
PERAHIA: CBS

Sonata for Piano (1926)
One of the most frequently performed of Bartók's solo piano works; in three movements. It is angular, dissonant, and powerful.

BISHOP-KOVACEVICH: Philips
KALICHSTEIN: Vanguard
KOCSIS: Denon (CD)

Out of Doors Suite (1926)
A tremendously effective cycle of five pieces, very difficult to play: *With Drums and Pipes, Barcarolla, Musettes, Night's Music,* and *The Chase.*

PERAHIA: CBS
SÁNDOR: Turnabout

Mikrokosmos, Six Volumes—
153 Progressive Pieces (1926–37)

A precious folk treasury for the young. Bartók carves out the pianist's gradual growth through pieces which progressively present an ever-widening awareness of compositional devices and pianistic problems.

> MASSELOS: MHS
> RÁNKI: Telefunken

Fifteen Hungarian Peasant Songs

This is a cycle characteristic of Bartók's folk settings.

> KOCSIS: Denon (CD)
> RICHTER: CBS/Melodiya

Piano Concerto No. 1 (1926)

Bartók's three piano concerti are classics of the twentieth-century concerto repertoire. No. 1 utilizes a large percussion battery and needs an excellent conductor.

> POLLINI, Abbado/Chicago Symphony: DG (CD)
> P. SERKIN, Ozawa/Chicago Symphony: RCA

Piano Concerto No. 2 (1932)

The Second Concerto is a technical *tour de force*, with a splashy and dissonant orchestral part. The most dashing of the three concerti.

> ASHKENAZY, Solti/London Philharmonic: London
> POLLINI, Abbado/Chicago Symphony: DG (CD)
> WEISSENBERG, Ormandy/Philadelphia: RCA

Piano Concerto No. 3 (1945)

The Third Concerto is the least taxing technically, the least complex orchestrally, and the easiest to grasp on first hearing. The slow movement, Adagio religioso, is an unearthly chant.

> ANDA, Fricsay/Berlin Symphony: DG
> ASHKENAZY, Solti/Chicago Symphony: London (CD)

> KATCHEN, Kertesz/London Symphony: London
> RÁNKI, Ferencsik/Hungarian State: Hungaroton (CD)

LUDWIG VAN BEETHOVEN
1770–1827 — Germany

The Thirty-two Piano Sonatas

Beethoven's piano sonatas form one of the great contributions to the musical art. Each of the thirty-two is a landmark in the history of the sonata form.

> ARRAU: Philips
> ASHKENAZY: London
> BACKHAUS: London
> BARENBOIM: DG (CD)
> BRENDEL: Philips (CD)
> GULDA: Amadeo (CD)
> KEMPFF: DG
> KUERTI: Odyssey
> SCHNABEL: Seraphim (a finer British pressing exists on EMI)

Sonata No. 1 in F minor,
Op. 2, No. 1 (1795)

The first three sonatas are fittingly dedicated to Haydn. They are all in four movements, a rarity in eighteenth-century piano sonatas. The F minor Sonata is composed for the specific qualities of the piano, unlike many of Haydn's sonatas which are still reminiscent of harpsichord writing. The slow movement is the height of graciousness, the minuet is courtly, but the storms of the first and fourth movements announce that the world of music will soon change under Beethoven.

> GOULD: CBS
> GRINBERG: Melodiya

Sonata No. 2 in A major,
Op. 2, No. 2 (1795)

A work of great complexity, demanding well-developed technique. Beethoven here substitutes the scherzo for the minuet. Pianist Denis Matthews wrote of the work: "The time-scale is luxurious, the harmonic progress leisurely; its humor ranges from the playful to the ferocious, with a few challenging outbursts of virtuosity that are offset by the surprisingly gentle ending of the final movement."

GILELS: DG (CD)
HORSZOWSKI: Nonesuch (CD)

Sonata No. 3 in C major, Op. 2, No. 3 (1795)

Here Beethoven writes a muscular sonata which outdoes Clementi's C major Sonata for virtuosity. Beethoven himself often played it. The Adagio is a heavenly movement in E major, showing how Romantic the early Beethoven could sound.

GILELS: Melodiya
GOULD: CBS
RICHTER: CBS
RUBINSTEIN: RCA

Sonata No. 4 in E-flat major, Op. 7 (1796)

The longest of the early sonatas, or of any eighteenth-century sonata, requiring a half-hour for performance of its four movements. The slow movement in C major demands a perfect rhythmic awareness. John Gillespie calls the rondo finale "a landmark in perfection for this form. It has seldom been equaled, never surpassed." This sonata is not nearly known or played enough.

GRINBERG: Melodiya
HUNGERFORD: Vanguard (CD)
MICHELANGELI: DG
PERAHIA: CBS
SHERMAN: Sine Qua Non

Sonata No. 5 in C minor, Op. 10, No. 1 (1796–98)

Great intensity of expression is needed in this first of the three sonatas composed in C minor. Louis Kentner thinks it "a remarkably

good 'key' to Beethoven's style, a gate through which the student may enter this world better than through any other."

BISHOP-KOVACEVICH: Philips
GOULD: CBS
HUNGERFORD: Vanguard (CD)
NIKOLAYEVA: Melodiya

Sonata No. 6 in F major, Op. 10, No. 2 (1796–98)

The first movement bubbles with Haydnesque merriment, but there is sarcasm, too. The second movement is an Allegretto, and the finale is in sonata form; the fugal opening is a surprise. This movement needs good broken octaves, deft fingerwork, and a crisp staccato.

GILELS: DG
GOULD: CBS

Sonata No. 7 in D major, Op. 10, No. 3 (1796–98)

Frequently performed, the D major Sonata is in four movements, the crown of the work being the slow movement, Largo e mesto, in D minor. Its tragic content and emotional power make it one of the great movements in early Beethoven.

HOROWITZ: RCA
RICHTER: Angel
SHERMAN: Pro Arte
YABLONSKAYA: Melodiya

Sonata No. 8 in C minor, Op. 13, "Sonate pathétique" (1798–99)

The most famous of the early sonatas. The first movement is preceded by an introduction marked Grave. With this page, Beethoven stands at the threshold of nineteenth-century Romantic emotionalism. The slow movement is an exquisite love song. The rondo finale must be played with a penetrating sadness.

LUPU: London
RICHTER: Melodiya
RUBINSTEIN: RCA
R. SERKIN: CBS

Sonata No. 9 in E major, Op. 14, No. 1 (1798–99)

Beethoven transcribed the work for string quartet. The first movement is pure quartet writing for the piano; the second movement is an Allegretto; the finale a Rondo: Allegro commodo.

GOULD: CBS
GRINBERG: Melodiya
RICHTER: CBS

Sonata No. 10 in G major, Op. 14, No. 2 (1798–99)

A pastel work of great charm. The first theme of the first movement is unforgettable. The second movement is a set of variations on a marchlike tune. Schumann must have loved it. The finale is a delightful Allegro assai.

GOULD: CBS
MERZHANOV: Melodiya
RICHTER: Melodiya

Sonata No. 11 in B-flat major, Op. 22 (1800–01)

This sonata greatly pleased Beethoven. It seems to sum up his ideas on sonata form at the moment. It's a wonderful, untroubled, extroverted work in four movements.

PERAHIA: CBS
R. SERKIN: CBS

Sonata No. 12 in A-flat major, Op. 26 (1800–01)

An unconventional work in four movements, it was one of the most popular sonatas during the nineteenth century. Chopin, who was not sympathetic to Beethoven, played at least its first movement, a set of variations. The work contains a Funeral March as well, subtitled *Sulla morte d'un eroe.*

GILELS: DG
RICHTER: RCA (CD)
ROBERTS: Nimbus (CD)

Sonata No. 13 in E-flat major, Op. 27, No. 1, "Sonata quasi una Fantasia" (1800–01)

A masterpiece which has been neglected because of its sister sonata, Op. 27, No. 2—the celebrated *Moonlight.* In both of these works, Beethoven breaks new ground; here and in the Op. 27, No. 2 he felt compelled to add the subheading *Sonata quasi una Fantasia.*

The first movement is highly unusual in that the tempo is slow, with an insertion of a quick section which is part dance, part drama. The following movement is a storm-filled Allegro molto e vivace in C minor, in the form of a scherzo, which sets the stage for one of those eloquent Adagios which can only be termed Beethovenian. The finale is glorious; the ending presents the Adagio movement's theme again, but as Wilhelm Kempff says, "not rising from twilight depths but on a higher and brighter level, a song of thanksgiving such as only Beethoven could create."

BILSON (fortepiano): Nonesuch
CHERKASSKY: Nimbus
GILELS: DG
ROSEN: Nonesuch

Sonata No. 14 in C-sharp minor, Op. 27, No. 2, "Sonata quasi una Fantasia"— "Moonlight" (1801)

One of the most popular of the sonatas. Its evocative title was given by Ludwig Rellstab, the Berlin critic who saw in the first movement moonlight over Lake Lucerne. The first movement was truly something new, the emotion expressed having nothing in common with anything written previously. Ernest Hutcheson felt "the least-disciplined fingers can easily play the notes, but only profoundest feeling can give expression to its yearning anguish."

The second movement is an Allegretto, which Liszt called "a flower between two abysses." It is neither a scherzo nor a minuet, yet it contains elements of both. It is a perfect resting place for the demons waiting to appear in the third-movement Presto agitato. Eric

Blom wrote, "Few of Beethoven's contemporaries grasped such music as this, stuck fast as they still were in eighteenth-century conventions." This movement is not a rondo, but a surging sonata form. It was surely the wildest music of the time, with its heated and frenzied upward arpeggio theme. The *Pathétique* Sonata introduced palpitating anxiety to music; this sonata brings to music an element of ruthlessness.

A. FISCHER: Angel
GILELS: DG
H. NEUHAUS: Melodiya
NOVAES: Vanguard
RUBINSTEIN: RCA
SOLOMON: Seraphim

Sonata No. 15 in D major, Op. 28, "Pastorale" (1801)

Published in 1802, this sonata was given the title *Pastorale* by the publisher. The title works well for this pantheistic four-movement score in which Beethoven shows himself at one with nature. He once wrote, "In the country it seems as if every tree said to me: 'Holy! Holy!' Nature is a glorious school for the heart." The *Pastorale* is spacious, disarmingly unpretentious, magnificently gentle. The Andante in D minor was a favorite movement of the composer's.

FOLDES: DG
GRINBERG: Melodiya
MORAVEC: Connoisseur Society
SOFRONITSKY: Melodiya

Sonata No. 16 in G major, Op. 31, No. 1 (1801–02)

Seldom played among Beethoven's piano sonatas. Fresh, bold, clever, the first movement in particular is all frolic, while the slow movement is an Adagio grazioso that is unlike any other. Alfred Brendel feels "it's like an ironic comment on something old-fashioned. . . . There is a mixture of love and irony that is very strange and if the player can manage to

convey it, it can be very effective." Kempff thinks "the piano assumes the role of a prima donna, glittering with enchanting graces. The Rondo finale is based on a gavotte-like theme. In this movement, there is humor and even Beethoven's sense of the grotesque."

BASHKIROV: Melodiya
GRINBERG: Melodiya
ROSEN: Nonesuch

Sonata No. 17 in D minor, Op. 31, No. 2, "Tempest" (1801–02)

Composed in the fateful key of D minor, it has become known as the *Tempest*. Beethoven was once asked for the mood to this work, and told the questioner to read Shakespeare's *Tempest*. The slow introductory passages of the first movement are the calm before the storm, filled with dark, foreboding tensions. The Adagio is a sonata movement with an exposition and recapitulation, but no development section. The finale in 3/8 meter is an Allegretto and again in a sonata structure. The movement is based upon unbroken sixteenth notes which pass to a throbbing, heart-piercing mordent. Louis Kentner says the movement is "like a wistful farewell to youth."

BILSON (fortepiano): Nonesuch
GOLDSMITH: MHS
GRINBERG: Melodiya
HASKIL: Philips (CD)

Sonata No. 18 in E-flat major, Op. 31, No. 3 (1801–02)

Edwin Fischer called the *Tempest* Beethoven's "masculine psyche," and this E-flat Sonata his "feminine psyche." The brilliant four-movement work is filled with light, grace, and vigor. The first theme is full of gentle questioning, leading to a motive that is pregnant with joy. Beethoven is absolutely bursting with happiness. The second movement is not the usual slow movement but a rocking scherzo, in a 2/4 pulse rather than the usual 3/4 meter. This is followed by a gracious and old-fashioned minuet. The finale is a perpetual motion in sonata form with an invigorating sense of movement.

> ASHKENAZY: London (CD)
> BADURA-SKODA (1815 piano): Astrée (CD)
> HASKIL: Philips (CD)

Sonata No. 19 in G major, Op. 49, No. 1 (1795)
Sonata No. 20 in G minor, Op. 49, No. 2 (1795)

Beethoven composed these two-movement sonatas in the middle 1790s, the time of composition of his Op. 2. These pieces were published without Beethoven's sanction. It is fortunate that they were, for as Sir Donald Francis Tovey says, "we might otherwise have been deprived of the two most beautiful sonatinas within the range of small hands and young players." For Brendel, "they are beautifully finished, graceful works in which Beethoven comes nearer to Mozart than in any other of the piano sonatas. They are very exposed. Every note is lying bare. . . . I admire the pianist who can play them well."

> BRENDEL: Philips
> FRANK: RCA

Sonata No. 21 in C major, Op. 53, "Waldstein" (1803–04)

Dedicated to Beethoven's patron Count Waldstein, the C major Sonata is a perfect masterpiece. For the performer, it requires the utmost in technical brilliance and rhythmic control of a large structure. The sonata is cast in a two-movement form with a twenty-eight-bar Adagio molto Introduzione occupying the place of the slow movement. In Kempff's words, it is "a flash of genius, illuminating the twilight between minor and major. The Rondo theme is as radiant as a temple in the first light of dawn." This sonata was the first to benefit from the extra notes available to Beethoven on the enlarged keyboard of the piano given to him by the Erard piano firm in 1803.

> ARRAU: Philips (CD)
> AX: RCA
> BACKHAUS: Fonit-Cetra (CD)
> BAR-ILLAN: Audiofon
> FIRKUŠNÝ: London
> A. FISCHER: Angel
> GILELS: DG (CD)
> HOROWITZ: CBS

Sonata No. 22 in F major, Op. 54 (1804)

This curious two-movement work has been overshadowed by the colossal *Waldstein* and *Appassionata,* which, respectively, precede and follow it. The first movement is a large and stylized "In tempo d'un menuetto," and is unprecedented as a musical form. The finale is a remarkably transparent and strange perpetual motion moving through various keys.

> GRINBERG: Melodiya
> RICHTER: RCA
> YUDINA: Melodiya

Sonata No. 23 in F minor, Op. 57, "Appassionata" (1804–05)

If Beethoven's Fifth Symphony epitomizes this composer for the general public, so his *Appassionata* is the piano sonata that defines Beethoven within this spectrum of his art. It is music of burning passion, the greatest musical explosion for keyboard up to its time.

The work is in three movements; both outer movements are in sonata form. The middle movement, Andante con moto, is a theme and variations which leads to the pulsating violence of the finale. After this depiction of a mighty struggle, Beethoven seems to have lost interest in the piano sonata. Five years passed before he composed his next works in the form.

> ARRAU: Philips (CD)
> GILELS: DG (CD)
> HOROWITZ: CBS (CD)
> MEDTNER: Melodiya

Ogden: MCA Classics (CD)
Richter: RCA (CD)
Rubinstein: RCA
R. Serkin: CBS (CD)
Watts: Angel (CD)
Weissenberg: Angel

Sonata No. 24 in F-sharp minor, Op. 78 (1808–09)

Published in 1809, this two-movement work is tender and graceful, small-scaled but far more subtle than it looks on the page. There is perfection in its economy of means. It is also difficult. Beethoven was particularly fond of this sonata.

Brendel: Philips (CD)
R. Casadesus: CBS
A. Fischer: Angel
H. Neuhaus: Melodiya
Nikolayeva: Melodiya
Ránki: Fidelio (CD)

Sonata No. 25 in G major, Op. 79 (1809)

This is a three-movement work of exquisite gaiety and rambunctiousness. The opening subject of springlike joy is expressed in the form of a German peasant dance, marked Presto alla tedesca. Mendelssohn must have loved the Andante. Technically, it is one of the easiest of the Beethoven sonatas.

Backhaus: Fonit-Cetra (CD)
Demus: Vanguard
Goode: Book-of-the-Month Records (CD)
Keene: Protone
Pollack: Melodiya

Sonata No. 26 in E-flat major, Op. 81a, "Les Adieux" (1809–10)

This sonata is often performed and is technically treacherous. The work depicts Beethoven's patron the Archduke Rudolf's departure from Vienna as the Napoleonic armies were moving into the city. The second movement is the period of his absence, and the joyous finale marks his return. Beethoven would have four unhappy years before he composed another piano sonata.

Arrau: Philips (CD)
Cliburn: RCA
Gilels: DG (CD)
Goode: Book-of-the-Month Records (CD)
Moravec: Connoisseur Society
Novaes: Vanguard
Rubinstein: RCA
R. Serkin: CBS

Sonata No. 27 in E minor, Op. 90 (1814)

Kempff calls this introspective masterpiece "a lone wanderer." In fact, Beethoven's world was now growing completely silent due to his deafness. With this two-movement composition, Beethoven enters uncharted territory. He's now on the threshold of his "late" period. The first movement is an impassioned confession. The finale in E major is a quest for purity and peace.

Backhaus: London
Badura-Skoda (1815 piano): Astrée
Moravec: Connoisseur Society
Richter: Melodiya
Solomon: Seraphim

Sonata No. 28 in A major, Op. 101 (1816)

Beethoven's last five sonatas show his ever-growing creativity from 1816 to 1822. They form the summit of his sonata writing and, together with the *Diabelli* Variations, they present, in James Friskin's words, "the most profound and subtle interpretative problems encountered in the work of any composer for the pianoforte. The musical ideas themselves are invested with a depth of emotion and almost prophetic exaltation that ask for exceptional qualities of dedication and musical insight, if any adequate performance is to be attained. There are no compositions which so greatly repay the pianist's lifelong study."

The Sonata Op. 101 is of an excruciating emotional quality and fiendish technical difficulty. The first movement has an indescribable yearning, an almost Wagnerian *melos*. This two-page opening movement is the shortest of his sonata career. There follows an almost brutish, ironic march that must have startled Schumann. Later in the sonata, Beethoven turns to a slow movement, which serves as an introduction to the fugal finale—one of the most magical pieces of contrapuntal writing. In his late music, Beethoven incorporated into his vast compositional equipment a counterpoint inspired by and absorbed from Bach, yet which he made entirely his own.

BISHOP-KOVACEVICH: Philips
LUVISI: Rivergate
POLLINI: DG (CD)
R. SERKIN: CBS
SOLOMON: Turnabout

Sonata No. 29 in B-flat major, Op. 106, "Hammerklavier" (1817–18)

The *Grosse Sonate für das Hammer-Klavier* is the longest of the sonatas, taking approximately forty-five minutes. The word is merely German for pianoforte, but the sound has a certain grim grandeur, which is appropriate. Beethoven's life was unhappy during these years and the sonata was a creative action towards reconciling his lonely, soundless world with a new and developing inner freedom. The "ego" growth of the Romantic movement and his own quest for immortality gave birth to this lofty, abstract work. It was to be his most monumental and most difficult sonata. Beethoven wrote to his publisher Artaria, exclaiming: "Now you have a sonata that will keep the pianists busy when it is played fifty years hence!" Charles Rosen thinks that "with this work, the emancipation of piano music from the demands of the amateur musician was made official, with a consequent loss of responsibility and a greater freedom for the imagination." Almost from the first, the score had about it an air of mythic solitude. "The immensity of this composition," wrote Hutcheson, "cannot fail to strike us with awe. We gaze at its vast dome

like pygmies from below, never feeling on an intellectual or moral level with it."

Its slow movement is the longest and most sublime in the history of instrumental art. In his entire output, Beethoven never repeated himself, and the fugue finale of the Op. 106 was once again a new departure. It remains startling to contemporary ears; it must have been incomprehensible to its few listeners in Beethoven's day. J. W. N. Sullivan wrote, "The fugue of the *Hammerklavier* Sonata is an almost insensate outburst of unconquerable self-assertion." Friskin says, "The combined musical and technical demands of this sonata make the most exacting of all tasks that a pianist can undertake. The difficulty for the listener is no less."

AITKEN: Delos
ASHKENAZY: London
BIRET: Finnadar
ESCHENBACH: DG
GILELS: DG (CD)
GRINBERG: Melodiya
NÁDAS: Period
NAT: Pathé
PETRI: Westminster
POLLINI: DG
P. SERKIN: Pro Arte (CD)
R. SERKIN: CBS
WEBSTER: Dover
YUDINA: Melodiya

Sonata No. 30 in E major, Op. 109 (1820)

In Op. 109, Beethoven has left the battleground of the *Hammerklavier* for human warmth. The first movement is a concentrated sonata form of incomparable subtlety in its structure and lyricism. One can compare Beethoven's immense formal elasticity with Clementi's greatest sonata, in G minor, also written in 1820, whose structure is earthbound and scholastic. Beethoven's flexibility is now so great that each work is an entirely new invention that cannot be classified under any genre; authority and freedom in form are now welded together.

The work is composed of two sonata-form movements, the second being a Prestissimo. Brendel called this sonata "an angel with a demon in its middle." The finale is an irresistible and elaborate theme and variations, in which the theme returns to close the sonata on an ethereally serene note.

ARRAU: Philips (CD)
DOHNÁNYI: Everest
GILELS: DG (CD)
HESS: Seraphim
HUNGERFORD: Vanguard

Sonata No. 31 in A-flat major, Op. 110 (1821)

Often performed in the concert hall, it is in some respects technically less demanding than Op. 109. Its expressivity, lyricism, and unity of design have never been equaled, while the second movement brings us Beethoven's overpowering humor. The smoothly wrought fugue could not be more different from the earth-shaking fugue of Op. 106. Beethoven's passion is now deep and humane. He sings on the piano; he becomes lovable.

BADURA-SKODA (1824 piano): Astrée
GILELS: DG (CD)
POLLINI: DG (CD)
R. SERKIN: CBS
SHURE: Audiofon
SOLOMON: Turnabout

Sonata No. 32 in C minor, Op. 111 (1821–22)

The last of the thirty-two sonatas is in two movements. The distance traveled from 1795 to 1822 cannot be gauged in years alone. Beethoven seems to have exhausted the possibilities of the sonata form, and the second movement, a set of variations, is beyond the power of words to describe. Some writers use terms such as "spiritual elevation," or "suprastates of consciousness." Louis Kentner writes: "The contrast between the two movements could not be more pronounced. The first, sombre, chaotic, passionate, the second all tranquillity, peace ('all passion spent') with a crystalline ending of trills suggesting the starry firmament. This contrast is so striking that one well-known musician went so far as to say that there are two kinds of pianist: those who can play the first movement of Opus 111, and those who can play the second; none can play both."

BISHOP-KOVACEVICH: Philips
GULDA: Philips (CD)
HUNGERFORD: Vanguard
KATCHEN: London
LATEINER: RCA
MICHELANGELI: London
NAT: Pathé
ROSEN: CBS
SCHNABEL: RCA

Variations and Fugue in E-flat major, Op. 35, "Eroica"

An important and large set of variations. The theme is taken from Beethoven's *Prometheus* ballet score, which Beethoven also used in the finale of the *Eroica* Symphony. The work is comparable in difficulty to middle-period sonatas such as Op. 31, No. 2 and Op. 53. The Variations are cerebral and demonstrate a wonderful use of the bass. The Fugue is most effective and original.

AX: RCA
CURZON: London
RICHTER: JVC/Melodiya (CD)
ROBERTS: Nimbus (CD)

Thirty-two Variations on an Original Theme in C minor (without opus number)

The most often played of Beethoven's twenty-two sets of variations for solo piano. Beethoven, however, was reputed to have disowned them, for reasons which are hard to imagine. The form is that of a passacaglia, and it has often been stated that these variations lie midway between Bach's violin

Chaconne and the finale of the Brahms Symphony No. 4.

ARRAU: Philips (CD)
GILELS: Angel (CD)

Thirty-three Variations on a Waltz by Diabelli in C major, Op. 120

In 1823 the publisher and composer Anton Diabelli asked fifty-one composers to write a variation on his theme. Beethoven called the tune a "cobbler's patch," but found it so rich with variational possibility that he created thirty-three. They remain the fundamental set of variations of the Classical epoch and equal in greatness Bach's *Goldberg* Variations. The work, nearly an hour in length, asks for interpretive power of the widest range.

AITKEN: Delos
BRENDEL: Philips (CD)
KATCHEN: London
RICHTER-HAASER: Seraphim
R. SERKIN: CBS
SHURE: Audiofon

Six Bagatelles, Op. 126

The greatest of his three sets of Bagatelles (the others being Opp. 33 and 119). These are beautiful and profound, with all the introspective characteristics of the late-Beethoven style. They form the master's farewell to the piano.

ASHKENAZY: London (CD)
GOLDSMITH: MHS
GOULD: CBS
KATCHEN: London
KEMPFF: DG

The Five Piano Concerti

Each of the Beethoven piano concerti is a masterpiece of the form.

BRENDEL, Levine/Chicago Symphony: Philips (CD)
FLEISHER, Szell/Cleveland: CBS (CD)

Piano Concerto No. 1 in C major, Op. 15

No. 1 is an optimistic, outgoing work, wonderfully effective. The last movement has an irresistible swing.

ARGERICH, Sinopoli/Philharmonia: DG (CD)
POLLINI, Jochum/Vienna Philharmonic: DG (CD)
SHERMAN, Neumann/Czech Philharmonic: Pro Arte (CD)

Piano Concerto No. 2 in B-flat major, Op. 19

The Second Concerto, written in 1795, predates the First by three years. This is the least demanding, technically, of the five concerti; however, around 1819 Beethoven added a very difficult and superb cadenza to the first movement. The slow movement is beautifully proportioned, with a rollicking, humorous finale, in 6/8 meter.

ARGERICH, Argerich/London Sinfonietta: Denon (CD)
AX, Previn/Royal Philharmonic: RCA (CD)
BISHOP-KOVACEVICH, Davis/BBC Symphony: Philips
SCHNABEL, Sargent/London Symphony: Arabesque (CD)

Piano Concerto No. 3 in C minor, Op. 37

Beethoven, who had publicly performed Mozart's C minor Concerto, was certainly influenced by his predecessor in this 1800 work, which represents the emotional elements of Beethoven's second period. The slow movement is in the remote key of E major, and the rondo forms an exciting conclusion. It is technically richer and more difficult than the earlier concerti.

NEWMAN (fortepiano), Simon/Philomusica Antiqua of London: Newport Classic (CD)
PERAHIA, Haitink/Concertgebouw: CBS (CD)
SCHNABEL, Sargent/London Symphony: Arabesque (CD)

R. SERKIN, Bernstein/New York Philharmonic: CBS (CD)

Piano Concerto No. 4 in G major, Op. 58
The most lyrical of the five concerti. Beethoven created an unprecedented unity in its structure and material. Tovey wrote, "All three movements of Beethoven's G major Concerto demonstrate the aesthetic principles of concerto form with extraordinary subtlety." In the slow movement, Liszt heard Orpheus taming the wild beasts with his music. The Fourth Concerto is the most difficult interpretively of the five piano concerti.

KOCSIS, Lukács/Budapest Symphony: Fidelio (CD)
PERAHIA, Haitink/Concertgebouw: CBS (CD)
SCHNABEL, Sargent/London Symphony: Arabesque (CD)

Piano Concerto No. 5 in E-flat major, Op. 73, "Emperor"
Beethoven had given the first performances of his earlier piano concerti, including an excellent E-flat Concerto (preceding No. 1) composed when he was fourteen. By the time of the Fifth Concerto, however, Beethoven's playing had deteriorated as a result of his ever-increasing deafness. The first performance was given in Leipzig, late in 1811, with Friedrich Schneider as the soloist. The concerto was a great success, and a review of the time stated correctly: "It is without doubt one of the most original, imaginative, most effective but also one of the most difficult of all existing concertos." The reviewer could have added that it was the longest of all existing concertos. The Viennese premiere in 1812 was put in the hands of Beethoven's pupil Czerny. Curiously, this performance was a failure, perhaps due to Czerny's nervousness and consequently inhibited playing.

The Fifth Concerto remains the grandest of all Classical concertos. Its title, *Emperor,* supposedly comes from a French army officer at the Viennese premiere who was so moved by the musical might that he exclaimed, *"C'est l'Empereur."*

ARRAU, Davis/Dresden State: Philips (CD)
GILELS, Szell/Cleveland: Angel (CD)
POLLINI, Böhm/Vienna Philharmonic: DG (CD)
SCHNABEL, Sargent/London Symphony: Arabesque (CD)
R. SERKIN, Ozawa/Boston Symphony: Telarc (CD)

ALBAN BERG
1885–1935 — Austria

Sonata for Piano, Op. 1 (1908)
This is Berg's only solo piano work. It is brooding and hyperchromatic, keyless, and difficult to memorize. The entire piece emanates from the opening theme. It remains the most frequently played solo piano work of any Viennese composer of the first decade of the twentieth century.

BARENBOIM: DG
BIRET: Finnadar
CHERKASSKY: Nimbus (CD)

LUCIANO BERIO
b. 1925 — Italy

Cinque Variazioni per pianoforte (1952–53)
This is a sensitive, complex, lyric work, based on serial technique. Berio means the score to be a dramatic essay "whose action resides in the relation between the soloist and his own instrument."

BUCQUET: Philips
BURGE: Candide

297

ERNEST BLOCH
1880–1959 — Switzerland

Piano Sonata (1935)

Bloch's largest and most important work for solo piano. The brooding grandeur of so much of his music is felt throughout its three movements. The structure is dense, with a beautiful Pastorale slow movement. The first movement throbs with passion and barbaric frenzy; the finale is pessimistic and sarcastic.

NÁDAS: Dover
SHAULIS: CRI

PIERRE BOULEZ
b. 1925 — France

Sonata No. 1 (1946)
Sonata No. 2 (1948)
Sonata No. 3 (1957)

Boulez has attempted to extend serial technique into new and flexible regions. His piano sonatas, especially Nos. 1 and 2, have entered a "classic" status of the avant-garde. The critic Susan Bradshaw observes that the first two sonatas "show traces of his teacher Messiaen (in the rhythmic devices), of Debussy (in the use of pianistic color, per se) and of virtuoso keyboard writing in general. But they are extraordinarily forward-looking for the time at which they were written and virtually without models for their musical vision: their astonishing vitality, liberality of invention and technical confidence are of breathtaking impact, as is the virtuosity of the keyboard writing." The Third Sonata, begun in 1957, is entirely different. Of the five movements or formats intended, only two have been published, as Boulez has not yet found his solutions for the other three. Throughout the notation, he has come to give the performer freedoms and choices as to the order of the sections. The first movement is in four sections, and gives the pianist eight possibilities of order.

The First Sonata is in two movements, totaling about ten minutes, with much leaping around, mostly in a two-part counterpoint, which is fearsomely difficult to execute. The thirty-minute Second Sonata is one of the great pieces of sheer virtuosity in the history of pianism. Bradshaw feels that "the composer seems trapped by his compositional virtuosity into producing a dangerously overblown pianistic virtuosity—very much in the grand manner." For maximum pleasure, it is helpful to read from the scores when these two sonatas are being performed.

The first two movements, titled *Trope and Constellation,* from the Third Sonata are mathematical and mysterious, a work of creative pianism. Maurice Hinson thinks it "one of the greatest pianistic creations of this century." Charles Rosen, who recorded the piece in 1973, observes, "The freedom that Boulez's music demands is also a form of rubato, often a continuous one."

Sonata No. 1:
BURGE: Candide
MARKS: CRI
ROSEN: CBS
Y. TAKAHASHI: CP2

Sonata No. 2:
BIRET: Finnadar
BURGE: MHS
POLLINI: DG (CD)

Sonata No. 3:
HENCK: Wergo (CD)
ROSEN: CBS

JOHANNES BRAHMS
1833–1897 — Germany

James Huneker wrote of Brahms: "He was the greatest contrapuntist after Bach, the greatest architectonist after Beethoven—his contribution to the technics of rhythm is enormous. He has literally popularized the cross-relation, rediscovered the arpeggio and elevated it from the lowly position of an accompanying figure to an integer of melodic phrase. . . . He pours into the elastic form of the sonata hot romantic passion, and in the loosest textured smaller pieces he can be as immovable as bronze, as plastic as clay. He is sometimes frozen by grief and submerged by thought. . . . To me this is the eternal puzzle; that Brahms, the master of ponderous learning, can yet be so tender, so innocent of soul, so fragile, so childlike. He must have valiantly protected his soul against earthly smudging to keep it so pure, so sweet to the very end. . . . Above all, he is profoundly human and touches humanity at many contacts."

Sonata No. 1 in C major, Op. 1 (1852)
In his Op. 1, Brahms immediately pays tribute to Beethoven, outlining the rhythm of Beethoven's *Hammerklavier* Sonata during the first five measures of the opening statement. Even from his nineteenth year, the sonata possesses Brahms's characteristic dense sonority. This surely must be one of the finest Opus Ones in the annals of music. "Musical history," reflected Daniel Gregory Mason, "is a series of reactions between man's primal emotional impulse and his desire for intelligibility." That could have been Brahms's motto. As Huneker points out, "Just compare the Schumann *Abegg* Variations, Opus 1, with the slow movement of this Sonata and you may realize the superior educational advantages enjoyed by Brahms."

KATCHEN: London
STEIGERWALT: Centaur (CD)
ZIMERMAN: DG (CD)

Sonata No. 2 in F-sharp minor, Op. 2 (1853)
Like No. 1, this sonata is in four movements, but more diffuse. Brahms is all storm and stress here; the first movement is Brahms at his most fiercely Romantic. The finale shows the amazing originality of the twenty-year-old Brahms.

ARRAU: Philips
KATCHEN: London
LOESSER: Perennial
OLSHANSKY: Monitor
ZIMERMAN: DG (CD)

Scherzo in E-flat minor, Op. 4 (1854)
When Brahms visited Liszt at Weimar, the great pianist sight-read the manuscript of this difficult Scherzo with two trios. It is not played nearly enough, considering its value.

ARRAU: Philips
BISHOP-KOVACEVICH: Philips (CD)
KEMPFF: Decca

Sonata No. 3 in F minor, Op. 5 (1854)
In five movements, this is one of the largest sonatas in the active literature, taking around forty minutes. All that Brahms had attained in the previous two sonatas is now synthesized. He never again composed a piano sonata. It was not premiered until 1863, when Brahms himself performed it in Vienna. He prefaces the second movement with lines from the poet Sternau:

> *The Twilight*
> *glimmers, by moonbeams lighted,*
> *two hearts are here in love united*
> *and laced in blest embrace.*

Huneker realized that with this work "the most beautiful in the genius of Brahms had flowered. The Andante in A flat [is] the most exquisite lyrical thing he has ever penned for piano . . . the picture is magical in its tender beauty and suggestiveness. It harks back to the old world romance, to some moonlit dell, wherein love hovers for a night, and about all is the mystery of sky and wood." Claudio Arrau has said of the slow movement, "For me, it is the most beautiful love music after *Tristan*. And the most erotic—if you really let go, without any embarrassment. And if you play it *slowly* enough."

> ARRAU: Philips
> BAUER: IPA–Desmar
> CANIN: Spectrum
> CURZON: London
> KATCHEN: London
> KEMPFF: Decca
> KOCSIS: Hungaroton (CD)
> RUBINSTEIN: RCA (CD)

Variations on a Theme by Schumann in F-sharp minor, Op. 9 (1854)

Brahms is the greatest variationist after Bach and Beethoven. He was inspired by three sources: Bach's *Goldberg*, Beethoven's *Diabelli*, and Schumann's *Symphonic Etudes*. The *Schumann* is Brahms's earliest set of variations and far undervalued—it is the most subtle work he had written thus far. The theme is taken from Schumann's *Bunte Blätter*, Op. 99, No. 5, and leads into sixteen variations. Nos. 9, 13, and 14 are masterstrokes.

> BARENBOIM: DG
> MOYER: GM Recordings

Four Ballades, Op. 10 (1856)

No. 1 in D minor, the most famous, is inspired by the Scottish ballad "Edward." Brahms composed the Ballades in the year Schumann died, and they flow from the well of his inspiration. These works possess a lyric maturity, a soul-searching quality, a sense of foreboding and tragedy, which are astonishing from an artist in his early twenties.

> ARRAU: Philips
> GILELS: DG
> GOULD: CBS (CD)
> KATCHEN: London (CD)
> KEMPFF: DG

> MICHELANGELI: DG (CD)
> RUBINSTEIN: RCA (CD)
> WILD: Vanguard

Variations and Fugue on a Theme by Handel, Op. 24 (1862)

One of the masterpieces of variation writing. The Romantic exuberance of the early sonatas has been relentlessly replaced by organic necessity. The Fugue is magnificent in sonority and structure. Brahms had carefully absorbed *The Well-Tempered Clavier*.

> ARTYMIW: Chandos (CD)
> BOLET: London
> CLIBURN: RCA
> FLEISHER: Odyssey
> KATCHEN: London (CD)
> KLIEN: Turnabout
> SCHUB: Vox Cum Laude
> R. SERKIN: CBS
> SOLOMON: EMI

Variations on a Theme by Paganini, Books I and II, Op. 35 (1866)

"The Brahms-Paganini," as they are called, are a legend in the piano literature. Pianists speak of them in a reverential tone. To instill life in them, a pianist must have artistry surpassing merely a good technique. They are far more difficult to play than they sound. "Brahms and Paganini! Was ever so strange a couple in harness?" asks Huneker. "Caliban and Ariel, Jove and Puck. The stolid German, the vibratile Italian! Yet fantasy wins, even if brewed in a homely Teutonic kettle. . . . These diabolical variations, the last word in the technical literature of the piano, are also vast spiritual problems. To play them requires fingers of steel, a heart of burning lava and the courage of a lion."

> ANIEVAS: Seraphim
> CHERKASSKY: Nimbus (CD)
> KATCHEN: London (CD)
> MERZHANOV: Monitor
> MICHELANGELI: EMI
> OHLSSON: Angel

VLASENKO: Melodiya
WILD: Vanguard

Sixteen Waltzes, Op. 39 (1865)

This is Brahms as charmer. The set also comes in piano duet form. In general, these waltzes are the easiest of his piano pieces. The Schubertian style of waltz is here transformed into miniatures of far more subtlety. No. 15 in A-flat is celebrated.

BISHOP-KOVACEVICH: Philips (CD)
FLEISHER: Odyssey
KATCHEN: London

Eight Klavierstücke, Op. 76 (1879)

These eight pieces marked Brahms's return to solo piano music after a gap of thirteen years. A sense of intimacy pervades—the piano becomes his confidant. No. 1, Capriccio in F-sharp minor, contains stressful arpeggiation and is gloomy even when ending in the major. No. 2, Capriccio in B minor, is a staccato piece with a magical modulation. Bruce Hungerford wrote, "The piece is one of the shortest rondo-sonata movements in all music." No. 3, Intermezzo in A-flat, exudes sweetness and peace. No. 4, Intermezzo in B-flat, may have been inspired by a John Field nocturne, although it is far more complex. No. 5, Capriccio in C-sharp minor, is one of the more difficult of Brahms's shorter pieces, containing complicated rhythms and a fiery style. No. 6, Intermezzo in A major, is blissful and has lovely curves. No. 7, Intermezzo in A minor, is simple in statement, somewhat pessimistic, gray in color. No. 8, Capriccio in C major, has wonderful key relationships.

BISHOP-KOVACEVICH: Philips (CD)
GIESEKING: Seraphim
HUNGERFORD (Nos. 2 & 6): Vanguard
KATCHEN: London

Two Rhapsodies, Op. 79, Nos. 1 and 2 (1880)

Although titled Rhapsodies, they are formal in construction. No. 1 in B minor is a rondo-sonata form, and No. 2 in G minor is in sonata form. Both works are magnificent; No. 2 is one of Brahms's best-known piano works, with its rich coloration in the second theme.

CLIBURN: RCA
GIESEKING: Seraphim
GOULD: CBS (CD)
HUNGERFORD: Vanguard
KATCHEN: London
RUBINSTEIN: RCA

Seven Fantasies, Op. 116 (1892)

After the Rhapsodies, Brahms again left the field of solo piano music for a dozen years. Arthur Rubinstein wrote: "It is with the late piano works, Opus 116 through 119, that we reach Brahms's most personal music for his chosen instrument. . . . Brahms in his final years produced serene and nostalgic music that was ever more inward in mood. . . . As his own notations in the scores indicate, they are so intensely intimate that one cannot really convey their full substance to a large audience. They should be heard quietly, in a small room, for they are actually works of chamber music for the piano."

No. 1, Capriccio in D minor, has restless syncopations. James Friskin says, "The legato diminished seventh arpeggios in octaves for the left hand can only be tackled easily by one with a large span." Of No. 2, Intermezzo in A minor, Huneker wrote, "It is another of those vaporish mysteries, those shadowy forms seen at dusk near the grey, thin edges of forests." On the technical side, Friskin warns: "The flickering broken octaves of the middle section are not easy to present with accuracy and delicacy." No. 3, Capriccio in G minor, is an agitated movement full of power. No. 4, Intermezzo in E major, the longest of these selections (four minutes), creates an ineffable mood. It is a work of the utmost beauty. No. 5, Intermezzo in E minor, is marked Andante con grazia ed intimissimo sentimento. Huneker thinks this elusive composition is "more like a sigh, a half-uttered

301

complaint of a melancholy soul. To play it you must first be a poet, then a pianist." No. 6, Intermezzo in E major, is simpler to play than the others; it has a fine melody. Huneker heard it as a minuet. No. 7, Capriccio in D minor, a brilliant close to the set, is less difficult than it sounds, with cadenza-like material.

GIESEKING: Seraphim
GILELS: DG (CD)
KATCHEN: London
OLSHANSKY: Monitor

Three Intermezzi, Op. 117 (1892)

No. 1 in E-flat is a lullaby of unsurpassed simplicity, with a folklike quality. No. 2 in B-flat minor is one of the most often played of these late works, tenderly passionate and tightly constructed in a sonata form based on the two-note phrase that opens the piece. No. 3 in C-sharp minor is exotically colored and beautifully textured.

BISHOP-KOVACEVICH: Philips
GOULD: CBS (CD)
KATCHEN: London
LUPU: London

Six Klavierstücke, Op. 118 (1893)

Analysis will uncover the myriad compositional devices that Brahms's genius unites so deceptively yet rigorously into these miraculous works. No. 1, Intermezzo in A minor, is an exultant one-and-a-half-minute piece, with the tonality revealed only at the very end. No. 2, Intermezzo in A major, is one of the longest of the late lyric pieces (5:30). It is often programmed because of its radiantly gracious melody. No. 3, Ballade in G minor, is a stirring piece with a quiet middle section. No. 4, Intermezzo in F minor, is breathtaking and contains canonic writing with a beautifully contoured episode in A-flat. Of No. 5, Romanze in F major, Hungerford wrote: "An idyllic work, its stately, gracious theme is heard from the outset in double counterpoint. The middle section, a delectable Pastorale in D major, is based on a four-bar theme above a kind of basso ostinato, repeated over and over. With each return the theme is most beautifully varied." No. 6, Intermezzo in E-flat minor, is a work of visionary beauty and mystery. The tempo marking is Andante, largo e mesto. It expresses despair and grief, a desire for atonement. A middle section beginning piano, sotto voce, gradually mounts to a marchlike theme which bursts into a powerful climax.

BACKHAUS: London
GIESEKING: Seraphim
HUNGERFORD: Vanguard
LUPU: London

Four Klavierstücke, Op. 119 (1893)

No. 1, Intermezzo in B minor, is a bittersweet Adagio. No. 2, Intermezzo in E minor, is a work of extreme loveliness. Huneker says, "Its poco agitato is the rustling of the leaves in the warm west wind, but they are flecked by the sunshine. A tremulous sensibility informs this andantino, and its bars are stamped by genius." No. 3, Intermezzo in C major, only one-and-a-half minutes, is marked "giocoso"; it is a study in cross-rhythms and the theme is in the middle voice. Its three pages are unrivaled in all of Brahms for rhythmic elasticity and sheer happiness. No. 4, Rhapsody in E-flat major, is Brahms the conqueror. It has a massive, Schumann-like quality, and its middle part includes a legato melody with staccato accompaniment. The last piano piece written by Brahms, it contains similarities to his early works. From the beginning to the end of his career, Brahms was Brahms.

CICCOLINI: Pathé
CLIBURN: RCA
FIRKUŠNÝ: Sugano (CD)
GIESEKING: Seraphim
KATCHEN: London
R. SERKIN: CBS

Piano Concerto No. 1 in D minor, Op. 15 (1858)

The Concerto in D minor was premiered by Brahms, with Joseph Joachim conducting, on January 22, 1859. The work occupied Brahms for more than five years. Tovey called the opening "the mightiest utterance since Beethoven's Ninth Symphony." The D minor is one of the glories of the piano concerto literature. Along with the Brahms Second Concerto, at fifty minutes it is the longest concerto in the literature. Abraham Veinus wrote, "Schumann's tragic attempt at suicide haunted Brahms during the initial sketching of the concerto. The grim and turbulent heroism of the first movement bears the imprint of the event; and the slow movement . . . is an instrumental requiem." The colossal rondo-finale is, unlike so many concerto last movements, in no way inferior to the rest of the work.

ARRAU, Giulini/Philharmonia: Angel (CD)
ARRAU, Haitink/Concertgebouw: Philips (CD)
AX, Levine/Chicago Symphony: RCA (CD)
CURZON, Szell/London Symphony: London
FLEISHER, Szell/Cleveland: Odyssey
KATCHEN, Monteux/London Symphony: London
POLLINI, Böhm/Vienna Philharmonic: DG (CD)
RUBINSTEIN, Reiner/Chicago Symphony: RCA
SCHNABEL, Szell/London Philharmonic: Rococo
P. SERKIN, Shaw/Atlanta Symphony: Pro Arte (CD)
R. SERKIN, Szell/Cleveland: CBS (CD)
ZIMERMAN, Bernstein/Vienna Philharmonic: DG (CD)

Piano Concerto No. 2 in B-flat major, Op. 83 (1881)

One of the greatest of all concertos, the work is also one of the most awkward pianistically and very demanding physically. It is cast in four movements, Brahms having added a passionate scherzo in D minor, which he called "a tiny-tiny wisp of a Scherzo." Brahms himself was soloist at the premiere on November 9, 1881, with Hans von Bülow conducting.

ARRAU, Haitink/Concertgebouw: Philips
BACKHAUS, Böhm/Vienna Philharmonic: London
E. FISCHER, Furtwängler/Berlin Philharmonic: Turnabout
FLEISHER, Szell/Cleveland: Odyssey
GILELS, Reiner/Chicago Symphony: RCA (CD)
HOROWITZ, Toscanini/NBC Symphony: RCA
POLLINI, Abbado/Vienna Philharmonic: DG
RICHTER, Leinsdorf/Chicago Symphony: RCA (CD)
RUBINSTEIN, Ormandy/Philadelphia: RCA
R. SERKIN, Szell/Cleveland: CBS (CD)
ZIMERMAN, Bernstein/Vienna Philharmonic: DG (CD)

FRANK BRIDGE
1879–1941 — England

Piano Sonata (1925)

This is arguably the finest English piano sonata of the 1920s and demands imagination and sympathy from the pianist. The work is Bridge's reaction to the horrors of World War I. Harsh, nervous, introspective, it is at times agonizing in its tragic import. In it, he moves away from the English musical nationalism of the period. There are three movements, totaling a half-hour.

GÜNEYMAN: Finnadar

FERRUCCIO BUSONI

1866–1924 — Italy

Seven Elegies (1908)

Deep feeling pervades the remarkable set of Elegies, which are among Busoni's finest piano music. They are masterfully designed for the hands and are more difficult than they look on the page. The two best-known are No. 2, *All'Italia,* a theme he also uses in his Piano Concerto, and the captivating No. 4, *Turandots Frauengemach* ("Turandot's Boudoir"), based on the English tune "Greensleeves." The fifth elegy, *Die Nächtlichen,* is fluttery, diaphanous, with an almost Godowskian aroma, a waltz danced among shadows. The seventh elegy, *Berceuse,* is a transcription of one of Busoni's orchestral pieces. With its asperities, it will never become a popular lullaby.

> BEAN (Nos. 1–6): RCA
> JOHANSEN: Artist Direct
> JONES: Argo
> WALDOFF (No. 4): MHS

Six Sonatinas (1910–20)

These works offer a variety of mood and difficulty. No. 1 is the easiest. No. 2 is seven minutes long, with two movements of intense music and great difficulty. No. 6 was composed in 1920, and is an exposé on themes from *Carmen.*

> JACOBS (Nos. 1–6): Nonesuch
> LOESSER (No. 2): IPA–Desmar
> VON ZADORA (No. 6): IPA–Desmar

Variations on a Chopin Prelude (1922)

A nine-minute work based on the famous and somber C minor Prelude, Op. 28, No. 20. The nine variations are masterly in style, a superb mixture of melodic, harmonic, and polyphonic variation technique. This rigorous work is piano writing of genius and should be better known.

> JOHANSEN: Artist Direct
> OGDON: Seraphim

The Complete Solo Piano Music :
> MADGE: Philips (CD)

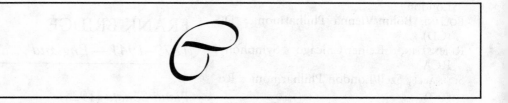

ELLIOTT CARTER

b. 1908 — United States

Piano Sonata (1945–46)

One of the most impressive contemporary piano works, the Piano Sonata launched Carter to the forefront of American composi- tion. It is in the two complicated movements of this work that Carter's exploring sense of rhythm became his hallmark. Wilfrid Mellers, the British critic and composer, finds that it "combines elements from the piano sonatas of both Ives and Copland, while achieving a powerful individuality. . . . There is nothing in European music to which one can compare it, except possibly the combination of madrigalian polyphonic rhythm with jazz syncopation in the later music of Michael Tippett."

JACOBS: Nonesuch
ROSEN: Epic; Etcetera
WEBSTER: Dover; Desto

Piano Concerto (1965–66)

The Concerto is pure Carter; it is purged of all outside influence. One of the most difficult piano concertos, it is far more intricate than the Piano Sonata. Some consider it the most important modern American concerto, yet few have the nerve or technical fiber to tackle and conquer it. The composer states, "It employs no pre-established form, but is a series of short, usually overlapping episodes, mosaics of fragments that derive from parts of the basic material." The Concerto is dense, unfriendly, and intellectual, but nevertheless it is a work of tremendous energy. The recording by Jacob Lateiner and Leinsdorf is from the actual world premiere performances of January 6 and 7, 1967.

LATEINER, Leinsdorf/Boston Symphony: RCA
OPPENS, Gielen/Cincinnati Symphony: New World (CD)

EMMANUEL CHABRIER
1841–1894 — France

Dix Pièces pittoresques (1880)

Chabrier was one of the creators of the modern French school. After the premiere of the *Pièces pittoresques,* César Franck declared, "We have just heard something extraordinary. This music links our era with that of Couperin and Rameau." Poulenc thought these ten pieces as important to French music as the later Debussy Preludes. Indeed, Chabrier was loved and assimilated by Debussy and Ravel. Satie admired him, and his conscious adoption of a music-hall style prompted *Les Six* to follow that path in some of their work.

Chabrier is somewhat uneven, but at his most inspired he is unpretentious, chaste, or tender. His harmony, with its ninth chords, has zest and there is always *joie de vivre.* Vincent d'Indy defined him as a person "open to every tender affection and exquisite in every way." Chabrier can also be bawdy, insouciant, and rhythmically unpredictable. He was known as a bumptious, rollicking pianist. Alfred Bruneau said, "He played the piano as no one had before him."

The ten pieces are *Paysage, Mélancolie, Tourbillon, Sous-bois, Mauresque, Idylle, Danse villageoise, Improvisation, Menuet pompeux,* and *Scherzo-valse.*

D'ARCO: Calliope
J. CASADESUS: Odyssey
CICCOLINI: Seraphim

Bourrée fantasque (1891)

Chabrier's final piano piece is a synthesis of all his music. The strutting, the seduction, the Lautrec night life, the mock sentimentality, are all here. Arthur Loesser speaks of its "Parisian proletarian flavor." Robert Casadesus felt that with this six-minute piece the modern French school was born.

CICCOLINI: Seraphim
JOHANNESEN: Vox
LOESSER: IPA–Desmar

CARLOS CHÁVEZ
1899–1978 — Mexico

Piano Concerto (1942)

The Chávez Concerto was not well received at its premiere given by Eugene List in 1942. At the time it was considered cacophonous. Nearly a half-century later, we hear a work filled with color and which evokes landscapes of ferocious power. The piano part is very demanding; List called it "the most difficult composition I have ever tackled." The high-spirited, motorized energy of the finale requires unusual muscle. Chávez left many piano works of marked originality both in idea and keyboard conception. His *Invención* and six piano sonatas should be investigated by contemporary pianists. Chávez was indisputably Mexico's greatest composer.

Piano Concerto:
List, Chávez/Vienna State Opera: Westminster
Rodriguez, Mata/New Philharmonia: RCA

FRÉDÉRIC CHOPIN
1810–1849—Poland

Andante spianato and Grand Polonaise for Piano and Orchestra, Op. 22 (1830)

Written in Chopin's twentieth year, this is a marvelous display piece. The sumptuous Polonaise is ceremonial, the Andante spianato (i.e., with smoothness) is a liquid-toned gem demanding a poet's reading. The orchestral part is paltry, but has its flavor; many have dispensed with it altogether, permitting this work to be performed on the recital stage.

Ax: RCA
Cherkassky: Nimbus (CD)
Davidovich, Marriner/London Symphony: Philips
Hofmann (Golden Jubilee concert, 1937; Casimir Hall recital, 1938): IPA–Desmar
Rubinstein: RCA (CD)
Zimerman: DG

Ballade No. 1 in G minor, Op. 23 (1836)

The first of the Four Ballades is a glowing masterpiece. James Huneker called this epic narrative "the odyssey of Chopin's soul." The great lyric theme, stated in three different forms, is intoxicating. The First Ballade is summed up with a coda of elemental power, culminating in a chilling downward chromatic passage in octaves, which will electrify any receptive listener.

Backhaus: London
Cortot (Ballades Nos. 1–4; recorded 1926): Music and Arts (CD)
Gilels: Melodiya
Hofmann: IPA–Desmar
Horowitz: RCA
Rubinstein (Nos. 1–4): RCA (CD)

Ballade No. 2 in F major, Op. 38 (1838)

Schumann had dedicated his *Kreisleriana,* Op. 16, to Chopin, who returned the honor by dedicating the Second Ballade to his German champion. A work of perfect proportion, it opens with a slow and magical episode which turns into a tempest, Presto con fuoco, a wild, magnificent outburst. In the words of the composer Alan Rawsthorne, at the end of the coda the Andantino theme becomes "a whispered reminder of the very opening," which "vibrates in the memory."

Ashkenazy (Nos. 1–4): London
Moravec (Nos. 1–4): Connoisseur Society
Pogorelich: Capriccio (CD)
Richter: CBS/Melodiya

Ballade No. 3 in A-flat major, Op. 47 (1841)

The Third Ballade is the essence of charm and warmth, with a sense of irony surrounding the second subject. Frederick Niecks, Chopin's first important biographer in English, says "a quiver of excitement runs through the whole piece. . . . There is suffused a most exquisite elegance." The slender second subject becomes a development section, "one of the most powerful Chopin ever composed," says Rawsthorne, "one is quite staggered to look back at its winsome origins." The coda, he continues, ends "in a blaze of light."

ASHKENAZY (Nos. 1–4): London
FRIEDMAN: Danacord
NOVAES (Nos. 3 & 4): Vanguard
DE PACHMANN: Pearl
SOFRONITSKY: Melodiya

Ballade No. 4 in F minor, Op. 52 (1842)

The Fourth Ballade is generally agreed to be one of the sublime works of Romantic music. For John Ogdon, it is "the most exalted, intense and sublimely powerful of all Chopin's compositions. . . . It is unbelievable that it lasts only twelve minutes, for it contains the experience of a lifetime." Huneker calls its chief theme a "melody which probes the very coverts of the soul." He compares it to the Mona Lisa, while Ogdon speaks of Scott Fitzgerald's *Last Tycoon,* inviting us to a "Romantic communion of unbelievable intensity."

The Fourth Ballade remains a narrative but has an inimitable feeling of intimacy and Slavonic coloring, and demands of the interpreter a delicate rubato and a virtuoso technique. It culminates in a coda of bone-crushing technical severity.

ASHKENAZY (Nos. 1–4): London
HOFMANN: IPA–Desmar
KENTNER (Nos. 1–4): Saga
MALCUZYNSKI (Nos. 1–4): Angel
RICHTER: DG/Melodiya
SOLOMON: EMI
VÁSÁRY (Nos. 1–4): DG

Barcarolle in F-sharp major, Op. 60 (1845–46)

One of Chopin's greatest compositions. It has been the despair of many fine artists, being difficult to interpret successfully. It is easy to sound affected, as does Arrau, or nervous, as does Horowitz, or too plain, as did Gieseking. Chopin must have been its ideal interpreter. At his very last Paris recital, in 1848, Charles

Hallé heard the frail master who now "played it from the point when it demands the utmost energy, in the opposite way, *pianissimo,* but with such wonderful nuances that one remained in doubt if this new rendering were not preferable to the accustomed one."

The Barcarolle displays Chopin's ornamental genius in full bloom. Ravel wrote, "Chopin was not content merely to revolutionize piano technique. His figurations are inspired. Through his brilliant passages one perceives profound, enchanting harmonies. Always there is the hidden meaning which is translated into poetry of intense despair. . . . The Barcarolle is the synthesis of the expressive and sumptuous art of this great Slav." André Gide finds the Barcarolle to express "languor in excessive joy."

ARGERICH: DG (CD)
ASHKENAZY: London
LIPATTI: Odyssey; Angel (CD)
RUBINSTEIN: RCA (CD)
SOFRONITSKY: Melodiya

Berceuse in D-flat major, Op. 57 (1844)

A cradle song which is a *tour de force* of exquisite filigree. A virtually unchanged tonic pedal in D-flat in the bass continues throughout its seventy magical measures. But "no analysis," says Sir Lennox Berkeley, "can give any idea of its compelling grace and charm."

BAUER: IPA–Desmar
DARRÉ: Vanguard
HOFMANN: RCA; International Piano Archives
NOVAES: Vanguard
PERAHIA: CBS (CD)
RUBINSTEIN: RCA
SOLOMON: EMI

Piano Concerto No. 1 in E minor, Op. 11 (1830)

The concerto is a grand harvest of perfect piano writing. It has retained a special place in the hearts of concert pianists, though conductors have far less to do in it than in other concertos. The slow movement is an exquisite, luxuriant nocturne.

ARGERICH, Abbado/London Symphony: DG (CD)
AX, Ormandy/Philadelphia: RCA
BRAILOWSKY, Ormandy/Philadelphia: Odyssey
CLIBURN, Ormandy/Philadelphia: RCA
CZERNY-STEFANSKA (formerly attributed to Lipatti): Seraphim
H. NEUHAUS, Gauk/Moscow Radio Symphony: Melodiya
NOVAES, Perlea/Bamberg Symphony: Vox
POLLINI, Kletzki/Philharmonia: Angel (CD)
RUBINSTEIN, Wallenstein/Los Angeles Philharmonic: RCA
RUBINSTEIN, Skrowaczewski/New Symphony of London: RCA (CD)
ZIMERMAN, Giulini/Los Angeles Philharmonic: DG (CD)

Piano Concerto No. 2 in F minor, Op. 21 (1829)

The Second Concerto, composed when Chopin was nineteen, predates No. 1, and is more subjective than the latter. Though equally popular, it is more elusive musically. The slow movement of the F minor Concerto is as breathtaking a poetic effusion as that of the First Concerto.

ASHKENAZY, Gorzynski/Warsaw Philharmonic: Angel
HASKIL, Markevitch/Lamoureux Orchestra: Philips (CD)
HOFMANN: International Piano Archives
LICAD, Previn/London Philharmonic: CBS (CD)
NOVAES, Klemperer/Vienna Symphony: Vox
POGORELICH, Abbado/Chicago Symphony: DG (CD)
RUBINSTEIN, Ormandy/Philadelphia: RCA
TS'ONG, Maag/London Symphony: Westminster
WEISSENBERG, Skrowaczewski/Paris Conservatoire: Angel (CD)

Twelve Etudes, Op. 10 (1829–31)
Twelve Etudes, Op. 25 (1830–34)

The Chopin Etudes are the most important pieces in the genre and formed the basis for all future concert etudes. The Op. 10 are dedicated *"A son ami,"* Franz Liszt.

Op. 10, No. 1 in C major: Arpeggios based on wide extension. Huneker considers it "the new technique in all its nakedness, new in the sense of figure, design, pattern, web, new in a harmonic way. . . . The nub of modern piano music is in the study."

Op. 10, No. 2 in A minor: The study is an expansion of the Moscheles Etude Op. 70, No. 3, in chromatic scale passages for the third, fourth, and fifth fingers of the right hand, with chords in the right hand for the first and second fingers.

Op. 10, No. 3 in E major: An exquisite aria for cantabile playing. A middle section features widely extended double-notes. When teaching the work to his pupil Adolf Gutmann, the composer cried out, "Oh, my homeland!"

Op. 10, No. 4 in C-sharp minor: An etude of lightness in high velocity for both hands.

Op. 10, No. 5 in G-flat major: The so-called *Black Key* Etude. Accuracy of chords in the left hand with exquisitely designed figuration on the black keys calls for a combination of finger technique with rotary action and supple wrists.

Op. 10, No. 6 in E-flat minor: A slow but restless chromatic study; it is difficult musically and needs a luscious touch for its melancholic, even anguished cantabile. For Henry T. Finck, "the etude seems as if it were in a sort of double minor . . . much sadder than ordinary minor."

Op. 10, No. 7 in C major: A toccata requiring strong fingers for quick changing on the same note with the first finger and thumb of the right hand. There is further need to articulate the melodic line in the fifth finger. Huneker asks, "Were ever Beauty and Duty so mated in double harness?"

Op. 10, No. 8 in F major: Brilliant finger passagework, sweeping the keyboard up and down more than four octaves for development of smoothness in thumb movements; a left-hand melody needs subtle pedaling. Von Bülow called it "a bravura study *par excellence.*"

Op. 10, No. 9 in F minor: A left-hand figure of wide extension, needing endurance (especially for small hands), and a developed rotational freedom in the forearm; its portamento right-hand melody is feverish. The composer marked this etude Allegro, molto agitato. It is less difficult than many others.

Op. 10, No. 10 in A-flat major: James Friskin describes this as "a tiring Etude for the right hand, which has a continuous octave position with rotation from single notes for thumb to sixths for second and fifth fingers. There are ingenious variations of touch and rhythm." John Ogdon feels that in its cross-rhythms, "Chopin's influence on Brahms may be clearly seen here." Von Bülow attests, "He who can play this study in a really finished manner may congratulate himself on having climbed to the highest point of the pianist's Parnassus." Musically, Chopin takes us to heights of Romantic poetry with breathtaking modulations.

Op. 10, No. 11 in E-flat major: Both hands play in extended arpeggios of chords, harplike in effect or, in Huneker's words, "as if the guitar had been dowered with a soul." Perching on top of these arabesques is a melody needing delicate tonal balance and phrasing.

Op. 10, No. 12 in C minor: Almost universally called the *Revolutionary* Etude, it is a complex left-hand study in continuous sixteenth notes. The right-hand theme requires tonal discrimination. Moritz Karasowski

wrote of this popular work that "the image is evoked of Zeus hurling thunderbolts at the world." Huneker called the opening "the crack of creation."

Op. 25, No. 1 in A-flat major: This is often called the *Aeolian Harp.* The weak fifth finger encounters a singing melody above a web of melting textures. A work of melodic magic, and one of the less taxing of the Etudes.

Op. 25, No. 2 in F minor: A study in cross-rhythms, requiring delicate finger articulation for its characteristic Chopinesque whisper.

Op. 25, No. 3 in F major: Theodor Kullak tells us that its "kernel lies in the simultaneous application of four different little rhythms to form a single figure." Ogdon hears it as "a study in the precise rhythmic values of ornaments," and Friskin wrote: "A light and independent action from the wrist for each beat constitutes an appropriate technique."

Op. 25, No. 4 in A minor: Ronald Smith says of this study, "A leaping staccato left hand throughout is combined with subtly varied, syncopated right-hand chords." The left hand is devilishly difficult to attain accuracy in.

Op. 25, No. 5 in E minor: Once called the *Wrong Note* Etude because of the piquant grace notes. The study demands variations of touch. This is one of the few Etudes with a middle section: a melody in the tenor register with an effective right-hand figuration. The effect is Thalbergian. The little recitativo coda with trills in both hands is the highest level of pianistic imagination.

Op. 25, No. 6 in G-sharp minor: The most hazardous study in thirds in the literature of the instrument. Louis Ehlert concludes, "Chopin not only versifies an exercise in thirds, he transforms it into such a work of art that in studying it one could sooner fancy himself on Parnassus than at a lesson."

Op. 25, No. 7 in C-sharp minor: Ronald Smith calls the form "a Sarabande which links the harmonic worlds of Bach and Wagner." Von Bülow thought of it as a duet for cello and flute. It is a study in touches calling for discreet tonal balance.

Op. 25, No. 8 in D-flat major: An etude in sixths which can be harmful to a small hand if not practiced with care. Von Bülow thought it "the most useful exercise in the whole range of the Etude literature. . . . As a remedy for stiff fingers and preparatory to performing in public, playing it six times through is recommended, even to the most expert pianist." But I warn, not six times at top speed.

Op. 25, No. 9 in G-flat major: Rather aptly termed the *Butterfly* Etude. Good wrist octaves and endurance are necessary for the projection of this puckish creation.

Op. 25, No. 10 in B minor: A fierce study in legato octaves in both hands. Frederick Niecks calls it "a real pandemonium." It is fearsome in its demand for endurance and can tax a small hand. The etude possesses for the sake of both musical and physical relief a middle section in B major of lyrical beauty.

Op. 25, No. 11 in A minor: Known as the *Winter Wind.* The left hand has a stately marchlike theme; the right hand projects an immense canvas with complex chromaticism. One of the most turbulent of the set, it asks for tremendous hand malleability.

Op. 25, No. 12 in C minor: An etude requiring powerful weight control and balance for arpeggios in both hands. A work of great majesty and starkness, it has often been called the *Ocean* Etude.

Etudes, Opp. 10 and 25:
ANIEVAS: Seraphim
ASHKENAZY: Melodiya; London (CD)
CORTOT: Pathé
FRIEDMAN (four etudes): Danacord
GINZBURG: Melodiya

KUERTI (Op. 25 only): Monitor
LORTIE: Chandos (CD)
POLLINI: DG (CD)
SAPERTON: IPA–Desmar
SLOBODYANIK: Melodiya/Angel
VÁSÁRY: DG
VERED: Connoisseur Society
ZAYAS: Spectrum

Trois Nouvelles Etudes (without opus number) (1840)

These were written for a piano method published by Moscheles. They make a fine six-minute set. No. 1 in F minor has a long melody of restrained passion, its technical use being three notes in the right hand to be played against four in the left hand. No. 2 in A-flat is all sweetness in its polyrhythmic movement. No. 3 in D-flat is a wickedly difficult study which asks for the playing of legato and staccato simultaneously in the same hand.

ASHKENAZY: London
AX: RCA
RUBINSTEIN: RCA (CD)

Fantaisie in F minor, Op. 49 (1841)

This large-scaled composition is considered one of Chopin's masterpieces. The Fantasy opens with a solemn and mysterious marchlike introduction leading to a passionate drama with a central chorale, Lento sostenuto, of unusual serenity. Niecks felt "Chopin's genius had now reached the most perfect stage of its development and was radiating with all the intensity of which its nature was capable."

ARRAU: Philips (CD)
GIMPEL: Genesis
PERAHIA: CBS (CD)
RUBINSTEIN: RCA (CD)

Four Impromptus

Impromptu No. 1 in A-flat major, Op. 29: The First Impromptu is carefree as a lark. George Du Maurier had poor Trilby sing it under the tutelage of Svengali. Jean Kleczynski wrote, "Here everything totters from the foundation to summit, and everything is, nevertheless, so beautiful and so clear."

Impromptu No. 2 in F-sharp major, Op. 36: The greatest and most difficult of the Impromptus, it resembles a Chopin Ballade. An elusive work demanding the utmost delicacy in the delivery of the passagework.

Impromptu No. 3 in G-flat major, Op. 51: A little-known piece, with some rather difficult double-notes. The theme has a serpentine, even morbid quality. But Huneker declares that "the Impromptu flavor is not missing, and there is allied to delicacy of design a strangeness of sentiment; that strangeness which Poe declared should be a constituent element of all great art." The improvisatory element must be brought out for a performance to succeed.

Impromptu No. 4 in C-sharp minor, Op. 66 (posth.), "Fantaisie-Impromptu": Countless pianists of all persuasions have attempted the *Fantaisie-Impromptu*. It was composed in 1834, and predates the other Impromptus. The opening, in its Bellinian coloratura, is alluring. The trio is a bit too long and mawkish. The coda uses the trio theme in an ingenious manner.

Four Impromptus:
CZIFFRA: Connoisseur Society
GINZBURG: Melodiya
PERAHIA: CBS (CD)
RUBINSTEIN: RCA (CD)
VÁSÁRY: DG

The Mazurkas

The sixty mazurkas are based on the dance's three main forms: the mazur, oberek, and kujawiak. One-half of them are composed in major keys, the other half in minor, with many moments of modality. The Chopin mazurkas form one of the great libraries of ethnically inspired art music. They are difficult to interpret; besides their own specific rhythms, they require a fine sense of rubato. The English critic of Chopin's day, Henry Chorley, wrote, "They lose half their meaning if played without a certain freedom and license, impossible to imitate, but irresistible if the player at all feels the music." Liszt remarked that "to do justice to the mazurkas, one would have to harness a new pianist of the first rank to each one of them." These works explore a harmonic kingdom which is unusual even for Chopin. Some are modal, with many subtleties in contrapuntal treatment. Arthur Hedley observed, "The Mazurkas contain beauties which Chopin reserved for these intimate tone-poems alone. Every kind of light and shade, of gaiety, gloom, eloquence and passion is to be found in them."

In the epoch-making four mazurkas of Op. 6, the twenty-year-old Chopin announces to the world his unique Slavic genius. Jean Kleczynski says, "In these first mazurkas at once appears that national life from which, as from an inexhaustible treasury, Chopin drew his inspirations."

Mazurka in F-sharp minor, Op. 6, No. 1: It begins with the triplet rhythm, a characteristic of the mazurka. It possesses a slight sadness in tonality but is filled with a sweet country bloom. "The third section," wrote Huneker, "with the appoggiaturas, realizes a vivid vision of country couples dancing determinedly." Chopin leaves the score without tempo marking. Already apparent in this first mazurka is a deep psychological content which becomes fused with the folk spirit to create an art of universal significance.

Mazurka in C-sharp minor, Op. 6, No. 2: It opens in shrouded mystery with a drone bass; the trio, marked "gajo" (merrily), is a fine example of Chopin's tonal ambiguity. It could be E major or in the Lydian mode. This mazurka is a masterpiece by one who had, as a child, assimilated the spiritual qualities of this Polish national dance. Jean Kleczynski speaks of "a song so sad, heartfelt, naive, diversified and caressing."

Mazurka in E major, Op. 6, No. 3: This mazurka is ninety measures long, but as usual Chopin is prodigal with his material. After a four-measure drone bass, there follows a four-measure phrase in the bass with the right hand crossing over the left hand. This is used four times in the piece. Chopin goes on to paint a village scene in an upward-moving theme which outlines the key of E major. After two more themes there appears in measures 47–48 an exotic unison, marked stretto, leading to yet another theme. The rustic theme is repeated, and all ends merrily in a four-measure coda.

Mazurka in E-flat minor, Op. 6, No. 4: In twenty-four highly compressed measures, with measures 9–24 repeated, the mazurka is laden with sorrow. The ending floats away.

Mazurka in B-flat major, Op. 7, No. 1: A scherzando theme proclaims the happiest mazurka thus far—a village dance for rosy-cheeked partners. The trio, marked sotto voce, has a drone bass using an exotic scale with an augmented second. The Op. 7, No. 1 is one of the best known of all the mazurkas.

Mazurka in A minor, Op. 7, No. 2: A pretty mazurka, though less original than the preceding ones.

Mazurka in F minor, Op. 7, No. 3: Guitarlike chords accompany this masterful work. At one point, the left hand presents a solo which sings from the heart, with the right hand accompanying in simple chords. One of the finest of the early mazurkas.

Mazurka in A-flat major, Op. 7, No. 4: Far more complex than it seems on first hearing, this mazurka is harmonically interesting, while lacking the melodic fragrance of the preceding one.

Mazurka in C major, Op. 7, No. 5: Twenty measures long, as if a strain of a folk mazurka from Chopin's childhood had crept into his consciousness. It has a carefree happiness with lusty overtones.

Mazurka in B-flat major, Op. 17, No. 1: Huneker calls this mazurka "bold and chivalric." Niecks also finds here "the marked chivalrous element that distinguishes the Polish character."

Mazurka in E minor, Op. 17, No. 2: Niecks thinks that in this mazurka "all the arts of persuasion are tried, from the pathetic to the playful, and a vein of longing, not unmixed with sadness, runs through the whole, or rather forms the basis of it."

Mazurka in A-flat major, Op. 17, No. 3: Pessimistic but not gloomy, this inward-looking composition is one to be played in solitude, rather than on the recital stage.

Mazurka in A minor, Op. 17, No. 4: This long, languid mazurka opens as it ends, with chords in the left hand for three measures, pursuing a vague triplet in measure four. In shaping his mazurka theme, Chopin uses more aristocratic and decorative figuration than usual. But the trio is earthier, with an almost grating quality; a marvelous unison passage leads back to the main theme.

Mazurka in G minor, Op. 24, No. 1: An attractive and exotic piece, of little technical difficulty.

Mazurka in C major, Op. 24, No. 2: Highly original, with its exotic use of the Lydian mode for fifteen bars.

Mazurka in A-flat major, Op. 24, No. 3: A work of delicate charm with a coda that seems to die away in the breeze.

Mazurka in B-flat minor, Op. 24, No. 4: The finest and most elaborate of the Op. 24. Huneker calls it "a beautiful and exquisitely colored poem. . . . It sends out prehensile filaments that entwine and draw us into the centre of a wondrous melody, laden with rich odors, odors that almost intoxicate. The figuration is tropical." A complicated work; its form is A B A C D A with coda.

Mazurka in C minor, Op. 30, No. 1: A beautiful specimen, short in time, long in emotional significance. The "con anima" section "stabs with its pathos," in Huneker's phrase.

Mazurka in B minor, Op. 30, No. 2: A sprightly mazurka of less importance.

Mazurka in D-flat major, Op. 30, No. 3: Has a characteristic lilt, with marvelous details. Another fine "con anima" section. The term as used by Chopin means "with heart."

Mazurka in C-sharp minor, Op. 30, No. 4: One of Chopin's supreme works in the form. Paul Hamburger speaks of "the tragic heroism of this Mazurka." Often noted are the extraordinary descending seventh chords before the ending. Schumann, who first reviewed the set when it was published in 1835, wrote, "Chopin has elevated the mazurka to an art form; he has written many, yet few among them resemble each other." One is reminded of Shelley's line, "Our sweetest songs are those that tell of saddest thought."

Mazurka in G-sharp minor, Op. 33, No. 1: A plaintive mazurka, less complex than many of the others. One of its themes is marked "appassionato," the only use of that marking in all of the mazurkas.

Mazurka in D major, Op. 33, No. 2: A delightful specimen; bright, cheerful, and popular.

Mazurka in C major, Op. 33, No. 3: A heartfelt little piece demanding that unique Chopinesque rubato, which was so new, fragrant, and wayward in Chopin's own playing. Chopin was furious with Meyerbeer when the opera composer accused him of playing this piece in 4/4 instead of 3/4 time.

Mazurka in B minor, Op. 33, No. 4: Among the longest of the mazurkas, it was once a popular favorite. In dull hands the work can sound repetitious, as the first theme returns eight times. Schumann wrote of the Op. 33 set that Chopin's "forms seem to grow ever brighter and lighter."

Mazurka in C-sharp minor, Op. 41, No. 1: Of the four mazurkas contained in Op. 41, the thirty-year-old Chopin wrote to the pianist Julius Fontana, "I have four new mazurkas. They seem to me pretty, as the youngest children usually do when the parents grow old." However, pretty is hardly the word for these four minutes with their depth, complexity, and passion. This is one of the great mazurkas, universal in its impact but Polish to the core, despite Schumann's complaint that in the later mazurkas Chopin was losing his Sarmatian skin. This mazurka is symphonic in scope and breadth. Huneker declares that "here is the very apotheosis of rhythm."

Mazurka in E minor, Op. 41, No. 2: There is an almost unbearable nostalgia in this mazurka, which rises to an outcry near the end, when the theme becomes fortissimo and sostenuto.

Mazurka in B major, Op. 41, No. 3: A fascinating dance, seldom played, ending with the same piquant melody that introduced it.

Mazurka in A-flat major, Op. 41, No. 4: Filled with light, good will, and the radiance of youth. There is an almost valse-like lilt.

Mazurka in G major, Op. 50, No. 1: The set of three mazurkas of Op. 50, composed in 1841, shows an ever-growing subtlety of style, both harmonically and structurally. No. 1 in particular is melodious and good-humored.

Mazurka in A-flat major, Op. 50, No. 2: Here is the embodiment of graciousness. Huneker calls it "a perfect specimen of the aristocratic mazurka." The D-flat trio is fetching.

Mazurka in C-sharp minor, Op. 50, No. 3: One of Chopin's great essays in the form. Hamburger sees in the mazurkas in C-sharp minor (Op. 30, No. 4; Op. 41, No. 1; and Op. 50, No. 3) "a common mood of nostalgia—more than that, of almost regal bitterness over the passing of Poland's glory." Henry T. Finck wrote, "His love for his country was exceeded only by his devotion to his art." Chopin, writing to a friend, remarked: "Oh, how sad it must be to die in a foreign country." In this mazurka, Romantic patriotism is wedded to high art. Chopin's study of Bach is also finely integrated in a complicated structure ending with a wondrous coda.

Mazurka in B major, Op. 56, No. 1: Critics such as Niecks, Huneker, and others were less attracted to the later mazurkas, which have since come to be understood as among Chopin's greatest works. For Niecks, these pieces had lost the *beautés sauvages*: "They strike us rather by their propriety of manner and scholarly elaboration." The B major work, writes James Friskin, is "interesting for its succession of keys: B–E-flat (i.e., D-sharp, the mediant)—B–G (sub-mediant)—B." The mazurka is elaborate and refined, with the E-flat section a chain of finely spun leggiero passagework.

Mazurka in C major, Op. 56, No. 2: Thomas Fielden wrote, "Performers should bear in mind the saying that 'an Eastern European is born with a violin in his hand.' In every Mazurka there is a violin atmosphere." Fielden feels "this Mazurka is in the form of a dialogue between a violin and a cello." Chopin here displays his ever-growing contrapuntal imagination.

Mazurka in C minor, Op. 56, No. 3: Huneker thinks "it is composed with the head, not the heart, nor yet the heels." The very long C minor Mazurka is symphonic in breadth, serious, beautiful, mature; its coda is glorious. Here Chopin brings the form to its most elevated state.

Mazurka in A minor, Op. 59, No. 1: A long work of astounding genius; the greatest of the six mazurkas in A minor. It reminded Huneker of "some strange glade wherein the flowers are rare in scent." The chromaticism is dense, with considerable contrapuntal activity. The trio in A major is complex. There follows the mazurka's main theme heard in G-sharp minor.

Mazurka in A-flat major, Op. 59, No. 2: Sir William Henry Hadow goes so far as to call this "perhaps the most beautiful of all the mazurkas." Friskin calls attention to "an astonishing passage of chromatic harmony leading to a delightful coda."

Mazurka in F-sharp minor, Op. 59, No. 3: A pungent work. Huneker feels that "Chopin is at the summit of his invention. Time and tune, that wait for no man, are now his bond slaves. Pathos, delicacy, boldness, a measured melancholy and the art of euphonious presentment of all these, and many factors more, stamp this mazurka a masterpiece."

Mazurka in B major, Op. 63, No. 1: The last set of Chopin's mazurkas, Op. 63, was published in 1847, and for all the hidden complexity, there is a return to the earlier feeling of charming simplicity so apparent in the mazurkas of his youth. The B major work is vivacious, with a fascinating contour.

Mazurka in F minor, Op. 63, No. 2: Two pages of music of a lingering sadness.

Mazurka in C-sharp minor, Op. 63, No. 3: By far the best known of this group. It possesses an eloquent lyricism and concludes with a display of Chopin's contrapuntal skill. "A more perfect canon at the octave," wrote Louis Ehlert, "could not have been written by one who has grown grey in the learned art." But Huneker slyly observes that "Chopin wears his learning lightly."

There remain the posthumous mazurkas, written in various years; four are gathered in Op. 67, the best being No. 4 in A minor. Exotic in coloration, it is often played. Op. 68 contains four mazurkas; the last, in F minor, from 1849, is Chopin's last work. It is subdued, morbid, and intensely chromatic. Finck calls it of "heartrending sadness and exquisite pathos." The desperately dying composer hardly had the strength to write it out. Also of interest is the seldom played Mazurka in A minor from 1841. The A major section is all in octaves, and the piece ends with a ten-measure trill.

BRAILOWSKY (51 mazurkas): CBS
FRIEDMAN (12): Danacord
HOROWITZ (6): CBS
KAPELL (18): International Piano Archives at Maryland (IPA is housed at the University of Maryland)
KAPELL (10): RCA (CD)
MAGALOFF (51): London
MALCUZYNSKI (13): Angel
MICHELANGELI (10): DG (CD)
NOVAES (9): Vox
RUBINSTEIN (51): RCA (CD)

The Nocturnes

The nocturne represents one of the great genres of Romantic art. Chopin inherited the species from John Field and proceeded to obliterate Field's charming naiveté with his own highly chromatic and sultry genius. It is said that Field, upon hearing Chopin's first three nocturnes, exclaimed: "Chopin's talent is of the sick-room." The last critic to prefer Field seems to have been the German anti-Chopinist Ludwig Rellstab: "Where Field smiles, Chopin makes a grinning grimace; where Field sighs, Chopin groans; where Field puts some seasoning into the food, Chopin empties a handful of pepper. . . . If one holds Field's charming nocturnes before a distorting, concave mirror, one gets Chopin's work."

The Chopin night-pieces bewitched countless nineteenth-century composers, and soon this category of music became so stereotyped as to cause Moscheles to exclaim: "What antidotes have we here for all these morbid moanings and over-wrought effects! . . . A composer brought me a nocturne of so restless a description that it threatened to disturb my nocturnal rest." Although Chopin had an instant success with many of them, the Nocturnes are generally the worst-played pieces of his output. Yet they remain critical works for the pianist in the development of a fine cantilena, the shaping of phrases, and tonal balance. Louis Kentner thinks that if pianists neglect the Nocturnes, they "are guilty of peevish discrimination, for if these pieces are 'too sweet,' or not very 'relevant' to our cheerless age, they are still expressive of another, happier age, and therefore entitled to bring pleasure to us poor deprived humans."

The lure of the Nocturnes does remain powerfully potent; few poet-pianists have failed to lavish their best efforts on them. Chopin, in these atmospheric works, let flow the full power of his voluptuous melodic gift, in piano writing that remains remarkable to this day. They are love-poems of the finest ardor, and within each one an intimate human drama is explored. Henry T. Finck declares, "Mendelssohn in *A Midsummer Night's Dream* and Weber in *Oberon* have given us glimpses of dreamland, but Chopin's nocturnes take us there bodily, and plunge us into reveries more delicious than the visions of an opium eater." Daniel Gregory Mason writes, "Chopin is one of the supreme masters in the coloristic use of the dissonance. His nocturnes may fairly be said to inaugurate by this means a new era in music, comparable in many respects to the era of impressionism in painting."

Nocturne in B-flat minor, Op. 9, No. 1: Composed when Chopin was twenty-two years old. A work of sumptuous phraseology, already it offers an elongation of the Field nocturne in the long-limbed opening theme. Charles Willeby wrote, "What could be more *triste* than the phrase in D-flat . . . marked legatissimo." The middle section is quite long and, in Huneker's words, "of exceeding charm. As a melody it has all the lurking voluptuousness and mystic crooning of its composer. . . . There is passion peeping out in the coda." For Jean Kleczynski, this nocturne "exhibits a thrilling sadness, together with a novel eloquence of construction." In the middle section he feels "as though the soul were sinking beneath the weight of thought and the heat of a summer's night." The B-flat minor Nocturne is a work of significance and is seldom played.

Nocturne in E-flat major, Op. 9, No. 2: The most famous of the nocturnes; indeed, it ranks high in celebrity among all of Chopin's works. It has been played rotten with sentimentality and now deserves a respite. One can still feel the suave, glamorous atmosphere of the fashionable Parisian salon which pervades this work.

Nocturne in B major, Op. 9, No. 3: Chopin's love for great singing must ever be in the interpreter's mind when performing the nocturnes. The B major Nocturne is luscious, with ornamental vocalization on the piano. The ghostlike theme is deeply penetrating, while the middle section is turbulent and convulsive. This nocturne is a masterful early work and is rather unknown. The Op. 9 set was fittingly dedicated to the bewitching pianist Mme. Camille Pleyel, née Moke. All who heard her play fell in love, among them Berlioz, Ferdinand Hiller, and Liszt.

Nocturne in F major, Op. 15, No. 1: The three nocturnes of this opus were dedicated to Ferdinand Hiller. The F major Nocturne is played less often than the Op. 15, No. 2; however, it is a gem, with its serene and tender Andante theme, followed by a trio marked Con fuoco, magnificently planned in double-notes. H. Barbedette, a writer who often heard Chopin perform, perceives "a calm and beautiful lake, ruffled by a sudden storm and becoming calm again." Finck rightfully complains that "few know how to use the pedal in such a way as to produce the rich uninterrupted flow of tone on which the melody should float."

Nocturne in F-sharp major, Op. 15, No. 2: One of the popular nocturnes; it is of a ravishing beauty, exhibiting a heavenly melody. Niecks says "the fioritura flit about us lightly as gossamer threads." The middle section, Doppio movimento, shows Chopin's command of pianistic notation. No composer had thus far been so explicit and original in showing to the pianist, on the page, what was needed. The increased motion of the middle section, with its novel figuration in quintuplets, possesses a burning passion.

Nocturne in G minor, Op. 15, No. 3: The first theme is marked "languido e rubato" with the second section marked "religioso." The G minor work is a slow-moving, feverish piece, of less value than the two preceding nocturnes. Huneker tells of a performance by Anton Rubinstein where "in the fourth bar, and for three bars, there is a held note, F, and I heard the Russian virtuoso, by some miraculous means, keep this tone prolonged. . . . Under Rubinstein's fingers it swelled and diminished, and went soaring into D, as if the instrument were an organ."

Nocturne in C-sharp minor, Op. 27, No. 1: The critic Alan Rich considers this nocturne "one of the most personal utterances in the entire realm of piano music." Finck feels that "it embodies a greater variety of emotion and more genuine dramatic spirit on four pages than many popular operas on four hundred." The work is tragic, menacing, at times hopeless. The form is A B A and coda. The central section marked Più mosso has a restless, vehement power. The coda once again reminds the listener of Chopin's seemingly inexhaustible prodigality.

Nocturne in D-flat major, Op. 27, No. 2: This exquisite piece, in one continuous mood, is the essence of *fioritura*. It is a favorite nocturne but demands a highly developed technical skill. Professor Niecks was fearful of the power of this luscious work: "Nothing can equal the finish and delicacy of execution, the flow of gentle feeling lightly rippled by melancholy, and spreading out here and there in smooth expansiveness. But all this sweetness enervates, there is poison in it. We should not drink in these thirds, sixths, etcetera, without taking an antidote of Bach or Beethoven." Lennox Berkeley writes, "A close study of this piece reveals the individuality of Chopin's piano writing; the proliferation of the arabesques that embellish the theme are of a kind that is his own invention, bearing little resemblance to the work of any other composer." The melody is violinistic, yet to transcribe the piece is to destroy its very essence. It can only be sung upon the piano.

Nocturne in B major, Op. 32, No. 1: A nocturne of less importance, though characteristic in design and melodic contour. However, a surprising coda of amazing originality completely shocks the listener out of reverie. Berkeley calls it an ending that "defies analysis, but compels acceptance." To Huneker, this little recitativo "is like the drum-beat of tragedy."

Nocturne in A-flat major, Op. 32, No. 2: A long, gracious melody with a balletic middle section. Indeed, the work is important in the ballet *Les Sylphides*, choreographed to Chopin's music. The A-flat Nocturne, though attractive, is less important than other members of this species.

Nocturne in G minor, Op. 37, No. 1: Also of lesser importance. Karasowski says it "keeps up a ceaseless sad thought, until interrupted by a church-like atmosphere in chords."

Nocturne in G major, Op. 37, No. 2: Once far more popular than at present. Its main theme in euphonious thirds and sixths gives it a barcarolle, Venetian flavor. The Victorian

Niecks finds "a beautiful sensuousness; it is luscious, soft, rounded, and not without a certain degree of languor. But let us not tarry too long in the treacherous atmosphere of this Capua—it bewitches and unmans." The view of Chopin's music as a dangerous aphrodisiac was once prevalent. Kentner warns us that the nocturnes should not "suffer critical degradation because sentimental young ladies used them, in days long gone by, to comfort their repressed libido."

Nocturne in C minor, Op. 48, No. 1: In grandeur of conception, the C minor Nocturne is unrivaled among its companions. The work, composed in 1841, finds Chopin's genius blooming, reaching new vistas of emotional power. The Doppio movimento section has an almost Beethovenian ethical ring. For Kullak, "the design and poetic contents of this nocturne make it the most important one that Chopin created; the chief subject is a masterly expression of a great powerful grief."

Nocturne in F-sharp minor, Op. 48, No. 2: A subtle and recondite nocturne. It is interpretively difficult, with a discursive middle section in D-flat which is a kind of recitative. The main theme is chaste and transparent, and of an unusual length, with a veiled passion throughout.

Nocturne in F minor, Op. 55, No. 1: Teachers often prescribe this nocturne for students grappling with Chopin's style. It is technically easier than many, though it lacks the melodic distinction of its companion nocturnes. Huneker calls it "a nice nocturne, neat in its sorrow."

Nocturne in E-flat major, Op. 55, No. 2: A work of striking beauty and exquisite intricacy. Berkeley notes, "Here no analysis can explain the natural growth of the melodic line." In the last twenty years, the E-flat Nocturne has become recognized by pianists as a spiritualization of the form. One has only to compare the Field-like E-flat Nocturne of

Op. 9, No. 2 to understand how far Chopin had traveled in pianistic layout and harmonic plenitude based on a personal contrapuntal approach, and a rarefication of melody. The coda is again a passage of breathtaking inspiration.

Nocturne in B major, Op. 62, No. 1: A work of pure luxuriance; the main theme is profusely adorned with difficult chain trills. In his book on Chopin, Camille Bourniquel writes: "The last Nocturnes complete the redemption of the genre and its final liberations—they possess a unique freedom." Gerald Abraham feels they "illustrate the principle of motive-generated melody in continuous cantabile form."

Nocturne in E major, Op. 62, No. 2: The eighteenth nocturne and the last one published during Chopin's life; a luminous and melting composition. It foreshadows Fauré's work in the nocturne genre. Ernest Hutcheson wrote, "This is one of Chopin's sostenuto melodies, warm and luscious like the G string of a violin." The middle section is agitated.

Nocturne No. 19 in E minor, Op. 72, and *Nocturne in C-sharp minor,* Op. posth.: The E minor Nocturne is the earliest piece by Chopin in nocturne form, composed when he was seventeen, and it is still played often. The popular C-sharp minor is a pastiche of his nocturne style, with passages from his F minor Concerto. Friskin describes it as "a poverty-stricken nocturne." It is now published in most Nocturne editions, although Chopin did not title the piece.

The Nocturnes:
Arrau: Philips (CD)
Ashkenazy: London (CD)
Barenboim: DG (CD)
Fou Ts'ong: CBS
Katin: Unicorn
Lima: Arabesque
Moravec: Connoisseur Society
Novaes: Vox

Ohlsson: Angel
Rubinstein: RCA (CD)
Weissenberg: Angel

Separate Nocturnes of note:
Busoni (Op. 15, No. 2): International Piano Archives
Flier (Op. 62, No. 2): Westminster
Friedman (Op. 55, No. 2): Danacord
Hofmann (Op. 15, No. 2): RCA; IPA
Loesser (Op. 9, No. 3): IPA
De Pachmann (Op. 37, No. 2): Pearl
Pogorelich (Op. 55, No. 2): DG
Rachmaninoff (Op. 9, No. 2, and Op. 15, No. 2): RCA
P. Serkin (Op. 48, No. 2): RCA
Solomon (Op. 9, No. 2): EMI

The Polonaises

From the first, the polonaise was important in Chopin's creative life. At the age of seven, he composed his first one, in B-flat major, and throughout his career he made the form exclusively his own, overshadowing the early examples by Oginski, Kurpinski, and Meyseder.

Chopin's mature polonaises form a heroic national epic. The dance, or more rightly the processional, is in triple time with an unmistakable rhythm featuring an eighth note and two sixteenths, followed by four eighths. Liszt felt that "this dance is designed above all to draw attention to the men and to gain admiration for their beauty, their fine airs, their martial and courteous appearance."

In these works, Chopin's Romantic patriotism envisions Poland's former greatness and chivalric deeds. The form also became a means of expressing his most violent and angry emotions concerning his nation's struggle. The Polonaises, with their "cannon buried in flowers," in Schumann's words, have become symbolic and poignant evocations of an oppressed people.

There are sixteen polonaises, of which nine were composed before Chopin left Poland at twenty-one. These are charming, especially the Op. 71, No. 3 in F minor. But only in Paris, idealizing his country from afar, could Chopin's genius for the polonaise ripen. His seven mature examples are thrilling in their splendor, rancor, and pianistic invention.

Polonaise in C-sharp minor, Op. 26, No. 1: It opens with an arrestingly grand statement, but the main character of the work is lyric. Once played frequently, the C-sharp minor Polonaise ought to be revived. The Meno mosso section is exquisite, in Huneker's words "tender enough to woo a princess."

Polonaise in E-flat minor, Op. 26, No. 2: A tragic tone poem which requires depth of expression on the part of the pianist to fulfill its savage, brooding character. The E-flat minor Polonaise is sometimes called *The Siberian Revolt.* The discontent of the work, its wild anger, makes this neglected polonaise one of Chopin's most realistic compositions. Janáček must have loved this Slavonic masterpiece.

Polonaise in A major, Op. 40, No. 1: Often called the *Military;* a world-famous piece, splendid in its pomp and glory, its chivalry and lean muscularity.

Polonaise in C minor, Op. 40, No. 2: Anton Rubinstein saw in this a gloomy picture of Poland's downfall, just as the Polonaise in A major was a portrait of her former greatness. The C minor Polonaise is seldom played. It is an enigmatic yet noble composition.

Polonaise in F-sharp minor, Op. 44: A raw and overwhelming work when played properly. Huneker asks us to "consider the musical weight of the work, the recklessly bold outpourings of a mind almost distraught! There is no greater test for the poet-pianist." Liszt called it the "lurid hour that precedes a hurricane," while John Ogdon sees in it a "Goya-like intensity." The central section is a mazurka preceded by two pages of the strangest monotony,

reverberating madly. The psychological impact is shattering. This work finds Chopin's spirit far from the elegant world of the Parisian salon.

Polonaise in A-flat major, Op. 53: One of the world's most famous pieces of music, it never fails to thrill. It is Chopin dreaming of an all-powerful Poland. The A-flat Polonaise is the very picture of the martial spirit. It has been called the *Heroic* Polonaise, and its majestic octave episode in E major resounds with the hooves of a proud cavalry. After "this central episode," wrote Ogdon, "Chopin's return to the main section is a *tour de force:* few composers would have dared and achieved so apparently wayward and capricious a return in so grandiose a work." Huneker cautions, "None but the heroes of the keyboard may grasp its dense chordal masses, its fiery projectiles of tone."

Polonaise-fantaisie in A-flat major, Op. 61: This late work, published in 1846, ranks with the master's most sublime creations. Chopin had said all he had to say in the form of the polonaise; he was now groping for a new, expansive, and more personal structure— hence the title *Fantaisie.* It took decades for it to be properly understood. Even Liszt was confused by it, saying, "Such pictures as these are of little value to art. They only serve to torture the soul, like all descriptions of extreme moments." The weaving of five themes, the impressionist harmony, the total mystery and profundity present one of the most absorbing interpretive problems in the Chopin canon.

Selected Polonaises:
ASHKENAZY: London (CD)
BERMAN: DG
CHERKASSKY: DG
FRANKL: Turnabout
MALCUZYNSKI: Angel
OHLSSON: Angel
POLLINI: DG (CD)
RUBINSTEIN: RCA (CD)

Individual Polonaises of interest:
ARGERICH (Opp. 53 & 61): DG
AX (Op. 61): RCA
CHERKASSKY (Op. 53): Mercury
FLIER (Op. 26): Westminster
HOFMANN (Op. 26): International Piano Archives; (Op. 40, No. 1): RCA
HOROWITZ (Opp. 53 & 61): CBS; (Op. 44): CBS (CD)
LHÉVINNE (Op. 53): RCA
NEUHAUS (Op. 61): Melodiya
PENNARIO (Op. 53): Angel
P. SERKIN (Op. 61): RCA

Twenty-four Preludes, Op. 28

Within these very small frames, Chopin captures a universe of feeling and mood. There is a prelude for each major and minor key; many of them demand high virtuosity. James Friskin writes, "Perhaps no other collection of piano pieces contains within such a small compass so much that is at the same time musically and technically valuable." Schumann thought them "eagle's feathers, all strangely intermingled. But in every piece we find his own hand—Frédéric Chopin wrote it. One recognizes him in his pauses, in his impetuous respiration. He is the boldest, the proudest, poet-soul of his time." Finck feels that "if all piano music in the world were to be destroyed, excepting one collection, my vote should be cast for Chopin's Preludes. There are among Chopin's preludes a few which breathe the spirit of contentment and grace, or of religious grandeur, but most of them are outbreaks of the wildest anguish and heart-rending pathos. If tears could be heard, they would sound like these preludes."

Prelude No. 1 in C major: An exquisite example of Chopin's devotion to Bach. Pulsating and agitated, it is over in half a minute, leaving the listener yearning for more.

No. 2 in A minor: Slow, indeed perversely morbid, in its musical makeup, but unforgettable.

No. 3 in G major: The right-hand melody is a puff of air. Ernest Hutcheson wrote, "It takes fairy fingers to compass the sun-kissed ripples of the left hand." And Robert Collet exclaims of its difficulties that "the Prelude in G major I regard as one of the most dangerous little pieces ever written."

No. 4 in E minor: A slender melody over a rich, slow-moving chordal accompaniment. Huneker wrote, "Its despair has the antique flavor." It was fittingly played, with Nos. 6 and 20, by the famous organist Lefébure-Wély, at Chopin's funeral service at the Madeleine Church in Paris. Mozart's Requiem was also performed.

No. 5 in D major: Very short, with cross-rhythms, intricate and iridescent.

No. 6 in B minor: A cello melody in the left hand; very sad and slow. A famous piece.

No. 7 in A major: Three lines, a skeletonized mazurka, used prominently in the ballet *Les Sylphides*. Even more famous than No. 6.

No. 8 in F-sharp minor: The right-hand melody is played by the thumb. Chopin writes the chromatic inner voice in smaller notation. This feverish vision is one of the greatest of the preludes.

No. 9 in E major: A work of only twelve measures but also of infinite grandeur.

No. 10 in C-sharp minor: It's over in a blink, and needs the lightest fingers.

No. 11 in B major: Concentrated grace and poetry. Huneker says, "Another gleam of the Chopin sunshine."

No. 12 in G-sharp minor: A powerful and despairing work. Technically treacherous.

No. 13 in F-sharp major: A nocturne-like prelude with a middle section. This is a pearl of lyric serenity.

No. 14 in E-flat minor: A unison study of a moment of gloom.

No. 15 in D-flat major: The so-called *Raindrop* Prelude is the longest of these pieces, with a dramatic middle section. The work has always been popular.

No. 16 in B-flat minor: Perilous right-hand fingerwork as the left hand becomes more explosive. A *tour de force* for the virtuoso.

No. 17 in A-flat major: A richly colored romance concluding with eleven low A-flats reminiscent of a bell. Mendelssohn wrote, "I love it! I cannot tell you how much or why; except perhaps that it is something which I could never at all have written."

No. 18 in F minor: A difficult prelude in fiery, recitativo style.

No. 19 in E-flat major: Marked Vivace, a beautiful and difficult piece. To play it through unscathed is an achievement.

No. 20 in C minor: Twelve bars of chords. George Sand had this funereal prelude in mind when she aptly stated that "one prelude of Chopin contains more music than all the trumpetings of Meyerbeer." Rachmaninoff and Busoni used it as the basis for sets of variations.

No. 21 in B-flat major: A nocturne-type prelude with a double-note accompaniment.

No. 22 in G minor: Short and stormy, with left-hand octaves.

No. 23 in F major: Ending on a dominant seventh chord, this prelude has the bliss of a perfect June day. Huneker rhapsodizes: "This prelude is fashioned out of the most volatile stuff. Aerial, imponderable, and like a sun-shot spider-web oscillating in the breeze of summer . . ."

No. 24 in D minor: It is a discharge of tremendous emotion marked Allegro appassionato. The turbulent left hand never relents.

Three solo D's in the bowels of the piano make for a foreboding conclusion.

Twenty-four Preludes:
ARGERICH: DG (CD)
BAKST: Westminster
CORTOT: Music and Arts (CD)
ESCHENBACH: DG
FELTSMAN: CBS (CD)
FLORENTINO: Saga
FREIRE: CBS
MORAVEC: Connoisseur Society
PERAHIA: CBS

Prelude in C-sharp minor, Op. 45

A seldom played work of great improvisational beauty. The composition contains far-flung modulations and needs imagination for its presentation. It has nothing in common with the Op. 28 Preludes (although some of the recordings include it).

POGORELICH: DG (CD)

Four Scherzos

Chopin composed four of his greatest creations under the title *Scherzo*, a word that means "a joke." Was Chopin being ironic? Schumann was baffled; when reviewing the B minor Scherzo, he asked, "How are seriousness and gravity to be clothed if jest is to go about in such dark-colored garments?" The title seems appropriate only for No. 4.

The Scherzos are epics among Chopin's works, and their instrumental brilliance has made them staples of the concert hall; each of them demands a highly finished technique.

Scherzo No. 1 in B minor, Op. 20: The First Scherzo was composed most likely in 1834, and first published in 1835. Later, when it was issued in England under the title *The Infernal Banquet,* Chopin, always a purist and opposed to any literary or pictorial allusions, had a fit. The opening must have shocked his contemporaries. Indeed, its almost repellent realism still astonishes. Niecks asks: "Is this not like a shriek of despair?" The material is feverishly restless and tragic in nature. The middle section, marked Molto più lento, is based on a Polish Christmas carol, "Sleep, Jesus Sleep" (one of Chopin's few uses of actual folk material). The section is worked out in the dreamiest manner until the Scherzo's opening chord interrupts the dream. The first section, which is then repeated, ends in a coda of barbaric splendor, which closes with furious chromatic scales.

Scherzo No. 2 in B-flat minor, Op. 31: The Second Scherzo is the favorite. Schumann compared it to a Byronic poem, "so overflowing with tenderness, boldness, love and contempt." According to Wilhelm von Lenz, a pupil of Chopin, the composer said that the renowned sotto voce opening was a question and the second phrase the answer: "For Chopin it was never questioning enough, never soft enough, never vaulted (*tombé*) enough. It must be a charnel-house." The melody, marked "con anima," is repeated three times during the lengthy proceedings, the last time bringing us to the coda in a magnificent key change. The gorgeous melody overlies a six-note-per-measure left-hand accompaniment of exceeding richness. The trio, filled with longing, takes on a pianistic complexity. Huneker exults, "What masterly writing, and it lies in the very heart of the piano! A hundred generations may not improve on these pages."

Scherzo No. 3 in C-sharp minor, Op. 39: The Third Scherzo opens with an almost Lisztian introduction, leading to a subject in octaves of pent-up energy. The key changes to D-flat major, with a chorale-like subject, interspersed with delicate falling arpeggios. Louis Kentner thinks of it as "a Wagnerian melody of astonishing beauty, recalling the sound of tubas, harps and all the apocalyptic orchestra of Valhalla." This is the most terse, ironic, and tightly constructed of the four scherzos, with an almost Beethovenian grandeur. The finger-bursting coda rises to emotional heights, bringing the score to a rhetorical ending.

Scherzo No. 4 in E major, Op. 54: An ethereal composition bathed in light, which ripples over the expanse of the keyboard. It is Chopin in a blessed moment, improvising and happy. His nerves are calm, and his deadly disease in check. Even the long trio in E minor, of seraphic lyric beauty, has no sign of *morbidezza*. The passagework is elegant; the coda is a picture of pastel beauty.

Four Scherzos:
ASHKENAZY: London (CD)
CHERKASSKY: HNH
DARRÉ: Vanguard
FREIRE: Teldec
RICHTER: CBS/Melodiya
RUBINSTEIN: RCA (CD)
RUBINSTEIN (1932): Seraphim
SIMON: Turnabout
VÁSÁRY: DG

Notable single Scherzos:
AX (Nos. 2, 4): RCA
BARÈRE (No. 3): Vanguard
CLIBURN (No. 2): RCA
HOROWITZ (No. 1): CBS
NOVAES (No. 3): Vox
ZIMERMAN (No. 4): DG

Sonata No. 2 in B-flat minor, Op. 35, "Funeral March"
Chopin wrote three piano sonatas. No. 1 in C minor (1827) was written for his teacher Elsner as a compositional problem. Academic and difficult, it holds almost no interest for pianists. Its third movement is an early example of 5/4 meter.

The Second Sonata is resplendent. Composed in 1838, it is one of the staple items of the pianist's repertory and contains the world's most famous Funeral March.

This work expresses a life-and-death struggle. The opening movement begins with a portentous motive, leading directly into a

Doppio movimento. The grandeur of the conception leads to a lean and inevitable development section. The second movement, a scherzo, echoes the first movement's conflagrations. The *Marche funèbre* is placed as the third movement with extraordinary effect; its trio must not be played sweetly. The finale, composed in unison, is a shudder of grief. This sonata was a specialty of Liszt and Anton Rubinstein; the latter called it "night winds sweeping over church-yard graves." John Ogdon says, "The finest recording of it is still Rachmaninoff's magnificent, unforgettable performance." Alan Walker wrote, "There are fewer great interpretations of this Sonata than there are great pianists."

ARGERICH: DG (CD)
GODOWSKY: IPA–Desmar
HOROWITZ: CBS
KAPELL: RCA (CD)
KATZ: Pye
NOVAES: Vox
POGORELICH: DG (CD)
RACHMANINOFF: RCA
RUBINSTEIN: RCA (CD)

Sonata No. 3 in B minor, Op. 58

Not as stark as the Second Sonata, No. 3 almost bursts its form in the first movement, so rich are the themes, so vital and ornamental. In this late masterpiece, Chopin is charting new formal and harmonic paths. As in the Second Sonata, he breaks out of the Viennese tradition of sonata form. The recapitulation begins with the second subject, which must be one of the most beautiful melodies ever composed within the confines of sonata form. The second movement is a blithe scherzo in E-flat major, with a chiseled and strange trio. The third movement opens with a funereal introduction leading to one of Chopin's greatest meditations, music that leaves one spellbound. The movement is worked out with formal genius and the last page calls for great profundity of feeling. The

agitated finale, Presto, ma non tanto, is a volcanic conception, utilizing only two subjects, worked out on a grand scale. It is a triumph of primordial power.

ANIEVAS: Angel
ARGERICH: DG (CD)
ARTYMIW: Chandos
CHERKASSKY: Nimbus (CD)
CLIBURN: RCA
CORTOT: Seraphim
FIRKUŠNÝ: Capitol
HOFMANN (first movement): RCA
HUNGERFORD: Vanguard
KAPELL: RCA (CD)
LIPATTI: Angel (CD)
NOVAES: Vox
RUBINSTEIN: RCA (CD)
SOREL: Monitor
VERED: London
WEISSENBERG: EMI

The Waltzes

Chopin's Waltzes are among the world's most often played piano music. They fall into two styles: gracious and brilliantly decorated, or melancholy. John Ogdon calls them "the brightest jewels in the greatest salons of the time."

The Waltzes are peculiarly Chopinesque. The Viennese waltzes of the day as exemplified by those of Lanner and the elder Johann Strauss were anathema to Chopin's rarefied nature, and after his stay in Vienna he reported: "I have acquired nothing of that which is specially Viennese by nature, and accordingly I am still unable to play valses." The true precursor of the Chopin waltz style is Weber's *Invitation to the Dance*. Arthur Hedley wrote, "The Chopin Waltzes were never meant to be danced by ordinary mundane creatures of flesh and blood."

Grande Valse brillante in E-flat major, Op. 18: One of Chopin's most extroverted works. Insouciant, teasing, high-stepping, it is beloved by the virtuoso. Berlioz spoke of its "divine delicacies." Some of its fetching passages must have inspired Offenbach. Schumann saw it "enveloping the dancers deeper and deeper in floods."

Valse brillante in A-flat major, Op. 34, No. 1: Chopin composed three waltzes in 1838, under the generic title *Trois Valses brillantes.* This waltz is akin in spirit to the *Grande Valse brillante,* Op. 18, but with even more delightful colors. A true ballroom creation, it is marked Vivace, and Chopin is happy and at ease with the aristocratic veneer of the salon. There is such sparkling life throughout that it feels as though it were improvised at a Dionysian revel.

Valse brillante in A minor, Op. 34, No. 2: The composer Stephen Heller related that Chopin called this slow (Lento) waltz his favorite. When Heller told the Pole that he, too, loved it best, Chopin immediately invited him for lunch at a fashionable café. Frederick Niecks wrote of this piece: "The composer evidently found pleasure in giving way to this delicious languor, in indulging in these melancholy thoughts full of sweetest, tenderest loving and longing."

Valse brillante in F major, Op. 34, No. 3: A witty and little-known waltz. Huneker calls it "a whirling wild dance of atoms." The themes are less distinguished, but the perpetual-motion flavor with its bracing appoggiaturas casts its own spell.

Waltz in A-flat major, Op. 42: A case may be made for the Op. 42 as Chopin's most perfect valse. After the first measures of trill, a call to the dance, there is a melody with a rare lilt composed in double-time, with the triple-time of the waltz in the left hand. Schumann remarked that "like his earlier waltzes it is a salon piece of the noblest kind." The composition, Schumann feels, should be danced to only by "countesses at least." This waltz is the most demanding technically of the series.

Waltz in D-flat major, Op. 64, No. 1: This all-time favorite of Chopin's waltzes is called the *Minute* Waltz because of its perpetual-motion attitude. However, it must not be played in that time period. Chopin himself was often compelled to play it, the London society ladies repeatedly exclaiming that it sounded "like water"—a phrase that annoyed the composer.

Waltz in C-sharp minor, Op. 64, No. 2: Huneker declares, "It is the most poetic of all. The first theme has never been excelled by Chopin for a species of veiled melancholy. It is a fascinating, lyrical sorrow." Delicate passagework ensues, followed by a D-flat major section of vocal beauty.

Waltz in A-flat major, Op. 64, No. 3: Seldom performed, because of the popularity of the two preceding waltzes, although it is shapely and finely made. The last of Chopin's waltzes, it has a deft charm. Niecks speaks of its "exquisite serpentining melodic lines, and other beautiful details." The middle section in C major is perfectly poised.

Waltz in A-flat major, Op. 69, No. 1: Published posthumously with the B minor Waltz in 1855. The manuscript has the inscription *"Pour Mlle Marie."* Chopin wrote this waltz in 1835, while courting Marie Wodzinska. He had fallen in love with the young and beautiful countess and had proposed marriage to her. As a poor musician, however, Chopin was not considered suitable marriage material by Marie's parents and he was rejected. His Waltz in A-flat was given to Marie just before his departure for Paris. Marked Lento, this beautiful dance-poem has often been called *L'Adieu.*

Waltz in B minor, Op. 69, No. 2: This often played work was composed when Chopin was nineteen. The composer wanted it and others of his early works burned, but they were issued posthumously. The piece has three themes; the opening is distinctively Chopinesque in its pensive melancholy.

Other posthumously issued works include three waltzes in Op. 70, all attractive pieces. The best known, No. 1 in G-flat, is a brilliant specimen, and the E minor Waltz, without opus number, composed in 1829, is deservedly popular.

The Waltzes:
ANIEVAS: Angel
CICCOLINI: Seraphim
CORTOT: Seraphim
LIPATTI: Odyssey; Angel (CD)
NOVAES: Vox
PENNARIO: Angel
PIRES: Erato (CD)
RACHMANINOFF (various waltzes): RCA
RUBINSTEIN: RCA (CD)
ZIMERMAN: DG

Other Works

Among Chopin's miscellaneous works, mention should be made of the *Variations brillantes* on an air from an opera by Hérold, Op. 12, which shows how Chopin applied his art to the then popular custom of composing variations on opera themes. Arthur Loesser called it "a masterpiece in its way."

A Bolero in C major, Op. 19, dates from 1833. Chopin turns this Spanish form into a rather Polish-sounding affair. In the proper hands, it can be elegant and gallant. The Tarantelle in A-flat, Op. 43, has spirit, though it lacks the native frenzy of the dance. Schumann praised it too highly when he found it "in Chopin's most daring manner." But the work has always been played.

In the Introduction and Rondo in E-flat, Op. 16, a Weber-like opening leads to a brilliant and engaging rondo, which is overly long. Perhaps more characteristic is the 1827 *Rondo à la mazur*, Op. 5, with its florid passages exuding a Slavic flavor.

MUZIO CLEMENTI
1752–1832 — Italy

Sonata in B minor, Op. 40, No. 2
  (1802)
This formidable sonata certainly shows why Beethoven admired Clementi. The plan is in two movements, both opened by slow, remarkable recitativo sections.

BERMAN: CBS

Sonata in C major, Op. 34, No. 1
  (1795)
Similar in muscularity to Beethoven's Op. 2, No. 3. An effective concert sonata in three movements.

GILELS: Melodiya

Sonata in B-flat major, Op. 24, No. 2
Sonata in G minor, Op. 50, No. 3, "Didone abbandonata"
The B-flat major Sonata bears a striking resemblance to the opening theme of the overture to Mozart's *The Magic Flute*. In the late G minor Sonata from 1820, Clementi achieves the emotional depth he was always striving for.

Both are played in a fine selection of Clementi sonatas on two records. Volume 1 contains, in addition to the G minor work, Sonatas Op. 33, No. 1 in A major; Op. 33, No. 3 in C major; and Op. 26, No. 2 in F-sharp minor. The B-flat Sonata is on the second record along with Op. 40, No. 2 in B minor; Op. 25, No. 4 in A major; and Op. 2, No. 3 in G minor.

CROWSON: L'Oiseau-Lyre

Six Sonatinas, Op. 36; *Three Sonatinas,* Op. 37; *Three Sonatinas,* Op. 38
These are the most frequently played sonatinas in history. Musical children can't resist their classical purity.

ENTREMONT: Columbia
FOSTER: MHS

Piano Concerto in C major (1790)
An excellent Classical concerto. Clementi adapted it from his own C major Sonata Op. 33, No. 3, which Horowitz has recorded (on RCA) with splendor and gusto. (Other Horowitz performances of Clementi sonatas are Op. 34, No. 2 in G minor; Op. 14, No. 3 in F minor; and Op. 26, No. 2 in F-sharp minor.)

BLUMENTAL, Zedda/Prague Chamber Orchestra: Turnabout
DRENIKOV, Sofia Chamber Orchestra: Fidelio (CD)

AARON COPLAND
b. 1900 — United States

Piano Variations (1930)
Copland has been a decisive figure in contemporary American music. Although he has composed relatively little for the piano, his contributions are significant. His set of Piano Variations—Theme, Twenty Variations, Coda—remains as rugged and abstract as on the day it was finished. The composer William Flanagan wrote: "No one who is familiar with the history of modern American music has to be told that Copland's Piano Variations is a legend in its own right and a work of prime significance in the composer's musical development. Its status as a sort of granitic masterwork has been questioned by virtually no cultivated musician—no matter what his stylistic allegiance—since its composition."

COPLAND: New World
KALISH: Nonesuch (CD)
MASSELOS: Odyssey
SHIELDS: Vox
SMIT: CBS
TOCCO: Pro Arte (CD)

Piano Sonata (1939–41)
Copland premiered the work in Buenos Aires in 1941. It is in three ample movements. The "Coplandesque" chords remind us of the impact he has had on American music. He consciously intended "writing a music—a serious concert music—that a European would recognize as having been written by an American."

BERNSTEIN: New World
FLEISHER: Epic
SMIT: CBS
SOMER: CRI

Piano Fantasy (1955–57)
This is one of Copland's great works, dedicated to the memory of the pianist William Kapell. It was premiered by William Masselos. The composer states: "The Fantasy belongs in the category of absolute music. It makes no use whatever of folk or popular music materials. The musical framework of the entire piece is based upon a sequence of ten different tones of the chromatic scale.... The Piano Fantasy is by no means rigorously controlled twelve-tone music, but it does make liberal use of devices associated with that technique."

MASSELOS: Odyssey
SMIT: CBS

Piano Concerto (1927)
The Concerto, in two movements, without break, is a finely integrated work that stands as one of the best jazz-inspired pieces in any musical genre. The piano part is effective and demanding; the orchestration, large and colorful.

COPLAND, Bernstein/New York Philharmonic: Columbia
SMIT, Copland/Rome Radio Symphony: Varèse/Sarabande
WILD, Copland/Symphony of the Air: Vanguard

GEORGE CRUMB
b. 1929 — United States

Makrokosmos, Volume 1 – Twelve Fantasy-Pieces After the Zodiac for Amplified Piano
Makrokosmos, Volume 2 — Twelve Fantasy-Pieces After the Zodiac for Amplified Piano

Crumb gets his inspiration from many sources, and the symbolic plays a large role in his compositions. The composer notes his debt to Bartók and Debussy, but says, "The spiritual impulse of my music is more akin to the darker side of Chopin, and even to the childlike fantasy of early Schumann." The twenty-four *Makrokosmos* take about seventy minutes in toto, comprising a work of modern Romanticism, and an uncharted journey to new musical lands. There are extensive extra pianistic "happenings" such as singing, shouting, whispering, whistling, as well as a type of notation in which most pianists would be lost. The composer is ever-present, asking the pianist to be "tremulous," "subliminal," as if "suspended in endless time," "desireless," "fantasmic," and on and on. Each one of the series has a different title. The first twelve were written for David Burge and the latter set for the pianist Robert Miller.

> BURGE (Volume 1): Nonesuch
> MILLER (Volume 2): Odyssey

LUIGI DALLAPICCOLA
1904–1975 — Italy

Quaderno musicale di Annalibera
(1953)

Dallapiccola is one of the best-known contemporary Italian composers. A practitioner of the twelve-tone method, he nevertheless expresses a great deal of warmth and sensuous feeling in his music. In the *Quaderno musicale* or "Musical Notebook for Annalibera," one of the tempo markings is Andantino amoroso. This quiet group of eleven pieces is one of the most profoundly respected piano works of tone-row music.

> BURGE: Candide
> MAXIMILIEN: CRI

Sonatina Canonica on Paganini Caprices
(1942–43)

A landmark piano work of the 1940s. Paganini themes are the foundation for this canonic, polytonal, touching, humorous piece in four movements.

> MAXIMILIEN: CRI

CLAUDE DEBUSSY
1862–1918 — France

One of the seminal figures in twentieth-century music. He composed the most original body of piano music since Liszt.

Although Debussy occasionally performed some of his own music, he was not a concert pianist. He did, however, give a great deal of advice to many pianists, who were eager to enter the secret garden of his compositions. "In playing his own music," Léon Paul Fargue remarked, "he appeared to be giving birth to the piano. He cradled it, talked softly to it." Nadia Boulanger told Bruno Monsaingeon: "You only need to have heard Debussy play once. I don't mean that he played better than others. He played otherwise, he had his own tone, his unique tone." Marguerite Long, who worked on all of his major works with him, wrote in her book *At the Piano with Debussy* that he "was an incomparable pianist. How could one forget his subtleness, the caress of his touch while floating over the keys with a curiously penetrating gentleness. There lay his secret, the pianistic enigma of his music. There lay Debussy's individual technique; gentleness in a continuous pressure gave the color that only he could get from his piano."

Debussy added a new dimension to the piano's expressive and evocative power. Through the century, his work has remained vitally fresh and intriguing to pianists and audiences alike. Debussy is the most exportable of all modern French composers. The originality of his music is such that Claudio Arrau says "it is like the music of another planet." It offers a new world, inspired less by the European music of the past than by Symbolist poetry, nature, Impressionist painting, indeed, sheer impulse itself, and the exoticism of the Javanese gamelan orchestra that he had heard in Paris. In Boulez's phrase, Debussy was to "break the circle of the Occident." Debussy's pianism contains layers of exquisite "chording," harmonies hovering unresolved in the most rarefied, intoxicating air. New concepts in pedaling and minute rhythms governing microspacing and a range of atmospheric tonal problems necessitate the highest sensitivity and elasticity that a pianist can possess.

With Debussy, the chord became freed of its necessity to move; a chord became a sensuous experience in itself. With this concept, harmonic progression was no longer required in the traditional sense. Yet his music is not a formless mass, relying on mere sensation. Debussy is a subtle builder of form, with an uncanny ability to write pieces that were neither too long nor too short, in the way that Pissarro, Monet, or Cézanne never painted a picture on the wrong size canvas.

Unfortunately, as the most exportable of French piano composers, he has been subjected to many untenable performances. He may be the most poorly played composer, generally speaking, after Chopin.

Suite bergamasque (1890)
A tribute to the seventeenth- and eighteenth-century French *clavecinistes,* the suite is in four movements: Prelude, Menuet, the celebrated *Clair de lune,* and Passepied. It is a great advance stylistically over his two well-known Arabesques, and over the several other short pieces composed in or before 1890, such as the Ballade and Nocturne, all of which are charming but lack the individuality of the *Suite bergamasque.*

CICCOLINI: Seraphim
GIESEKING: Seraphim
KOCSIS: Philips (CD)
RICHTER: Columbia
ROUVIER: Denon (CD)
VÁSÁRY: DG
WEISSENBERG: DG (CD)

Pour le piano (1901)
Debussy had become master of the orchestra before he achieved similar mastery over the

piano. *Pour le piano* was his first piano work in a decade. It was premiered by Ricardo Viñes. Debussy had not yet reached the apex of his powers in this work, but through its stunning effects, whole-tone scales, and neo-Classic purity, it has gained a place in the international repertory. The three movements are: Prelude, with glissando effects, Sarabande, and an exhilarating Toccata.

BACHAUER: Mercury
BÉROFF: Angel
GIESEKING: Angel
HEIDSIECK: Cassiopée
MORAVEC: Connoisseur Society
PERLEMUTER: Nimbus (CD)

Estampes: Pagodes, La Soirée dans Grenade, Jardins sous la pluie 1903
First performed by Viñes, these works inaugurate a new era in piano writing. *Estampes* are "images printed from engraved copper or wood plates." The pianist E. Robert Schmitz wrote, "Years of gestation purified these visions to the pungency of an essence." The stimulus for *Pagodes* is the Javanese gamelan orchestra that Debussy fell in love with. In *Evening in Granada,* a habanera rhythm permeates fine, short themes. Manuel de Falla thought it "contain[ed] in a marvelously distilled way the most concentrated atmosphere of Andalusia." *Gardens in the Rain* is a pure impressionistic evocation of raindrops with two French nursery songs woven into the framework.

BADURA-SKODA: Harmonic (CD)
R. CASADESUS: Columbia
FIRKUŠNÝ: Sugano (CD)
GIESEKING: Columbia; Angel
JACOBS: Nonesuch
MORAVEC: Vox Cum Laude (CD)
RICHTER: DG
WEISSENBERG: DG

L'Isle joyeuse (1904)
This is a Bacchanalian masterpiece, inspired by Watteau's most famous painting, *The Embarkment for Cythère*. It was always a favorite of the composer, who said, "That piece seems to assemble all the ways to attack a piano." Marguerite Long calls it a "Feast of Rhythm." It was premiered by Viñes, whose playing of it, Long says, was "made of light that burst from all sides in a simultaneously vertiginous and precise fantasy."

BASHKIROV: Melodiya
CLIBURN: RCA
FERBER: Saga
GIESEKING: Angel
HOROWITZ: Columbia
WEISSENBERG: RCA

Images (First Series): *Reflets dans l'eau, Hommage à Rameau, Mouvement* (1905)
Images (Second Series): *Cloches à travers les feuilles, Et la Lune descend sur le temple qui fut, Poissons d'or* (1907)
Debussy believed the First Series would "take their place in piano literature . . . to the left of Schumann or the right of Chopin." *Reflections in the Water* is one of the miracles of musical impressionism. *Hommage à Rameau* is a stately sarabande, and *Mouvement* is a perfect study in motion. In the Second Series, Debussy uses three staves for the clarification of his exquisite notation. Both *Cloches à travers les feuilles* ("Bells Heard Through the Leaves") and *La Lune descend sur le temple qui fut* ("The Moon Goes Down on the Ruined Temple") are among the most difficult interpretive problems in Debussy. Their transparency demands expert and imaginative pedaling. The best known of the Second Series is *Poissons d'or* ("Goldfish"), in which, Schmitz says, the performer must "be convinced that the body of a goldfish is luminous and almost transparent, and that it displaces itself quite suddenly by dashes of rapid timing."

R. CASADESUS: Columbia
DEMUS: MHS

GIESEKING: Angel
HENKEMANS: Epic
JACOBS: Nonesuch
MICHELANGELI: DG (CD)

Children's Corner Suite (1908)

This is a masterful production of satire, tenderness, and humor. It begins with *Doctor Gradus ad Parnassum,* which, in Debussy's words, "is a sort of hygienic and progressive gymnastics; it should therefore be played every morning, before breakfast, beginning at 'modéré' and winding up to 'animé.' " No. 2, *Jimbo's Lullaby,* is also humorous. Jimbo is a toy elephant belonging to Debussy's daughter. No. 3, *Serenade for the Doll,* is legato and staccato in a whimsical setting. No. 4, *The Snow Is Dancing,* is technically the most exacting of the set. No. 5, *The Little Shepherd,* is simplicity itself. No. 6, *Golliwog's Cakewalk,* is a piece in which Debussy indulges in the syncopation of the minstrel groups he heard, with an irreverent quote from Wagner's *Tristan und Isolde.*

R. CASADESUS: Columbia
FRANKL: Turnabout
GIESEKING: Odyssey
HORSZOWSKI: Nonesuch (CD)
JOHANNESEN: Vox
MICHELANGELI: DG (CD)

Twenty-four Preludes

The Preludes furnished the piano with a new vocabulary, never before heard in music. Marguerite Long has written, "The content of these two books is of an order not to be confused with any other." Schmitz affirmed, "Only a man with a magnificent wealth of knowledge, of experience, of intuition could characterize so sharply and so briefly the infinite array and range of subjects of these twenty-four works, which whirl through legends, literature, vaudeville, painting, architectural landmarks, archaeological objects, natural phenomena, a multitude of scenes and of personages, each individualized, crystallized, in the moment of Debussy's creations." Laurence Davies comments, "They recall no one so much as Monet, with his dissolving canvasses in which the scene almost begins to change before one's eyes. . . . Debussy gave to music a whole new encyclopedia of sensations."

Twelve Preludes, Book I (1910)

Danseuses de Delphes ("Delphi Dancers"): Debussy himself played the first performance in 1910. At the Louvre, the composer had seen a fragment from a Greek pillar depicting three dancers. He was often inspired by Hellenic sources, as in *Chansons de Bilitis* or *Danses sacrée et profane.* This archaic, slow-moving prelude uses modal, diatonic, pentatonic, and chromatic elements, which possess a graveness of tone. "Yet," says Schmitz, "this gravity is enveloped by a lightness of touch, as if the dancers were clad in veils or enfolded by curving wraps of incense."

Voiles ("Veils," "Sails"): Debussy also premiered this prelude. The work uses the whole-tone scale to great effect. Debussy told Marguerite Long that some pianists played it with too much color, losing the insubstantial feeling he wanted. Debussy himself saw "sailing boats anchored to a fixed pedal-point" as well as "mysterious veils enveloping palpitating feminine forms, hiding eyes which fan desire by their devious glances." The composer Edgard Varèse said the piece was inspired by the diaphanous veils used by the American dancer Loïe Fuller, then famous in Paris.

Le Vent dans la plaine ("The Wind on the Plain"): A nature study, in an arpeggio figure, broken by violent gusts. "The invisibility of the wind," notes the critic Edward Lockspeiser, "is meant above all to be mysterious and on a long suspended B-flat, the piece ultimately disappears into thin air."

Les Sons et les parfums tournent dans l'air du soir ("The Sounds and Perfumes Swirl in the Evening Air"): Inspired by a line in Baudelaire's poem "Harmonie du Soir" from *Les Fleurs du mal*. The Fourth Prelude calls for creative interpreters. It is "poignant and sensuous," in Long's words, "rich with beguiling nocturnal vibrations and the ephemeral languor of human life avid for the raptures of Tomorrow." Debussy once said, "It is only the pleasures of the moment that matter."

Les Collines d'Anacapri ("The Hills of Anacapri"): A bright work with bell sounds, tarantella rhythm, frenzied dancing. Debussy told Long that a pianist had once played it with a gypsy feeling and that it should rather be Neapolitan. The score closes with Debussy asking the pianist to play luminously, as the sun bursts in the piano's upper registers.

Des Pas sur la neige ("Footsteps in the Snow"): An incomparable psychological masterpiece. With only a few notes, he has created a feeling of total desolation. Debussy said it should have the aural value of a melancholy, snowbound landscape. Arrau speaks of "a sadness, an intolerable dilemma."

Ce qu'a vu le vent d'ouest ("What the West Wind Saw"): Technically the most demanding of the preludes from Book I. A work embodying the unleashed power of the West Wind, which is a horribly destructive phenomenon, gathering force over the Atlantic and crashing in on the coasts. "Here," writes Schmitz, "Debussy is no longer the poet of tenderness, the painter of the exquisite. . . . It exhibits a passionate fascination for evil. . . . Debussy asks the player to be *en dehors et angoissé*—outside and anxiously." A lone and tragic human voice is almost silenced by the oceanic turbulence of the score. Lockspeiser thinks that Debussy, who was a great admirer of Shelley, may have been inspired by his "Ode to the West Wind."

La Fille aux cheveux de lin ("The Girl with the Flaxen Hair"): Inspired by a poem of Leconte de Lisle. A slender and supple melody about a girl who sang to herself in a field of clover with lips cherry-red. One of the most popular of the Preludes.

La Sérénade interrompue ("The Interrupted Serenade"): A portrait of a Spanish guitarist trying to sing his love song. But, alas, he is interrupted and lightly scorned. Debussy himself said, "Poor fellow, he keeps on being interrupted."

La Cathédrale engloutie ("The Engulfed [Submerged] Cathedral"): A work bathed in mystery, echoing with the sound of ancient bells. Based on an old Breton legend of the Cathedral of Ys engulfed in water because of impiety but rising at sunrise. Debussy may also have been inspired by Monet's paintings of the Rouen Cathedral. The prelude was premiered by Debussy in 1910, and stands as one of his most purely "impressionist" scores. "After sunrise, its watery grave is still," writes Long, "but Debussy tears away the submarine fabric of the city with a superb theme which surges up to form a kind of cupola."

La Danse de Puck ("Puck's Dance"): This tiny, capricious character from *A Midsummer Night's Dream* is portrayed here in one of the most delightful Shakespearean depictions in music. Schmitz wrote, "Tripping lightly, sliding, vanishing, reappearing, our nimble elf has a mocking laugh." This prelude is not an easy one to play well.

Minstrels: A music-hall piece of broad humor inspired by the American cakewalk. Minstrel shows were becoming popular around 1900, and Debussy put such a scene into a prelude with a foppish rhythmic appeal and which awakens a whole set of images.

Twelve Preludes, Book II (1913)
Brouillards ("Mists"): A piece of musical impressionism with the mysterious quality of

fog—vaporous and enigmatic. It demands, in the words of Maurice Hinson, "exquisite control" from the executant.

Feuilles mortes ("Dead Leaves"):   "This is the Rite of Autumn," wrote Schmitz, "in which the falling leaves are a signal of the suspension of life, creating a static expectancy, a mood of intense regrets of a past now so far gone, of great sadness and the poignant melancholy of fall. Debussy had once written of golden leaves celebrating the glorious agony of the trees."

La Puerta del vino ("The Gateway to the Vineyard"):   Manuel de Falla sent Debussy a postcard depicting the famed gate of the Alhambra Palace in Granada, to which Debussy responded with a tonal masterpiece infused with the habanera rhythm. Debussy asks the interpreter to play "with brusque oppositions of extreme violence and impassioned sweetness." The work exudes a haunting sensuousness. "What riotous sounds, what lasciviousness," wrote Marguerite Long.

Les Fées sont d'exquises danseuses ("The Fairies Are Exquisite Dancers"):   The pianist Ernest Ulmer wrote that this prelude "is dedicated to the ephemeral charm of fairy-tale sylphs."

Bruyères ("Heather"):   A pastoral picture—a scene of the moors of Scotland. One of the easiest preludes technically, and reminiscent of *La Fille aux cheveux de lin*.

General Lavine—Eccentric: In the style and rhythm of a cakewalk. Debussy, in this prelude, depicts the once-famous American clown and juggler Edward Lavine, who seemed to be nine feet tall. Debussy loved seeing this entertainer perform. He called him "wooden . . . he hid with humor and with pirouettes a too sensitive heart." The piece is similar to *Minstrels* from Book I and has a flavor of ragtime.

La Terrasse des audiences du clair de lune ("The Terrace for Moonlight Audiences"):   The composer was inspired by a letter published in *Le Temps* on the coronation of George V as emperor of India. "The hall of victory, the hall of pleasure, the garden of the sultanesses, the terrace for moonlight audiences." This prelude demands the highest concentration and tonal control from an interpreter. The work is ethereal, languorous, yet touched by a nameless anxiety.

Ondine: The seductive water nymph of Debussy differs greatly from the elegant Ondine of Ravel. Ravel's Ondine is a mature siren who lures sailors to her watery palace, and to death. Debussy's Ondine is young, capricious, and tempting, and, in Paul Jacobs's words, "is merely a sprite whose music is shimmering laughter." *Ondine* is technically and tonally a difficult piece.

Hommage à S. Pickwick, Esq. P.P.M.P.C.:   Debussy was always fascinated by England, and this is a tribute to Dickens. The prelude begins with "God Save the King" and is rich in humor. As with many Debussy preludes, the score is filled with psychological twists.

Canope: A *canope* is the covering of an Egyptian funeral urn. Canope, also, was a city of ancient Egypt on the Nile. This is a piece of tender sadness.

Les Tierces alternées ("Alternating Thirds"):   The only prelude without a descriptive title. An abstract etude of a purely pianistic intent, which anticipates Debussy's Etudes.

Feux d'artifice ("Fireworks"):   A magnificent fireworks display on Bastille Day is captured in the most illuminating and evocative piano writing. In the last measures the *Marseillaise* floats through the night air. This may be the most technically difficult of the entire series of preludes, a masterpiece of color, animation, and kaleidoscopic pattern making. Schmitz wrote of the Preludes, "One has run the gamut of emotions from youth to death, candor to furor to melancholy. An exacting pianistic technique has been developed to match the rich effects of a multiplicity of rhythms, melodies, harmonies, the like of which respond to our wildest dreams of treasure chests in Baghdad." Lockspeiser adds: "Soon one is aware of the symbolism in this piano writing. There is a visual aspect of this music and often a subtle psychological aspect. There is no doubt that Debussy shows himself in the Preludes to be not only a clairvoyant but a clairaudient. The music allows the listener to see things and to hear things in a new way. Debussy's mysterious conception of the tactile properties of music is equally remarkable, and there are pages which bring music to the borders of an odoriferous or even—so completely are we regaled by this music of the senses—a soporific art."

It is interesting to note that Debussy put the titles of the Preludes at the end of each piece. Perhaps he was reminded of the Symbolist poet Stéphane Mallarmé's dictum: "To name an object sacrifices three-quarters of the enjoyment. To suggest it—that is our dream."

Twenty-four Preludes:
ARRAU: Philips (CD)
R. CASADESUS: Columbia
CIANI: DG
GIESEKING: Odyssey; Angel
HAAS: DG
HEIDSIECK: Cassiopée
JACOBS: Nonesuch (CD)
KARS: London
MICHELANGELI (BOOK I): DG (CD)
ULMER: Protone

Twelve Etudes (1915)
These Etudes, dedicated to the memory of Chopin, are a monument of the technical literature. As Marguerite Long wrote: "Debussy made use of a special alchemy in his Etudes. He worked at his craft like a refined lover." Although drier and more objective than the impressionist Preludes, the Etudes did not receive the attention they deserve until the last generation, and in fact are now receiving

complete performances in concert by such superior technicians as Pollini. In the composer's words, "These Etudes hide a rigorous technique beneath harmonic flowers." Debussy wrote no fingerings for this complicated task, asking the player to prove "those eternal words: 'One is never better served than by oneself.' Let us seek our fingerings." Each Etude presents a different problem.

No. 1:   *Pour les "cinq doigts" d'après Monsieur Czerny* (Study for Five Fingers)
No. 2:   *Pour les tierces* (Study in Thirds)
No 3:   *Pour les quartes* (Study in Fourths)
No. 4:   *Pour les sixtes* (Study in Sixths)
No. 5:   *Pour les octaves* (Study in Octaves)
No. 6:   *Pour les huit doigts* (Study for Eight Fingers without Thumbs)
No. 7:   *Pour les degrés chromatiques* (Study in Chromatic Steps)
No. 8:   *Pour les agréments* (Study in Ornaments)
No. 9:   *Pour les notes répétées* (Study in Repeated Notes)
No. 10: *Pour les sonorités opposées* (Study in Opposed Sonorities)
No. 11: *Pour les arpèges composés* (Study for Composite Arpeggios)
No. 12: *Pour les accords* (Study for Chords)

DI BONAVENTURA: Connoisseur Society
GIESEKING: Angel
JACOBS: Nonesuch (CD)
LORIOD: MHS
ROSEN: Epic

ERNÖ VON DOHNÁNYI
1877–1960—Hungary

Variations on a Nursery Song for Piano and Orchestra (1913)
This ingenious score keeps Dohnányi alive in the international repertoire. The composer

commented that it was made "for the enjoyment of lovers of humor, and the annoyance of others." After its portentous introduction, we hear the French nursery air *"Ah, vous dirai-je, maman,"* and then we are treated to eleven variations of impressive inventiveness. They are an example of remarkable piano writing. The Waltz Variations possess an incomparable insouciance.

> DOHNÁNYI, Boult/Royal Philharmonic: Angel
> SCHIFF, Solti/Chicago Symphony: London (CD)
> WILD, C. von Dohnányi/New Philharmonia: Quintessence

PAUL DUKAS
1865–1935 — France

Variations, Interlude, and Finale on a Theme by Rameau (1901–02)
One of the finest works in variation form. Norman Demuth aptly states, "Had these *Rameau* Variations been written by a Teutonic composer they would have undoubtedly become established long ago in the regular repertoire and would have been taken as much for granted as are Brahms' *Handel* Variations, and equally reverenced; but it is only quite recently that the French genius has been recognised as consisting of something more than Impressionism and Pictorial Romanticism." A noble, precise composition with intricate part writing, difficult to play well in its seventeen-minute duration. It takes more than one hearing to appreciate its subtle beauties.

> D'ARCO: Calliope
> JOHANNESEN: Candide

Sonata in E-flat minor (1899–1900)
A vast work of deeply warm spirit in four movements, lasting upwards of forty-five min-

utes. It received its premiere in 1901, by Edouard Risler. The work is more Franckian in its fervor than Dukas's more neo-Classic variations, which spring from the French clavecin tradition. It may be considered one of the few important French sonatas. The scherzo movement has some similarity to Dukas's more popular work, *The Sorcerer's Apprentice.*

> PLESHAKOV: Orion
> THINAT: MHS

JAN LADISLAV DUSSEK
1760–1812 — Czechoslovakia

Sonata in F minor, Op. 77, "L'Invocation" (1812)
One of the pinnacles of Czech Classical music, *L'Invocation* is Dussek's last, longest, and perhaps his finest creation. It has the breadth of great art and is deserving of a place in the hierarchy of the Classical sonata. The work is a massive four-movement structure cut from granite and far too little known.

> FIRKUŠNÝ: Candide
> HNAT: Supraphon
> MARVIN: Genesis

Sonata in B-flat major, Op. 35, No. 1 (1797)
Sonata in C minor, Op. 35, No. 2 (1798)
Sonata in F-sharp minor, Op. 61, "Elégie harmonique sur la mort du Prince Louis Ferdinand" (1806)
The Sonata in C minor is a distinguished work. Beethoven may have been influenced by it in his Op. 13 *Sonate pathétique*, composed soon after. Frederick Marvin writes that the second movement, Adagio patetico et espressivo, is "one of the great inspirations of

Dussek and I feel [it] is not paralleled by an adagio written before 1798 in its depth and tragic expressiveness." The Sonata in B-flat, in a two-movement format, is technically more difficult than most of the sonatas of the era. Its finale is absolutely irresistible. The Sonata in F-sharp minor is also in two movements. The first movement is a striking utterance, filled with drama. One can hear the pre-Lisztian gesture as Dussek rolls up the diminished seventh chords, and Brahms certainly knew the syncopated finale when he wrote his own Sonata in F-sharp minor, Op. 2. One other sonata of Dussek, Op. 70 in A-flat, with the title *Le Retour à Paris,* must be considered important. It is a beautifully planned, highly pianistic work. A critic of the day felt it would "retain its value as long as music provided good pianos and accomplished pianists." There is no adequate recording of the composition, however.

KEENE (Op. 61): Protone
MARVIN: Genesis

HENRI DUTILLEUX
b. 1916 — France

Piano Sonata (1947)
Dutilleux's three-movement Sonata was premiered by Geneviève Joy, to whom it was dedicated. It has become a classic of its period. The composer wrote, "I tried to create a certain internal pulsation, a type of lyrical tension and also this 'sonorous abundance' that the piano, better than any other instrument, can translate by virtue of its harmonic richness and variety of its timbres." The Sonata is marvelously conceived for the piano and is stated with lucid restraint.

AMATO: Archduke (CD)
SIEGEL: Orion

MANUEL DE FALLA
1876–1946 — Spain

Cuatro Piezas españolas (1907)
Composed at the same time Albéniz was working on *Iberia,* the *Cuatro Piezas—Aragonesa, Cubana, Montañesa,* and *Andaluza*—should not be underestimated. They are a high point of Spanish nationalism. Although they demand rhythmic flexibility and sophistication, they are by no means as note-heavy as Albéniz's *Iberia.*

ACHUCARRO: RCA
DE LARROCHA: London (CD)
RICHARD: Nonesuch
SANCHEZ: Estereo (Euroclass)

Fantasía baética (1919)
The *Fantasía baética* (Baestis being the Roman name for Andalusia) is the longest, most difficult of Falla's works for piano. Composed

335

for Arthur Rubinstein, it is more primitive and stark than the *Cuatro Piezas,* representing a searing, almost parched landscape. It has never received the attention it deserves. It is daring in the simplicity of the score's harmonic layout.

ACHUCARRO: RCA
DE LARROCHA: London (CD)
RICHARD: Nonesuch
SANCHEZ: Estereo (Euroclass)

Nights in the Gardens of Spain—Symphonic Impressions for Piano and Orchestra (1918)

The greatest of all Spanish works for piano and orchestra. It is a glowing, bewitching, youthful score, which conjures up the perfumes of night. Falla called the composition "evocations in sound." The piano part is ingenious and brilliant, but deceptively simple on the page with its many unison passages.

ACHUCARRO, Mata/London Symphony: RCA
ARGERICH, Barenboim/Orchestre de Paris: Erato (CD)
DE LARROCHA, Comissiona/Suisse Romande: London
DE LARROCHA, Burgos/London Philharmonic: London (CD)
ENTREMONT, Ormandy/Philadelphia: CBS
HASKIL, Markevitch/Lamoureux Orchestra: Philips (CD)
RUBINSTEIN, Ormandy/Philadelphia: RCA
SORIANO, Burgos/Paris Conservatoire: Angel (CD)

GABRIEL FAURÉ
1845–1924—France

"Fauré's feline melody and chaste pianism," wrote Norman Demuth, "contain all the lyrical slenderness and lightness hitherto absent from French piano music. . . .

Fauré's music sings as that of no earlier French piano composer ever sang, but it lacks the extreme limpidity of Chopin's Nocturnes and therefore does not lend itself so easily to abuse. . . . It is sentimental only if the player makes it so." A taste for Fauré must be developed and nurtured. His reflective gentleness and general reticence become more beautiful with repeated listening; he makes his impact by steps. His art has often been described as Hellenic in its serenity. His forms are entirely Chopinesque, into which are assimilated the influences of Schumann and Mendelssohn. He was a great master of piano writing. James Gibb notes that in the Ninth Barcarolle, "canonic imitation amid arpeggios is managed with a nonchalance that would have been the envy of Thalberg, the inventor of the 'three-handed' trick." Fauré's music can be voluptuous, frolicsome, ingratiating, and a hundred other things. It is, nevertheless, too contemplative to recommend itself to the average virtuoso, who may find its beauty too rarefied.

The Complete Piano Music

Laurence Davies wrote: "His large corpus of piano music stands along those of Debussy and Ravel, at the very summit of his nation's achievements in that sphere. . . . The gentle swerve of his melodies, the amazingly poised and delicate harmonies of which he was such a master, the apparently effortless flow of his scales and arpeggios—these features combined to make him a kind of musical Bonnard or Vuillard, and an unequalled exponent of his nation's graces."

CROCHET: Vox
JOHANNESEN: Golden Crest

Thirteen Barcarolles (1883–1921)

No. 1 in A minor, Op. 26 (1883): Three graceful melodies. Fauré made a piano roll of it in 1913 for the Welte Company.

No. 2 in G major, Op. 41 (1885): More difficult than No. 1; again, with three motives.

No. 3 in G-flat major, Op. 42 (1885): Two themes, with arpeggios serving the rocking motion. The longest of these works (duration: 7:30).

No. 4 in A-flat major, Op. 44 (1886): A peaceful, simple work.

No. 5 in F-sharp minor, Op. 66 (1895): More experimental and enigmatic than any of the earlier examples. Emile Vuillermoz wrote of these pieces: "Until now the Barcarolle had only sailed on lakes or lagoons. The No. 5 seems to carry us off to the open sea."

No. 6 in E-flat major, Op. 70 (1896): An amiable and smoothly wrought work.

No. 7 in D minor, Op. 90 (1906): This short composition (3:00) takes us into the more subterranean, austere style of the composer.

No. 8 in D-flat major, Op. 96 (1908): There is a rare loud ending in this charming, animated work.

No. 9 in A minor, Op. 101 (1910): A sadly meditative work lasting four minutes.

No. 10 in A minor, Op. 104, No. 2 (1913): Introspective; the melody is rather stagnant, the harmonic progression interesting.

No. 11 in G minor, Op. 105, No. 1 (1914): Wonderful technique exhibited by the composer in his use of short repetitive motives.

No. 12 in E-flat major, Op. 105, No. 2 (1916): The barcarolle motion is especially gentle.

No. 13 in C major, Op. 116 (1921): Fauré was seventy-six and deaf when he concluded this series, begun by his fortieth year, with a piece of springtime freshness.

Thirteen Barcarolles:
COLLARD: Angel (CD)
DOYEN: MHS

Thirteen Nocturnes (1883–1922)

The Nocturnes are among Fauré's greatest flights of creativity. They display an enormous range of mood and harmonic progression, and are generally more complex than the Barcarolles.

No. 1 in E-flat minor, Op. 33 (1883): Very original in its piano setting; full of sorrow and heaviness.

No. 2 in B major, Op. 33, No. 2 (1883): Vuillermoz wrote, "It is pleasant, carefree, a bit capricious, and permits itself at times the graceful freedom of an impromptu."

No. 3 in A-flat major, Op. 33, No. 3 (1883): More Chopinesque than any of the other nocturnes, and among the most frequently played.

No. 4 in E-flat major, Op. 36 (1884): Direct, without any of Fauré's shy mystery; bell effects.

No. 5 in B-flat major, Op. 37 (1884): A pastoral setting; the second theme, in Evelyne Crochet's phrase, "shows more anxiety than genuine emotion."

No. 6 in D-flat major, Op. 63 (1894): A span of a decade separates the Fifth and Sixth Nocturnes. In this nine-minute work, the once luxuriant form becomes a psychological drama of emotional depth. It is one of the great masterpieces of French piano music.

No. 7 in C-sharp minor, Op. 74 (1898): Ten minutes long, this is interpretively more difficult than No. 6. The beauties are more severe, the austerity entering the realm of grief. The ending is in a calm D major.

No. 8 in D-flat major, Op. 84, No. 8 (1902): The Eighth Nocturne, the shortest by far of the thirteen (2:30), is also the eighth piece of Fauré's *Huit Pièces brèves*. But this light and amiable work is always included in the complete nocturnes as well.

No. 9 in B minor, Op. 97 (1908): Evelyne Crochet wrote, "The Ninth Nocturne has one of the most beautiful of Fauré's piano themes; a phrase of exquisite purity modulates into B major and bursts into a resonant chorale."

No. 10 in E minor, Op. 99 (1909): A serious work, full of asperities, which needs very skillful musicianship.

No. 11 in F-sharp minor, Op. 104 (1913): "A sad and moving song," wrote Crochet. "As in the Requiem, a detached serenity, surely and starkly expressed, makes itself felt through the grief."

No. 12 in E minor, Op. 107 (1916): Harmonically interesting; a gloomy work.

No. 13 in B minor, Op. 119 (1922): Fauré's last piece for the piano; a work of sad nobility, rising to a great climax but ending in a calm despair.

> *Thirteen Nocturnes:*
> COLLARD: Angel (CD)
> DOYEN: MHS
> HEIDSIECK: HMV

Nine Preludes, Op. 103 (1911)

The Preludes sound best played as a set. Their aftereffect lures a listener back. It almost seems that all of Fauré is condensed here in twenty minutes.

> R. CASADESUS (Nos. 1, 3, 5): Columbia
> CROSSLEY: CRD (CD)
> FERBER: Saga
> HEIDSIECK: Cassiopée

Theme and Variations, Op. 73 (1897)

The longest of Fauré's piano works (fifteen minutes), it is a peak in French piano music, and perhaps the most played set of French variations. The theme is original. In the Variation No. 11, Fauré endows the score with all of his tender-heartedness, allied to a fine variational skill.

> COLLARD: Angel (CD)
> DEMUS: Westminster
> DOYEN: MHS
> FERBER: Saga

Ballade for Piano and Orchestra in F-sharp major, Op. 19 (1881)

This is perhaps the most poetic smaller work for piano and orchestra in the literature, with long lyric lines rising to a climax, then subsiding to Fauré's usual soft close. The work was originally composed for piano solo, and in that setting may be the most difficult of Fauré's piano writings.

> R. CASADESUS, Bernstein/New York Philharmonic: Columbia
> CROSSLEY (solo version): CRD (CD)
> HEIDSIECK, Benzi/Festival du Grand Rué: Cassiopée
> JOHANNESEN, Froment/Luxembourg Radio: Turnabout
> JOHANNESEN (solo version): Golden Crest
> WILD, Gerhardt/Metropolitan Symphony: Quintessence

CÉSAR FRANCK
1822–1890 — Belgium

Symphonic Variations for Piano and Orchestra (1885)

One of Franck's richest works, a staple of the repertoire, the *Variations symphoniques* is a masterpiece of variational technique. In fifteen minutes, Franck presents an introduction in which he creates six variations, and a finale. Franck also composed a neglected but effective and beautiful work for piano and orchestra, *Les Djinns,* based on a poem by Victor Hugo.

> *Symphonic Variations:*
> R. CASADESUS, Ormandy/Philadelphia: Odyssey
> COLLARD, Plasson/Toulouse Capitole: Angel (CD)
> CURZON, Boult/London Symphony: London
> WATTS, Leinsdorf/London Symphony: Columbia
> WEISSENBERG, Karajan/Berlin Philharmonic: Angel (CD)

Prelude, Chorale, and Fugue (1884)
A majestic score of nearly twenty minutes. The technical demands are heavy. Harvey Grace wrote, "It is a kind of epitome of the Franckian mood and method. . . . Like so much of his music, it is over-chromatic in places—notably in the interludes of the Chorale on its first appearance—but that is a small blemish on a work which in construction, thematic development, polyphony, command of keyboard technique, and above all in sustained musical interest, is among the masterpieces of pianoforte literature."

CHERKASSKY: Nimbus (CD)
CICCOLINI: Pathé
MALCUZYNSKI: Seraphim
MORAVEC: Connoisseur Society
RICHTER: Monitor
RUBINSTEIN: RCA (CD)

Prelude, Aria, and Finale (1886–87)
This is less valuable than the Prelude, Chorale, and Fugue but nevertheless an important work in the history of French piano music. Franck's last piano work, it lies in a dangerous domain, hovering on the verge of vulgarity and sentimentality. Norman Demuth wrote, "I have heard the first section made to sound like a military march, and the second like Gounod at his feeblest." Demuth also gives the key to the interpretation of Franck's works: "Pianists try to make them sound 'holy.' Franck was simply a good man who made his faith the mainstay of his existence; he was no more 'holy' than was Bach. His Romanticism is neither sanctimonious nor priggish. The music is introvert and subjective, but it should not be given the air of spiritual isolation. It must be approached in a broad manner."

It should be noted that Harold Bauer made a superb transcription for piano of Franck's Prelude, Fugue, and Variation for Organ, which is ten minutes long and less difficult than the two original Franck piano works.

Prelude, Aria, and Finale:
D'ARCO: Calliope
CROSSLEY: L'Oiseau-Lyre
DEMUS: MHS

GEORGE GERSHWIN
1898–1937 — United States

Three Preludes (1926)
The longer No. 2 is a beautiful blues work, falling between the two shorter, syncopated, jazz-derived pieces. Gershwin also composed arrangements of his own popular songs; these wonderfully pianistic adoptions have long fascinated pianists.

BOLCOM: Nonesuch
LEVANT: CBS (CD)
PENNARIO: RCA

Rhapsody in Blue (1924)
The most popular of all American orchestral works, the *Rhapsody in Blue* has instant ap-

peal. The piano writing abounds in graceful play. With its rhythmic audacity and delicious melodies, it seems to epitomize the Jazz Age of the 1920s. The work spurred a flood of jazz-inspired compositions. There is an interesting album made from Gershwin's own 1925 piano roll, with the orchestral part in the original Ferde Grofé instrumentation, performed by the Columbia Jazz Band and directed by Michael Tilson Thomas. The Gershwin tempi are faster and fresher than we are used to hearing.

> BERNSTEIN, Bernstein/Columbia Symphony: CBS (CD)
> GERSHWIN (piano roll), Thomas/Columbia Jazz Band: CBS (CD)
> KATCHEN, Kertesz/London Symphony: London
> LEVANT, Ormandy/Philadelphia: CBS (CD)
> PREVIN, Previn/London Symphony: Angel (CD)
> WILD, Fiedler/Boston Pops: RCA (CD)

Piano Concerto in F (1925)

The Concerto in F is probably the most often played American concerto. At thirty minutes, it is double the length of the *Rhapsody,* and structurally not as sound as the tightly packed earlier work. It has all the Gershwin traits, as Paul Rosenfeld notes, "some of them being popularly American in essence or gaily, brightly Yiddish, and others impressionistic or vaguely grand-operatic, or reminiscent of the melodramatic emphasis and *fioritura* of Liszt or Chopinesque."

> PREVIN, Previn/Pittsburgh Symphony: Philips (CD)
> SIEGEL, Slatkin/St. Louis Symphony: Vox Cum Laude (CD)
> SZIDON, Downes/London Philharmonic: DG
> WILD, Fiedler/Boston Pops: RCA (CD)

ALBERTO GINASTERA
1916–1983 — Argentina

Sonata No. 1 (1952)

This piano sonata in four short movements is dazzling in its laconic compositional virtuosity. In addition to an atonal Presto, of folk material endowed with a sense of mystery, it has a passionate slow movement, and a vital finale, Ruvido ed ostinato, which has made this one of the best-known contemporary sonatas. Ginastera has an exceptional knowledge of piano sonority. His Sonatas Nos. 2 and 3 are less rewarding.

> BEAN: Westminster
> NISSMAN: Desto
> RODRIGUEZ: Elan (CD)
> SOMER: Desto
> WILLE: DG

Piano Concerto No. 1 (1961)

Both Ginastera piano concerti are landmarks of the South American concerto literature. The First Concerto is more complex than the Sonata in its structure and dissonance. It is rewarding listening, with its occasional rhapsodic moments and fluttering atonality.

> MARTINS, Leinsdorf/Boston Symphony: RCA
> SOMER, Maerzendorfer/Vienna Philharmonic: Desto

Piano Concerto No. 2 (1972)

The composer speaks of the tragic and fantastic nature of this concerto. Technically more arduous than No. 1, it is in four movements, the first being thirty-two variations on a single chord by Beethoven, that of measure 208 of the fourth movement of the Ninth Symphony. The second movement is a scherzo for left hand alone, and displays opposing colors. The third movement of microsounds, Quasi una fantasia, is the emotional heart of this dense score, and the fourth movement, Cadenza e finale, uses eleven notes from the finale of Chopin's *Funeral March* Sonata, "The Wind over the Graves."

SOMER, Cassuto/UCI Symphony: Orion

ENRIQUE GRANADOS
1867–1916 — Spain

Granados was an astute explorer of the piano's resources. He had a wonderful feel for sonority and color, which culminated in his breathtaking masterpiece, the *Goyescas*. One of the first to appreciate him was the English critic Ernest Newman, who wrote, "The texture of Granados' music . . . is of the kind that makes you want to run your fingers over it, as over some exquisite velvet; the flavor of it is something for the tongue almost, as well as the ear. . . . To play through some of his pages is like a joyous wading knee-deep through beds of gorgeous flowers—always with a sure way through and the clearest of light and air around us."

Granados's last appearance as a virtuoso took place at the White House, where he performed for President Wilson. While returning to Spain, Granados and his wife were killed at sea by a German submarine.

The Complete Piano Music
Granados wrote twenty-four titles, which consist of either single pieces or suites. Except for a few of the *Goyescas* and the Fifth Spanish Dance, much of Granados's output is still not well known. His music conveys a highly Romantic imagery, ranging from Spanish nationalism to the ever-present influence of Chopin and Schumann. He had his salon side, and he was a master of small forms and of the various Spanish dances.

DOSSE: Vox

Twelve Danzas españolas
Some of his finest purely Spanish writing. Many are not difficult to execute, but such pieces as the celebrated No. 5, *Andaluza,* or the *Zarabanda, Jota,* and *Asturiana,* call for a certain rhythmic knack.

DE LARROCHA: London (CD)
SORIANO: Connoisseur Society

Seis Piezas sobre cantos populares españoles
The Six Pieces on Spanish Folk Songs are again in an exclusively Spanish frame of reference. They are full-blooded, richly textured, and more difficult than the *Danzas españolas*.

DE LARROCHA: Turnabout; London (CD)

Valses poéticos (1887)
Danza lenta
The suite of dances is the earliest mature work of the composer. It contains an introduction followed by seven waltzes, with the first waltz repeated as the coda. Almost unknown, this suite—influenced by Schumann and Schubert—has a beauty all its own. Each melody is more fragrant than the last, and the morning dew of the first waltz is unforgettable. The technical requirements are modest. The *Danza lenta,* with its elaborate growth of trilled figures, is a very late piece, probably composed after the *Goyescas*.

DE LARROCHA: Turnabout or MHS

Allegro de concierto
In C-sharp major, this is glorious music. Written for a piano competition and dedicated to Maláts, it is Lisztian pianism in a Spanish mode.

DE LARROCHA: London (CD)
ITURBI: Angel

Escenas románticas
A suite of six pieces totaling twenty-four minutes, and including a lovely Mazurka. *The Poet and the Nightingale* is wonderfully real-

ized. This passionate score is sadly neglected and ranks with the finest of Granados's work. It asks of the performer a wide variety of tone, imaginative use of rubato, and a Romantic nature.

DE LARROCHA: MHS; London (CD)

Goyescas (1911)

The *Goyescas* are the fullest expression of Granados's genius, which possessed many visual elements. He was immersed in Francisco Goya's world of *majas* and *majos*, their gallantry and turbulence, their sensuality and coquetry. This maze of impressions, filtered through his acute, visual sensibility, produced music of an extempore quality—fragmented, luxuriant, and moody. In *El Amor y la muerte,* the bells toll in the bass, representing the hovering presence of death, which culminates in the *Dies Irae,* used in the middle of *The Specter's Serenade.* The suite calls for the richest of virtuoso equipment and a feel for the dramatic atmosphere of the Iberian peninsula. Granados wrote, "In *Goyescas* I intended to give a personal note, a mixture of bitterness and grace . . . that are typically Spanish; and a sentiment suddenly amorous and passionate, dramatic and tragic, such as is seen in the works of Goya." The collection of six pieces is subtitled *Los Majos enamorados* ("The Enraptured Lovers").

1. Los Requiebros ("Flatteries"): A difficult piece; melodies move between the hands with difficult double-notes. The main theme is a jota, a Spanish dance from Aragon. The work starts and stops with a fateful intensity. (The work is dedicated to Emil von Sauer.)

2. Coloquio en la reja ("Love Duet"; "Conversation in the Jailhouse"): Technically diffuse, a work requiring great ardor. Joan Brown writes, "The atmosphere is one of love and tragedy. Here Granados heard the guitar in the piano's bass and the human voice in the melody. Man and woman and all they can mean to each other are in the amorous last *copla,* or theme." (The work is dedicated to Edouard Risler.)

3. El Fandango de candil ("The Fandango by Lantern Light"): A work of the utmost pianistic elegance and harmonic richness. The fandango rhythm is used with incomparable allure. (The work is dedicated to Ricardo Viñes.)

4. Quejas, o la maja y el ruiseñor ("Laments, or The Maiden and the Nightingale"): A supremely Romantic improvisation and the most celebrated of the *Goyescas.* In the final page, the nightingale bursts forth, in the words of the composer, "with the jealousy of a wife, not with the sadness of a widow." (The work is dedicated to Amparo Gal.)

5. El Amor y la muerte ("Ballade—Love and Death"): The longest of the *Goyescas,* asking the pianist for flights of imagination and a command of complex textures, as well as artistic use of the pedals. The composer brings back with exquisite and painful effect the great theme from No. 4, *The Maiden and the Nightingale.* The work possesses the highest dramatic impact and is indispensable to the psychology of the entire set. (The work is dedicated to Harold Bauer.)

6. Epílogo (*Serenade of the Specter*): A perfect ending. A ghostly atmosphere envelops the listener, as a skeleton strums on an eerie guitar. (The work is dedicated to Alfred Cortot.)

Goyescas:
AYBAR: Connoisseur Society
CICCOLINI: Seraphim
DE LARROCHA: London (CD)
KYRIAKOU: Turnabout

El Pelele (*The Strawman*)

This is a sparkling late piece, which Granados incorporated into his ill-fated opera, *Goyescas,* based on the piano suite.

DE LARROCHA: Turnabout; London (CD)

EDVARD GRIEG
1843–1907 — Norway

Grieg was a good pianist who appeared often in public, mostly in the accompaniments of his songs or in collaboration in his violin sonatas. He made a few piano rolls. Of his seventy-four opus numbers, thirty-two are groups of solo piano pieces. The most enduring are the ten sets of *Lyric Pieces,* sixty-six in number. Their tart lyricism has survived the changing currents of fashion, notwithstanding Debussy's sarcastic quip: "pink bonbons filled with snow."

Grieg began as a disciple of Schumann and Chopin (von Bülow wrongly dubbed him the Chopin of the North), but early in his career he came under the influence of the fervent Norwegian nationalist composer Rikard Nordraak, who died at the age of twenty-four, in 1866. Grieg assumed his mantle.

Grieg is the greatest of the Norwegian composers and is beloved throughout his homeland. His pianism is based on Liszt's muscular system in the large works, such as the Ballade, Op. 24, and the great A minor Concerto. While not exactly awkward for the hands, much of Grieg can be inconvenient to play.

Ballade in the Form of Variations on a Norwegian Folk Song in G minor, Op. 24 (1875)

The Ballade was written from the depth of Grieg's heart. It is the finest set of Scandinavian variations of the nineteenth century. It is also Grieg's most technically difficult solo work, filled with his strangest, most adventurous chromatic harmony. It is not easily brought off in concert, but pianists have always felt its appeal. It was in the repertoires of Rachmaninoff, Hofmann, and Percy Grainger.

DAVIS: Audiofon (CD)
GODOWSKY: International Piano Archives
KLIEN: Turnabout
LAVAL: Seraphim

MERZHANOV: Melodiya
RUBINSTEIN: RCA

Holberg Suite, Op. 40 (1844)

Subtitled *From Holberg's Time* and in four movements, headed by a Praeludium. Grieg is charming in his attempt to wed a northern spirit to Baroque forms.

DAVIS: Audiofon (CD)
KLIEN: Turnabout
WIKSTROM: Swedish Society Discofil

Lyric Pieces, Opp. 12, 38, 43, 47, 54, 57, 62, 65, 68, 71

The sixty-six *Lyric Pieces* are virtually a repository of Norwegian music. They retain their freshness and portray both sides of Grieg's mind and heart, which often fluctuated between the elegiac and a joyous elfin spirit.

GIESEKING (31 pieces): Seraphim
GILELS (20 pieces): DG (CD)
GOLDENWEISER (complete): Melodiya
KOCSIS (14 pieces): Philips
RUBINSTEIN (11 pieces): RCA

Norwegian Peasant Dances (Slåtter), Op. 72 (1902)

Arrangements of dances transcribed from the Hardanger fiddle, these neglected pieces are far more daring than the *Lyric Pieces.* They represent a side of Grieg that is fascinating, and harmonically stark. Wilfrid Mellers thinks they "can be legitimately compared with the folk-song arrangements of Bartók. . . . He transfers the sharp, crackling sound of the village fiddler with miraculous skill to the piano."

MOURAO: Vox

Piano Concerto in A minor, Op. 16 (1868)

One of the most popular concertos of all time. It lacks the excessive difficulty of other Romantic concertos and consequently it has been overplayed by students and amateurs. The

343

work was inspired by Schumann's A minor Concerto. It retains its youthful freshness. The overall Norwegian color, and the peasant dance of the last movement, never fail to delight an audience.

FLEISHER, Szell/Cleveland: Odyssey
FRIEDMAN, Gaubert: Danacord
LIPATTI, Galliera/Philharmonia: Odyssey
LUPU, Previn/London Symphony: London (CD)
RUBINSTEIN, Wallenstein/RCA Symphony: RCA (CD)
SOLOMON, Menges/Philharmonia: EMI
ZIMERMAN, Karajan/Berlin Philharmonic: DG (CD)

CHARLES TOMLINSON GRIFFES

1884–1920 — United States

Griffes, who died at thirty-six, was the most sensitive impressionist tone poet America ever produced. Though not prolific, he wrote music of uniformly high quality both in craft and content. His later work took on a harsher tone.

Unusual for an American of the day, his affiliations were French, Debussy and Ravel being his mainstays. His interests also took him to exotic subjects.

The *Three Tone Pictures*, Op. 5, from 1915 (including the perfect *Night Wind*), and the exquisite set of *Four Roman Sketches,* Op. 7 (which include *The Fountain of the Acqua Paola* and Griffes's best-known work, *The White Peacock*), represent the peak of American impressionism.

Piano Sonata (1917–18)

The Sonata is Griffes's masterwork. He was a lonely figure during a particularly sterile period in American music. Wilfrid Mellers says, "This disturbingly powerful Sonata is an American parable in musical terms, telling us what happens to the ego alone in the industrial wilderness. . . . Griffes' Sonata is an astonishing and frightening work; its Orientalism is not an escape into dream but a consequence of desperation such as could have occurred only in a spiritually barbarous world." The work is pianistically a marvel, Griffes having a magnificent ear for sonority and color. The Sonata possesses sensuousness and a raw, seething energy, as well as its own Romanticism, exploding into soaring ecstasy near the end. The performer must get deep inside the work's most painful and frenzied regions. His Three Piano Preludes (1919) continue to lead Griffes in new directions.

Piano Sonata:
HAMBRO: Lyrichord
KEENE: Protone
STARR: Orion
TOCCO (complete piano music): Gasparo (CD)

ROY HARRIS
1898–1979 — United States

Sonata, Op. 1 (1928)

Harris wrote a quantity of fine music. His Op. 1, written in France when he was studying with Boulanger, has a Prelude (Maestoso con bravura), Andante ostinato (Misterioso), and Scherzo. Harris flexes his muscles here and finds them strong. Still fresh today, the score must have been a revelation to the American musical scene in 1928, its primitivism and pioneer spirit coupled with a distinctly Anglo-American hymnody and jazziness in the scherzo.

    CORBATÓ: Orion
    SHIELDS: Vox

JOSEPH HAYDN
1732–1809 — Austria

Although Haydn research has made large strides since the invention of the LP, few of his sonatas have been assimilated into concert life, and not more than half a dozen are well known. Ironically, Haydn—considered by all to be one of music's immortals—still lives in the shadow of his friend Mozart, and of his student Beethoven. The appellation "Papa" Haydn has presented the world with the picture of a benevolent grandfather, who always writes good-humored, happy music. Never has a superficial image done more harm to a man of such original genius.

Unlike Mozart and Beethoven, he was not a virtuoso, displaying his wares in public. By his own reckoning, however, he was "not a bad pianist." Some of the early sonatas were probably written for his students. He once lamented, "I spent eight long, wretched years teaching youngsters." Haydn's sonatas, written from 1760 until the final three sonatas of 1794, are a measure of his growth. Here, we can see clearly the evolution of a long, hard-working career.

The Piano Sonatas

Haydn's sonatas are not as easy to listen to as those of Mozart. They are diffuse, often brusque, wilder—indeed, experimental. Martin Cooper contrasts the masters: "The vocal element that plays a strong part in Mozart's keyboard sonatas—the cantabile of aria or lied in slow movements and the operatic bustle of many finales—is almost entirely absent from Haydn's keyboard sonatas, whose inspiration is purely instrumental and for that very reason often less immediately enchanting." Indeed, the new search for bel canto on the piano left Haydn and his hero, C. P. E. Bach, behind. It was J. C. Bach's *galant* vocal style that was to influence the Mozart, Clementi, Dussek, and Beethoven slow movements. But Haydn was not interested in singing on the piano so much as in pure expression. In many ways he has more in common with Beethoven than with Mozart. In Haydn, there is an earthy passion; the slow movements suggest the peasant, rather than the courtier, and of

345

course his devastating humor is incomparable.

The numbering of the sonatas has caused endless confusion. Each edition had its own numbering. It is best for contemporary pianists to use two classifications in listing: the Christa Landon numbering (Vienna Urtext, published by Universal), and the Hoboken number (Anthony van Hoboken).

Most Haydn sonata readings today are on the modern grand. According to John McCabe, who has recorded the Sonatas, "That the instruments of Haydn's day have certain coloristic and technical features not to be found on modern instruments is not in doubt. But I firmly believe that the full color and subtlety of the music can be better realized on a modern piano of suitable character, and I also believe that Haydn's writing, even in his early days, is essentially *pianistic* in conception." Still, an authentic instrument can bring hidden textures to life in Haydn's keyboard music.

The Complete Sonatas and various pieces:
BUCHBINDER: Telefunken
MCCABE: London

Selected Sonatas:
BACKHAUS: London
BILSON (fortepiano): Titanic
BRENDEL: Philips (CD)
GOULD: CBS (CD)
HOROWITZ: CBS; Seraphim
KALISH: Nonesuch
NÁDAS: Ashland
SVIRSKY: Monitor

Variations in F minor
One of Haydn's most deeply felt piano works. It is a masterpiece of eighteenth-century variation writing.

DE LARROCHA: London
KALISH: Nonesuch
RUBINSTEIN: RCA

Piano Concerto in D major, Hob. XVIII/2 (1782)
The D major Concerto of Haydn is the finest of his various keyboard concerti, and the only one to have entered the repertoire. Especially captivating is the finale, a Rondo all'ongarese.

GILELS, Barshai/Moscow Chamber Orchestra: Columbia/Melodiya
MICHELANGELI, de Stoutz/Zurich: Angel

HANS WERNER HENZE
b. 1926 — Germany

Piano Concerto No. 2 (1967)
A fifty-minute concerto of massive dimension, needing much rehearsal; the virtuosic orchestral writing has stretches without the piano's intervention. The piano part, though difficult, with much martellato playing, is restricted compared with the orchestral requirements. The effect is bold, fantastic, windy, scattered; it is music of great mournfulness as well.

ESCHENBACH, Henze/London Philharmonic: DG

PAUL HINDEMITH
1895–1963 — Germany

Suite "1922," Op. 26
Suite "1922" consists of four parts: *Marsch, Schimmy, Nachtstück,* and *Ragtime.* A highly effective work, with an ironic and sarcastic use of dance forms. The composer asks the performer to "use the piano as an interesting kind of percussion instrument and treat it accordingly."

BILLETER: MHS
CARNO: GSC
KUBALEK: Golden Crest

Sonatas Nos. 1, 2, and 3

All three sonatas were composed in 1936. No. 1, in five movements, needs especially a firm grasp of chord playing. No. 2 is the shortest of the three sonatas, eleven minutes, and offers much easier, brighter, and more rewarding recital material. The Third Sonata, in four movements, is the weightiest of these works, with a concluding double fugue.

The Three Sonatas:
GOULD: CBS (CD)

Sonata No. 1:
BADURA-SKODA: Westminster
BILLETER: MHS

Sonata No. 2:
BILLETER: MHS
TURINI: RCA

Sonata No. 3:
SIEGEL: Orion
YUDINA: Melodiya

Ludus Tonalis (1942)

The high point in Hindemith's piano writing, based upon concepts of expanded tonality espoused in his *The Craft of Musical Composition*. He calls the *Ludus Tonalis* "studies in counterpoint, tonal organization and piano playing." There are, he continues, "Twelve Fugues, in as many keys, connected by interludes in free lyric and dance forms, old and new, and framed by a Prelude and Postlude that have more in common than meets the casual ear." Hindemith is one of the great neo-Classicists. This score is rewarding for those seeking intellectual refreshment: for pianists, it is fascinating to work on. For listeners, at first, it may be somewhat acrid, but its geometry becomes increasingly interesting on repeated hearings.

CARLSON: MHS
LARETEI: Philips

CHARLES IVES
1874–1954 — United States

Ives was the first American composer to venture into the uncharted regions of sound. It is amazing to think of his work being composed against the background of the genteel establishment composers of his time. If ever a man was frustrated with the music of his day, it was Ives. He wanted to "kick out the softy ears!" He shouted: "Stand up and use your ears like a man." Finally, after more than a half-century, we are listening to the freshness of his immense vision. Polytonality, clusters, aspects of atonality, and quarter-tones are now commonplace, but Ives used them far in advance of most others. His best music, including his two mammoth piano sonatas, must be ranked among the most outstanding creations of twentieth-century art.

Sonata No. 1 (1902–09)

The First Sonata presents a multitude of polyrhythmic problems for the pianist to solve. Of an exhausting forty-minute duration, it demands a tremendous technique, a dedicated spirit, humor, and fearlessness. Ives used hymn tunes in each of the five movements to project the spirit of America as he perceived it at the turn of the century. Like all of his works, this sonata requires great interpretive flux. Only a searching artist can convey its impressionistic manner, shifting moods, and boldness of utterance. The pianist must be able to capture the essence of the ragtime movements in all of their exuberance, fierce clutter of "wrong" notes, and drunken revelry.

> COBB: Spectrum
> LEE: Nonesuch
> MASSELOS: Odyssey

Sonata No. 2, "Concord, Mass., 1840–1860" (1909–15)

For the creative pianist, this is one of the most intriguing works in the repertoire. Since Lawrence Gilman dubbed it "the greatest music composed by an American," the *Concord, Mass.* Sonata has acquired legendary status, with more and more performers applying themselves to its awesome demands. Ives, however, never wrote anything that he himself considered technically impossible. He viewed the performer as a partner. "In fact," he wrote, "these notes, marks and near pictures of sounds, etc., are for the player to make his own speeches on."

The work is a vast musical canvas of the spirit of Transcendentalism, conceived in four movements: *Emerson, Hawthorne, The Alcotts, Thoreau.* Ives continuously revised the work over thirty years. There is no definitive edition, and the serious pianist must do considerable research and make many choices. As the pianist Hadassah Sahr puts it: "The *Concord* Sonata is, finally, inexhaustible. . . . The suggested bits of melodies and rhythms bring with them a kind of nostalgic emotion; frequently they sound like a reflection of Americana. The theme from Beethoven's Fifth Symphony is heard in so many different contexts it seems embedded into the very core of the music." It is more difficult to achieve a cohesive conception of the *Concord* than of the First Sonata.

> KALISH: Nonesuch
> KIRKPATRICK: CBS
> MIKHASHOFF: Spectrum
> SZIDON: DG

LEOŠ JANÁČEK
1854–1928 — Czechoslovakia

In the Mist (1912)
The great Czech composer left only a few works for solo piano. They are stamped with his unique understanding of Moravian folk music and speech patterns, and with his highly fluid tonality. The music is not pianistic by conventional standards. *In the Mist* is a cycle of four somber and episodic pieces without titles.

CROWSON: Angel or Vanguard
FIRKUŠNÝ Sugano (CD)
KUBALEK: Golden Crest
MORAVEC: Nonesuch

Sonata in E-flat minor, "October 1, 1905"
In two movements, inspired by a tragic political event—a university uprising in Prague. The first movement is titled *Foreboding,* Con moto, and the second is titled *Death,* Adagio. It is a heartbreaking piece of music, tense and throbbing.

FIRKUŠNÝ: DG
MORAVEC: Nonesuch

Concertino for Piano, Strings, and Winds (1925)
A masterpiece characteristic of Janáček's mature work. Its opening idea is pregnant, and Janáček develops it ingeniously. The work is inspired by the composer's love for animals and nature. It was originally called *Spring.*

CROWSON, Melos Ensemble: Angel or Vanguard
FIRKUŠNÝ, Kubelik/Bavarian Radio Symphony: DG
KLIEN, Chamber Orchestra: Turnabout

ERNST KŘENEK
b. 1900 — Austria

Sechs Vermessene, Op. 168 (1958)
Křenek has been a potent force in the music of our time. Ranging from jazz to twelve-tone, his music has been controversial and much studied by other composers. The *Sechs Vermessene* (meaning "measurements") are totally "serialized." The rhythmic difficulties are very great, though the music is slow-moving.

  BURGE: Candide

Sonata No. 3, Op. 92, No. 4 (1943)
Sonata No. 4 (1947)
Two important sonatas. No. 3 is in four movements: a sensitive Allegretto piacevole;

Theme, Canons, and Variations; Scherzo; and Adagio. A work demanding intelligence from the interpreter.

The Fourth Sonata is a work of skill and imagination, using twelve-tone techniques together with older forms. In the first movement, three motives are exposed and exploited in differing tempi. The second movement, Andante sostenuto, con passione, is a big expressionist drama. The third movement is a Rondo, vivace. Speedy, humorous, with trills, it's a spiritual descendant of a Mendelssohn scherzo. The finale is a Tempo di minuetto, molto lento, with three variations, a short section bringing back the motive of the first movement, and a fourth variation with a quiet ending.

  BURGE (Sonata No. 4): MHS
  GOULD (Sonata No. 3): CBS (CD)

FRANZ LISZT
1811–1886 — Hungary

Busoni made the assumption that Bach was the foundation of piano playing, and Beethoven was the summit, and the two make Liszt possible. Within this enigmatic remark lies an essence. As Alan Walker puts it: "Liszt was the first modern pianist. The technical 'breakthrough' he achieved during the 1830s and '40s was without precedent in the history of the piano. All subsequent schools were branches of his tree. Rubinstein, Busoni, Paderewski, Godowsky and Rachmaninoff—all those pianists who together formed what historians later dubbed 'the golden age of piano playing'—would be unthinkable without Liszt. It was not that they copied his style of playing; that was inimitable. Nor did they enjoy close personal contact with him; not one of them was his pupil. Liszt's influence went deeper than that. It had to do with his unique ability to solve technical problems. Liszt is to piano playing what Euclid is to geometry. Pianists turn to his music in order to discover the natural laws governing the keyboard. It is impossible for a modern pianist to keep Liszt out of his playing—out of his biceps, his forearms, his fingers—even though he may not know that Liszt is there, since modern piano playing spells Liszt."

James Friskin stated: "No pianist who desires to develop a complete equipment can ignore the compositions of Liszt. . . . On the musical side they exhibit declamatory—one might say, histrionic—qualities that call for a corresponding approach from the executant. . . . The sentiment is sometimes superficial and the rhetoric, at its worst, becomes exaggerated and even vulgar; but when that has been admitted we have to realize that both sentiment and rhetoric give an opportunity for the development of freedom of expression and the discarding of hampering inhibitions that has undeniable value. At the same time Liszt asks for extremes of sonority and brilliance which tax all the player's muscular resources to the limit, and which have their own peculiar glitter."

Six Etudes d'exécution transcendante d'après Paganini

The *Paganini Etudes* were an epoch-making event in the history of virtuosity. They are based on Paganini's breathtaking Caprices (No. 3, *La Campanella*, is from the rondo of the B minor Violin Concerto). In addition to divining Paganini's infernal talents, Liszt took advantage of the piano's recent improvements in physical power, backed by iron, and of the increased flexibility of the Erard mechanism. A piece such as *La Campanella* would have been unthinkable in 1820. The *Paganini Etudes* were completed in 1838, and dedicated to Clara Wieck. Their difficulties were unseemly, and Liszt simplified them, without compromising their brilliance, in 1851; this later version is the one now performed. Humphrey Searle notes, "The difference is that between experimentation and mature mastery." The works are *Tremolo, Octaves, La Campanella, Arpeggios, La Chasse,* and *Theme and Variations.* In this last, Liszt used Paganini's Twenty-fourth Caprice, the theme which was also used by Brahms in his variations, and by Rachmaninoff in his *Rhapsody.*

ANIEVAS: Angel
DARRÉ: EMI (French)
JOHANSEN: Artist Direct
KENTNER: Vox
WATTS: CBS; Angel (CD)

Douze Etudes d'exécution transcendante

These twelve works constitute one of the most exciting cycles in music. They stand as a monument to Romanticism and a miraculous exploration of piano mechanism. Liszt produced a set of twelve in 1826 which contained the germ of the later edition. These earlier etudes are still boyhood works based on a Czerny technique. The second version was virtually unplayable, except by Liszt. A comparison of this version with Liszt's final setting, the one that is now used, reveals the genius of crystallization, a fabulous assimilation of idea and technique. These *Transcendental Etudes*, in their final form, opened new horizons for the instrument. It is significant that they are dedicated to Czerny, Liszt's only teacher. As Busoni said, "The final improvements are to be found in a greater ease and smooth playableness and a corresponding amount of impressive effect and character." 351

For Busoni, No. 1, *Preludio,* "is less a prelude to the cycle than a prelude to test the instrument and the disposition of the performer after stepping onto the concert platform." It is an invigorating piece—daring the pianist to begin the extraordinary cycle. No. 2, untitled, is all devilry, a madcap work for which Paganini was surely the inspiration. No. 3, *Paysage* ("Landscape"), provides a pastoral setting in which passion lurks. No. 4, *Mazeppa,* is a programmatic work inspired by Victor Hugo's poem of the same title; it portrays a Cossack tied to a wild stallion, and is one of the most exhausting works in the literature, a monumental workout for wrist and arm. No. 5, *Feux follets* ("Will o' the Wisps"), is in a class with Chopin's double-note etudes and the Schumann Toccata; Mendelssohn's fairy world is shimmeringly Lisztified. No. 6, *Vision,* is a work of impressive pomp. John Ogdon notes its "Berliozian splendour." On the technical side, Friskin refers to its "powerful chords embedded in sweeping arpeggios [and] double-note tremolandos." No. 7, *Eroica,* is more grandiose than heroic. No. 8, *Wilde Jagd* ("Wild Chase"), requires split-second reflexes and taxes the strength of the hand with tireless chords. Searle wrote, "In *Wilde Jagd* we have all the feeling of the romantic nocturnal hunt, celebrated in all German music from Weber onwards."

No. 9, *Ricordanza* ("Remembrance"), presents an excruciating, ripe sentiment embedded in ardent ornamentation, perfectly calculated, "with a richness of tonal effect that comes from an exact appreciation of the special qualities of the piano's different registers," as Friskin put it. Busoni felt *Ricordanza* "gives the impression of a packet of yellowed love letters." No. 10, marked Allegro agitato molto, is untitled, and the most often played of the set. It is feverish and charged with breathless tension. No. 11, *Harmonies du soir* ("Evening Harmonies"), is nearly ten minutes long. It "looks forward," in Ogdon's words, "to the evanescent textures of Debussy and the massive chordal writing of Rachmaninoff. [It is] highly sustained, almost ecstatic in its lyricism." It gushes with the perfumes of a summer evening. No. 12, *Chasse-neige* ("Snowscape"): technically the melody and tremolando accompaniment need the utmost care in tonal balance. As Louis Kentner states: "Many Lisztians look upon the concluding piece as the greatest of the studies. Indeed, it is unique in its mood of desolation. It is as if the softly falling snowflakes gradually covered the whole world, burying man and beast, while the wind moans." Busoni goes so far as to say that *Chasse-neige* is "the noblest example, perhaps, amongst all music of a poetising nature." It is amazing that this work is still little known among pianists.

ARRAU: Philips (CD)
BERMAN: Columbia/Melodiya
BOLET: London (CD)
CLIDAT: Vega
CZIFFRA: Angel
JOHANSEN: Artist Direct
KENTNER: Vox
SHERMAN: Vanguard

Trois Etudes de concert
No. 1, *Il Lamento,* is long, ten minutes, and displays a cloying sentiment. No. 2, *La Leggierezza,* is popular, with its graceful, decorative chromaticism; a perfect piece of piano writing. In No. 3, *Un Sospiro,* "one sigh" is expressed in cross-hand effects within ascending and descending arpeggiation. It is a fine example of Liszt's utilization of Thalberg's three-handed effects.

ARRAU: Philips
BOLET: L'Oiseau-Lyre
JOHANSEN: Artist Direct
LORTIE: Chandos (CD)

Deux Etudes de concert (1862–63)
Both pieces—No. 1, *Waldesrauschen* ("Forest Murmurs"), and No. 2, *Gnomenreigen* ("Dance of the Gnomes")—are among the most frequently played of Liszt's etudes. Ravel

352

surely knew the shimmering pianistic layout of *Waldesrauschen,* a magical scene in a wooded glade. *Gnomenreigen* is Mendelssohn turned diabolic, a goblin scherzo in which the salient feature, according to Friskin, is "delicate hand staccato. . . . The alternative theme is a searching test of finger technique and rotational freedom."

BOLET: L'Oiseau-Lyre
KENTNER: Vox
WILD: Etcetera (CD)

Liebesträume—Three Nocturnes
These are transcriptions of Liszt's own songs. No. 3, a passionate love poem, is one of the most famous piano pieces ever written.

BARENBOIM: DG (CD)
CLIDAT: PG
CURZON (No. 3): London
RUBINSTEIN (No. 3): RCA

Six Consolations
There is a quasi-religious feel to these short sketches, all of which are lyric in character and among the easiest of Liszt's piano works. No. 3, in D-flat, is popular and often heard without its companions.

BARENBOIM: DG
BOLET: Ensayo (CD)
HOROWITZ (No. 3): RCA
KATIN: London
RUBINSTEIN (No. 3): RCA
THIBAUDET: Denon (CD)

Berceuse (1862)
Inspired by Chopin's Berceuse, and also in D-flat. A first version (1854) is quite simple in statement and sentiment; in the ensuing years, Liszt turned his earlier version into a ten-minute score that was quite startlingly different. The melodic line became profusely embellished with the most gorgeous ornamentation. The work is, unfortunately, all but unknown.

CLIDAT: PG
CURZON: London

Ballade No. 2 in B minor (1853)
There is a growing interest in this fascinating score, so different in nature from the Chopin Ballades. Sacheverell Sitwell feels Liszt is here "concerned, as it were, less with personal suffering than with great happenings on the epical scale, barbarian invasions, cities in flames—tragedies of public, more than private, import."

ARRAU: Philips
BAR-ILLAN: Audiofon
HOROWITZ: RCA (CD)
LEWENTHAL: Angel
MARVIN: Genesis
NYIREGYHÁZI: IPA—Desmar
WILD: Quintessence

Mephisto Waltz No. 1 (1860)
Liszt composed four *Mephisto Waltzes* and a *Mephisto Polka.* No. 1 is one of his greatest works; every measure is bold. The work was inspired by Lenau's *Faust* and is subtitled *The Dance in the Village Inn.* The scene is played out by Faust, Mephistopheles, and Marguerite. The opening, "the Devil tuning up his fiddle," writes Kentner, "is surely one of the most daring things created by any pre-Bartók composer." The middle-section theme and its working out in the seductive key of D-flat greatly influenced Scriabin. For James Huneker, it is "one of the most voluptuous episodes outside the *Tristan* score. That halting, languorous, syncopated theme is marvelously expressive."

ASHKENAZY: London
BAR-ILLAN: Audiofon
BOLET: Everest
BROWNING: Seraphim
GUTIÉRREZ: Angel
KAPELL: RCA
KATSARIS: Telefunken
RÁNKI: Denon (CD)
RUBINSTEIN: RCA
WILD: Vanguard

Bénédiction de Dieu dans la solitude (No. 3 of "Harmonies poétiques et religieuses")

Funérailles (No. 7 of "Harmonies poétiques et religieuses")

The complete *Harmonies poétiques et religieuses* is an imposing but uneven set of ten pieces, of which Nos. 3 and 7 are masterworks. "The *Bénédiction*," writes Searle, "is indeed almost unique among Liszt's works in that it expresses that feeling of mystical contemplation which Beethoven attained in his last period, but which is rarely found elsewhere in music." Liszt used the ecstatic Lamartine poem for inspiration: "Whence comes, O God, this peace that overwhelms me? Whence comes this faith with which my heart overflows?" *Funérailles,* with its tumultuous octaves for the left hand, was dedicated to the memory of Chopin. It has the blackness of despair, the clangor of bells, and a grandeur in the piano scoring that is unforgettable.

Bénédiction:
ARRAU: Philips
BRENDEL: Philips
DUCHABLE: Erato
E. LEVY: Unicorn
OHLSSON: Angel
ROSE: Vox

Funérailles:
BARÈRE: Turnabout
BERMAN: Melodiya
CHERKASSKY: Nimbus (CD)
HOROWITZ: RCA (CD); Seraphim
OHLSSON: Angel

Années de pèlerinage (1836–77)

Liszt's *Years of Pilgrimage* consist of twenty-six pieces: *First Year: Switzerland; Second Year: Italy;* and *Third Year,* a compilation of works from his later period. These pieces occupied him sporadically from 1836 to 1877 and constitute a characteristic achievement of musical Romanticism. All facets of Liszt's many-sided personality are revealed. His love for nature is magnificently illustrated in the

Suisse years. "The Swiss pieces are pure nature," writes Kentner, "lakes, springs, cowbells, church-bells, Alpine horn—all these effects appear, drawn with astonishing precision by the hand of a master."

In Book II, *Italie* (1846–49), Liszt's inspiration comes from his contemplation of great painting, sculpture, poetry, and literature. *Sposalizio,* No. 1, was derived from Raphael's famous painting. No. 2, *Il Penseroso,* was inspired by Michelangelo, while the three *Sonetti* are passionate musical translations of Petrarch sonnets. The *Third Year* (1867–77) exhibits Liszt the pioneer harmonist opening new musical paths, as in the impressionist *Les Jeux d'eaux à la Villa d'Este.* Alice Levine Mitchell wrote: "The individual pieces in the *Années de pèlerinage* . . . by virtue of their programmatic orientation, their poetic inspiration, and their relationship to the natural landscape, give voice to the distinctive language of Romantic musical art. The collection may be considered in effect an encyclopedia of Romantic expression."

Années de pèlerinage (*complete*):
BERMAN: DG
CZIFFRA: Connoisseur Society
ROSE: Vox

First Year: Switzerland:
BARENBOIM: DG (CD)
VILLA: Second Hearing (CD)

Vallée d'Obermann (No. 6 of First Year: Switzerland)

Inspired by Etienne de Senancour's novel and by far the longest of the Swiss set of the *Années,* this is a voluptuous Byronic work involving thematic transformation.

ARRAU: Philips

Au bord d'une source (No. 4 of First Year: Switzerland)

A difficult and evocative piece. One can hear each drop of water in this exquisite and perfect work.

HOROWITZ: RCA

Tre Sonetti del Petrarca (Nos. 4, 5, and 6 of Second Year: Italy)

The *Sonetti* are highly charged love poems. Liszt transcribed these for solo piano from his own songs. The *Sonnet No. 47* is the weakest, but *104* and *123* are masterful works expressing erotic passion in settings of superb pianistic beauty.

BARENBOIM: DG
BROWNING: Delos (CD)
HOROWITZ: RCA
LIPATTI: EMI
WEISSENBERG: Connoisseur Society

Après une lecture de Dante—Fantasia quasi sonata (No. 7 of Second Year: Italy)

The *Dante Sonata*, the largest work of the second volume of the *Années*, is a massive chordal composition; a grim, Luciferian tone poem with a love scene, chaos, and redemption. In a great performance, it is an exalted work.

ARRAU: Philips (CD)
BAR-ILLAN: RCA
BEAN: Westminster
BERMAN: DG
BRENDEL: Turnabout
BROWNING: Delos (CD)
KENTNER: EMI Odéon

Les Jeux d'eaux à la Villa d'Este (from Third Year of "Années de pèlerinage")

In later years, Liszt lived at the Villa d'Este at Tivoli, near Rome, overlooking the celebrated fountains. Liszt evokes an impressionism which is ecclesiastical yet with a marked sensuality; one of the masterpieces of his late period.

ARRAU: Philips
BRENDEL: Philips
KENTNER: EMI Odéon

Fantasia and Fugue on the Name B–A–C–H (1855)

Originally an organ work, which Liszt transcribed for piano in 1870. It is music of tremendous power, nobility, and theatricality.

BEAN: Westminster
BRENDEL: Philips
CZIFFRA: Philips
PONTI: HK (CD)

Variations on a Theme of Bach (1862)

An important and virtually unknown work of impressive concentration, based on a theme from Bach's cantata *Weinen, Klagen, Sorgen, Zagen.*

BRENDEL: Philips
JOHANSEN: Artist Direct
PONTI: HK (CD)
SILVERMAN: Orion

Deux Légendes (1863)

Liszt's genius for descriptive writing is nowhere better realized than in his two Franciscan *Legends*. No. 1, *Saint Francis of Assisi Preaching to the Birds,* makes use of the keyboard's upper register, combining trills and melody in the same hand. In the wrong hands No. 2, *Saint Francis of Paolo Walking on the Waves,* can be merely bombastic; in sympathetic hands, however, it is a monumental work.

BRENDEL: Philips (CD)
CZIFFRA (No. 2): Philips
DUCHABLE: Erato (CD)
HEIDSIECK: Cassiopée
JOHANSEN: Artist Direct
KARS (No. 2): London
KEMPFF (No. 1): DG
VÁSÁRY (No. 2): DG

Valse impromptu (1850)

A wonderful piece of fluff—this is a perfect encore number, on which Moszkowski modeled some of his work.

LYMPANY: Angel
RUBINSTEIN: RCA
WEISSENBERG: EMI

Quatre Valses oubliées (1881–85)

These late works express a curious languor, nostalgia, and amorousness in a forward-looking harmonic scheme. The *Valse oubliée* No. 1 in F-sharp major is the best known of Liszt's late music.

FARNADI: Westminster
HOROWITZ (No. 1): DG (CD)
JOHANSEN: Artist Direct

Polonaise No. 2 in E major

No. 1 in C minor is easier and more poetic than No. 2 but is unknown. The E major Polonaise was once popular but has now slipped from the repertoire. There is a sense of pageantry in this very un-Chopinesque work.

CHERKASSKY: Mercury
GRAINGER: Pearl
RACHMANINOFF: RCA
WILD: Etcetera (CD)

Rhapsodie espagnole (1863)

One of the earliest musical excursions into Spain, based on two Spanish themes, the *Spanish Rhapsody* is a grandiose piece which cries out for pianists in the old heroic mold. At sixteen minutes it is an impressive concert piece, and should be far better known. Busoni transcribed it for piano and orchestra. During the 78 era it was recorded by Egon Petri with Dmitri Mitropoulos conducting.

ARRAU: Desmar
BERMAN: Columbia/Melodiya
CZIFFRA: Angel
LELCHUK: Telarc (CD)
MARSH, Freeman/London Philharmonic (arr. Busoni): MMG (CD)

The Nineteen Hungarian Rhapsodies

With these works, Liszt opened the way for a flood of works in national costume. The Rhapsodies exhibit Liszt's histrionic, virtuoso nature, and unfortunately the once-excessive popularity of a few of them has caused his reputation far more harm than good. They remain a unique literature, requiring from the pianist a high temperament, sense of color, and gregariousness. Each Rhapsody is a showpiece which abounds in spine-tingling pianistic effects, and their gypsy flavor is irresistible to audiences.

CAMPANELLA: Philips
CZIFFRA: Connoisseur Society
KENTNER: Vox
RUBINSTEIN (Nos. 3, 10, 12): RCA
SZIDON: DG

Individual Rhapsodies:
No. 2:
FRIEDHEIM: IPA–Desmar
FRIEDMAN: Arabesque
HOFMANN: IPA–Desmar
HOROWITZ (his own arrangement): RCA
RACHMANINOFF (with his own cadenza): RCA

No. 6:
HOROWITZ: RCA
LEVITZKI: Arabesque

No. 9:
GILELS: Melodiya

No. 11:
KAPELL: RCA

No. 13:
BUSONI: Arabesque

No. 14:
HAMBOURG: Arabesque

No. 15:
GRAINGER (abbr.): IPA–Desmar
HOROWITZ (his own arrangement): RCA
SOLOMON: Arabesque

No. 19:
HOROWITZ (his own arrangement): CBS

Sonata in B minor (1852–53)

Premiered by von Bülow in 1857, the Sonata is one of the glories of the piano literature and Liszt's greatest achievement as a musical architect. Never before or after was he able to develop and sustain his thought on such an inspired and flawless level within a large form. The B minor Sonata was dedicated to Schumann, who had dedicated his own C major Fantasy, Op. 17, to Liszt. William S. Newman affirms, "The two nineteenth century masterpieces . . . stand almost alone in the heat and inspiration of their full-bloomed Romanticism." When Wagner heard Liszt's pupil, Karl Klindworth, play this work, he wrote to Liszt: "The Sonata is beautiful beyond all belief, great, lovable, deep, and noble, just as you are." The writer Peter Yates asserts that "Liszt's Piano Sonata in B minor stands isolated as the most successful formal organization of the nineteenth century stylistic conglomerate. . . . He spread the single-movement sonata form over an entire large Sonata, somewhat in the manner of Schubert's *Wanderer* Fantasy, without breaks to distinguish movements." The large expanse covered by Liszt was based on his own concept of thematic transformation. The entire work germinates from five themes. Sharon Winklhofer has written a valuable book, *Liszt's Sonata in B minor: A study of Autograph Sources and Documents.*

ARRAU: Philips
BARÈRE: Turnabout
BRENDEL: Philips (CD)
BROWNING: Delos (CD)
CHERKASSKY: Nimbus (CD)
CLIBURN: RCA
CURZON: London
DARRÉ: Vanguard
FLEISHER: Epic
GABOS: DG
GILELS: RCA
GUTIÉRREZ: Angel
HOROWITZ: Seraphim
KUERTI: Aquitaine
E. LEVY: Unicorn
WEISSENBERG: Angel

Piano Concerto No. 1 in E-flat major
Liszt's First Concerto, with its dashing opening theme followed by heraldic antiphonal octaves, is in one continuous movement with four sections. Imagine being in Weimar in 1855 for its premiere—with Liszt as soloist and Berlioz conducting. Although the concerto has always been popular, it has acquired a musically poor reputation because of the many vulgar, exhibitionistic performances it has received. Nevertheless, it is a masterpiece.

ARRAU, Ormandy/Philadelphia: CBS
BERMAN, Giulini/Vienna Symphony: DG
DE GREEF, Ronald/Royal Albert Hall: Opal
GUTIÉRREZ, Previn/London Symphony: Angel
JANIS, Kondrashin/Moscow Philharmonic: Mercury
MARSH, Freeman/London Philharmonic: MMG (CD)
RICHTER, Kondrashin/London Symphony: Philips (CD)
RUBINSTEIN, Wallenstein/RCA Symphony: RCA (CD)
SAUER, Weingartner: Turnabout
WATTS, Bernstein/New York Philharmonic: CBS

Piano Concerto No. 2 in A major
The Second Concerto, described by critic William Apthorp as "The Life and Adventures of a Theme," is Romantically successful and poetic, less showy and more diffuse than No. 1. The orchestration in both works is original and filled with piquant touches.

BOLET, Zinman/Rochester Philharmonic: Vox Cum Laude
CLIBURN, Ormandy/Philadelphia: RCA
DUCHABLE, Conlon/London Philharmonic: Erato (CD)
FRANÇOIS, Silvestri/Philharmonia: Seraphim
VÁSÁRY, Prohaska/Bamberg Symphony: DG

Totentanz for Piano and Orchestra (1859)
This masterly set of variations on the *Dies Irae* was inspired by Andrea Orcagna's frescoes, *The Triumph of Death,* which Liszt first saw when he was twenty-seven. This work has a chilling impact when played by a dramatic

pianist. The virtuosic writing is a good example of Liszt's genius for creating electrifying effects that are always more manageable than they look on the page or sound.

BÉROFF, Masur/Leipzig Gewandhaus: Angel
BRAILOWSKY, Ormandy/Philadelphia: Odyssey
FREIRE, Kempe/Munich Philharmonic: Columbia
JANIS, Reiner/Chicago Symphony: RCA
WATTS, Leinsdorf/London Symphony: CBS

Hungarian Fantasy
Also known as Fantasia on Hungarian Folk Tunes, this work uses the same material as the Hungarian Rhapsody No. 14.

CAMPANELLA, Ceccato/Monte Carlo Opera: Philips
CHERKASSKY, Karajan/Berlin Philharmonic: DG
SOLOMON, Susskind/Philharmonia: EMI

Malédiction for Piano and Strings (1840)
Almost unknown, this early work has an intriguing Romantic sensibility. Of *Malédiction* (under a curse), Robert Collet observes: "The work has much charm; the mingling of Byronic defiance, great tenderness and a touch of religious sentiment is very characteristic."

BÉROFF, Masur/Leipzig Gewandhaus: Angel
BRENDEL, Gielen/Vienna Symphony: Turnabout

Arrangements, Transcriptions, Paraphrases
These were the stock-in-trade of virtuosi during much of the nineteenth century. Liszt, in spite of his startling originality as a composer, seemed almost compelled—sometimes with good intentions, sometimes not—to re-create other composers' music in his own image, or, at the very least, to translate it into piano terms. His was very much an experimental mind, and he approached many of his "tran-scriptions" with the utmost seriousness, subjecting some of them to constant revision. The opera fantasies are especially intriguing, for in these he gave himself free rein to exploit the instrument in ways he never quite permitted himself in his original piano music. Without knowing the operatic fantasies, one cannot appreciate the full impact of Liszt's technical system, which brought the resources of both the instrument and the player to a degree of development previously undreamed of, and which raised pianistic effects (even "tricks") to a level of sheer wizardry. In recent years, many pianists have once again been finding these works fascinating.

Mozart-Liszt: Réminiscences de "Don Juan" (1814)
The *Don Juan* Fantasy, based on Mozart's *Don Giovanni,* is one of the legendary pieces in the literature. Even when Liszt's reputation was in decline, there were pianists around to confront the "Don." Its title is perfect, too, for this is a true reminiscence of the great opera, interpreted by a nineteenth-century mind. Technically, it is abominably difficult; unlike other works by Liszt, it is even more difficult than it sounds. Harold Schonberg once wrote, "I have come to the conclusion that to play Liszt well you have to have in your breast a good-sized dollop of original sin." To play this work requires technical amplitude and a temperament yearning to let loose its pandemonium.

BARÈRE: Remington
BOLET: L'Oiseau-Lyre
OGDON: Seraphim
ROSEN: Epic
WILD: Vanguard

Bellini-Liszt: Réminiscences de "Norma" (1841)
Liszt extracts the essence of Bellini's opera. Kaikhosru Sorabji even remarked that "Bellini's themes never had, by themselves, the

grandeur and magnificence that Liszt is able to infuse into them." Of the B major section, Busoni felt "anyone who had listened to or played [it] . . . without being moved has not yet arrived at Liszt." Liszt took Thalberg's pedaling and three-handed effect and instilled new sonorous developments into them. Ivan Davis has written, "For me, this is one of Liszt's greatest creations as well as one of the most stupendously difficult, both technically and architecturally."

BRENDEL: Turnabout
DAVIS: Audiofon
LEWENTHAL: RCA

Donizetti-Liszt: "Lucia di Lammermoor" Paraphrase (1836)

This paraphrase is based only on the famous sextet at the close of the second act of *Lucia di Lammermoor*. Just compare any one of the many other transcriptions of this slice of the opera with Liszt's to fully understand Liszt's musical ways and means.

BOLET: RCA
BRENDEL: Turnabout

Verdi-Liszt: "Rigoletto" Paraphrase (1863)

The *Rigoletto* concert paraphrase is by far the best known of Liszt's works based on Verdi. Here, he expands the celebrated quartet from the opera.

ARRAU: Philips
BOLET: RCA
CHERKASSKY: Mercury
CZIFFRA: Connoisseur Society or EMI Pathé
GINZBURG: Melodiya
VÁSÁRY: DG

Meyerbeer-Liszt: Réminiscences de "Robert le diable"—Valse infernale (1841)

Meyerbeer was the most successful composer of grand opera in Europe during the 1830s and 1840s. Liszt penned four works based on

his hits: *Illustrations de "l'Africaine," Illustrations du "Prophète," Grande Fantaisie sur "Les Huguenots,"* and this Valse. The *Valse infernale* is raucous and racy. When Wagner heard Liszt play it, he wrote: "Someday Liszt will be obliged in heaven to play before the assembled angels his Fantasia on the Devil! But probably for the last time." It demands the strength and endurance of a giant with the right dose of mockery and fun. There was a time when to play one of these maligned creations was almost certainly to invite hostile reviews. Audiences might quiver with delight while listening to one of these ingenious transformations, but Liszt was always accused of tampering with the genius of others.

WILD: Vanguard

Gounod-Liszt: Valse de l'opéra "Faust" (1861)

In his approach to Mephistopheles, Liszt is unique. This work, built on Gounod's *Faust*, is one of the best waltz paraphrases ever contrived. Sacheverell Sitwell felt Liszt brought the trivial tune "to a higher spiritual plane than it could ever aspire to on its own merits."

BARÈRE: Turnabout
GINZBURG: Melodiya
PETRI: Westminster
WILD: Vanguard

Berlioz-Liszt: Symphonie fantastique (1833)

Liszt produced this piece as an act of support for the unknown avant-garde Berlioz. His objective in such a transcription, in contrast to his *réminiscences* and paraphrases, was to translate the composer's intention more or less faithfully to the piano, which in the case of Berlioz's glowing orchestration is a seemingly impossible task. In his memoirs, Charles Hallé noted that following a performance of the "March to the Scaffold" from the symphony conducted by Berlioz, Liszt "played his own arrangement for piano alone of the same piece, with an effect even surpassing that of the full orchestra, and creating an indescribable furor."

BIRET: Finnadar

Mendelssohn-Liszt: Wedding March and Dance of the Elves from "A Midsummer Night's Dream"

This has always been played, but Horowitz's version, with his own touches, surpasses the original in brilliance.

CZIFFRA: Connoisseur Society
HOROWITZ: RCA
KENTNER: Turnabout
PETRI: Westminster

Tchaikovsky-Liszt: Polonaise from "Eugene Onegin" (1880)

A marvelous composition; Liszt's only paraphrase of any Tchaikovsky work. Tatiana's love theme is used as well.

CZIFFRA: Connoisseur Society

Beethoven-Liszt: Adelaide

A free transcription of a Beethoven song, marvelously made for the piano.

PETRI: Westminster
VILLA: Spectrum

Beethoven-Liszt: Symphony No. 5 in C minor

Liszt transcribed all of the Beethoven symphonies for the piano, somehow achieving all the finer points of detail. Characteristic of these is his version of the most famous symphony in history, No. 5; it is an amazing re-creative act.

GOULD: Columbia

Wagner-Liszt: Overture to "Tannhäuser"

Liszt produced twelve Wagner adaptations; the largest is the *Tannhäuser* overture. (The erotic, trembling *Liebestod*, splendidly "re-orchestrated" for the piano, is the best known of this group.)

BOLET: RCA
CZIFFRA: Connoisseur Society
KERER: Melodiya
SMITH: Unicorn

The Lieder Literature

Liszt was especially fond of transcribing the song literature. Sometimes he is quite faithful to the original, and other times he can be far more fanciful. In 1838 he transcribed twelve Schubert lieder, including the famous "Erlkönig," "Der Wanderer," "Ave Maria," "Du bist die Ruh," "Gretchen am Spinnrade," and "Auf dem Wasser zu singen." These are freer than his later renderings of the *Schwanengesang* and *Winterreise* cycles.

Liszt's transcriptions of Schumann's "Widmung" and "Frühlingsnacht" are among his best, and the Mendelssohn-Liszt *Auf Flügeln des Gesanges* ("On Wings of Song") is well known. The transcriptions of six Chopin songs come under the heading *Six Chants polonais;* the two best known of these are *The Maiden's Wish* and *My Joys.* The former is played by Hofmann (RCA) with indescribable pianism. *My Joys,* a nocturne of exquisite beauty, is played magnificently by Rosenthal (RCA).

The Late Music

Liszt's late music has come into its own only in the last few decades. Many of his contemporaries thought these works were merely the eccentric toying of a disillusioned man who had once known the glories of the world. In these later works, he opened a new vista, using whole-tone scales, chords in fourths, ambiguous tonality; the music, it seemed, was abandoned in mid-measure. He moved toward both impressionism and expressionism. How far Liszt had traveled from his showiest Rhapsodies to music that would later amaze Debussy, Stravinsky, and Bartók! According to

John Ogdon, "Liszt was responsible for breaking the Germanic stranglehold on nineteenth century composers, and scattering the seeds of modern music almost literally to the four winds. His music shows an avant-garde attitude to the problems of composing which was without parallel in the nineteenth century."

Some of the most extraordinary of these pieces are:

Elegy No. 2:
KENTNER: Turnabout

Unstern, Sinistre, Disastro;
Csárdás macabre;
Schlaflos, Frage und Antwort:
BRENDEL: Philips

Nuages gris;
La Lugubre Gondola No. 1:
KARS: London

La Lugubre Gondola No. 2:
BRENDEL: Turnabout; Philips (CD)

En rêve:
BAR-ILLAN: Audiofon
WATTS: Angel (CD)

EDWARD MACDOWELL
1861–1908 — United States

MacDowell wrote the most distinctive music by any American during the 1890s. As Virgil Thomson states, he is "our nearest to a great master before Ives. His short works for piano still speak to us." He was a master at producing music with a sweet, nostalgic lyricism. Living in an emerging industrial America, he yearned for the romance of the old sagas. H. E. Krehbiel wrote: "MacDowell aimed at depicting the mood of things and the moods awakened by things rather than the things themselves. He was fond of subjects and titles which . . . smack of the woods—not the greenwood of the English ballads, but the haunted forests of Germany, in which nymphs and dryads hold their revels and kobolds frolic."

Until at least 1925, MacDowell was considered the preeminent American composer. "However," wrote Gilbert Chase, "he does not mark the beginning of a new epoch in American music, but the closing of a fading era, the *fin de siècle* decline of the genteel tradition which had dominated American art since the days of Hopkinson and Hewitt."

Twelve Virtuoso Studies, Op. 46 (1894)
The best of these pieces—such as *Moto Perpetuo, Wild Chase, Elfin Dance, Burlesque,* and *Bluette*—are treasures, showing MacDowell at his best. MacDowell also wrote a set of Twelve Etudes, Op. 39, the best known being

361

the *Shadow Dance*, while the very effective *Etude de concert*, Op. 36, and the *Hexentanz*, Op. 17, No. 2, are scintillating encore pieces.

Twelve Virtuoso Studies:
FRAGER: New World
JOCHUM: Golden Crest

Eight Sea Pieces, Op. 55 (1900)
The *Sea Pieces*—with titles such as *In Mid-Ocean, From a Wandering Iceberg, Starlight, Nautilus*—reflect the graver side of MacDowell. Little fingerwork is required for this slowly paced music.

BENNETTE: Grenadilla
SWEM: Orion

First Modern Suite, Op. 10 (1881)
Second Modern Suite, Op. 14 (1883)
Both of these suites have musical interest, especially No. 1, with its rolling Praeludium and the finely spun staccato study of the Presto movement. The fugue finale begins in an academic vein but quickly turns to bravura.

FIERRO (First Suite): Nonesuch
SWEM (Second Suite): Orion

Ten Woodland Sketches, Op. 51 (1896)
Some of MacDowell's most glowing writing. *To a Wild Rose* is his most celebrated piece, based on an Iroquois Indian melody. *To a Water-Lily* is exquisite.

DRAKE: Genesis
LYTHGOE: Philips
RIVKIN: Westminster

Sonata No. 1 in G minor, Op. 45, "Tragica" (1893)
Sonata No. 2 in G minor, Op. 50, "Eroica" (1895)
Sonata No. 3 in D minor, Op. 57, "Norse" (1900)
Sonata No. 4 in E minor, Op. 59, "Keltic" (1901)
MacDowell's are the most significant of Romantic American sonatas of the nineteenth century. In them he strove, perhaps too much, for "greatness." The piano style acquired a turbid thickness. His ideas, often excellent in themselves, stagnate in the context of the large form. But "whatever his limitations," wrote William S. Newman, "performers are likely to return to one or another of his Sonatas again and again. . . . The Sonatas abound in frank songful melody, in opportunities to emote with judicious abandon, and in piano writing that makes good sounds and pleasurable technical challenges." The Sonata No. 1 is the noblest of the four. The *Sonata Eroica* contains some of MacDowell's most beautiful pages. The Third and Fourth Sonatas are dedicated to Grieg, whom MacDowell loved and had much in common with.

The Four Sonatas:
TOCCO: Gasparo (CD)

Sonata No. 1:
CORBATÓ: Orion
RIVKIN: Westminster

Sonata No. 2:
LYTHGOE: Philips

Sonata No. 3:
MANDEL: Desto

Sonata No. 4:
BATES: Orion
FIERRO: Nonesuch
MITCHELL: Vanguard

Piano Concerto No. 1 in A minor, Op. 15
Though overshadowed by the finer Second Concerto, the Op. 15 has heaping handfuls of chords and a surging appeal which make it an entertaining showcase. The Andante tranquillo is imbued with, as James Lyons puts it, "the demi-tinted landscaping which was to be MacDowell's hallmark."

LIST, Chávez/Vienna State Opera: Westminster
RIVKIN, Dixon/Vienna State Opera: Westminster

Piano Concerto No. 2 in D minor, Op. 23 (1890)

The Second Concerto is the only nineteenth-century concerto by an American to have even a small place in the international repertoire. It was dedicated to Teresa Carreño, who also popularized it. It is a striking example of a Romantic concerto in the grand heroic manner.

CLIBURN, Hendl/Chicago Symphony: RCA
SZIDON, Downes/London Philharmonic: DG
WILD, Freccia/National Philharmonic: Quintessence

FRANK MARTIN
1890–1974—Switzerland

Martin wrote music of lasting value. He combines a French clarity of texture with German harmonic idioms. From 1933 on, Martin integrated some of Schoenberg's twelve-tone system into his own highly charged chromaticism. Martin's rhythms are often original, as is his passionate musical diction. He left only a small output for piano, but each work is important.

Eight Preludes (1948)

The Eight Preludes, twenty-one minutes in length, composed for Dinu Lipatti, are considered by Maurice Hinson to be "one of the major contributions to the twentieth century piano literature."

SILVERMAN: Orion

Guitare—Quatre Pièces brèves (1933)
Clair de lune (1952)
Esquisse (1965)
Etude rythmique (1965)
Fantaisie sur des rythmes flamenco (1973)

Guitare is dedicated to Segovia and was composed in 1933. The composer transcribed it for piano in the late 1950s, and it sounds magnificent. The Four Pieces are titled *Prélude, Air, Plainte,* and *Comme une gigue. Clair de lune* is the sparest of the works and the easiest to play. *Esquisse* was composed for a Munich piano competition; marked Allegretto tranquillo, it was intended as a test of sight-reading skill. The *Etude rythmique* is an homage to the composer Jacques Dalcroze. In it, a 9/8 meter in the right is pitted against a 3/4 meter in the left. The *Fantaisie sur des rythmes flamenco* is one of Martin's most amazing creations in any genre. Composed on a commission from Paul Badura-Skoda, it was also intended to be danced by the composer's daughter, Anne-Thérèse, a flamenco dancer. The four sections, totaling sixteen minutes in length, are *Rumba lente, Rumba rapide, Soleares,* and *Petenera.* Regarding the flamenco dance, Martin wrote: "I had been fascinated more by the mixture of tragedy, dignity in the face of destiny, and joy which this art expresses, than by its complexity and richness of rhythms."

LA BRECQUE: Opus One

Concerto No. 2 for Piano and Orchestra

The Second Concerto does not have immediate appeal. It lacks the concentration of the solo piano pieces, although it has a forcefulness all its own. The three movements are Con moto, Lento, and Presto. It was premiered in 1970 by Paul Badura-Skoda, for whom it was conceived.

BADURA-SKODA, Martin/Luxembourg Radio: Candide

NICOLAI MEDTNER
1880–1951—Russia

Medtner is an important piano composer who has remained on the fringes of the performing repertoire. He has had his boosters, including Rachmaninoff, whom he often resembles superficially. There are pianists, of the mighty caliber of Gilels, who believe in him and program him regularly. Medtner's work is often of great beauty in thematic shape, but the subtlety of his designs has little immediate appeal, as compared with Rachmaninoff. "His music," states Ernest Newman, "is not always easy to follow at first hearing, but not because of any extravagance of thought or confusion of technique, it is simply because this music really does go on thinking from bar to bar, evolving logically from its premises."

Medtner was basically a composer involved with sonata principles—"he was born with sonata form," uttered his delighted teacher, the academic-minded Sergei Taneyev. But with all of his contrapuntal expertise and rhythmical ingenuity, there is a certain cerebral quality, which for stretches provides a dry effect within his Romantic context.

Piano Concerti Nos. 1, 2, and 3
Medtner's three piano concerti are of interest. Concerto No. 1 in C minor (1918) is in one brilliantly conceived movement and has much to recommend it. The composer plays it beautifully, along with a moving performance of his *Sonata tragica,* Op. 39, No. 5.

The massive Concerto No. 2 in C minor (1927) is dedicated to Rachmaninoff. This is a work of forty-three minutes, in three movements: Toccata, Romance, and Divertissement. There is much complicated piano scoring.

The Concerto No. 3 in E minor, *Ballade* (1940–42), is the finest of the three concerti in overall content. The piano writing is elaborate but less thickly constructed. It runs to half an hour.

Concerto No. 1, Op. 33:
MEDTNER, Weldon: Melodiya
ZHUKOV, Dmitriev/Moscow Radio Symphony: Melodiya/EMI

Concerto No. 2, Op. 50:
SHATSKES, Svetlanov/USSR State Symphony: Melodiya

Concerto No. 3, Op. 60:
MEDTNER: Melodiya
NIKOLAYEVA, Svetlanov/Moscow Radio Symphony: Melodiya
PONTI, Cao/Luxembourg Radio: Candide

Sonata in G minor, Op. 22 (1911)
This is a coherent work, with a great many tempo changes. It's a very good recital sonata and its seventeen minutes are of considerable pianistic interest.

GILELS: Odyssey/Melodiya
PONTI: Candide

Sonata in C minor, Op. 25, No. 1, "Fairy Tale"
The first of the three movements is marked Allegro abbandonamente. One of Medtner's characteristics is his use of unexpected cross-rhythms.

AXELROD: Melodiya
BINNS: HNH

Improvisation, Op. 31, No. 1
This is Medtner at his best. It has a haunting, lyric theme, which is subjected to cobweb elaborations. It needs virtuosity to bring it to life.

MEDTNER: Melodiya
WILD: RCA

Sonata-reminiscenza in A minor, Op. 38, No. 1 (1914)
Gilels, in a recording of a 1969 recital at Carnegie Hall, plays up the sonata's introspective side. He says this work is "very Romantic, and brings together Russian and Western traditions."

GILELS: MHS or Melodiya/Angel

Sonata romantica in B-flat minor, Op. 53,
   No. 1   (1930)
The *Romantica* is the penultimate of Medtner's fourteen solo piano sonatas. In four
movements, it is a complex and dreamlike
work, with swirls of polyphony. All the main
themes of the work return for a final appearance in the coda.

GRAHAM: MHS

Fairy Tales
Medtner composed twenty-eight pieces that
he called *Fairy Tales,* and these small works
are among his best productions. Leonid Sabaneyev wrote, "In his *Fairy Tales,* Medtner is
neither heavenly nor ethereal, nor in the
clouds, but earthy, subterranean."

GRAHAM (Op. 26, Nos. 1–4; Op. 20, Nos. 1
   & 2; Op. 8, Nos. 1 & 2): MHS
SHATSKES (Op. 8, No. 1; Op. 42, No. 1; Op.
   48, No. 2; Op. 14, No. 1; Op. 34, Nos. 3
   & 4): Melodiya

FELIX MENDELSSOHN
1809–1847 — Germany

The word *dated,* which was once applied to
a large amount of Mendelssohn's writing, has
now practically disappeared from discussions
of his work. This is mainly the result of a more
thorough knowledge of historical style; also,
recordings have been kind to Mendelssohn's
varied output. His better piano music is unrivaled in its evocation of the Kingdom of
Oberon, an enchanted fairyland of elves and
sunlight. Ernest Hutcheson had in mind the E
minor Scherzo, the *Spinning Song, Rondo
capriccioso,* and other works of scherzando
origin when he wrote: "These pieces dart or
hover on gossamer wings. Transformed into a
dragonfly or hidden by an invisible cap, Felix
must have stolen into meetings of the little

people." Mendelssohn's largest contribution
to the literature is his set of forty-eight *Songs
without Words,* which, as pianist Karl Engel
noted, "are really sketches of a traveler, written for the delectation of those who had
stayed home." George Bernard Shaw advised:
"They are too easy for our young lions, but
really, I suspect, because they are too difficult.
If you want to find out the weak places in a
player's technique . . . ask him to play you ten
bars of Mozart or Mendelssohn."

The Complete Solo Piano Music
Daniel Gregory Mason has best summarized
Mendelssohn's art: "Violence of contrast, dramatic trenchancy of expression, the over-
emphasis   of   hysterical   eloquence,   he
punctiliously avoids; he is always clear, unper-
turbed, discreet, harmonious. The lavish sensuousness of Schubert, the impulsive sincerity
of Schumann, are impossible if not distasteful
to this Addisonian temperament; personal sentiment, self-revelation, the autobiographic appeal, he avoids as the purist in manners avoids
a blush, an exclamation, or a grimace. If he is
romantic in his love of the picturesque, in his
sense of color, and in his fondness for literary
motives, his emotional reticence is entirely
classic. He is more observant than introspective, and his art is more pictorial than passionate."

JONES: Nimbus (CD)

Forty-eight Songs without Words, Opp.
   19, 30, 38, 53, 62, 67, 85, 102
These pieces were the joy of Victorian parlor
pianists and were among the world's best-
loved music. The most famous piece Mendelssohn composed, the *Spring Song,* became
hackneyed almost beyond repair. Many of the
titles were given by publishers. The *Volkslied,
May Breezes,* the tender, loving *Duetto,* the
Spinning Song, Consolation, and *Hunting
Song* are indispensable works of German Romanticism. In all, there is that special fastidi-

365

ousness which makes Mendelssohn the Beau Brummell of composers.

BARENBOIM: DG (CD)
BATTERSBY: MHS
DORFMANN: RCA
FRIEDMAN (10 pieces): Danacord
GIESEKING (17 pieces): Angel
KYRIAKOU: Vox
NOVAES (14 pieces): Vox

Variations sérieuses in D minor, Op. 54
One of the great sets of variations of the period. Brimming with compositional skill and emotional intensity, the work was never equaled by Mendelssohn for its remarkable cohesion of form and passion. It reveals his great capacity for original and idiomatic keyboard figuration.

ARTYMIW: Chandos
DE LARROCHA: London
HOROWITZ: RCA
KEENE: Laurel/Protone
PERAHIA: CBS (CD)
SIMON: Turnabout
SOFRONITSKY: Melodiya

Six Preludes and Fugues, Op. 35
In the Fugues, Mendelssohn puts his admiration for Bach and Handel to good use, especially in the finest of these pieces, No. 1 in E minor, which in the Prelude is also a good example of the Thalbergian three-handed effect.

D'ARCO: MHS
KYRIAKOU: Vox
PERAHIA (No. 1): CBS (CD)

Fantasy in F-sharp minor, Op. 28
Perhaps second only to the Variations sérieuses in importance, this work is unduly neglected. Dedicated to Moscheles, it is sometimes known as the Sonate écossaise. It is in three movements, and is slightly marred by a tepid but not unattractive Allegro con moto functioning as the middle movement. The first movement is in two alternating tempi, with

recitative-like cadenzas and a central climax of intense feeling. The finale is bursting with perilous and fiery passagework.

ARTYMIW: Chandos (CD)
CHERKASSKY: Vox Cum Laude
KEENE: Laurel/Protone
KUERTI: Monitor

Three Fantasies or Caprices, Op. 16
No. 2 of the set, in E minor (Scherzo), is two minutes of staccatissimo delight. It is often called The Trumpeter. Of the last piece in the set, Mendelssohn wrote: "It runs so slowly and peacefully, a trifle boring in its simplicity, that I have played it to myself every day and become quite sentimental in so doing."

ALPENHEIM: Philips
ARTYMIW: Chandos (CD)

Three Etudes, Op. 104
Marvelously crafted works; No. 3 in A minor is particularly ingenious in its use of the two thumbs. Rachmaninoff can be heard in a stunning performance of Nos. 2 and 3 in Volume 3 of his complete RCA recordings. It also includes his rightfully famous rendering of the Spinning Song.

KEENE: Laurel/Protone

Andante and Rondo capriccioso, Op. 14
One of the most popular of Mendelssohn's solo works, it is completely representative of his airy genius. There is hardly a pianist who has not worked on it, with its perennial freshness. The piece concludes in a paroxysm of blind octaves.

ALPENHEIM: Philips
ARTYMIW: Chandos (CD)
KATCHEN: London
KUERTI: Monitor

Capriccio in A minor, Op. 33, No. 1
A slow introduction is followed by tempestuous material in Mendelssohn's best vein. The

two other Caprices in Op. 33 are also typical of his style.

DE LARROCHA: London

Scherzo a capriccio in F-sharp minor
This taxing work of seven minutes, without opus number, needs flexible wrists and untiring staccato in chords and single notes. Although neglected, it is one of Mendelssohn's greatest works for piano, glowing with inspiration and formal elegance.

HOROWITZ: RCA
KUERTI: Monitor

Piano Concerto No. 1 in G minor, Op. 25
The three movements are without break. The G minor Concerto was once the ultimate "conservatory" concerto; Berlioz dreamed that pianos at the Paris Conservatoire played the piece late at night without aid of the pianists. The work is dazzlingly conceived for the piano, and the orchestration is piquant.

FIRKUŠNÝ, Froment/Luxembourg Radio: Turnabout
OUSSET, MARRINER/LONDON SYMPHONY: Angel (CD)
PERAHIA, Marriner/Academy of St. Martin: CBS (CD)
R. SERKIN, Ormandy/Columbia Symphony: Columbia

Piano Concerto No. 2 in D minor, Op. 40
The last movement is the best, with its sunny good nature. This concerto, though much less difficult technically than No. 1, is seldom played in public.

KATIN, Collins/London Symphony: London
PERAHIA, Marriner/Academy of St. Martin: CBS (CD)

Capriccio brillant in B minor for Piano and Orchestra, Op. 22
Rondo brillant in E-flat major, Op. 29
These smaller works for piano and orchestra show Mendelssohn at his most lighthearted,

and the idiomatic piano writing could not be more grateful or fun to practice. The themes are gracious, and the constructions are finely integrated, revealing an incomparable mastery and clarity. Mendelssohn's influence in such works as these can be heard in the productions of many composers who followed him.

Capriccio brillant:
GRAFFMAN, Munch/Boston Symphony: RCA
ORTIZ, Atzmon/Stuttgart Radio Symphony: Pantheon (CD)
R. SERKIN, Ormandy/Philadelphia: CBS

Rondo brillant:
KYRIAKOU, Swarowsky/Vienna Pro Musica: Turnabout
OGDON, Ceccato/London Symphony: Klavier
ORTIZ, Atzmon/Stuttgart Radio Symphony: Pantheon (CD)

OLIVIER MESSIAEN
b. 1908 — France

Messiaen is without a doubt one of the most influential composers since the war. He has many personalities: a religious ecstatic who writes mystical music; a Romantic, who calls himself a "sound color" composer; a student of ornithology, who translates bird song into music of amazing complexity; a theorist, who spawned much new thought; the teacher of Boulez; a student of musics past, from plainsong to Hindu ragas. Messiaen's work is often shrouded in symbolism. The length of his scores is unprecedented: such cyclic compositions as the *Vingt Regards* and the *Catalogue d'oiseaux* take over two hours for complete presentations. With these works, Messiaen broke new ground in the evolution of piano timbre and time-values. Indeed he created a new sense of form, which is no longer based on classic Western standards but seems not to

367

be bound by time at all. The *Vingt Regards,* in a sense, could go on forever. With his "super chords," Messiaen has gone past Debussy's sensory world, inducing almost trance states. He is the last notch on the ladder of French Romanticism begun by Berlioz. The multiplicity of pianistic textures and contrapuntal voicings present the pianist with a new and incandescent language to master.

Vingt Regards sur l'Enfant Jésus (1944)

The composer wrote, "More than in all my preceding works I have sought a language of mystic love, at once varied, powerful and tender, sometimes brutal, in a multi-colored ordering." The work was dedicated to and premiered by his wife Yvonne Loriod, a pianist of extraordinary gifts, who has been a constant inspiration to Messiaen. Her 1950s Westminster monos were considered the last word in avant-garde pianism, and they remain great performances in and of themselves, as well as pioneering recordings which moved other pianists to explore these daunting works. Since that time Messiaen has continuously attracted the efforts of major pianists. The *Twenty Contemplations of the Infant Jesus* include motives representing the Cross, the Virgin, the Star, the Angels, and God, all viewing the infant. The cycle has been excerpted by many pianists with striking effect. Indeed, so unusual are his works that Norman Demuth warned, "An evening of Messiaen's exultant piano music can do more harm than good and may antagonize the listener, who is left baffled and bewildered. The rich chords, the harmonic intensities, the ample figuration, the constantly changing tonalities, the wealth of detail and comparative lack of repose, when spread over a two-hour concert are too much for human receptivity."

BÉROFF: Pathé or Connoisseur Society
DE OLIVEIRA-CARVALHO: Vox
LORIOD: Westminster or Adès (CD)
OGDON: Argo
P. SERKIN: RCA

Catalogue d'oiseaux (1956–58)

This work, even longer than the *Vingt Regards,* is also more advanced in its rhythms and sonorities. It is an enormous undertaking of thirteen works in seven books, celebrating Messiaen's lifelong interest in bird song. He has translated the calls of such birds as the alpine chough, golden oriole, blue rock thrush, buzzard, and others into a uniquely conceived musical canvas. Messiaen, of course, does not attempt merely imitative sounds on the piano, as the instrument, being divided only into semitones, cannot translate the many "micro"-tones of bird call. The premiere took place in 1959, played by Yvonne Loriod.

DE OLIVEIRA-CARVALHO: Vox
JOHNSON: Argo

Eight Preludes (1928–29)

These short works are early Messiaen, with his instinct for chiaroscuro fully developed. They reveal Debussy's art as his prime inspiration at that time. Especially fine is the Sixth Prelude, *Cloches d'angoisse et larmes d'adieu* ("Bells of Anguish and Tears of Farewell"), "in sumptuous draperies of violet, orange and royal purple," as described by the composer.

LORIOD: MHS
CROSSLEY (Nos. 5 & 6, and selections from the two cycles): L'Oiseau-Lyre

Quatre Etudes de rythme (1949–50)

These pieces were very influential in the serialism of the 1950s. Etude No. 1 is *Ile de feu I* ("Island of Fire"), dedicated to the people of Papua, New Guinea. In explanation, Messiaen wrote, "The themes have the violence of the magic cults of that country." No. 2 is *Mode de valeurs et d'intensités* ("Mode of Values and Intensities"): according to the composer, "this utilizes a pitch-mode (36 tones), a value-mode (24 note-lengths or durations), an attack-mode (12 kinds of attacks), and an intensity-mode (12 shades of intensity)." No. 3, *Neumes rythmiques,* was composed while considering the different shapes of the neumes used for notating plainsong. No. 4 is *Ile de feu II*, which is often performed.

JACOBS: Nonesuch
LORIOD: MHS

FEDERICO MOMPOU
1893–1987 — Spain

Twelve Canciones y danzas
Impressiones intimas (1911–14)
Charmes (1920–21)
Suburbis (1916–17)
Eleven Preludes (1927–60)
Variaciones sobre un tema de Chopin

Mompou's fleeting sketches are charming and often poignant, possessing their own perfume. The scope of his work as a Spanish nationalist has been confined to a distillation of Catalan folk material. He seldom uses bar-lines, and though he is often technically easy, subtleties of pedaling, as well as interpretive imagination, are called for. The critic Emile Vuillermoz, decades ago, wrote of Mompou: "He searches in music for enchantments and spells wherewith to compound his magic songs. His formulas are short, concise, concentrated, but they possess a weird, hallucinating power of evocation . . . no matter how minutely we analyze Mompou's score, we cannot discover his secrets. This music which is so gentle and peaceful, reaches out to unexplored regions of the subconscious."

Mompou made five records of his complete piano music in 1974. So much of his music is static that only small doses are recommended for maximum effect. Mompou's playing echoes the spirit of his music; in some of his preludes, the *Trois Variations, Dialogues,* and *Charmes,* he produces a trancelike state. When the dance elements come to the fore, however, he plays rhythmically. Mompou has a beautiful and, at times, a liquid touch with a great deal of sensitivity at the fingertips. He nurtures his music. A most appealing novelty is the long (twenty minutes) set of variations on the Chopin Prelude in A major.

The Complete Piano Music:
MOMPOU: Ensayo or MHS

Selected Piano Music:
DE LARROCHA: London
MOMPOU: Ensayo (CD)

WOLFGANG AMADEUS MOZART
1756–1791 — Austria

The Classical piano concerto was, in Mozart's time, virtually in its infancy. Through his genius for balance, Mozart arrived at a partnership of piano and orchestra that has never been equaled.

Mozart wrote thirty-six cadenzas for various of his twenty-five solo concerti. Most often they are rather sketchy, and they are not always used by performers. Many pianists—including Hummel, Beethoven, Brahms, Reinecke, Saint-Saëns, Godowsky, Gulda, Casadesus, Magaloff, Landowska, Foldes, Badura-Skoda, and others—have composed their own. Some of Busoni's are quite startling.

Performance of these concerti on the modern piano presents many problems. Mozart occasionally used a shorthand in his notations, expecting himself or the performer to fill in and embellish. As Wanda Landowska notes: "What today would be described as the taking of 'peculiar liberties' was in Mozart's time the *sine qua non* of every performer. No virtuoso would have dared play certain phrases of Mozart as Mozart wrote them. . . . Those performances which we respect today for their literal devotion would have been called ignorant and barbaric by Mozart's contemporaries,

369

for it was in his art of ornamentation that the eighteenth century interpreter submitted himself to his audience to be judged an artist of good or poor taste."

Landowska also insists that "for a true understanding of these works and of the multiplicity of sonorous and expressive means Mozart had at his disposal, it is of prime importance for all present day pianists to study the resources and effects of eighteenth century keyboard instruments, as well as the manner of manipulating them. . . . Under the expert touch of a knowing performer, it is possible to obtain from [the modern piano] the color and particularities of the Forte-Piano. The gray and neutral tone of the modern piano can be set ablaze and yield hitherto unsuspected colors."

The Twenty-five Piano Concerti
In these recordings of the complete Mozart concerti and in the individual performances to be cited, the listener will be treated to the greatest variety of style, timbre, and performing attitudes, as well as great variability in the cadenzas used.

ANDA, Anda/Salzburg Mozarteum: DG
BRENDEL, Marriner/Academy of St. Martin: Philips (CD)
PERAHIA, Perahia/English Chamber Orchestra: CBS (CD)

Piano Concerti Nos. 1–4, K. 37, 39, 40, 41 (1767)
These were written when Mozart was eleven. The composer called them "pasticci." They are based on sonata movements by contemporary composers, including Johann Christian Bach, and were performed on the tours Mozart made as a child prodigy.

PERAHIA, Perahia/English Chamber Orchestra: CBS (CD)

Piano Concerto No. 5 in D major, K. 175 (1773)
Composed when he was seventeen, this was thus far the finest piano concerto of the Classical era. It is scored for one of Mozart's largest orchestras, using oboes, trumpets, horns, and timpani along with the strings. Mozart remained fond of the work, performing it and teaching it throughout his life. He wrote his own cadenzas for the first and second movements. If it were played more frequently, it would undoubtedly attain popularity through its brilliant and elegant pianism and dashing thematic material.

BILSON (fortepiano), Gardiner/English Baroque Soloists: DG Archiv (CD)
ENGEL, Hager/Salzburg Mozarteum: Telefunken
FRANKL, Fischer/Vienna Volksoper: Turnabout

Piano Concerto No. 6 in B-flat major, K. 238 (1776)
Composed early in 1776, this work calls for a small orchestra. The rondo offers a charming technical display.

ASHKENAZY, Schmidt-Isserstedt/London Symphony: London
Galling, Maga/Hungarica Philharmonia: Turnabout

Piano Concerto No. 8 in C major, K. 246 (1776)
The Piano Concerto No. 7 is for three pianos, a far weaker work than any of the solo concerti. The technical requirements of No. 8 are milder than those of either No. 5 or 6. The rondo, a Tempo di minuetto, has touches of Mozartian humor.

ASHKENAZY, Kertesz/London Symphony: London
BILSON (fortepiano), Gardiner/English Baroque Soloists: DG Archiv (CD)
KEMPFF, Leitner/Berlin Philharmonic: DG
R. SERKIN, Abbado/London Symphony: DG (CD)
TIPO, Chailly/London Philharmonic: Ricordi (CD)
VERA, de Waart/Rotterdam Philharmonic: Philips

Piano Concerto No. 9 in E-flat major, K. 271 (1777)

In January 1777, the twenty-one-year-old Mozart composed what Alfred Einstein called his *Eroica*. It was unprecedented in Mozart's already formidable output, and remains one of his greatest works. Charles Rosen devotes seventeen pages to an analysis of this score in his book *The Classical Style*. Maurice Hinson calls it "a daring work on a majestic scale . . . one of the greatest of all the concertos." Because of its early chronology, the concerto is still not as well known as later examples.

ASHKENAZY, Kertesz/London Symphony: London
BILSON (fortepiano) Gardiner/English Baroque Soloists: DG Archiv (CD)
BRENDEL, Marriner/Academy of St. Martin: Philips
BUCHBINDER, Teutsch/Warsaw Chamber Orchestra: Telefunken
HESS, Casals/Perpignan Festival: Columbia
PERAHIA, Perahia/English Chamber Orchestra: CBS (CD)
PIRES, Guschlbauer/Gulbenkian Chamber Orchestra of Lisbon: MHS or Erato (CD)
R. SERKIN, Schneider/Marlboro Festival: Odyssey
Ts'ONG, Priestman/Vienna Radio: Westminster
WEISSENBERG, Giulini/Vienna Symphony: Angel

Piano Concerto No. 11 in F major, K. 413 (1782)

The Tenth Concerto in E-flat, K. 365, for Two Pianos, was composed for his sister and himself. It is not quite on the level of his Sonata for Two Pianos, K. 448. The Eleventh to Thirteenth Concerti were written in quick succession during the winter of 1782–83. Mozart had moved to Vienna in the summer of 1781, intent on creating a livelihood as a public pianist and teacher. The F major Concerto is the smallest in scale, possessing little pianistic brilliance, but plenty of charm.

PERAHIA, Perahia/English Chamber Orchestra: CBS (CD)
R. SERKIN, Schneider/Marlboro Festival: CBS

Piano Concerto No. 12 in A major, K. 414 (1783)

The K. 414 was a favorite of Mozart's, and he often taught it. The themes have wonderful appeal, and the technical problems are only slightly greater than those of K. 413.

R. CASADESUS, Szell/Columbia Symphony: Columbia
DE LARROCHA, Zinman/London Sinfonietta: London
LUBIN (fortepiano), Lubin/Mozartean Players: Arabesque (CD)
LUPU, Segal/English Chamber Orchestra: London
R. SERKIN, Schneider/Marlboro Festival: CBS

Piano Concerto No. 13 in C major, K. 415 (1783)

K. 415 uses bassoons, trumpets, and timpani. Most of its technical brilliance is in the first movement; there are strokes of genius throughout the finale.

BARENBOIM, Barenboim/English Chamber Orchestra: Angel
FRAGER, Festival Sinfonia: Fidelio (CD)
HASKIL, Paumgartner/Lucerne Festival Strings: DG
MICHELANGELI, Giulini/Rome Radio and Television: Fonit-Cetra (CD)

Piano Concerto No. 14 in E-flat major, K. 449 (1784)

Starting with K. 449, six more piano concerti (Nos. 14–19) were composed between February and December of 1784. Of these six, four were written within a two-month period. This is amazing enough, but during the same time span, Mozart also produced six major works of chamber music. The Piano Concerto No. 14 is an exhilarating work, described by its composer as "a concerto of quite another kind."

BARENBOIM, Barenboim/English Chamber Orchestra: Angel
MORAVEC, Vlach/Czech Chamber Orchestra: Quintessence
PERAHIA, Perahia/English Chamber Orchestra: CBS (CD)
P. SERKIN, Schneider/English Chamber Orchestra: RCA (CD)
R. SERKIN, Schneider/Columbia Symphony: CBS
VÁSÁRY, Vásáry/Berlin PHILHARMONIC: DG

Piano Concerto No. 15 in B-flat major, K. 450 (1784)

This concerto is very tricky technically, as Mozart gives new scope to the left hand. He believed that this and the next concerto, in D, would "make the performer sweat."

BERNSTEIN, Bernstein/Vienna Philharmonic: London
R. CASADESUS, Szell/Cleveland: Columbia
HAEBLER, Davis/London Symphony: Mercury
MICHELANGELI, Gracis/I Pomeriggi Musicali di Milano: EMI
P. SERKIN, Schneider/English Chamber Orchestra: RCA (CD)

Piano Concerto No. 16 in D major, K. 451 (1784)

The thematic material of No. 16 lacks the general inspiration characteristic of this set of concerti, yet it is a work of the finest planning.

HAEBLER, Davis/London Symphony: Mercury
KLEIN, Angerer/Vienna Volksoper: Turnabout
P. SERKIN, Schneider/English Chamber Orchestra: RCA (CD)

Piano Concerto No. 17 in G major, K. 453 (1784)

K. 453 is a masterpiece of the rarest beauty. The slow movement makes incomparable use of the woodwinds, while the finale is an outstanding set of variations. The orchestra called for is small and the technical difficulties are far below Nos. 15 and 16. Many pianists have been attracted to its golden youthfulness.

ASHKENAZY, Ashkenazy/Philharmonia: London
R. CASADESUS, Szell/Cleveland: Columbia
GOODE, Orpheus Chamber Orchestra: Nonesuch (CD)
PREVIN, Previn/Vienna Philharmonic: Philips (CD)
RUBINSTEIN, Wallenstein/RCA Symphony: RCA
R. SERKIN, Schneider/Columbia Symphony: CBS

Piano Concerto No. 18 in B-flat major, K. 456 (1784)

K. 456 is much less known, though its piano part is most gracious. The slow movement in G minor is a set of variations, and there are several audacious modulations in the finale.

ASHKENAZY, Ashkenazy/Philharmonia: London (CD)
BRENDEL, Marriner/Academy of St. Martin: Philips
R. CASADESUS, Szell/Columbia Symphony: Odyssey
ENGEL, Hager/Salzburg Mozarteum: Telefunken

Piano Concerto No. 19 in F major, K. 459 (1784)

K. 459 has practically no prominence for the soloist. The slow movement, usually an adagio or andante, is instead a captivating Allegretto.

ASHKENAZY, Ashkenazy/Philharmonia: London (CD)
BILSON (fortepiano) Gardiner/English Baroque Soloists: DG (Archiv (CD)
BRENDEL, Marriner/Academy of St. Martin: Philips
HAEBLER, Rowicki/London Symphony: Philips

POLLINI, Böhm/Vienna Philharmonic: DG (CD)

R. SERKIN, Szell/Columbia Symphony: CBS (CD)

Piano Concerto No. 20 in D minor, K. 466 (1785)

The next six concerti, Nos. 20–25, are universally considered to be among the most honored works in the concerto literature. The group spans the period from February 1785 to December 1786. During this time, *The Marriage of Figaro* was also composed. No. 20 is the first of all the piano concerti to be written in a minor key. Its reception was slightly less favorable than Mozart was accustomed to with his concerti. Perhaps the dark, brooding first movement was too demonic for his polite late-eighteenth-century audience. (Within a decade, Beethoven would play the work and write cadenzas for it.) The middle movement is entitled "Romanza," of which Beethoven told his student Ries, "We will never get an idea like that." And the exciting finale, with its many themes, is enchanting.

ASHKENAZY, Schmidt-Isserstedt/London Symphony: London

R. CASADESUS, Szell/Columbia Symphony: CBS

HASKIL, Paumgartner/Vienna Symphony: Mercury

HASKIL, Markevitch/Lamoureux Orchestra: Philips (CD)

MATTHEWS, Swarowsky/Vienna State Opera: Vanguard

RUBINSTEIN, Wallenstein/RCA Symphony: RCA

SCHNABEL, Susskind/Philharmonia: Turnabout

R. SERKIN, Szell/Columbia Symphony: CBS (CD)

UCHIDA, Tate/English Chamber Orchestra: Philips (CD)

Piano Concerto No. 21 in C major, K. 467 (1785)

K. 467 is majestic. The piano part is one of the most complex of the series. The Andante, with its magnificent cantilena, is understandably popular—a lovely, dreamlike slow movement.

BADURA-SKODA, Badura-Skoda/Prague Chamber Orchestra: Supraphon

BISHOP-KOVACEVICH, Davis/London Symphony: Philips

R. CASADESUS, Szell/Cleveland: CBS (CD)

A. FISCHER, Sawallisch/Philharmonia: EMI or Price-Less (CD)

GULDA, Abbado/Vienna Philharmonic: DG

R. LHÉVINNE, Morel/Juilliard: CBS

LIPATTI, Karajan/Lucerne Festival: Angel

LUPU, Segal/English Chamber Orchestra: London

RUBINSTEIN, Wallenstein/RCA Symphony: RCA

SCHNABEL, Sargent/London Symphony: Angel

R. SERKIN, Schneider/Columbia Symphony: Odyssey

UCHIDA, Tate/English Chamber Orchestra: Philips (CD)

WEISSENBERG, Giulini/Vienna Symphony: Angel

Piano Concerto No. 22 in E-flat major, K. 482 (1785)

K. 482 receives many concert performances. At the premiere, the Andante had such instant appeal that the audience demanded that Mozart play it again. The concerto is thirty-five minutes long and incomparable for its breadth, humor, and pathos.

R. CASADESUS, Szell/Columbia Symphony: CBS

DE LARROCHA, Segal/Vienna Symphony: London (CD)

A. FISCHER, Sawallisch/Philharmonia: EMI or Price-Less (CD)

E. FISCHER, Barbirolli: Turnabout

KEMPFF, Klee/ Bavarian Radio Symphony: DG

LANDOWSKA, Rodzinski: IPA–Desmar

RICHTER, Muti/Philharmonia: Angel (CD)

R. SERKIN, Casals/Perpignan Festival: CBS

UCHIDA, Tate/English Chamber Orchestra: Philips (CD)

ZACHARIAS, Zinman/Dresden State: Angel (CD)

Piano Concerto No. 23 in A major, K. 488 (1785)

K. 488 is one of the most popular of the concerti. Its opening movement is radiant. The slow movement is a Siciliana—touching and transparent. It is the only movement in F-sharp minor in all of Mozart's compositions. The finale is euphoric, "though not without that after-tang of sadness," writes Eric Blom, "which is always liable to make one suddenly feel that Mozart, even in his most lighthearted moods, is fundamentally never a singer of ingenuous happiness."

R. CASADESUS, Szell/Columbia Symphony: CBS

CURZON, Kertesz/London Symphony: London

HASKIL, Paumgartner/Vienna Symphony: Mercury

HOROWITZ, Giulini/La Scala: DG (CD)

KEMPFF, Leitner/Bamberg Symphony: DG

POLLINI, Böhm/Vienna Philharmonic: DG (CD)

RUBINSTEIN, Wallenstein/RCA Symphony: RCA

ZACHARIAS, Zinman/Dresden State: Angel (CD)

Piano Concerto No. 24 in C minor, K. 491 (1786)

K. 491 touches the sublime. It is Mozart's only minor-keyed concerto besides No. 20 in D minor. The first movement is structurally elaborate. Mozart employed his largest orchestra, and the demands placed on the soloist are great.

R. CASADESUS, Szell/Cleveland: CBS (CD)

CURZON, Kertesz/London Symphony: London

E. FISCHER, Fischer/Danish Chamber Orchestra: Turnabout

HASKIL, Markevitch/Lamoureux Orchestra: Philips (CD)

PERAHIA, Perahia/English Chamber Orchestra: CBS (CD)

SCHNABEL, Susskind/Philharmonia: Turnabout

ZACHARIAS, Wand/North German Radio Symphony: Angel (CD)

Piano Concerto No. 25 in C major, K. 503 (1786)

K. 503 rivals No. 24 in complexity and grandeur. Mozart's contrapuntal skill here reaches its peak. The work asks for intellectual insight from its interpreters.

BERNSTEIN, Bernstein/Israel Philharmonic: Columbia

BISHOP-KOVACEVICH, Davis/London Symphony: Philips

DE LARROCHA, Solti/London Philharmonic: London

E. FISCHER, Krips/Philharmonia: Turnabout

FLEISHER, Szell/Cleveland: CBS (CD)

KATCHEN, Münchinger/Stuttgart Chamber Orchestra: London

R. SERKIN, Szell/Columbia Symphony: Odyssey

ZACHARIAS, Zinman/Bavarian Radio Symphony: Angel (CD)

Piano Concerto No. 26 in D major, K.537 (1788)

After the Twenty-fifth Concerto, Mozart lived only five more years, writing two more piano concerti. K. 537 has often been called the *Coronation* Concerto, because he played it during the coronation of Leopold II.

R. CASADESUS, Szell/Columbia Symphony: CBS

KLIEN, Maag/Vienna Volksoper: Turnabout

LANDOWSKA, Goehr: Seraphim

PIRES, Guschlbauer/Gulbenkian Chamber Orchestra of Lisbon: Erato (CD)

Piano Concerto No. 27 in B-flat major, K. 595 (1791)

K. 595 was composed when Mozart had only eleven months to live. He was already ill, and in the preceding several years he had been beset with many disappointments. He wrote to his father, "I have now made a habit of being prepared in all affairs of life for the worst." Yet this last piano concerto is sparkling, full of childlike spontaneity, optimism, and humor along with suppressed tears. It was being composed as he sketched the Requiem.

R. CASADESUS, Szell/Columbia Symphony: CBS

CURZON, Britten/English Chamber Orchestra: London (CD)

DE LARROCHA, Solti/London Philharmonic: London

GILELS, Böhm/Vienna Philharmonic: DG (CD)

R. SERKIN, Ormandy/Philadelphia: CBS

The Piano Sonatas
The study of the Mozart solo sonatas is indispensable to the pianist and to our understanding of eighteenth-century style. Listed are complete recordings of exceptional merit.

ESCHENBACH: DG

GIESEKING (complete solo piano music): Seraphim

GOULD: CBS

KLIEN: Vox

KRAUS: Odyssey

Sonatas Nos. 1–6
The first six sonatas, composed in 1775–76, in C, F, B-flat, E-flat, G, and D (K. 279–284), have their charms, but do not approach the magnitude of those to follow later. The slow movement of K. 281 is marked Andante amoroso, the only such marking in Mozart's sonatas.

Sonata No. 1 in C major, K. 279:
UCHIDA: Philips (CD)

Sonata No. 2 in F major, K. 280:
HASKIL: DG

ZIMERMAN: DG

Sonata No. 3 in B-flat major, K. 281:
BILSON (on a Stein fortepiano): Golden Crest

GILELS: DG (CD)

Sonata No. 4 in E-flat major, K. 282:
ARRAU: Philips (CD)

BACKHAUS: London

DE LARROCHA: London (CD)

LANDOWSKA: RCA

Sonata No. 5 in G major, K. 283:
BACKHAUS: London

LANDOWSKA: RCA

RÁNKI: Hungaroton (CD)

Sonata No. 6 in D major, K. 284:
UCHIDA: Philips (CD)

Sonata No. 7 in C major, K. 309
An excellent work, large in design, showing Mozart with a new confidence within the solo sonatas.

UCHIDA: Philips (CD)

Sonata No. 8 in A minor, K. 310
One of the greatest works for solo piano from the Classical period. Eva Badura-Skoda wrote: "Suddenly, with the A minor Sonata, a new world opens up.... The opening theme is indeed majestic.... The texture is orchestral in fullness, and the relentless pulsing of the accompanying chords suggests majesty of a demonic and sinister kind. The second movement ... displays a restrained passion.... The Presto is one of the darkest movements Mozart ever wrote, with its remarkable fluctuations between resignation and defiance."

ARRAU: Philips (CD)

ASHKENAZY: London

BRENDEL: Philips (CD)

GILELS: DG (CD)

LIPATTI: Angel (CD)

MATTHEWS: Vanguard

SCHIFF: London (CD)

UCHIDA: Philips (CD)

375

Sonata No. 9 in D major, K. 311

This is an exuberant sonata. The first movement reflects the sonorities of the celebrated orchestra of Mannheim, where this work was composed. The Andante, unlike those in the previous two sonatas, is not elaborate. It was composed for a young pianist, Rosa Cannabich, of whom Mozart reported: "She is a sweet, pretty girl, just like the Andante." The rondo finale is an exceptionally brilliant movement.

DE LARROCHA: London
LANDOWSKA: RCA
RÁNKI: Hungaroton (CD)
ZIMERMAN: DG

Sonata No. 10 in C major, K. 330

Mozart took particular care with the dynamic and phrase markings in this robust and happy work.

BILSON (on a Stein fortepiano): Golden Crest
CLIBURN: RCA
DE LARROCHA: London (CD)
HOROWITZ: DG (CD)

Sonata No. 11 in A major, K. 331

One of the most popular of the sonatas. None of its three movements is in sonata form. The opening variations are lovable; the minuet is typical of its form, and the Rondo alla turca is renowned.

BILSON (on a Stein fortepiano): Golden Crest
DE LARROCHA: London (CD)
HOROWITZ: CBS
SCHIFF: London (CD)
UCHIDA: Philips (CD)

Sonata No. 12 in F major, K. 332

A popular masterpiece and a perfect recital work. The first movement has lyricism and drama; the slow movement is the very essence of grace. The finale is one of Mozart's most virtuosic movements, a brilliant perpetual motion.

BILSON (on a fortepiano): Nonesuch
DE LARROCHA: London (CD)

HOROWITZ: RCA
LANDOWSKA: IPA–Desmar

Sonata No. 13 in B-flat major, K. 333

This sonata is favored in public with its lyrical first movement, serious slow movement, and large-scale rondo finale, which introduces, at bar 171, a cadenza—normally a feature of the concerto, not of the sonata.

ARRAU: Philips (CD)
BILSON (on a fortepiano): Nonesuch
BRENDEL: Philips
HOROWITZ: DG (CD)
MATTHEWS: Vanguard
MORAVEC: Connoisseur Society
SCHIFF: London (CD)

Sonata No. 14 in C minor, K. 457

Six years separate this, composed in 1784, from the previous sonata. It is Mozart's second minor-key sonata, and one of his greatest piano works. It is often played, preceded by the C minor Fantasia K. 475, with which it has a deep affinity in mood as well as in key. Eva Badura-Skoda states: "The C minor Sonata . . . offers a shattering expression of personal anguish, and a new language which sets it at the beginning of an epoch. This is the work which made the deepest impression on Mozart's direct contemporaries and successors, especially on the young Beethoven. . . . It is the first truly monumental work in the Sonata repertory, designed for acoustics more spacious than those of drawing rooms."

ARRAU: Philips
KLIEN: Turnabout
MATTHEWS: Vanguard
SCHIFF: London (CD)
P. SERKIN: RCA
SHIRK: Classic Masters (CD)
UCHIDA: Philips (CD)

Sonata No. 15 in C major, K. 545

The so-called *Sonata facile* is the most frequently played sonata of the Classical era, and almost certainly the first Mozart sonata that the young piano student attempts. It seems as though no amount of hackneyed playing can dull its delights.

DE LARROCHA: London
ESCHENBACH: DG
ESTRIN: Connoisseur Society
GOULD: CBS
NOVAES: Vox
PIRES: Denon (CD)

Sonata No. 16 in B-flat major, K. 570

This is a gracious work, a model of sonata design, with simple contrapuntal interest.

BILSON (on a Stein fortepiano): Golden Crest
MORAVEC: Connoisseur Society
SCHNABEL: Seraphim
P. SERKIN: Pro Arte (CD)

Sonata No. 17 in D major, K. 576

The last Mozart piano sonata, it is often called the *Hunt* or *Trumpeter,* and is one of the most difficult technically of the sonatas.

ARRAU: Philips (CD)
ASHKENAZY: London
BADURA-SKODA: Astrée (CD)
DE LARROCHA: London
JOHANNESEN: Golden Crest
KLIEN: Turnabout
P. SERKIN: Pro Arte (CD)

Rondo in A minor, K. 511

James Friskin wrote, "Among Mozart's pianoforte compositions there is nothing more beautiful than the Rondo in A minor, nor any more finished example of his art."

BADURA-SKODA: Astrée (CD)
RUBINSTEIN: RCA
SCHNABEL: Seraphim
R. SERKIN: CBS
UCHIDA: Philips (CD)

Rondo in D major, K. 485

This sparkling work is actually a sonata form with one subject.

BILSON (on a fortepiano): Nonesuch
DE LARROCHA: London
P. SERKIN: Pro Arte (CD)

Adagio in B minor, K. 540

A work of deep expressiveness. One of Mozart's most profound utterances, and demanding of the interpreter true musical and structural insight.

ARRAU: Philips (CD)
BADURA-SKODA: Astrée (CD)
BRENDEL: Philips

Fantasia in C minor, K. 396

This is a fine work, actually in sonata form.

BRENDEL: Vanguard
JOHANNESEN: Golden Crest
LORIOD: Adès (CD)

Fantasia in D minor, K. 397

One of the most often played of Mozart's piano works. It opens with beautifully laid-out slow arpeggios, followed by an Adagio, and closing with a surprising Allegretto in D major.

BADURA-SKODA: Astrée (CD)
DE LARROCHA: London
GILELS: DG (CD)
GOULD: CBS
HORSZOWSKI: Nonesuch (CD)
KLIEN: Turnabout

Fantasia in C minor, K. 475

The Fantasy is often performed alone, as well as in conjunction with the C minor Sonata. Its range of emotional freedom is unprecedented in Mozart's solo piano music.

EGOROV: Peters
GOULD: Columbia
KEMPFF: DG
MATTHEWS: Vanguard
MORAVEC: Supraphon
NEWMAN (fortepiano): Newport Classic (CD)

Variations on "Ah, vous dirai-je, maman," K. 265

This is the most popular of Mozart's variations, with pretty melodic decorations on the famous nursery tune.

BADURA-SKODA: Astrée (CD)
BUCHBINDER: Teldec
HASKIL: DG
PREVIN: CBS (CD)

MODEST MUSSORGSKY

1839–1881 — Russia

Pictures at an Exhibition

Mussorgsky was considered a competent pianist, and during his short and turbulent life he left two dozen piano pieces that generally show little gift for piano writing. Yet his masterwork for the instrument, in fact the greatest piano work of the Russian nationalists, *Pictures at an Exhibition,* is music of stupendous originality. This group of ten tableaux, linked by a Promenade, was inspired by a memorial exhibition of drawings and paintings by the composer's friend Victor Hartmann. But, as Martin Last writes, "it is . . . disappointing to see Hartmann's drawings from the perspective of Mussorgsky's music: the music is so much bigger, so much wilder, so much more visceral."

The work has been even more popular in the orchestral transcription by Ravel, though in this form the score sounds more like a showcase of brilliant effects. The original piano writing, however, has often been criticized as being unpianistic and awkward. Horowitz accepted this judgment when he made his own version, which enriches Mussorgsky's sound, and is played with tremendous tension and shattering climaxes. It is Horowitz at his most elemental. Richter's recording, from a live concert at Sofia, Bulgaria, in 1958, has been treasured by all aficionados of the original version of the score.

ASHKENAZY: London
BERMAN: DG
BROWNING: Delos (CD)
FIRKUŠNÝ: DG
HOROWITZ: RCA
RICHTER: Odyssey or Melodiya, or Philips (CD)
ROUVIER: Denon (CD)
SMITH: Unicorn
YERESKO: Melodiya

CARL NIELSEN

1865–1931 — Denmark

Symphonic Suite, Op. 8 (1894)
Chaconne, Op. 32 (1915)
Theme and Variations, Op. 40 (1916)
Suite, Op. 45 (1919)
Three Piano Pieces, Op. 59 (1928)

Nielsen, the best known of all Danish composers, was a violinist who forged a distinct and personal piano style, though it is awkward to play. His piano works are typical of his original and gritty music. The *Symphonic Suite,* Op. 8, is thick and cumbersome pianism, with loud Brahmsian overtones. The Five Piano Pieces, Op. 3, remind one of Schumann and Grieg, as do the Six Humoresque-Bagatelles, Op. 11. But the Chaconne, Op. 32, is music with a power and logic of its own. The Theme and Variations, Op. 40, is subtle and sparse, while the Suite Op. 45, sometimes known as the *Luciferian,* is a significant contribution to the literature and, in fact, the greatest of any Scandinavian piano work of the twentieth century, and should be better known. Written for Artur Schnabel, it is in six movements, twenty-two minutes long. It has the rugged but careful workmanship of a master who thinks and feels deeply. Near the end of his life, Nielsen composed *Twenty-five* *Pieces for Young and Old,* Op. 53, each based on the pentatonic scale, and using five-finger positions in varied ways. His Three Pieces, Op. 59, are brilliant in design, the middle piece a beautifully generated Molto adagio.

BÄRTSCHI (Suite Op. 45): Ex Libris (CD)
OGDON (Chaconne, Suite, Three Pieces): RCA
WESTENHOLZ (complete piano music): BIS

FRANCIS POULENC
1899–1963 — France

Poulenc was an eclectic. Ned Rorem wrote, "Take Chopin's dominant sevenths, Ravel's major sevenths, Fauré's straight triads, Debussy's minor ninths, Mussorgsky's augmented fourths. Filter them, as Satie did, through the added sixth chords of vaudeville (which the French call *le music-hall*), blend in a pint of Couperin to a quart Stravinsky, and you get the harmony of Poulenc." Virgil Thomson thought Poulenc "incontestably the greatest writer of melodies in our time." Poulenc, himself, thought less of his solo music than of his song accompaniments. Yet the piano music is certainly typical of the Poulenc whom the public has come to love—breezy, tongue-in-cheek, flippant, and openly sentimental. The composer wrote: "It is with my piano music that I suffer the most fraudulent interpretations, especially since I myself have set a very precise instrumental conception. . . . The major technical errors disfiguring my piano music . . . are these: Rubato, stinginess with the pedal; and too clear articulation of certain arrangements of chords and arpeggios that should, on the contrary, be played hazily." He goes on to say, "The use of pedals is the great secret of my piano music and often its true drama. One can never use enough pedals. When I hear certain pianists interpret me, I want to yell at them, put the butter in the sauce! Why play as though you were on a diet." (Nadia Boulanger differed with him and thought Poulenc overpedaled.)

Poulenc's own piano teacher Ricardo Viñes gave the premiere of the *Mouvements perpétuels* of 1918, to this day Poulenc's most popular piano work. His best piano music includes the little three-movement Suite (1920), the felicitous Toccata, written for Horowitz, the haunting A-flat Intermezzo, the set of Eight Nocturnes, the *Napoli* Suite, Five Impromptus, and the *Improvisations.*

Les Soirées de Nazelles (1930–36)
The work consists of a Preamble, Eight Variations, Cadence, and Finale. The Variations

are musical portraits of friends. Laurence Davies, a great believer in the quality of the work, heard in it "some of the most limpid music the instrument has inspired since Schumann. . . . It is probably the composer's best piano work and a worthy successor to the great keyboard suites of Debussy and Ravel."

> FÉVRIER: Pathé
> RANCK: International Piano Archives

Suite française (1935)
Seven French dances of the sixteenth century, "after Claude Gervaise," dressed in Poulenc's own freshly tailored, sophisticated clothing. The Suite is one of Poulenc's best-known piano works.

> JOHANNESEN: Golden Crest
> POULENC: Odyssey
> TACCHINO: Angel

Aubade for Piano and Eighteen Instruments (1929)
A choreographic poem based on the myth of the goddess Diana. Opening with a Toccata, it has seven movements, totaling twenty-one minutes, played without interruption. The work is strongly neo-Baroque, spare and brilliantly brittle.

> DUCHABLE, Conlon/Rotterdam Philharmonic: Erato (CD)
> FÉVRIER, Baudo/Lamoureux Orchestra: Nonesuch
> KRAJNY, Prague Chamber Orchestra: Supraphon
> TACCHINO, Prêtre/Paris Conservatoire: Angel

Piano Concerto (1949)
Poulenc premiered the Concerto in Boston. The third movement is a Rondo à la français, but the naughty genie in Poulenc manages to quote "Swanee." The first movement is urbane and slightly mischievous, but the slow movement is less successful than the Larghetto of the inspired Concerto for Two Pianos and Orchestra.

> DUCHABLE, Conlon/Rotterdam Philharmonic: Erato (CD)
> ORTIZ, Frémaux/Birmingham Symphony: Angel
> TACCHINO, Prêtre/Paris Conservatoire: Angel

SERGEI PROKOFIEV
1891–1953 — Russia

The Complete Solo Piano Music

Nine Sonatas
Four Etudes, Op. 2   (1909)
Four Pieces, Op. 3   (1907–11)
Four Pieces, Op. 4   (1913)
Toccata, Op. 11   (1912)
Ten Episodes, Op. 12   (1913)
Five Sarcasms, Op. 17
Twenty Visions fugitives, Op. 22   (1915–17)
Four Tales of an Old Grandmother, Op. 31   (1918)
Four Pieces, Op. 32   (1918)
Chose en soi (Things in Themselves), Op. 45a and 45b   (1928)
Sonatine in E minor, Op. 54, No. 1   (1931)
Sonatine in G major, Op. 54, No. 2
Three Pensées, Op. 62   (1933–34)
Music for Children (Twelve Pieces)

Several of Prokofiev's piano sonatas are frequently played, but the small pieces—outside of a few famous ones such as *Suggestion diabolique,* Op. 4, No. 4, and the Toccata, Op. 11—are little known. In addition to the solo pieces listed above, there are: the Divertissement, Op. 43b, consisting of four pieces arranged by the composer from other media; Six Transcriptions, Op. 52; Ten Pieces from the *Romeo and Juliet* Ballet, Op. 75; and the *Peter and the Wolf* score, Op. 67.

Prokofiev himself listed the principal elements of his art: "1) Classicism—an affinity for forms indigenous to the Baroque and Classic periods; 2) Innovation—a striving for a new harmonic language and the means for expressing stronger emotions; 3) the Toccata or Motor element—where rhythmic vitality plays an important role; 4) the Lyric element; 5) an element of either Grotesqueness, Jesting or Mockery."

SÁNDOR (complete solo piano music): Vox
BOUKOFF (Sonatas Nos. 1–9): Westminster
NISSMAN (Sonatas Nos. 1–9): Newport Classic (CD)

Sonata No. 1 in F minor, Op. 1 (1909)
This one-movement sonata-allegro structure is almost full-fledged Prokofiev, a highly charged, Romantic drama. Influenced somewhat by Scriabin.

PETROV: Melodiya

Sonata No. 2 in D minor, Op. 14 (1912)
The twenty-one-year-old composer's Second Sonata, in four laconic movements, is a masterpiece. The scherzo, with its hand-crossing, tickles the ear. Prokofiev uses staccato technique in a way that makes him a direct descendant of Mendelssohn.

BERMAN: DG
BIRET: Finnadar
GILELS: Melodiya
GRAFFMAN: Columbia
JOSELSON: RCA
KRAINEV: Melodiya

Sonata No. 3 in A minor, Op. 28 (1917)
The sonata form was Prokofiev's main genre of composition, and the one-movement Third Sonata, wrote Irwin Freundlich in his edition of the Sonatas, "may be viewed as an essay in classic motivic development." It is a brilliant seven-minute score, which was once played more often than it is at present.

GRAFFMAN: Columbia; RCA
KERER: Melodiya
POLLACK: Melodiya

Sonata No. 4 in C minor, Op. 29 (1917)
This three-movement sonata is seldom played, but it is vintage Prokofiev. The Andante assai middle movement was marvelously recorded by the composer on Angel. The finale has dashing lift, a very choreographic work.

MALININ: Melodiya or Angel
ZAK: Melodiya

Sonata No. 5 in C major, Op. 38/Op. 135
This gentle gem of neo-Classicism has caused confusion. Originally composed in 1923, it was revised in 1953. The second edition is now used, as in the performances of Grinberg, Sándor, and Novitskaya. Loesser, however, used parts of each version, stating: "In my not too humble estimation, the composer's revisive afterthoughts do not, for the most part, constitute improvements on the original, except, however, for the very end, which definitely sounds more satisfactorily finale-like in the later version. Thus, what you will hear will be Opus 38 almost entirely; but the last five pages will be Opus 135." Performers approaching this score should compare both editions.

GRINBERG: Melodiya
LOESSER: International Piano Archives
NOVITSKAYA: Melodiya/Angel

Sonata No. 6 in A major, Op. 82
Composed during the Second World War, this is one of Prokofiev's most massive scores and the longest of the sonatas. If No. 5 was neo-Haydn with a dash of Hindemithian utilitarianism, then No. 6 demands tremendous emotional resources from the pianist and the audience. It is tonal but bitter in its dissonant impact. It is the most difficult technically of the sonatas, using, as Freundlich observes, "double notes, arpeggio sweeps, interlocking thumbs, repeated notes, quick skips, percussive chords (col pugno, with the fist), screaming passages in extreme upper register." The third movement is a long waltz. The composer

381

himself premiered the sonata in Moscow on radio in 1940.

CLIBURN: RCA
MERZHANOV: Melodiya
POGORELICH: DG (CD)
RICHTER: Columbia
SILVERMAN: Orion
SLOBODYANIK: Melodiya

Sonata No. 7 in B-flat major, Op. 83 (1942)

In three movements, the best known of the nine sonatas was premiered by Richter, who is astonishing in his playing of it. Horowitz gave it the American premiere. The first movement has a characteristic wiry athleticism contrasted with a lyric vein; it is a magnificently constructed movement. The slow movement has a ripe, melodic appeal, while the third movement rivals Prokofiev's own Toccata in its tremendous energy.

ASHKENAZY: London
GOULD: Columbia
HOROWITZ: RCA
NÁDAS: Dover
POLLINI: DG (CD)
RICHTER: Artia or Melodiya
SOKOLOV: Melodiya
TORADZE: Angel (CD)

Sonata No. 8 in B-flat major, Op. 84

Gilels premiered the Eighth Sonata, which he continued to champion heartily. In recent years it has attracted numerous advocates. In three movements, half an hour in length, this is the most introspective and lyrical of the sonatas. Eric Salzman finds that "there is little that would lead one to suspect that its composition spans almost exactly the period of World War II. The opening Andante dolce has an almost Schubertian calm and transparency, troubled only in passing by the agitations of the development and coda. The second movement, Andante sognando, is the most Schubertian of all. The third movement with its triplet flow and scherzo-ish

middle section has a Haydn-Schubert finale feeling in a modern context." Many hear the heartbeat of Mahler in the Andante movement.

ASHKENAZY: London
BERMAN: DG
GILELS: Columbia/Melodiya
JOSELSON: RCA
RICHTER: DG
ZELTSER: Columbia

Sonata No. 9 in C major, Op. 103 (1947)

With this sonata, Prokofiev closes a nearly forty-year span in his piano sonata writing. The work was given its premiere in 1951, by Richter. It is far less difficult than the three preceding sonatas, and is full of delightful turns and jolly twists.

KALICHSTEIN: Vanguard
RICHTER: Monitor

Piano Concerto No. 1 in D-flat major, Op. 10 (1911–12)

The five Prokofiev piano concerti are all original and vital creations, the most often played of twentieth-century piano concertos and the most recorded. No. 1 in D-flat was played by the twenty-one-year-old composer as his graduation piece from the St. Petersburg Conservatory. He scandalized the jury by not using a prescribed Classic or Romantic concerto. The work is in a modified sonata design, the jubilant opening statement returning to close the work. Maurice Hinson thinks "this may be the most important single-movement concerto since Liszt's Concerto No. 2 in A."

ASHKENAZY, Previn/London Symphony: London
BROWNING, Leinsdorf/Boston Symphony: RCA
GAVRILOV, Rattle/London Symphony: Angel
GRAFFMAN, Szell/Cleveland: Columbia

Katz, Boult/London Philharmonic: PRT (CD)

Kerer, Kondrashin/Moscow Philharmonic: Melodiya

Richter, Kondrashin/Moscow Philharmonic: Odyssey

Piano Concerto No. 2 in G minor, Op. 16 (1913; revised 1923)

In four movements, the Second Concerto is a dynamite showpiece, with a panoramic piano part. It is among the most difficult technical challenges in the standard repertoire. When Prokofiev introduced it to Russian audiences, they were indignant, calling him the piano's cubist and futurist. Today we hear it as a colorful Romantic work. Poulenc once called Prokofiev the Russian Liszt.

Ashkenazy, Previn/London Philharmonic: London

Baloghova, Ancerl/Czech Philharmonic: Supraphon or Artia

Bolet, Cox/Nuremberg Symphony: Genesis

Frager, Leibowitz/Paris Conservatoire: RCA

Henriot-Schweitzer, Munch/Boston Symphony: RCA

Joselson, Ormandy/Philadelphia: RCA

Tacchino, Froment/Luxembourg Radio: Candide

Piano Concerto No. 3 in C major, Op. 26 (1921)

The Third Concerto is a perfect work of art. It is the most often played of the Prokofiev concerti. The piano part is of exceptional brilliance; the visual aspect of the virtuosity—the choreography of the hands upon the keyboard—is extremely striking. Prokofiev played the premiere in Chicago in 1921. His own recording is a must-hear for those interested in a composer's interpretation of his own work. Prokofiev was a startling pianist. In his day it was said that his playing was like his music—he was called an "Age of Steel" pianist. Our ears now hear how lyrical he could be both as pianist and composer. All of the performances listed offer virtuosity of a high order.

Argerich, Abbado/Berlin Philharmonic: DG (CD)

Browning, Leinsdorf/Philadelphia: Seraphim

Cliburn, Hendl/Chicago Symphony: RCA (CD)

Gilels, Kondrashin/USSR Symphony: Melodiya

Graffman, Szell/Cleveland: Columbia

Janis, Kondrashin/Moscow Philharmonic: Mercury

Joselson, Mata/Dallas Symphony: RCA

Judd, Lazarev/Moscow Philharmonic: Chandos

Kapell, Dorati/Dallas Symphony: RCA

Margalit, Maazel/New Philharmonia: London

Prokofiev, Coppola/London Symphony: Angel

Weissenberg, Ozawa/Orchestre de Paris: Angel

Concerto No. 4 in B-flat major for Piano, Left Hand Alone, and Orchestra, Op. 53 (1931)

The Left Hand Concerto was commissioned by Paul Wittgenstein, who had lost his right arm in World War I. He commissioned the great Ravel concerto, as well as works by Schmidt, Korngold, Bortkiewicz, Hans Gál, and others. Unfortunately, he didn't care for Prokofiev's and did not play it. It was neglected until Siegfried Rapp, who lost his arm in the next world war, played it in 1956. In 1958, Rudolf Serkin gave the American premiere. The work is in four movements, neo-Classic and transparent in content, thematically delightful.

Ashkenazy, Previn/London Symphony: London

R. Serkin, Ormandy/Philadelphia: Columbia

Piano Concerto No. 5 in G major, Op. 55 (1932)

No. 5, in five movements, is a dark horse which is a winner in performance, full of sparkling wit, daring pianism, and loads of themes.

BRENDEL, Sternberg/Vienna State Opera: Turnabout
HOLLANDER, Leinsdorf/Boston Symphony: RCA

RICHTER, Maazel/London Symphony: Angel
RICHTER, Rowicki/Warsaw Philharmonic: DG (CD)

SERGEI RACHMANINOFF
1873–1943 — Russia

A good deal of Rachmaninoff's piano music continues to be widely played, especially several of the concerti. The pianism, based on his own large hands and sublime capability, is extremely taxing for the muscles. His scores are often loaded—at times, overloaded—with complicated textures and note-spinning. The result, however, is always idiomatic, the sonorities potent and bell-like. Rachmaninoff at his best has a unique appeal, with his gift for emotional melody and his nostalgic late Russian Romanticism.

Five Pieces, Op. 3 (1892)
Seven Pieces, Op. 10 (1894)
The earlier of these two sets of character pieces includes the notorious Prelude in C-sharp minor, Op. 3, No. 2—the "It" Prelude, so described by the composer because every audience expected him to play "It." Its appeal, however, is real. Rachmaninoff recorded it three times, never bombastically. (Other pieces recorded by Rachmaninoff are *Mélodie, Polichinelle, Sérénade, Barcarolle,* and *Humor-*

esque, to be found in Volumes 1 and 2 of his complete recorded performances on RCA.)

LAREDO: CBS

Six Moments musicaux, Op. 16 (1896)
Drenched in Russian languor, this important and technically treacherous set of concert pieces is far more difficult than the preceding ones. Only the mournful B minor is easily playable. A merely good technique is not enough—these works call for high virtuosic equipment. Rachmaninoff's own performance of Op. 16, No. 2 in E-flat minor (in Volume 2) makes child's play of this thickly packed piece and demonstrates the meaning of aristocratic pianism.

BERMAN: DG
JONES: Nimbus
PONTI: Vox
HOROWITZ (OP. 16, NO. 2): RCA

Variations on a Theme by Chopin, Op. 22 (1903)
On February 10, 1903, Rachmaninoff premiered the *Chopin* Variations in a recital with some of the Op. 23 Preludes. It was his first large-scale work for solo piano and is dedicated to Leschetizky. Its basis is the famous

Chopin C minor Prelude, Op. 28, No. 20, which Busoni, too, would later use for variation purposes. Though it has quality and fine logic, this neglected work lacks appealing melodies like those of the Second Concerto, which would have made it more popular.

LAREDO: Columbia
PONTI: Vox
SHELLEY: Hyperion

Ten Preludes, Op. 23 (1903–04)
Thirteen Preludes, Op. 32 (1910)

In these twenty-three pieces, we encounter the finest of Rachmaninoff's piano music, with beguiling melodic appeal and lush keyboard texture. Rachmaninoff could easily span a twelfth, and he asks here for thick chords. His left hand was invincible, and he charted his left-hand figuration with new and wondrous formations, making use of bass sonorities that have a physical, almost guttural impact. The technical range of the Preludes is enormous, the most difficult of all being perhaps the Op. 23, No. 9—a double-note study that can ruin the muscles if practiced poorly. Op. 23, No. 5, Alla marcia, in G minor is the best-known prelude of the two sets, and the Lento B minor, Op. 32, No. 10, is one of Rachmaninoff's most powerful creations. We are fortunate in having recordings by Rachmaninoff himself of seven preludes: Op. 23, Nos. 5 and 10, and Op. 32, Nos. 3, 5, 6, 7, and 12. They should be heard by anyone interested in Rachmaninoff. Nobody has ever approached him in playing the G major Prelude, Op. 32, No. 5, with its antique flavoring.

RACHMANINOFF: RCA
ANIEVAS: Angel
ASHKENAZY: London (CD)
KATIN: Olympia (CD)
KEENE: Protone (CD)
LYMPANY: Everest
RICHTER (six from Op. 23, seven from Op. 32): MHS or JVC/Melodiya (CD)
WEISSENBERG: RCA

Sonata No. 1 in D minor, Op. 28 (1907)

The sonata is in three mammoth-sized movements totaling thirty-five minutes, the best being the Lento middle movement with its vast melancholia. Robert Offergeld declares, "The idiom is the all-out, head-on, non-ironic representationalism of the grand Romantic manner."

LAREDO: CBS
OGDON: RCA
PONTI: Vox
YERESKO: Chant du Monde (CD)

Sonata No. 2 in B-flat minor, Op. 36 (1913; revised 1931)

This sonata is in three concise movements. It is even more difficult than the Sonata No. 1. Indeed, it is brutal, even after revisions by Rachmaninoff to trim some of the difficulty. Some Rachmaninoff devotees consider it a masterpiece. The Second Sonata desperately needs sympathetic interpreters, for the phraseology is dense, fragmented, and filled with a wild despair. The finale must be counted as one of the composer's most electrifying works. In 1940, Rachmaninoff approved a version by Horowitz which combined both the original and condensed versions, and which Horowitz plays on his two recordings.

BROWNING: Delos (CD)
CLIBURN: RCA
COLLARD: Connoisseur Society
HOROWITZ: CBS; RCA
LAREDO: CBS
OGDON: RCA
SOREL: MHS

Nine Etudes-tableaux, Op. 33 (1911)
Nine Etudes-tableaux, Op. 39 (1916–17)

Of the title Etudes-tableaux, the composer, when questioned, responded, "I do not believe in the artist disclosing too much of his images. Let them paint for themselves what it most suggests." The eighteen etudes are more chro-

385

matic and difficult than the preludes. They are invariably beautiful in their writing, though lacking in some cases the immediate melodic appeal of the preludes. As compensation, however, they possess an added rhythmic virility, sometimes with an almost barbaric thrust.

ASHKENAZY (OP. 39): London
COLLARD: Connoisseur Society
HOROWITZ (three etudes): Columbia
LAREDO (Opp. 33 & 39): Columbia
NASEDKIN: Melodiya
RACHMANINOFF (Op. 33, Nos. 2 & 7; Op. 39, No. 6): RCA
SOFRONITSKY (Op. 33, Nos. 2 & 5; Op. 39, Nos. 4–6): Melodiya
WEBSTER: Dover

Variations on a Theme by Corelli, Op. 42 (1931)

The composer premiered his *Corelli* Variations in Montreal. The theme, "La Folia," was believed at the time to be by Corelli, but it is in fact a Spanish folk melody that has been used by many composers. This was Rachmaninoff's final piece of solo piano music. It had been fourteen years since the Op. 39 Etudes, during which time he had produced only the Fourth Piano Concerto, Op. 40, and Three Russian Songs for Chorus and Orchestra, Op. 41. His constant touring practically brought his creative work to a standstill. After the *Corelli* Variations, however, he would write three of his most important works: the *Rhapsody on a Theme of Paganini*, Op. 43; the Third Symphony, Op. 44; and the *Symphonic Dances*, Op. 45. As a composer, he had felt far from the mainstream of current musical thought, and critics of his day thought him an anachronism. But with the *Corelli* Variations, one may say Rachmaninoff entered a new period in his work. In these last compositions, he remains true to himself, but there is a paring down of excess, both in his emotionalism and in the density of the music. The sobbing and often indulgent Slavic melancholy is drastically diminished. The *Corelli* Variations and

the *Rhapsody* are of considerable difficulty, but in both, the structure and the ideas have a new transparency, as well as a more urbane harmonic language.

ASHKENAZY: London
CHERKASSKY: Nimbus (CD)
COLLARD: Connoisseur Society
SHELLEY: Hyperion
YERESKO: Melodiya

Piano Concerto No. 1 in F-sharp minor, Op. 1 (1891)

The Rachmaninoff concerti continue to be the most regularly performed of any Romantic concertos. No. 1 is dedicated to Alexander Siloti. The concerto was a favorite work of Rachmaninoff's and he revised it in 1917. It has all of his strong points, including melodic appeal and brilliant piano writing. The first movement's cadenza is very strong and taxing. The work is generally squarer than either No. 2 or 3.

JANIS, Reiner/Chicago Symphony: RCA
KOCSIS, de Waart/San Francisco Symphony: Philips (CD)
RACHMANINOFF, Ormandy/Philadelphia: RCA (CD)
VÁSÁRY, Ahronovitch/London Symphony: DG
WILD, Sanderling/Royal Philharmonic: Odyssey

Piano Concerto No. 2 in C minor, Op. 18 (1901)

No. 2 is, after the Tchaikovsky Concerto No. 1, the world's most beloved piano concerto. The piano writing is luxuriant, the orchestration subtle but colorful. The concerto is gratefully dedicated to Dr. Nicholas Dahl. Rachmaninoff had been deeply depressed and was creatively blocked until he went for therapy to Dr. Dahl.

CLIBURN, Reiner/Chicago Symphony: RCA (CD)
JANIS, Dorati/Minneapolis Symphony: Mercury
KAPELL, Steinberg/Robin Hood Dell Orchestra: RCA

KRAINEV, Ivanov/Moscow Radio Symphony: Melodiya/Angel

LYMPANY, Sargent/Royal Philharmonic: EMI

RACHMANINOFF, Stokowski/Philadelphia: RCA (CD)

RICHTER, Kondrashin/Moscow State Philharmonic: Everest

RUBINSTEIN, Reiner/Chicago Symphony: RCA (CD)

VÁSÁRY, Ahronovitch/London Symphony: DG (CD)

WEISSENBERG, Karajan/Berlin Philharmonic: Angel (CD)

Piano Concerto No. 3 in D minor, Op. 30 (1909)

The Third Concerto has become the ultimate measure of technical prowess and emotional projection. Dedicated to Josef Hofmann, who never played it, it is the most difficult concerto, technically, in the standard repertoire. Such a superlative technician as Gary Graffman wishes he had learned it as a young student: "Probably the only time I could have learned that magnificent knucklebreaker would have been when I was still too young to know fear."

ASHKENAZY, Fistoulari/London Symphony: London

BERMAN, Abbado/London Symphony: CBS (CD)

CLIBURN, Kondrashin/Symphony of the Air: RCA (CD)

GILELS, Cluytens/Paris Conservatoire: Angel

HOROWITZ, Coates/London Symphony: Seraphim

HOROWITZ, Reiner/RCA Symphony: RCA

JANIS, Munch/Boston Symphony: RCA

MERZHANOV, Anosov/USSR Symphony: Monitor

MOGILEVSKY, Kondrashin/Moscow Philharmonic: Melodiya/Angel

RACHMANINOFF, Ormandy/Philadelphia: RCA (CD)

WATTS, Ozawa/New York Philharmonic: CBS

WEISSENBERG, Prêtre/Chicago Symphony: RCA

Piano Concerto No. 4 in G minor, Op. 40 (1927)

This concerto is by far the least played of the series, lacking the melodic invention of the other works. Michelangeli, however, has always been a partisan of the score, and he conjures up its spirit with a gorgeous sound. The brooding Largo has material reminiscent of the nursery tune "Three Blind Mice."

KOCSIS, de Waart/San Francisco Symphony: Philips (CD)

MICHELANGELI, Gracis/Philharmonia: Angel

VÁSÁRY, Ahronovitch/London Symphony: DG (CD)

WILD, Horenstein/Royal Philharmonic: Quintessence

Rhapsody on a Theme of Paganini, Op. 43 (1934)

A popular concert-hall staple, the Rhapsody is based on the theme of Paganini's celebrated Twenty-fourth Caprice for solo violin. The Dies Irae is also integrated into the score.

GRAFFMAN, Bernstein/New York Philharmonic: CBS (CD)

KAPELL, Reiner/Robin Hood Dell Orchestra: RCA

PENNARIO, Leinsdorf/Los Angeles Philharmonic: Seraphim

RACHMANINOFF, Stokowski/Philadelphia: RCA (CD)

RUBINSTEIN, Reiner/Chicago Symphony: RCA (CD)

Transcriptions

Rachmaninoff composed a group of effective transcriptions, which have been played by many pianists, though none to equal his own playing. They are scattered throughout RCA's three volumes of Rachmaninoff's complete recordings:

Bizet-Rachmaninoff: Minuet from *L'Arlésienne* Suite No. 1 (in Volume 1)

Kreisler-Rachmaninoff: *Liebesfreud* (in Volumes 2 & 3); *Liebesleid* (in Volume 1)

Mendelssohn-Rachmaninoff: Scherzo from *A Midsummer Night's Dream* (in Volume 2) (Rachmaninoff's distillation of Mendelssohn's shimmering orchestration is inimitable.)

Mussorgsky-Rachmaninoff: Hopak from *The Fair at Sorochinsk* (in Volume 2)

Rachmaninoff—transcriptions of his songs for piano solo: *Daisies* (in Volume 2); *Lilacs* (in Volumes 1 & 2)

Rimsky-Korsakov–Rachmaninoff: *The Flight of the Bumblebee* (in Volume 2)

Schubert-Rachmaninoff: *The Brooklet* (in Volume 2)

Tchaikovsky-Rachmaninoff: *Lullaby* (in Volume 2)

MAURICE RAVEL
1875–1937 — France

Ravel was one of the great composers of the twentieth century and his piano music, though its quantity is not large, is played wherever piano recitals are given. Ravel brought to the piano many new technical devices. Though he was older than Ravel, Debussy's greatest piano music was written only after he discovered Ravel's *Jeux d'eau*. Alfred Cortot described the essential difference between the two composers: "Where Debussy would have described the sensations caused by viewing an object, Ravel describes the object itself."

The Complete Solo Piano Music
"The unique contribution of Ravel," for Laurence Davies, "lay in his power to retain a certain firmness of line, while at the same time capturing that fluidity we have come to associate with Impressionism." Walter Gieseking spoke of this body of work as "the most pianistic ever written, making the most perfect

and universal use of the resources of the modern piano."

R. CASADESUS: Odyssey
CROSSLEY: CRD
ENTREMONT: CBS
FRANÇOIS: Seraphim
GIESEKING: Angel
HELFFER: Harmonia Mundi
PERLEMUTER: Vox
SIMON: Vox

Pavane pour une infante défunte (1899)
The *Pavane for a Dead Princess* is one of Ravel's best-known works, and offers little technical difficulty. The key, G major, is not dark, as one might expect from a funeral pavane. It has, rather, that peculiarly Ravelian melancholy which seems to be bathed in white light. The composer himself thought the Chabrier influence on this work was too "obtrusive."

R. CASADESUS: Odyssey
COLLARD: Angel (CD)
ENTREMONT: CBS
GILELS: MHS
PENNARIO: Angel

Jeux d'eau (1901)
This exquisite score, dedicated to Ravel's teacher Fauré, paved a new road in piano technique with use of seconds, major sevenths, dominant ninths, and eleventh chords. Cortot called the work "liquid poetry." Its antecedents were Liszt's *Jeux d'eaux à la Villa d'Este* and *Au bord d'une source*. "It is by imitating that I innovate," Ravel once proudly said. Ricardo Viñes gave the world premiere.

CORTOT: Seraphim
GILELS: MHS
RICHTER: RCA
ROGÉ: London
ROSENBERGER: Delos (CD)
THIBAUDET: Denon (CD)

Sonatine (1905)
An unsurpassed masterwork exhibiting polish and perfection of detail. The texture is thin,

with an admirable use of the keyboard's upper register. The movements are marked Modéré, Mouvement de Menuet, and Animé. In his notation and markings, the composer took special pains to make his intention understood.

Argerich: DG
R. Casadesus: Odyssey
Cortot: Seraphim
François: Seraphim
Gieseking: Angel
Moravec: Connoisseur Society
Perlemuter: Nimbus (CD)
Ránki: Hungaroton (CD)

Miroirs (1905)

Miroirs contains five pieces: *Noctuelles* ("Night Moths"), *Oiseaux tristes* ("Mournful Birds"), *Une Barque sur l'océan* ("A Ship on the Ocean"), *Alborada del gracioso* ("Aubade/ Morning Song of the Jester"), *La Vallée des cloches* ("The Valley of the Bells"). The works are seldom played in public as a complete set. Each piece offers a unique excursion into impressionism and symbolism, opening new avenues of harmonic color. Leon Vallas pictured *Noctuelles* as "an inextricable mass of curves drowned in a sonorous flood of audacious intervals which interrupt the fluttering of nocturnal butterflies." *Oiseaux tristes* does not demand as much technically as it does in the imaginative portrayal of the sadness of birds lost in a forest in extreme summer heat. *Une Barque sur l'océan* uses sweeping arpeggio forms to summon the image of water, which symbolizes the vicissitudes of fate. *Alborada del gracioso* is the best known of the five pieces and offers, as well, the most treacherous battle with the keyboard. Only a very good piano will be adequate for the work's rapidly insistent, repeated-note technique. In this piece Ravel has integrated the glamour of a Liszt Hungarian Rhapsody into a Hispanic framework. This jester and his insinuating guitar strains are hypnotically molded with a sardonic smile and an extreme technical cru-

elty, especially in the double glissandos in fourths. *La Vallée des cloches* is a superb work which evokes a sense of ritual.

François: Seraphim
Gieseking: Angel
Laredo: CBS
Perlemuter: Nimbus (CD)
Rogé: London
Toradze: Angel (CD)

Gaspard de la nuit (1908)

The suite was inspired by the Aloysius Bertrand triptych, *Gaspard de la nuit.* The three parts are *Ondine, Le Gibet,* and *Scarbo.* The work was launched in public by the indefatigable Ricardo Viñes. Cortot proclaimed, "These three poems enrich the piano repertoire . . . with one of the most extraordinary examples of instrumental ingenuity which the industry of composers has ever produced."

In *Ondine,* Ravel portrays the water nymph attempting to seduce a mortal as she tries to lure him to her palace in the depths of the lake. The work is bewitching in its powers of evocation. Edward Lockspeiser finds that "nowhere in music, and seldom in the Impressionist paintings of this period, have the iridescent images of glistening, transparent water been so convincingly conveyed." The climax is surely one of Ravel's most seductive, with its sprays of glimmering water surging ever upward. *Ondine* was dedicated to Harold Bauer. *Le Gibet,* the gallows, is a study in suspense, evoking an eerie, static, half-lit scene. Ravel asks the pianist to play "sans expression" at one point. Of *Scarbo,* Charles Stanley says, "Words cannot describe the complexities and difficulties of *Scarbo,* which demands wrists of steel, fingers with eyes in them." "In *Scarbo,*" James Gibb asserts, "the macabre terrors of a harrying goblin hurtle the composer beyond the diabolic extremes of virtuosity in Liszt and Balakirev. All laughter is sardonic and cruel. . . . Even its silences are frightening and the vicious elusiveness of the goblin is expressed in startling harmonies.

Scarbo is a unique masterpiece in the literature of piano virtuosity." It has become a badge of mastery for pianists worldwide. *Scarbo* is dedicated to Rudolph Ganz.

ARGERICH: DG
ASHKENAZY: London (CD)
AX: RCA
BACHAUER: Mercury
BROWNING: RCA
DE LARROCHA: CBS
FRANÇOIS: Seraphim
MICHELANGELI: Rococo
POGORELICH: DG (CD)
SIMON: Turnabout
WILD: Audiofon

Valses nobles et sentimentales (1911)
Ravel wrote that these pieces were an expression of "my intention of composing a chain of waltzes following the example of Schubert." Yet with their perfectly carved, needlelike detail and ironic overtones, these seven waltzes and an epilogue are worlds apart from the naive spirit of Schubert's waltzes. On the title page, Ravel quotes a line from Henri de Régnier: "The delicious and always new pleasure of a useless occupation."

AX: RCA
DE LARROCHA: CBS
MICHELANGELI: Rococo
RÁNKI: Hungaroton (CD)
RUBINSTEIN: RCA (CD)

Le Tombeau de Couperin (1917)
This suite consists of six movements: Prelude, Fugue, Forlane, Rigaudon, Menuet, Toccata. Ravel said: "In reality, it is a tribute not so much to Couperin himself as to eighteenth century music in general." During the dark days of World War I, Ravel, master of logical construction, looked back yearningly to that earlier age of logic and aristocratic grace. He dedicated each piece to a friend killed in the war. The final piece, Toccata, is a repeated-note moto perpetuo with a golden halo. When Ravel later orchestrated the suite, even

with his unique mastery of the orchestra he did not touch the Toccata, which is so perfectly tailored to the piano that a separation from its original medium would be ruinous.

BROWNING: RCA
PERLEMUTER: Nimbus (CD)
STARR: Orion
THIBAUDET: Denon (CD)
WEISSENBERG: Connoisseur Society

La Valse (1920)
Ravel transcribed his great *La Valse* for solo piano himself, though few pianists know of the existence of the transcription. The work was written for Diaghilev. When the composer played it for him, the impresario rightly called it "a masterpiece, but it is not a ballet, it is a portrait of a ballet." It is also a portrait of a dead era. *La Valse* is an apotheosis of the Viennese waltz; desperately nostalgic in its depiction of a city and a dance with their aura of dissipation. It is a wail of misty, ghostlike suffering. The piece is irresistibly effective when played with an almost unruly abandon.

LAREDO: CBS
PENNARIO: Angel

Piano Concerto in G major (1931)
During the first stages of composition, Ravel thought of naming the work *Divertissement*. He noted that the concerto "is written in the spirit of Mozart and Saint-Saëns. I believe that the music of a concerto can be gay and brilliant, and that it need not pretend to depths nor aim at dramatic effects." Ravel's wonderful ability to assimilate styles of music is nowhere more perfectly displayed than in this concerto. The use of alternating hand technique is perfection. The composer borrows some jazz elements, yet the concerto is purely Gallic in spirit and still exerts an influence over French musical composition. The 1930s recording by Marguerite Long and

Ravel shows the grace and polish of Long's very French pianism.

BERNSTEIN, Bernstein/Columbia Symphony: Columbia

COLLARD, Maazel/Orchestre National de France: Angel (CD)

ENTREMONT, Ormandy/Philadelphia: Columbia

LONG, RAVEL: Seraphim

MICHELANGELI, Gracis/Philharmonia: Angel

ROGÉ, Dutoit/Montreal Symphony: London (CD)

WEISSENBERG, Ozawa/Orchestre de Paris: Angel

Concerto for the Left Hand and Orchestra in D major (1931)

The concerto is a miracle of technical know-how. For Maurice Hinson, this is "one of Ravel's most powerful and dramatic works; [it] contains a curious combination of Hispanic, jazz, and modernist (modal and polytonal) influences; [it is] a long way from the Impressionistic and neoclassic qualities so frequently associated with Ravel's style. The resources of the hand are greatly taxed. Power and technical dexterity are called for all over the keyboard. Careful balancing of tone (melody and accompaniment in one hand) is a *sine qua non*."

BROWNING, Leinsdorf/Philadelphia: Seraphim

R. CASADESUS, Ormandy/Philadelphia: Columbia

CICCOLINI, Martinon/Orchestre de Paris: Angel

COLLARD, Maazel/Orchestre National de France: Angel (CD)

DE LARROCHA, Foster/London Philharmonic: London (CD)

ENTREMONT, Boulez/Cleveland: Columbia

FLEISHER, Comissiona/Baltimore Symphony: Vanguard (CD)

KATCHEN, Kertesz/London Symphony: London

ROGÉ, DUTOIT/MONTREAL SYMPHONY: London (CD)

MAX REGER
1873–1916 — Germany

Reger was essentially a post-Romantic, with a penchant for Baroque and Classical forms. He wrote nearly two hundred piano pieces, many of which are stuffed with notes and accidentals, making for a fearsome-looking page. He is still highly regarded in Germany, though his music has not traveled very well.

Variations and Fugue on a Theme by Telemann, Op. 134

Reger was the most interesting variationist after Brahms. The set of *Telemann* Variations is among his finest works, and there have always been pianists around attracted by its merits. The theme is a minuet from Telemann's *Tafelmusik*, which is similar, in its variational possibilities, to the Handel tune that Brahms used in his great set of Variations and Fugue, Op. 24. The Reger stems from that work, reaching a massive conclusion in its Fugue.

BOLET: London

Variations and Fugue on a Theme by J. S. Bach, Op. 81

The *Bach* Variations, based on a theme from the Cantata No. 128, are far more chromatically intense than the *Telemann* Variations. Some consider this Reger's greatest work.

LAUGS: MHS

R. SERKIN: CBS (CD)

Aus meinem Tagebuch (From My Diary), Op. 82

This treasure trove shows us a relaxed, harmonically conservative Reger. There are four books, totaling thirty-five pieces. Some pieces remind one of Schubert, Brahms, or Schumann. Some are rollicking; others are intimate. The work is homophonic, without the

391

obsessive contrapuntalizations one often finds in Reger.

LAUGS: MHS

Piano Concerto in F minor, Op. 114

The Concerto is in three movements: Allegro moderato, Largo con gran espressione, and Allegro con spirito. It is a brilliant, warm, and emotional work, and the first movement is masterful in design and texture. The Concerto was rescued from oblivion by Rudolf Serkin, who gave the American premiere in 1945, and who takes the music firmly to his heart.

MAYER, Bour/The Hague Philharmonic: Leonarda
R. SERKIN, Ormandy/Philadelphia: Columbia

ALBERT ROUSSEL

1869–1937 — France

Roussel was not a virtuoso player himself, nor was he really at home with the piano. He did, however, contribute several major works to the repertoire. His style is awkward to play, but "meaty," vigorous, and individual, with a rugged quality. It is French to the core, but not Parisian. Roussel is a composer who wears well, but will never be as popular as, say, Debussy, Ravel, or Poulenc.

Trois Pièces pour piano, Op. 49
Suite pour piano, Op. 14
Sonatine, Op. 16
Prélude et fugue, Op. 46

In the Suite, Op. 14, one may hear Roussel's mastery of dance forms. The movements are: Prelude, Sicilienne, Bourrée, and Rondo. The last is a masterly virtuoso piece. The *Sonatine* is planned in two sections, with subdivisions. Its square pianism becomes more interesting with repeated hearing. The Prelude and Fugue is a splendid edifice from 1932, comprising a somewhat savage prelude and a fugue built on the letters of Bach's name. The *Trois Pièces*, dedicated to Robert Casadesus—*Toccata*, *Valse lente*, and *Scherzo et trio*—are more conducive to performance.

DOYEN: MHS
JOHANNESEN (Sonatine): Golden Crest
PETIT (Trois Pièces, Suite, Sonatine): L'Oiseau-Lyre

Piano Concerto (1927)

This is one of the best French piano concertos of the century. Because of its concertante style, pianists are not prone to sacrifice the hours needed to learn its biting pianism. It is in three short, dry, bitter movements. The slow movement has an austere beauty. There is not an excess note in this superbly developed work, and it exploits the bass range in an important way.

KRAJAY, Macura/Prague Chamber Orchestra: Supraphon
LITTAUER, Springer/Hamburg Symphony: Turnabout

CAMILLE SAINT-SAËNS
1835–1921 — France

Saint-Saëns composed piano music throughout his long career, but he left no solo sonata or other weighty structure. At his best he composed elegantly crafted salon music where the keyboard sparkles and bubbles. His tunes are memorable, his harmony is arresting, and his rhythms are infectious. He wears his heart on his sleeve; and his wit, sophistication, and lucidity seldom fail to charm. Daniel Gregory Mason has aptly put it: "Saint-Saëns is always the onlooker, the man of the world, never the mystic who contemplates in his own heart the forces that underlie the universe."

The Complete Solo Piano Music
The very best of Saint-Saëns's solo piano music is: the *Allegro appassionato,* Op. 70; the Toccata and Valse from the *Album for Piano,* Op. 72; the gloriously fetching *Etude en forme de valse,* No. 6 of the admirable Six Etudes of Op. 52, as well as the sixth and last Etude from Op. 111, *Toccata;* several of his flirtatious valses—the *Valse nonchalante, Valse langoureuse,* and *Valse gaie;* and lastly, the lengthier, twelve-minute *Caprice sur les airs de ballet d' "Alceste."*

DOSSE: Vox

Concerto No. 1 in D major, Op. 17 (1865)
Concerto No. 2 in G minor, Op. 22 (1868)
Concerto No. 3 in E-flat major, Op. 29 (1869)
Concerto No. 4 in C minor, Op. 44 (1873)
Concerto No. 5 in F major, Op. 103 (1895)

These represent the best-known French concertos of the nineteenth century. The composer was often heard as soloist. The concerti are slick and facile, with some electrifying pianistics and deftly colored orchestration. No. 2 is the most frequently played. Sigismund Stojowski said that it "opened like Bach, and ended like Offenbach." No. 4, in C minor, is the masterpiece; all of the best of Saint-Saëns is contained in this work, which is brilliantly clever in its construction. No. 5, in F, called the *Egyptian* Concerto, is delightful and lightweight. No. 1, in D, is lots of fun and has an effective slow movement. No. 3, in E-flat, on the other hand, is overloaded with molasses and trite figurations, yet it still possesses a kind of entertaining virtuosity.

The Five Concerti:
CICCOLINI, Baudo/Orchestre de Paris: Angel (CD)
ROGÉ, Dutoit/Royal Philharmonic: London (CD)
TACCHINO, Froment/Luxembourg Radio: Vox

Concerto No. 1:
ENTREMONT, Plasson/Toulouse Capitole: CBS

Concerto No. 2:
DAVIDOVICH, Järvi/Concertgebouw: Philips (CD)
RUBINSTEIN, Ormandy/Philadelphia: RCA

393

WILD, Freccia/National Philharmonic:
    Quintessence

Concerto No. 3:
DARRÉ, FOURESTLER: Pathé

Concerto No. 4:
CASADESUS, Bernstein/New York Philharmonic: CBS
COLLARD, Previn/Royal Philharmonic:
CORTOT, Munch: Pathé

Concerto No. 5:
ENTREMONT, Plasson/Toulouse Capitole:
    CBS
RICHTER, Kondrashin/Moscow Philharmonic: Monitor

ERIK SATIE
1866–1925 — France

Often associated with such movements as
Dadaism and Surrealism, Satie occupies a
pivotal position in French music. He detested
Wagnerism and Germanic "giantism," and
created instead a music devoid of heroics or
heavy emotionalism, music which indeed
mocked such sentiments. In the preface to his
Sports et divertissements, he wrote: "Turn the
pages of this book with an amiable and smiling
hand; for this is a work of fantasy and does
not pretend to be anything else. For those who
are dried up and stultified, I have written a
chorale which is serious and respectable. This
chorale is a sort of bitter preamble, a kind of
austere and unfrivolous introduction. I have
put into it everything I know about boredom.
I dedicate this chorale to those who do not like
me—and withdraw."

Satie's aesthetic was so new and guileless
that on first hearing it sounded as preposterous
as his titles. Laurence Davies wrote of "Satie's
own terrifying willingness to disrobe, shedding
all those aids to beauty which the ordinary
composer finds indispensable." The music of

Erik Satie, said James Gibb, "came in like the
voice of a child, saying outrageous things with
complete, honest calm." While Virgil Thomson extols: "It wears no priestly robes; it
mumbles no incantations; it is not painted up
by Max Factor to terrify elderly ladies or to
give little girls a thrill. Neither is it designed to
impress orchestral conductors or to get anybody a job teaching school. It has literally no
devious motivation. It is as simple as a friendly
conversation and in its better moments exactly
as poetic and as profound."

Satie's music for the piano is mostly thin-textured, of moderate or even simple demands
technically, but it is deceptively difficult to
play with simplicity and without caricature.
"Satie's habit of writing his pieces in groups of
three," noted Constant Lambert, "was not
just a mannerism. It took the place in his art of
dramatic development, and was part of his
peculiarly sculpturesque view of music. When
we pass from the first to the second *Gymno-pédie,* or from the second to the third *Gnos-sienne,* we do not feel that we are passing from
one object to another."

The Piano Music
Some of Satie's best works are: *Trois
Sarabandes* (1887); *Trois Gymnopédies*
(1888); *Trois Gnossiennes* (1890); *Trois
Préludes* (1891); *Heures séculaires et
instantanées* (1914); *Chapitres tournés en
tous sens* (1913); *Embryons desséchés*
(1913); *Trois Valses distinguées d'un
précieux dégoûté* (1914) (all sets of three);
Pièces froides (1897); *Véritables Préludes
flasques* (1912); *Sonatine bureaucratique* (a
parody of Clementi's C major Sonatina);
Sports et divertissements (1914—twenty
small pieces); and *Cinq Nocturnes* (1919).

CICCOLINI (complete piano music): Angel
GLAZER (complete piano music): Vox
MASSELOS: RCA
ROGÉ: London (CD)
Y. TAKAHASHI: Denon (CD)
VARSANO: CBS

394

DOMENICO SCARLATTI
1685–1757 — Italy

Scarlatti was the chief Italian keyboard composer of the eighteenth century, producing nearly six hundred pieces in a simple, binary form, which he called sonatas. Maurice Hinson has written, "Scarlatti gave the binary form a variety and expressive range that has never been surpassed by any other composer."

Most of this enormous literature of four-minute pieces was produced during the last fifteen years of his life. Scarlatti was himself a great harpsichordist, and most of his output was inspired by the high skills of his pupil, Maria Barbara, Queen of Spain. Wanda Landowska wrote: "Spain fired the imagination of the great Neapolitan. . . . When we hear Scarlatti's music, we know that we are in the climate of sunlight and warmth. It is Italy, it is Spain—the spirit of the Latin countries and the god of the Mediterranean." Scarlatti has the genuine nobility, the heroism, and the audacity of a Don Quixote. The Scarlatti scholar, biographer, and harpsichordist Ralph Kirkpatrick states: "There is hardly an aspect of Spanish life, of Spanish popular music and dance, that has not found itself a place in the microcosm that Scarlatti created with his sonatas. . . . He has captured the click of castanets, the strumming of guitars, the thud of muffled drums, the harsh bitter wail of Gypsy lament, the overwhelming gaiety of the village band, and above all, the wiry tension of the Spanish dance."

The Sonatas
Alessandro Longo and Ralph Kirkpatrick have both catalogued Scarlatti. The Kirkpatrick numbers are more correct chronologically, but the Longo edition, in eleven volumes published by Ricordi, seems to be used more often internationally for the sonatas. Sacheverell Sitwell made certain helpful divisions for some of the sonatas he knew. His groupings are:

Tarantellas: L. 241, 233, 95, 125, 475.

Neapolitan Sonatas: L. 388–486, 387, 384, 375, 461, 13, 103, 263, 414, 463, 385.

Siciliennes: L. 487, 452, 218.

Bell Sounds: L. 369, 218, 196.

Dances (not of Spanish character): L. 357, Suppl. 36 (K. 42), 168, 315, Suppl. 40 (K. 172), 178, Suppl. 39 (K. 441), 82, Suppl. 21 (K. 554).

Military Sonatas: L. 107, Suppl. 10 (K. 335), 400, 23, Suppl. 2 (K. 420), 205, 193, 255, 86.

High Speed "Velocity" Sonatas: L. 345, 215, 364, 272, 380, 470, 385.

Adagio Sonatas: L. 383, 423, Suppl. 7 (K. 34), 261, 382, 403, 33, 64, 4, 59, 27, 468, Suppl. 9 (K. 287), 61, 248, 332, Suppl. 27 (K. 328), 18, 443, 438, 99, 12, 187, 497, 312.

Pastoral or Bucolic Sonatas: L. 138, 344, 354, 439, 198, 132, Suppl. 41 (K. 489), 206.

"Hunting" Sonatas: L. 107, 364, 228, 192, 95, 302, 470, 290, 164, 287, 475.

The Virtuoso Sonatas: L. 356, 233, 232, 308, 65, 470. L. 273, 199, 328, 7, 255 with glissando passages.

From Sitwell's list of *Spanish Sonatas* by Scarlatti: L. 479, 413, 368, 449, 373, 478, 29, 241, 356, 58, 465, 317, 204, 474, 138, 407, 415, 232, 457, 282, 224, 107, 422, 349, 376, 179, 104, 412, 429, 498, 257, 371, 238, 428, 135, 165, 323, 273, 309, 199, 308, 27, 381, 305, 466, 328, 57, 161, 9, 454, 400, 172, 240, 263, 23, 134, 284, 65, 208, 213, 310, 279, 128, 286, 361, 109, 319, 418, 294, 338, 324, 340, 206, 164, 14, 196, 113, 311, 1, 255, 266, 116, 475, 408, 458, 200, 327, 223, 395, 11, 293, 497, 500, 312, 404.

Scarlatti himself wrote in the preface to the only group of these pieces (called *Esercizi*) that was published during his lifetime: "Reader, whether you are a dilettante or a professor, do not expect to find in these compositions any profound intention, but rather, an ingenious gesting of the art, to prepare you for bold playing on the harpsichord. . . . Show yourself more human than critical, and thus you will increase your own pleasure. . . . Live happily!''

Scarlatti created not only a citadel of humanity, but also one of the most compressed arts in history, with a technical audacity that still astounds. Scarlatti might have played upon a very early pianoforte at the Madrid court, but the instrument would hardly have interested him at that time. It is in the best interest of contemporary players essaying these works on the piano to familiarize themselves with harpsichord versions, such as those of Landowska, Pinnock, Kirkpatrick, Valenti, George Malcolm, and others. The harpsichord sonority and its varied registration may help the pianist to hear the works with more authenticity than the eleven-volume Longo edition does, with its Romantic curvature of phrasing, tempi, and accent. I have noted some of the performances by pianists who have most thoroughly adapted and assimilated Scarlatti to the piano:

DI BONAVENTURA (L. 17, 463, 420, 373, 433, 479, 422, 369, 41, 380, 385, 266, 487, 109, 33, 388, 462, 486, 384, 370, 413, 104, 395): Connoisseur Society

R. CASADESUS (L. 463, 395, 411, 263, 465, 413, 487, 449, 387, 22, 486): CBS

CICCOLINI (L. 5, 413, 14, 23, 33, 41, 58, 103, 104, 263, 281, 288, 366): Seraphim

DECHENNE (L. 401, 186, 188, 413, 108, 366, 103, 375, 450, 457, 422): MHS

DE LARROCHA (From the 1738 Thirty Esercizi: Nos. 9, 6, 10, 8, 13, 11, 28): London

DRZEWIECKI (L. 352, 422, 23, 375, 413, 495, 424, 241, 188, 383, 349, 465): Muza

GIESEKING (L. 23, 275, 413, 424, 443): EMI (Italian)

GILELS (L. 104, 449, 487, 23, 345): Monitor

GOULD (L. 463, 413, 486): CBS

HASKIL (L. 256, 388, 182, 457, 386, 171, 475, 483, 33, 255, 278): Westminster

HESS (L. 352, 387): Angel

HOROWITZ (K. 33, 39, 54, 55, 96, 146, 162, 198, 322, 380, 455, 466, 474, 481, 491, 525, 531): CBS (CD)

HOROWITZ (six sonatas): RCA

SCHIFF (K. 17, 27, 96, 162, 208, 322, 394, 420, 427, 491, 518, 519): Hungaroton (CD)

WEISSENBERG (K. 8, 13, 20, 87, 107, 109, 132, 184, 193, 233, 247, 450, 481, 531, 544): DG (CD)

ARNOLD SCHOENBERG
1874–1951 — Austria

Three Piano Pieces, Op. 11 (1908)
Six Little Piano Pieces, Op. 19 (1911)
Five Little Piano Pieces, Op. 23 (1924)
Suite, Op. 25 (1924)
Piano Piece, Op. 33a, and *Piano Piece,* Op. 33b (1932)

Although Schoenberg's complete solo piano music fits snugly on one LP, Paul Jacobs is convinced "that these five books of pieces are as important to contemporary piano technique as the Chopin Etudes were to that of the nineteenth century." Glenn Gould remarks: "Schoenberg does not write *against* the piano, but neither can he be accused of writing *for* it. There is not one phrase in his keyboard output which reveals the least indebtedness to the percussive sonorities exploited in an overwhelming percentage of contemporary keyboard music." Regarding the Three Piano Pieces, Op. 11, Gould adds, "Perhaps no other composition was as crucial to Schoenberg's future. . . . Opus 11 was the first major test of the possibilities of survival in a musical universe no longer dominated by a triadically centered harmonic orbit."

The set of Six Little Piano Pieces, Op. 19, continues Schoenberg's experiments in atonality while giving new meaning to musical brevity. The pieces range from nine bars to only eighteen in length, and spawned a whole miniaturist movement, headed by Webern. The Five Pieces, Op. 23, are similar in texture to Op.

11, but they are far more thoroughly developed. The last of these pieces, a Waltz, was Schoenberg's first totally organized work based on a row of the twelve tones. It is interesting that Schoenberg's departure from harmonic practice still allowed him to integrate the beloved dance form of his native Vienna.

Of the Suite, Op. 25, Gould reports, "I can think of no composition for solo piano from the first quarter of this century which can stand as its equal. . . . For all its reliance on binary dance forms and its sly digs at pre-classical convention, it is among the most spontaneous and wickedly inventive of Schoenberg's works." The Suite consists of a Präludium, Gavotte with Musette, Intermezzo, Minuet with Trio, and Gigue. Each movement is arrived at through the use of the same row. The Two Piano Pieces, Op. 33a and 33b, are freer examples of Schoenberg's expressionistic idiom; both are marvelously developed, concentrated, and expressive.

Schoenberg's musical evolution stemmed from his early post-Wagnerian epigonism and culminated in the twelve-tone method, in which all twelve notes of the chromatic scale are arranged in a special sequence. This method has still not achieved anything like wide public acceptance, though many musicians consider his work to be the classicism of twentieth-century music, a body of work which revitalized an exhausted harmonic system. The historian Frederic Morton felt Schoenberg "would not just revolutionize music but reinvent it." Many have felt that Schoenberg concocted a new methodology in a quest for originality or expressionist ugliness. But Ernest Hutcheson writes: "The system is no more complicated or empirical than the polyphony of a Bach fugue or the harmonic and formal structure of a Beethoven Sonata, though it has been accused of being involved, mechanical, and cerebral. It is simply a technique of composition, and works written within it must, like all others, be judged primarily by the value and perceptibility of their ideas."

Each of the pianists listed gives perceptive readings. Schoenberg's piano music is overly stocked with interpretive indications, and his metronome markings can be confusing.

The Complete Solo Piano Music:
GOULD: CBS
HELFFER: MHS
JACOBS: Nonesuch
POLLINI: DG
Y. TAKAHASHI: Denon

Piano Concerto, Op. 42 (1942)

The Concerto is somewhat easier to grasp on first hearing than other works of this composer; there is a reflective, mellow quality in it. It was Oscar Levant who suggested to Schoenberg that he write a piano concerto. It was premiered by Edward Steuermann, and the NBC Symphony with Stokowski conducting, in 1944. Schoenberg, in describing the work, wrote: "Life was so easy (Andante), but all of a sudden hate broke loose (Molto allegro); the situation became grave (Adagio) but life has to go on (Giocoso)."

BRENDEL, Kubelik/Bavarian Radio: DG
GOULD, Craft/CBC Symphony: Columbia
P. SERKIN, Ozawa/Chicago Symphony: RCA

FRANZ SCHUBERT
1797–1828 — Austria

Schubert had one of the least public careers of any of the great musicians. Though he played the piano well, he never gave a concert and, in fact, was lucky even to have a piano at his disposal for composing. Yet Schubert is one of the progenitors of Romantic piano style and his influence was great—not as much in his solo piano music as in his accompaniments to more than six hundred songs (virtually a new art form in European music). In these songs he made the piano an equal partner with the voice and, more important, he developed an art of description inspired by the poetic text; this would have far-reaching influence on the small character pieces for solo piano of the Romantic composers. Unlike his piano music, some of Schubert's songs were comparatively well known, even during his lifetime. Liszt and Schumann were the first to realize that a poetic piano style existed in these accompaniments. It was not for nothing that Liszt transcribed more than fifty of Schubert's songs. Schubert played the accompaniments of his own songs, as well as his solo piano music, for his friends and was pleased when complimented on his "singing tone."

In 1822 he composed his famous *Wanderer Fantasy*, a work whose structure influenced Liszt in his later experiments with "thematic transformation." Technically, this work was one of the most muscular ever written up to that time and must certainly have strained the light mechanisms of the Viennese pianos to their limits (though there is no record of Schubert expressing dissatisfaction with the pianos of his time, as Beethoven did). Schubert himself had a hard time with the work and once stopped during a performance, shouting that perhaps the devil could play it, but he could not.

He was unhappy with the pianists in Vienna during his day, calling them "thumpers." He wrote no "bravura" variations or "fugitive pieces" for public consumption or easy digestibility; Schubert composed for himself from a seemingly ever-flowing magic fountain. His own playing must have had that kind of purity which is engendered by unworldliness. His solo works, especially the sonatas (those visionary scores, the last voice of Viennese Classicism), were almost totally neglected. They were criticized for not being of the "Beethovenian Sonata-type." Not until the 1930s did Schubert's Classicism make its impact. It was inevitable that so great a literature as these sonatas could not remain unknown. As with the Mozart concerti, pianists since the mid-1950s have been passionately exploring

Schubert, and these masterpieces have finally become repertory staples.

The ordering of the Schubert piano sonatas has always been confusing. Many of the twenty-three sonatas were left incomplete. The only unfinished work performed in public is the C major Sonata, D. (Deutsch listing) 840, in two movements. Eleven complete sonatas are part of the international repertory. Only three of these, the late A minor, D. 845, the D major, D. 850, and the G major, D. 894, were published during Schubert's lifetime. Traversals of the complete and incomplete sonatas have been accomplished by Kempff (DG) and by Klien (Vox). These artists are both finely attuned to Schubert. The incomplete works have interest for all those following Schubert's evolution as a composer of sonatas.

Sonata in A minor, D. 537 (1817)
In three movements, this is the earliest of the Schubert sonatas to have received somewhat regular performance in concert, though it is hardly in the same musical sphere as his other two sonatas in A minor.

KATIN: Olympia (CD)
MICHELANGELI: DG (CD)

Sonata in E-flat major, D. 568 (1817)
This work, in four movements, is very difficult for the pianist to hold together. It harks back to Haydn, and is redolent of the Viennese countryside.

FEDOROVA: Melodiya
KEMPFF: DG
P. SERKIN: RCA
WEICHERT: Accord (CD)

Sonata in B major, D. 575 (1817)
In four movements. The Andante is high Schubert lyricism; the rest of the score, except for a good scherzo, is not well organized.

KEMPFF: DG
KLIEN: Vox
WEICHERT: Accord (CD)
WÜHRER: Vox

Sonata in A major, D. 664 (1819)

The best known of the sonatas and the easiest for the performer to make intelligible. The outer movements have a youthful freshness, while the Andante can only be called Schubertian in its bittersweet beauty.

ARRAU: Philips
ASHKENAZY: London
BADURA-SKODA: RCA
HESS (recorded 1928): Pearl
KRAUS: Vanguard
RICHTER: Angel; MMG (CD)
WATTS: CBS

Sonata in A minor, D. 784 (1823)

Schubert had not composed a piano sonata for several years when he wrote this three-movement work, and his structural prowess had grown considerably in the interim. The first movement shows a sparseness of notes and an awkwardness in the pianism. The finale, with its octave passage at the end, shows Schubert's characteristic disregard for what was playable. Yet the musical quality of this work is the highest thus far in the sonatas. The opening movement is majestic, and the finale's triplet figure has an autumnal flavor.

ASHKENAZY: London
BRENDEL: Philips
DEMUS: MHS
LUPU: London
MAISENBERG: Orfeo
RICHTER: MMG (CD)
WATTS: CBS

Sonata in C major (unfinished), D. 840 (1825)

In two movements, this is by far the finest of the incomplete sonatas. Sketches for the unfinished movements exist. The C major Sonata is as complete as is the *Unfinished* Symphony and stands as a masterpiece of structural and emotional content. Only now, however, is it beginning to be appreciated by a larger public.

BARENBOIM: DG
BRENDEL: Philips

KALISH: Nonesuch
RICHTER: Monitor; Philips (CD)

Sonata in A minor, D. 845 (1825)

Its four perfect movements show a complete mastery of large form. After a noble first movement featuring Schubertian dotted rhythms in contrast to lyric material, there is a springy set of variations, with much brilliant writing and contrapuntal interest. The scherzo and trio have a typically Schubertian innocence, while a finale of slender material is imbued with an interior restlessness.

BRENDEL: Philips
FIRKUŠNÝ: Sugano (CD)
HASKIL: Music and Arts (CD)
LUPU: London (CD)
POLLINI: DG (CD)
RICHTER: Monitor

Sonata in D major, D. 850 (1825)

This is a giant of a work in four movements, over forty minutes long, calling for a tremendous grasp of large form on the part of the pianist, and a Schubert-loving audience to appreciate what Schumann dubbed the "heavenly lengths" of Schubert's larger works. The slow movement has, with its melodic beauty, a marvelous subtlety of syncopation and harmonic boldness. The work was composed in the country in three weeks. Schubert wrote, "The environs . . . are truly heavenly and deeply moved and benefited me, as did its inhabitants." The sonata is filled with the song and dance of the people, as well as the sounds of their yodeling.

ASHKENAZY: London
CURZON: London
RICHTER: Monitor
SCHNABEL: Arabesque

Sonata in G major, D. 894, "Sonata-Fantasy" (1826)

In four movements, this is a work of the most lovable lyricism. Schumann called it Schubert's "most perfect" sonata in form and spirit. In view of its leisurely qualities, the interpreter must be on guard to keep the audience awake. Schumann was wary of those who lacked "the imagination to solve its riddles."

ARTYMIW: Chandos
ASHKENAZY: London
DEMUS: MHS
LUPU: London (CD)
P. SERKIN: RCA

Sonata in C minor, D. 958 (1828)
The C minor Sonata joins the late A major, D. 959, and the B-flat major, D. 960, among the great sonatas of the Classical age. Published posthumously in 1838, they were composed within weeks before Schubert's death, which could not have been more untimely. Schubert had grown from being a prodigal, spontaneous fountain of melody to a profound and fully matured thinker whose contribution to sonata form was entirely his own, not bound by the sonata idea as defined by Beethoven. These last works—the String Quintet, the Ninth Symphony, and the last sonatas—exhibit a new grandeur of intention, a power of creative execution, a cumulative flow, a new fierceness in the ideas, as well as a peacefulness that go beyond Romantic subjectivity. The Sonata in C minor and its two companions were composed in less than four weeks. Their psychological import is becoming better understood by discriminating pianists not merely attracted to virtuosity. The C minor Sonata is more somber than dramatic. In this late work, it is interesting that Schubert still uses the old-fashioned Minuetto.

ARRAU: Philips
BRENDEL: Philips
GRAFFMAN: Columbia
RICHTER: Columbia/Melodiya
SHURE: Audiofon

Sonata in A major, D. 959 (1828)
The most astonishing of this sonata's four movements is the second, an Andantino which, as Denis Matthews attests, "has the greatest, most alarming, surprise of all: a plaintive song, harmonized in F-sharp minor and A major respectively, is invaded by a cataclysmic passage of bravura recitative in which key as such ceases to exist." The sonata as a whole is musically and structurally completely different from the C minor or the B-flat Sonata.

BRENDEL: Philips (CD)
ESCHENBACH: DG
HUNGERFORD: Vanguard
LUPU: London
OLSHANSKY: Monitor
SCHNABEL: EMI Electrola
R. SERKIN: CBS

Sonata in B-flat major, D. 960 (1828)
For contemporary pianists, this work has become one of their greatest musical goals. It is the most often played of the last three sonatas. It is cast in four movements, and takes over forty minutes. Maurice Hinson calls the B-flat Sonata "a transcendental work of unique individuality." It is music of ravishing and visionary beauty. The Andante sostenuto ranks with the greatest slow movements ever written.

BISHOP-KOVACEVICH: Hyperion (CD)
CURZON: London (CD)
HAUTZIG: Monitor
HOROWITZ: RCA
KEMPFF: DG
RUBINSTEIN: RCA (CD)
SCHNABEL: Angel or EMI Electrola
R. SERKIN: CBS

Fantasia in C major, D. 760, "Wanderer" (1822)
Known as the *Wanderer* Fantasy. Each movement is thematically derived from Schubert's song "Der Wanderer." It is a highly successful work of thematic unification in a four-movement plan. The Fantasia is the most virtuosic work of Schubert piano music, and is technically taxing. Liszt saw its possibilities as

a work for piano and orchestra and, knowing that Schubert undertook no concerto writing, he made an effective transcription of it, which is occasionally performed.

Bashkirov: Melodiya
Graffman: Columbia
Perahia: CBS (CD)
Pollini: DG (CD)
Richter: Angel
Rubinstein: RCA (CD)
Watts: CBS

Four Impromptus, D. 899 (1827)

No. 1 in C minor is the longest of the set, and needs careful planning for its effect. No. 2 in E-flat is extremely popular; brilliant passage-work needed in the right hand leads to a trio of contrasting material. No. 3 in G-flat, writes James Friskin, "is by reason of its melodic inspiration and harmonic magic, a supreme test of the player's power to sing on his instrument." No. 4 in A-flat is one of the best-loved of Schubert's piano pieces, "with those poetic garlands of sound," as Curzon called them. Schnabel used to say they made him think of "a dance in the moonlight—with the feet scarcely touching the ground."

Barenboim: DG
Curzon (Nos. 3 & 4): London
E. Fischer: EMI Pathé
Gieseking: Seraphim
Kempff: DG
Lipatti (Nos. 2 & 3): Angel
Perahia: CBS (CD)
Rubinstein (Nos. 3 & 4): RCA (CD)
Schnabel (Nos. 2 & 4): Seraphim

Four Impromptus, D. 935 (1828)

No. 1 in F minor is long. The dialogue with the left hand crossing back and forth is almost Italianate in its bel canto. No. 2 in A-flat is the easiest technically of the eight impromptus, but requires meticulous phrase punctuation. No. 3 in B-flat is popular, a set of variations of a particularly Viennese cast. No. 4 in F minor is especially difficult in its scale work, staccato, and thirds.

Brendel: Philips (CD)
Buchbinder: Teldec (CD)
E. Fischer: EMI Pathé
Gieseking: Seraphim
Kempff: DG
Lupu: London (CD)
Perahia: CBS (CD)
R. Serkin: CBS

Drei Klavierstücke, D. 946 (1828)

These are impressive pieces, which are now becoming known. They contain much rhythmic and harmonic interest.

Brendel: Philips
Buchbinder: Teldec (CD)
Firkušný: Sugano (CD)
Gieseking: Seraphim
Kalish: Nonesuch

Six Moments musicaux, D. 780

Very subtle phrasing is needed in most of these miniatures. No. 3 in F minor is by far the best known. No. 4 in C-sharp minor consists of passagework of a Bachian tone based on broken chords, with a beautiful middle section, artful in its syncopated rhythm. No. 5 in F minor is chordal. Nos. 2 and 6, both in A-flat, are gems from the deep well of Schubert's lyric genius.

Curzon: London (CD)
Gilels: Mobile Fidelity (CD)
Hautzig: Monitor
Kempff: DG
Luvisi: Rivergate
Schnabel: Seraphim

Allegretto in C minor, D. 915 (1827)

An example of the later Schubert, it is veiled and subtle.

Arrau: Philips
Goldsmith: MHS
Schnabel: Angel

401

Waltzes

Schubert wrote more than four hundred dances for solo piano. Most of them were waltzes, *Ländler,* German dances, and the like. These were played by him at gatherings, while his friends danced. They are mostly harmonically simple, and are usually a student's first encounter with the composer.

The Complete Waltzes:
BORDONI: Seraphim

Waltzes as fillers:
ASHKENAZY (with Schubert's beautiful Hungarian Melody in B minor, D. 817): London
BRENDEL (Twelve German Dances, D. 790; Sixteen German Dances, D. 783): Philips
HAUTZIG: Turnabout
WATTS: Columbia

ROBERT SCHUMANN
1810–1856 — Germany

For contemporary performers, Schumann's great piano cycles, such as the *Carnaval, Davidsbündlertänze, Kreisleriana, Fantasy,* and *Humoreske,* represent one of the supreme tests in the art of the pianist. In these works Schumann weaves a dense contrapuntal tapestry, interlaced with fragmented melody. No other music ever sounded like his, and it even looked different on the printed page.

Schumann has fared especially well since the invention of the long-playing recording, which has shaped a new listener better able to cope with Schumann's wide-ranging forms. Through this medium, one has the means to listen over and over to Schumann's highly personal and psychological formal shapes. It takes many hearings to travel through the webs of, say, the *Humoreske* or *Novelletten.* In the past, pianists would often program parts of Schumann's cycles; for example, several of the *Fantasiestücke* Op. 12, or a group of the *Davidsbündlertänze,* or two or three of the *Kreisleriana.* That is now becoming rarer. Indeed, pianists are now including Schumann's five variation outcasts from the *Symphonic Etudes.*

For the pianist, Schumann is often a difficult riddle to solve. More than with any other Romantic master, the interpreter needs to be a true re-creator and must possess a special empathy for Schumann the man and troubled creator. Often, the deeper the pianist goes into the "twilight zone" of Schumann's imagination, the deeper he or she may get tangled within the labyrinth. It must never be forgotten that Schumann throughout his life was desperately holding back the gates of madness. Public performance of his music is always problematic. His art is so unpublic, and although his music is often technically difficult, there is never a shred of virtuosity or easy appeal. Roland Barthes feels that "the piano as a social instrument has undergone for a century a historical evolution of which Schumann is the victim. The human subject has changed: intimacy and solitude have lost their value, the individual has become increasingly gregarious, he wants collective, massive, often paroxysmal music, the expression of *us* rather than of *me;* yet Schumann is truly the musician of solitary intimacy, of the amorous and imprisoned soul that *speaks to itself . . .* of the child who has no other link than to the mother. . . . To play Schumann implies an innocence very few artists can attain. . . . Schumann lets his music be fully heard only by someone who plays it, even badly. . . . It is because Schumann's music goes much farther than the ear; it goes into the body, into the muscles through its rhythm. . . . It is as if on each occasion the piece was written only for one person, the one who plays it; the true Schumannian pianist—*c'est moi.*"

It is a pity that some of Schumann's most radical thoughts were watered down by his own hand in final revisions, years after the outpourings of the early manifestations of his genius. Charles Rosen writes: "Many of them came out of the revising process badly mauled. If anyone except Schumann himself had done this work, these revisions would be repudiated today with indignation."

More often than not, performers use the last edition of Schumann. But as Rosen states: "With a composer like Schumann, terrified of insanity . . . the changes are, almost without exception, deplorable. . . . One might say that Schumann misunderstood his own genius, at least at moments when he lacked confidence . . . he sometimes attempted to remove from his own scores those qualities most idiosyncratic, to attenuate everything which made him so different from his contemporaries." It remains incumbent upon Schumann interpreters to compare Schumann's original versions.

Schumann's career as a pianist was demolished when his fourth finger became partially paralyzed after he used a contraption to strengthen it. He composed for the piano, however, a body of music of the utmost beauty and originality.

From the age of twenty, Schumann's genius glowed for ten years. The piano was his sole friend, and to it he poured out the most susceptible soul of any of the Romantics. He invented the Romantic piano suite, the tying together of smaller musical units into a large form, such as the *Carnaval, Papillons,* or *Kinderscenen.* Like many Romantics', his music has literary implications and, in his case, a fierce autobiographical content.

Schumann was a complex man with more than one personality. He has been called the most Romantic of the Romantics. His music formed the springtime of German Romanticism. His early piano works, wrote Daniel Gregory Mason, "conceived with most daring originality and executed with inimitable verve, . . . rank with . . . the very supreme and perfect attainments of the Romantic spirit in music. Their exuberant vitality, their prodigal wealth of melodic invention, their rhythmic vigor and harmonic luxuriance, their absolutely novel pianistic effects, their curious undercurrent of fanciful imagery and extra-musical allusion, the peculiarly personal, even perverse, idiom in which they are couched, all conspire to make them unique even among their author's works, and in some respects more happily representative of him than the later productions in which he was more influenced by conventional or borrowed ideals. In them we have the wild-flavored first fruits of his genius, fresh with all the aroma and bloom of unsophisticated youth."

Variations on the Name Abegg, Op. 1 (1830)

The *Abegg* Variations is an astonishing opus one. In four variations and a finale, the piano writing reflects something of Weber and Hummel. Yet enough magic is displayed so that the work is frequently played. It already contains the characteristic Schumann in embryo.

ARRAU: Philips
ESCHENBACH: DG
GINZBURG: Melodiya
HASKIL: Philips
KEENE: Protone

Papillons, Op. 2 (1831)

The first of Schumann's character suites; his youthful imagination soars. In this eleven-minute score of twelve tiny dance movements, Schumann is on his chosen path, fiercely inspired by literature—in this case, his beloved Jean Paul Richter, whose novels Schumann typically credits with teaching him more counterpoint than any theoretical treatise. "The clamour of the carnival dies away, the clock in the tower strikes six," is written on the last line of the score. The dancers disappear to Schumann's striking pedal effect.

ARRAU: Philips
CORTOT: Seraphim
EGOROV: Angel
KEMPFF: DG

403

PERAHIA: CBS (CD)
RICHTER: Melodiya
SCHIFF: Denon (CD)
SOFRONITSKY: Melodiya

Six Studies after Caprices by Paganini, Op. 3 (1832)

Based on the Paganini Caprices for solo violin. These pieces are interesting, difficult, and almost never played. Teachers might use these with profit instead of, say, the usual Czerny studies.

DEMUS: MHS
FRANKL: Vox

Intermezzi, Op. 4 (1832)

Composed when Schumann was twenty-two, this is a neglected and significant work, living in the shadow of the more famous cycles. It throbs with the true Schumann spirit. Each of the five pieces is in song form with trio. They must be played as a cycle.

BASHKIROV: Melodiya
ESCHENBACH: DG
JOHANNESEN: Golden Crest

Impromptus on a Theme of Clara Wieck, Op. 5 (1833; revised 1850)

This set of variations has never found much favor, and is played even less than Op. 4. Anyone thinking of working on this composition should examine the first version, which is vastly more original and inspired than Schumann's final thoughts.

COLLARD: Connoisseur Society
ROSEN: Nonesuch

Davidsbündlertänze, Op. 6 (1837)

The title literally means "Dances of the League of David." (Actually, few of these are dances.) Schumann and his friends were "Davidites," as they called themselves, waging war against Philistinism. Robert Haven Schauffler suggests the pieces be called "Eighteen Studies in the Psychology of Autobiography." Schumann af-

fixed to each piece an "F" or an "E": if proud and passionate, it was the production of the Florestan side of his nature; if pensive and dreamy, it was Eusebius emerging. The Op. 6 is pure, unalloyed Schumann, a helter-skelter work of whimsy and tenderness. His heart is sensitive and easily wounded. On the title page are the words "Delight is linked with pain forever and ever." Schumann wrote to Clara Wieck that the pieces "originated in the most joyful excitement that I can ever recall. . . . If ever I was happy at the piano, it was while composing these."

ARRAU: Philips
ARTYMIW: Chandos
CORTOT: EMI
FIRKUŠNÝ: Sugano (CD)
PERAHIA: CBS
ROSEN: Nonesuch

Toccata in C major, Op. 7 (1833)

This is one of the wonder works in the double-note literature. The Toccata is indispensable; no pianist should avoid working at it. Its structure is a modified sonata-allegro design, bracing and energetic. Schumann had first composed it in the key of D, but transposed it to C, in which, as he said, it was "no longer so wild, but much better behaved." Clara Wieck Schumann called it the Toccata of Toccatas— "Toccata Toccatarium." The work is a colorful amplification of the Czerny Toccata. These days it is not played as much as it once was when Lhévinne, Hofmann, and Barère thrilled audiences with it.

BARÈRE: Varèse/Sarabande
GILELS: Melodiya
GINZBURG: Melodiya
HOROWITZ: CBS (CD)
LHÈVINNE: RCA
RICHTER: DG

Allegro in B minor, Op. 8 (1831)

Occasionally dusted off by pianists, the *Allegro* is self-conscious and difficult technically, but contains a great deal of fanciful music.

DE LARROCHA: London
FEINBERG: Melodiya

Carnaval, Op. 9 (1834–35)

Carnaval is subtitled *Scènes mignonnes sur quatre notes.* This suite is Schumann's most frequently played large work. The richness of its material and pulsating life make it one of the great half-hours of human fantasy. *Carnaval* is composed of twenty pieces, opening with a preamble and closing with a march in 3/4 time, and presents us with a scene of perpetual youth, the Davidsbund against the Philistines. At the Carnival, Schumann meets Pierrot, Pantalon and Columbine, Harlequin, Chiarina (the sixteen-year-old Clara Wieck—not yet his wife), and his current romantic interest, Estrella (Ernestine von Fricken—whose native town, Asch, is spelled with four letters which are also in Schumann's name and which correspond to the four notes that the work is based on: A, E-flat, C, and B [German A, Es, C, and H]). Schumann himself makes a dual appearance as Florestan and Eusebius (the two opposing sides of his nature). Paganini appears in a violinistic movement of treacherous difficulty. Chopin shows up in heated nocturne style, and so forth. In this great orgiastic ballroom scene, Schumann reveals his secrets to his assembled friends and lovers.

MICHELANGELI: DG (CD)
NOVAES: Turnabout
RACHMANINOFF: RCA
RUBINSTEIN: RCA (CD)
SOFRONITSKY: Melodiya
SOLOMON: Seraphim

Twelve Concert Etudes after Caprices of Paganini, Op. 10 (1833)

Schumann said, "These Etudes are of the greatest difficulty throughout, every one in a different way." Of this set, Op. 10, No. 2 was also transcribed by Liszt. Schumann here ex-

pands his vision of transcription from his Op. 3 series, and gives himself far more freedom in adapting the Caprices to the piano.

DEMUS: MHS
FRANKL: Vox

Sonata in F-sharp minor, Op. 11 (1835)

The sonata is in four movements totaling thirty-five minutes. The introduction radiates Romantic beauty, the slow movement, an Aria, is filled with yearning. Throughout the other movements, there is much infectious gaiety. On the title page is a dedication to Clara with a note stating that the sonata was composed by Florestan and Eusebius. When Liszt played the work to Schumann in 1840, the composer reported that his performance "moved me strangely. Although his reading differed in many places from my own . . ." Clara Schumann performed it as early as 1837, and Brahms did so in 1867. Anton Rubinstein, Paderewski, and Josef Hofmann were great advocates of this work. To say that it is one of the most problematic compositions in the Romantic literature would be to understate its myriad problems of organization, not the least of which is to maintain an audience's interest through the compositional maze. From the great introduction, with its trembling of the soul, throughout, the score is fantastic, poetic, thrilling.

ARRAU: Philips
BERMAN: Columbia/Melodiya
GILELS: Monitor
POLLINI: DG (CD)
ROSEN: Nonesuch

Fantasiestücke, Op. 12 (1837)

One of Schumann's most popular collections, and the epitome of German Romanticism. The eight pieces are: (1) *Des Abends* ("In the Evening")—Schumann lulls us on a fragrant spring evening, using cross-rhythms. (2) *Aufschwung* ("Soaring")—passionate optimism; the Florestan part of his nature is fully exhibited. (3) *Warum?* ("Why?")—one of Schumann's most poetic pieces. (4) *Grillen* ("Whims")—the tempo marking only says "with humor," and its humor is uniquely Schumann's. (5) *In der Nacht* ("In the Night")— Schumann said the piece contains the story of Hero and Leander. *In der Nacht* is one of the glorious pages in Schumann's output. It is also technically demanding. (6) *Fabel* ("Fable")—a whimsical piece with alternating moods. (7) *Traumeswirren* ("Dream Visions")—filled with gorgeous patterns and one of Schumann's most difficult pieces, calling for strong fingers and good rotation. (8) *Ende vom Lied* ("Song's End")—Schumann wrote to Clara, "At the close my painful anxiety about you returned, so that it sounds like wedding- and funeral-bells commingled."

ARGERICH: CBS
ARRAU: Philips
AX: RCA
BRENDEL: Philips (CD)
GULDA: Philips (CD)
JOHANNESEN: Golden Crest
PERAHIA: CBS
RUBINSTEIN: RCA (CD)
STARR: Orion

Symphonic Etudes, Op. 13 (1834)

The *Symphonic Etudes* were also called by Schumann *Etudes en forme de variations.* They are based on a somber theme of great elegiac beauty, composed by Baron von Fricken, an amateur flutist and the father of Schumann's first fiancée. (Etudes 3 and 9 and the finale are not derived from this theme.) This is Schumann at his most brilliant, dazzling in its splendor and sonority, making harsh technical demands. Brahms was deeply affected by the *Etudes,* and they are the inspiration for his own *Handel* and *Paganini* Variations. Fauré, also, modeled his Theme and Variations, Op. 73, on them. The last etude, a regal finale, is built from a theme in Heinrich Marschner's opera *Der Templer und die Jüdin.* Schumann warned Clara not to play the whole work in public, because of its length. Indeed, he suppressed five variations which were later published posthumously and which are now often included by contemporary pianists. Although Schumann's instinct was to pare down the work for the overall good of the form, the material of these additional etudes is of such astounding beauty that not to include them is to deprive the listener of the fullness of Schumann's treatment. The work is dedicated to the English composer William Sterndale Bennett, who reported to Schumann that he played it successfully in England; however, the work began coming into its own in performances by Anton Rubinstein.

ANDA: DG
ARRAU: Philips
ASHKENAZY: London (CD)
GRAINGER: Philips (Australia)
GRINBERG: Melodiya
HESS: Seraphim
NOVAES: Turnabout
PERAHIA: CBS
POLLINI: DG (CD)
SOFRONITSKY: Melodiya
WEISSENBERG: Connoisseur Society

Sonata in F minor, Op. 14 (1836)

Schumann originally called the second of his three sonatas *Concerto sans orchestre.* It is in four movements, the third being an Andantino—a set of four variations on a theme by Clara Wieck. The work is the least known of Schumann's sonatas, but it is as inspired as the others. Arthur Loesser states, "It seems to me that Op. 14 is more consistent, more even, in quality than Op. 22. It is an outstanding ebullition of German Romanticism, bursting with excess visceral emotion, now fiery, now dreamy." Unfortunately, it has become a commonplace among critics to call the F minor Sonata the inferior sister of the F-sharp minor and G minor sonatas. This great work is scandalously neglected.

COLLARD: Connoisseur Society
HOROWITZ: RCA

KUERTI: London
LOESSER: International Piano Archives
ROSE: Turnabout

Kinderscenen (Scenes of Childhood), Op. 15 (1838)

Since their creation, these thirteen pieces have been played around the world, by virtuosi and amateurs alike. No. 7 is one of the all-time favorite melodies, *Träumerei* ("Dreaming"). Alban Berg once analyzed the piece, showing how complex it actually is. Schumann wrote to Clara that "these scenes are peaceful, tender and happy, like our future. . . . You will enjoy them; but of course, you have to forget that you are a virtuoso." Each piece is touched with refinement and tenderness and shows the restraint Schumann was capable of in his youth.

HOROWITZ: CBS (CD)
KEMPFF: DG
MOISEIWITSCH: (American) Decca
NOVAES: Turnabout

Kreisleriana, Op. 16 (1838)

These eight untitled fantasies, running to thirty-five minutes, are dedicated to Chopin, who abhorred Schumann's music. Schumann wrote, "Kreisler is a creation of E. T. A. Hoffmann's, an eccentric, wild, clever conductor. You will like much about him." For the uninitiated, this may be Schumann's most bewildering maze of fragments and textures. After finishing the work, he wrote: "My music now seems to me so wonderfully complicated, for all its simplicity, so eloquent from the heart." The *Kreisleriana* vibrates with disturbing and mysterious chords. Here are the composer's darker aspects, yet Schumann combines them, as only Schumann can, with a childlike innocence that goes deeper than even the *Kinderscenen*. Never has a poet so poured out his heart. To Clara he said, "Play my *Kreisleriana* once in a while. In some passages there is to be found an utterly wild love, and your life and mine."

ARGERICH: DG (CD)
ARRAU: Philips

ASHKENAZY: London
CORTOT: EMI Pathé
DE LARROCHA: London
EGOROV: Peters
HOROWITZ: CBS (CD); DG (CD)
MOISEIWITSCH: (American) Decca
RUBINSTEIN: RCA (CD)
SOFRONITSKY: Melodiya

Fantasia in C major, Op. 17 (1836)

Dedicated to Franz Liszt, in three movements, the Fantasy is universally regarded as a towering achievement in Romantic art. Harold Bauer wrote, "It would be hard to point to any composition in the entire literature of the piano wherein an expression of intense personal feeling is projected with such compelling and vivid power." In the Fantasy, Schumann has reached the very essence of his genius. Schumann himself thought he "had never composed anything as impassioned as this first movement," which he labeled Fantastico ed appassionato. The second movement, March, is one of the most majestic pages in Schumann. It demands a big mechanism and powerful chord playing, and is famous for its skips in the coda. Of this coda, William Newman writes: "One can take a transcendental approach; one can throw oneself into the laps of the gods while gambling on superhuman effort!" The finale, a slow movement, is one of the most beautiful meditations in music. On the title page of the score is a motto by the poet Friedrich von Schlegel: "Through all the varied sounds which fill the world's many-colored dreams, one whispered tone may be barely heard for those who listen in secret."

ARGERICH: CBS
BASHKIROV: Melodiya
FLIER: Melodiya
GIMPEL: Genesis
GOODE: Nonesuch
HOROWITZ (Carnegie Hall comeback): CBS
RICHTER: Angel
RUBINSTEIN: RCA (CD)
SOFRONITSKY: Melodiya

Arabeske in C major, Op. 18 (1839)

The *Arabeske* is very well known and not terribly difficult. This piece was once played to death by parlor pianists. It is the most Mendelssohnian-sounding of all Schumann's piano music, and the Victorian and Edwardian English loved it. Its suave opening theme is unforgettable, and Schumann conceives a rondo-type form that is fascinating.

HOROWITZ: CBS (CD)
KEMPFF: DG
NOVAES: Turnabout
RUBINSTEIN: RCA
SOFRONITSKY: Melodiya

Blumenstück, Op. 19 (1839)

The title means "Flower Piece." It is a pleasant sectional lyric work, but not one of Schumann's greater pieces. Still, it is not difficult and is a good place for students to explore Schumann's style.

DEMUS: MHS
HOROWITZ: CBS (CD)

Humoreske, Op. 20 (1839)

It is becoming apparent that this long and loosely made work is one of Schumann's finest scores. The composer called it "the Great *Humoreske.*" It is in six sections without interruption. For years, Sviatoslav Richter's performance taught pianists what this work could be like in the hands of a creative interpreter. The younger generation is now realizing the *Humoreske*'s potency, vernal freshness, and effectiveness in the concert hall (though it lasts nearly half an hour). The title highlights only the humorous aspects of the work, but many emotions are revealed in this superb creation.

ARRAU: Philips
ASHKENAZY: London
AX: RCA
DAVIDOVICH: Philips
GOODE: Nonesuch
HOROWITZ: RCA
RICHTER: Monitor
SCHIFF: Denon (CD)

Novelletten, Op. 21 (1838)

Of these eight works, Schumann said, "They are intimately interrelated, were written with enormous zest, are by and large gay and superficial, with the exception of places where I got right down to fundamentals." Actually, they play better in groups or separately. No. 8 in F-sharp minor is long, discursive, and simmers with hot passion; it is one of Schumann's most characteristic works, in two sections connected by a poetic passage that Schumann marked "Voice from Afar." All the Novelettes are masterful. No. 4 is an exuberant, syncopated waltz, and No. 5 is an animated polonaise.

ARRAU: Philips
WEBSTER: Dover

Sonata in G minor, Op. 22 (1830–38)

In four movements, this is the most concise of the sonatas, a work of vintage Schumann. In the first movement one finds his celebrated tempo markings, beginning with "As fast as possible." In the coda, he urges the performer to go "faster," and finally, he demands "still faster." The Andantino is one of Schumann's loveliest lyrical pages, followed by a miniature scherzo. The finale is based on a broken octave theme and is squarer in proportion than the original Presto passionato finale which it replaced. As a whole, the G minor is the easiest of Schumann's sonatas to give an adequate performance of.

ARGERICH: DG
ARRAU: Philips
BERMAN: Columbia/Melodiya
GRAINGER: Philips (Australia)
RICHTER: Angel
RYCE: Everest
STARR: Orion

Nachtstücke, Op. 23 (1839)

These are in C major, F major, D-flat major, and again F major. This last is by far the best known of the four, with its purity and melodic charm.

ARRAU: Philips
GILELS: Mobile Fidelity (CD)
HOROWITZ (Nos. 3 & 4): RCA

Faschingsschwank aus Wien, Op. 26 (1837)

The title means "Carnival Jest (Prank) from Vienna." The work contains five movements; the longest is the first, marked Allegro. It is a chain of loosely developed ideas, one of which is Schumann's sly use of the *Marseillaise*, which was illegal in Vienna, where he composed the piece. There is an introspective, wistful Romanze; a purely Schumannish Scherzino; and the finest movement, a turbulent song without words, Intermezzo in E-flat minor. The finale is in sonata form, parading a carnival atmosphere. The work falls just short of Schumann's best.

BARENBOIM: DG
DAVIS: Audiofon
MICHELANGELI: DG (CD)
RICHTER: Angel

Three Romances, Op. 28 (1838)

Schumann thought highly of the Three Romances, but only the luscious No. 2 in F-sharp major ever achieved renown. Nos. 1 and 3 are interesting but somewhat dry.

ARRAU: Philips
KEMPFF: DG

Scherzo, Gigue, Romanze, and Fughetta, Op. 32 (1839)

These are bits of choice Schumann. They would be the last piano works of the furiously productive first decade of Schumann's twenty-year creative life. After his marriage in 1840, he turned to writing songs, making use of the piano in a masterly way. Later, his piano writing would be more interesting in his chamber works than in his solo piano music. Some of the spirit and most of the adventure vanished, and Schumann's deepening interest in Bach and counterpoint produced such monotonous works as the Four Fugues, Op. 72, and several works for the now-obsolete pedal piano. There are also the fairly interesting Four Marches, Op. 76.

DEMUS: MHS

Album for the Young, Op. 68

These are forty-three pieces with wonderful titles, the greatest of children's musical storybooks, and the prototypes for countless children's pieces since. All that is lovable and tenderhearted in Schumann's nature is found here. Youngsters should start playing them as soon as possible. Adults find them rather harder to play than they look on the page.

DEMUS: MHS
ENGEL: Telefunken
FRANKL: Vox
WEISSENBERG: EMI or Connoisseur Society

Waldscenen, Op. 82 (1849)

Nine "Forest Scenes" of moderate difficulty. The most inspired is No. 7, *The Prophet Bird*, which has gained popularity on its own. This set is filled with many reminders of earlier Schumann. Of less importance in Schumann's output is the set of Fourteen Pieces, Op. 99, called *Bunte Blätter* ("Colored Leaves"). The collection covers an assortment of pieces from 1839 through 1849. Richter and Haskil have recorded them.

BACKHAUS: London
HASKIL: Philips
KEMPFF: DG
P. SERKIN: RCA

Fantasiestücke, Op. 111 (1851)

There are flashes here of Schumann at his best. Unlike Op. 12, the pieces are untitled. They make a good group. No. 1 is stormy; No. 2, lyric; No. 3, a march.

In 1853 he wrote *Three Sonatas for the Young,* Op. 118. There are also the *Albumblätter,* Op. 124, a collection of twenty pieces from various years. Here and there, the old Schumann shines through. Op. 126 contains seven pieces in fughetta form that are dry and rather boring. Although 1853 was a year of anguish for Schumann, his contrapuntal craft is astonishing. Schumann's swan song from that year—*Gesänge der Frühe* ("Songs of Dawn"), Op. 133—has touching moments. He composed a bit after 1853. There is a Theme and Variations, without opus number. Schumann told people that the theme was dictated to him by angels. But thereafter the angels turned into devils, as Schumann drifted into complete madness.

ARRAU: Philips
HOROWITZ: RCA

Piano Concerto in A minor, Op. 54 (1845)

The Schumann Concerto is a staple of the repertoire. It is perfect music, of beauty and lucidity, a classic of the concerto literature. Schumann is mellow, serene, and joyous, with none of the mental turmoil evident in the earlier poetic cycles. There is not a superfluous note in the score. The Concerto eschews virtuosity for its own sake. Schumann wrote to Clara: "I cannot write a concerto for virtuosi; I must think of something else." Schumann also composed for piano and orchestra a *Konzertstück* in G major, Op. 92, a very pretty work which is not as difficult as the first movement of the A minor Concerto. The *Introduction and Allegro* in D minor, Op. 134, has some vigor and strength of ideas.

BISHOP-KOVACEVICH, Davis/BBC Symphony: Philips (CD)
FIRKUŠNÝ, Froment/Luxembourg Radio: Turnabout
HASKIL, van Otterloo/The Hague Philharmonic: Philips

HESS, Schwartz/Philharmonia: Seraphim
ISTOMIN, Walter/Columbia Symphony: CBS (CD)
LIPATTI, Galliera/Philharmonia: Odyssey
LUPU, Previn/London Symphony: London (CD)
RUBINSTEIN, Giulini/Chicago Symphony: RCA (CD)
R. SERKIN, Ormandy/Philadelphia: Columbia
SOLOMON, Menges/Philharmonia: EMI
ZIMERMAN, Karajan/Berlin Philharmonic: DG (CD)

ALEXANDER SCRIABIN
1872–1915 — Russia

Scriabin was widely discussed during his lifetime. He appealed to a *fin de siècle* public receptive to the newest movements in the art world. Through his own mercurial playing, which was blessed with a delectable and rarefied sense of rubato, his newest music was accepted instantly.

While in his thirties, he became enmeshed in esoteric, mystic ideas, which harmonized with his highly ecstatic nature. He wrote: "I am transported with gladness that is in me. If the world could only partake of an atom of the joy that is mine, the world would suffocate in bliss."

In his last years, Scriabin believed that he was a messiah, and that through his music (a final incantation was to be called *The Mysterium*) a new and higher world order would appear. He said: "I shall not die, I shall suffocate in ecstasy after *The Mysterium.*" Unfortunately, he died at forty-three, with only sketches for the culminating work written. After his death, his art suffered an eclipse, as his philosophic ideas became increasingly unattractive. The impending Russian Revolution, with its populist cultural climate, did not look kindly upon his egomania or his innovative harmonic system. Outside of Russia, the younger emigrés, Prokofiev and Stravinsky, took center stage. In Germany, musical composition was assuming a neo-Classic stance, and Schoenberg's twelve-tone method would soon influence many young composers. The great Scriabin players, Heinrich Neuhaus and Vladimir Sofronitsky, were contained within Russian frontiers, and his early advocates Rachmaninoff, Josef Hofmann, and Arthur Rubinstein, who gave the London premiere of the Fifth Sonata, soon abandoned his work. Very little was written about him in English after his death, save by Alfred J. Swan and by Eaglefield Hull, who perceived him as "the most remarkable spiritual phenomenon in all music." No full-length biography appeared until Faubion Bowers published one in 1970.

Fortunately, Horowitz, who was taken to play for Scriabin as a boy, sustained an interest in him, and during a protracted sabbatical he began learning more of his work. By the 1970s, Scriabin had taken his rightful place as the greatest of all Romantic Russian composers of piano music. Horowitz has said: "Scriabin is super-Romantic, super-sensuous, super-everything." Scriabin's music, wrote Wilfrid Mellers, "depends on the pedal effects of the modern grand piano, which dominates all Scriabin's musical thought."

From Op. 1 through approximately Op. 28, Chopin was his predominant influence. "But Scriabin," as Swan attests, "is far from being a mere imitator. He is Chopin's rightful successor, and, as such, carries to an extreme certain peculiarities of Chopin's style. What lay in the background with Chopin comes to the fore in Scriabin: the music grows in nervousness; the tissue becomes closer and more compact, the writing neater and more scrupulous than even Chopin's. . . . But above all it is the prevalence of soaring ecstatic moods that unveils the true Scriabin from his Chopinesque coverlet."

The works from Op. 30, the Fourth Sonata, through the Fifth Sonata, Op. 53, may be called his middle period. The music is more languorous and erotic, the pianism more widely spaced, while major and minor triads appear less and less as he constructs harmony in quartal blocks. Yet his ninth chords in all their modifications are still basically treated as dominant harmony waiting patiently to be resolved into the home key. After the Fifth Sonata, however, key centers almost totally disappear, and the composer dispenses with key signatures. The music now dissolves into atonality, the idiom becoming ever more incandescent, intoxicated, and fevered. The music speaks of secret rites and fabulous sins. Pulsations and convulsions mark the rubatoed meter. The composer's favorite word was "sensations." In his last works, he became obsessed by fire, which for him symbolized purification.

Except for a single piano concerto and five symphonies, Scriabin's music is all for piano solo. There are upwards of two hundred pieces, including ninety preludes (generally very short), twenty-seven etudes, twenty-three mazurkas, twenty poems (with various names attached), nine impromptus, five waltzes, four nocturnes, ten sonatas, several concert pieces (of which the longest is the Fantasy, Op. 28), and various pieces with descriptive titles.

Etude in C-sharp minor, Op. 2, No. 1

Composed when he was fourteen years old, this Andante is one of Scriabin's best-known pieces. It is richly colored and already shows his passionate nature.

HOROWITZ: CBS (CD); DG (CD)
LAREDO: Connoisseur Society
SOFRONITSKY: Melodiya

Ten Mazurkas, Op. 3 (1893)
Nine Mazurkas, Op. 25 (1899)
Two Mazurkas, Op. 40 (1904)

Nine of the Ten Mazurkas of Op. 3 are in minor keys. The content is gracious, with some commonplace material; they are strongly influenced by Schumann and Chopin. The Nine Mazurkas are far more Scriabinic—tense, miniature dance-poems, capricious and fragile.

FEINBERG (Op. 3; Op. 25): Melodiya
SOFRONITSKY (Op. 25, Nos. 3, 7, 8; Op. 40): Melodiya

Allegro appassionato in E-flat minor (1887–92)

Heavy-handed, with some interesting color, this work is important because in it a Lisztian influence breaks through in Scriabin's harmonic thinking.

PONTI: Vox

Twelve Etudes, Op. 8 (1895)

One of the finest late-nineteenth-century sets of concert etudes. They present many technical demands and contain polyrhythms. The best of the set are No. 2 in F-sharp minor; No. 3, Tempestoso in B minor; No. 4, Piacevole in B major; the well-known No. 5 in E; the furious No. 7 in B-flat minor; and No. 9 in G-sharp minor, the crowning work of the set. The longest of these etudes, marked Alla ballata, it exploits octave passages. No. 10 in D-flat is famous for its right-hand double-notes. No. 11 in B-flat minor is a "touch" study of Russian melodic beauty. No. 12 in D-sharp minor, marked Patetico, is Scriabin's most famous work; its rhapsodic declamation never fails to thrill. Louis Biancolli wrote, "Whoever plays it feels momentarily like a god. To have composed that etude is to have married the piano."

ESTRIN: Connoisseur Society
HOROWITZ (Nos. 2, 8, 10–12): CBS (CD)
MERZHANOV: Melodiya/Angel
SOFRONITSKY (Nos. 2, 4–9, 11): Melodiya

Eight Etudes, Op. 42 (1904)

Although highly Romantic, these are fine examples of Scriabin's middle period, exhibiting more advanced harmonic schemes and concentrated musical emotion. As studies, they feature irregular cross-rhythms, such as five against three, three against two, four against three. No. 3 is a measured trill study. Marked Prestissimo, it has often been called *The Mosquito*. No. 4 is a sweet melody with a gentle throb in the accompaniment. The largest in emotional scope is No. 5 in C-sharp minor, marked Affannato (breathlessly); it is one of the most smoldering of Scriabin's works, gorgeously colored.

BERMAN: Melodiya
HOROWITZ (Nos. 3–5): CBS (CD)
LAREDO: Connoisseur Society
RICHTER (Nos. 2–6): Melodiya

Three Etudes, Op. 65 (1908)

No. 1 is in ninths, No. 2 in sevenths, and No. 3 in fifths. These are amazing works from his later period. The Richter recording also includes the tiny Presto Etude in 2/8 time, Op. 56, No. 4.

KUERTI: Monitor
RICHTER: Melodiya

Nocturne in D-flat major for the Left Hand Alone, Op. 9, No. 2

A ravishing encore number, long a popular favorite. Scriabin composed it when he injured his right hand trying to outdo Josef Lhévinne. It soon became a Josef Lhévinne specialty. The Prelude in C-sharp minor for Left Hand, Op. 9, No. 1, is not as well known; technically simpler, it nevertheless has a lyric beauty.

S. NEUHAUS: Melodiya
RUTSTEIN: Orion
SOMER: Mercury

Twenty-four Preludes, Op. 11 (1897)

A high-water mark in early Scriabin, the Preludes represent all sides of the composer's personality in cameo. They follow the circle of fifths and proclaim all the major and minor keys. These remarkable works in Scriabin's Chopinesque manner are a cavalcade of technical finesse and melodic appeal. Rachmaninoff only recorded one piece by his friend Scriabin—the F-sharp minor Prelude No. 8, marked Allegro agitato, which he manages to make convincing at a very slow tempo. It is to be found in Volume 2 of his complete recordings.

Twenty-four Preludes:
BACHAUER: Capitol
DEYANOVA: Nimbus (CD)
GAVRILOV: Angel (CD)
LAREDO: Desto
LEWENTHAL: Westminster
SOFRONITSKY: Melodiya

Other collections of Preludes:
BASHKIROV (eight preludes from Opp. 16, 17, 22, 33, 37): Melodiya
HOROWITZ (Op. 11, Nos. 1, 3, 9, 10, 13, 14, 16; and nine others, representing each period): RCA (CD)
RUTSTEIN (four preludes from Op. 22): Orion
SOFRONITSKY (sixteen preludes from Opp. 11, 13, 15, 16, 22; four preludes from Op. 31): Melodiya

Five Preludes, Op. 74 (1914)

Scriabin's last music is ominous, painfully intense. Donald Garvelmann wrote, "Opus 74 is psychologically jarring, shattering. All the sadness and troubles of the world are encapsulated in these few pages."

BIRET: Finnadar
KUERTI: Monitor
LEWENTHAL: Westminster
S. NEUHAUS: Melodiya

Fantasia in B minor, Op. 28 (1901)

The Fantasy is a gloriously rich apotheosis of all the Chopinesque and Lisztian elements of Scriabin's early work.

BERMAN: Melodiya
FEINBERG: Melodiya
SOFRONITSKY: Melodiya

Valse in A-flat major, Op. 38 (1904)

M. Montagu-Nathan describes this waltz as "exquisitely feathered" and says, "We have now to deal rather with a Chopinesque Scriabin, than, as previously, with a Scriabinesque Chopin." The composer asks the pianist to play it "as if you were dreaming."

BASHKIROV: Melodiya
DAVIDOVICH: Melodiya (CD)
WALDOFF: MHS

Two Poems, Op. 32, Nos. 1 and 2 (1904)

No. 1 is one of Scriabin's better-known pieces, a beguiling work. No. 2 is the diabolic Scriabin.

BECKMAN-SCHERBINA (No. 1): Melodiya
HOROWITZ: CBS (CD)
SOFRONITSKY: Melodiya

Poème satanique, Op. 36 (1903)

An effective work presenting a false sweetness and ironic insincerity; the diabolic streak in Scriabin comes to the surface in many of his works. Swan says, "Devilish fits continued to pester Scriabin."

SOFRONITSKY: Melodiya or Westminster

Poème tragique, Op. 34 (1904)

The ninth chord with sharpened fifth is characteristic of this period in Scriabin's work. A chordal work with widely spaced figuration in the middle section.

SOMER: Mercury

Poème-nocturne, Op. 61 (1913)

A subtle piece in which Scriabin's mysticism and liquid poetry are wrapped in a form of great flexibility. A neglected masterpiece of Scriabin's later manner.

SOFRONITSKY: Melodiya
SOMER: Mercury

Two Poems, Op. 69 (1912–13)

Two delicate pieces, both marked simply Allegretto. Thomas Frost hears "the introverted fantasy, and the solipsism that are typical of Scriabin's mature works."

HOROWITZ: CBS (CD)

Vers la flamme, Op. 72 (1914)

If one had to know only one work of Scriabin's late music, I would recommend the hypnotic *Towards the Flame*. It has often been described as psychedelic. In it, Scriabin was setting his soul on fire, and an acrid odor is suggested. It is surely one of the most powerful of Scriabin's works.

HOROWITZ: CBS (CD)
S. NEUHAUS: Melodiya
SOFRONITSKY: Melodiya

Two Dances, Op. 73 (1914)

The penultimate works: *Guirlandes* and *Flammes sombres*. *Garlands* is incomparably beautiful; *Dark Flames* is less turbulent than *Towards the Flame,* but it has an undercurrent of danger.

ASHKENAZY: London
SOFRONITSKY: Melodiya

The Ten Piano Sonatas

Scriabin was, at root, a miniaturist, but he attempted to fit his music into an appropriate larger frame. As a harmonist, he was a great innovator. He tried to mold the sonata idea to his formal needs. From the Fifth Sonata through the Tenth, his solution was to shape all elements of the sonata into a one-movement scheme. Mellers wrote that "by 1903 . . . the wealth of higher chromatic discords in Scriabin's music had made [the] sonata form anachronistic. A conflict of keys is impossible unless tonality is at first clearly defined." Aaron Copland feels that the Sonatas are "one of the most extraordinary mistakes in music. . . . The quality of his thematic material was truly individual, truly inspired.

But Scriabin . . . had the fantastic idea of attempting to put this really new body of feeling into the straight jacket of the old classical sonata form, recapitulation and all."

Such criticism notwithstanding, Scriabin's ten sonatas are so infused with coloristic sensation, gorgeous figuration, spiritual aspiration, erotic palpitation, and new facets of pianistic resource that they have come to have an honored place in the piano's literature. In addition, they offer a magnificent view of Scriabin's astounding development.

LAREDO (complete sonatas): Nonesuch
SOFRONITSKY (Sonatas Nos. 3–5, 8–10):
    Chant du Monde (CD)
SZIDON (complete sonatas): DG

Sonata No. 1 in F minor, Op. 6 (1892)

The longest of the sonatas; in four movements, No. 1 concludes with a funeral march. The influence of Tchaikovsky and also Schumann is apparent, but signs of individuality appear throughout, especially in the Presto third movement.

ASHKENAZY: London (CD)
BERMAN: Columbia/Melodiya
ZHUKOV: Melodiya/Angel

Sonata No. 2—Sonata Fantasy in G-sharp minor, Op. 19 (1892–97)

"The first of its two movements—an Andante," wrote Swan, "is perhaps the most gorgeously fanciful and capricious of all Scriabin's early works. . . . Its melodic elaboration is stupendous: one little melodic wave chases another in poetic playfulness. The accompaniment, thickly woven on broad lines, is all nerve and refinement." The second movement, a Presto, is much shorter, in triplets, and it sprouts a theme of sweeping impetuousness.

ASHKENAZY: London (CD)
FEINBERG: Melodiya
SOFRONITSKY: Melodiya
ZHUKOV: Melodiya/Angel

Sonata No. 3 in F-sharp minor, Op. 23 (1898)

In four movements; the first, Drammatico, is the hardest of any Scriabin movement to hold together convincingly. Glenn Gould wrote, "It's an expansive and declamatory Sonata-Allegro in which the bittersweet nostalgia of the secondary thematic group is held in check by the foreboding double-dot interpretations of the primary theme's chief rhythmic component. It's 'music-to-read-*Wuthering Heights*-by'—a hypnotic, self-centered piece of doom-foretelling."

GOULD: CBS (CD)
HOROWITZ: RCA (CD)
SOFRONITSKY: Melodiya
SOKOLOV: Melodiya

Sonata No. 4 in F-sharp major, Op. 30 (1903)

A masterpiece, the most original of the earlier sonatas. The first of its two movements is a liquid, evanescent, shimmering Andante; the second movement is marked Prestissimo volando, in 12/8 meter. This vertiginous dance quickens the pulse. It exudes a sexual energy which culminates in jubilant repeated chords, triple fortississimo. A pianist must feel the heated inner core of this music.

ASHKENAZY: London
FEINBERG: Melodiya
GAVRILOV: Angel (CD)
RUTSTEIN: Orion
VILLA: Second Hearing (CD)
ZHUKOV: Melodiya/Angel

Sonata No. 5 in F-sharp major, Op. 53 (1907)

By the Fifth Sonata, Scriabin begins to purge his art of any outside influences. This sonata, an outgrowth of his Symphony No. 4 (*Poem of Ecstasy*), is a mystic impressionist poem. The most frequently performed in public of the ten sonatas, "the Fifth Sonata," Swan wrote, "has been likened to a piece of wiz-ardry, a deed of black magic, illumined by the rays of a black sun. Its impetuosity alternating with a caressing languor, the legerdemain of the Prestos in their radiant mixture of B major and F-sharp major, and the wild orgiastic rhythm of the Allegros, combine to produce an uncanny impression."

ASHKENAZY: London
GOULD: CBS (CD)
HOROWITZ: RCA (CD)
MERZHANOV: Monitor
RICHTER: DG (CD)
VILLA: Second Hearing (CD)
ZHUKOV: Melodiya

Sonata No. 6, Op. 62 (1911–12)

No. 6 is more involved, complex, and mysterious than its companions. Scriabin never played the work in public; it has been said that he feared it. The premiere was given by Beckman-Scherbina in 1912.

ASHKENAZY: London (CD)
KUERTI: Monitor
RICHTER: Melodiya
ZHUKOV: Melodiya/Angel

Sonata No. 7, Op. 64 (1912)

Scriabin loved this creation, which he called *The White Mass.* He considered it holy and played it often. Never had his work had such "lift" or flight. The vibratory qualities of this sonata stem from a magnificent use of trills. Referring to one portion of the piece, Scriabin said, "This is real vertigo!" He beseeches the pianist to play "with radiant and ecstatic voluptuousness." It is one of the most luminous works in the repertoire and, perhaps, the most difficult technically of all Scriabin's sonatas. Near the sonata's end, he writes a twenty-three-note rolled chord.

ASHKENAZY: London
V. BUNIN: Melodiya
VILLA: Second Hearing (CD)
ZHUKOV: Melodiya/Angel

Sonata No. 8, Op. 66 (1913)

The longest of the one-movement sonatas, with two development sections. Donald Garvelmann wrote: "The gorgeous harmonies hypnotize, kaleidoscopic shifting shapes and colors draw us in. . . . The Eighth Sonata is a walk through a crystalline floral labyrinth." It may be difficult to find one's way around, but the view is always bewitching and beautiful.

ASHKENAZY: London (CD)
ZHUKOV: Melodiya/Angel

Sonata No. 9, Op. 68 (1913)

If, for Swan, the Eighth Sonata was "a divine azure vault, the happiest and most careless of inspirations, a phantom woven of delicate cobwebs," then the Ninth Sonata was for him "a veritable picture of Dorian Gray!" Couched in the most hideous, grimacing harmonies, No. 9 was shocking even to Scriabin himself. He called it *The Black Mass*—it expressed for him a falling from grace. In its eight minutes Scriabin compressed all of the dark elements in his being. The Ninth Sonata is along with the Fourth and Fifth Sonatas the best known.

ASHKENAZY: London
HOROWITZ: CBS (CD)
SOFRONITSKY: Melodiya

Sonata No. 10, Op. 70 (1913)

A blazing spectacle, No. 10 has been dubbed the *Trill* Sonata. The composer called it a Sonata of Insects, and said it was "born from the sun." He played the premiere himself in Moscow. The composer asks many things of the performer, one of which is to play in "a sweet drunkenness."

BIRET: Finnadar
HOROWITZ: CBS (CD)
H. NEUHAUS: Melodiya
SOFRONITSKY: Melodiya

Concerto in F-sharp minor, Op. 20 (1896)

Often performed by Scriabin, this concerto is in three movements, the middle movement being a simple set of variations. The style is refined, with Scriabin's early brand of nervosity.

ASHKENAZY, Maazel/London Philharmonic: London
BASHKIROV, Kondrashin/USSR Symphony: Melodiya
H. NEUHAUS, Golovanov/Moscow Radio Symphony: Melodiya
S. NEUHAUS, Dubrovski/USSR Symphony: Melodiya
RUSKIN, Epstein/MIT Symphony: Pantheon (CD)

ROGER SESSIONS
1896–1985 — United States

One of the most influential composers in the United States, Sessions has taught two generations of composers, including Milton Babbitt. His music is serious, forceful, and wonderful to practice because of its emotional durability. The composer Andrew Imbrie has said, "Sessions is neither a system builder nor a preserver of inherited values. . . . [His] distrust of both systems and polemics has enabled him to respond to outside influence without becoming eclectic: the increasing influence of Schoenberg can combine with the diminishing influence of Stravinsky without either of them touching the essential quality of Sessions' own language."

Sonata No. 1 (1930)
Sonata No. 2 (1946)
Sonata No. 3 (1965)

The three sonatas are tremendous contributions to the literature. They all offer complicated problems in musicianship and technique. Rebecca La Brecque once said to the composer that she thought No. 1 was the most difficult of the three. Sessions responded: "If I practiced nothing else for two years, I could probably play my Third Sonata. If I practiced nothing else for one year, I could play my Second Sonata. If I wanted to play the First, I would have to be sixteen years old, maybe fourteen, and practice only Czerny, Chopin, and Bach for the next twenty years." La Brecque adds, "As with all of Sessions' music, the greatest performance problem is the separation of the two to five voices going on at any particular moment." The expressive range of the First Sonata is enormous, and the opening Andante, heartrending. The Second Sonata, wrote Maurice Hinson, "is a challenge to the finest pianist and is probably one of the most important piano sonatas by an American composer of this century." The Second Sonata is the most completely chromatic and insistent in its harmonic tension. La Brecque feels it "is the most direct of the three, and yet has the most potential for being misunderstood. . . . The Second Sonata defies its surroundings, and I've rarely heard a performance by anyone (including me) that has shown the performer to have the courage and the stamina to hold this conflict in balance." The Third Sonata is the capstone of La Brecque's experiences as a musician; she says that "the Sonata means more to me than any other music I have ever played, heard, or come in contact with." The work is indeed one of the very finest products of Sessions's world.

The Three Sonatas:
LA BRECQUE: Opus One

Sonata No. 1:
HELPS: CRI

Sonata No. 2:
HODGKINSON: New World
MARKS: CRI

Sonata No. 3:
HELPS: New World

DMITRI SHOSTAKOVICH
1906–1975 — Russia

The most extensively performed Soviet composer of the twentieth century. His greatest works are his symphonies and string quartets. He composed in all genres. Shostakovich was himself an excellent pianist, a classmate of Sofronitsky and Yudina at the St. Petersburg Conservatory.

Twenty-four Preludes, Op. 34
   (1932–33)
These miniatures are a gold mine for exploring the many ramifications of Shostakovich's style. They follow the Chopin grouping of using the circle of fifths, and vary technically from easy to taxing.

> BERMAN: DG
> DEYANOVA: Nimbus (CD)
> HAVLIKOVA: Supraphon
> WIKSTROM: RCA

Twenty-four Preludes and Fugues, Op. 87
   (1951)
These are Shostakovich's major contribution to the literature of his instrument. In 1950, for the commemoration of the bicentennial of Bach's death, Shostakovich visited Leipzig, where he undertook to write a modern *Well-Tempered Clavier.* His own Twenty-four Preludes and Fugues occupy Volume 40 of the forty-two volumes of his collected works. Another interesting piano piece by Shostakovich is the 1922 *Three Fantastic Dances,* Op. 5. These were once very popular. His Sonata No. 1, Op. 12, is biting and dissonant.

> *Twenty-four Preludes and Fugues:*
> NIKOLAYEVA: Melodiya
> SHOSTAKOVICH: Melodiya
> WOODWARD: RCA

> *Selected Preludes and Fugues:*
> GILELS (Nos. 1, 5, 24): Seraphim
> RICHTER (Nos. 4, 12, 14, 15, 17, 23): Philips   417

Sonata No. 2 in B minor, Op. 61 (1943)

More conservative than No. 1, the sonata is in three movements, the finale being a set of nine variations.

D'ARCO: MHS
GILELS: RCA
RUTSTEIN: Orion
YUDINA: Melodiya

Piano Concerto No. 1, with Trumpet and Strings, Op. 35 (1933)

This has become one of the best-known piano concertos in the contemporary literature. It blazes with a youthful brazenness and sarcastic, vulgar flavor, but the slow movement has touching moments. Eugene List gave the American premiere with Stokowski and the Philadelphia Orchestra in 1934.

D'ARCO, Paillard/Paillard Chamber Orchestra: MHS
GRINBERG, Rozhdestvensky: Westminster
LIST, M. Shostakovich/Moscow Radio Symphony: Columbia/Melodiya
OGDON, Marriner/Academy of St. Martin: Argo
ORTIZ, Berglund/Bournemouth Symphony: Angel
PREVIN, Bernstein/New York Philharmonic: CBS
ROSENBERGER, Schwarz/Los Angeles Chamber Orchestra: Delos (CD)
SHOSTAKOVICH, Cluytens/ORTF: Seraphim

Piano Concerto No. 2, Op. 101 (1957)

This is a capital work on all accounts, not overly difficult, and musically a delight in its three movements. The slow movement's melody is captivating. The finale in 7/8, with a section based on a famous Hanon five-finger exercise, will make the listener smile.

BERNSTEIN, Bernstein/New York Philharmonic: CBS
LIST, M. Shostakovich/Moscow Radio Symphony: CBS/Melodiya

OGDON, Foster/Royal Philharmonic: Angel
ORTIZ, Berglund/Bournemouth Symphony: Angel
SHOSTAKOVICH, Cluytens/ORTF: Seraphim

KARLHEINZ STOCKHAUSEN
b. 1928 — Germany

Klavierstücke I–XI

Stockhausen is among the most fascinating experimenters in music. He has composed electronic music and early in his career he used total serialization. He has written: "In a world bombarded by images the function of music is to awaken the inner man." He has also said, "From time to time I have concentrated again on 'Piano Pieces,' on composing for a single instrument, for ten fingers, with minute nuances of timbres and structures. They are my 'drawings.' " The *Klavierstücke* vary greatly in length—No. III is 27 seconds long, No. VI lasts 25:22 minutes, No. IX is 9:40 minutes, and No. X is 22:19 minutes. Marie-Françoise Bucquet is convincing in her reading of No. IX, played in exactly 9:40 minutes, the same timing as Kontarsky's. She has said, "If I tried to persuade someone that music is time experienced through sound I would choose Stockhausen's *Klavierstück IX*."

BUCQUET (Nos. IX & XI): Philips
HENCK (complete): Wergo (CD)
A. KONTARSKY (complete): CBS
KÖRMENDI (No. IX): Hungaroton (CD)

IGOR STRAVINSKY
1882–1971 — Russia

Stravinsky once stated, "Composing begins for me as the feeling of intervals in my fingers."

He also made the assumption that "the piano is an instrument of percussion and nothing else." He took an anti-Romantic stance, showing contempt for the cult of the performer, asking for performances of objectivity. Of course, Stravinsky was trying to assure more straightforward performances and a spirit of modernity, as well as a respect for the composer's intentions, which was at a low ebb in the performance practices of his own youth.

Stravinsky's piano music covers a wide range of his stylistic traits, including the Tchaikovskian Russianism displayed in the early Sonata in F-sharp minor (1903), composed ten years before *The Rite of Spring*. In 1908 he continued along a Romantic but leaner vein in the marvelous Four Etudes, Op. 7, which show some of Scriabin's influence. During the next decade, he left the piano for other media. Then, in 1919, he produced the extraordinary *Piano Rag Music*, and in 1921 the artful *Les Cinq Doigts* for young students. He moved from simplicity to the ultimate in pianistic color when he wrote for Arthur Rubinstein the startling *Trois Mouvements de Petrouchka*, based on three scenes from his great ballet score. In the twenties Stravinsky was occupied with his so-called neo-Classical or "back to Baroque" phase. The dry and beautifully modeled Concerto for Piano and Wind Instruments dates from 1924, as does the Piano Sonata, with its decorative Adagietto. The year 1925 saw the publication of the *Sérénade en la,* and 1929, the terse *Capriccio.* Another work of shorter duration, based on a twelve-tone row, *Movements* for Piano and Orchestra, stems from 1959. His post-Webern permutations showed his constant sense of experimentation and open-mindedness.

Four Etudes, Op. 7 (1908)

These treats are rather neglected. This is Stravinsky as part of the virtuoso tradition of pianism. No. 1 pits quintuplets against triplets and duplets. No. 2 is a pattern of six against three, six against four, and six against five.

No. 3 is a contrasting slow-touch study; and No. 4 in F-sharp major is a volatile study in perpetual motion of legato against staccato.

JACOBS: Nonesuch
LEE: Nonesuch
OZOLINS: Aquitaine
RINGEISSEN: Adès (CD)

Piano Rag Music (1919)

A dissonant work of serious quality, using ragtime as a basis for Stravinsky's highly sophisticated technical prowess.

JOHANNESEN: Golden Crest
LEE: Nonesuch
LIVELY: DG
STRAVINSKY: Seraphim

Les Cinq Doigts (The Five Fingers) (1921)

These are wonderful examples of the use of limitation. With the melodic material confined within the range of five notes, each piece fits the span of a young student's hand. Full of characteristic twists and turns, they achieve a simple charm.

BIRET: Finnadar

Trois Mouvements de Petrouchka (1921)

This is a masterpiece. In a good performance it cannot fail—the interest never wanes. The score is dedicated to Rubinstein, who never recorded it, though he played it in public with incomparable panache.

BACHAUER: Mercury
BIRET: Finnadar
CHERKASSKY: Nimbus (CD)
POLLINI: DG (CD)
RÁNKI: Telefunken
TORADZE: Angel
VERED: London
WEISSENBERG: Connoisseur Society

Sonata (1924)

Ten precious minutes in three movements. The first movement is Bachian counterpoint, the second is ornate. The third is subtle toccata writing, the essence of Stravinskian neo-Classicism. The composer said, "I have used the term *sonata* in its original sense, deriving from the word *sonare,* to sound."

LEE: Nonesuch
NÁDAS: Dover
RÁNKI: Telefunken
RINGEISSEN: Adès
P. SERKIN: New World (CD)

Sérénade en la (1925)

The spirit of the Serenade in A echoes that of the eighteenth century. It is one of the important piano works of the 1920s. Stravinsky himself plays the work sympathetically; his opening *Hymne* is full of life.

LEE: Nonesuch
RÁNKI: Telefunken
STRAVINSKY: Seraphim

Concerto for Piano and Winds (1924)

The work was composed for Stravinsky's own use as a pianist. Its dry, nonlegato figures, with ever-changing metrics, are intriguing. Stravinsky's synthesis of piano and wind sound is unique.

BÉROFF, Ozawa/Orchestre de Paris: Angel
BISHOP-KOVACEVICH, Davis/BBC Symphony: Philips
ENTREMONT, Stravinsky/Columbia Symphony: Columbia
MAGALOFF, Ansermet/Suisse Romande: London

Capriccio for Piano and Orchestra (1929)

This is a brilliant and highly successful composition. Only Stravinsky could have written it. The piano and orchestra are seamlessly molded together.

BÉROFF, Ozawa/Orchestre de Paris: Angel
ENTREMONT, Craft/Columbia Symphony: Columbia
OGDON, Marriner/Academy of St. Martin: Argo

STRAVINSKY, Ansermet/Concerts Straram: Seraphim

Movements for Piano and Orchestra (1958–59)

Balanchine created a ballet from this score, which is in five movements. The work is in the intellectual manner of the composer's late works. Here he acknowledges the influence of Webern.

BÉROFF, Ozawa/Orchestre de Paris: Angel
ROSEN, Stravinsky/Columbia Symphony: Columbia

Le Sacre du printemps (The Rite of Spring), transcribed for solo piano by Sam Raphling and by Dag Achatz

The great ballet score may be said to be the most influential single work of the first quarter of the century. Raphling wrote his transcription in the early 1970s, and it is a tremendous work of transformation, while also remaining true to the music.

ACHATZ (Achatz transcription): BIS
ATAMIAN (Raphling transcription): RCA

KAROL SZYMANOWSKI
1882–1937 — Poland

Szymanowski was the most renowned Polish composer of the first half of the twentieth century; his keyboard works are among the finest in his varied output. He was also a persuasive pianist of his own work and has been interpreted by artists of the caliber of Heinrich Neuhaus, Jacob Gimpel, Richter, Arthur Rubinstein, Malcuzynski, Jan Smeterlin, and, most recently, Emanuel Ax. Nevertheless, Szymanowski has never really entered the repertoire in a big way. Possibly this is because his music is difficult to categorize. His earliest music betrays many influences—Chopin, a touch of Brahms, Richard Strauss, and Scriabin, whose piano style he studied as minutely as he did Chopin's. The influence of Reger on his early style can be heard in the dense Prelude and Fugue and the Second Piano Sonata. Szymanowski's middle works, especially the *Masques* and *Métopes*, reveal a rarefied feeling for piano sonority and texture. These tone poems breathe an Oriental atmosphere, with their hypnotic rhythms, floating improvisations, and gossamer textures. For the executant, they lack the severe structural cohesiveness of their model, Ravel's *Gaspard de la nuit*, and they demand an even more highly developed creative imagination.

A third and more ascetic period in Szymanowski's evolution began in the 1920s, with his assimilation of indigenous Polish music in a highly personalized manner. His leading works in this idiom are the Twenty Mazurkas, Op. 50, and the *Symphonie concertante*.

Selected Piano Music

Szymanowski has created a vivid and florid art; his exquisite and capricious pianistic carvings, contemplative lyricism, and soaring line should be examined by pianists looking for a literature of great importance which has been unduly neglected. As Mark Swed has written: "By nursing a Romantic soul and feeding an anti-Romantic intellect, he produced works of delicious sensuality, overwhelming beauty, and profound sophistication."

Preludium and Fugue in C-sharp minor;
Preludes, Op. 1, Nos. 7–9;
Twelve Etudes, Op. 33 (1916–18);
Shéhérazade (Masques, Op. 34, No. 1);
Mazurkas, Op. 50, Nos. 3, 8, 13, 15;
Two Mazurkas, Op. 62:
ROMANIUK: MHS

Masques, Op. 34 (Shéhérazade, Tantris the Buffoon, Don Juan's Serenade)
(1915–16);
Twelve Etudes, Op. 33;
Four Etudes, Op. 4 (1903):
ROSENBERGER: Delos

Masques, Op. 34;
Fantasy in F minor, Op. 14 (1905);
Four Etudes, Op. 4;
Métopes, Op. 29 (L'Isle des sirènes, Calypso, Nausicaa) (1915):
JONES: Argo

Sonata No. 1, Op. 8 (1905)
Sonata No. 2, Op. 23 (1912)
Sonata No. 3, Op. 36 (1916–19)
The Piano Sonatas are dense, intellectual, and lush. Each is capped by a fugue and offers difficult matters of interpretation. No. 3 is perhaps the most successful, with its one-movement form. No. 2 (which was premiered by Rubinstein) overflows its form.

FEDER (Sonata No. 3): Protone
GRAHAM (Sonatas Nos. 1 & 3): MHS
PLESHAKOV (Sonata No. 2): Orion
UTRECT (Sonata No. 3): MUZA

Symphonie concertante for Piano with Orchestra, Op. 60 (1932)

A significant nationalist work whose material is marvelously fused into a complicated, stylized contemporary idiom. The piano functions as a partner, not as a soloist, but the pianism is brilliant nevertheless. Szymanowski gave the premiere in 1932.

BLUMENTAL, Kord/Polish Radio Symphony of Katowice: Unicorn
EKIER, Rowicki/National Philharmonic: Muza

Twenty Mazurkas, Op. 50 (1923–29)

These are highly original. They have nothing in common with the Chopin Mazurkas. Swed thinks they are "some of his most exquisite jewels . . . as subtle and elliptical as late-Beethoven bagatelles."

HESSE-BUKOWSKA (nine mazurkas from Op. 50): Muza
ROSENBERGER (Twenty Mazurkas, Op. 50, and Two Mazurkas, Op. 62): Delos
RUBINSTEIN (four mazurkas from Op. 50): RCA (CD)

T

PETER ILYICH TCHAIKOVSKY
1840–1893 — Russia

Tchaikovsky "remains to this day," as Glenn Gould observed, "Russian music's chief tourist attraction." Although mainly concerned throughout his career with opera and orchestral forms, Tchaikovsky, surprisingly, left something over one hundred piano pieces, many of them permeated by his unique melodic magic.

The Complete Piano Music
Musically speaking, the most striking revelation of Tchaikovsky's piano writing is what might be called the "normalcy" of his expressive intentions. In the solo keyboard music, we encounter virtually no Tchaikovskian hysteria; at the piano, it would seem, he almost never reveled in morbidity. Instead, there is much cheer, more major keys than minor ones, a smattering of the exotic, bits of the barbaric, rustic dancing, and echoes from the composer's beloved world of ballet. There is also far more of Schumann's influence than Tchaikovsky would have allowed in his orchestral creations. Tchaikovsky was himself only an adequate pianist, and his gifts were by no means pianistic. The music is not always well-molded for the hand, but everywhere we discern the personal authenticity that has touched so many hearts.

PONTI: Vox

Sonata in G major, Op. 37
The Sonata is Tchaikovsky's largest piano canvas. The opening movement is indebted to Schumann's F-sharp minor Sonata. There is loveliness in the long slow movement; the scherzo is characteristic in 6/16 time, and the effective finale is easier than it sounds—a rush of brilliant figuration, a lush tune, all *à la russe*. It was dedicated to Karl Klindworth; its first performance by Nikolai Rubinstein gave Tchaikovsky one of the most glorious evenings of his life.

CROSSLEY: Philips
RICHTER: Monitor

Six Pieces, Op. 19
In addition to the famous Nocturne, which is No. 4, this opus contains a wonderful set of variations, buried in it as No. 6. Tchaikovsky loved the variation form although, unlike Brahms, he more often than not limited himself to exploring the diverse charms of a given melody. Historically, the work is of interest because it was the model for numerous sets of variations by other Russian composers—by Liapunov, by Glazunov, and two by Liadov, to mention a few examples.

GILELS: Melodiya

Six Pieces on One Theme, Op. 21
Another strong set. Wilhelm Backhaus used to program these, but they have enjoyed no such formidable advocacy in many decades. The music is ingeniously contrived to achieve a wide range of moods with a single theme. The Six Pieces are: Prelude, Fugue, Impromptu,

Funeral March, Mazurka, Scherzo. The Impromptu is a real golden nugget.

NIKOLAYEVA: Melodiya

Dumka, Op. 59

This is a later work, subtitled *A Scene from Russian Life*—a kind of Lisztian Hungarian Rhapsody with a Volga accent.

HOROWITZ: RCA

Piano Concerto No. 1 in B-flat minor, Op. 23 (1874–75)

This most popular of all concertos was given its world premiere by Hans von Bülow in Boston on October 25, 1875. In 1891, with Tchaikovsky conducting and Adèle aus der Ohe as soloist, it was the first concerto ever heard in Carnegie Hall. There have been dozens of recordings devoted to its ripe and spirited measures.

ARGERICH, Kondrashin/Bavarian Radio Symphony: Philips (CD)
BERMAN, Karajan/Berlin Philharmonic: DG
CLIBURN, Kondrashin: RCA (CD)
CURZON, Solti/Vienna Philharmonic: London
GILELS, Reiner/Chicago Symphony: RCA
HOROWITZ, Toscanini/NBC Symphony: RCA
JANIS, Menges/London Symphony: Mercury
POGORELICH, Abbado/London Symphony: DG (CD)
RUBINSTEIN, Leinsdorf/Boston Symphony: RCA (CD)
SGOUROS, Weller/London Philharmonic: Angel (CD)
WEISSENBERG, Karajan/Orchestre de Paris: Angel (CD)

Piano Concerto No. 2 in G major, Op. 44 (1881)

In three movements, a colorful, high-caliber work which has nevertheless been perpetually in the shadow of No. 1. Quite long, it is most often played in Siloti's composer-approved edition, which excised a good deal of material from the slow movement. The score has been heard to great advantage in Balanchine's *Ballet Imperial*.

CHERKASSKY, Kraus/Berlin Philharmonic: DG
CHERKASSKY, Susskind/Cincinnati Symphony: Vox Cum Laude
GILELS, Kondrashin/Leningrad Philharmonic: Baroque or Olympic
GRAFFMAN, Ormandy/Philadelphia: CBS

Piano Concerto No. 3 in E-flat major, Op. 75 (1893)

In one movement, with three subjects and a long cadenza, No. 3 is dedicated to the French virtuoso Louis Diémer. The work is not as difficult as its predecessors. Balanchine also choreographed a ballet to this concerto.

GRAFFMAN, Ormandy/Philadelphia: Columbia
ZHUKOV, Rozhdestvensky/USSR Symphony: Melodiya/Angel

Concert Fantasy for Piano and Orchestra, Op. 56 (1891)

A work written for Annette Essipova and first played in the United States in the 1890s by Julie Rivé-King. The cadenza is perhaps the longest ever composed. The Concert Fantasy is difficult and clumsy to play, but unduly neglected.

KATIN, Boult/London Philharmonic: London
PONTI, Kapp/Prague Symphony: Turnabout
ZHUKOV, Rozhdestvensky/USSR Symphony: Melodiya

HEITOR VILLA-LOBOS
1887–1959—Brazil

Villa-Lobos, by general consent, is Brazil's greatest composer. He wrote voluminously—1,500 works in all. The piano was never neglected. His music speaks directly; one always feels the pull of an unusual musical mind and personality. He was affected by the Indian folk material of his country, by impressionism, and by exotic and strange rhythms. He knew how to strike the barbaric chord, and he could be lovable.

Bachianas Brasileiras No. 3 for Piano and Orchestra (1938)

Villa-Lobos composed nine works titled *Bachianas Brasileiras,* of which No. 3 is scored for piano and orchestra. The composer saw parallels in certain Bachian melodic contours and Brazilian folk melodies, and these are brilliantly amalgamated into works of a very special flavor. The movements of No. 3 are Preludio, Fantasia, Aria, and Toccata (titled *Picapao*—which is a musical description of the sound of a woodpecker-like bird).

ORTIZ, Ashkenazy/New Philharmonia: Angel

Rudepoêma (1926)

Villa-Lobos's most extensive piano work; the title means "Rough-Poem." It was premiered in Paris in 1927 by Arthur Rubinstein, who early on had befriended the composer. Villa-Lobos wrote to the pianist: "I do not know whether I have been successful in capturing all your soul in this *Rudepoêma,* but I swear with all my heart, that I believe I have imprinted a picture of your personality on my memory and that I put it down on paper like an intimate camera. Thus, if I have succeeded, you will always remain the true author of this work." Rubinstein never recorded it, but thought Roberto Szidon played the piece "magnificently." The score is in one movement, with great torrents of sound.

BEAN: RCA
FREIRE: Telefunken
SZIDON: DG

Próle do bébé (1918)

The impressionist fabric is well contrasted with the more percussive note. These are among the most popular of Villa-Lobos's many piano pieces.

FREIRE: Telefunken
RUBINSTEIN: RCA (CD)

CARL MARIA VON WEBER
1786–1826 — Germany

Weber's piano music includes eight sets of variations, the four sonatas, and the separate pieces, *Momento capriccioso*, Op. 12; *Grande Polonaise*, Op. 21; *Rondo brillante*, Op. 62; *Polacca brillante*, Op. 72; and *Invitation to the Dance*, Op. 65. The variations are the weakest of the output; however, they do exploit most effectively Weber's always splendid piano technique, which often requires a large span. The best of these sets is the sparkling *Dorina Bella* Variations, Op. 7.

Sonata No. 1 in C major, Op. 24 (1812)
Sonata No. 2 in A-flat major, Op. 39 (1814–16)
Sonata No. 3 in D minor, Op. 49 (1816)
Sonata No. 4 in E minor, Op. 70 (1819–22)

The four sonatas constitute Weber's most important works for piano solo. They offer a unique blend of Weber the virtuoso and the operatic master forging a new epoch in German music. They all possess bold themes and the mysterious Romanticism of his opera *Der Freischütz*. Each one has indelibly refreshing qualities. The finale of the First Sonata is the dashing Perpetuum Mobile. No. 2 was loved by many Romantic pianists; its third movement, marked Presto assai, is tremendous fun with the spirit of a forest goblin. The Third Sonata's best movement is the finale, Allegro di bravura. The Sonata No. 4 has a first movement of early Romantic melancholia, a beautiful Andante, a fiendishly difficult minuet, and ends with a whirling tarantella.

D'ARCO (Sonatas Nos. 3 & 4): L'Oiseau-Lyre
BAR-ILLAN (Sonata No. 2): Audiofon
CIANI (Sonatas Nos. 2 & 3): DG
FLEISHER (Sonata No. 4): Epic
KANN (Sonatas Nos. 1–4 and complete solo piano music): Vox
OHLSSON (Sonatas Nos. 1–4 and solo piano music): Arabesque (CD)
WEBSTER (Sonatas Nos. 1 & 2): Dover

Invitation to the Dance (1819)
The ever-youthful *Invitation to the Dance* is history's first great ballroom waltz. It was perhaps the most often attempted piano work of its time.

DE LARROCHA: MHS
FLEISHER: Epic
SCHNABEL: Seraphim

Konzertstück for Piano and Orchestra (1821)
Piano Concerti Nos. 1 and 2 (1810–11)
Today the Weber *Konzertstück* and his two piano concerti are seldom performed, but they are the link between the Classical concerto (Beethoven had, by the time of Weber's First Concerto, completed his five examples) and those of Chopin, Mendelssohn, and Liszt. Weber wrote an octave glissando in the *Konzertstück* which is seldom attempted on the contemporary keyboard; it was far easier for Weber on his own light-action Brodmann.

Gottschalk was known to have a bloody keyboard whenever he played the piece. The *Konzertstück* is a remarkably advanced composition for 1821, and it became a war-horse for Liszt and Gottschalk; in fact, few Romantic virtuosi failed to achieve success with it.

John Warrack wrote of these three scores: "In true Romantic fashion the highest store is set upon personal sensation as the most reliable artistic guide and upon the virtuoso artist as the most brilliant and eloquent voice of sensations shared by all."

Konzertstück:
ARRAU, Galliera/Philharmonia: Seraphim
BRENDEL, Abbado/London Symphony: Philips (CD)
R. CASADESUS, Szell/Cleveland: CBS
FRANTZ, Menuhin/Royal Philharmonic: Big Ben (CD)
KELLER, Köhler/Berlin Symphony: Turnabout

The Two Concerti:
FRAGER, Andreae/North German Radio Symphony: RCA
KELLER, Köhler/Berlin Symphony: Turnabout

ANTON WEBERN
1883–1945 — Austria

Variations for Piano, Op. 27 (1936)
Webern is surely one of the main influences on musical thinking after World War II. His Piano Variations, dedicated to Edward Steuermann, is a work that anyone interested in serial music should study. Eric Salzman comments: " 'Systemic' and 'minimal' are catch-words in the advanced art world today, but thirty and forty years ago Webern evolved an intense, aphoristic, late-Romantic, expressionist-psychological style in a geometry of musical space where ideas and their expression become identicals, where the minimum materials are endowed with their maximum meaning and where ideas themselves and the 'systemic' form and expression become identical."

BIRET: Finnadar
POLLINI: DG (CD)
Y. TAKAHASHI: Denon
WEBSTER: Dover

Most of the preceding compositions form the nucleus of the literature of the piano that is most frequently performed and recorded. For serious students, however, there remains much more that is worth examination and study. The following composers are by no means an exhaustive list of those who have made contributions to piano music, but all of these are composers of special quality who have explored the piano with high ideals and particularly understand the instrument's resources.

JEAN ABSIL
1893–1974 — Belgium

A rewarding composer. His *Passacaille,* Op. 101 (1959), and Variations, Op. 93, find him at his best.

WILLIAM ALBRIGHT
b. 1944 — United States

He is an excellent pianist who has often exploited the ragtime idiom in his work, which can be complex, dissonant, and improvisatory, as in *Pianoagogo* (1966). The composer described his *Grand Sonata in Rag* (1968) as "the perhaps impossible synthesis of ragtime textures with 'classical' structures."

WILLIAM ALWYN
1905–1985 — England

A modern Romanticist who writes clever and effective piano music. Especially fine are the Twelve Preludes and the *Fantasy* Waltzes.

DAVID AMRAM
b. 1930 — United States

His Sonata (1965) is representative of its composer's merging of popular styles with classical form.

GEORGE ANTHEIL
1900–1959 — United States

It is a shame so little of Antheil's piano music is played. The early works retain their radical spirit; the later ones, with much motivic writing, tend to be more conservative. He left four sonatas, of which the Sonata No. 2, *The Airplane* (1922), has a wonderfully brash lilt.

ANTON ARENSKY
1861–1906 — Russia

Many gems can be found among his numerous piano pieces. Arensky had a suave lyricism

427

and a talent for the instrument, best exhibited in his Twelve Etudes.

GEORGES AURIC
1899–1983 — France

A member of the celebrated group *Les Six,* he wrote well for the piano. His most important score is the Sonata (1931).

MILTON BABBITT
b. 1916 — United States

One of the leading American composers. His piano music, such as *Three Compositions for Piano* (1947) and *Partitions* (1963), has found many performances. His music is intellectually demanding.

GRAZYNA BACEWICZ
1913–1969 — Poland

An important composer whose Ten Studies and Second Sonata are powerful and well-written scores.

CARL PHILIPP EMANUEL BACH
1714–1788 — Germany

The greatest talent among J. S. Bach's children. C. P. E. Bach's place in music history is secure, for he helped formulate the principles of the Classical sonata. Much of his huge output is original, ebullient, and florid. The slow movements are especially interesting.

HENK BADINGS
1907–1987 — Netherlands

A composer of substance, writing in highly structured forms. His works for piano, especially the sonatas, are weighty but accessible.

JEAN BARRAQUÉ
1928–1973 — France

His 1950–52 Piano Sonata is considered one of the most important French sonatas of the century. It runs to forty minutes and is daunting technically. Maurice Hinson says, "Few pianists will be able to handle this work successfully."

MARION BAUER
1887–1955 — United States

Bauer was a refined talent. Her music mingles American and French traits. She composed nineteen titles for the piano, from an Elegy (1909) to the *Summertime* Suite (1953). Her most extensive piano work is the *Dance Sonata* (1935). The Four Piano Pieces, Op. 21 (1930), are an exceptional set; the pianistic demands are varied, the material is hard-edged and elegantly worked out.

ARNOLD BAX
1883–1953 — England

Some of Bax's finest work is for the piano. At his best, he is capable of a haunting beauty. The four solo sonatas ask for a complete pianism. The Sonata No. 1 in F-sharp minor (1922) is in one movement, melodramatic and infused with Irish folk flavor as well as Lisztian thematic transformation.

MRS. H. H. A. BEACH (AMY MARCY CHENEY)
1867–1944 — United States

A shining talent whose music is among the best of American Romanticism. Her work abounds in melting, honest lyricism. Her writing for the instrument is grateful and coloristic. Her longest piano work, the Variations on Balkan Themes, Op. 60, reveals Beach as an astute variationist.

RICHARD RODNEY BENNETT
b. 1936 — England

An inventive composer; his Piano Sonata and Five Studies display an affinity for the piano.

WILLIAM BOLCOM
b. 1938 — United States

An accomplished pianist whose piano music shows various influences. He has delved deeply into ragtime style. Paul Jacobs recorded his *Graceful Ghost Rag*. Bolcom's Twenty-four Etudes exploit many pianistic problems.

SERGEI BORTKIEWICZ
1877–1952 — Russia

An attractive composer. His music exhibits an amazing gift for Chopinesque and Lisztian piano writing. The Ten Etudes Op. 15 and Sonata Op. 9 are delightful to work on.

PIERRE DE BRÉVILLE
1861–1949 — France

An exceptional composer. His Sonata (1923) and the *Suite stamboul* are vital and ingratiating compositions for the piano. Although he began his career under the influence of Franck, his music became very individual, yet quite French in feeling.

JOHN CAGE
b. 1912 — United States

Cage has had a vital influence on many composers, with his interest in Oriental philosophy, his creative collaboration with the pianist David Tudor (where the performer engages in a new partnership with the composer), his constant explorations into new sounds, and, for the piano, his invention of the "prepared piano," which has given the percussiveness of the instrument new outlets of expression. His belief in all sounds as equal, his play with chance and randomness, have given to many composers an extended outlook on form and color. He has wanted to depersonalize music, but instead, through his screws and bolts, added new and distinctive sonorities to the art.

His early, "tamer" music includes *Bacchanale* (1938), the first piece in which he used the prepared piano. Cage said, "The need to change the sound of the instrument arose through the desire to make an accompaniment, without employing percussion instruments, suitable for the dance by Syvilla Fort, for which it was composed." The sounds are effective in their pristine percussion. *Bacchanale* is melodic. Other pieces for prepared piano, of more interest, are *Music for Marcel Duchamp, Prelude for Meditation, The Perilous Night,* and *Suite for Toy Piano,* a 7½-minute *tour de force* on nine white keys. The twangs and vibrations are often delicate. *Dream,* created for Merce Cunningham, is for "plain piano": a straight line of single melody, some open harmony, and the most traditionally "beautiful" piece he wrote. The Concerto for Prepared Piano (1951) is high in interest in Cage's catalogue of music; within its dissonant world there is a finely knit delicacy. Other works include *Sonatas and Interludes,* which comes with a kit to prepare the piano.

JOHN ALDEN CARPENTER
1876–1951 — United States

He left some fine piano music, including a delightfully sweet and saucy Concertino for Piano and Orchestra (1915). Percy Grainger gave the premiere.

ROBERT CASADESUS
1899–1972 — France

The great pianist was a prolific composer, who wrote impeccably for the piano. His Piano Concerto in E major, Op. 37, is a skillful and thoroughly Gallic concerto in the tradition of Saint-Saëns and Ravel. The slow movement is a gem. There are also four difficult sonatas, twenty-four preludes, and eight etudes.

ALFREDO CASELLA
1883–1947 — Italy

He was a serious piano thinker, leaving a library of music both stimulating in its search for formal coherence and an adequate expression of his eclectic personality. In some respects, he reminds one of the restlessness of Busoni's creative faculty. He partook of Bachian influence within a neo-Classic scheme, experimented with polytonality and atonality, and in an outstanding work like *A notte alta* (1917), he bows to the seduction of impressionism. In such scores as the two *Ricercari on the Name Bach* (dedicated to Gieseking), he is dark and intense.

JUAN JOSÉ CASTRO
1895–1968 — Argentina

Castro and his gifted brothers, José María (1892–1964) and Washington (b. 1909), are interesting creators, all producing piano music well worth playing. José María's *Sonata de primavera* (1939) is fascinating. Juan José welds elements of twelve-tone technique to a folkloristic idiom. His Five Tangos have been recorded by Grant Johannesen.

PAUL COOPER
b. 1926 — United States

His short piano pieces, such as *Cycles* (1969), show a creative mind and an ingenious use of the pedal. His Piano Sonata (1962) should be noted as significant. Ronald Rogers played the work brilliantly.

JOHN CORIGLIANO
b. 1938 — United States

This composer has an appeal for many. His piano music, such as the Etude-Fantasy, is splashy, and the four-movement Piano Concerto has a theatrical core. Corigliano is not afraid to express his emotions.

HENRY COWELL
1897–1965 — United States

He may be called the father of the "tone cluster." Cowell was an early experimenter in "extra-finger technique." For example, *Piece for Piano Paris* (1924) uses strumming, plucking, damping, and hitting strings inside the piano, in addition to fist, forearm, and palm clusters. Doris Hays plays Cowell's music to maximum effect.

RICHARD CUMMING
b. 1928 — China

He came to the United States in 1941 and studied with Bloch and Sessions. He has written a piano sonata and a set of twenty-four preludes in a neo-Romantic idiom. They were written, says the composer, to "express my own joy and respect for that lyric, noble, and dynamic instrument I dearly love, the piano." The entire set takes half an hour. They range from fairly easy to very difficult, and from "café to strict twelve-tone," with one each for

left hand alone and right hand. Nos. 3 and 4 are lyric diamonds.

ARTHUR CUSTER
b. 1923 — United States

See especially *Rhapsodality Brown* (1968). The title is unexplained, though halfway through this twelve-minute score someone screams out "Rhapsodality." After that unexpected outburst, with some drumlike tapping, the music becomes jazzier and orgiastic, leading to impressioned textures and closing with slow, bleak chords dying off. The work is finely spaced, dissonant and improvisatory. It has been recorded by Dwight Peltzer, whose playing of contempoary music is always fastidious, intelligent, and textually respectful.

ABEL DECAUX
1869–1943 — France

Nothing in Decaux's output could have presaged his *Clairs de lune* (1900–07). They are titled *Midnight Strikes the Alley, The Cemetery,* and *The Sea.* They represent the most advanced compositional procedures of the day. They also have a phantomlike emotional content.

NORMAN DELLO JOIO
b. 1913 — United States

Dello Joio's piano music combines many influences. His Third Sonata (1948) is a good example of his directness and his melodic and rhythmic immediacy.

DAVID DIAMOND
b. 1915 — United States

His piano music is invariably interesting and well-made. The Piano Sonata (1947) is well worth investigating, as is the Piano Concerto (1950), a work of richness and virtuosity, exhibiting the contrasting elements of Diamond's musical personality. Thomas Schumacher premiered it. The most recent piano work by Diamond is the Prelude, Fantasy, and Fugue, dedicated to and performed by William Black.

ANTONÍN DVOŘÁK
1841–1904 — Czechoslovakia

The great Czech master was better suited to other media, but he composed more than a hundred solo piano pieces which are often beautiful, and filled with Czech nationalism. His best pieces are the thirteen *Poetic Tone Pictures,* Op. 85, the Suite in A major, Op. 98, and the eight Humoresques, Op. 101. His G minor Piano Concerto, Op. 33, is always a treat.

KLAUS EGGE
1906–1979 — Norway

His piano music has freshness and intensity. Compositionally, Egge uses a free tonality with much contrapuntal skill. His Piano Sonata No. 2 (*Patética*), Op. 27, is a work of high value. He also composed two piano concerti.

GOTTFRIED VON EINEM
b. 1918 — Austria

Neo-Classic influence in his solo piano music. A Piano Concerto, Op. 20 (1956),

is a marvelous score and should be well known.

GEORGES ENESCO
1881–1955 — Rumania

The great violinist wrote beautifully for the piano, including a virtuoso transcription of his own celebrated Roumanian Rhapsody No. 1. His Suite for Piano, Op. 10, and the Piano Sonatas Nos. 1 and 3 reveal a complex and sensitive composer.

LUIS GIANNEO
1897–1968 — Argentina

He wrote many worthy piano pieces. A charming Sonatina (1938) is dedicated to Arrau. His B-flat minor Piano Sonata is a subtle work in three movements; graceful, some bitonality, and use of Argentine folk song. The third movement builds to an imposing climax.

ALEXANDER GLAZUNOV
1865–1936 — Russia

A beguiling composer who has held to the edge of the repertoire. Beauties abound in catchy melodies, piquant harmony, and an exceptional ease in handling a late-nineteenth-century pianism. The two piano sonatas are quite impressive, ranking with the best of his eight symphonies. The critic Stassov called the Second Sonata, Op. 75, a "grandiose, magnificent masterpiece." Gilels loved it and played it with all the plumage and color that can be lavished upon it. Glazunov's Variations in

F-sharp minor, Op. 72 (1900), is one of his finest compositions.

MORTON GOULD
b. 1913 — United States

An American master. He has given the piano many works containing a deep knowledge of the instrument. One may look at the *Abby* Variations, the Prelude and Toccata, and *Rag-Blues-Rag*. The Sonatina is especially effective and the *Boogie-Woogie* Etude is often played by Shura Cherkassky. Gould's *Interplay* for Piano and Orchestra was premiered by José Iturbi.

CAMARGO GUARNIERI
b. 1907 — Brazil

He devoted a great many works to the piano. His five sonatinas are subtle, neo-Classical, yet nationalistic works. His *Ponteios* (Preludes) are fifty in number, composed from 1939 to 1959, and explore many sentiments.

REYNALDO HAHN
1875–1947 — France

A charming composer, better known for his songs. The piano music is airy and urbane.

IAIN HAMILTON
b. 1922 — Scotland

His Piano Sonata, Op. 13 (1951), shows Bartók's influence. The Nocturnes with Ca-denzas (1963) are serial in their structure but impressionistic. They are a good cycle for concert performance. The *Palinodes* (1972), inspired by Rimbaud, are imaginative pieces, seven in number, with clusters, glissandos, and all sorts of technical requirements.

ROBERT HELPS
b. 1928 — United States

An outstanding concert pianist who studied with Abby Whiteside. Helps plays such works as the Sessions Sonata No. 1 with the utmost expression and technical know-how. His own music shows how thoroughly conversant he is with the instrument and its heritage.

ARTHUR HONEGGER
1892–1955 — Switzerland

His Concertino for Piano and Orchestra (1924) is a clever piece, slender, jazzy, perky orchestration, with music-hall seductiveness; it is characteristic of the 1920s. The Toccata and Variations (1916) and *Sept Pièces brèves* (1920) are grainy, chordal, polyphonic in texture.

ALAN HOVHANESS
b. 1911 — United States

A ceaselessly prolific composer. Oriental elements and Armenian folk music characterize his work, which often sounds improvisatory but in fact is tightly organized. There is a quality of mysticism in Hovhaness's music. His very personalized idiom is heard to advantage in the Fantasy, Op. 16, producing string vibrations and atmospheric gong effects inside

433

the piano. Hovhaness is an ideal exponent of his music. He has written: "Composer, publisher and performer unite in beautiful cooperation for altruism of a better civilization. The composer, as in Old China, joins heaven and earth with threads of sound, the publisher promptly prints the music; the performer promptly plays the music and the world promptly receives the benediction."

KAREL HUSA
b. 1921 — Czechoslovakia

His Sonatina, Op. 1 (1943), is a delight, with real humor. The First Sonata, Op. 11 (1949), in three movements, is expressive and dissonant. The Second Sonata, composed in 1975, is a stunning work—three movements of virtuosic, imaginative piano scoring, with use of the sostenuto (middle) pedal and some inside-the-piano technique. A highly charged composition.

JACQUES IBERT
1890–1962 — France

A composer of charm and wit. Les Rencontres and Petite Suite en quinze images are breezy and a delight to play. His best-known set is Histoires, ten pieces of which Le Petit Ane blanc, "The Little White Donkey," became a favorite.

VINCENT D'INDY
1851–1931 — France

An important composer who wrote a great deal of piano music. His best-known work is his Symphony on a French Mountain Air for Piano and Orchestra, Op. 25 (1886). Of particular interest is the Thème varié, fugue, et chanson, Op. 85. Le Poème des montagnes, Op. 15, contains three colorful and lyrical nature studies of moderate difficulty. The Sonata in E minor (1907) is d'Indy's most significant composition, a work, above all, of high intellectual quality, cyclic construction, and musical substance. The pianism is ungrateful, and novel figuration plays a small role. Yet the score has a subtlety that penetrates with repeated study. The structure of the three movements is fused from three generating themes. D'Indy was also a smooth contrapuntist, and his knowledge of music's past in many guises is transmitted in this sonata alongside plenty of moments of cool, sensuous lyricism. It could only have been written by a French composer.

JOHN IRELAND
1879–1962 — England

His piano music is among Ireland's best work. It is mildly modern, often impressionistic, mingling modal English folk song. Of his descriptive works, the Decorations are best known, consisting of The Island Spell, with its bell-like sonorities, Moon-glade, and The Scarlet Ceremonies, with its trills. The Sonatina is terse; the Ballade, gloomy; the Rhapsody, big-climaxed. The Piano Sonata (1918-20) has power and architectural solidity in its three-movement plan; the work bristles with technical inventiveness and is harmonically adventurous. Ireland's 1930 Piano Concerto in E-flat has had a number of advocates: Curzon, Bachauer, Lympany, Eileen Joyce, who gave its premiere, Sondra Bianca, and Eric Parkin.

ADOLF JENSEN
1837–1879 — Germany

A composer with a real lyric gift most splendidly felt in his songs and small piano pieces, such as his etudes. His Sonata in F-sharp minor, Op. 25, is Jensen's largest work, an interesting attempt to cope with sonata form tied to a Romantic rhetoric.

HUNTER JOHNSON
b. 1906 — United States

Pianists on the lookout for a major American sonata may look seriously at the Johnson Piano Sonata (1948). John Kirkpatrick, who has performed it often, has said that Johnson's Piano Sonata is to the South what the Charles Ives *Concord* Sonata is to the North. The Johnson sonata, however, is only twenty minutes in length. The form is cyclic, in three movements, changing meters, difficult, and requiring an absorbing concentration. The composer wrote: "My spirit was teeming defiantly with America. It is an intense expression of the South. . . . The nostalgia, dark brooding, frenzied gaiety, high rhetoric and brutal realism are all intermingled."

ANDRÉ JOLIVET
1905–1974 — France

He wrote persuasively for the piano, especially in the two piano sonatas. The 1950 Piano Concerto is an important work, using exotic themes based on music of Africa, Asia, and Polynesia. It is heavy on percussion, complex in ensemble, and difficult to play.

DMITRI KABALEVSKY
1904–1987 — Russia

A good pianist who wrote brilliantly for the instrument. He has written abundantly for children in a charming and invariably interesting manner, with constant little twists and a taut harmony here and there. Representative are the *Twenty Pieces for Children* Op. 27 and the *Twenty Pieces for Children* Op. 39. The Sonatina in C major, Op. 13, No. 1, has attained "classic" status among students for its wit and light heart. The Twenty-four Preludes, Op. 38 (1943), form a tremendous fund of ethno-Russian folk material using many keyboard techniques. The Third Sonata and the Piano Concerto No. 2 in G minor are both remarkable syntheses of Kabalevsky's intentions as a Soviet composer of the highest taste and craft working within the guidelines of the Prokofiev mold.

ARAM KHACHATURIAN
1903–1978 — Armenia

The most famous of Armenian composers. At his finest, he sings his colorful musical heritage with an authenticity which has compelled an international audience beyond the Soviet Union. Khachaturian's Piano Concerto, which was once played often, retains its glamor as a colorful bravura work. His solo piano music occupies a small but attractive place in his output. There is a pleasant and often amusing capriciousness to this music, which abounds in sharp rhythms and colorful timbres. His characteristic use of the intervals of the major and minor second, as well as a frequently static bass, make for a distinctive pianism entirely his own. His *Poem* (1927) is pungent and discursive. The Toccata (1932) is the best known of his solo pieces; it is sonorous, with a short middle section of Oriental atmosphere. The Sonatina (1959) is laconic, fresh, neo-Classic, and finely cut. The 1961 Sonata is full of objective and outgoing energy.

LEON KIRCHNER
b. 1919 — United States

His Piano Sonata (1948) is one of the best piano works of its period. Five tempo markings combine for a concentrated, turbulent work, high in dissonant content, with an underlying expressivity that blossoms in the Adagio. Hinson says, "The whole work pulsates with rubato." Leon Fleisher, a surgically precise artist, integrates his recorded performance with temperamental intensity. Robert Taub plays it on a more recent recording.

THEODOR KIRCHNER
1823–1903 — Germany

A composer with flashes of high talent. He wrote hundreds of miniatures in a Schumann-esque and Brahmsian style. Edward Dannreuther wrote: "Though sheltered under Schumann's cloak, many minor points of style and diction are Kirchner's own, and decidedly clever." Adrian Ruiz revived some of these pieces on a recording.

HALFDAN KJERULF
1815–1868 — Norway

A composer of genuine talent and high standards. Grieg greatly admired him. His piano music, mostly small character pieces, is tinged with Nordic sound and the fragrance of Schumann and Mendelssohn's Romanticism. He had a vein of abundant melody and a true naturalness.

ZOLTÁN KODÁLY
1882–1967 — Hungary

His Nine Piano Pieces, Op. 3, are beautifully conceived impressionistic music. The Seven Piano Pieces, Op. 11 (1910–18), are a superb set. The pianist David Burge has recorded them with an extraordinary sensitivity and command of rhythm. He wrote of the Op. 11, "Its theatrical rhetoric is elemental and its moments of high grandeur and despairing pathos are unembarrassed by excessive sophistication."

The *Marosszek Dances* (1927) is a splendid piano work, also orchestrated by Kodály. Here Kodály's lavish style and passionate lyricism leave the world of impressionism and move toward his more characteristic use of the Magyar folk heritage. The composer, in differentiating his dances from the Brahms Hungarian dances, said the latter "are typical of urban Hungary around 1860. . . . My Marosszek dances have their roots in a much more remote past, and represent a fairyland that has disappeared."

CHARLES KOECHLIN
1867–1951 — France

A renowned teacher, who as a composer was held in respect by Fauré, Roussel, Milhaud, and Poulenc. His music for piano is individual and is an unexplored avenue of beauties. The composer Henri Sauguet wrote, "His music is like no other . . . it takes many an unexpected, refined and even surprising detour and leads one to discover whole new landscapes." In recent years, the Israeli pianist Boaz Sharon has done much to bring Koechlin's piano music to attention.

JOSEPH LAMB
1887–1960 — United States

Along with Joplin and James Scott, Lamb is one of the big three of classic ragtime. "Lamb," wrote Rudi Blesh, "developed a very personal sensitivity into the most haunting chromatic harmonies and exquisitely Chopinesque *morbidezza* in all ragtime literature. It is impossible to conceive of the classic Missouri Valley black ragtime without its rounding out in the work of this white Eastern genius." Lamb's music is all freshness and subtlety, and pianists will be charmed by his *Ethiopia Rag, American Beauty,* and the *Ragtime Nightingale* (1915), a masterpiece of this genre.

CONSTANT LAMBERT
1905–1951 — England

A brilliant figure in the musical life of England during the thirties and forties. His book, *Music Ho!,* remains provoking. His Concerto for Piano and Nine Players (1930) is problematic but of superior quality and craft; neo-Classic designs combine with jazz and "blue" harmony. It is pianistically vital. Lambert's major work for solo piano is his Piano Sonata in three very serious movements: Allegro molto marcato, with exuberant syncopation; Nocturne, a blues, ragtime movement; and the long finale with its very convincing ending. The work is Lambert's summation of the jazz elements that so intrigued him. His *Elegiac Blues* for piano, composed in memory of the blues singer Florence Mills, is expressively melancholic and fragrant of that period.

BENJAMIN LEES
b. 1925 — China

An American composer whose piano music is serious and often exuberant. The 1953 Fantasia, six ornamental etudes, and the *Sonata breve* and Sonata No. 4 show a composer who loves to write for the instrument.

ANATOL LIADOV
1855–1914 — Russia

A talented composer of fastidious salon music, as well as the larger-scaled Variations on a Theme of Glinka, Op. 35, a work of fetching musicality and pianistic delight.

SERGEI LIAPUNOV
1859–1924 — Russia

M. D. Calvocoressi wrote of Liapunov: "He remains, with Liadov, the most attractive of the minor poets of Russian music." The influence of Liszt, and of Liapunov's mentor Balakirev, is apparent. The twelve *Etudes d'exécution transcendante,* Op. 11, dedicated to Liszt, are the most important concert etudes to come out of the Balakirev school. Besides the *Etudes,* which are a gold mine of inventive figuration and Russian nationalism, Liapunov wrote a Toccata and Fugue, a Sonata, Op. 27, and a *Sonatine*, Op. 65. Both his Piano Concerto No. 2 in E major, Op. 38, and the *Rhapsody on Ukrainian Themes* for Piano and Orchestra are attention-provoking works. In the concerto, suavely lyric themes are developed with deftness: double-notes, heavy Lisztian octaves and glissandi. The full-blown *Rhapsody* is dressed in lavish Oriental regalia.

BOHUSLAV MARTINŮ
1890–1959 — Czechoslovakia

An intriguing, uneven, and prolific composer. He often uses his Czech folk lineage, as well as bitonality and neo-Classicism, with a skillful eclecticism. His etudes and polkas (sixteen pieces) have color and considerable keyboard ingenuity. His works for piano and orchestra deserve performance. In the Piano Concerto No. 3 (1948) and the Piano Concerto No. 4 (*Incantation*), we have some of Martinů's best work.

NIKOLAI MIASKOVSKY
1881–1950 — Russia

He is little known in the West, but in the Soviet orbit Miaskovsky is very respected. He wrote nine piano sonatas, along with many smaller pieces. The Piano Sonata No. 2 in F-sharp minor, Op. 13 (1912), is pure Russian Romanticism, a strong, turbulently gloomy statement in one movement. The Sonata No. 3 in C, Op. 19, is even more brooding and grave, but with touches of the heroic. The Piano Sonata No. 4 in C minor, Op. 27, is in three movements; less intense than the earlier ones, it contains a dazzling finale.

438

FRANCISCO MIGNONE
1897–1986 — Brazil

A richly satisfying composer whose piano music is particularly colorful. One may look at his Sonata No. 1 (1941), Four Sonatinas (1951), and the *Lenda brasileira*, a set of four pieces.

DARIUS MILHAUD
1892–1974 — France

He wrote much piano music within his staggering output. It is invested with many styles and devices: folk song, polytonality, jazz, and an all-embodying rhythmic genius. Much of Milhaud's piano music is casual in manner. His best-known piano pieces are the 1920 *Saudades do Brasil*, which have retained their spontaneous freshness. They are constructed with Brazilian rhythms; each piece is two pages long. The Piano Concerto No. 1 (1933) was composed for Marguerite Long, who recorded it on 78s with Milhaud conducting. In three short movements, all of it is sheer pleasure. The Concerto No. 2 (1941) is also a wonderful score, in two movements. It moves from ragtime to South America and to the Paris music-hall, too.

ROBERT PALMER
b. 1915 — United States

The *Toccata Ostinato* was played a good deal during the 1950s. The Piano Sonata No. 2 (1948) is a two-movement conception. The work asks for formidable fingers. The composer has written: "I love the way nineteenth-century composers used the instrument, especially Chopin. I hoped to achieve something of the spacious sound that he and other composers achieved, but in my own twentieth-century language." The sonata was recorded by Yvar Mikhashoff, a formidable champion of American composers.

HECTOR CAMPOS-PARSI
b. 1922 — Puerto Rico

His finest piano music is the Sonata in G (1952–53). It combines a freely tonal, biting neo-Classicism with a stylization of the island's traditional music. The first movement is marked Mesto and is emotional; a Vivo finale is relieved by a sad "chorale" but sails on to a brilliant conclusion.

GEORGE PERLE
b. 1915 — United States

A composer of great purity. He has been an influential theorist, and he writes in a personal "twelve-tone tonality." Perle has always taken special interest in the piano. Michael Boriskin, who has recorded five of Perle's works, wrote: "Perle's music is elegant, poised, lucid, effervescent. His instrumental writing is resourceful and idiomatic." His Six Etudes are brilliant and demanding. Bradford Gowen has recorded them. Robert Miller has recorded his fascinating Toccata, and Robert Helps the Six Preludes. The Six New Etudes (1984) are concerned with the exploration of problems of rhythm, pedaling, and tonal balance.

VINCENT PERSICHETTI
1915–1987 — United States

He was an excellent pianist and a great teacher. Persichetti's works for piano, especially the eleven sonatas, form a valuable library of music that should not be neglected. His music displays a deep knowledge of the instrument. His two volumes of *Poems,* Opp. 4 and 5 (1939), had frequent performance.

GABRIEL PIERNÉ
1863–1937 — France

An extremely artful composer. The peak of his piano music is in the large-scale and difficult Variations in C minor, Op. 42 (1918). A much earlier Piano Concerto, Op. 12 (1887), finds expansive piano writing and ripe tunes; instead of a slow movement, there is a deft scherzo, of a Saint-Saëns type of brilliance.

WILLEM PIJPER
1894–1947 — Netherlands

One of the leading Dutch composers of his time. His three *sonatines* show a variety of moods. His Piano Concerto (1927), a thirteen-minute work, is built in seven tiny movements. Insinuating dance rhythms, Stravinskian neo-Classics, a whimsical, stylish, "swanky" air pervade the score. It was recorded by Hans Henkemans, a pianist-composer who studied with Pijper.

MANUEL PONCE
1886–1948 — Mexico

An expressive composer. There is a strong Sonata No. 2, as well as *Twenty Easy Pieces for Piano* and a *Preludio trágico.*

MARCEL POOT
b. 1901 — Belgium

He studied piano with the famed Belgian Arthur de Greef. He is a composer who can be entertaining, with rhythmic vitality and pianistic ingenuity. See especially the Sonata in C (1927), the four-movement Suite (1943), and the cheery *Sonatine* (1945). His Piano Concerto was compulsory for the 1960 Queen Elizabeth competition. The material is sparse, charming, and often exhilarating.

JOACHIM RAFF
1822–1882 — Switzerland

He left about 150 piano pieces. Raff was a fecund melodist with a conventional harmonic palette. At his best, he is dashing and humorous. His Piano Concerto in C minor, Op. 185 (1870–73), is a melodic concoction that invited performance for three decades after its premiere by von Bülow. It has fresh qualities that deserve revival.

PHILIP RAMEY
b. 1939 — United States

He studied with Alexander Tchérépnin. His Fourth Sonata is nondevelopmental, using the title as "sound-piece." It is very atmospheric, inspired by bells, with no bar-lines, nontonal, with giant clusters ending the work. The *Leningrad Rag, or Mutations on Scott Joplin,* uses Joplin's *Gladiolus Rag* as a palimpsest. His largest score for piano is the (1969–72) Piano Fantasy. It is harsh, emotive, decorative, and difficult. It has been recorded by John Atkins and Bennett Lerner.

ALAN RAWSTHORNE
1905–1971 — England

A refined and sensitive temperament comes through in Rawsthorne's music. He was an eclectic; at times his music is atonal. The best of his compositions for piano are the *Four Romantic Pieces* (1953), the Sonatina (1949), and two piano concerti. The First Concerto (1938) is strongly dissonant; the Concerto No. 2 (1951) was played by Curzon and is by far a more immediately attractive work, with lyric passages as well as lighter sections.

GEORGE ROCHBERG
b. 1918 — United States

There are twelve Bagatelles in twelve-tone idiom, a Sonata-Fantasia in three movements, and the *Carnival Music* (1970), a twenty-three-minute work of which the composer wrote: "I chose the overall title to suggest the side-by-side presence in both living reality and cultural reality of the 'lighter' and 'heavier,' the 'popular' and the 'serious.' " It is a work of highly charged opposites, stirring textures; the first-movement Fanfares and March is especially vital and bumptious. The whole composition is tinged with many subconscious strands of sounds and semi-forgotten tunes.

NED ROREM

b. 1923 — United States

Rorem is one of America's best-known composers. At his finest, he is highly communicative. His 1949 Three Barcarolles are in A B A form, No. 3 being the most brilliant. The Piano Sonata No. 2 is an ingratiating score (1949), French-influenced in its mood and clarity. The composer calls it "a garland of four happy songs." The first movement is sad and yearning, then come a bubbling Tarantella, a Nocturne, and a Toccata. Julius Katchen played it joyously. Rorem's set of Etudes, written for and performed by Emanuel Ax, is difficult and makes a good concert piece. His Piano Concerto in six movements is imaginative throughout. The first movement is for right hand alone.

HILDING ROSENBERG

1892–1985 — Sweden

The major Swedish composer of his time. His Sonata No. 2 (1925) uses many devices popular during the twenties, such as bitonality. The Sonata No. 3 (1926) is worth performance, as is the Theme and Variations (1941).

GIOACCHINO ROSSINI

1792–1868 — Italy

The great opera composer left nearly 150 piano pieces, suffused with a little of everything, and lumped together as *Sins of My Old Age,* "dedicated to fourth-rate pianists, to whom I have the honor to belong." The titles are pre-Satie, such as *Italian Innocence, French*

Candor, Harmless Prelude, and *Oh! the Green Peas.* They are spunky, delectable, and radiant. A pity this literature is hardly known.

CARL RUGGLES

1876–1971 — United States

Ruggles left only twelve works, each one a milestone in twentieth-century music and each often studied. *Evocations (Four Chants for Piano)* (1937–43), ten minutes in duration, is his only piano work. They are: Largo, Andante con fantasia, Moderato appassionato, Adagio sostenuto. Each is tightly compressed and heavily chromatic; every note is of prime importance. The pianist must gently prick the inner tendrils of these slow-moving pieces. John Kirkpatrick exerts a deep spell in these chants of loneliness.

FREDERIC RZEWSKI

b. 1938 — United States

His piano music has been well-received, especially his fifty-minute set of variations, *The People United Will Never Be Defeated* (*Thirty-six Variations on a Chilean Song*), composed in 1965 and dedicated to Ursula Oppens, who plays it to the hilt with remarkable flair and technique. Besides slamming the lid on the piano, crying out, whistling, and so on, there are many conventional variations also, with popular elements and diverse, unexpected turns, in this surprise package. The *Four North American Ballads* are lengthy (twenty-six minutes) and difficult, composed for Paul Jacobs, whose recording is enthralling from first to last. All are based on American work songs. The fourth piece, *Winnsboro Cotton Mill Blues,* is the most original in its

441

soundscape, depicting the life of the textile mills. The heart pounds louder as the music becomes ever more relentless.

Another of Rzewski's piano works is the Variations on *No Place to Go but Around*. Of it, Eric Salzman wrote, "It is a twenty-minute, super-tonal, wonderfully eclectic Mahlerian structure.... A big contrapuntal super-structure is woven out of themes that represent the various classes of society.... Rzewski has here turned his creative and pianistic skills in an astonishing direction, fashioning a piano work with impact that is 'monumental' in the old-fashioned sense." The composer, a pianist of devastating power, has recorded his own work.

CYRIL SCOTT
1879–1970 — England

An interesting figure in English music. He wrote books on occult subjects and health matters. He was once described as the "English Debussy." *Lotus Land,* Op. 47, was once popular. His Piano Concerto No. 1 in C major (1913–14) is around forty minutes and is one of the best English piano concertos of its time. It was premiered by Beecham, with Scott as soloist. The work gets bogged down in an undergrowth of tangled harmony and, as in many of his scores, Scott's weakness is a lack of forward motion; but he has a distinct individuality, with many peculiarly colored harmonies and shimmering textures.

Of the Piano Concerto, which John Ogdon recorded, the composer wrote: "It is simply what I intended it to be, not a deep work but just an enlivening one.... It is as if Scarlatti had lived in China! In the last movement I unashamedly used a sort of neo-Handelian idiom." Scott's most adventurous work for solo piano is the Piano Sonata No. 1, Op. 66 (1909), which was recorded by Martha Ann Verbit.

DÉODAT DE SÉVERAC
1873–1921 — France

The composer of a small and gracious output. He loved the Southern French region of his birth. His instrument was the piano, and his method of writing was spontaneous and improvisatory. He once stated: "It matters little whether it is written vertically, horizontally or in other ways one might discover—but it must say well what it has to say." Séverac had a remarkable visual sense, and his music is alive with field, mountain, and stream, as well as the people of the land. His masterpiece, the *Cerdaña* Suite (1908–11), *Cinq Etudes pittoresques,* inspired by the Cerdagne region, best sums up his work and is a fine evocation of the full scope of French impressionist techniques. In some ways, it is related to Albéniz's *Iberia,* but with a far more limited pianistic inventiveness. Other important cycles are *En vacances* (eleven pieces), *Sous les lauriers roses* (ten pieces), and *Le Chant de la terre* (seven pieces). There are also a few individual works of interest, such as *Baigneuses au soleil* ("Women Bathers in the Sunlight"), dedicated to Cortot. "What the title implies," the composer wrote, "the music makes specific—a sort of pagan vision of beautiful nude bodies, dripping wet in the sea air and bathed in Mediterranean light."

Much of his music was first given to the world by Blanche Selva. Aldo Ciccolini has recorded the entire *oeuvre* and is well aware of the airy and carefree nature of the music, in addition to giving it proper underpinning by accenting exuberantly and discreetly.

RODION SHCHEDRIN
b. 1932 — USSR

His piano music possesses virtuosity, humor, melody, and craft. Shchedrin is a fine pianist, who worked with Yakov Flier. His early Piano Concerto No. 1 (1954) in four short, irresistible movements was the composer's graduation piece from the Moscow Conservatory. With all the exuberance of youth, he put everything he liked into its gleaming measures—Prokofiev, Poulenc, and a dab of Gershwin and plump Russian folk themes. It is a virtuoso vehicle with a sensational grandiose opening theme returning at the end for an even bigger effect. The Third Piano Concerto (1973) is stylistically a galaxy away. It has a raging intensity that never lets up.

Shchedrin's Piano Sonata No. 1 (1962) is dedicated to Dmitri Bashkirov, who plays it brilliantly. The finale, a Rondo-Toccata, with its unison passagework interspersed with jarring, jabbing, repeated chords, is a thriller with audiences. The *Twenty-five Polyphonic Tetrad* (1972), fifty-five minutes, are polyphonic studies which show tremendous knowledge and skill. Some are very austere, others are humorous. Bach is the constant inspiration.

JEAN SIBELIUS
1865–1957 — Finland

The giant of Finnish music was a violinist. Seventeen opus numbers, from his total of 119, include nearly one hundred piano pieces, with nothing approaching anything like the greatness of the Fourth Symphony. Yet one easily detects in these works always something of the composer's genius. Of interest are the three *Sonatines,* Op. 67, which Glenn Gould recorded. Gould wrote that they "demonstrate he discovered, through the development of Haydnesque textures and pre-Classical contrapuntal forms, a means by which to extract the best of the piano without placing the instrument in a disadvantageously competitive position vis-a-vis those orchestral sonorities

which, in his day, were deemed to constitute the sonic norm." In the early Sonata, Op. 12, however, Sibelius is hankering for the orchestral sonority of his early symphonies, and in the end it sounds like an unsuccessful piano reduction.

ELIE SIEGMEISTER
b. 1909 — United States

His *American* Sonata (1944) in three movements is rhythmic in the first and last movements, with an "Americana" quality. The 1967 Theme and Variations No. 2, however, is a bricklike, abstract work of spare sonority throughout. *On This Ground* (1971) is a five-movement expressionistic suite. In No. 5, *Mr. Henry's Monday Night,* Siegmeister transmits ragtime rhythms and ballad tunes into a dissonant tangle, depicting a barroom scene.

CHRISTIAN SINDING
1856–1941 — Norway

This Norwegian composer wrote much more than *Rustle of Spring,* Op. 32, No. 3, which was one of the most popular pieces of the late nineteenth century and which can still manage a sigh when used as an encore by Shura Cherkassky. Sinding wrote a B minor Sonata, Op. 91, a set of Variations in D minor, and dozens of smaller works which show a fine melodist and an original touch here and there. His Piano Concerto in D-flat, Op. 6 (1887–88), is a real conglomerate, from Brahms to Franck, with the Wagnerian impulse standing out.

NIKOS SKALKOTTAS
1904–1949 — Greece

The best-known Greek composer, he wrote personal and sensitively conceived atonal music. Skalkottas studied with two Busoni students, Philipp Jarnach and Kurt Weill, in Berlin, and later with Schoenberg. His piano music includes Fifteen Little Variations, four piano suites, a moving Berceuse, and a Passacaglia, all revealing a potent musical mind.

BEDŘICH SMETANA
1824–1884 — Czechoslovakia

Although operas and symphonic poems loom large in his work, Smetana has composed some attractive keyboard music. His polkas and Czech dances are his abiding contribution to the literature, and they are often physically and technically taxing. Also to be noted are the *Six Rêves* ("Dreams"), composed in 1875 after Smetana lost his hearing. Many of these works, such as *Faded Happiness,* have golden ideas.

KAIKHOSRU SORABJI
1892–1988 — England

Surely Sorabji is one of the most unusual cases in music history. Throughout the century, musicians of the highest caliber praised his work, but because of his own ban (in 1936) on performance of his music, he became a mystery man of music. Sorabji, however, published a great deal, and many of his scores are among the most fearsome in all of music. Often their duration alone brings them to the limits of human participation. His *Opus Clav-*icembalisticum, by Sorabji's own admission "the most important work for piano since *The Art of the Fugue,*" takes over two hours. The score is 252 pages. Sorabji's idiom is sometimes redolent of impressionism and Scriabin, while complex polyphony flows through most of his music. The extravagance of the figuration seems unending and asks of the pianist dedication probably beyond the call of duty. There is no doubt that Sorabji's keyboard imagination is prodigious. Learning his scores is literally a note-by-note procedure. In later years, the composer relaxed his outlawing of performance in favor of Yonty Solomon, Michael Habermann, and Victor Sangiorgio, who have mastered and recorded some of his music, such as the *Fantaisie espagnole* and *Introito and Preludio-Corale* (1929–30).

EUGEN SUCHON
b. 1908 — Czechoslovakia

His music is expansive, rhapsodic in nature, and rhythmically inventive. His *Metamorphosen* (1953) is a long work, intensely personal and bittersweet, with irregular phrase groups. The *Balladeske,* Op. 9 (1935), is less stylized and more folk-oriented.

JOSEF SUK
1874–1935 — Czechoslovakia

An outstanding composer who wrote convincing post-Romantic music. He left twenty or so cycles and individual pieces. By far Suk's most popular piece is the 1893 *Love Song,* Op. 7, No. 1. Perhaps the most stimulating of his piano music is the half-hour cycle *Things Lived and Dreamed,* music that is cryptic, subtle harmonically, and original in piano textures. Each piece ends in *pp* or *ppp*.

CARLOS SURINACH
b. 1915 — Spain

A significant representative of Spanish music. His 1951 *Trois Chansons et danses espagnoles* each begin with a quiet opening, followed by faster music, which is rhythmically exciting. There is a dynamic *Sonatine* from 1943, and the suite *Acrobats of God*. The 1974 Piano Concerto, written for de Larrocha, is a sophisticated tapestry based on the eight-note flamenco scale, with many transpositions.

LOUISE TALMA
b. 1906 — France

She grew up in the United States. Talma studied piano with Isidor Philipp. Her piano works are few in number but of impressive musical value and beautifully composed. The Six Etudes (1953–54) are filled with virtuoso and expressive worth. Beveridge Webster has recorded them. The *Alleluia in Form of Toccata* (1947) is a five-minute work that shines brilliantly and possesses rhythmic bite and an exciting buildup. It should be well known. Sahan Arzruni recorded it. The fifteen-minute Piano Sonata No. 1 is highly rhythmic. Virginia Eskin, who recorded it, thinks Talma's music is "reminiscent of certain sky-scrapers such as the Chrysler Building." Herbert Rogers recorded the Talma Sonata No. 2. The composer wrote: "My Second Piano Sonata was composed to unite tonal and serial elements in one work. The first movement, a tonic to freshen ears, is flooded with fresh currents of optimism."

ALEXANDER TANSMAN
1897–1986 — Poland

A composer who wrote much finely conceived piano music in many forms. The Sonata No. 5 was dedicated to the memory of Bartók. The 1930 *Sonatine transatlantique* is based on the fox-trot, blues, and Charleston. His two sets of mazurkas, as well as the four nocturnes, should be looked at; these short pieces need sympathetic interpreters.

ALEXANDER TCHÉRÉPNIN
1899–1977 — Russia

A good part of his career took place in the United States. Tchérépnin's music stems from many sources and influences: Russian nationalism, Chinese music, Prokofiev, French textures and polyphony. His large supply of piano music can be difficult, exciting, varied, and worthwhile exploring. Tchérépnin was an excellent pianist and understood the instrument well. He can be heard in high-caliber playing of his own Second and Fifth Piano Concerti. His most famous piano pieces are the Ten Bagatelles, Op. 5. Virgil Thomson wrote, "His work has at all periods been filled with poetry and bravura."

VIRGIL THOMSON
b. 1896 — United States

He has composed a good deal of piano music, including about 170 portraits, the average length of each being less than two minutes. The composer states: "The musical style of the pieces varies with the personality of the subject . . . an effort has been made to catch in all cases a likeness recognizable to persons acquainted with the sitter." Each portrait is titled. Thomson's music is essentially diatonic, witty, folkish, and always has a touch of originality. His Ten Etudes (1943–44) and Nine New Etudes (1954) are designed around specific keyboard problems, very sagaciously packaged. There are a fingered glissando, a ragtime bass, a music-box lullaby for weaker fingers, parallel chords, and chromatic double-harmonies pivoting on the thumb. All are imaginative.

MICHAEL TIPPETT
b. 1905 — England

One of England's foremost composers. The three Tippett piano sonatas show him to great advantage. The First Sonata requires varied facility; the shortest, No. 2, about twelve minutes, is one movement and predominantly in a lyric frame. The form is interesting, as there is no development in the usual sense. The Third Sonata is dedicated to the pianist Paul Crossley, who has recorded it. The Tippett Piano Concerto was premiered in 1956, with Louis Kentner as soloist. The composer wrote: "I felt moved to create a Concerto which once again the piano may sing. . . ." Of course, Tippett's singing on the piano is very different from that of Chopin.

JOAQUÍN TURINA
1882–1949 — Spain

His piano music is varied and beautifully made for the instrument. Always Turina offers authentic Spanish color. His sixteen-minute suite *Danzas fantásticas* is one of the best examples of his highly pictorial talent. De Larro-

cha, who is engrained with the idiom, has recorded the three movements—*Exaltación* ("Ecstasy"), *Ensueño* ("Daydream"), and *Orgía* ("Revel")—to rousing effect. The *Sanlucar de Barrameda* (*Sonata pintoresca*, Op. 24, 1922) is also made for de Larrocha's sound. For piano and string orchestra there is a small ten-minute work, *Rapsodia sinfónica* (1933), a charming score in two sections, with a piano part of only medium difficulty. Although Turina was a regionalist, he studied with d'Indy in Paris and post-Franckian methods sew up many of his works.

GEORGE WALKER
b. 1927 — United States

Walker is a good pianist who worked with Rudolf Serkin and Robert Casadesus. His 1975 Piano Concerto is stark, lyric, and wrapped in drama in three movements. The slow movement is "a personal and musical memorial to Duke Ellington" in Walker's own idiom. Natalie Hinderas recorded the work. Works for solo piano include three piano sonatas. No. 1 (1953) is in three movements. In quartal harmony, the first movement simmers with restlessness; the second movement is Variations on a Kentucky Folk Song. The Second Sonata (1957) is ten minutes of concentrated music. Sonata No. 3 (1976) is freer in style, bleak and serious.

BEN WEBER
1916–1979 — United States

Weber's music uses a free twelve-tone vocabulary. His work is expressive and made with a fine hand. His Fantasia, Op. 25 (nine minutes), is difficult and brooding. The Piano

Concerto (1961) is rather dark. The second movement is an emotional passacaglia with five variations and a coda.

STEFAN WOLPE
1902–1972 — Germany

He studied with Busoni and Webern. His music for piano is an important part of his total output. His early pieces for piano stem from 1924. The 1929 *Presto agitato* is German expressionism, and the 1959 *Form* is serial. There is also *Form IV* (1969), composed for Robert Miller. The Passacaglia is perhaps his most daring work pianistically. Peter Serkin has played Wolpe's piano music often. Wolpe had a deep influence on many younger composers.

Index

Abraham, Gerald, 68, 318
Absil, Jean:
  compositions of, 427
  Passacaille, 427
  Variations, 427
Achatz, Dag, 420
Adam, Louis, 29, 32, 147
Adamowski Trio, 253
Adler, Clarence, 29, 252
Adni, Daniel, 29
Agosti, Guido, 29
Aitken, Webster, 29, 230
Albéniz, Isaac, 51, 117, 213
  Azulejos, 282
  Cantos de España, 282
  compositions of, 281–82
  Evocation, 149
  Iberia, 34, 50, 70, 83, 173,
    240, 281–82, 335, 442
  Malagueña, 75
  Navarra, 223–24
  Sequidillas, 75
  La Vega, 282
Albert, Eugene d', 22, 29–30,
    32, 36, 40, 47, 63, 136,
    169, 217, 219, 230, 271
  Tiefland, 30
Albright, William:
  compositions of, 427
  Grand Sonata in Rag, 174,
    427
  Pianoagogo, 42
Aldrich, Richard, 196
Alexeev, Dmitri, 30
Alice Tully Hall, 96, 250
Alkan, Charles Valentin, 19, 20,
    21, 30–32, 50, 79, 82, 167,
    206, 217, 226, 247, 275
  Aesop Variations, 160
  Barcarolle, 159–60

compositions of, 283–84
  Grande Sonate, 31, 159–60,
    192, 247, 283
  Shorter Pieces, 283
  Sonatine, 159–60, 247, 283
  Twelve Etudes in All the Ma-
    jor Keys, 283–84
Alkan the Enigma (Smith), 31
Alwyn, William:
  compositions of, 427
  Fantasy Waltzes, 427
  Twelve Preludes, 427
Amateur at the Keyboard, An
    (Yates), 61
Amram, David, Piano Sonata,
    427
Anda, Géza, 31–32, 85
Andersen, Hans Christian, 167,
    223
Anderson, Lucy, 32
Anderson, Margaret, 172
Anievas, Agustin, 32, 174
Ansorge, Conrad, 32
Antheil, George, 252
  compositions of, 427
  Sonata No. 2 (*The Airplane*),
    427
Anton Rubinstein Prize, 40, 43,
    97, 160, 207
Apthorp, William, 357
Arbos, Fernández, 82
Arco, Annie d', 32
Arensky, Anton:
  compositions of, 427–28
  Twelve Etudes, 250, 428
  Waltz, 100
Argerich, Martha, 32–33, 55,
    162, 202
Arlington National Cemetery,
    197

Around Music (Sorabji), 31
Arrau, Claudio, 7, 33–36, 63,
    78, 154–55, 214, 231,
    250, 279, 285, 300, 307,
    328
Artaria, 294
*Art du chant appliqué au pi-
    ano, L'* (Thalberg), 256
Arthur Rubinstein Competition,
    38
Art of Pedaling, The
    (Gebhard), 101
Art of Piano Playing, The
    (Neuhaus), 188
Arzuni, Sahan, 445
Ashkenazy, Vladimir, 9, 36–38,
    121, 192, 234, 248
Askenase, Stefan, 38, 230, 262
Aspen Music Festival, 164, 252
Atkins, John, 440
At the Piano with Debussy
    (Long), 171, 328
At the Piano with Fauré
    (Long), 171
Auer, Leopold, 127
Aurelius, Marcus, 13
Auric, Georges, Piano Sonata,
    428
Avery Fisher Award, 199
Avery Fisher Hall, 191, 244,
    266
Ax, Emanuel, 38–39, 187, 420,
    441

Babbitt, Milton, 416
  compositions of, 428
  Partitions, 428
  *Three Compositions for Pi-
    ano,* 428

Babin, Victor, 39, 265
Bacewicz, Grazyna:
  compositions of, 428
  Sonata No. 2, 247, 428
  Ten Studies, 428
Bach, Carl Philipp Emanuel,
  39, 42, 104, 345
  compositions of, 428
  Piano Sonata No. 1 (*Würt-
    temberg* Sonata No. 1),
    115
Bach, Johann Christian, 39–40,
  70, 166, 185, 345, 370
Bach, Johann Sebastian, 18, 20,
  33, 34, 39–40, 44–45, 49,
  62, 64, 68, 70, 73, 77, 79,
  100, 101, 103, 113–14,
  122, 144, 149–150, 166,
  226–27, 227, 232, 237,
  251, 268, 272, 294, 310,
  314, 317, 320, 339, 366,
  392–93, 397, 401, 409,
  419–20, 424, 428, 430,
  443
  Aria with Thirty Variations
    (*Goldberg* Variations), 23,
    112, 114, 151, 156–57,
    175, 187, 218, 228, 231,
    240, 262, 286, 296, 300
  The Art of the Fugue, 61,
    154, 218–19, 444
  Chaconne for Violin, 295–96
  Chromatic Fantasia and
    Fugue in D minor, 53, 55,
    60, 94, 228, 261, 285
  compositions of, 285–86
  Concerto in the Italian Style
    (*Italian* Concerto), 285,
    286
  English Suite in A minor,
    228
  Fantasia in C minor, 228
  Fifteen Three-Part Inventions,
    114, 286
  Fifteen Two-Part Inventions,
    114, 175, 286
  Jesu, Joy of Man's Desiring,
    124, 163
  Mass in B minor, 170
  Partita in B-flat major, 163,
    228
  Partita in G major, 112
  Prelude and Fugue in C ma-
    jor, 61
  Prelude and Fugue in
    C-sharp minor, 168

  Saint Matthew Passion, 178,
    286
  Six *English* Suites, 114, 203,
    285–86
  Six *French* Suites, 114, 170,
    203, 285–86
  Six Partitas, 175, 285–86
  Toccata and Fugue in D mi-
    nor, 255
  Toccata in C major, 133
  Triple Concerto, 247
  *Weinen, Klagen, Sorgen, Za-
    gen*, 355
  *The Well-Tempered
    Clavier*—Books I and II—
    Forty-eight Preludes and
    Fugues, 45, 58, 84, 94,
    114, 139, 157, 171, 175,
    178, 187, 205, 215, 217,
    228, 262, 286, 300, 417
Bachauer, Gina, 40, 74, 434
Backer-Grøndahl, Agathe, 59
Backhaus, Wilhelm, 23, 40–41,
  43, 197, 279, 422
Badings, Henk, 428
Badura-Skoda, Eva, 375–76
Badura-Skoda, Paul, 41, 47,
  94, 363, 369
Baily, Richard, 211
Bakst, Ryszard, 261
Balakirev, Mily, 14, 247, 271,
  389, 437
  compositions of, 286–87
  Islamey-Oriental Fantasy, 34,
    43, 55, 66, 97–98, 139,
    161, 212, 239, 286–87
  Sonata in B-flat minor, 152,
    287
Balanchine, George, 420, 423
Baldwin Wallace University,
  268
Balogh, Ernö, 42
Balsam, Artur, 42
Barbedette, H., 316
Barber, Samuel, 264
  compositions of, 287
  Excursions, 139
  Piano Concerto, 56, 287
  Sonata in E-flat minor, 56,
    72, 133, 138, 204, 287
  Souvenirs, 157
Barberi, Amerigo, 243
Barenboim, Daniel, 42, 94
Barère, Simon, 42–43, 51, 90,
  161, 279, 404
Bargiel, Woldemar, 105

Bar-Illan, David, 43, 99
Barnum, P. T., 109, 124
Barraqué, Jean, Piano Sonata,
  428
Barraud, Henri, Piano Con-
  certo, 232
Barth, Karl Heinrich, 43, 59,
  151, 214, 222, 255
Barthes, Roland, 402
Bartlett, Homer, *Grand polka
  de concert*, 82
Bartók, Béla, 23, 42, 43, 50,
  85, 96, 146–47, 150,
  154, 187, 193, 205, 213,
  228–29, 232, 257, 273,
  327, 343, 353, 360, 433,
  445
  compositions of, 287–88
  Fifteen Hungarian Peasant
    Songs, 288
  Fourteen Bagatelles, 287
  Improvisations, 200, 219,
    287
  Mikrokosmos, Six
    Volumes—153 Progressive
    Pieces, 288
  Out of Doors Suite, 287
  Piano Concerto No., 1, 229,
    241, 243, 288
  Piano Concerto No. 2, 88,
    152, 229, 268, 288
  Piano Concerto No. 3, 31,
    229, 241, 288
  Sonata for Piano, 287
  Three Etudes, 287
Bashkirov, Dmitri, 443
*Basic Principles in Piano-forte
  Playing* (Lhévinne), 160
Battersby, Edmund, 109
Baudelaire, Charles, 331
Bauer, Harold, 44, 78, 84, 100,
  184, 244, 339, 342, 389,
  407
Bauer, Marion:
  compositions of, 428
  Dance Sonata, 428
  Elegy, 428
  Four Piano Pieces, 428
  Summertime Suite, 428
Bax, Sir Arnold, 73
  compositions of, 429
  Sonata No. 1 in F-sharp mi-
    nor, 429
Beach, Mrs. H. H. A. (Amy
  Marcy Cheney), 199
  compositions of, 429

Beach, Mrs. H.H.A.,
  continued
  Variations on Balkan
    Themes, 90, 429
Beatles, 113
Beaux Arts Trio, 207
Bechstein, Carl, 57
Beckman-Scherbina, Elena, 44,
  240, 415
Beckwood, Peter, 70
Beecham, Sir Thomas, 130, 442
Beecke, Ignaz von, 186
Beethoven, Ludwig van, 18, 20,
  22, 24, 34–38, 44–47, 51,
  52, 64, 65, 67, 70–71, 77,
  87, 93, 96, 119, 125, 139–
  140, 150, 159, 165, 174,
  184, 186, 198, 213, 215,
  216, 232, 245, 251, 272,
  275–76, 280, 317, 322,
  345, 350, 354, 369, 373,
  376, 397–98
  "Adelaide," 360
  "Ah! perfido," 46
  Bagatelles, Op. 33, 115
  Choral Fantasy, 46
  compositions of, 288–97
  *The Creatures of
    Prometheus,* 295
  Fidelio, 183
  Five Piano Concerti, 104,
    187, 242–43, 268, 296–
    297, 425
  Für Elise, 203
  Mass in C major, 46
  Missa Solemnis, 73
  Piano Concerto No. 1 in C
    major, 45, 74, 181, 188,
    212, 242
  Piano Concerto No. 2 in B-
    flat major, 74, 95, 112,
    149
  Piano Concerto No. 3 in C
    minor, 63, 73–74, 112,
    206
  Piano Concerto No. 4 in G
    major, 30, 46, 54, 60, 63,
    74, 81–82, 103, 112, 129,
    152, 178, 190, 206, 224,
    242
  Piano Concerto No. 5 in E-
    flat major (*Emperor* Con-
    certo), 46, 54, 60, 63, 74,
    79, 97, 105, 125–26, 133–
    134, 157–58, 160, 188,
    227, 237, 243

  Piano Trio in B-flat major
    (*Archduke* Trio), 74
  Six Bagatelles, Op. 126, 155,
    157, 296
  Sonata Op. 2, No. 1 in F
    minor, 54
  Sonata Op. 2, No. 2 in A
    major, 40, 45, 152
  Sonata Op. 2, No. 3 in C
    major, 152, 325
  Sonata Op. 7 in E-flat major,
    54, 181, 199
  Sonata Op. 8 in C minor
    (*Pathétique*), 46–47, 78,
    134, 216, 224, 242, 334
  Sonata Op. 10, No. 2 in F
    major, 54, 115, 152
  Sonata Op. 10, No. 3 in D
    major, 134, 199, 212
  Sonata Op. 14 in E major,
    152
  Sonata Op. 22 in B-flat ma-
    jor, 54, 199, 203
  Sonata Op. 26 in A-flat ma-
    jor, 216
  Sonata Op. 27, No. 1 in E-
    flat major (*Sonata quasi
    una Fantasia*), 152
  Sonata Op. 27, No. 2 in C-
    sharp minor (*Moonlight*),
    47, 54, 85, 111, 134, 190,
    197, 224, 242
  Sonata Op. 28 in D major
    (*Pastoral*), 183
  Sonata Op. 31, No. 1 in G
    major, 54
  Sonata Op. 31, No. 2 in D
    minor (*Tempest*), 108,
    203, 212, 217
  Sonata Op. 31, No. 3 in E-
    flat major, 224
  Sonata Op. 53 in C major
    (*Waldstein*), 38, 43, 54,
    108, 117, 128, 134, 152,
    161, 163, 190–91, 224,
    249
  Sonata Op. 54 in F major,
    152
  Sonata Op. 57 in F minor
    (*Appassionata*), 38, 47, 49,
    54, 117, 134, 152, 212,
    224, 242, 249
  Sonata Op. 78 in F-sharp
    minor, 54
  Sonata Op. 79 in G major,
    54, 204

  Sonata Op. 81a in E-flat ma-
    jor (*Les Adieux*), 54, 107,
    190, 199, 217, 224, 237
  Sonata Op. 90 in E minor,
    54, 152, 200, 203, 224,
    233
  Sonata Op. 101 in A major,
    50, 54, 89, 134, 152, 237,
    242
  Sonata Op. 106 in B-flat ma-
    jor (*Hammerklavier*), 23,
    29, 37, 41, 47, 89, 105,
    160, 168, 200, 205, 217–
    218, 234, 237, 268, 283,
    299
  Sonata Op. 109 in E major,
    112, 125, 152, 201, 212
  Sonata Op. 110 in A-flat ma-
    jor, 31, 54, 108, 125, 152,
    199, 201
  Sonata Op. 111 in C minor,
    54, 115, 117, 157, 181,
    190, 200, 203, 212, 221,
    233, 248
  Symphony No. 3 in E-flat
    major (*Eroica*), 295
  Symphony No. 5 in C minor,
    46, 115, 292, 348, 360
  Symphony No. 6 in F major,
    46
  Symphony No. 9 in D minor,
    243, 303, 340
  Thirty-three Variations on a
    Waltz by Diabelli in C ma-
    jor (*Diabelli Variations*),
    42, 50, 53, 55–56, 97,
    233, 241, 243, 296, 300
  Thirty-two Piano Sonatas,
    14, 23, 29, 36, 42, 49, 54,
    58–59, 75, 81, 84, 94,
    103, 118, 122, 141, 185,
    187, 217, 233, 267, 288–
    295 (discussed)
  Thirty-two Variations on an
    Original Theme in C mi-
    nor, 133–34, 237, 295–96
  Turkish March, 130
  Variations and Fugue in E-
    flat major (*Eroica*), 53, 78,
    160, 295
  Violin Concerto in D major,
    276
*Beethoven and the Voice of
  God* (Mellers), 46–47
Beethoven Centennial, 233
Behr, Therese, 233

450

Belgiojoso, Christina, Princess, 256
Belleville-Oury, Anna Caroline de, 47
Belli, Vincenzo:
  Norma, 82, 160, 202, 358–359
  La Sonnambula, 97
Benedict, Julius, 267
Bennett, Richard Rodney:
  compositions of, 429
  Five Studies, 429
  Piano Sonata, 429
Bennett, Sir William Sterndale, 47–48, 176, 182, 406
  Piano Sonata No. 3 (The Maid of Orleans), 48
Berg, Alban, 407
  Sonata for Piano, 42, 49, 66, 112, 116, 155, 297
  Berger, Ludwig, 48, 68, 177, 272
  Grand Sonata, 48
Beringer, Oscar, 48, 108, 167, 255
Berio, Luciano, 59, 241
  Cinque Variazioni per pianoforte, 297
Berkeley, Sir Lennox, 307
Berlin Hochschule, 105
Berlin Philharmonic, 33, 63, 112, 151, 175
Berlioz, Hector, 31, 69, 95, 109, 120, 122, 166–68, 170, 202, 283, 316, 323, 357, 367–68
  Orchestral Setting of Weber's Invitation to the Dance, 95
  Symphonie fantastique, 49, 165, 359–60
  Symphonie funèbre et triomphale, 284
Berman, Lazar, 48, 107
Bernhardt, Sarah, 50
Bernstein, Leonard, 48–49, 112, 115, 260, 264, 265–66
  Symphony No. 2 for Piano and Orchestra (The Age of Anxiety), 48–49
  Touches, 66
Béroff, Michel, 49
Bertini, Henri, 49
Bertrand, Aloysius, 389
Besançon Festival, 164
Bianca, Sondra, 434
Biancolli, Louis, 412

Bigot, Marie, 49
Bilson, Malcolm, 49
Bird, John, 117–18
Biret, Idil, 49
Bischoff, Hans, 49, 155
Bishop-Kovacevich, Stephen, 49–50, 234
Bizet, Georges, 102, 174
  L'Arlésienne, 387
  Carmen, 62, 138, 304
  Variations chromatiques, 115–16
Black, William, 432
Blahetka, Marie Leopoldine, 50
  Konzertstück for Piano and Orchestra, 50
Blake, William, 283
Blanchet, Émile, 50
Blesh, Rudi, 437
Bliss, Sir Arthur:
  Piano Concerto, 248
  Piano Sonata, 180
Bloch, Ernest, 14, 431
  compositions of, 298
  Piano Sonata, 187, 298
Bloch, Joseph, 50, 283–84
Block, Michel, 50, 268
Blom, Eric, 290–91, 374
Bloomfield Zeisler, Fannie, 50, 184
Blumenfeld, Felix, 42–43, 50–51, 118, 130, 188
  Etude for the Left Hand, 43
  Sonata-Fantasy, 51
  Twenty-four Preludes, 50–51
Blumental, Felicja, 51, 86
Bocklet, Carl Maria von, 51
Boehm, Mary Louise, 148
Boks family, 127
Bolcom, William, 145
  compositions of, 429
  Graceful Ghost Rag, 429
  Twenty-four Etudes, 429
Bolet, Jorge, 51–52, 184, 230, 236, 243, 279
Bologna Conservatory, 175
Bomtempo, João Domingos, 52
Bonaventura, Anthony Di, 52
Bonnard, Pierre, 336
Boriskin, Michael, 439
Borodin, Alexander, 212
Bortkiewicz, Sergei, 52, 214, 383, 429
  Sonata Op. 9, 429
  Ten Etudes, 429
Borwick, Leonard, 52–53

Bösendorfer Hall, 232
Boston Symphony, 149, 151
Boukoff, Yuri, 53, 188
Boulanger, Nadia, 59, 153, 162, 164, 205, 328, 379
Boulez, Pierre, 23, 59, 219, 328, 367
  compositions of, 298
  Sonata No. 1, 298
  Sonata No. 2, 205, 261, 298
  Sonata No. 3, 298
Boult, Sir Adrian, 85
Bourniquel, Camille, 318
Bowen, York, 53, 80, 176
Bowers, Faubion, 411
Boyle, George, Piano Concerto in D minor, 53
Bradshaw, Susan, 298
Brahms, Johannes, 31, 35–37, 41, 50, 52–53, 71, 77, 88, 93, 97, 103, 118, 147, 149, 153, 176, 222, 228, 230, 239, 257, 264, 267, 284, 309, 369, 378, 405, 421–22, 436, 443
  arrangement of Gluck's Gavotte, 130
  Capriccio in B minor, 43
  compositions of, 299–303
  Concerto in A minor for Violin and Cello, 74
  Eight Klavierstücke, 301
  Ein deutsches Requiem, 73
  Four Ballades, 36, 104, 115, 150, 300
  Four Klavierstücke, 302
  Intermezzo in A major, Op. 118, No. 2, 141
  Intermezzo in B-flat minor, Op. 117, No. 2, 136
  Piano Concerto No. 1 in D minor, 44, 53, 55, 60, 84, 95, 115, 125, 136, 193, 205, 225, 243, 268, 303
  Piano Concerto No. 2 in B-flat major, 48, 53, 55, 91, 101, 120, 125, 136, 142, 187, 205, 215, 225, 229, 242–43, 249, 261, 268, 279, 303
  Scherzo in E-flat minor, 36, 151, 299
  Seven Fantasies, 301–2
  Six Klavierstücke, 302
  Sixteen Waltzes, 301

Brahms, Johannes, *continued*
  Sonata No. 1 in C major, 237, 299
  Sonata No. 2 in F-sharp minor, 33, 36, 299, 335
  Sonata No. 3 in F minor, 36, 44, 62, 78, 118, 125, 150–151, 171–72, 224, 275, 299
  Symphony No. 4 in E minor, 296
  Three Intermezzi, 302
  Two Rhapsodies, 115, 301
  Variations and Fugue on a Theme by Handel (*Handel Variations*), 32, 95, 150, 243, 249, 300, 334, 391, 406
  Variations on a Theme by Paganini, Books I and II (*Paganini* Variations), 36, 40, 53, 109, 150, 161, 179, 181, 193, 206, 244, 253, 300–301, 351, 406
  Variations on a Theme by Schumann in F-sharp minor (*Schumann* Variations), 42, 300
  Waltz No. 15 in A-flat major, 136
Brailowsky, Alexander, 53–54, 230
Brassin, Louis, 54, 118, 156, 183, 226, 229
  Transcription of Wagner's *Magic Fire Music*, 54, 130
Breithaupt, Rudolf, 168
Brendel, Alfred, 54, 94, 234, 291–92, 295
Bréville, Pierre de:
  compositions of, 429
  Sonata, 429
  Suite stamboul, 429
Bridge, Frank, 14
  compositions of, 303
  Piano Sonata, 303
Britten, Benjamin, 118
  Diversions, 272
Brodsky, Vera, 156
Bronfman, Yefim, 56
Brown, Joan, 342
Browning, John, 56, 198, 212, 287
Bruce, Neely, 248
Bruckner, Anton, 284
Brumberg, Leonid, 56

Bruneau, Alfred, 305
Brussels Beethoven Competition, 201
Brussels Conservatoire, 118, 144, 202, 226
Bucharest Conservatory, 162
Bucquet, Marie-Françoise, 418
Bülow, Hans von, 20, 30–31, 36, 40, 47, 56–59, 121, 123, 153, 169, 185, 222, 233, 270, 286, 303, 309–310, 356, 423, 440
Buonamici, Giuseppe, 59
Burge, David, 59, 327, 436
Burne-Jones, Sir Edward, 196
Burney, Charles, 39, 235
Busch, Adolf, 241
Busoni, Ferruccio, 22, 29, 30, 31, 32, 47, 50, 59–62, 92, 101, 117, 121, 123, 133, 136, 143–45, 170, 187, 200, 211, 225, 229–30, 247, 261, 321, 350–52, 356, 359, 369, 385, 430, 444, 447
  arrangement of Bach's Chaconne for Violin, 181, 224
  compositions of, 304
  Fantasia contrapuntistica, 61–62, 200, 280
  Piano Concerto, 61, 120, 192–93, 200
  reduction of Liszt's *Mephisto Waltz*, 201
  Seven Elegies, 62, 252, 304
  Six Sonatinas, 62, 304
  Sonatina No. 2, 171
  Sonatina No. 6 (*Super Carmen*), 274
  Toccata, 62
  Turandots Frauengemach, 185
  Variations on a Chopin Prelude, 304
Busoni International Competition, 32, 54, 179, 192–93, 206, 253–54, 274
Bussotti, Sylvano, *Five Piano Pieces for David Tudor*, 261
Byron, George Gordon, Lord, 18, 21, 69, 166, 322, 354

Cage, John:
  Bacchanale, 430
  compositions of, 429–30

Concert for Piano and Orchestra, 261
Concerto for Prepared Piano, 430
Dream, 430
Music for Marcel Duchamp, 430
The Perilous Night, 430
Prelude for Meditation, 430
Sonatas and Interludes, 430
Suite for Toy Piano, 430
Calvocoressi, M. D., 437
Campanella, Michele, 62
Campos-Parsi, Hector:
  compositions of, 439
  Sonata in G major, 229, 439
Canabich, Rosa, 376
Canin, Martin, 62, 228
Carl Alexander, Grand Duke of Weimar, 170
Carnegie Hall, 30, 40, 74, 91, 100, 103, 130–33, 137, 161, 164, 172, 175, 184, 192, 214–15, 222, 231, 244, 254, 261, 264, 270, 273, 364, 423
Carnegie Recital Hall, 97
Carpenter, John Alden:
  compositions of, 430
  Concertino for Piano and Orchestra, 430
Carreño, Teresa, 32, 62–63, 73, 176, 200, 230, 363
Carter, Elliott:
  compositions of, 304–5
  Night Fantasies, 143, 219
  Piano Concerto, 164, 305
  Piano Sonata, 268, 304–5
Caruso, Enrico, 22, 190
Casadesus, Gaby, 63–64
Casadesus, Jean, 63–64
Casadesus, Robert, 63–64, 84, 144, 217, 279, 305, 369, 392, 446
  compositions of, 430
  Piano Concerto in E major, 430
Casagrande Competition, 202
Casals, Pablo, 14, 70, 73–74
Casella, Alfredo, 64–65
  compositions of, 430
  A notte alta, 430
  Ricercari on the Name Bach, 430
Castro, José María, 144
  Sonata de primavera, 430

Castro, Juan José, 430
  Five Tangos, 430
  Sonatina española, 250
Castro, Washington, 430
Catholic University, 174
CBC, 112
Cervantes, Ignacio, 65
  Danzas cubanas, 65
Cesi, Beniamino, 175
Cézanne, Paul, 328
Chabrier, Emmanuel, 14, 70,
  144, 223
  Bourrée fantasque, 217, 305
  compositions of, 305
  Dix Pièces pittoresques, 63,
  305
Chaminade, Cécile, 65–66
Chase, Gilbert, 361
Chasins, Abram, 51, 65, 128,
  151
  Narrative, 65
Chateaubriand, François René
  de, 166
Chávez, Carlos, 176
  compositions of, 305–6
  Invención, 306
  Piano Concerto, 164, 305–6
  Polignos, 250
  Sonatas, 306
Cherkassky, Lydia, 65
Cherkassky, Shura, 65–67,
  195, 212, 230, 236, 433,
  443
Cherubini, Luigi, 46
Chevalier de l'Ordre des Arts et
  des Lettres, 33
Chiafarelli, Luigi, 189
Chiapusso, Jan, 261
Chicago Musical College, 101
Chopin, Frédéric, 19–21, 23,
  29–38, 40–41, 50, 53, 55–
  56, 63, 65, 67–69, 70–71,
  73–74, 82–83, 87, 96,
  102–3, 105, 112–14, 120–
  123, 125, 128, 144–47,
  155, 167, 173, 176, 180,
  183–84, 187, 193–94,
  207–8, 213, 215, 217–19,
  236, 247, 253, 256, 261–
  262, 267–69, 271, 273,
  275, 280, 290, 327, 328–
  329, 337, 340–41, 343,
  352, 354, 356, 360, 379,
  405, 407, 411–13, 417,
  425, 429, 437, 439, 446
  Allegro de concert, 66

Andante spianato and Grand
  Polonaise for Piano and
  Orchestra, 129, 135,
  306
Ballade No. 1 in G minor,
  129, 135, 181, 270, 306
Ballade No. 2 in F major, 37,
  306
Ballade No. 3 in A-flat major, 29, 66, 99, 159, 190,
  306–7
Ballade No. 4 in F minor,
  35, 97, 129, 135, 161,
  188, 190, 249, 307
Ballades, 38, 76, 81, 88–89,
  97, 182–83, 224, 353
Barcarolle in F-sharp major,
  37, 76, 80, 95, 135, 164,
  199, 219, 225, 234, 241,
  307
Berceuse in D-flat major, 44,
  76, 224, 307, 353
Boléro in C major, 66, 225,
  325
compositions of, 306–25
Etude Op. 10, No. 1 in C
  major, 220
Etude Op. 10, No. 5 in G-
  flat major (Black Key
  Etude), 61, 98
Etude Op. 10, No. 7 in C
  major, 98–99
Etude Op. 10, No. 12 in C
  minor (Revolutionary
  Etude), 85, 98, 135, 198
Etude Op. 25, No. 1 in A-
  flat major (Aeolian Harp
  Etude), 69, 309
Etude Op. 25, No. 6 in G-
  sharp minor, 98, 161
Etude Op. 25, No. 7 in C-
  sharp minor, 36
Etude Op. 25, No. 9 in G-
  flat major (Butterfly
  Etude), 98, 195
Etude Op. 25, No. 10 in B
  minor, 161
Etude Op. 25, No. 11 in A
  minor (Winterwind Etude),
  161
Etude Op. 25, No. 12 in C
  minor (Ocean Etude), 160
Fantaisie in F minor, 35, 76,
  97, 212, 224, 249, 310
Four Impromptus, 38, 76,
  92, 140, 224, 310–11

Four Scherzos, 34–35, 81,
  212, 224, 321–22
Impromptu No. 1 in A-flat
  major, 134
Impromptu No. 2 in F-sharp
  major, 190
Introduction and Rondo in
  E-flat major, 212, 325
Maiden's Wish, 129
Mazurka Op. 50, No. 3 in
  C-sharp minor, 164
Mazurkas, 37–38, 69, 99,
  145, 149, 181, 188, 191,
  212, 220, 225, 248, 311–
  315, 421
My Joys, 220
Nocturne Op. 9, No. 3 in B
  major, 129, 171
Nocturne Op. 15, No. 2 in
  F-sharp major, 134–35
Nocturne Op. 27, No. 2 in
  D-flat major, 129, 164
Nocturne Op. 48, No. 1 in C
  minor, 97, 266
Nocturne Op. 48, No. 2 in
  F-sharp minor, 241
Nocturne Op. 55, No. 1 in F
  minor, 135
Nocturne Op. 55, No. 2 in
  E-flat major, 99, 135, 203
Nocturne Op. 62, No. 2 in E
  major, 66
Nocturne Op. 72, in E mi-
  nor, 134–35
Nocturnes, 35, 68, 107, 142,
  150, 183, 190, 193, 202,
  221, 224, 269, 315–18,
  336
Piano Concerti, 38
Piano Concerto No. 1 in E
  minor, 60, 66–67, 72, 79,
  92, 109, 126, 129, 139–
  140, 147, 162, 188, 193,
  205, 220, 225, 244, 268,
  307–8
Piano Concerto No. 2 in F
  minor, 36, 67, 81, 121–22,
  126, 129, 139, 151, 190,
  204, 225, 266, 268, 308
Polonaise-fantaisie in A-flat
  major, 35, 38, 97, 135,
  188, 241
Polonaise Op. 26, No. 2 in
  E-flat minor (The Siberian
  Revolt Polonaise), 96,
  129

453

Chopin, Frédéric, *continued*
  Polonaise Op. 40, No. 1 in A
    major (*Military* Polonaise),
    129, 135
  Polonaise Op. 40, No. 2 in C
    minor, 203
  Polonaise Op. 44 in F-sharp
    minor, 135, 203
  Polonaise Op. 53 in A-flat
    major (*Heroic* Polonaise),
    98, 135, 161, 219, 225,
    229, 255
  Polonaises, 69, 80, 193, 203,
    212, 224–25, 318–20
  Prelude in C-sharp minor,
    Op. 45, 76, 203
  Prelude No. 7 in A major,
    369
  Prelude No. 13 in F-sharp
    major, 66
  Prelude No. 16 in B-flat mi-
    nor, 161
  Prelude No. 19 in E-flat ma-
    jor, 99
  Prelude No. 20 in C minor,
    304, 385
  Prelude No. 24 in D minor,
    76, 201
  Rondo à la mazur, 325
  Rondo in C minor, 67
  Scherzo No. 1 in B minor,
    135
  Scherzo No. 2 in B-flat mi-
    nor, 181, 225
  Scherzo No. 3 in C-sharp
    minor, 37, 190, 203, 212,
    225
  Scherzo No. 4 in E major,
    38, 134, 227
  Sonata No. 1 in C minor, 66
  Sonata No. 2 in B-flat minor
    (*Funeral March* Sonata),
    21, 33, 86, 99, 107, 118,
    135, 190–91, 199, 203,
    211–12, 224, 266, 322–
    323, 341
  Sonata No. 3 in B minor, 14,
    33, 64, 72, 86, 93, 104,
    117, 129, 141, 149, 164,
    190, 199, 203, 212, 220,
    224, 230, 234, 269, 323
  Les Sylphides, 317, 320
  Tarantelle in A-flat major,
    66, 202, 212, 225, 325
  Trois Nouvelles Etudes, 76,
    310

  Twenty-four Etudes, Opp. 10
    and 25, 34, 40–41, 68, 71,
    76, 80, 86, 88, 106–7,
    109, 126, 134, 165, 182,
    184, 190, 200, 205–6,
    214, 225, 242, 244, 263–
    264, 274, 308–10, 396
  Twenty-four Preludes, 35,
    52, 75, 81, 89, 151–52,
    183, 190, 194, 199–201,
    205, 225, 232, 244, 320–
    321
  Variations brillantes, 171,
    325
  Variations on Mozart's "La
    ci darem la mano" from
    Don Giovanni in B-flat
    mjor, 66–68, 237
  Waltzes, 32, 34, 76, 81, 182,
    212, 225–26, 241, 249,
    323–25
  Waltz in D-flat major
    (*Minute* Waltz), 129
  Waltz in E minor, 164
Chopin International Competi-
  tion, 32, 36, 50, 79, 81,
  86, 96, 121, 125, 162,
  192–93, 202, 205, 262–
  263, 275
Chopin Playing (Methuen-
  Campbell), 199
Chorley, Henry, 311
Christian VIII, King of Den-
  mark, 213
Ciampi, Marcel, 70, 171, 194
Ciani, Dino, 74
Ciccolini, Aldo, 70, 442
Clara Haskil Competition,
  108
Clark, Alfred Corning, 127
*Classical Style: Haydn, Mozart,
  Beethoven, The* (Rosen),
  218, 371
Clauss-Szarvady, Wilhelmine,
  70
Clemenceau, Georges, 197
Clemens, Clara, 100
Clementi, Muzio, 18, 42, 46,
  48, 51, 68, 70–71, 76–77,
  86, 88, 91, 140, 167,
  170, 177, 181, 183, 186,
  345
  compositions of, 325–26
  Gradus ad Parnassum, 71
  Piano Concerto in C major,
    326

Six Sonatinas, Op. 36, 96,
  325
Sonata in B-flat major, 325
Sonata in B minor, 48, 133–
  134, 325
Sonata in C major, 104,
  133–34, 289, 325
Sonata in F-sharp minor,
  133–34
Sonata in G minor, 294–325
Three Sonatinas, Op. 37, 325
Three Sonatinas, Op. 38, 325
Cleveland Institute of Music,
  39, 144, 170, 225–26
Cleveland Orchestra, 116, 243
Cleveland Press, 170
Cliburn, Van, 71–72, 202, 204
Clidat, France, 73, 159
Cluytens, André, 105
Coates, Albert, 137
Coates, Helen, 48
Cohen, Harriet, 73, 176
Coleridge, Samuel Taylor, 280
Collard, Jean-Phillipe, 73
Colles, H.C., 48
Collet, Robert, 320, 358
Columbia University, 114
*Complete Theoretical and Prac-
  tical Course of Instruction
  on the Art of Playing the
  Pianoforte, A* (Hummel),
  140–41
Congress of Vienna, 184
Conservatoire of Lyon, 122
Cooper, Frank, 86, 129
Cooper, Martin, 345
Cooper, Paul:
  compositions of, 430–31
  Cycles, 430
  Piano Sonata, 430–31
Copeland, George, 73
Copland, Aaron, 14, 149–50,
  169, 176, 304, 414
  compositions of, 326
  Four Piano Blues, 247
  Piano Concerto, 326
  Piano Fantasy, 149, 326
  Piano Sonata, 48, 95, 326
  Piano Variations, 144, 268,
    326
Corelli, Arcangelo, 386
Corigliano, John:
  compositions of, 431
  Etude Fantasy, 260, 431
  Piano Concerto, 250, 431
Cornell University, 200

454

Cortot, Alfred, 23, 53, 73–76, 84, 96, 121–22, 162, 172, 200, 229, 254, 279–80, 342, 388–89, 442
Couperin, Franqois, 18, 285, 305, 379, 390
Covent Garden, 120, 188
Cowell, Henry, 193
compositions of, 431
Piece for Piano Paris, 431
Craft of Musical Composition, The (Hindemith), 347
Cramer, Johann Baptist, 68, 71, 76–77, 85, 140, 167, 183, 272
Crankshaw, Edward, 233
Craxton, Harold, 77, 176
Creston, Paul, Piano Concerto, 270
Cristofori, Bartolomeo, 17–18, 24
Crochet, Evelyne, 337–38
Crumb, George:
compositions of, 327
Makrokosmos, Volume 1, 327
Makrokosmos, Volume 2, 327
Cubiles, José, 193
Cumming, Richard, 56
compositions of, 431
Piano Sonata, 431
Twenty-four Preludes, 431
Cunningham, Merce, 430
Curtis Institute of Music, 22, 51–52, 56, 117, 122, 127, 139, 155, 157, 164, 187, 230, 240, 242, 246, 264
Curzon, Sir Clifford, 78–79, 170, 249, 401, 434, 440
Custer, Arthur:
compositions of, 431
Rhapsodality Brown, 431
Czerny, Carl, 19–20, 39, 45–47, 68, 78–79, 84–85, 140, 155, 158, 165, 167, 180, 186, 202, 217, 297, 351, 404, 417
Sonata in A-flat major, 250
Variations on La Ricordanza, 133–34
Czerny-Stefanska, Halina, 79, 81, 86, 261
Cziffra, György, 80, 85

Dachs, Joseph, 80, 195, 264

Dahl, Nicholas, 386
Calcroze, Jacques, 363
Dale, Kathleen, 80
Dallapiccola, Luigi, 59
compositions of, 327
Quaderno musicale di Anna-libera, 327
Sonatina Canonica on Pagan-ini Caprices, 327
Dallas Symphony, 264
Damrosch, Leopold, 57
Damrosch, Walter, 209
Dannreuther, Edward, 58, 81, 100, 184, 228, 436
Dante, 166
Darré, Jeanne-Marie, 81, 171, 201, 264
Davidovich, Bella, 79, 81, 142
Davies, Fanny, 80, 81–82, 214
Davies, Laurence, 330, 336, 380, 388, 394
Davis, Ivan, 82, 359
Davison, J. W., 105
Debussy, Claude, 17, 23, 34, 35, 49, 52–53, 69, 70, 73, 97, 102, 117, 119, 122, 143, 168, 171, 173–74, 181, 183, 190–91, 204, 205, 213, 215, 223, 226, 263–64, 268, 281–82, 287, 298, 305, 327, 336, 343–44, 352, 360, 368, 379–80, 388, 392, 442
Children's Corner Suite, 44, 64, 266, 330
Clair de lune, 172
compositions of, 328–33
Estampes: Pagodes, La Soirée dans Grenade, Jardins sous la pluie, 329
Etude No. 11: Pour les arpèges composés, 138
Images (First Series): Reflets dans l'eau, Hommage à Rameau, Mouvement, 329–30
Images (Second Series): Cloches à travers les feuilles, Et la lune descend sur le temple qui fut, Poissons d'or, 329–30
L'Isle joyeuse, 138, 329
Pour le piano, 328–29
Reflets dans l'eau, 172
Reverie, 44
Serenade for the Doll, 138

Suite bergamasque, 328
Twelve Etudes, 206, 219
Twelve Preludes (1915), 333
Twelve Preludes, Book I, 75, 330–31
Twelve Preludes, Book II, 331–33
Twenty-four Preludes, 330
Decaux, Abel:
Clairs de lune, 431
compositions of, 431
Delaborde, Élie Miriam, 82, 227
Delacroix, Eugène, 31
De Larrocha, Alicia, 82–83, 174, 279, 445–46
Delius, Frederick, Piano Concerto in C minor, 108
Dello Joio, Norman:
compositions of, 431
Sonata No. 3, 431
Demus, Jörg, 83–84, 94, 188
Demuth, Norman, 65, 334, 336, 339, 368
Dent, Edward J., 60
Denver Symphony, 88
Descombes, Émile, 73
Detroit Symphony, 100, 112
Dett, Nathaniel, In the Bottoms Suite, 117
Diaghilev, Sergei, 390
Diamond, David:
compositions of, 432
Piano Concerto, 432
Piano Sonata, 432
Prelude, Fantasy, and Fugue, 432
Dichter, Misha, 84
Dickens, Charles, 332
Diémer, Louis, 63–64, 70, 84, 97, 159, 174, 188, 217, 232, 252, 423
Dieren, Bernard van, 283
Dittersdorf, Karl Ditters von, 186
Doguereau, Paul, 270
Döhler, Theodor, 84
Dohnányi, Ernö von, 84, 93, 95, 121, 123, 152, 159, 191, 212, 238, 263
compositions of, 333–34
Piano Concerto in B minor, 85
Variations on a Nursery Song for Piano and Orchestra, 85, 232, 333–34

Donizetti, Gaetano:
  Don Pasquale, 257, 271
  Lucia di Lammermoor,
    359
Door, Anton, 85, 96, 253
Dorfmann, Ania, 85, 201
Dorn, Heinrich, 48, 177
Downes, Olin, 100, 132, 161
Doyen, Jean, 85, 162
Draeseke, Felix, 200
Dreyschock, Alexander, 19, 80,
    85–86, 260, 271
  Konzertstück, 86
Drzewiecki, Zbigniew, 86, 121,
    247, 273
Dubois, Théodore, 174
Dubuc, Alexander, 86, 264,
    276
Duchable, François-René, 86
Dukas, Paul, 144, 162, 281
  compositions of, 334
  Sonata in E-flat minor, 217,
    334
  The Sorcerer's Apprentice,
    229, 334
  Variations, Interlude, and
    Finale on a Theme by
    Rameau (Rameau Varia-
    tions), 217, 334
Dürer, Albrecht, 242
Dussek, Jan Ladislav, 86–87,
    151, 175, 267, 272, 345
  compositions of, 334–35
  La Consolation, 87
  Piano Concerto No. 12, 123
  Sonata in A-flat major (Le
    Retour à Paris), 335
  Sonata in B-flat major, 334–
    335
  Sonata in C minor, 334–35
  Sonata in F minor (L'Invoca-
    tion), 87, 93, 334
  Sonata in F-sharp minor, 87,
    334–35
Dutilleux, Henri:
  compositions of, 335
  Piano Sonata, 146, 245, 335
Duvernoy, Victor Alphonse,
    87
Dvořák, Antonin, 156
  compositions of, 432
  Humoresques, 432
  Piano Concerto in G minor,
    120, 432
  Poetic Tone Pictures, 432
  Suite in A major, 93, 432

Eastman School of Music, 101
Echaniz, José, 88
Ecole du mecanisme du piano
    (Le Couppey), 153
Ecole Normale de Musique, 74
Edison, Thomas, 130
Egge, Klaus:
  compositions of, 432
  Piano Sonata No. 2 (Paté-
    tica), 432
Egorov, Youri, 88, 274
Ehlert, Louis, 309, 314
Eibenschütz, Ilona, 88
Einem, Gottfried von, Piano
    Concerto, 432
Einstein, Alfred, 187, 371
Eisenberger, Severin, 88
Ekier, Jan, 88
Elgar, Sir Edward, Concert Al-
    legro, 82
Eliot, George, 167
Elizabeth Sprague Coolidge
    Medal, 246
Ellington, Duke, 446
Elsner, Joseph, 322
Elvira Madigan, 32
Embarkment for Cythère, The
    (Watteau), 329
Enesco, Georges, 162
  compositions of, 432
  Roumanian Rhapsody No. 1,
    432
  Sonata No. 1, 432
  Sonata No. 3, 163–64, 432
  Suite for Piano, 432
Engel, Karl, 201, 365
Entremont, Philippe, 76, 88–
    89, 171
Epstein, Julius, 89, 101, 156
Epstein, Lonny, 215, 789
Epstein, Richard, 89
Erard, Sébastien, 19, 183
Ertmann, Dorothea, 89
Eschenbach, Christoph, 89
Eskin, Virginia, 89–90, 445
Essays in Musical Analysis
    (Tovey), 260
Essipova, Annette, 21, 42, 65,
    90, 121, 207, 261, 264,
    423
Estrin, Morton, 90
Euclid, 351

Falkowska, Janina, 109
Falla, Manuel de, 174, 223,

264–65, 281, 329, 332
  compositions of, 335–36
  Cuarto Piezas españolas, 335
  Fantasia baética, 335–36
  Nights in the Gardens of
    Spain—Symphonic Impres-
    sions for Piano and Or-
    chestra, 83, 88, 149, 225,
    265, 336
  Ritual Dance of Fire, 224
Fargue, Léon Paul, 328
Farnadi, Edith, 90
Farrenc, Louise, 90–91
Fauré, Gabriel, 14, 17, 73–74,
    144, 150, 171, 190, 223,
    254, 257, 271, 281, 318,
    379, 387, 388, 436
  Ballade for Piano and Or-
    chestra in F-sharp major,
    64, 338
  Barcarolle in B minor, 138
  Complete Piano Music, 336
  compositions of, 336–38
  Huit Piéces brèves, 337–38
  Impromptu No. 2 in F mi-
    nor, 146
  Impromptu No. 5 in F-sharp
    minor, 138
  Nine Preludes, 64, 338
  Theme and Variations, 338,
    406
  Thirteen Barcarolles, 336–37
  Thirteen Nocturnes, 337–38
  Valse-caprice in D-flat major,
    227
Faust (Goethe), 166–67, 178
Faust (Lenau), 353
Fay, Amy, 91, 111, 169, 255
Feinberg, Samuel, 91, 107, 240
Feltsman, Vladimir, 91
Ferber, Albert, 91
Fétis, François Joseph, 202
Février, Jacques, 91, 217
Field, John, 13, 29, 67–68, 71,
    86, 91–92, 154, 158, 167,
    177, 179, 188, 253, 301,
    315, 317–18
Fielden, Thomas, 314
Filtsch, Karl, 92
Finck, Henry T., 190, 196,
    308, 314–16
Finzi, Gerald, Grand Fantasy
    and Toccata, 150
Fiorentino, Sergio, 92
Firkušný, Rudolf, 93, 155
Fischer, Annie, 85, 93

Fischer, Edwin, 34, 55, 94–95, 154, 187, 214, 216, 228, 247, 279, 291
Fischer-Dieskau, Dietrich, 182
Fitzgerald, F. Scott, 307
Flanagan, William, 326
Fleisher, Leon, 95, 148, 265, 436
Fleurs du mal, Les (Baudelaire), 331
Flier, Yakov, 81, 95, 142, 443
Flonzaley Quartet, 100
Florida State University, 152
Foldes, Andor, 85, 95–96, 369
Fontana, Julius, 313
Forbidden Childhood (Slenczynska), 246
Fort, Syvilla, 430
Foster, Sidney, 96, 230, 264
Fou Ts'ong, 86, 96
Frager, Malcolm, 96
Franck, César, 257, 275, 305, 429, 443, 446
  compositions of, 338–39
  Les Djinns, 338
  Prelude, Aria, and Finale, 75, 339
  Prelude, Chorale, and Fugue, 44, 75, 173, 183, 223, 339
  Prelude, Fugue, and Variation for Organ, 84, 339
  Symphonic Variations for Piano and Orchestra, 64, 75, 84, 118, 338
Francke, August, 96
François, Samson, 74, 96
Frank, Claude, 96, 126, 148
Frankenstein (Shelley), 19
Frankfurt Conservatory, 89
Frankl, Peter, 97, 171
Frederick II (the Great), King of Prussia, 18, 39
Freire, Nelson, 97
Freundlich, Irwin, 228, 381
Frey, Emil, 97, 101
Fricken, Baron von, 406
Fricken, Ernestine von, 405
Friedberg, Carl, 89, 96, 97, 141, 156, 176
Friedheim, Arthur, 22–23, 72, 97–98, 136, 145, 169, 220–21, 230
Friedman, Ignaz, 21, 98–99, 145, 158, 162, 184, 197, 234, 279
  Elle danse, 98

Six Viennese Dances, 98
Friskin, James, 81, 100, 156, 260, 293–94, 301, 309, 314, 318, 320, 351–53, 377, 401
Froberger, Johann Jakob, 285
Frost, Thomas, 414
Fuleihan, Anis, 149
Fuller, Loïe, 330
Fumagalli, Adolfo, 100
  Les Clochettes, 100
Furtwängler, Wilhelm, 42

Gabrilowitsch, Ossip, 21, 100, 184
Gál, Amparo, 342
Gál, Hans, 383
Gallico, Paolo, 101
Galuppi, Baldassare, 181
Ganz, Rudolph, 50, 101, 184, 193, 214, 245, 390
Garbo, Greta, 113
Garvelmann, Donald, 413, 416
Gaspard de la nuit (Bertrand), 389
Gát, József, 263
Gavrilov, Andrei, 101
Gebhard, Heinrich, 48, 101
Gelatt, Roland, 14
Gelinek, Abbé Joseph, 101
Geneva Conservatoire, 163, 173
Geneva International Piano Competition, 33, 153, 180, 217, 247, 262
Genhart, Cecile Staub, 101, 200
George IV, King of England, 165–67
George V, King of England, 332
Géricault, Théodore, 31
Gerke, Anton, 101
  Ten Characteristic Pieces, 101
Gershwin, George, 121, 150, 245, 443
  compositions of, 339–40
  Piano Concerto in F major, 158–59, 207, 270, 340
  Porgy and Bess, 270
  Rhapsody in Blue, 48, 82, 158, 207, 266, 270, 339–340
  Three Preludes, 339
Gervaise, Claude, 380

Gianneo, Luis:
  compositions of, 432
  Sonata in B-flat minor, 432
  Sonatina, 432
Gibb, James, 281–82, 336, 389, 394
Gibbons, Orlando, 112, 115
Gide, André, 76, 133, 307
Gieseking, Walter, 91, 102–3, 279, 307, 388, 430
Gilels, Emil, 103–5, 188, 215, 248, 279, 382, 432
Gillespie, John, 286, 289
Gilman, Lawrence, 348
Gimpel, Jacob, 420
Ginastera, Alberto, 52
  compositions of, 340–41
  Piano Concerto No. 1, 175, 250, 340
  Piano Concerto No. 2, 250, 340–41
  Sonata No. 1, 250, 340
  Sonata No. 2, 340
  Sonata No. 3, 189, 340
Ginzburg, Gregory, 105
Giulini, Carlo, 134
Glazunov, Alexander, 42, 422
  compositions of, 432–33
  Sonata No. 2, 432
  Variations in F-sharp minor, 432–33
Glenn Gould Reader, The (Gould), 116
Glinka, Mikhail, 92
Gluck, Christoph Willibald:
  Gavotte, 130
  Orfeo, 159, 243
Goddard, Arabella, 105
Godowsky, Leopold, 22–23, 29, 51, 65, 105–7, 126, 145, 162, 188, 195, 197, 226, 229–30, 247, 279, 351, 369
  Arrangement of Weber's *Invitation to the Dance*, 51
  Symphonic Metamorphosis on Themes from Johann Strauss's Künstlerleben, 212, 271
  Transcription of Strauss's *Die Fledermaus*, 246
  Transcription of Strauss's *Wine, Women, and Song*, 66
Goedicke, Alexander, 226

Goethe, Wolfgang von, 141,
178, 253
Goetz, Hermann, 59, 154
Goldenweiser, Alexander, 48,
107, 142, 189, 194, 209,
239–40, 245, 273
Goldsand, Robert, 108
Goldsmith, Harris, 108, 234
Golinelli, Stefano, 108
Twelve Etudes, 108
Twenty-four Preludes, 108
Goode, Richard, 108
Goodson, Katharine, 108, 145
Goria, Alexander, 108, 275
Etudes, 108
Gorodnitzki, Sascha, 109, 192,
252, 253
Gottschalk, Louis Moreau, 1,
63, 65, 109–12, 123, 164,
174, 251, 426
Bamboula, 109
Le Bananier, 109
The Banjo, 110–11
The Dying Poet, 110
Fantasy on the Brazilian Na-
tional Hymn, 191
Grand Scherzo, 82
La Jota aragonesa, 109
The Last Hope, 110–11
Manchega, 82, 109
Minuit a Séville, 109
Morte, 111
Ojos criollos, 111
La Savane, 109
Souvenir de Porto Rico, 110
Tournament Galop, 82,
110
L'Union, 110, 198
Gould, Glenn, 112–16, 232,
234, 279–80, 396–97,
415, 443
So You Want to Write a
Fugue, 115
Gould, Morton:
Abby Variations, 433
Boogie-Woogie Etude, 433
compositions of, 433
Interplay for Piano and Or-
chestra, 433
Prelude and Toccata, 433
Rag-Blues-Rag, 433
Sonatina, 433
Gounod, Charles, 339
Faust, 105, 271, 359
Gosseau, Lélia, 159
Gowen, Bradford, 439

Goya, Francisco de, 83, 319,
342
Grace, Harvey, 339
Graf, Hans, 116
Graffman, Gary, 117, 264, 387
Grainger, Percy, 22, 29, 117–
118, 140, 156, 184, 194,
206, 343, 430
Country Gardens, 118
Handel in the Strand, 118
Mock Morris, 118
Molly on the Shore, 118
Spoon River, 118
Granados, Enrique, 23, 69,
174, 208, 257, 282
El Amor y la muerte, 83
Andaluza, 250
Asturiana, 250
Complete Piano Music, 341
compositions of, 341–42
Danza lenta, 83
Goyescas, 83, 342
Jota, 250
El Pelele, 342
Seis Piezas sobre cantos pop-
ulares españoles, 341
Twelve Danzas españolas,
83, 341
Valse poéticos, 83, 341–42
Zarabanda, 250
Granados Academy, 174
Grand Prix du Disque, 54
Grant, Mark W., 245
Greef, Arthur de, 54, 118, 144,
440
Greig, Edvard, 14, 40, 184,
269, 362, 378, 436
Ballade in the Form of Varia-
tions on a Norwegian Folk
Song in G minor, 51, 107,
139, 144, 180, 212, 223,
343
Brooklet, 146
compositions of, 343–44
Holberg Suite, 343
Lyric Pieces, 103, 105, 223,
343
Norwegian Peasant Dances,
343
Piano Concerto in A minor,
72, 117, 120, 163, 169,
188–89, 208, 212, 225,
343–44
Piano Sonata in E minor, 66,
116
Violin Sonata in C minor, 212

Griffes, Charles Tomlinson,
121, 176, 260
compositions of, 344
Four Roman Sketches, 344
Piano Sonata, 151, 344
Three Piano Preludes, 344
Three Tone Pictures, 344
Grinberg, Maria, 51, 118, 142,
381
Grofé, Ferde, 340
Piano Concerto, 229
Groot, Cor de, 118
Groote, Steven de, 119
Grove, Sir George, 238
Grünfeld, Alfred, 119
Guarnieri, Camargo:
compositions of, 433
Ponteios, 433
Guerrero, Alberto, 112
Guide to the Pianist's Repetoire
(Hinson), 126
Gulda, Friedrich, 32, 119, 369
Gutiérrez, Horacio, 119, 174
Gutmann, Adolf, 308
Gyrowetz, Adalbert, 67

Haas, Monique, 119, 159
Haberbier, Ernst, 119–20
Etudes, 120
Habermann, Michael, 444
Hadow, Sir William Henry,
314
Haebler, Ingrid, 120
Haggin, B. J., 128
Hahn, Reynaldo:
compositions of, 433
Piano Concerto, 254
Sonatina, 254
Haien, Jeannette, 199
Hall, Denis, 228
Hall, Elsie, 120
Hallé, Sir Charles, 19, 69, 109,
120, 122, 307, 359–60
Hallé Orchestra, 120
Halm, Anton, 122
Hambourg, Mark, 120, 158
Hambro, Leonid, 121
Hamburger, Paul, 313–14
Hamilton, H. V., 231
Hamilton, Iain:
compositions of, 433
Nocturnes with Cadenzas,
433
Palinodes, 433
Piano Sonata, 433

Handel, George Frideric, 77, 103, 122, 178, 243, 285, 366, 442
  Chaconne in G major, 94, 96
  Harmonious Blacksmith, 44
  Piano Concerto, 93
Hanon, Charles Louis, 121, 418
Hanslick, Eduard, 13, 58–59, 219, 237–38, 255, 260
Hans von Bülow Medal, 33
Harasiewicz, Adam, 86, 121
"Harmonie du Soir" (Baude-laire), 331
Harriet Cohen Medal, 73, 82, 246
Harris, Roy:
  compositions of, 345
  Sonata, 345
Harrison, Sidney, 121
Hartmann, Thomas de, 90, 121
Hartmann, Victor, 378
Hartvigson, Fritz, 121
Harvard University, 218
Haskil, Clara, 74, 121–22, 409
Hassler, Johänn:
  Grande Gigue, 122
  Sonata-Fantasy, 122
Hauptmann, Moritz, 272
Hautzig, Walter, 122
Haydn, Joseph, 39, 46, 52, 75, 94, 177–78, 181, 213, 215, 232, 265, 272, 288, 381–82, 398, 443
  compositions of, 345–46
  Piano concerto in D major, 104, 346
  Piano Sonata in B minor, 203
  Piano Sonata in C major (*English* Sonata), 115, 119, 266
  Piano Sonata in E-flat major, 115, 133
  Piano Sonata in F major, 133
  Piano Sonatas, 41–42, 49, 55, 224, 345–46
  Variations in F minor, 224, 346
Haydn, Michael, 266
Hays, Doris, 431
Hedley, Arthur, 128, 311, 323
Heidsieck, Eric, 76, 122
Heifetz, Jascha, 132, 198
Heine, Heinrich, 84–85, 167
Heller, Stephen, 19, 120, 122, 167, 201, 324

L'Avalanche, 122
Helps, Robert, 433, 439
Henahan, Donal, 204
Henderson, W. J., 126, 161, 190, 211, 251
Henkemans, Hans, 122, 439
Henriot, Nicole, 171
Henschel, Sir George, 183, 269
Henselt, Adolf von, 39, 48, 122–23, 167, 184, 206, 236–37, 276
  Etude (*Were I a Bird*), 123
  Etudes, 101, 123, 237
  Piano Concerto in F minor, 60, 160, 226, 237
Henze, Hans Werner:
  compositions of, 346
  Piano Concerto No. 2, 346
Hernádi, Lajos, 85, 97, 123, 263
Hérold, Ferdinand, 325
Herz, Henri, 51, 79, 109, 111, 123–24, 167, 180, 202, 207, 236
  Variations on "No più mesta" from Rossini's *La Cenerentola,* 271
Hess, Dame Myra, 49, 124–25, 163, 176, 230, 249, 250, 260, 279
Hesse-Bukowska, Barbara, 125
Hétu, Jacques, Variations, 116
Hewitt, James, 361
Heyman, Katherine Ruth, 125
Hiller, Ferdinand, 19, 125–26, 167, 169, 178, 232, 316
Hilsberg, Ignace, 90, 230, 264
Hilton, James, 139
Hindemith, Paul, 214, 273
  compositions of, 346–47
  Ludus Tonalis, 347
  Sonatas Nos. 1, 2, and 3, 116, 347
  Suite "1922," 346
Hinderas, Natalie, 446
Hinson, Maurice, 122, 126, 298, 332, 363, 371, 382, 391, 395, 400, 417, 428, 436
Hinton, Arthur, Piano Con-certo, 108
Hipkins, Alfred J., 123, 126, 198
History of the Sonata Idea, A (Newman), 189

Hitchcock, Daniel L., 257
Hobson, Ian, 126
Hochschule für Musik, Der, 116
Hoffman, Ludwig, 126, 171
Hoffman, Richard, 110, 126, 183
  Chromaticon for Piano and Orchestra, 127
  Dixiana, 82, 126
  Impromptu in C minor, 126
  In Memorian L. M. G., 126
Hofmann, Casimir, 126
Hofmann, E. T. A., 407
Hofmann, Josef, 22–23, 51, 53, 65–66, 67, 105, 112, 126–130, 162, 184, 190, 197, 209, 212–13, 221–22, 246, 279, 343, 387, 404–6, 411
Hollander, Lorin, 130
Homer, 166
Honegger, Arthur:
  compositions of, 433
  Concertino for Piano and Orchestra, 433
  Sept Pièces brèves, 433
  Toccata and Variations, 433
Hoover, Herbert, 65
Hopekirk, Helen, 130
Hopkinson, Francis, 361
Horowitz, Vladimir, 15, 23, 51, 53, 98, 114, 117, 130–139, 143, 173, 184, 239–240, 242, 262, 279–80, 307, 326, 360, 378–79, 382, 385, 411
Horszowski, Mieczyslaw, 119, 139–40, 158, 164, 175, 199, 240
Hovhaness, Alan:
  compositions of, 433–34
  Fantasy, 433–34
Howard, Leslie, 140
Howe, Tina, 113
How People Change (Wheelis), 215
Hubeau, Jean, 159
Hughes, Edwin, 109, 140, 285
Hugo, Victor, 31, 166, 168, 338, 352
Hull, Eaglefield, 411
Hume, Paul, 112
Hummel, Johann Nepomuk, 19–20, 45–46, 67–68, 79, 125, 140–41, 148, 151,

Hummel, Johann Nepomuk, *continued*
183, 217, 238, 253, 256–257, 267, 369, 403
Piano Concerto in A minor, 42, 140
Piano Concerto in B minor, 32, 60
Piano Septet in D minor, 140
Sonata Op. 81, in F-sharp minor, 140
Sonata Op. 106, 140
Twenty-four Etudes, 141
Huneker, James, 13, 21, 30, 63, 98, 102, 123, 135, 146, 190, 195, 219–20, 299–302, 308–9, 311–14, 316–17, 319–22, 324, 353
Hungerford, Bruce, 141, 301–2
Hünten, Franz, 141, 236
Hurok, Sol, 215
Husa, Karel:
compositions of, 434
Sonata No. 1, 434
Sonata No. 2, 434
Sonatina, 434
Hutcheson, Ernest, 65, 141, 143, 214, 227, 286, 290, 294, 318, 320, 365, 397
Huxley, Aldous, 19
Hyman, Dick, 145

Ibert, Jacques:
compositions of, 434
Histoires, 434
Petite Suite en quinze images, 434
Les Rencontres, 434
Igumnov, Konstantin, 81, 118, 142, 192–94, 240, 245, 276
Imbrie, Andrew, 416
Indiana University, 50, 96, 207, 260
Indy, Vincent d', 31, 305, 446
compositions of, 434
Le Poème des montagnes, 434
Sonata in E minor, 240, 434
Symphony on a French Mountain Air for Piano and Orchestra, 64, 434
Thème varié, fugue, et chanson, 434
In Search of Chopin (Cortot), 74

Introduction to the Performance of Bach, An (Tureck), 262
I Really Should Be Practicing (Graffman), 264
Ireland, John:
Ballade, 434
compositions of, 434
Decorations, 434
Piano Concerto in E-flat major, 434
Piano Sonata, 434
Rhapsody, 434
Sonatina, 434
Istomin, Eugene, 142, 234
Istomin-Stern-Rose trio, 142
Italian Opera (London), 70
Iturbi, Amparo, 142
Iturbi, José, 142, 252, 433
Ives, Charles, 23, 283, 304
compositions of, 347–48
Sonata No. 1, 176, 348
Sonata No. 2, "Concord, Mass., 1840–1860," 153, 348, 435

Jacobs, Paul, 143, 268, 332, 396, 429, 441
Jaëll, Alfred, 143
Jaëll, Marie, *La Touche,* 143
Janáček, Leos, 319
Capriccio for Left Hand and Orchestra, 93
compositions of, 349
Concertino for Piano, Strings, and Winds, 93, 349
In the Mist, 93, 183, 349
On an Overgrown Path, 93
Sonata in E-flat minor, "October 1, 1905," 93, 349
Tema con variazioni, 93
Jandó, Jenö, 146
Janis, Byron, 15, 143, 174
Janotha, Natalia, 143
Mountain Scenes, 143
Jarnach, Philipp, 444
Jasinski, Andrzej, 275
Jensen, Adolf:
compositions of, 435
Sonata in F-sharp minor, 435
Joachim, Joseph, 260, 303
Johannesen, Grant, 64, 144, 430
Johansen, Gunnar, 59, 98, 144

Johnson, Hunter:
compositions of, 435
Piano Sonata, 435
Jolivet, André:
compositions of, 435
Piano Concerto, 435
Jonás, Alberto, 144–45
Master School of Modern Piano Playing and Virtuosity, 144–45
Jonas, Maryla, 145, 230
Jones, Martin, 145
Joplin, Scott, 145, 437
Elite Syncopation, 145
The Entertainer, 145
Gladiolus Rag, 145, 440
Maple Leaf Rag, 145
Ragtime Dance, 145
School of Ragtime, 145
Joseffy, Fafael, 13, 63, 106, 145–46, 183, 213, 219–221, 255
School of Advanced Playing, 145
Joselson, Tedd, 174
Joseph II, Holy Roman Emperor, 186
Joubert, Joseph, 277
Joy, Geneviève, 146, 188, 335
Joyce, Eileen, 146, 172, 176, 434
Joyce, James, 222
Judson, Arthur, 130
Juilliard School, 10, 22, 32, 38, 50, 56, 62, 65, 72, 85, 89, 105, 109, 119, 129–30, 141, 146–47, 157, 159–160, 164, 172, 174, 187, 192–93, 204, 213–15, 228, 246, 252–53, 268, 273

Kabalevsky, Dmitri:
compositions of, 435
Piano Concerto No. 2 in G minor, 174, 435
Sonata No. 2, 139
Sonata No. 3, 133, 138–39, 274, 435
Sonatina in C major, 435
Twenty-four Preludes, 95, 435
Twenty Pieces for Children, Op. 27, 435
Twenty Pieces for Children, Op. 39, 435

Kabos, Ilona, 146, 245
Kacso, Diana, 109
Kadosa, Pál, 146–47, 153–54, 231
    Piano Concerto No. 3, 146–47
    Sonata No. 4, 146–47
Kalichstein, Joseph, 147
Kalish, Gilbert, 245
Kalkbrenner, Friedrich, 19, 21, 50, 68, 87, 105, 109, 120, 123, 139, 147–48, 183, 194, 202, 226, 236, 238, 250–51, 256, 267, 275
    Effusio musica, 148
    Etudes, 148
    Grande sonate brillante, 148
    Piano Concerto No. 1 in D minor, 148
    Sonate pour la main gauche principale, 148
Kallir, Lilian, 148, 264
Kangaroo-Pouch Free Music Machine, 118
Kanner-Rosenthal, Hedwig, 218
Kapell, William, 142, 148–50, 153, 172, 227, 279, 326
Karajan, Herbert von, 86, 112
Karasowski, Moritz, 309, 317
Katchen, Julius, 150, 218, 230, 441
Katin, Peter, 150
Katz, Mindru, 150
Kedra, Wladyslaw, 86
Keene, Constance, 65, 151
Keller, Roland, 251
Kempff, Wilhelm, 78, 122, 151–52, 163, 216, 262, 290–92, 398
Kennedy, Daisy, 196
Kentner, Louis, 47, 152, 289, 291, 295, 315, 317, 322, 352–54, 446
Kessler, Johann, 152
Keys to the Keyboard (Foldes), 96
Kezeradze, Alicia, 202–3
Khachaturian, Aram, 148, 150
    compositions of, 435–36
    Lullaby, 158
    Piano Concerto, 83, 149, 158, 192, 198, 435
    Poem, 435
    Sabre Dance, 158
    Sonata, 436

Sonatina, 436
    Toccata, 435–36
Kiev Conservatory, 188, 261, 263
Kilenyi, Edward, 85, 152
Kirchner, Leon:
    compositions of, 436
    Piano Sonata, 436
Kirchner, Theodor, compositions of, 436
Kirkpatrick, John, 153, 435, 441
Kirkpatrick, Ralph, 141, 395–396
Kjerulf, Halfdan, compositions of, 436
Kleczynski, Jean, 310–11, 316
Kleeberg, Clotilde, 153
Klein, Jacques, 153
Klemperer, Otto, 42
Klien, Walter, 153, 398
Klindworth, Karl, 57–58, 153, 217, 357, 422
    Polonaise-fantaise, 153
Knorr, Julius, 153, 272
Kocsis, Zoltán, 146, 153–54
Kodály, Zoltán, 152, 187, 229, 263
    compositions of, 436
    Marosszek Dances, 436
    Nine Piano Pieces, 436
    Seven Piano Pieces, 436
Koechlin, Charles, compositions of, 436–37
Kohler, Louis, 154, 214
Kondrashin, Kiril, 32, 72
Kontarsky, Aloys, 418
Kontski, Antoine de, *The Awakening of the Lion*, 154
Korngold, Erich von, 383
Koussevitzky, Serge, 149
Kraus, Lili, 154
Krause, Martin, 33–34, 94, 154–55, 213–14
Krehbiel, H. E., 361
Kreisler, Fritz, 212, 407
    Liebesfreud, 387
    Liebesleid, 387
Křenek, Ernst:
    compositions of, 350
    Piano Concerto No. 2, 273
    Sechs Vermessene, 350
    Sonata No. 3, 116, 350
    Sonata No. 4, 350
Kreutzer, Leonid, 155, 235
Kuerti, Anton, 155, 234

Kuhlau, Friedrich, 88
Kullak, Franz, 184, 188, 192, 200, 317
    School of Octaves, 155
Kullak, Theodor, 40, 49, 119, 155–56, 226, 230, 309
Kurpinski, Karl, 318
Kurz, Ilona, 183
Kurz, Vilém, 93, 155
Kvapil, Radoslav, 156
Kwast, James, 117, 156, 160

La Brecque, Rebecca, 416–17
Lack, Théodore, 174
Ladies' Home Journal, 127
Laires, Fernando, 156
Lamartine, Alphonse de, 166, 354
Lamb, Joseph, 437
    American Beauty, 437
    Ethiopia Rag, 437
    Ragtime Nightingale, 437
Lambert, Alexander, 156, 184, 225
Lambert, Constant, 394
    compositions of, 437
    Concerto for Piano and Nine Players, 437
    Elegiac Blues, 437
    Piano Sonata, 437
Lamennais, Félicité Robert de, 166
Lamond, Frederic, 144, 191
Lamoureux Orchestra, 73
Landon, Christa, 346
Landowska, Wanda, 77, 114, 156–57, 180, 228, 369–370, 395–96
Laplante, André, 109
Lara, Adelina de, 157
Laredo, Ruth, 157
Lassimonne, Denise, 125
Last Tycoon, The (Fitzgerald), 307
Lateiner, Jacob, 157, 264, 305
Lavine, Edward, 332
Lebert, Siegmund, 157
Leconte de Lisle, Charles Marie, 331
Le Couppey, Félix, 65, 157–58
Lee, Noel, 158
Leeds Competition, 172, 193, 199, 208, 262
Lees, Benjamin:
    compositions of, 437

Lees, Benjamin, *continued*
  Fantasia, 437
  Sonata breve, 437
  Sonata No. 4, 117, 457
Lefébure, Yvonne, 74–75
Lefébure-Wély, Louis James, 320
Legge, Walter, 163
Leginska, Ethel, 204
Legion of Honor, 158, 174, 213, 251, 275
Legouvé, Ernest, 166
Lehmann, Lotte, 212
Leimer, Karl, 102
Leinsdorf, Erich, 215, 305
Leipzig, University of, 57
Leipzig Conservatory, 40, 154, 183–84, 199, 202, 213, 247, 252, 256, 265, 269, 270
Leipzig Gewandhaus Orchestra, 213
Leningrad Philharmonic, 104
Lenz, Wilhelm von, 69, 123, 255, 322
Leopold II, Holy Roman Emperor, 374
Lerner, Bennett, 440
Lerner, Tina, 194
Leschetizky, Theodor, 20–21, 23, 50, 53, 65, 79, 88, 90, 92, 98–101, 108, 120, 130, 139–40, 158, 177, 179, 182, 193, 195–96, 207, 221, 232, 234–38, 244–46, 264, 272, 274, 285, 384
Lettvin, Theodore, 158
Lev, Ray, 254
Levant, Oscar, 158–59, 252, 397
Leventritt Award, 72, 96, 142, 147, 155, 268
Levin, Sophia Brilliant, 261
Levitzki, Mischa, 22–23, 85, 159, 161, 243
Levy, Ernst, 159
Lévy, Lazare, 119, 159, 171, 263
Lewenthal, Raymond, 31, 159–160, 227, 283–84
Lewis, C. Day, 233
Lhévinne, Josef, 22–23, 72, 98, 109, 160–62, 174, 184, 213, 221, 226, 236, 239, 246, 276, 404–6, 412

Lhévinne, Rosina, 56, 62, 84, 90, 160–62, 164, 174, 192–93, 204, 226, 245, 264
Liadov, Anatol, 422
  compositions of, 437
  Variations on a Theme of Glinka, 437
Liapunov, Sergei, 194, 422
  compositions of, 437–38
  Piano concerto No. 2 in E minor, 438
  Rhapsody on Ukrainian Themes for Piano and Orchestra, 438
  Sonata, 428
  Sonatine, 438
  Toccata and Fugue, 438
  Twelve *Etudes d'exécution transcendante,* 152, 437
Library of the Performing Arts, Lincoln Center, Tureck Archive at, 261
Liceo Musicale, 243
Lieberson, Peter:
  Bagatelles, 241
  Piano Concerto, 241
Life of Beethoven (Schindler), 183
Ligeti, Gyorgy, 52
Lima, Arthur Moreira, 162
Lincoln, Abraham, 110
Lind, Jenny, 109
Lipatti, Dinu, 74, 79, 150, 162–64, 199, 279, 363
  Concertino in the Classic Style, 163
  Fantasy for Piano Trio, 163
  Sonatina for the Left Hand, 163
Lipkin, Seymour, 164
Lipman, Samuel, 164
Lisbon Conservatory, 201
List, Eugene, 164, 227, 305–6, 418
Liszt, Adam, 164
Liszt, Franz, 13, 19–24, 29–34, 38–39, 47, 58–59, 63–63, 67, 69, 73–74, 77–78, 83–84, 90–92, 94, 102, 109, 119, 123, 134, 136–37, 144–45, 148, 154–56, 160–61, 164–70, 177–79, 180, 182, 184, 192, 194, 196, 200, 206, 208, 214–215, 217–18, 222, 223,

227, 230, 236–39, 241, 243, 251–53, 254, 256–257, 260, 267, 270–71, 273, 290, 297, 299, 308, 311, 316, 318–19, 322–323, 328, 335, 340, 343, 383, 389, 400–401, 405, 407, 413, 423, 425–26, 429, 437–38
Années de pèlerinage, 48, 55, 263, 354
Après une lecture de Dante—Fantasia quasi sonata (Dante Sonata), 52, 211, 268, 355
Arrangement of Wagner's Overture to *Tannhäuser,* 42, 51, 207
Arrangements, Transcriptions, and Paraphrases, 138, 172, 212, 358–60, 398
Au bord d'une source, 136, 354, 388
Ballade No. 2 in B minor, 36, 43, 52, 136, 152, 175, 353
Bénédiction de Dieu dans la solitude, 36, 55, 159, 354
Berceuse, 353
La Campanella, 98
compositions of, 350–61
Consolation No. 3 in D-flat major, 136
Dance of the Gnomes, 78
Deux Etudes de Concert, 352–53
Deux Légendes, 55, 263, 355
Don Sanche, 165
Douze Etudes d'exécution transcendante (Transcendental etudes), 24, 36, 48, 52, 79, 101, 152, 165, 168, 192, 200, 244, 351–352
Etude de concert No. 2 in F minor (*La Leggierezza*), 197
Etude in E-flat major (*Paganini* Etude), 266
Fantasia and Fugue on the Name *B-A-C-H,* 55, 355
Feux-follets, 216
Funérailles, 43, 133, 136, 193, 204, 224, 354
Grand Concert Solo, 175

Hexaméron, 160, 202
Hungarian Fantasy, 249, 358
Hungarian Rhapsody No. 2, 98, 136
Hungarian Rhapsody No. 6, 136, 159
Hungarian Rhapsody No. 9, 36
Hungarian Rhapsody No. 11, 149
Hungarian Rhapsody No. 12, 52, 136, 224
Hungarian Rhapsody No. 15 (Rakoczy March), 136, 249
Hungarian Rhapsody No. 19, 136
Les Jeux d'eaux a la Villa d'Este, 36, 355, 388
Late Music, 360–61
Légende—Saint Francis of Paolo Walking on the Waves, 80, 151
Die Legende von der Heiligen Elisabeth, 73
Liebesträum—Three Nocturnes, 42, 78, 353
Lieder Literature, 360
Maiden's Wish, 129
Malédiction for Piano and Strings, 358
Mephisto Waltz No. 1, 43, 97, 136, 149, 193, 201, 224, 229, 353
My Joys, 220
Nineteen Hungarian Rhapsodies, 80, 84, 118, 152, 232, 356, 389
Paraphrase on Gounod's Faust, 105, 271
Paraphrase on Saint-Saëns's Danse macabre, 138
Paraphrase on Verdi's Ernani, 245
Paraphrase on Verdi's Rigoletto, 42, 66, 105
Piano Concerto No. 1 in E-flat major, 72, 118, 139, 159, 174, 216, 224–25, 265–66, 357
Piano Concerto No. 2 in A major, 60, 64, 72, 88, 97, 139, 216, 275, 357, 382
Polonaise No. 2 in E major, 356
Quatre Valses oubliées, 78, 216, 356

Reminiscences de Don Juan de Mozart (Don Juan Fantasy), 43, 52, 66, 97, 218–219, 239, 246, 263
Reminiscences de La Sonnambula de Bellini, 97
Reminiscences de Norma de Bellini, 82, 160, 202
Rhapsodie espagnole, 34, 43, 356
Six Consolations, 52, 353
Six Etudes d'exécution transcendante d'après Paganini (Paganini Etudes), 168, 237, 351
Sonata in B minor, 30, 33, 36–37, 42–43, 52–53, 55, 57, 66, 72, 75, 78, 81, 83, 85, 94, 97, 105, 136, 140, 153, 155, 159, 192, 212, 216, 229, 266, 269, 279, 356–57
Sonetto 104 del Petrarca, 136, 163
Spring Night, 162
Totentanz for Piano and Orchestra, 80, 143, 185, 266, 357–58
Transcription of Beethoven's Symphony No. 5 in C minor, 115
Transcription of Berlioz's Symphonie fantastique, 49
Transcription of Schubert's "Der Wanderer," 60
Tre Sonetti del Petrarca, 42, 355
Trois Etudes de concert, 352
Vallée d'Obermann, 36, 136, 354
Valse impromptu, 224, 355
Valse infernale, 271
Valse oubliée No. 1, 136, 224
Variations on a Theme of Bach, 355
Liszt Academy, 123, 231, 245
Liszt Prize, 33, 95
Liszt's Sonata in B minor: A Study of Autograph Sources and Documents (Winklhofer), 357
Literature of the Piano, The (Hutcheson), 141

Litolff, Henri, 170
Concertos symphoniques, 170
Scherzo, 198
Lloyd George, David, 197
Lockspeiser, Edward, 330–31, 333, 389
Loesser, Arthur, 19, 59, 79, 111, 155, 170–71, 189, 213, 252, 286, 305, 325, 381, 406
London, 70–71
Long, Kathleen, 171
Long, Marguerite, 32, 53, 81, 85, 88, 91, 96–97, 162, 171, 217, 328–32, 390–391, 438
Longo, Alessandro, 171, 395
Loriod, Yvonne, 159, 171, 368
Los Angeles Philharmonic, 82
Louis Ferdinand, Prince of Prussia, 87, 267
Louis Philippe, King of France, 183
Lowenthal, Jerome, 172
Lucca, Pauline, 196
Luening, Otto, 60
Luke, Guthrie, 75
Lupu, Radu, 172
Luvisi, Lee, 240
Lympany, Moura, 172, 434
Lyons, James, 362

McCabe, John, 177, 346
Fantasy on a Theme of Liszt, 177
McCabe, Robin, 29
McClellan, George, 198
MacDowell, Edward, 130, 260
compositions of, 361–63
Eight Sea Pieces, 362
First Modern Suite, 362
Piano Concerto No. 1 in A minor, 362–63
Piano Concerto No. 2 in D minor, 72, 270, 363
Second Modern Suite, 362
Sonata No. 1 in G minor (Tragica), 362
Sonata No. 2 in G minor (Eroica), 362
Sonata No. 3 in D minor (Norse), 362
Sonata No. 4 in E minor (Keltic), 362
Ten Woodland Sketches, 362

MacDowell, Edward, *continued*
Twelve Virtuoso Studies, 96, 361–62
McGreevy, John, 115
McKenna, Marian, 176
Madrid Conservatory, 144, 250
Maffei, Scipione, 18
Magaloff, Nikita, 173, 201, 369
Toccata, 173
Mahler, Gustav, 97, 196, 209, 284, 382, 442
Maier, Guy, 173, 198
Maláts, Joaquin, 142, 173, 208
Serenade, 173
Malcolm, George, 231, 396
Malcuzynski, Witold, 173, 261, 420
Malinin, Yevgeny, 174, 202
Mallarmé, Stéphane, 333
Mana-Zucca, 66
Valse brillante, 156
Mandel, Alan, 174
Manhattan School of Music, 108, 151
Mannes College of Music, 214, 244
Mannheim Orchestra, 376
Marcus, Adele, 32, 174
Marguerite Long-Jacques Thibaud Competition, 91, 218, 254, 273–74
Maria Barbara, Queen of Spain, 395
Marlboro School of Music, 242
Marmontel, Antoine, 21, 65, 84, 87, 171, 174, 270, 275
Marsch, Ozan, 174
Marschner, Heinrich, *Der Templer und die Jüdin,* 406
Marshall, Frank, 82, 174
Martin, Anne-Thérèse, 363
Martin, Frank:
Clair de lune, 363
compositions of, 363
Concerto No. 2 for Piano and Orchestra, 363
Eight Preludes, 363
Esquisse, 363
Etude rythmique, 363
Fantaisie sur des rythmes flamenco, 363
Guitare—Quatre Pièces brèves, 363
Martins, João Carlos, 175

Martinů, Bohuslav:
compositions of, 438
Piano Concerto No. 2, 93
Piano Concerto No. 3, 438
Piano Concerto No. 4 (Incantation), 438
Martucci, Giuseppe, 175
Piano Concerto in B-flat minor, 175
Marvin, Frederick, 48, 175, 334–35
Marx, Joseph, 52, 241
Marxsen, Eduard, 53
Maryland, University of, International Piano Archives at, 214
Masaniello (Tomasso Aniello), 256
Mason, Daniel Gregory, 299, 315, 365, 393, 403
Mason, William, 111, 169, 175
Silver-Spring, 82
Touch and Technic, 175
Mason and Hamlin, 175
Masselos, William, 176, 326
Masters of the Keyboard (Wolff), 272
Mathias, Georges, 63, 69, 176, 201, 208, 231, 267, 271
Matthay, Tobias, 53, 73, 124, 146, 172, 176, 230
Matthews, Denis, 176–77, 192, 247, 400
Maurana-Press, Vera, 90
Mayer, Charles, 92, 177
Valse-étude in D-flat, 177
Mazeppa (Hugo), 352
Medtner, Nicolai, 105, 120, 212, 226, 271
compositions of, 363–65
Fairy Tales, 139, 365
Improvisation, 364
Piano Concerto No. 1 in C minor, 364
Piano Concerto No. 2 in C minor, 364
Piano Concerto No. 3 in E minor (*Ballade*), 364
Sonata in C minor (*Fairy Tale* Sonata), 364
Sonata in G minor, 364
Sonata-reminiscenza in A minor, 364
Sonata romantica in B-flat minor, 365
Mehlig, Anna, 177

Mehta, Zubin, 91
Melbourne Academy of Music, 194
Melcer, Henrik, 177
Piano Concerto No. 1, 177
Mellers, Wilfrid, 46, 166, 284, 304–5, 343–44, 411, 414
Memoirs of an Amnesiac (Levant), 158
Memories of a Musical Life (Mason), 111, 175
Memories of Liszt (Siloti), 245
Men, Women, and Pianos (Loesser), 170
Mendelssohn, Fanny, 90, 179
Mendelssohn, Felix, 13, 19, 47–48, 52, 109, 123, 126, 140, 145, 151, 165, 167, 169, 177–79, 183, 202, 212, 213, 227, 251, 267, 269–70, 293, 321, 336, 350, 352–53, 360, 381, 408, 425, 436
Andante and Rondo capriccioso, 155, 179, 200, 366
Boat Song, 99
Capriccio brillant in B minor for Piano and Orchestra, 237, 367
Capriccio in A minor, 83, 366–67
Complete Solo Piano Music, 365
compositions of, 365–67
Duetto, 99, 191
Fantasy in F-sharp minor (*Sonate ecossaise*), 155, 366
Forty-eight Songs without Words, 42, 79, 85, 99, 103, 111, 134, 178–79, 191, 365–66
Hunting Song, 99
May Breezes, 191
A Midsummer Night's Dream, 177, 193, 211, 315, 360, 388
Octet in E-flat major, 177
Piano Concerto No. 1 in G minor, 60, 172, 178, 199–200, 243, 367
Piano Concerto No. 2 in D minor, 367
Piano Trio No. 1 in D minor, 74

Prelude and Fugue in E minor, 200, 257
Rondo brillant in E-flat major, 367
Scherzo a capriccio in F-sharp minor, 134, 367
Scherzo in E minor, 179
Six Preludes and Fugues, 366
Sonata Op. 6, 200
Spinning Song, 179, 191
Spring Song, 134, 191
Three Etudes, 366
Three Fantasies or Caprices, Op. 16, 366
Variations sérieuses in D minor, 75, 83, 134, 200, 366
Venetian Boat Song, 99
Wedding March, 138
Mennin, Peter, 192
Menotti, Gian Carlo, 270
Piano Concerto, 270
Menter, Sophie, 179, 229
Réminiscences des Huguenots, 179
Menuhin, Hephzibah, 70
Merlet, Michel, Twenty-four Preludes, 122
Mérö, Yolanda, 179, 184
Merrick, Frank, 179
Merzhanov, Victor, 15, 179–80
Messiaen, Olivier, 23, 143, 171, 298
Catalogue d'oiseaux, 368
compositions of, 367–69
Eight Preludes, 368
Quatre Etudes de rythme, 368–69
Vingt Regards sur l'Enfant Jésus, 49, 192, 241, 368
Mes Voyages en Amérique (Herz), 124
Methode de piano du Conservatoire (Adam), 29
Méthode pour apprendre le piano à l'aide du guidemains (Kalkbrenner), 251
Methuen-Campbell, James, 66, 75–76, 161, 171, 176, 199
Metropolitan Opera House, 97, 126
Mewton-Wood, Noel, 180
Meyendorff, Olga von, 179, 227
Meyer, Leopold de, 124, 180
Meyerbeer, Giacomo, 69, 313, 321

L'Africaine, 359
Les Huguenots, 257, 359
Le Prophète, 359
Robert le diable, 359
Miaskovsky, Nikolai:
compositions of, 438
Sonata No. 2 in F-sharp minor, 438
Sonata No. 3 in C major, 438
Sonata No. 4 in C minor, 438
Michalowski, Aleksander, 156, 159, 180, 188, 213, 253
Michelangeli, Arturo Benedetti, 32, 153, 180–82, 183, 205, 279, 387
Michelangelo, 113, 222, 354
Midsummer Night's Dream, A (Shakespeare), 331
Mignone, Francisco:
compositions of, 438
Four Sonatinas, 438
Lenda brasileira, 438
Sonata No. 1, 438
Mikhashoff, Yvar, 439
Mikuli, Karl, 176, 180, 182, 219–20
Milan Conservatory, 100, 204, 205
Milhaud, Darius, 436
compositions of, 438
Piano Concerto No. 1, 438
Piano Concerto No. 2, 438
Saudades do Brasil, 438
Miller, Robert, 327, 439, 447
Mills, Florence, 437
Mills, Sebastian Bach, 182
Mills College, 200
Mitchell, Alice Levine, 354
Mitropoulos, Dimitri, 148, 356
Mitropoulos Piano Competition, 32
Moiseiwitsch, Benno, 21, 158, 182, 207, 279
Mompou, Federico:
Charmes, 369
compositions of, 369
Eleven Preludes, 369
Impressiones intimas, 369
Suburbis, 369
Twelve Canciones y danzas, 369
Variaciones sobre un tema de Chopin, 369

Monet, Claude, 132, 328, 330–331
Moniuszko, Stanislaw, *Halka,* 255
Monsaingeon, Bruno, 328
Montagu-Nathan, M., 413
Montreal International Competition, 192, 202
Moore, Gerald, 182, 249
Moravec, Ivan, 183
Morawetz, Oskar, Fantasy, 116
Morton, Frederic, 397
Moscheles, Ignaz, 47–48, 50, 54, 68–69, 77, 81, 126, 139, 143, 145, 156, 158, 168, 170, 175, 177–78, 180, 182–84, 199, 202, 206, 213, 247, 252, 256, 265, 310, 315, 366
Etude Op. 70, No. 3, 308
Piano Concerto in G minor, 184
Sonate mélancolique, 184
Twenty-four Etudes, 184
Variations on the *Alexander March,* 184
Moscow Central School of Music, 202
Moscow Conservatory, 36, 85, 91, 97, 103, 107, 142, 153, 160, 162, 172, 179, 188, 189, 192–94, 202, 209, 214, 226, 239, 246, 273–74, 276, 443
Moszkowski, Moritz, 127, 155, 184–85, 190, 212, 232, 264, 355
Etincelles, 138
Etude in A-flat major, 138
Etude in F major, 138
Piano Concerto in E major, 43
Spanish Caprice, 129
Waltz in E major, 171
Motta, José Vianna Da, 59, 185, 225
Vals caprichosa, 185
Mottl, Felix, 73
Mozart, Franz Xaver, 198
Mozart, Leopold, 185
Mozart, Maria Anna, 185
Mozart, Wolfgang Amadeus, 17–20, 34–35, 39, 41, 44–45, 46–47, 52, 56, 68, 70–71, 72, 75, 77, 82–83, 86–87, 101, 113–15, 119–

Mozart, Wolfgang Amadeus, *continued*
120, 122–23, 139–40, 144, 149, 153, 166, 170, 177, 181, 185–87, 199, 202, 204, 206, 208, 213–214, 219, 227, 229, 231–232, 238, 251, 264, 272, 275, 280, 292, 345, 365, 390
Adagio in B minor, 134, 377
"Là ci darem la mano," 66–68, 237
La Clemenza di Tito, 45
compositions of, 369–76
Don Giovanni, 43, 52, 66–68, 97, 218–19, 239, 246, 263, 358
Fantasia in C minor, K. 396, 377
Fantasia in C minor, K. 475, 95, 377
Fantasia in D minor, 35, 241, 377
The Magic Flute, 325
The Marriage of Figaro, 178, 373
Piano Concerto No. 1 in F major, 185
Piano Concerto No. 2 in B-flat major, 185
Piano Concerto No. 3 in D major, 185
Piano Concerto No. 4 in G major, 185
Piano Concerto No. 5 in D major, 185
Piano Concerto No. 12 in A major, 60
Piano Concerto No. 15 in B-flat major, 48
Piano Concerto No. 17 in G major, 108, 148
Piano Concerto No. 18 in B-flat major, 198
Piano Concerto No. 20 in D minor, 94, 178, 201
Piano Concerto No. 21 in C major, 32, 162, 253
Piano Concerto No. 22 in E-flat major, 94
Piano Concerto No. 23 in A major, 108, 132, 134, 264
Piano Concerto No. 24 in C minor, 296

Piano Concerto No. 25 in C major, 78, 94
Piano Sonatas, 49, 55, 89, 133, 157, 214, 375–77
Requiem in D minor, 67, 320, 375
Rondo in A minor, 35, 224, 243, 262, 377
Rondo in D major, 134, 241, 377
Sonata No. 8 in A minor, 37, 154, 163
Sonata No. 10 in C major, 134
Sonata No. 11 in A major, 134
Sonata No. 12 in F major, 134
Sonata No. 13 in B-flat major, 134
Sonata No. 14 in C minor, 35, 243
Sonata No. 16 in B-flat major, 183
Twenty-five Piano Concerti, 23, 31, 49, 64, 78, 89, 103, 123–25, 154, 157, 186–87, 201, 207, 214, 233, 241–43, 272, 370–75 (discussed), 398
Variations on "Ah, vous dirai-je, maman," 377
Munch, Charles, 75, 162
Munich Competition, 208
Münz, Mieczyslaw, 38, 187
Murchie, Guy, 43
Musical Memories (Upton), 111
Musical Ornamentation (Dannreuther), 81
Musical Thoughts and Afterthoughts (Brendel), 54
Musicescu, Florica, 150, 162
Music for Piano and Orchestra (Hinson), 126
Music Ho! (Lambert), 437
Music-Study in Germany (Fay), 91
Musique française de piano, La (Cortot), 74
Mussorgsky, Modest, 17
compositions of, 378
The Fair at Sorochinsk, 388
Pictures at an Exhibition, 93, 137, 149, 180, 216, 253, 378

My Many Years (Rubinstein), 222
My Young Years (Rubinstein), 222

Nádas, István, 187
Naples Conservatory, 92, 171, 175
Napoleon I, Emperor of France, 18–19, 87, 166, 219
Nasedkin, Alexei, 188
Nat, Yves, 53, 84, 146, 188, 228
National Gallery, 124
Naumburg Award, 51, 148, 151, 158, 174, 246
NBC Symphony, 252, 270, 397
Neate, Charles, 188
Neefe, Gottlob, 44–45
Neuhaus, Heinrich, 51, 56, 103–4, 106, 156, 172, 188, 201, 205, 212, 214, 216, 246, 274, 411, 420
Neuhaus, Stanislav, 142, 174, 188
Neupert, Edmund, 188–89, 238
New England Conservatory, 158, 173, 238, 244
Newman, Ernest, 83, 341, 364
Newman, William S., 87, 148, 189, 357, 362, 407
New Orleans, La., 109
New Orleans Philharmonic, 88
New York College of Music, 96
New York Philharmonic, 52, 67, 91, 112, 121, 130, 137, 143, 148, 180, 268
New York Sun, 161, 190
New York Times, 72, 132, 161, 204, 215
Ney, Elly, 189, 230
Nicholas I, Czar of Russia, 166
Nicolaiev, Leonid, 189, 214, 226, 248, 273
Niecks, Frederick, 306, 310, 312, 316–17, 321, 324
Nielsen, Carl, 248
Chaconne, 378–79
compositions of, 378–79
Suite, 378–79
Symphonic Suite, 378–79
Theme and Variations, 378–379

Three Piano Pieces, 378–79
Twenty-five Pieces for Young and Old, 379
Nijinsky, Waslaw, 113
Nikisch, Arthur, 224
Nikolayeva, Tatiana, 107, 189
Nineteenth Century Piano Music (Dale), 80
Nineteenth Century Piano Music (Long), 171
Nissman, Barbara, 189
Nojima, Minoru, 189
Nono, Luigi, 52, 205
Notes of a Pianist (Gottschalk), 110
Novaes, Guiomar, 189–91, 201
Novitskaya, Yekaterina, 381
Novotný, Jan, 191
Nyiregyházi, Ervin, 191

Oborin, Lev, 36, 142, 192
"Ode to the West Wind" (Shelley), 331
Offenbach, Jacques, 324, 393
Offergeld, Robert, 110–11, 385
Ogdon, John, 31, 37, 192, 309, 319, 323, 352, 361, 442
Oginski, Michal, 318
Ohe, Adèle aus der, 192, 423
Ohlsson, Garrick, 109, 192–93
On Piano Playing (Sándor), 229
Oppens, Ursula, 193, 441
Orcagna, Andrea, 357
Orchestra Hall, Chicago, 113
Orlov, Nicolas, 193
Ormandy, Eugene, 42, 130, 137, 157, 229
Ornstein, Leo, 193
À la chinoise, 193
Sonata No. 4, 193
The Three Moods, 193
Orozco, Rafael, 193–94
Ortiz, Cristina, 194
Osborne, George A., 69, 147, 194
La Pluie des perles, 194
Ousset, Cécile, 70, 194
Ozawa, Seiji, 214

Pabst, Louis, 107, 117, 194
Pabst, Paul, 66, 142, 194–95, 206
Paraphrase on Tchaikovsky's *Eugene Onegin,* 66

Pachmann, Vladimir de, 21, 23, 24, 80, 106, 195, 197, 220, 246
pactytion, 124
Paderewski, Ignacy Jan, 21–22, 44, 90, 98, 132, 145, 158, 173, 190, 195–98, 205, 220–22, 230–31, 234, 237, 246, 251–53, 351, 405
Manru, 196
Minuet in G, 90, 196
Piano Concerto in A minor, 90, 270
Polish Fantasy, 214
Sonata in E-flat minor, 192
Symphony in B minor, 196
Variations and Fugue, 196
Paderewski Medal, 82
Paganini, Niccolò, 19, 67, 137, 165–67, 181, 351–52
Capricci per violino solo, 166, 266, 404–5
Caprice No. 24 for Violin, 351, 387
Palmer, Robert:
compositions of, 438–39
Sonata No. 2, 438–39
Toccata Ostinato, 438
Paradis, Maria Theresa, 198
Paris Conservatoire, 21, 29, 30, 51, 63–65, 70, 73–74, 81, 84, 86–88, 90, 108–9, 123, 141, 147, 153, 157, 159, 171, 173–74, 176, 188–89, 200, 201, 206–8, 217, 218, 227–28, 231–232, 235, 240, 252, 254, 263–64, 267, 271, 275, 367
Parish-Alvars, Elias, 257
Paris Opera, 130, 165
Parkin, Eric, 434
Pasternak, Alexander, 239
Patti, Adelina, 190
Pattison, Lee, 173, 198
Pauer, Ernst, 154, 179, 198, 275
Pauer, Max, 146, 198
Pavlova, Anna, 98
Peabody Conservatory, 95, 156
Pearl Records, 197
Pennario, Leonard, 198, 264
Perabo, Ernst, 199, 269
Perahia, Murray, 199–200

Perle, George:
Ballade, 108
compositions of, 439
Serenade, 164
Six Etudes, 439
Six New Etudes, 439
Six Preludes, 439
Toccata, 439
Perlemuter, Vlado, 74, 200, 264
Perry, Edward Baxter, 200
Perry, John, 200
Persichetti, Vincent, 52, 149
compositions of, 439
Poems, 439
Petrarch, 354
Petri, Egon, 22, 23, 31, 59, 144, 159, 174, 192, 200–201, 270, 280, 356
Philadelphia Orchestra, 151, 157, 172, 418
Philharmonic Society of London, 32, 188
Philipp, Isidor, 81, 153, 156, 176, 190–91, 201, 227, 253, 267, 445
Phillips Gallery, 112
Pianistes cèlébres (Marmontel), 174
Pianist's Problems, The (Newman), 189
Piano Pedagogy (Rubinstein), 226
Piano Works of Claude Debussy, The (Schmitz), 232
Pierné, Gabriel:
Piano Concerto, 439
Variations in C minor, 439
Pijper, Willem:
compositions of, 439
Piano Concerto, 439
Pinnock, Trevor, 396
Pires, Maria João, 201
Pishna, Johann, 201
Pissarro, Camille, 328
Pixis, Johann Peter, 201–2
Plaidy, Louis, 57, 202
Planté, Francis, 21, 174, 202
Plato, 166
Pleyel, Camille, 202
Pleyel, Maria Félicité Moke, 147, 202, 316
Poe, Edgar Allen, 283, 311
Pogorelich, Ivo, 283, 202–4
Poland, 197–98, 318, 319
Pollack, Daniel, 72, 204

Pollini, Francesco, 204
  *Trentadue esercizi in forma
    di toccata,* 204
Pollini, Maurizio, 55, 205–6,
  234, 262, 333
Pommier, Jean-Bernard, 206
Ponce, Manuel:
  compositions of, 440
  Preludio trágico, 440
  Sonata No. 2, 440
  *Twenty Easy Pieces for Pi-
    ano,* 440
Ponti, Michael, 31, 170, 177,
  206, 255, 257
Poot, Marcel:
  compositions of, 440
  Piano Concerto, 440
  Sonata in C major, 440
  Sonatine, 440
  Suite, 440
Potter, Cipriani, 182, 206,
  275
Pouishnov, Lev, 90, 207
Poulenc, Francis, 144, 163,
  223, 254, 264–65, 305,
  436, 443
  Aubade for Piano and Eigh-
    teen Instruments, 380
  compositions of, 379–80
  Concerto for Two Pianos
    and Orchestra, 91
  Pastourelle, 138
  Piano Concerto, 380
  Les Soirées de Nazelles, 379–
    380
  Suite française, 83, 380
  Toccata, 138
Powell, John, 207
  Rapsodie nègre for Piano and
    Orchestra, 207
  Sonata Teutonica, 207
Practicing the Piano (Merrick),
  179
Pradère, Louis, 123, 141, 207
Prague Conservatory, 240
Presidential Medal of Freedom,
  132
Pressler, Menahem, 207
Pressman, Matvei, 226
Preston, Robert, 109
Previn, André, 207
Princeton University, 218
Prokofiev, Sergei, 23, 53, 90,
  147, 148–49, 150, 189,
  203, 207, 211, 215, 223,
  229, 411, 443, 445

  Complete Solo Piano Music,
    380–81
  compositions of, 380–84
  Concerto No. 4 in B-flat ma-
    jor for Piano, Left Hand
    Alone, and Orchestra, 43,
    243, 272, 383
  Piano Concerto No. 1 in D-
    flat major, 207, 382–83
  Piano Concerto No. 2 in G
    minor, 96, 383
  Piano Concerto No. 3 in C
    major, 33, 56, 72, 117,
    207, 253, 268, 383
  Piano Concerto No. 5 in G
    major, 383–84
  Romeo and Juliet, 33
  Sonata No. 1 in F minor, 381
  Sonata No. 2 in D minor,
    117, 381
  Sonata No. 3 in A minor,
    117, 204, 381
  Sonata No. 4 in C minor, 381
  Sonata No. 5 in C major, 381
  Sonata No. 6 in A major, 72,
    138, 204, 247, 381–82
  Sonata No. 7 in B-flat major,
    116, 133, 138, 187, 382
  Sonata No. 8 in B-flat major,
    48, 103, 138, 382
  Sonata No. 9 in C major,
    216, 382
  Toccata, 138
Proksch, Josef, 208
Proust, Marcel, 113, 222
Pruckner, Dionys, 208
Prudent, Émile, 208, 275
  Piano Concerto in B-flat ma-
    jor, 208
Pugno, Raoul, 159, 176, 208,
  235
  Les Nuits, 208
  Sonata, 208
Pujol, Juan, 173, 208, 264

Queen Elizabeth Competition,
  36, 86, 95, 96, 103, 179,
  440
Queffelec, Anne, 208

Rachmaninoff, Sergei, 13, 22–
  23, 37, 44, 53, 67, 69,
  98–99, 113–14, 117, 123,
  126, 128, 136, 139, 148,

  160, 161–62, 182, 184,
  195, 197, 206, 209–12,
  217, 221, 243, 245–46,
  255, 270–71, 276, 279,
  321, 323, 343, 352, 364,
  366, 411, 413
  compositions of, 384–88
  Etude-tableau in C major,
    137, 248, 268
  Etude-tableau in E-flat mi-
    nor, 137, 248, 268
  Five Pieces, 384
  Nine Etudes-tableaux, Op.
    33, 385–86
  Nine Etudes-tableaux, Op.
    39, 385–86
  Piano Concerto No. 1 in F-
    sharp minor, 73, 143, 216,
    222, 245–46, 263, 386
  Piano Concerto No. 2 in C
    minor, 52, 101, 142, 149,
    209, 222, 225, 263, 386–
    387
  Piano Concerto No. 3 in D
    minor, 15, 40, 48, 72–74,
    83, 95, 105, 119, 130,
    137, 143, 149–50, 154,
    179, 193–94, 209, 222,
    244, 246, 263–64, 266,
    268, 387
  Piano Concerto No. 4 in G
    minor, 181, 222, 246, 263,
    387
  Prelude in C-sharp minor,
    209
  Prelude in G minor, 129, 137
  Preludes, 90, 151, 216, 245
  *Rhapsody on a Theme of
    Paganini,* 32, 149, 157,
    225, 351, 387
  Seven Pieces, 384
  Six Moments musicaux, 48,
    384
  Sonata No. 1 in D minor,
    269, 385
  Sonata No. 2 in B-flat minor,
    56, 72, 133, 137–38, 174,
    250, 385
  Ten Preludes, 385
  Thirteen Preludes, 385
  Transcription of Scherzo
    from Mendelssohn's *A
    Midsummer Night's
    Dream,* 211
  Transcriptions, 387–88
  Variations on a Theme by

Chopin (*Chopin* Variations), 91, 384–85
Variations on a Theme by Corelli (*Corelli* Variations), 386
Raff, Joachim:
compositions of, 440
La Fileuse, 250
Piano Concerto in C minor, 143, 440
Suite in D minor, 90
Raieff, Josef, 213
Ramann, Lina, 168
Rameau, Jean-Philippe, 305
Ramey, Philip:
compositions of, 440
Leningrad Rag, or Mutations on Scott Joplin, 440
Piano Fantasy, 440
Sonata No. 4, 440
Ránki, Dezsö, 146, 213
Raphael, 163, 354
Raphling, Sam, 420
Rapp, Siegfried, 383
Ravel, Maurice, 53, 83, 91, 96, 102–3, 117, 118–19, 150, 157, 193, 200, 215, 228, 246, 264, 271, 287, 305, 307, 336, 344, 352–53, 378–80, 392, 430
Alborada del gracioso, 163
Complete Solo Piano Music, 388
compositions of, 388–91
Concerto for the Left Hand and Orchestra in D major, 56, 75, 268, 272, 383, 391
Gaspard de la nuit, 37, 40, 41, 49, 102, 181, 204, 268, 389–90, 421
Jeux d'eau, 75, 388
Le Gibet, 204
Miroirs, 389
Ondine, 44, 172, 204, 332
Pavane pour une infante défunte, 388
Piano Concerto in G major, 42, 48, 81, 88, 171, 181, 390–91
Scarbo, 39, 101, 139, 204, 286–87
Sonatine, 64, 75, 183, 388–389
Le Tombeau de Couperin, 56, 390
La Valse, 390

Valses nobles et sentimentales, 39, 223, 390
Ravina, Jean Henri, 213, 275
Etude de style, 213
Rawsthorne, Alan, 306–7
compositions of, 440
Four Romantic Pieces, 440
Piano Concerto No. 1, 152, 440
Piano Concerto No. 2, 440
Sonatina, 440
Reger, Max:
Aus meinem Tagebuch, 391–392
compositions of, 391–92
Piano Concerto in F minor, 243, 392
Variations and Fugue on a Theme by J. S. Bach (*Bach* Variations), 243, 391
Variations and Fugue on a Theme by Telemann (*Telemann* Variations), 52, 391
Régnier, Henri de, 390
Reichardt, J. F., 46
Reinagle, Alexander, 213
Reinecke, Carl, 81, 141, 154, 156, 180, 213–14, 217–218, 238, 252, 256, 265, 271, 369
Piano Concerto No. 1 in F-sharp minor, 214
Reinecke, Johann Peter, 213
Reiner, Fritz, 103, 127, 134, 137, 224
Reisenauer, Alfred, 52, 154, 169, 214
Reisenberg, Nadia, 108, 214, 253
Reisenstein, Franz, 214
Rellstab, Ludwig, 68, 168, 178, 290, 315
"Remembering Rachmaninoff," (Baily), 211
Renard, Rosita, 214
Rhoads, Shirley, 149
Rich, Alan, 316
Richner, Thomas, 214
Richter, Hans, 73, 220
Richter, Jean Paul, 403
Richter, Sviatoslav, 188, 214–216, 248, 280, 378, 382, 408–9, 412, 420
Richter-Haaser, Hans, 216
Ricordi, 171, 395
Riefling, Robert, 216–17

Ries, Ferdinand, 45, 51, 165, 217, 373
Piano Concerto No. 3 in C-sharp minor, 217
Rifkin, Joshua, 145
Rimbaud, Arthur, 433
Rimsky-Korsakov, Nicolai, 139
The Flight of the Bumblebee, 80, 388
Ringeissen, Bernard, 171, 217
Ringold, Berthe, 103
Risler, Édouard, 73, 84, 91, 217, 334, 342
Ritter, Théodore, 217
Les Courriers, 217
Rivé-King, Julie, 213, 217–18, 423
Robert, Richard, 218, 241
Robinson, Francis, 212
Rochberg, George:
Bagatelles, 440
Carnival Music, 440
compositions of, 440
Sonata-Fantasia, 440
Rodriguez, Santiago, 174
Rogé, Pascal, 218
Rogers, Herbert, 445
Rogers, Ronald, 431
Ronald, Sir Landon, 195
Roosevelt, Franklin D., 197
Rorem, Ned, 150
compositions of, 441
Piano Concerto, 172, 441
Sonata No. 2, 441
Three Barcarolles, 441
Rose, Jerome, 218, 245
Rosellen, Henri, 218
Rosen, Charles, 23, 218–19, 286, 294, 298, 403
Rosenberg, Hilding:
compositions of, 441
Sonata No. 2, 441
Sonata No. 3, 441
Theme and Variations, 441
Rosenfeld, Paul, 125, 193, 340
Rosenthal, Moriz, 22–23, 108, 161, 167, 169, 176, 218, 219–20, 230, 279, 360
Carnaval de Vienne, 220
Rossini, Gioacchino:
The Barber of Seville, 257
La Cenerentola, 271
compositions of, 441
Moses, 257
Semiramide, 271
Sins of My Old Age, 441

Rostropovich, Mstislav, 244
Roussel, Albert, 144, 436
  compositions of, 392
  Piano Concerto, 392
  Prélude et fugue, 392
  Sonatine, 392
  Suite for Piano, 240, 392
  Trois Pièces pour piano, 392
Royal Academy of Music, 48,
  108, 121, 126, 154, 172,
  176, 180, 198, 247, 275
Royal Albert Hall, 105
Royal College of Music, 171,
  200
Royal Manchester College of
  Music, 192, 252
Royal Philharmonic Society, 77
Royal Toronto Conservatory,
  112
Rózsa, Miklós, Piano Concerto,
  198
Rubin Academy, 56, 214
Rubinstein, Anton, 21–22, 24,
  42, 48, 50, 57–58, 63, 69,
  100, 111, 120, 123, 126–
  128, 140, 167, 175, 205,
  209, 212, 220–22, 226,
  232–33, 236, 257, 260,
  264–65, 286, 316, 319,
  323, 351, 405–6
  Arrangement of Beethoven's
    Turkish March, 130
  Kamenoi-Ostrow, 222
  Melody in F major, 222
  Piano Concerto No. 4 in D
    minor, 67, 127, 129, 158,
    222
  Piano Concerto No. 5 in E-
    flat major, 60, 160
  Romance in E-flat major, 222
  Symphony No. 2 *(Ocean),*
    222
Rubinstein, Arthur, 23, 30, 34,
  43, 53, 62, 69, 78, 86, 91,
  105, 107, 128, 202, 205,
  211, 217, 222–25, 227,
  239, 253, 269, 279, 301,
  336, 411, 419, 420, 424
Rubinstein, Beryl, 156, 225–26
Rubinstein, Joseph, 80
Rubinstein, Nikolai, 226, 230,
  245, 286, 422
Rudolf, Archduke of Austria,
  293
Rudorff, Ernst, 105
Ruggles, Carl, *Evocations (Four*

Chants for Piano), 441
Ruiz, Adrian, 436
Rummel, Franz, 226
Rummel, Walter, 226
Ruskin, John, 19
Rzewski, Frederic:
  compositions of, 441–42
  *Four North American Bal-
    lads,* 441–42
  *The People United Will
    Never Be Defeated (Thirty-
    six Variations on a Chilean
    Song),* 193, 441
  Variations on "No Place to
    Go but Around," 442

Sabaneyev, Leonid, 365
Safonov, Vassily, 54, 160, 162,
  189, 226
Sahr, Hadassah, 348
Said, Edward, 114
St. Louis Symphony, 101
St. Patrick's Cathedral, 197
St. Petersburg Conservatory,
  90, 100, 189, 193, 207,
  214, 221, 229, 248, 264,
  273, 382, 417
Saint-Saëns, Camille, 21, 70,
  102, 105, 168, 226–27,
  243, 251, 254, 369, 390,
  430, 439
  Allegro appassionato, 194,
    227
  *Caprice sur les airs de ballet
    d'Alceste,* 212
  Complete Solo Piano Music,
    393
  compositions of, 393–94
  Concerto No. 1 in D major,
    227, 393
  Concerto No. 2 in G minor,
    67, 81, 225, 227, 393
  Concerto No. 3 in E-flat ma-
    jor, 82, 227, 393
  Concerto No. 4 in C minor,
    64, 74–75, 85, 227, 393
  Concerto No. 5 in F major,
    84, 227, 393
  Danse macabre, 138
  Etude en forme de valse,
    198, 227
  Five concerti, 393–94
  The Swan, 107
  Toccata, 227
Salieri, Antonio, 165, 186

Salle Noblesse, 127
Salzman, Eric, 382, 426, 442
Samaroff, Olga, 50, 82, 148,
  159, 227–28, 250, 261,
  268
Samuel, Harold, 81, 228
Sancan, Pierre, 228
Sand, George, 30, 67, 69,
  321
Sanders, Samuel, 228
Sándor, György, 189, 228–29,
  381
Sangiorgio, Victor, 444
Sanromá, Jesus María, 229
Santa Cecilia Academy, 64–65
Sapellnikov, Vassily, 54, 229
Saperton, David, 51, 96, 150,
  229–30, 246
Satie, Erik, 70, 441
  compositions of, 394
  Piano music, 394
Sauer, Emil von, 22–23, 29,
  38, 53, 123, 145, 174,
  226, 230, 235
Sauguet, Henri, 436–37
Scaramuzza, Vincenzo, 32
Scarlatti, Domenico, 18, 23,
  43, 64, 70, 82, 121, 133,
  138, 170, 171, 176, 181,
  184, 212, 266, 268, 274,
  285, 442
  compositions of, 395–96
  Sonatas, 43–44, 52, 104,
    133, 203, 395–96
Scharrer, Irene, 176, 230
Scharwenka, Xaver, 155, 160,
  185, 206, 230–31
  Piano Concerto No. 1 in B-
    flat minor, 230–31, 270
  Polish Dance in E-flat minor,
    230–31
  Theme and Variations, 231
Schauffler, Robert Haven, 404
Schein, Ann, 187
Schelling, Ernest, 176, 184, 231
  *Impressions from an Artist's
    Life* for Piano and Orches-
    tra, 231
  Nocturne à Ragaze, 231
Schiff, Andras, 146, 231–32
Schiller, Friedrich von, 19, 167
Schindler, Anton Felix, 183
Schioler, Victor, 144
Schlegel, Friedrich von, 407
Schmidt, Franz, 383
Schmitt, Aloys, 232

Schmitz, E. Robert, 232, 329–333

Schnabel, Artur, 23, 29, 34, 36, 39, 47, 55, 77, 94, 95, 96, 120, 123, 146, 154, 158, 163, 173–74, 180, 187, 192, 198, 205, 213, 228–229, 232–35, 245, 262, 265, 267, 272, 279, 379, 401

Schnabel, Karl Ulrich, 235

Schneider, Alexander, 243

Schneider, Friedrich, 297

Schnitzer, Germaine, 184, 235

Schoenberg, Arnold, 143, 157–158, 193, 205, 213, 219, 363, 416, 444
compositions of, 396–97
Five Little Piano Pieces, 396–397
Piano Concerto, 38, 116, 241, 252, 397
Piano Piece, Op. 33a, 396–397
Piano Piece, Op. 33b, 396–397
Six Little Piano Pieces, 396
Suite, 116, 396–97
Three Piano Pieces, 396–397

Schola Cantorum, 240

Schonberg, Harold, 128, 212, 230, 233, 358

Schröter, Johann Samuel, 235

Schub, André-Michel, 235

Schubert, Franz, 17, 23, 32, 34–35, 41, 46, 51, 55, 59, 77–78, 94, 103, 144, 148, 152, 158, 167, 172, 188, 218, 231–34, 237, 260, 266, 268, 272–73, 341, 365, 382, 390–91
Allegretto in C minor, 401
Brooklet, The, 388
compositions of, 397–402
Drei Klavierstücke, 93, 401
Fantasia in C major (Wanderer Fantasy), 34, 37, 151, 187, 199, 216, 224, 357, 398, 400–401
Four Impromptus, D. 899, 401
Four Impromptus, D. 935, 401
Impromptu No. 1 in C minor, D. 899, 238

Impromptu No. 2 in E-flat major, D. 899, 134, 146
Impromptu No. 3 in B-flat major, D. 935, 134, 170
Impromptu No. 3 in G-flat major, D. 899, 134, 163
Impromptu No. 4 in A-flat major, D. 899, 134, 212
Lieder, 212, 360
Marche militaire, 134
Piano Trio in B-flat major, 74
Six Moments musicaux, 41, 105, 401
Soirée de Vienne, 134
Sonata in A major, D. 664, 67, 205, 399
Sonata in A major, D. 959, 84, 141, 205, 243, 400
Sonata in A minor, D. 537, 398
Sonata in A minor, D. 784, 93, 205, 249, 399
Sonata in A minor, D. 845, 93, 154, 205, 216, 399
Sonata in B-flat major, D. 960, 35, 42, 84, 89, 108, 121, 133–34, 154, 205, 216, 224, 243, 248, 400
Sonata in B major, D. 575, 398
Sonata in C major (Unfinished Sonata), D. 840, 216, 399
Sonata in C minor, D. 958, 35, 117, 205, 216, 400
Sonata in D major, D. 850, 37, 78, 142, 205, 399
Sonata in E-flat major, D. 568, 241, 398
Sonata in G major (Sonata-Fantasy), D. 894, 37, 84, 205, 263, 268, 399–400
Waltzes, 402
"Der Wanderer," 60, 400

Schulhoff, Julius, 235–36, 260
Le Chant du berger, 235–36

Schulz-Evler, Adolf, 236

Schumacher, Thomas, 432

Schumann, Clara Wieck, 20, 52, 57–58, 81–82, 97, 103, 123, 143, 157, 178, 200, 233, 236–38, 255, 257, 264, 270, 351, 404–407, 410

Schumann, Elisabeth, 212

Schumann, Robert, 13–14, 19–20, 31–32, 41, 44, 47–48, 52, 55–56, 59, 64, 66–67, 69, 77, 81–82, 87–89, 90–91, 111, 122–24, 126, 140, 147–48, 157, 167–168, 171, 176–78, 184, 198, 202, 211, 215, 218–219, 251, 253, 260, 265, 266–67, 270, 294, 302–3, 313, 318, 320–21, 324–325, 327, 329, 336, 341, 343, 365, 378, 380, 391, 399–400, 412, 414, 436
Des Abends, 197
Album for the Young, 409
Allegro in B minor, 404–405
Arabeske in C major, 135, 201, 408
Blumenstück, 408
Bunte Blätter, 300
Carnaval, 13, 36, 42, 64, 66–67, 75, 82–83, 97, 107, 152, 181–82, 184–185, 190, 212, 222, 229, 244, 248–50, 268, 405
compositions of, 402–10
Davidsbündlertänze, 35–36, 75, 151, 404
Fantasia in C major, 53, 78, 83, 95, 135, 199, 216, 224, 237, 248, 357, 407
Fantasiestücke Op. 12, 35, 40, 144, 199, 224, 405–6
Fantasiestücke, Op. 111, 409–10
Faschingsschwank aus Wein, 181, 409
Humoreske, 35, 82–83, 108, 133, 135–36, 216, 408
Impromptus on a Theme of Clara Wieck, 404
In der Nacht, 224
Intermezzi, 89, 404
Kinderscenen, 75, 97, 103, 136, 151, 182, 407
Kreisleriana, 33, 75, 83, 129, 135, 151, 229, 306, 407
Lieder, 360
Nachstücke, 408–9
Novellette, No. 8 in F-sharp minor, 82
Novelletten, 408
Papillons, 75, 151, 190, 199, 403–4

471

Schumann, Robert, *continued*
  Piano Concerto in A minor,
    60, 72, 74–75, 125, 154,
    163, 190, 225, 270, 344,
    410
  Piano Trio No. 1 in D mi-
    nor, 74
  Presto passionato, 135
  The Prophet Bird, 190, 241
  Quintet in E-flat major, 100
  Scherzo, Gigue, Romanze,
    and Fughetta, 409
  Six Studies after Caprices by
    Paganini, 404
  Sonata in F minor, 136, 155,
    406–7
  Sonata in F-sharp minor,
    205, 405, 422
  Sonata in G minor, 33, 118,
    216, 408
  Spring Night, 162
  Symphonic Etudes, 35, 37,
    67, 75, 97, 118, 125, 151,
    199, 203–4, 244, 269,
    300, 406
  Three Romances, 409
  Toccata in C major, 43, 135,
    161, 204, 238, 352, 404
  Träumerei, 136
  Traumeswirren, 135
  Twelve Concert Etudes after
    Caprices of Paganini, 405
  Variations on the Name
    Abegg (*Abegg* Variations),
    89, 299, 403
  Waldscenen, 241, 268, 409
  Warum?, 197
Schunke, Ludwig, 238
Schütt, Eduard, 232, 238
Schwalb, Miklos, 238
Schwarzkopf, Elisabeth, 116,
  182
Schweitzer, Albert, 113–14
Schytte, Ludvig, 238–39
  Piano Concerto, 239
Scott, Cyril, 192
  compositions of, 442
  Lotus Land, 442
  Piano Concerto No. 1 in C
    major, 442
  Sonata No. 1, 117, 442
Scriabin, Alexander, 23, 44, 91,
    123, 125, 174, 193, 213,
    215, 221, 226, 239–40,
    250, 253, 274, 276, 353,
    381, 419, 421, 444

Allegro appassionato in E-flat
  minor, 412
compositions of, 410–16
Concerto in F-sharp minor,
  188, 209, 416
Eight Etudes, 412
Etude Op. 2, No. 1 in C-
  sharp minor, 138, 411
Etude Op. 8, No. 11 in B-flat
  minor, 138
Etude Op. 8, No. 12 in D-
  sharp minor, 43, 239
Etude Op. 42, No. 5 in C-
  sharp minor, 138
Fantasia in B minor, 48, 107,
  209, 413
Five Preludes, 413
Flames sombres, 248
Guirlandes, 248
Nine Mazurkas, 411–12
Nocturne in D-flat major for
  the Left Hand Alone, 239,
  412
Poème-nocturne, 248, 413
Poème satanique, 248, 413
Poème tragique, 413
Poems, 203
Sonata No. 2-Sonata Fantasy
  in G-sharp minor, 81, 203
Sonata No. 3 in F-sharp mi-
  nor, 116, 138
Sonata No. 4 in F-sharp ma-
  jor, 188, 248
Sonata No. 5 in F-sharp ma-
  jor, 116, 133, 138, 179,
  209, 211, 216, 224, 248
Sonata No. 6, 37, 155, 216
Sonata No. 9 (*The Black
  Mass*), 133, 138, 248
Sonata No. 10 (*Trill* Sonata),
  133, 138, 248
Symphony No. 4 (*Poem of
  Ecstasy*), 138, 415
Ten Mazurkas, 411–12
Ten Piano Sonatas, 206,
  414–16
Three Etudes, 412
Twelve Etudes, 90, 155, 412
Twenty-four Preludes, 40,
  101, 412–13
Two Dances, 414
Two Mazurkas, 411–12
Two Poems, Op. 32, 413
Two Poems, Op. 69, 138,
  414
Valse in A-flat major, 413

Vers la flamme, 138, 414
Searle, Humphrey, 351–52,
  354
Sebök, György, 240
Seeling, Hans, 240
  Barcarolle, 240
  Concert Etudes, 240
  Lorlei, 240
  Memories of an Artist, 240
Segall, Bernardo, 246
Seidlhofer, Bruno, 97
Seiss, Isidor, 240
Selva, Blanche, 240, 442
Sembrich, Marcella, 127, 190
Senancour, Etienne de, 354
Serkin, Peter, 240–41, 447
Serkin, Rudolf, 56, 108, 117,
  142, 155, 157, 158, 164,
  175, 194, 218, 235, 240–
  243, 250, 279, 383, 392,
  446
Serov, Alexander, 167
Sessions, Roger, 431
  compositions of, 416–17
  Sonata No. 1, 416–17, 433
  Sonata No. 2, 416–17
  Sonata No. 3, 416–17
Seven Mysteries of Life, The
  (Murchie), 43
Séverac, Déodat de, 264, 282
  Baigneuses au soleil, 442
  Cerdaña Suite, 442
  Le Chant de la terre, 442
  Cinq Etudes pittoresques,
    442
  compositions of, 442
  En vacances, 442
  Sous les lauriers roses, 442
Seyfried, Ignaz von, 45
Sgambati, Giovanni, 52, 243
  "Melody" from Gluck's *Or-
    feo,* 159, 243
  Piano Concerto in G minor,
    243
Sgouros, Dimitris, 244
Shakespeare, William, 291, 331
Sharon, Boaz, 437
Shattuck, Arthur, 244
Shaw, George Bernard, 17, 81,
  118, 120, 229, 238, 251,
  365
Shchedrin, Rodion:
  compositions of, 442–43
  Piano Concerto No. 1, 443
  Piano Concerto No. 3, 443
  Sonata No. 1, 443

472

Twenty-five Polyphonic Tet-
  rad, 443
Shelley, Mary, 19
Shelley, Percy Bysshe, 313
Sheridan, Frank, 244
Sherman, Russell, 244
Sherwood, William, 244–45
Shorr, Lev, 164
Shostakovich, Dmitri:
  compositions of, 417–18
  Piano Concerto No. 1, with
    Trumpet and Strings, 118,
    164, 418
  Piano Concerto No. 2, 48,
    418
  Prelude No. 5 in D major,
    149
  Sonata No. 2 in B minor,
    418
  Twenty-four Preludes and
    Fugues, 189, 207, 273,
    417
Shure, Leonard, 174, 218, 245
Sibelius, Jean, 116
  compositions of, 443
  Sonata, 443
  Sonatines, 443
  Symphony No. 4 in A minor,
    284, 443
Siegel, Jeffrey, 245
Siegmeister, Elie, 174
  American Sonata, 443
  compositions of, 443
  On This Ground, 443
  Theme and Variations No.,
    2, 443
Sieveking, Martin, 245
Siki, Béla, 245
Silbermann, Gottfried, 18, 39
Siloti, Alexander, 22, 107, 142,
  167, 169, 209, 213, 226,
  245–46, 276, 386, 423
Simon, Abbey, 230, 246
Sinding, Christian, 172
  compositions of, 443
  Piano Concerto in D-flat ma-
    jor, 443
  Rustle of Spring, 107, 443
  Sonata in B minor, 443
  Variations in D minor, 443
Sitwell, Sacheverell, 166, 353,
  359
Skalkottas, Nikos:
  Berceuse, 444
  compositions of, 444
  Fifteen Little Variations, 444

Passacaglia, 444
Sketch of a New Esthetic of
  Music (Busoni), 61
Slaughterhouse Five, 116
Slenczynska, Ruth, 74, 246
Slivinski, Josef, 246
Slobodyanik, Alexander, 246–
  247
Smattering of Ignorance, A (Le-
  vant), 158
Smendzianka, Regina, 86, 247
Smetana, Bedřich, 208
  compositions of, 444
  Faded Happiness, 444
  Six Reves, 444
Smeterlin, Jan, 247, 420
Smit, Leo, 247, 264
Smith, Logan Pearsall, 25
Smith, Ronald, 31, 247, 283–
  284, 309–10
Smith, Sydney, 183, 247–48
  Galop de concert, 248
  La Reine des fées, 248
  Tarantelle in E minor, 248
Society for the Prevention of
  Cruelty to Children, 127
Sofronitsky, Vladimir, 189,
  239–40, 248, 411, 417
Soler, Antonio, 82
Solomon, Yonty, 214, 248–50,
  444
Solti, Georg, 85
Some Musical Recollections of
  Fifty Years (Hoffman),
  110, 126
Somer, Hilde, 250
Sonata since Beethoven, The
  (Newman), 87
Sonate, La (Selva), 240
Sorabji, Kaikhosru, 31, 250,
  283, 358–59
  compositions of, 444
  Fantaisie espagnole, 444
  Introito and Preludio-Corale,
    444
  Opus Clavicembalisticum,
    444
Sorel, Claudette, 227, 250
Soriano, Gonzalo, 250
Sousa, John Philip, Stars and
  Stripes Forever, 138
Southern Illinois, University of,
  246
Spanish Order of Civil Merit,
  82
Spanuth, August, 229

Spender, Stephen, 218
Spitta, Philipp, 267
Spohr, Ludwig, 46, 67, 92
Stalin Prize, 215
Stamaty, Camille, 21, 50–51,
  109, 111, 147, 226
Souvenir du conservatoire,
  251
Stanley, Charles, 389
Starer, Robert, Piano Concerti,
  43
Stark, John, 145
Stassov, Vladimir, 167, 432
State Department, U.S., 265
Stavenhagen, Bernhard, 217,
  251
  Piano Concerto in B minor,
    251
Steibelt, Daniel, 68, 251, 272
  Etude No. 3, 251
  Etude No. 8, 251
  Piano Concerto No. 3, 251
  Piano Concerto No. 8, 251
Stein, Johann Andreas, 185–86
Steiner, George, 280
Steinway and Sons, 221
Steinway Hall, 182
Štepán, Paul, 251
Sternberg, Constantin von, 252
Stern Conservatory, 226
Stessin, Herbert, 252
Steuermann, Edward, 32, 60,
  154, 172, 244, 252, 397,
  426
  Suite for Piano, 252
Stevenson, Ronald, 252
  Passacaglia on D S C H,
    192, 252
Stockhausen, Karlheinz, 23
  compositions of, 418
  Klavierstücke I–XI, 418
  Kontakte, 261
Stojowski, Sigismund, 158–59,
  184, 227, 252, 393
  By the Brookside, 252
  Chant d'amour, 252
  Piano Concerto No. 1, 252
  Piano Concerto No. 2, 252
Stokowski, Leopold, 115, 252,
  397, 418
Stradal, August, 253
Stradivarius, Antonio, 17
Strasbourg Conservatory, 240
Strauss, Johann, Jr., 119, 220,
  230–31
  Die Fledermaus, 246

Strauss, Johann, Jr.,
  continued
  Künstlerleben, 212, 271
  One Only Lives Once, 255
  *On the Beautiful Blue
    Danube,* 236
  Wine, Women, and Song, 66
Strauss, Johann, Sr., 323
Strauss, Richard, 421
  Burleske for Piano and Or-
    chestra, 116, 243
  Ophelia lieder, 116
  Sonata in B minor, 116
Stravinsky, Igor, 143, 158, 187,
    213, 268, 360, 379, 411,
    416, 439
  Capriccio for Piano and Or-
    chestra, 267, 420
  Les Cinq Doigts, 419
  compositions of, 418–20
  Concerto for Piano and
    Winds, 420
  Danse russe, 138
  Four Etudes, 419
  Movements for Piano and
    Orchestra, 219, 420
  L'Oiseau de feu, 29
  Piano Rag Music, 419
  Le Sacre du printemps, 156–
    157, 420
  Sérénade en la, 420
  Sonata, 419–20
  *Trois Mouvements de Pe-
    trouchka,* 40, 55, 84, 105,
    138, 206, 225, 419
Stravinsky, Soulima, 253
Strong, George Templeton, 180
Stuttgart Conservatory, 157
Suchon, Eugen:
  Balladeske, 444
  compositions of, 444
  Metamorphosen, 444
Suh, Hai-Kyung, 109, 253
Suk, Josef:
  compositions of, 444–45
  Love Song, 444–45
  Things Lived and Dreamed,
    444–45
Sullivan, J. W. N., 294
Sullivan, Sir Arthur, 202
Sumbatyan, Anaida, 36, 273
Supervia, Conchita, 174
Surinach, Carlos:
  Acrobats of God, 445
  compositions of, 445
  Piano Concerto, 445

Sonatine, 445
*Trois Chansons et danses
  espagnoles,* 445
Swan, Alfred J., 239, 411,
    413–16
Swann, Jeffrey, 268
Swed, Mark, 421
Sweelinck, Jan Pieterszoon, 112
Székely, Arnold, 152
Szell, George, 56, 95, 112, 116–
    117, 137, 218, 243, 268
Szidon, Roberto, 253, 424
Szumowska, Antoinette, 180,
    253
Szymanowska, Maria, 68, 253
  Nocturne in B-flat major,
    253
  Selected Piano Music, 421
  Twelve Etudes, 253
  Twenty-Four Mazurkas, 253
Szymanowski, Karol, 14, 69,
    145, 188, 215, 224, 247,
    275
  compositions of, 420–21
  Sonata No. 1, 421
  Sonata No. 2, 421
  Sonata No. 3, 421
  Symphonie concertante for
    Piano with Orchestra, 51,
    421
  Twenty Mazurkas, 421

Tacchino, Gabriel, 254
Tagliaferro, Magda, 74, 194,
    205, 254
Takahashi, Aki, 254
Takahashi, Yuji, 254
Takemitsu, Toru, 241
Talleyrand, Charles-Maurice
    de, 87
Talma, Louise:
  Alleluia in Form of Toccata,
    445
  compositions of, 445
  Six Etudes, 445
  Sonata No. 1, 90, 445
  Sonata No. 2, 445
Taneyev, Sergei, 226, 364
Tanner, Allen, 190
Tansman, Alexander:
  compositions of, 445
  Sonata No. 5, 445
  Sonatine transatlantique, 445
Tarnowsky, Sergei, 130, 263
Tashi, 241

Taub, Robert, 436
Tauriello, Antonio, Piano Con-
    certo, 250
Tausig, Carl, 13, 21–22, 48,
    53, 57, 91, 134, 145, 153,
    160–61, 167, 169, 179,
    195, 219, 236, 254–55,
    260
  Adaptation of Weber's *Invi-
    tation to the Dance,* 182,
    255
  Arrangement of Bach's Toc-
    cata and Fugue in D mi-
    nor, 255
  Ballade (*The Ghost Ship*),
    255
  Concert Etudes, 255
  Daily Exercises, 255
  Fantasy on themes from Mo-
    niuszko's *Halka,* 255
  Paraphrase on Strauss's *One
    Only Lives Once,* 255
Taylor, Franklin, 255, 264
Tchaikovsky, Peter Ilyich, 32,
    204, 206, 226, 267, 414
  Complete Piano Music,
    422
  compositions of, 422–23
  Concert-Fantasy for Piano
    and Orchestra, 180, 423
  *Dumka (A Scene from Rus-
    sian Life),* 137, 423
  Eugene Onegin, 66, 194–
    195, 360
  Lullaby, 388
  Piano Concerto No. 1 in B-
    flat minor, 52, 57, 72, 77,
    82, 103, 117, 130, 137,
    142, 192, 225, 229, 232,
    248, 253, 268, 386, 423
  Piano Concerto No. 2 in G
    major, 43, 67, 104, 120,
    172, 180, 225, 229, 232,
    253, 268, 423
  Piano Concerto No. 3 in E-
    flat major, 172, 180, 225,
    232, 253, 268, 423
  Rêverie, 188
  Six Pieces, 422
  Six Pieces on One Theme,
    422–23
  Sonata in C-sharp minor,
    105
  Sonata in G major, 66, 214,
    216, 422
  Valse-caprice, 85, 188

Tchaikovsky International
    Competition, 37, 72, 84,
    101, 119, 192, 202, 204
Tchérépnin, Alexander, 440
    compositions of, 445
    Piano Concerto No. 2, 445
    Piano Concerto No. 5, 445
    Ten Bagatelles, 445
Tedesco, Ignace, 256, 260
Teichmüller, Robert, 213–14,
    256
Telemann, Georg Philipp,
    Tafelmusik, 391
Tempest, The (Shakespeare),
    291
Terminal Man, The, 116
Thalberg, Sigismond, 19–20,
    79, 105, 109–11, 123,
    147, 160, 167, 180, 183,
    202, 206, 256–57, 336,
    352, 359
    Fantasy on Donizetti's *Don
        Pasquale*, 257, 271
    Fantasy on Meyerbeer's *Les
        Huguenots*, 257
    Fantasy on Rossini's *Barber
        of Seville*, 257
    Fantasy on Rossini's *Moses*,
        257
    Fantasy on Rossini's *Semira-
        mide*, 271
    Piano Concerto in F minor,
        257
    Sonata in C minor, 257
    Variations on "Home, Sweet
        Home," 257
    Variations on "The Last
        Rose of Summer," 257
Theodore Thomas Orchestra,
    97
Thibaud, Jacques, 73–74
Thomán, István, 43, 84, 257
Thomas, Michael Tilson, 340
Thomson, Virgil, 50, 78, 143,
    149, 162, 232, 234, 361,
    379, 394
    compositions of, 445–46
    Nine New Etudes, 446
    Ten Etudes, 446
Timanoff, Vera, 260
Timbrell, Charles, 74
Time, 132
Times (London), 237
Tippett, Michael, 192, 305
    compositions of, 446
    Piano Concerto, 152, 446

Sonata No. 1, 446
Sonata No. 2, 446
Sonata No. 3, 446
Tocco, James, 260
Tomáschek, Johann, 45, 85–
    87, 157, 235, 260, 265
    Dithyrambs, 260
    Eclogues, 260
Toradze, Alexander, 260, 274
Toscanini, Arturo, 136–37,
    175, 242, 270
Tovey, Sir Donald Francis, 186–
    187, 243, 260, 292, 297
    Piano Concerto in A major,
        260
Town Hall, 50, 90, 108, 112,
    122, 152, 171, 244, 268
Triumph of Death, The (Orca-
    gna), 357
Trombini-Kazuro, Margherita,
    125
*True Art of Playing Keyboard
    Instruments, the* (Bach), 39
Tudor, David, 261, 429
Turczynski, Josef, 145, 173, 261
Tureck, Rosalyn, 227, 261–62
Turina, Joaquin:
    compositions of, 446
    Danzas fántasticas, 446
    Rapsodia sinfónica, 446
    *Sanlucar de Barrameda (So-
        nata pintoresca)*, 446
Turini, Ronald, 262
Twain, Mark, 100
Tzerko, Aube, 84, 262

Uchida, Mitsuko, 262
Ulmer, Ernest, 332
Unashamed Accompanist, The
    (Moore), 182
Ungar, Imre, 85, 263
Uninsky, Alexander, 263
Upton, George P., 111

Valen, Fartein, 217
Valenti, Fernando, 396
Vallas, Leon, 389
Van Cliburn International
    Competition, 72, 119, 172,
    189, 194, 235, 260, 264
van Gogh, Vincent, 113
Vardi, Arie, 56
Varèse, Edgard, 330
Vasari, Giorgio, 113

Vásáry, Tamás, 15, 263–64
Veinus, Abraham, 303
Vengerova, Isabelle, 48, 52, 80,
    90, 117, 157, 198, 247,
    264
Verbit, Martha Ann, 442
Verdi, Giuseppe:
    Ernani, 245
    Rigoletto, 42, 66, 105, 359
    Il Trovatore, 110
Vered, Ilana, 264
Verne, Adela, 264
Verne, Mathilde, 172, 228,
    248, 264
Versailles Conference, 197
Viardo, Vladimir, 264
Victoria, Queen of England,
    32, 51, 243
Vienna, University of, 219
Vienna Chamber Orchestra, 88
Vienna Conservatory, 56, 89,
    218, 253, 273
Vienna State Academy of Mu-
    sic, 122, 153
Vigny, Alfred de, 136
Villa-Lobos, Heitor, 223–24
    Bachianas Brasileiras No. 3
        for Piano and Orchestra,
        424
    compositions of, 424
    Momoprecoce for Piano and
        Orchestra, 254
    Piano Concerto No. 5, 51
    Próle do bébé, 424
    Rudepoema, 253, 424
Villoing, Alexander, 86, 226,
    264
    *Practical School of Piano
        Playing*, 264
Viñes, Ricardo, 208, 264–65,
    281, 329, 342, 379, 388
Vladigerov, Pantcho, 265, 268
Vogler, George Joseph, 45, 266
Vogrich, Max, 183, 213, 265
    Staccato-Caprice, 265
Voltaire, 18
Vorisek, Jan, 265
Vronsky, Vitya, 39, 265
Vuillard, Édouard, 336
Vuillermoz, Emile, 337

Wagner, Cosima, 57
Wagner, Richard, 13, 154, 167–
    168, 206, 222, 255, 310,
    322, 357, 359, 397, 443

Wagner, Richard,
continued
Dawn and *Siegfried's Rhine Journey*, 115
Götterdämmerung, 73, 115
Lohengrin, 57
Magic Fire Music, 54, 130
Die Meistersinger Prelude, 115
Overture to *Tannhäuser*, 42, 51, 207, 360
Parsifal, 73
Ring Cycle, 153
Siegfried Idyll, 115
Tristan und Isolde, 57, 153, 237, 239, 300, 330, 353
Die Walküre, 97
Waldoff, Stanley, 236
Waldstein, Ferdinand Ernst, Count of, 292
Walker, Alan, 350–51
Walker, George:
compositions of, 446
Piano Concerto, 446
Piano Sonatas, 446
Wallace, Robert K., 160
Walter, Bruno, 235
Warrack, John, 267, 426
Wars, The, 116
Warsaw Conservatory, 51, 67–68, 125, 173, 177, 195, 253, 261
Washington, George, 213
Watteau, Antoine, 329
Watts, André, 265–66
Weber, Ben, 176
compositions of, 446–47
Fantasia, 446
Piano Concerto, 446–47
Weber, Carl Maria von, 67, 79, 96, 148, 167, 177, 183, 237–38, 257, 266–68, 325, 352, 403
compositions of, 425–26
Invitation to the Dance, 51, 95, 182, 255, 267, 323, 425
Konzertstück for Piano and Orchestra, 60, 64, 81, 154, 166, 178, 267, 425–26
Oberon, 266–67, 315

Perpetuum Mobile, 250, 267
Piano Concerti Nos. 1 and 2, 425–26
Sonata No. 1 in C major, 267, 425
Sonata No. 2 in A-flat major, 43, 75, 267, 279, 425
Sonata No. 3 in D minor, 425
Sonata No. 4 in E minor, 95, 425
Weber, Dionys, 183
Webern, Anton, 205, 396, 419, 447
compositions of, 426
Variations for Piano, 112, 426
Webster, Beveridge, 50, 143, 201, 267–68, 445
Weill, Kurt, 444
Weingartner, Felix, 116, 230
Weiss-Busoni, Anna, 59
Weissenberg, Alexis, 193, 227–228, 265, 268–69
Welte Company, 336
Wenzel, Ernst, 269, 270
Werther (Goethe), 178
Wheelis, Allen, 215
Whiteside, Abby, 433
Wieck, Alwin, 270
Wieck, Friedrich, 20, 57, 236–237, 269–70
Wieck, Marie, 270
Wieniawski, Henri, 270
Wieniawski, Josef, 270, 275
Wigmore Hall, 222
Wild, Earl, 230, 243, 270–71
Grand Fantasy on Gershwin's *Porgy and Bess*, 270
Wilde, David, 271
Wilkomirska, Wanda, 132
Willeby, Charles, 315
Williams, Alberto, 176, 271
Sonata Argentina, 271
Williamson, Malcolm, 192
Wilson, Woodrow, 197, 341
Winding, August, 271–72
Winklhofer, Sharon, 357
Wisconsin, University of, 144
Wittgenstein, Paul, 272, 383
WNCN, 14, 113

Wodzinska, Marie, 324
Wolf, Hugo, 17, 58, 219
Wolff, Auguste Désiré, 272
Wolff, Konrad, 272
Wölfl, Joseph, 45–46, 206
Practical School for the Pianoforte, 272
Sonata Op. 25, 272
Sonata Op. 41, 272
Wollenhaupt, Hermann, 272
Wolpe, Stefan:
compositions of, 447
Form, 447
Form IV, 241, 447
Passacaglia, 241, 447
Pastorale, 241
Presto agitato, 447
Woodward, Roger, 86, 273
WQXR, 65
Wührer, Friedrich, 273

Xenakis, Iannis:
Herma, 254
Maeander, 254

Yablonskaya, Oxana, 107, 273
Yale University, 266
Yates, Peter, 61, 156–57, 357
Yudina, Maria, 189, 273, 417

Zadora, Michael von, 274
Zak, Yakov, 88, 260, 274
Zayas, Juana, 274
Zayde, Jascha, 235
Zecchi, Carlo, 82, 274
Zhukov, Igor, 274
Zichy, Géza, 274–75
Zimbalist, Efrem, 127
Zimerman, Krystian, 275
Zimmerman, Pierre, 21, 30, 32, 108–9, 174, 208, 218, 226, 270, 272, 275
Zimmermann, Agnes, 275–76
Sonata, 276
Zumpe, Johann, 18
Zverev, Nikolai, 86, 142, 209, 239, 245, 276
Zywny, Adalbert, 67–68

476

About the Author

DAVID DUBAL is music director of New York's classical music station WNCN. His six-part radio series, "Conversations with Vladimir Horowitz," received the George Foster Peabody Award in 1980, and in 1986 he was honored with the first ASCAP-Deems Taylor Broadcasting Award. A Steinway artist, he has himself recorded the piano music of more than thirty composers. He has performed and lectured throughout the United States and Europe, given master classes in Korea, and been a judge at various international piano competitions. Since 1983 he has been on the faculty of the Juilliard School, where he teaches piano literature. He is the author of *Reflections from the Keyboard: The World of the Concert Pianist.*